Oxford Studies in European Law

General Editors: Paul Craig and Gráinne de Búrca

FROM DUAL TO COOPERATIVE
FEDERALISM

From Dual to Cooperative Federalism

The Changing Structure of European Law

ROBERT SCHÜTZE

OXFORD
UNIVERSITY PRESS

OXFORD

UNIVERSITY PRESS

Great Clarendon Street, Oxford ox2 6DP
United Kingdom

Oxford University Press is a department of the University of Oxford.
It furthers the University's objective of excellence in research, scholarship,
and education by publishing worldwide. Oxford is a registered trade mark of
Oxford University Press in the UK and in certain other countries

© Robert Schütze 2009

The moral rights of the author have been asserted

First published in 2009
First published in paperback 2013

Impression: 1

British Library Cataloguing in Publication Data
Data available

Library of Congress Cataloging in Publication Data
Data available

ISBN 978-0-19-923858-3 (hbk)
ISBN 978-0-19-966494-8 (pbk)

Printed in Great Britain by
CPI Group (UK) Ltd, Croydon, CR0 4YY

Für Isolde und Dieter

Eltern, Vorbilder, Freunde – in Liebe, Bewunderung, Dankbarkeit

PREFACE TO THE PAPERBACK EDITION

I am very pleased that Oxford University Press has decided to publish a paperback edition of my "From Dual to Cooperative Federalism: The Changing Structure of European Law". The ideas behind the book have, I think, helped to re-kindle a serious debate on the 'federal' nature of the European Union in constitutional and philosophical circles.[1]

The book's central methodological aims were threefold. First, it tried to rehabilitate a comparative approach to the study of European law. A comparativist challenge to the *sui generis* 'theory' of the European Union will thereby not necessarily deny the Union's 'unique' character; yet its uniqueness is – like the uniqueness of a human being – not rooted in a different 'genus'. Thus: even if the European Union is a unique species of the federal genus, it forms part of the federal family and thus shares a family resemblance to earlier federal orders. And it is this resemblance that might provide us with conceptual keys to unlock the nature of the European Union and the structure of European law.

Second, much contemporary European constitutionalism is over-theorized. It is disheartening to see many a 'theorist' of European law identify the nature of that law by a casual reference to *Van Gend en Loos* and *Costa v ENEL*.[2] But did *Van Gend* encompass *Cassis de Dijon*;[3] and did *Costa* contain *Kadi*?[4] And even if *Costa* established the supremacy of European law, why was the doctrine originally not applied in the external sphere? Simplicity – not subtlety – often appears the theorists' specialty! But the character of the European Union can as little be explained by *two* cases, as the nature of humanity is distilled from Adam and Eve.[5] (For did not their chasing from paradise only make human nature *possible*?) The problem with all three-penny

---

[1] Cf. J. Habermas, *Zur Verfassung Europas – Ein Essay* (Suhrkamp, 2011), 66.

[2] Case 26/62, *Van Gend & Loos v Netherlands Inland Revenue Administration*, [1963] ECR 1; and Case 6/64, *Costa v ENEL*, [1964] ECR 585.

[3] Case 120/78, *Rewe-Zentral v Bundesmonopolverwaltung für Branntwein (Cassis de Dijon)*, [1979] ECR 649.

[4] Case C-402/05P, *Kadi and Al Barakaat International Foundation v Council and Commission*, [2008] ECR I-6351.

[5] And for a criticism that *Costa* was formed out of *Van Gend*'s 'rib', see: R. Schütze, *European Constitutional Law* (Cambridge University Press, 2012), 349.

theories of European law is that they are written by drinkers – and often: drunkards – of philosophical quintessences.[6] But constitutional law is *not* legal philosophy. Constitutional law is where political theory meets historical reality; and a constitutionalism without historical realities is a remote – and banal – legal formalism.[7]

Yet this is not to say that history must always trump over philosophy![8] On the contrary, the third methodological point behind the book was to show the determinative power of a philosophical theory over a constitutional text. For the changing structure of European law could have taken place without – or even despite – formal constitutional changes. The meaning of a constitutional provision will indeed often depend – like that of a poem – on the philosophical preconceptions of the interpreter. This is the story behind much American constitutional law.[9] In the European constitutional context, this philosophical independence from positive law is however less pronounced. For the gap between (constitutional) theory and (historical) reality has been regularly narrowed by constitutional amendments. The 'constitutionalisation' of cooperative federalism in the form of complementary competences is but one example.

Finally, a word on the substance of the book. Despite the coming into force of the Lisbon Treaty on 1 December 2009, very little of the original argument has lost its force. Much of the new constitutional text was indeed designed to consolidate past jurisprudence, and is thus likely to be interpreted in line with a cooperative federal philosophy. However, this might not necessarily be so: a changing text might always, with time, inspire the arrival of a new – or the revival of an old – constitutional philosophy. But even if there might be some textual signs in the new Treaties in favour of dual federalism, we must be patient and wait for another decade (or two) to see whether the Lisbon reforms will have significantly changed the structure of European law.

Durham, 1 December 2012

---

[6] On the pleasures, even for philosophers, of – occasionally – falling into the mire of everyday life, see: C. Baudelaire, *Paris Spleen – Loss of a Halo* (New Directions, 1970), 94.

[7] For a perfect example of this imperfect 'constitutionalism', see: N. Walker, Postnational Constitutionalism and the Problem of Translation, in: J. Weiler (et al, eds), *European Constitutionalism Beyond the State* (Cambridge University Press, 2003), 27. For an excellent critique of such an excessive theoretical endeavour, see: N. Krisch, Europe's Constitutional Monstrosity, [2005] 25 Oxford Journal of Legal Studies 321, esp. 326.

[8] In this – relativist – sense, consider Quentin Skinner's famous plea of "*less* philosophy, *more* history".

[9] Cf. B. Ackerman, *We the People – Transformations* (Harvard University Press, 2000).

PREFACE

This book was written in Brussels, Cambridge, Durham, Florence, Luxembourg, and Zwickau. In each of these cities, I was very fortunate to meet a remarkable number of remarkable people. For their advice or encouragement I wish to single out and thank Catherine Barnard, Michael Bohlander, Damian Chalmers, Marise Cremona, Holly Cullen, Alan Dashwood, Michael Dougan, Piet Eeckhout, Claus-Dieter Ehlermann, Amandine Garde, Daniel Halberstam, Adrienne Héritier, Francis Jacobs, Christian Joerges, Kaiyan Kaikobad, Jan Klabbers, Panos Koutrakos, Konrad Lachmayer, Jo Murkens, Ernst-Ulrich Petersmann, Boris Rotenberg, Wojciech Sadursky, Eleanor Spaventa, Takis Tridimas, Hanns Ullrich, John Usher, Neil Walker, Colin Warbrick, Steve Weatherill, and Bruno de Witte. Special thanks go to Gráinne de Búrca for all the support given during the first phase of this project, and to Antonis Antoniadis for his critical eye and friendship during the second. I am indebted to three 'classic' scholars of European constitutionalism: Hans-Peter Ipsen, Pierre Pescatore, and Eric Stein. Their constitutional and comparative wisdom have shaped my thinking about European law. On the editorial side, I want to thank Darcy Ahl and Alex Flach from Oxford University Press and the General Editors of this Series. Thanks equally go to Hart Publishing, Kluwer Law International, Oxford University Press, and Sweet & Maxwell for their kind permission to incorporate sections from previously published material. Finally, my warmest expression of gratitude to Isolde and Dieter Schütze. No words can do justice to what I owe them.

The 'thesis' behind this book was defended in 2005 at the European University Institute, where it received the *Obiettivo Europa* Prize. In the past three years, I have substantially restructured the original manuscript. Most importantly: a chapter on German federalism was dropped, and the chapter on 'Federal Tradition(s) and the European Union' was added. While part of my argument has already been published, this is not the book—to paraphrase Edgar Allan Poe—that is 'used up'. This book offers 'new' ideas and even those updated 'old' ones will assume a new meaning within the context of the overall story. Its parts should form a 'unity within diversity' and—I hope—the whole is much greater than the sum of its parts. In the days of 'theoretical' European constitutionalism, it may seem unusual for a constitutional argument to go into the mire of Europe's legislative and judicial practice. However, constitutional *law* is about extracting legal principles from specific rules. And: constitutional *theory* must always be about constitutional *practice*. Thus, a word of warning borrowed from Ezra Pound: 'The book is not addressed to those who have arrived at full knowledge of the subject without knowing the facts'.

Robert Schütze

March 2009

SUMMARY CONTENTS

CONTENTS

TABLE OF CASES

European Union Cases

US Supreme Court Cases

Other Jurisdictions

TABLE OF LEGISLATION

European Legislation

Regulations

Directives

Singular Legal Acts

Political Guidelines

European Council

Council

ABBREVIATIONS

CAP	Common Agricultural Policy
CCP	Common Commercial Policy
CFI	Court of First Instance
CFSP	Common Foreign and Security Policy
CMO	Common Market Organization
CT	Constitutional Treaty
COREPER	Committee of the Permanent Representatives
EAGGF	European Agricultural Guidance and Guarantee Fund
EC	European Community
ECB	European Central Bank
ECHR	European Convention on Human Rights
ECJ	European Court of Justice
ECR	European Court Reports
ECSC	European Coal and Steel Community
EDC	European Defence Community
EEA	European Economic Area
EEC	European Economic Community
EFTA	European Free Trade Association
EMU	European Monetary Union
EPC	European Political Community
EU	European Union
Euratom	European Atomic Energy Community
GATT	General Agreement on Tariffs and Trade
GATS	General Agreement on Trade in Services
ICJ	International Court of Justice
IGC	Intergovernmental Conference
ILO	International Labour Organization
JHA	Justice and Home Affairs
MEP	Member of the European Parliament
NATO	North Atlantic Treaty Organization
OECD	Organization for Economic Co-operation and Development
OEEC	Organization for European Economic Co-operation
OJ	Official Journal
PCIJ	Permanent Court of International Justice
PJCC	Police and Judicial Co-operation in Criminal Matters
QMV	Qualified Majority Voting
SEA	Single European Act

TEU	Treaty on European Union ('Maastricht Treaty')
TFEU	Treaty on the Functioning of the European Union
UN	United Nations
US	United States
WEU	Western European Union
WTO	World Trade Organization

INTRODUCTION

Coming to Constitutional Terms

Philosophical problems arise when language revels.[1] Constitutional problems arise when society revels. Each society—and each time—has 'its' constitutional law as each *legal* order will try to 'reflect the principles of the *social* order that it seeks to regulate'.[2] But what if society has moved on? Social changes may only slowly translate into constitutional ones. The relationship between a society and 'its' constitutional law may, then, at times follow the relation between 'existence' and 'essence': the former precedes the latter. Social changes precede constitutional ones. These are moments, when constitutionalism— the philosophical context to positive constitutional law—fails to explain or justify the existing social order. The cleavage between theory and reality—the difference between 'norms' and 'facts'—will fuel the search for a new constitutional paradigm.[3] This happened in the nineteenth century, when the democratization of European societies could no longer be explained on the basis of monarchic constitutionalism.

In the twentieth century, the philosophy behind classic international law became increasingly unable to provide an undistorted reflection of the changed social reality of international relations. The shockwaves of the First and Second World Wars blew away the blind belief in an international legal order founded on the idea of State sovereignty. The spread of multilateral cooperation pushed the frontiers of international law into new fields.[4] And the rise of international cooperation caused a fundamental transformation in the substance and structure of international law. 'The changing structure and scope of international relations demand[ed] a corresponding adjustment in the structure and scope of international law.'[5] The changed *reality* of international

[1] L Wittgenstein, *Philosophical Investigations*, §38 (translation—RS).
[2] WG Friedmann, *The Changing Structure of International Law*, 3 (emphasis added).
[3] On scientific paradigms, see: TS Kuhn, *The Structure of Scientific Revolutions*.
[4] G Schwarzenberger, *The Frontiers of International Law*.
[5] WG Friedmann (n 2 above) 365.

relations necessitated a change in the *theory* of international law.[6] International society had revelled and a new international 'constitutionalism' emerged: the theory of 'cooperative international law'. The transition from a law of 'co-existence' to a law of 'cooperation' changed the structure of international law 'from an essentially negative code of rules of abstention to positive rules of cooperation'.[7] The—solidified—expression of this new philosophy of cooperation was the spread of international organizations.

The European Union embodies this cooperative spirit on a regional international scale.[8] Originally, the Treaties of Paris (1951) and Rome (1957)

[6] C de Visscher, *Theory and Reality in Public International Law*. The theoretical re-evaluation of key concepts involved the very foundations of classic international law. First, the doctrine of sovereignty: had the classic doctrine of sovereignty placed the State *above* international law, the 'new' international doctrine defined the State as sovereign *under* international law (cf L Wildhaber, *Sovereignty and International Law*, 438 and 442). Secondly, international law enlarged its 'subjects': while the 'old' international law had considered that 'the right of entering into international engagements is an attribute of *State* sovereignty' (cf *SS Wimbledon*, (1923) Series A No 1, 15 at 25 (emphasis added)), the 'new' international doctrine has come to recognize the international personality and treaty-making capacity of international organizations (cf *Reparation for Injuries suffered in the Service of the United Nations*, (1949) ICJ Reports, 174). Thirdly, modern international law has enlarged its 'substance' (cf G Schwarzenberger (n 4 above)).

[7] WG Friedmann (n 2 above) 62. The international law of coexistence is defined as 'the traditional sphere of diplomatic relations represented by the classical system of international law'. 'The principal object of these rules of coexistence is the regulation of the conditions of mutual diplomatic intercourse and, in particular, of the rules of mutual respect for national sovereignty. The substance of these rules is found in the classic texts on international law: the rules regulating membership of the family of nations, including the regulation of new states and governments; the rules governing the limits of territorial jurisdiction; the jurisdictional and diplomatic immunities of foreign sovereigns; the principles of responsibility incurred by a state for injury done to the lives or properties of the subjects of another state; the adjustment of the rights of belligerent states and neutral states in the rules of war and neutrality, and the formal implementation of these principles by custom, treaty or adjudication.' (Ibid 60).

[8] Students of the European Union will first have to come to terms with the—confusing—terminology. Words and numbers seem in a process of constant change. The Merger Treaty had changed the terminology of the first European Community; the Maastricht Treaty changed the name of the European Economic Community into European Community and created the European Union; the Amsterdam Treaty renumbered all Treaty articles; and, if the Lisbon Treaty enters into force, the European Community will be re-baptized into the European Union and all Treaty articles will be renumbered again. The following study will use the term 'European Union' in its broadest sense, that is: as the all-embracing entity within which all European integration has taken place. Thus, even if much of the constitutional consolidation of Europe has taken place within the European *Community*—that is, within the first of the three pillars—the book will refer to the constitutional evolution of the European Union *writ large*. This is a purely linguistic convention. It should not be taken to imply that the European Union and the European Communities form one legal entity, but simply acknowledges a semantic evolution that would become official under the Lisbon Treaty.

formed part of international law, although the European Court of Justice was eager to emphasize that the European Union 'constitutes a *new* legal order of international law'.[9] 'By contrast with ordinary international treaties, the E[]C Treaty has created its own legal system which, on the entry into force became an integral part of the legal systems of the Member States and which their courts are bound to apply.'[10] While born with the genetic code of international law, the social reality of the European Union would soon pose serious conceptual problems to classic *and* cooperative international law. 'Community law was established on the most advanced frontiers of the law of peaceful co-operation, where in the past the rules of customs and economic unions began to develop'; indeed, the principles of solidarity and integration had taken it 'to the boundaries of federalism'.[11] But was the Union inside those federal boundaries or outside them? While the European Union was not a Federal State, it had assumed 'statist' features and thus combined—like a chemical compound—international and national elements.

How should one conceptualize this 'middle ground' between international and national law? In the absence of a theory of federalism beyond the State, European thought invented a new word—supranationalism—and proudly announced the European Union to be *sui generis*. The belief that Europe was incomparable ushered in the dark ages of European constitutional theory.[12] For the *sui generis* idea is not a theory. It is an *anti*-theory as it refuses to search for commonalities; yet, theory *must* search for what is generic.[13] In any event, the *sui generis* 'theory' only ever provided a thin veneer in times of constitutional peace. In times of constitutional conflict, Europe's philosophical heritage returned to the fore and would insist on the international foundations of the European Union. However, this conceptualization simply can no longer explain the social and legal reality inside Europe. How, then, shall we conceive the European Union? The answer suggested in this book is inspired by

---

    [9] Case 26/62 *NV Algemene Transport- en Expeditie Onderneming van Gend & Loos v Netherlands Inland Revenue Administration*, 12 (emphasis added).

    [10] Case 6/64 *Flaminio Costa v ENEL*, 593.

    [11] P Pescatore, *International Law and Community Law—A Comparative Analysis*, 182.

    [12] While the 'classics' of European law had actively searched for comparisons with international and national phenomena (cf E Haas, *The Uniting of Europe*), the legal comparative approach fell into a medieval slumber in the course of the 1980s. (For two remarkable exceptions to the rule, see: M Cappelletti, M Seccombe & J Weiler, *Integration Through Law: Europe and the American Federal Experience*; and K Lenaerts, *Le juge et la constitution aux États-Unis d'Amérique et dans l'ordre juridique européen*.) The same applies, *mutatis mutandis*, to European political studies, cf M Forsyth, *The Political Theory of Federalism: The Relevance of Classical Approaches*.

    [13] K Popper, *The Logic of Scientific Discovery*.

a constitutional comparison with another Union: the United States of America. Early on, American constitutionalism came to identify federalism with the very 'in-between' international and national organization. Standing on 'middle ground', federalism represented not an—absolute—norm but a—relative—principle.[14]

The objection that the European and the American Union are incomparable, because the former is not a State, is historically short-sighted. The American Union was not always considered—certainly not by Americans—to represent a Federal State. On the contrary, the American constitutional experience may give us the key to 'think' federalism beyond the State:

Filled with more than two centuries of history, American federalism offers a privileged ground to think federalism outside the theory of the Federal State. It is unique in its kind and profoundly different from European federal thought that followed a path trodden by German constitutional doctrine. American federalism constitutes an excellent illustration of a constitutional pragmatism that would not embrace theory for theory's sake. Today, this is the only method which may allow us to envisage a theory of federalism conceived of as an 'in between' Confederation of States and Federal State and that will also allow us to think differently about the problem of a European Constitution ... Starting from the experience of the union of the United States of America, it may be permitted to say that the concept of 'State'—as formed by European legal theory—will not tell us what federalism really is. Worse: European constitutional theory impedes this understanding, because it prohibits and censors the idea that in federations of States competences will necessarily be limited. And by thinking the federal phenomenon exclusively in terms of the State and always in relation to it, European constitutional theory has locked itself in a dead-end.[15]

Today, European constitutionalism is gradually unlocking itself from this dead end. This 'renaissance' of the federal principle and the idea of a 'Federation of States', allows us to analyse the European Union in federal terms and, finally, to ask what sort of federation the European Union is.

The idea behind federalism—unity within diversity—may express itself in different ways. Two major federal philosophies emerged in the evolution of the American Union. They became known under the names of dual and cooperative federalism. While both arrangements are based on the idea of dual

---

[14] On the relative nature of the federal principle, see: WS Livingston, *A Note on the Nature of Federalism*, 88: '[F]ederalism is not an absolute but a relative term; there is no specific point at which a society ceases to be unified and becomes diversified. The differences are of degree rather than of kind. All countries fall somewhere in a spectrum which runs from what we may call a theoretically wholly integrated society at one extreme to a theoretically wholly diversified society at the other'.

[15] E Zoller, *Aspects internationaux du droit constitutionnel. Contribution à la théorie de la fédération d'états*, 73 and 149 (translation—RS).

government, they differ in how the federal and the State governments relate
to each other. Each federal philosophy has 'its' constitutional *structure*. And
while dual and cooperative federalism are, in the United States, associated
with—respectively—State-rightism and nationalism; as federal models, they
are, strictly speaking, agnostic as regards the substantive federal balance.
Each model stands for a *method* of dividing sovereignty.

Dual Federalism

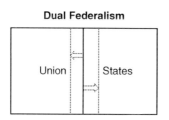

Cooperative Federalism

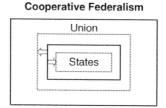

Dual federalism is based on the idea of dual 'sovereignty'. The Constitution
divides sovereignty into blocks of exclusive powers. The federal government
and the State governments are co-equals and operate independently in their
separate spheres. (Again: this will not tell us anything about the respective
size of these spheres; and, depending on the substantive balance struck, one
could envisage a 'nationalist' as much as a 'State-rightist' dual federalism.)
Cooperative federalism, on the other hand, stands for a philosophy in which
sovereignty is shared: 'the national and state governments work together in
the same areas, sharing functions and therefore power'.[16] '[T]he National
Government and the States are mutually complementary parts ... whose
powers are intended to realize the current purposes of government according
to their applicability to the problem at hand.'[17]

Which of the two federal philosophies inspires the European Union? The
answer may depend on what aspect of the Union one looks at. Federal philosophy may inspire the institutional and/or the functional dimension within a
compound polity. Thus, depending on whether the two governmental levels are
organizationally separate or mixed, we could speak of—respectively—a dual or
a cooperative structure.[18] Similarly, depending on whether the governmental

[16] MD Reagan, *The New Federalism*, 21.

[17] ES Corwin, *The Passing of Dual Federalism*, 19.

[18] The dual federalist solution—a federal legislator without a States chamber—has not been
adopted by American federalism. The Constitution requires the procedural involvement of the
States through the Senate for all legislation and treaty-making. American constitutionalism conceptualizes this phenomenon under the idea of the 'political safeguards of federalism'. Despite the

functions are divided into two exclusive spheres or not, we could speak of—respectively—a dual or a cooperative federalism. Focusing on the institutional dimension may lead us to prejudge the European Union as a cooperative federation: after all the Member States 'cooperate' in the Council of the European Union. However, this is *not* the perspective chosen for this book. We shall concentrate on the *functional* dimension within the European Union. The question to be answered is: what is the structure of European *law*?[19] Will the

significant power of the American States in the legislative process, German federal thought has, nonetheless, come to associate it with a *dual* (!) federal structure. Why? Because it insists on a distinction between two types of federal chambers—the American 'Senate' model as opposed to the German 'Council' model. The distinguishing characteristic between the two models is said to be that—after the Seventeenth Amendment (1913)—the (American) Senate is composed of representatives directly elected by the *people* of each State, whereas the (German) Council is composed of representatives of the State *governments*. However, the direct election of the Senators is, as such, *not* less protective of State rights: after all, it only ensures the direct representation of the political authority behind each State: its people. Admittedly, each American Senator can vote in full independence, whereas Article 51(3) of the German Constitution stipulates that '[t]he votes of each Land may be cast only as a unit and only by members present'. Thus, while the American system accepts a split vote for a State, the German system bundles the votes of each State into a uniform voice. Yet, whether this difference results in a stronger representation of the State, may be doubted (cf VD Amar, *Indirect Effects of Direct Elections: A Structural Explanation of the Seventeenth Amendment*).

[19] The book thus concentrates on the legislative function. However, long ago, and in a swift manner, the shift from dual to cooperative federalism seems to have taken place in the *judicial* sphere. In 1960, the European Court of Justice still found that the three Community treaties 'are based on the principle of strict separation between the powers of the Court on the one hand and the national courts on the other' from which it followed 'that there is no overlapping of the jurisdiction assigned to the different courts' (Case 6/60 *Jean-E Humblet v Belgian State*, 572). Yet, already in 1965, cooperative federalism had arrived and the sharing of judicial tasks between the European Court of Justice and the national courts was seen in the 'judicial cooperation under [Article 234] which requires the national court and the Court of Justice, both keeping within their respective jurisdiction, and with the aim of ensuring that Community law is applied in a unified manner, to make direct and complementary contributions to the working out of a decision' (Case 16/65 *Firma G Schwarze v Einfuhr- und Vorratsstelle für Getreide und Futtermittel*, 886).

As regards the executive function generally, we may also identify a change from a—predominantly—dual to a—more—cooperative federal arrangement. In the past decade, European administrative lawyers have indeed diagnosed a shift from 'the classic principle of separating between the implementation of European administrative law by the Commission (as an exception) and the implementation of Community law by national authorities (as the rule) on the one hand and the principle of co-operation between member State[s] and European authorities on the other hand' (J Schwarze, *European Administrative Law*, ccxxiv). And while Europe has increasingly established its own administrative structures, '[t]he outcome of the process of European integration in the administrative sphere of the EC legal order has not been a move from indirect to direct execution, but from indirect to forms of co-execution' (E Chiti, *The Emergence of a Community Administration: The Case of European Agencies*, 341). On the emergence of cooperative administrative law, see also: T Groß, *Die Kooperation zwischen europäischen Agenturen und nationalen Behörden*.

bodies of European and national law be separated blocks of legal rules or will they interact and cooperate? Has Europe's philosophy perhaps changed over time?

Unfortunately, even a focus on the functional dimension of Europe's federalism encounters terminological difficulties. An unfortunate degree of conceptual disharmony with American federal thought has been caused by German political scientists.[20] Focusing on the *executive* function, these authors have made their categorization dependent on whether federal law is executed directly by federal institutions or indirectly by the States. In the former scenario they speak of dual federalism, in the latter of cooperative federalism. From this perspective, the United States of America is said to represent a dual (!) federal structure, while the German Federal Republic would have a cooperative federal structure.[21] Formally, one may object that such a view—unthankfully—contradicts the self-understanding of the federal order from which these ideas have originated. (American constitutionalism thinks it has abandoned dual federalism.) Substantially, one must object that such a view—simplistically—suggests that a constitutional command addressed to the States to execute federal law represents, *ipso facto*, cooperative federalism. This is misleading: if we define federalism by the presence of *two independent*

---

[20] The German branch of European Studies has come to identify the American federal structure with dual federalism and the German federal structure with cooperative federalism. Emblematic for this approach is the work of T Börzel, *What Can Federalism Teach Us About the European Union? The German Experience.* According to Börzel, the United States constitutes a dualist federal system, ibid 248: 'For each sector, one level of government holds both legislative and executive powers. As a consequence, the entire government machinery tends to be duplicated, as each level manages its own affairs autonomously'. By contrast, German federalism is 'cooperative' (ibid 249): 'cooperative federalism, a concept for which Germany serves almost as a "prototype", is based on a functional division of powers among different levels of government: the central level makes the laws, while the federal units are responsible for implementing them'. The States' 'reduced capacity of self-determination is compensated, however, by strong participatory rights in the process of federal decision-making (mainly in the framework of the second chamber of the national legislature). Major policy initiatives usually require the consent of both the federation and a majority of the federal units'.

This terminological development is not part of German constitutional theory. German constitutionalism has traditionally subscribed—even if subconsciously—to a dual federal philosophy. This dual federalism expresses itself in two constitutional prohibitions: the 'double competence prohibition' (*Verbot der Doppelzuständigkeit*) and the 'mixed administration prohibition' (*Verbot der Mischverwaltung*). Cooperative federalism is thereby *not* identified with the decentralized execution of federal law, but with the constitutional developments that took place in the 1960s (cf G Kisker, *Kooperation im Bundesstaat: Eine Untersuchung zum kooperativen Föderalismus in der Bundesrepublik Deutschland*).

[21] Article 83 of the German Constitution states: 'The *Länder* shall execute federal laws in their own right insofar as this Basic Law does not otherwise provide or permit'.

governments, we must exclude instances when the States only act as *dependent administrations*. Where federal law asks a State 'slavishly' to apply federal law to the letter, the State is not acting as 'government'. In such a case, Saxony in Germany acts like Brittany in France. What, then, distinguishes the phenomenon of cooperative federalism from administrative decentralization? The answer suggested here lies in the distinction between *legislative* implementation and *executive* application.[22] The former involves the adoption of *generally* applicable rules that will allow a State to express a *political* choice for its population. A 'political' choice always concerns a 'we'—a collectivity. In regulating its 'people', the State acts as its 'government'. Thus, only where federal law allows *legislative* choices at the implementation level, should we speak of cooperative *federalism*. The controlling criterion for our distinction between dual and cooperative federalism, consequently, is—in line with American constitutional thought—the legislative function. Europe's constitutional choice to recruit the Member State administrations for the execution of European law will not *as such* signify a cooperative federal arrangement.

After all these terminological preliminaries, we can now return to our original question: 'What is the structure of European law?' Following the American connotations, the classification as dual or cooperative federalism depends on how legislative powers are divided in Europe's compound polity. Do the European Union and its Member States act in separate legislative spheres defined by policy areas; or do both act in the same areas but according to the size of the problem at hand? Has the federal philosophy underlying the structure of European law changed over time? This book serves my answer on the silver plate of its title.[23] But how exact must our map of European law be to 'prove' this thesis? A perfect picture of Europe's law would only emerge through the study of the European Union's *Official Journal*.[24] This we shall—to the reader's relief—not do. After all, it is the task of theory in science to

---

[22] On the distinction between legislative and executive acts, see: H Kelsen, *General Theory of Law and State*.

[23] The thesis advanced in this book is not absolute. It does not claim that there were no elements of cooperative federalism in the past or that there are no elements of dual federalism in the present. Nor does it deny that there exist countercurrents to the general move from dual to cooperative federalism. The book makes a relative claim: the *predominant* federal philosophy underlying the structure of European law has changed from one philosophy to the other. This relative claim is in line with Wheare's terminological convention for the concept of 'federation': a federation is a polity, in which the federal principle was not necessarily the 'only' but the 'dominant' structural principle (cf KC Wheare, *Federal Government*, 16).

[24] '[T]he answer to the standard question raised in the competence debate—"Who does what in Europe?"—can easily be found in the Official Journal' (F Mayer, *The Debate on European Powers and Competences: Seeing Trees but not the Forest?*, 24).

'abstract' and thereby reduce complexity to a 'bearable' size.[25] Our analysis will concentrate on the European Union's competences. However, an analysis at this abstract level would only be conclusive if we found a constitutional principle that stated that all Union competences are exclusive competences. But this is not the case; on the contrary, Europe's primary competence category—at least in its internal sphere—is that of shared power. But will this not in itself signal a choice in favour of cooperative federalism? This is not necessarily so: where European legislation automatically leads to the total exclusion of all State law within its sphere of application, it will be impossible to attribute a cooperative federal structure to European law. In order to prove our thesis, we must consequently look—at least to some degree—to the actual *exercise* of legislative power by the European Union.

In order to show Europe's transition from a—predominantly—dual to a—predominantly—cooperative federalism, the book adopts the following structure. It is divided into a general and a special part. The general part will try to clarify two things. It attempts to (re)establish that the European Union is a Federal Union in Chapter 1. This conclusion will allow us to compare it to the American Union—the United States of America. An analysis of the changing structure of American law follows in Chapter 2. This, in turn, provides us with a comparative map for analysing the changing structure of European law in the special part of the book. This special part begins by tracing the growth of the European Union's powers over the last decades. This growth has reduced the exclusive 'police powers' of the States to such an extent that one leading authority of European law has claimed that '[t]here simply is no nucleus of sovereignty that the Member States can invoke, as such, against the Community'.[26] However, this 'Europeanization' will not itself signal a move towards cooperative federalism. The latter required a reduction of—constitutional and/or legislative—exclusivity on the part of the European Union. The passing of dual federalism is illustrated in Chapters 3 and 4. What is striking about the transition from dual to cooperative federalism in the European legal order is that—unlike its American counterpart—this development has been 'constitutionalized'. The elevation

---

[25] The danger of a passion for precision is wonderfully captured by JL Borges in '*On Exactitude in Science*', which tells the story of an imaginary empire. 'In that Empire, the Art of Cartography attained such Perfection that the map of a single Province occupied the entirety of a City, and the map of the Empire, the entirety of a Province. In time, those Unconscionable Maps no longer satisfied, and the Cartographers Guilds struck a Map of the Empire whose size was that of the Empire, and which coincided point for point with it' (JL Borges, *Collected Fictions*, 325).

[26] K Lenaerts, *Constitutionalism and the Many Faces of Federalism*, 220.

of the principle of subsidiarity to a constitutional status and the emergence of 'complementary competences' will be discussed in Chapter 5. Foreign affairs will be separately discussed in Chapter 6.[27] In national legal orders they are traditionally regarded as 'exceptional' and consequently subject to distinct constitutional principles. This has also been the case for the external powers of the European Union. The dual federalist principles and reasons for their emergence will be discussed here. Finally, a Conclusion will provide a summary of the results and offer elements of a normative theory of cooperative federalism. Reading it immediately after this Introduction may be profitable in order to avoid the pitfalls of the hermeneutic circle and to install—from the beginning—a feeling for the unity in the diversity of the arguments presented in this book.

---

[27] However, the Community's Common Commercial Policy is already dealt with in Chapter 3—Section II. This arrangement reflects the fact that the policy allows for the adoption of internal as well as external measures.

GENERAL PART

Federalism in America and Europe

1

Federal Tradition(s) and the European Union

Introduction: Federalism and (Inter)national Law

Federalism is a philosophical and a constitutional problem. The federal principle has made a long 'journey through time in quest of a meaning'.[1] Its etymological origins lie in *'foedus'*—a word that signified 'contract'.[2] Contractual bonds are variously made; and the federal principle was open to a variety of conceptual directions. Early on, the federal idea became associated with legal arrangements between political communities. Yet, there was no theory of federalism in antiquity;[3] and in the medieval world, the federal principle found but little light to grow.[4] Modern federalism emerged with the rise of the European State system. Since then, the federal principle is associated with the political relations between States. In Federal Unions, authority is divided between a centre and a periphery. The federal principle comes to represent a legal structure which attempts to find 'unity in diversity'. However, not one but three traditions of federalism emerge in the modern era. The first section of this chapter will analyse each tradition and the semantic evolution of the federal principle through time.

Should we analyse the European Union through the federal lens; and if so, which one? Europe's legal structure is often portrayed as *sui generis*. This is a conceptually and historically short-sighted approach. The second section of this chapter aims to show that 'the older doctrines of federalism, while in no sense providing a blueprint for integration, do help us to understand what [European] integration is, and clarify the key issues that confront it now and

---

[1] SR Davis, *The Federal Principle: A Journey through Time in Quest of a Meaning.* Equally brilliant philosophical and constitutional histories of the federal principle are: O Beaud, *Théorie de la fédération*; E Deuerlein, *Föderalismus: Die historischen und philosophischen Grundlagen des föderativen Prinzips*; R Kosseleck, *Bündnis, Föderalismus, Bundesstaat*; M Forsyth, *Unions of States: The Theory and Practice of Confederations*; and B Voyenne, *Histoire de l'idée federalist: Les Sources.*

[2] The Latin term *'foedus'* is related to *'fides'*—a word that signified 'fidelity' and 'trust'. The Middle Ages preferred adding the prefix 'con' to 'federal'. This was a pleonasm designed to underline that an association was formed by men 'with' other men, cf B Voyenne, ibid 61.

[3] In Greek political philosophy, the federation or *koinon* is overshadowed by the city-state or *polis*, cf E Deuerlein (n 1 above) 307. In Imperial Rome, the *foedus* was a treaty of alliance by which imperial Rome secured its aggrandizement. The political communities sworn into alliance—the *con-federati*—would promise help in times of emergencies and crisis.

[4] Medieval universalism eulogized constitutional unity and marginalized theories that legitimized political diversity, cf SR Davis (n 1 above) 35.

in the future'.[5] We shall explore the structure of the European Union in the light of—respectively—the American and the European federal tradition. According to the American tradition, the European Union constitutes a Federal Union; and the analytical tools developed by this tradition will be shown to offer enormous conceptual potential for a legal analysis of the European Union. This will be contrasted with European federal theory. Concentrating on the locus of sovereignty, the analytical poverty of this tradition presents us with a black-or-white choice: the European Union is either an international organization or a Federal State. This theory is unable to explain, and thus ultimately collapses, in the face of a new legal society in a new time: the European Union.

I. The Federal Principle: Three Legal Traditions

Modern federalism emerges with the rise of the European State system. The normative heart of that system is the legal independence of each State.[6] This legal pluralism provides the conceptual background to all modern federal thought. It is the moment when federalism could come to refer to legal arrangements between territorially *distinct* political communities.

However, not one but three federal traditions emerge in the modern era. The meaning of the federal principle differs in each tradition. In a first stage, the dogma of State sovereignty relegates the federal principle to purely *international* and *contractual* relations between sovereign States. (Con)federal Unions are conceived as international organizations. By the end of the eighteenth century, this international format of the federal principle was over-shadowed by the American Union. In this second tradition, federalism came to represent the 'middle ground' between international and national organizational principles. This mixed format was, in turn, challenged in the course of the nineteenth century, when a third tradition insisted on a purely *national* and *constitutional* meaning of the federal principle. Federation here came to mean Federal State.

---

[5] M Forsyth, *The Political Theory of Federalism: The Relevance of Classical Approaches*, 25.

[6] E de Vattel, *The Law of Nations*, Preliminaries, §4: '*Nations*, or sovereign states, are to be considered as so many free persons living together in the state of nature'.

Semantic changes in constitutional concepts are not uncommon in the history of ideas.[7] They occur through 'speech acts' dealing with these ideas.[8] In analysing conceptual changes, two things must be borne in mind. First, history is not teleology.[9] There is nothing deterministic in the history of ideas. Secondly, each federal tradition has had a conceptual competitor in its time and place. We thus find an intellectual countercurrent accepting the idea of divided sovereignty in seventeenth-century and nineteenth-century Europe;[10] and also discover the dogma of undivided sovereignty in heated debates in the constitutional history of the United States.[11] These alternative voices will not be heard here as the following section concentrates on those views that became—justly or unjustly—the dominant intellectual currents in their time and place.

1. *The Classic Tradition: The 'International' Format of the Federal Principle*

The rise of the modern State system was a celebration of political pluralism. The apostles of State sovereignty denied the existence of supranational legal authority and introduced a distinction that would structure our modern legal imagination: the distinction between national and international law.

---

[7] An illustration of a similarly fundamental semantic change can be found in the intellectual biography of 'democracy'. Ancient political thought distinguished between three forms of government: monarchy, aristocracy, and democracy. In the seventeenth century, Hobbes defined the three types as follows (cf T Hobbes, *Leviathan*, 129): 'When the representative is One man, then is the Common-wealth a *Monarchy*: when an Assembly of All that will come together, then it is a *Democracy*, or Popular Common-wealth: when an Assembly of a Part onely, then it is called an *Aristocracy*.' The idea of democracy thus stood for 'a council which is made up of *all the citizens*, and in which every citizen has the right to vote'. By contrast, 'a council made up of *select citizen*' was an aristocracy (cf S Pufendorf, *On the Law of Nature and Nations*, Volume II, 1024–5). Our modern notion of democracy speaks of 'representative democracy'—a contradiction in terms for ancient philosophers. For them, the idea of representation of the people by a parliament would correspond to an (elective) aristocracy.

[8] On the theory of 'speech acts' generally: JL Austin, *How to do Things with Words*.

[9] K Popper, *The Poverty of Historicism*.

[10] The counter-current to the idea of undivided sovereignty in the seventeenth-century federal tradition was L Hugo's *De Statu Regionum Germaniae* (1708). Hugo applied the idea of double government and divided sovereignty to the German Empire. The nineteenth-century counter-current to the national federal tradition is represented by the work of G Waitz, *Das Wesen des Bundesstaates*, in: *Grundzüge der Politik* accepting the idea of divided sovereignty.

[11] The first century of the United States is aplenty with disputes over the question of sovereignty. The idea of undivided sovereignty could be found in both extremes: the international and the national format. The former was advocated in the writings of Calhoun; the latter was propagated in the works of Webster. For an excellent overview of the debate, see: F McDonald, *States' Rights and the Union: Imperio in Imperio*, 1776–1876.

The former was the sphere of subordination and compulsory law; the latter constituted the sphere of coordination and voluntary contract. From the perspective of classic international law, a 'civil law' between sovereigns was a contradiction in terms for it required an authority above the States; and if sovereignty was the defining characteristic of the modern State, there could be no such higher authority. All relations between States must be voluntary and, as such, 'beyond' any public legal force.[12]

How, then, did seventeenth-century international law explain 'Unions of States', like the Swiss Confederacy, the United Provinces of the Netherlands, and the German Empire? The classic tradition of the federal principle emerged in the discourse that tried to come to terms with these theoretical aberrations. In a pluralist system based on the idea of territorial sovereignty, Unions of States were constitutional oddities. These composed bodies raised serious conceptual problems in a normative world that prayed to the goddess State sovereignty. In order to bring Federal Unions into line with the new idea of State sovereignty, they were forced into a conceptual dichotomy: they were either an international (con)federation or a sovereign unitary State.[13] Thus, for Bodin the Swiss League was but a (con)federation in which the cantons had retained full sovereignty, while the German Empire was a unitary State governed by an aristocracy of princes.[14] The federal principle was

---

[12] Thence, the famous opening remarks by E de Vattel, *The Law of Nations* Preface, xiii: 'In the very outset of my work, it will be found that I differ entirely from Monsieur Wolf in the manner of establishing the foundations of that species of law of nations which we call *voluntary*. Monsieur Wolf deduces it from the idea of a great republic (*civitatis maximæ*) instituted by nature herself, and of which all nations of the world are members. According to him, the *voluntary* law of nations is, as it were, the civil law of that great republic. This idea does not satisfy me; nor do I think the fiction of such a republic either admissible in itself, or capable of affording sufficiently solid grounds on which to build the rules of the universal law of nations, which shall necessarily claim the obedient acquiescence of sovereign states. I acknowledge no other natural society between nations than that which nature has established between mankind in general. It is essential to every civil society (*civitati*) that each member have resigned a part of his right to the body of the society, and that there exist in it an authority capable of commanding all the members, of giving them laws, and of compelling those who should refuse to obey. Nothing of this kind can be conceived or supposed to subsist between nations. Each sovereign state claims, and actually possesses, an absolute independence on all the others.'

[13] O von Gierke, *The Development of Political Theory*, 263.

[14] J Bodin, *Method for the Easy Comprehension of History*, 165–6 and 207: 'But that all ambiguity be removed, we may ask whether governments federated among themselves can create one and the same state; for example, the city-states of the Swiss ... But to have exchange of goods, sanctity of contract, rights of intermarriage and of mutual entertainment, finally a firm bond of friendship does not create one and the same republic ... Thirteen Swiss city-states ... sealed a lawful alliance to the effect that they would not injure each other and that in their common peril they would fight their sword foes with mutual aid. But there is no common authority and no union .... Thus the

thus associated with *international* relationships between sovereign States.[15] A (con)federation was an international 'Union of States'. The most influential seventeenth-century treatise on the law of nations gave it the following definition:

[A Union of States] consists of several States bound to each other by a perpetual treaty, and which is usually occasioned by the fact that the individual States wished to preserve their [autonomy], and yet had not sufficient strength to repel their common enemies. *In this treaty there is commonly an agreement that one or other part of the supreme sovereignty should be exercised at the consent of all.* For a treaty that gives rise to a [federal] system seems to differ from those treaties which are otherwise most commonly drawn up between States, chiefly in this: That in the others each people of the league agrees to certain mutual performances, yet in such a way that they are on no account willing to make the exercise of that part of the sovereignty from which those performances flow dependent upon the consent of their associates, nor to limit in any degree their complete and unlimited power to conduct the affairs of their State. So also simple treaties have usually before their eyes only the particular advantage of the different States, as it happens to coincide, and do not produce any lasting Union in matters which concern the chief object of States. *The case is entirely different with the treaties that appear in [federal] systems, the purpose of which is that distinct States may intertwine for all time the prime interests of their safety, and on that score make the exercise of certain parts of the supreme power dependent upon the mutual consent of their associates.*[16]

This view recognized the difference between temporary and *permanent* treaties. In a Federal Union, sovereign States were bound together by a 'perpetual' treaty—the 'articles of confederation'. They would delegate powers that were of common interest to a 'council' and retain their independence for those matters that were 'of little or no interest, at least directly, to the rest'. In a 'regular' Federal Union, all the Member States would be equal and independent. This meant that they could 'voluntarily leave the league and administer their States to themselves'. A regular Union would fully respect the sovereignty of its members and thus operate by unanimity.

separate city-states of the Helvetians are bound by decrees of the others only so far as they voluntarily agree, as in private partnerships. On the contrary, in one and the same domination what pleases the majority binds all. A different opinion must be given about the . . . German imperial towns and provinces, which compose a state because they are subordinated to the same empire and the same emperor.' But since 'the princes have more power over the citizens than the emperor himself has' Germany was 'an aristocratic state'.

[15]   Locke therefore identified the 'federative power' as 'the power of war and peace, leagues and alliances, and all the transactions with all persons and communities without the commonwealth'; cf J Locke, *Two Treatises of Government*, § 146.

[16]   S Pufendorf, *The Law of Nature and Nations*, 1046–7 (emphasis added).

'For the liberty of a State, which is nothing other than the power to decide on its own judgement about matters pertaining to its self-preservation, is unintelligible in case it can be forced by another, acting with authority, to undertake something against its will.' 'For it is one thing if I say, "I will not exercise my right unless you are willing," and another to say, "You will have the right to require me to exercise my right, even though I be unwilling." The first, but not the second, is contained in the treaty of Union.' Where the unanimity principle was replaced by majority rule, the Federal Union became 'an irregular system, and one that approaches more closely to the nature of a State'.[17]

This view became the gold standard for modern international law. It resurfaces in *the* international law manual of the eighteenth century: de Vattel's 'Law of Nations'. 'Every nation that governs itself, under what form soever, without dependence on any foreign power, is a *Sovereign State*'; and a State that wishes to be part of international society must be a sovereign State.[18] Hence, in all of its relations with other States, it is fundamental to retain sovereignty.[19] This meant the following for Federal Unions:

§ 10. Of States forming a Federal Republic

Finally, several sovereign and independent States may unite themselves together by a perpetual confederacy, *without ceasing to be, each individually, a perfect State.* They will together constitute a federal republic: *their joint deliberations will not impair the sovereignty of each member, though they may, in certain respects, put some restraint on the exercise of it,* in virtue of voluntary engagements. A person does not cease to be free and independent, when he is obliged to fulfil engagements which he has voluntarily contracted. Such were formerly the cities of Greece; such are at *present* the Seven United Provinces of the Netherlands, and such the members of the Helvetic body.

§ 11. Of a State that has passed under the dominion of another.

But a people that has passed under the dominion of another is no longer a State, and can no longer avail itself directly of the law of nations. Such were the nations and kingdoms which the Romans rendered subject to their empire; the generality even of those whom they honoured with the name of friends and allies no longer formed

---

[17] Ibid 1050–2.

[18] E de Vattel, *The Law of Nations*, Book I, §4: 'To give a nation a right to make an immediate figure in this grand society, it is sufficient that it be really sovereign and independent, that is, that it governs itself by its own authority and laws.'

[19] In Book I, Chapter I of 'The Law of Nations', Vattel discusses the various relations between States, known at his time: States bound by unequal alliance (§5), States bound by treaties of protection (§6), States bound by tributary treaties (§7), States bound by feudal oaths (§8), States united under the same prince (§9); and finally States bound by federal treaty (§10).

real States. Within themselves they were governed by their own laws and magistrates; but without, they were in every thing obliged to follow the orders of Rome; they dared not of themselves either to make war or contract alliances; and could not treat with nations.[20]

A federal treaty was, unlike an ordinary international 'pact', designed to be enduring and would involve the establishment of a permanent diplomatic congress. Yet, the 'joint deliberations' among the Member States must not impair the sovereignty of each member. The obligations within the Union would be 'voluntary engagements' that allowed each member to remain a 'perfect State'. The Federal Union under international law ended, where a State 'passed under the dominion' of another. Such a subordinated body was 'no longer a State' and could 'no longer avail itself directly of the law of nations'.

But why would States wish to federalise? Two famous answers were given in the eighteenth century. The first offered a particular rationale, the second a universal rationale. In 'The Spirit of the Laws', de Montesquieu advanced a concrete reason for republics to federate. 'If a republic is small, it is destroyed by a foreign force; if it is large, it is destroyed by an internal vice.' To overcome this 'dual drawback', democracies would need to combine 'all the internal advantages of republican government and the external force of monarchy'. The solution was the creation of a 'federal republic'. 'This form of government is an *agreement* by which many political bodies consent to become citizens of the larger State that they want to form. It is a society of societies that make a new one, which can be enlarged by new associates that unite with it'.[21] Composed of small republics, the 'federal republic' thus 'enjoys the goodness of internal government of each one; and, with regard to the exterior, it has, by the force of the association, all the advantages of large monarchies'.[22] The confederated States would retain their sovereignty—this suggested unanimous decision-making;[23] and, in the event of a disagreement, the confederation could be dissolved.

A second—universalist—rationale came from the pen of the German philosopher Kant. In his 'Perpetual Peace—A Philosophical Sketch', Kant argued that the very idea of international *law* could only be achieved on the basis of a

---

[20] Ibid 3–4.

[21] Ch de Montesquieu, *The Spirit of the Laws*, 131.

[22] Ibid 132.

[23] '[C]omme chaque partie a conservé la souveraineté, il peut être fort bien établi que toutes les resolutions, pour être executés, soient unanimes' (Ch de Montesquieu, *Oeuvres complètes*, 1005). On this point, the final version of the 'Spirit of the Law' is more cautious. Book 9, Chapter III, dealing with '[o]ther things required in the federal republic' only states that provinces should not make alliances without the consent of the other provinces (ibid 133).

Federal Union of sovereign States.[24] For Kant, international society had remained in a state of nature. And the only solution to this sorry state of affairs was that 'peace must be *formally instituted*' on the basis of a federal treaty.[25] The second definitive article of such a treaty was entitled '[t]he Right of Nations shall be based on a Federation of Free States'. It is explained in the following way:

Each nation, for the sake of its own security, can and ought to demand of the others that they should enter along with it into *a constitution, similar to the civil one*, within which the rights of each should be secured. This would mean establishing a *federation of peoples. But a federation of this sort would not be the same thing as an international State.* For the idea of an international State is contradictory, since every State involves a relationship between a superior (the legislator) and an inferior (the people obeying the laws), whereas a number of nations forming one State would constitute a single nation. And this contradicts our initial assumption, as we are here considering the right of nations in relation to one another in so far as they are a group of separate States which are not to be welded together as a unit . . . But peace can neither be inaugurated nor secured without a general agreement between the nations; thus a particular kind of league, which we might call a *pacific federation (foedus pacificum)*, is required. It would differ from a *peace treaty (pactum pacis)* in that the latter terminates *one* war, whereas the former would seek to end *all* wars for good. *This federation does not aim to acquire any power like that of a State, but merely to preserve and secure the freedom of each State in itself, along with that of the other confederated States, although this does not mean that they need to submit to public laws and to a coercive power which enforces them, as do men in a state of nature.*[26]

The Federation of States was to be based on a constitutive treaty, the *foedus pacificum*. The treaty would be the basis of all international law as a *right* to peace. Yet, at the same time, the federal treaty would not provide the federation with 'any power like that of a State'. The States would not 'need to submit to public laws and a coercive power which enforces them'; and, in this way, their sovereignty was not restricted. A federation of peoples organized as States would thus not itself be an international State. (The latter would, according to Kant, turn national peoples into one single people.) While the idea of a world republic could be desirable in the distant future, the social

---

[24] I Kant, *Perpetual Peace*, in *Political Writings*, 103: 'It is therefore to be wondered at that the word *right* has not been completely banished from military politics as superfluous pedantry, and that no State has been bold enough to declare itself publicly in favour of doing so. For Hugo Grotius, Pufendorf, Vattel and the rest (sorry comforters as they are) are still dutifully quoted in *justification* of military aggression, although their philosophically and diplomatically formulated codes do not and cannot have the slightest *legal* force, since States as such are not subject to a common external constraint'.

[25] Ibid 98.

[26] Ibid 102 and 104 (emphasis added).

structure of international society was not ripe. In the light of the cultural diversity of mankind, a world republic would lead to international despotism.[27] Temporarily, Kant thus preferred the 'negative substitute' in the form of a federation of States. This practical optimum would better reflect the social structure of eighteenth-century society.

2. *The American Tradition: The 'Mixed' Format of the Federal Principle*

The international format of the federal idea prevailed at the time of the American Revolution. And it is only against the intellectual background of eighteenth-century federal thought that we can appreciate the semantic revolution that was to take place in America. The 'Articles of Confederation and Perpetual Union'—the first American Constitution—had still breathed the classic tradition of the federal principle. The Articles established a 'Confederacy' under the name of 'The United States of America'.[28] The thirteen States promised to 'hereby severally enter into a firm league of friendship with each other, for their common defense, the security of their liberties, and their mutual and general welfare, binding themselves to assist each other, against all force offered to, or attacks made upon them, or any of them'.[29] Within the confederacy, '[e]ach state retains its sovereignty, freedom, and independence, and every power, jurisdiction, and right, which is not by this Confederation expressly delegated to the United States, in Congress assembled'.[30] While not in perfect accord with eighteenth-century doctrine— the Articles allowed for majority voting—they had remained loyal to the classic idea of federalism as an international Union of sovereign States.[31]

   The semantic departure from the classic tradition came with the second American Union. The meaning of the federal principle would be forever changed by the most important 'speech act' in the history of constitutional federalism: the 1787 Constitution of the United States of America. Having realized the 'vices' and weaknesses of the old Union, deliberations on a 'more perfect union' began in 1787 by a Constitutional Convention meeting in Philadelphia. The Convention's draft proposed a more 'consolidated' Union. The project triggered a debate on the 'international' or 'national' character of

---

[27] I Kant, *Theory and Practice*, in I Kant, *Political Writings*, 90 and 92.

[28] Article I of the Articles of Confederation. The Articles were drafted in 1777, but would only enter into force in 1781 after the last State—Maryland—had ratified the treaty establishing the Union.

[29] Article III of the Articles of Confederation.

[30] Article II of the Articles of Confederation.

[31] SR Davis, *The Federal Principle: A Journey through Time in Quest of a Meaning*, 75.

the suggested constitutional structure. In the course of this debate, the old concept of federalism was rhetorically hijacked. Indeed, those advocating greater national consolidation styled themselves as 'federalists'; and the papers that defended the new constitutional structure would become known as 'The Federalist'.[32] By contrast, those insisting on the old 'international' nature of the American Union became—ironically—known as '*anti*-federalists'. The opponents of the new constitution complained that the Convention had been charged to 'preserve[] the *federal* form, which regards the Union as a *confederacy* of sovereign states'; 'instead of which, they have framed a *national* government, which regards the Unions as a *consolidation* of the States'. It was the response to this accusation that would provide the starting point of a completely new understanding of the federal idea. This new tradition would identify federalism with the 1787 constitutional compromise that placed the United States of America 'in between' an international and a national structure.

This new American tradition of the federal principle was immortalized by Madison. In the thirty-ninth paper of 'The Federalist', this grandmaster of constitutional analysis explored the 'federal' and/or 'national' characteristics of the proposed new legal order. ('Federal' still meant 'international', in the sense of respect for the sovereign equality of the States. 'National', by contrast, meant unitary, in the sense of one 'consolidated' central government.) Refusing to concentrate on the metaphysics of sovereignty, Madison singled out three analytical dimensions, which—for convenience—may be called: the foundational, the institutional, and the substantive dimension. The first relates to the origin and character of the new constitution; the second concerns the composition of its government; while the third deals with the scope and nature of the federal government's powers.

As regards the *foundational* dimension, the proposed 1787 Constitution was—like the 'Articles of Confederation'—a 'federal' act. What did this mean? It meant that the Constitution would be ratified 'by the people, not as individuals composing one entire nation, but as composing the distinct and independent States to which they respectively belong'. The '*unanimous* assent of the several States' that decide to become parties to it was required. The Constitution would thus result 'neither from the decision of a *majority* of the

---

[32] A Hamilton, J Madison & J Jay, *The Federalist*. On the rhetorical usurpation of the federal idea, see also: M Diamond, *The Federalist's View of Federalism*, 23: 'we must remember that the choice of *The Federalist* as the title of the essays was regarded by many as a shrewd and unwarranted usurpation of that term'.

people of the Union, nor from that of a *majority* of the States'.[33] 'Each State, in ratifying the Constitution, is considered as a sovereign body, independent of all others, and only to be bound by its own voluntary act.' Thus, 'the new constitution will, if established, be a *federal*, and not a *national* act'.[34] However, the new legal order differed from the old one in an important respect. While the Articles of Confederation had been ratified by the State *legislatures*, the proposed Constitution was to be validated by 'the assent and ratification of the several States, *derived from the supreme authority in each State, the authority of the people themselves*'.[35] Instead of the State *governments*—the delegates of the people—each State *people* itself would have to ratify the Constitution. This was the meaning behind the famous 'We, the people'. However, it was not the 'American people', but the people(s) of the several States that would ordain the 1787 Constitution.[36] The direct authority from the (State) people(s) would set the Constitution above the State *governments*. And in having the peoples of each State ratify the Constitution, the 1787 document would be a 'constitutional'—and not a mere 'legislative'—treaty.

---

[33] J Madison, *The Federalist No 39*, 184. To bring the point home, Madison continues (ibid 185): 'Were the people regarded in this transaction as forming one nation, the will of the majority of the whole people of the United States would bind the minority, in the same manner as the majority in each State must bind the minority; and the will of the majority must be determined either by a comparison of the individual votes, or by considering the will of the majority of the States as evidence of the will of a majority of the people of the United States. Neither of these rules have been adopted.'

[34] Ibid 185.

[35] Ibid 184 (emphasis added).

[36] The phrase 'We, the people of the United States' simply referred to the idea that the people(s) in the States—not the State legislatures—had ratified the Constitution. Thus, the preamble of the 1780 Massachusetts Constitution, to offer an illustration, read: 'We, therefore, the people of Massachusetts'. The original 1787 draft preamble indeed read: 'We, the people of the States of New Hampshire, Massachusetts, Rhode-Island and Providence Plantations, Connecticut, New-York, New-Jersey, Pennsylvania, Delaware, Maryland, Virginia, North-Carolina, South-Carolina, and Georgia, do ordain, declare and establish the following constitution for the government of ourselves and our posterity.' However, due to the uncertainty which of the thirteen States would succeed in the ratification (according to Article VII of the Constitution-to-be only nine States were required for the document to enter into force), the enumeration of the individuals States was dropped by the 'Committee of Style' (cf M Farrand, *The Framing of the Constitution of the United States*, 190–1). Even a staunch nationalist as Chief Justice J Marshall admitted that 'the people' had ratified the 1787 Constitution as 'state peoples' (cf *McCulloch v Maryland*, 17 US 316 (1819), 403): 'No political dreamer was ever wild enough to think of breaking down the lines which separate the States, and of compounding the American people into one common mass. Of consequence, when they act, they act in their States. But the measures they adopt do not, on that account, cease to be the measures of the people themselves, or become the measures of the State governments.'

What authority could amend the new Constitution once it had been 'ordained'? Unlike the Articles of Confederation, the 1787 Constitution would not require unanimity for amendment. The new amendment procedure was set out in Article V of the 1787 Constitution.[37] The provision stipulated that each proposed amendment would have to be ratified by three quarters of the States—represented by a State convention or by its State legislature.[38] Once the Constitution would enter into force, the power of amending it was thus 'neither wholly *national* nor wholly *federal*'. 'Were it wholly national, the supreme and ultimate authority would reside in the *majority* of the people of the Union; and this authority would be competent at all times, like that of a majority of every national society, to alter or abolish its established government. Were it wholly federal, on the other hand, the concurrence of each State in the Union would be essential to every alteration that would be binding on all'.[39]

Having analysed the origin and nature of the 1787 Constitution, Madison then moved to the second aspect of the new constitutional structure. In relation to the *institutional* dimension, the following picture emerged. The legislature of the new Union was composed of two branches. The House of Representatives was elected by all the people of America as individuals and therefore was the 'national' branch of the central government.[40] The Senate, on the other hand, would represent the States as 'political and

[37] Article V reads: 'The Congress, whenever two thirds of both Houses shall deem it necessary, shall propose Amendments to this Constitution, or, on the Application of the Legislatures of two thirds of the several States, shall call a Convention for proposing Amendments, which, in either Case, shall be valid to all Intents and Purposes, as part of this Constitution, when ratified by the Legislatures of three fourths of the several States, or by Conventions in three fourths thereof, as the one or the other Mode of Ratification may be proposed by the Congress; Provided that no Amendment which may be made prior to the Year One thousand eight hundred and eight shall in any Manner affect the first and fourth Clauses in the Ninth Section of the first Article; and that no State, without its Consent, shall be deprived of its equal Suffrage in the Senate'.

[38] The structure of the amendment power led Dicey to conclude that 'the legal sovereignty of the United States resides in the States' governments as forming one aggregate body represented by three-fourths of the several States at any time belonging to the Union' (cf AV Dicey, *Introduction to the Study of the Law of the Constitution*, 81).

[39] J Madison, *The Federalist No 39*, 186–7.

[40] The 'national' structure of the House of Representatives would not be immediately created by the 1787 Constitution. Article I, Section 4 stated: 'The Times, Places and Manner of holding Elections for Senators and Representatives, shall be prescribed in each State by the Legislature thereof; but Congress may at any time make or alter such Regulations, except as to the Place of choosing Senators.' In the words of H Wechsler (cf *The Political Safeguards of Federalism: The Role of States in the Composition and Selection of the National Government*, 546): 'Though the House was meant to be the "grand depository of the democratic principle of the government," as distinguished from the Senate's function as the forum of the states, the people to be represented with due reference to

coequal societies'.[41] And in respecting their sovereign equality, the Senate was viewed as a 'federal' organ. Every law required the concurrence of a majority of the people and a majority of the States. The President's authority, lastly, derived from a 'very compound source': it involved the States as political societies, but '[t]he votes allotted to them are in a compound ratio, which considers them partly as distinct and coequal societies, partly as unequal members of the same society'. Overall, the structure of the central government thus had 'a mixed character, presenting at least as many *federal* as *national* features'.[42]

Finally, 'The Federalist' analysed a third dimension of the new constitutional order. In terms of substance, the powers of the central government showed both federal and national characteristics. In relation to their *scope*, they were surely 'federal', since the idea of a national government implied competence over all objects of government. Thus, 'the proposed government cannot be deemed a *national* one; since its jurisdiction extends to certain enumerated objects only, and leaves to the several States a residuary and inviolable sovereignty over all other objects'.[43] However, unlike the Articles of Confederation, the *nature* of the powers of the central government was 'national' in character. The distinction between a (con)federation and a national government was that 'in the former the powers operate on the political bodies composing the Confederacy, in their political capacities; in the latter, on the individual citizens composing the nation, in their

their respective numbers were *the people of the states.*' The first national electoral law for the House would only be adopted in 1842.

[41] J Madison, *The Federalist No 39*, 185. In 'The Federalist No 62', Madison adds (ibid 301): 'In this spirit it may be remarked, that the equal vote allowed to each State is at once a constitutional recognition of the portion of sovereignty remaining in the individual States, and an instrument for preserving that residuary sovereignty. So far the equality ought to be no less acceptable to the large than to the small States; since they are not less solicitous to guard, by every possible expedient, against an improper consolidation of the States into one simple republic'.

[42] Ibid 185.

[43] Ibid 186. In comparison with the Articles of Confederation, the proposed Constitution would not significantly enlarge the enumerated powers of the central level, except for the added competence to regulate commerce. Thus, 'The Federalist No 45' could justly claim that '[t]he powers delegated by the proposed Constitution to the federal government, are few and defined', whereas '[t]hose which are to remain in the State governments are numerous and indefinite' (ibid 227). What about constitutional disputes between the federation and its States? Madison's answer was this (ibid, 186): 'It is true that in controversies relating to the boundary between the two jurisdictions, the tribunal which is ultimately to decide, is to be established under the general government. But this does not change the principle of the case. The decision is to be impartially made, according to the rules of the Constitution; and all the usual and most effectual precautions are taken to secure this impartiality'.

individual capacities'.[44] The 1787 Constitution allowed the central government to operate directly on individuals and thus fell on the national side.

In the light of these three constitutional dimensions, 'The Federalist' concluded that the overall constitutional structure of the 1787 Constitution was 'in strictness, neither a national nor a federal Constitution, *but a composition of both*'.[45] The central government was a 'mixed government'.[46] It stood on 'middle ground'.[47] And it was this *mixed* format of the reformed constitutional structure of the United States of America that would, in the future, be identified with the federal principle.

The American federal tradition came to Europe on board a French ship. The analysis by de Tocqueville brought the new ideas to a broader European audience.[48] His influential account of the structure of American society also described the Federal Union as a 'middle ground' between an international league and a national government. The mixed nature of the American Union was, according to de Tocqueville, particularly reflected in the composition of the central legislator. The Union was neither a pure international league, in which the States would have remained on a footing of perfect—sovereign—equality. Nor was it a national government; for if 'the inhabitants of the United States were to be considered as belonging to one and the same nation, it would be natural that the majority of the citizens of the Union should make the law'. The 1787 Constitution had chosen a 'middle course', '*which brought together by force two systems theoretically irreconcilable*'.[49] A middle ground had also been reached in relation to the powers of government: 'The sovereignty

---

[44] Ibid 185. In 'The Federalist No 15', we hear Hamilton say (ibid 67): 'The great and radical vice in the construction of the existing Confederation is in the principle of LEGISLATION for STATES or GOVERNMENTS, in their CORPORATE or COLLECTIVE CAPACITIES, and as contradistinguished from the INDIVIDUALS of which they consist. Though this principle does not run through all the powers delegated to the Union, yet it pervades and governs those on which the efficacy of the rest depends.' And in the words of the same author in 'The Federalist No 16' (ibid 74): 'It must stand in need of no intermediate legislations; but must itself be empowered to employ the arm of the ordinary magistrate to execute its own resolutions. The majesty of the national authority must be manifested through the medium of the courts of justice'.

[45] Ibid 187.

[46] 'The Federalist No 40'—Title.

[47] Letter of J Madison to G Washington of 16 April 1787: 'Conceiving that an individual independence of the States is utterly irreconcileable with their aggregate sovereignty; and that a consolidation of the whole into one simple republic would be as inexpedient as it is unattainable, I have sought for some middle ground, which may at once support a due supremacy of the national authority, and not exclude the local authorities wherever they can be subordinately useful'.

[48] A de Tocqueville, *Democracy in America*.

[49] Ibid 122–3.

of the United States is shared between the Union and the States, while in France it is undivided and compact'. 'The Americans have a Federal and the French a national Government'.[50] In fact, the unique aim of the 1787 Constitution 'was to divide the sovereign authority into two parts': 'In the one they placed the control of all the general interests of the Union, in the other the control of the special interests of its component States'.[51] The cardinal quality of the Union's powers was their direct effect: like a State government, the Union government could act directly on individuals. The American 'federal' arrangement thus differed from previous conceptions of federalism:

This Constitution, which may at first sight be confused with the federal constitutions that have preceded it, *rests in truth upon a wholly novel theory, which may be considered as a great discovery in modern political science*. In all the confederations that preceded the American Constitution of 1789 the States allied for a common object agreed to obey the injunctions of a federal government; but they reserved to themselves the right of ordaining and enforcing the execution of the laws of the union . . .

The human understanding more easily invents new things than new words, and we are hence constrained to employ many improper and inadequate expressions. When several nations form a permanent league and establish a supreme authority, which, although it cannot act upon private individuals like a national government, still acts upon each of the confederate States in a body, this government, which is so essentially different from all others, is called Federal. *Another form of society is afterwards discovered in which several peoples are fused into one with regard to certain common interests, although they remain distinct, or only confederate, with regard to all other concerns. In this case the central power acts directly upon the governed, whom it rules and judges in the same manner as a national government, but in a more limited circle. Evidently this is no longer a federal government, but an incomplete national government, which is neither exactly national nor exactly federal; but the new word which ought to express this novel thing does not yet exist.*[52]

But, instead of a 'new word' to define the new thing, it was the new thing that came to define the 'old' word. Abandoning the classic tradition of the federal idea, the 'novel theory' of federalism placed the federal idea on the middle ground between international and national law. The 1787 system itself became identified with 'federal' government and this speech act changed the semantic content of the federal principle forever. Sovereignty—while ultimately resting somewhere—was seen as delegated and divided between *two* levels of government. Each State had given up part of its sovereignty,[53]

---

[50] Ibid 128.

[51] Ibid 151.

[52] Ibid 162–4.

[53] 'The Federalist No 42' ridiculed the theory according to which the absolute sovereignty had remained in the States: 'the articles of Confederation have inconsiderately endeavored to

while the national government remained 'incomplete'. And because both governments enjoyed powers that were 'sovereign', the new federalism was identified with the idea that '[t]wo sovereignties are necessarily in presence of each other'.[54] Federalism implied *dual* government, *dual* sovereignty, and also *dual* citizenship.[55]

Importantly, in the early American tradition the Union was not identified with a Federal State. The Union was not referred to in the singular *United States*, but conceived as a plural—the United *States*.[56] The use of the plural form 'unwittingly expressed the *emotional* fact'. 'This habit of thinking and feeling state-by-state was slow to disappear'.[57] The turning point for the federal

accomplish impossibilities; to reconcile a partial sovereignty in the Union, with complete sovereignty in the States; to subvert a mathematical axiom, by taking away a part, and letting the whole remain' (A Hamilton, J Madison & J Jay, *The Federalist*, 206).

[54] A de Tocqueville, *Democracy in America*, 172.

[55] On the concept of dual citizenship in federal orders, see: O Beaud, *The Question of Nationality within a Federation: a Neglected Issue in Nationality Law*; as well as C Schönberger, *Unionsbürger: Europas föderales Bürgerrecht in vergleichender Sicht.*

[56] The Constitution itself uses the phrase 'United States' consistently as a plural (cf Article III, Section 3: 'Treason against the United States, shall consist only in levying war against *them*' (emphasis added)). While the linguistic convention was eventually to disappear in English, it still exists in French and German. Here, the 'United States' is still a plural noun: '*les* États-Unis' or '*die* Vereinigten Staaten'.

[57] DJ Boorstin, *The Americans: The National Experience*, 402–3. That the loyalty of the American people(s) would predominantly lie with their States, rather than the federal government, had been predicted by 'The Federalist No 17' (cf A Hamilton et al, *The Federalist*, 77): 'It is a known fact in human nature, that its affections are commonly weak in proportion to the distance or diffusiveness of the object. Upon the same principle that a man is more attached to his family than to his neighborhood, to his neighborhood than to the community at large, the people of each State would be apt to feel a stronger bias towards their local governments than towards the government of the Union; unless the force of that principle should be destroyed by a much better administration of the latter.' 'There is one transcendent advantage belonging to the province of the State governments, which alone suffices to place the matter in a clear and satisfactory light,–I mean the ordinary administration of criminal and civil justice. This, of all others, is the most powerful, most universal, and most attractive source of popular obedience and attachment. It is that which, being the immediate and visible guardian of life and property, having its benefits and its terrors in constant activity before the public eye, regulating all those personal interests and familiar concerns to which the sensibility of individuals is more immediately awake, contributes, more than any other circumstance, to impressing upon the minds of the people, affection, esteem, and reverence towards the government. This great cement of society, which will diffuse itself almost wholly through the channels of the particular governments, independent of all other causes of influence, would insure them so decided an empire over their respective citizens as to render them at all times a complete counterpoise, and, not unfrequently, dangerous rivals to the power of the Union.' That the loyalty to a national 'authority' was emotionally weaker than the loyalty owed to one's State was also de Tocqueville's conviction (cf *Democracy in America*, 175): 'The sovereignty of the Union is an abstract being, which is connected with but few external objects; the sovereignty of the States is perceptible by the senses, easily understood, and constantly active. The former is of recent creation,

equilibrium was the Civil War (1861–65). Prior to the Civil War, the term 'State' had been reserved for the parts of the Union. This would gradually change thereafter. 'In a very real sense, the constitutional bargain of 1787 was redefined by the Civil War, with that reformulation being marked by the Fourteenth Amendment and the creation of a national citizenship'.[58] After the Civil War emotional supremacy was gradually transferred to the American nation; and this evolution was one catalyst towards a more *united* American *State*.

3. *The European Tradition: The 'National' Format of the Federal Principle*

The American federal theory became known and influential in Europe. 'The Federalist' became the 'Magna Carta' of federal imagination.[59] However, a victim of the nineteenth century's obsession with sovereign States,[60] European federal thought came to reject the idea of a divided or dual sovereignty. Sovereignty was indivisible. It could lie with the States, in which case the Union was a voluntary international organization; or sovereignty would lie with the Union, in which case the Union was a 'State'. The 'new' federalism was thus thought of in terms of a sovereign State. The 'Federal State' was seen as the 'new world' that de Tocqueville had been searching for.

This statist redefinition of the federal principle gave birth to a third tradition: the national format of the federal idea. To distinguish between the 'old' international and the 'new' national format, European constitutional thought developed a conceptual distinction between two species of (con)federal organization by having recourse to the concepts of 'Confederation' and 'Federation'. Originally, the two concepts were synonyms.[61] But in comparing

the latter is coeval with the people itself. The sovereignty of the Union is factitious, that of the States is natural and self-existent, without effort, like the authority of a parent.'

[58] E Katz, *The Development of American Federalism, 1763-1865*, 48. Before the Civil War, it was the State citizenship that procured federal citizenship. The Fourteenth Amendment would invert this relationship. The 1868 Amendment states: 'All persons born or naturalized in the United States and subject to the jurisdiction thereof, are citizens of the United States and the State wherein they reside.' Since then, State citizenship derives from federal citizenship and the States lost their right to determine membership in their polity. On the changing relationship, see the brilliant analysis of C Schönberger (n 55 above) 61–80.

[59] E Deuerlein, *Föderalismus: Die historischen und philosophischen Grundlagen des föderativen Prinzips*, 54.

[60] M Koskenniemi, *From Apology to Utopia*, Chapter 4.

[61] M Diamond, *The Federalist's View of Federalism*, 1274: '*The Federalist* and the whole founding generation saw no more difference between confederalism and federalism than we see, say, between the words inflammable and flammable; nothing more was involved than the accidently presence of a nonsignifying prefix'.

the 1777 Articles of *Confederation* with the 1787 *Federation*, European thought distilled and juxtaposed two *different* constitutional principles. The two ideal-ized principles came to be known as the *confederal* principle and the *federal* principle. This semantic distinction enjoyed an immense success in European constitutional thought in the nineteenth century. The 'Confederation of States' was identified with the 'old' international format of the federal princi-ple, whereas the 'Federal State' became the 'new' national manifestation of the federal principle. The federal genus identified by the American tradition would gradually be forgotten.

Within this European tradition, federalism came to refer to the *constitu-tional* devolution of power within a sovereign nation.[62] A federation was a Federal State. This 'national' reduction of the federal principle censored the very idea of a 'Federation *of States*'. To understand this European tradition of the federal idea,[63] we will analyse the conceptual polarization that occured in nineteenth-century Europe, before presenting two early critics of the new European tradition.

a. Conceptual Polarization: 'Confederation' versus 'Federation'

European constitutionalism insisted on the indivisibility of sovereignty.[64] This *absolute* idea of sovereignty came to operate as a prism that would blind out all *relative* nuances within a mixed or compound legal structure. The result was a conceptual polarization expressed in a distinction between two idealized categories: *either* a Union of States was a 'Confederation of States' *or* it was a 'Federal *State*'. Both concepts constituted legal ideal-types.

---

[62] DJ Elazar, *Constitutionalizing Globalization: The Postmodern Revival of Confederal Arrangements*, 39: 'Federation, indeed, is federalism applied to constitutionally defuse power within the political system of a single nation. Federation became synonymous with modern federalism because the modern epoch was the era of the nation-state when, in most of the modern world, the ideal was to establish a single centralized state with indivisible sovereignty to serve single nations or peoples.'

[63] In the nineteenth century, Germany and Switzerland were Europe's 'federal' entities. Austria and Belgium would be added in the twentieth century. On the constitutional history of German federal thought, see: Deuerlein (n 59 above). On the constitutional history of Swiss federalism, see: A Kölz, *Neue Schweizerische Verfassungsgeschichte*.

[64] One British, one French and one German 'representative' will suffice to support this point: cf A Dicey, *Introduction to the Study of the Law of the Constitution*, 3: 'Parliament is, under the British Constitution, an absolutely sovereign legislature'; R Carré de Malberg, *Contribution à la théorie général de l'état*, 139–40: 'La souveraineté est entière ou elle cesse de se concevoir. Parler de souve-raineté restreinte, relative ou divisée, c'est commettre une *contradiction in adjecto* . . . Il n'est donc pas possible d'admettre dans l'État federal un partage de la souveraineté[.]'; and P Laband, *Das Staatsrecht des Deutschen Reiches*, 73: 'die Souveränität eine Eigenschaft absoluten Charakters ist, die keine Steigerung und keine Verminderung zuläßt'.

While American federalism accepted gradations on the spectrum between a (con)federation and a unitary State,[65] semantic fluidity was unacceptable to European conceptual legal science (*Begriffsjurisprudenz*). European federal thought followed a deductive approach, in which conceptual definition came to precede and prevail over empirical legal analysis. The conceptual distortion effected by the sovereignty prism would thereby downgrade all existing *weak* (con)federations to ordinary international organizations and upgrade all existing strong (con)federations to ordinary unitary States. Mixed features were aberrations, if not imaginations, and were interpreted away.[66] *Was nicht sein darf, das nicht sein kann!*

How did European federal thought define a 'confederation'? A (confederal) Union of States was said to have been formed on the basis of an ordinary international treaty. Because it was an international treaty, the States had retained sovereignty and, therewith, the right to nullification and secession. 'Nullification and secession, absolutely prohibited within a unitary or federal State, follow logically from the nature of the Confederation as a treaty creature. A sovereign State cannot be bound unconditionally and permanently.' 'The Confederation is a creature of international law. However, international law knows no other legal subjects than States. The Confederation is not a State and can, consequently, not constitute a subject of international law'.[67] Since the confederation was not a legal subject, it could not be the author of legal obligations; and it 'deductively' followed that the Member States *themselves* were the authors of the Union's commands.[68] The Union was thus regarded as possessing no powers of its own. It only 'pooled' and exercised

---

[65] The 1777 and the 1787 American constitutional structures were a mixture of 'international' and 'national' elements. J Madison readily admitted this in 'The Federalist No 40' (cf A Hamilton et al, *The Federalist*, 191): 'The truth is, that the great principles of the Constitution proposed by the convention may be considered less as absolutely new, than as the expansion of principles which are found in the Articles of Confederation. The misfortune under the latter system has been, that these principles are so feeble and confined as to justify all the charges of inefficiency which have been urged against it, and to require a degree of enlargement which gives to the new system the aspect of an entire transformation of the old'.

[66] The insistance on 'sharp' legal categories allowed for no gradations between 'confederation' and 'federal State'; and once sovereignty was the selected criterion, all conceptual nuances and semantic fluidity could be removed from the discussion as superficial social appearances that did not concern the legal essence of (con)federal unions. On the dynamics of conceptual polarization, see: G Jellinek, *Die Lehre von den Staatenverbindungen* 173; as well as C Schönberger, *Die Europäische Union als Bund*.

[67] G Jellinek (n 66 above) 175 and 178 (translation—RS).

[68] Ibid 176.

State power. From this international law perspective, the confederation was not an autonomous 'entity', but a mere 'relation' between sovereign States.

How did European federal thought define the concept of the 'Federal State'? The Federal State was regarded as a *State*; and, as such, it was sovereign—even if national unification had remained 'incomplete'. Because the Federal State was as sovereign as a unitary State, constitutional differences between the two States needed to be downplayed to superficial 'marks of sovereignty'. It indeed became the task of nationalist scholarship to make the imperfect Nation State look like its unitary sisters. This was achieved through ingenious feats of legal 'reasoning'. A first argument asserted that when forming the Union, the States had lost all their sovereignty. They had been 're-established' as '*Member* States' *by the federal constitution*. These Member States were non-sovereign States.[69] But if the criterion of sovereignty could no longer be employed as the emblem of statehood, what justified calling these federated units 'States'? The search for a criterion that distinguished 'Member *States*' from 'administrative units' led European federal thought to insist on the existence of exclusive legislative powers.[70] In the succinct words of one of the most celebrated legal minds of that day: 'To the extent that the supremacy of the Federal State reaches, the Member States lose their character as States.' And contrariwise: 'To the extent that the Member States enjoy an exclusive sphere, but only to this extent, will they retain their character as States'.[71]

Could European constitutionalism explain the legal transformation of a 'Confederation' to a 'Federal State'? The dominant view held that such a transformation was impossible; yet, this appeared to have happened when the German Confederation (1815) transformed itself into the German Imperial State (1871). The former had been created by an international treaty;[72]

---

[69] A Hänel, *Deutsches Staatsrecht*, 802–3.

[70] G Jellinek (n 66 above) 43–4: 'Das Wesen eines zu eigenem Rechte zustehenden Herrschaftsrechts besteht also darin, dass auf einem begrenzten Gebiete staatlicher Tätigkeit eine öffentlich-rechtliche Corporation berechtigt ist, innerhalb desselben die regelnden Normen in letzter Instanz, mit Ausschluß einer Controle einer höheren Macht, zu erlassen. Eine solche Corporation lässt ich nach dem Vorangehenden unter dem Begriff "Staat" juristisch subsumieren'.

[71] G Jellinek, *Allgemeine Staatslehre*, 771–2 (translation—RS).

[72] Cf Articles 1 and 2 of the Final Vienna Act (1820): 'The German Confederation is a union under international law of the sovereign German princes and free cities, for the preservation of the independence and inviolability of the States included in its Confederation and for the maintenance of the domestic and external security of Germany. This union exists domestically as a community of independent States, none dominated by another, with mutual equal rights and obligations by treaty, but externally as a whole power bound in political unity'.

the latter was founded by a constitution.[73] But if a State or its constitution could not legally emerge from an international treaty, how did European federal thought conceal its 'Achilles heel'?[74] It concealed it by claiming that the birth of a State and its constitution was altogether beyond legal analysis. 'All attempts to derive the creation of a Federal State from an international treaty between its members must fail, since it is impossible legally to construct the creation of a State. The State, as the precondition for a legal order, cannot be explained on the basis of a norm whose very sanction follows from that order.' 'Nation States come into being when a people, which feels and knows itself to be a unity, expresses this unity in organising its State.' 'The people, as a natural unity, precedes the State; but through the State the *factual* people *(Nation)* constitutes itself as a *legal* people *(Staatsvolk)*.' The legal order thereby created is the constitution. 'The creation of a State thus coincides with the creation of the constitution, and a State's first constitution is posited by its existence'.[75]

The very existence of a State was 'always a matter of fact'. 'The constitution of a newly formed State is, consequently, as much a matter of fact as the State itself. Neither can be legally construed'.[76] For the creation of a Federal State in particular this meant: even if an international treaty had initially brought sovereign States closer together, there was simply no legal causality between it and the foundation of the new Federal State. There could be no transformation from an international treaty to a national constitution. The latter emerged, together with the State, as a 'fact'—generated by a feeling of national unity.

Let us look at a last ingenious argument that was successfully developed to downplay the constitutional differences between a Federal State and a unitary State. In a Federal State powers are divided between the Federal State and its Member States. But if the characteristic element of a Member *State* was the possession of exclusive legislative power, how could the Federal State be said to be sovereign? The European answer to this question was that

---

[73] The Preamble of the 1871 Imperial Constitution stated: 'His Majesty the King of Prussia, in the name of the North German Confederation, His Majesty the King of Bavaria, His Majesty the King of Württemberg, His Royal Highness the Grand Duke of Baden, and His Royal Highness the Grand Duke of Hesse and the Rhine for those parts of the Grand Duchy of Hesse which are situated South of the Main, conclude an eternal alliance for the protection of the territory of the Confederation, and of the law of the same, as well as for the promotion of the welfare of the German people'.

[74] E Zoller, *Aspects internationaux du droit constitutionnel. Contribution à la théorie de la fédération d'états*, 52.

[75] G Jellinek, *Die Lehre von den Staatenverbindungen*, 265 (translation—RS).

[76] Ibid 262–6 (translation—RS).

all powers were ultimately derived from the Federal State, since it enjoyed 'competence-competence' *(Kompetenz-Kompetenz).*[77] This idea translated the unitary concept of sovereignty into a federal context: 'Whatever the actual distribution of competences, the Federal State retains its character as a sovereign State; and, as such, it potentially contains within itself all sovereign powers, even those whose autonomous exercise has been delegated to the Member States'.[78] If the Federal State is sovereign, it must be empowered to *unilaterally* amend its constitution. '[T]he power to change its constitution follows from the very concept of the sovereign State.' 'A State, whose existence depends on the good will of its members, is not sovereign; for sovereignty means independence'.[79]

The Federal State was, consequently, deemed to be empowered to 'nationalize' competences that were exclusively reserved to the Member States under the federal constitution—even against the will of the federated States. Through this process of 'unitarization', the Member States would gradually lose their 'statehood'; and since the power to unilaterally amend the constitution was unlimited,[80] the Federal State was said to enjoy the magical power of 'competence-competence' with which it could legally transform itself into a unitary State. 'The existence of the Member States in the Union is, as such, no absolute barrier to the federal will. Indeed, the option to transform the Member States into mere administrative units reveals, in the purest way, the sovereign nature of the Federal State.' 'The negation of this legal option to transform the Federal State into a unitary State by means of constitutional amendment entails with it the negation of the sovereign and, therefore, state *(staatlich)* character of the Federal State'.[81] In the final analysis, the European tradition of

---

[77] One of the best discussions of the concept of *Kompetenz-Kompetenz* can be found in: A Hänel, *Deutsches Staatsrecht,* 771–806.

[78] G Jellinek, *Die Lehre von den Staatenverbindungen,* 290–1 (translation—RS).

[79] Ibid 295–6 (translation—RS).

[80] A Hänel (n 77 above) 776: 'Die Kompetenz-Kompetenz des Reiches findet in der *Verfassung selbst* keine rechtliche Grenze.' Hänel proceeds to discuss the possibility of extra-constitutional limits imposed by the contractual nature of the Federation. However, the idea of a partial *Kompetenz-Kompetenz* is discarded. The Reich had been transformed into a State by the 'Constitutional Law' *(Verfassungsgesetz)* of the Empire; and therefore (ibid 779) 'steht dem Reiche die *volle Herrschaft über seine Kompetenz* zu—in dem nämlichen Sinne und Umfange wie dem Einheitsstaate im Verhältnis zu den ihm einverleibten gesellschaftlichen Organisationen'.

[81] G Jellinek (n 78 above) 304 and 306 (translation—RS). This has never been accepted by American constitutionalism, see: *Texas v White* (1868) 74 US 700 at 725: 'The Constitution, in all its provisions, looks to an indestructible Union composed of indestructible States.' The rejection of an omnipotent Federal State can now also be found in the modern German Constitution. According to its Article 79 (3) constitutional '[a]mendments to this Basic Law affecting the division

the federal principle thus equated the Federal State with a decentralized unitary State.[82] Federalism had become a purely 'national' phenomenon.

b. Early Criticism: The European Tradition and the (missing) Federal Genus

The conceptual polarization of the federal principle into two specific manifestations—confederation and federation—would structure much of the twentieth-century European debate. And yet, there were two remarkable early critics of that tradition. They could not be more different as regards their legal outlook. Kelsen *legally* approached the federal principle with the tools of his 'pure theory of law', while Schmitt concentrated on the *political* nature of federal orders.[83]

In 1920, Kelsen torpedoed the inconsistencies and tautologies inherent in European federal thought in a path-breaking analysis of the principle of sovereignty and the nature of international law.[84] While remaining loyal to the idea of indivisible sovereignty,[85] Kelsen attacked the categorical distinction between confederation and Federal State. Legally, they had a similar structure. What distinguished the one from the other was only their degree of (de)centralization:

Confederation and Federal State, these two main types of State relations, differ in the degree of centralization and decentralization only. In both cases, we are dealing with legal communities, whose legal order consists of norms that are valid throughout the federal territory and norms that are valid in only a part thereof. However, the scope and importance of objects regulated by central norms, and thus valid for the total federal territory, is in a Federal State—in contrast to a Confederation—greater than the objects regulated by local norms. Once the scope of the central competence reaches the threshold of a 'State', we refer to the former as a 'Federal State'; where it does not, we simply refer to the central legal order as a 'Confederation' of States . . .

The only way to justify that the difference between Federal State and Confederation is not a relative but an absolute distinction is to elevate the concept of 'State' itself to an absolute idea. But this absolute notion excludes the idea of other States 'inside'

of the Federation into *Länder*, their participation on principle in the legislative process . . . shall be inadmissible'.

[82]   H Triepel, *Unitarismus und Föderalismus im Deutschen Reiche*, 81.

[83]   None of these two brilliant critiques of traditional European federal thought enjoyed much influence outside Germany after the Second World War. This is perhaps not surprising in the light of Schmitt's disgraceful post-Weimar biography. In Kelsen's case, the reason may lie in the lack of a translation of 'Das Problem der Souveränität und die Theorie des Völkerrechts' and the disappointingly reductionist translation of the relevant chapter of his 'Allgemeine Staatslehre' in 'The General Theory of Law and State'.

[84]   H Kelsen, *Das Problem der Souveränität und die Theorie des Völkerrechts*.

[85]   Ibid 64–6.

a State as much as the idea of other States 'outside' it with whom the State is coordinated in a[n] [international] legal community, unless one posits the existence of a higher all-embracing whole that would turn these States into members and thereby deprive them of their sovereign quality. However, once we dissociate the concept of the 'State' from the idea of an absolute whole, once we relativize its meaning, then, the absolute distinction between Federal State and Confederation, insisted upon by traditional [European] constitutionalism, must also disappear. And that will permit us to refocus the analysis of Unions of States on the criterion that leads to the relative distinction between the two known types: the criterion of decentralization.[86]

A Federal State is simply a more 'consolidated' or 'centralized' union than a confederation. One federal species blends continuously into the other.[87] But what did this mean for the distinction between 'treaty' and 'constitution'? For Kelsen, 'treaty and constitution are not mutually exclusive concepts', since the content of a treaty may be a constitution. 'The Federal State may thus have a constitution and yet be founded on an international treaty as much as the confederation has its constitution that may also be created through a treaty'.[88] There was no objective or inherent distinction between 'treaty' and 'constitution' as regards their origin; what differed was the *emotional* feeling brought towards them. Sovereignty lay in the eye of the beholder; and for social communities, this was a question of social psychology. The community of onlookers decided which legal order was to be posited at the origin—the '*Grund*'. Sovereignty and supremacy were 'emotional' questions; and, as such, beyond empirical and normative analysis.[89] The categorical distinction between 'treaty' and 'constitution', which was advocated by the European federal tradition, was based on a *petitio principii*:

What matters is not, whether the treaty creates a legal order—every treaty does—but whether the legal order so created is considered as a partial legal order or as a total

---

[86] H Kelsen, *Allgemeine Staatslehre*, 194 (translation—RS).

[87] Ibid 195: 'eine Form *kontinuierlich* in die andere übergeht'.

[88] Ibid.

[89] This is the very essence of Kelsen's theory of sovereignty and the 'basic' norm, cf H Kelsen, *Das Problem der Souveränität und die Theorie des Völkerrechts*, 15: 'Weil Souveränität kein in der Außenwelt sozialer Tatsachen wahrnehmbares Faktum ist und solches nicht sein kann, sondern nichts anders als eine Annahme des Betrachters, eine Betrachtungs-, Wertungs-Voraussetzung ist, bedeutet die Frage: wann ist Souveränität gegeben: 1. Welches sind die *psychologischen* Bedingungen, unter denen ich—der Betrachter—die rechtslogische *Voraussetzung* der Souveränität mache, und 2. welches sind die psychischen, insbesondere die sozialpsychischen und sonstigen (etwa wirtschaftlichen, religiösen, politischen, aber immer wieder nur *sozialpsychisch* wirksamen) Ursachen, die zu einer Massenvorstellung von Souveränität, die zu der Tatsache führen, daß auch die Volksgenossen oder doch eine bestimmte Gruppe derselben die Vorstellung von der Souveränität ihres Gemeinwesens haben, mit ihrer Staatsordnung als mit einer höchsten, nicht weiter ableitbaren operieren'.

legal order. The decisive difference between the two lies in whether the juristic construction of the binding force of the treaty . . . is considered to derive from a 'higher', that is a more general, legal order—in our case: from the legal norm 'pacta sunt servanda' of the international legal order; or, whether the juristic construction posits the legal order created by the treaty itself as the highest source. In the latter case, the binding force of the treaty order is derived from an 'originality hypothesis'. Thereby, one must not overlook that the treaty as such, that is: a meeting of wills, is never 'constitutive'. 'Constitutive', that is: the final source of legal validity and force, is in the former case the 'international law hypothesis', in other words, the idea that above the contracting parties stands a higher international legal order; and in the latter case the 'originality hypothesis'.

When some refer to a treaty creating a Federal State as 'constitutive', this signifies nothing but a desire to dissociate the treaty from the international legal order—standing above all States and consequently also above the central legal order created by the Member States—by denying its foundational quality for the legal order of the Federal State. Better still: the hypothesis of the primacy of international law is rejected so as to posit the concrete treaty and the legal order it creates—a legal order, which from the perspective of international law, would only be a partial legal order—as sovereign, that is: as a State in the sense of the dominant sovereignty dogma. The primacy of this State legal order is thus presumed from the start . . . However, now there exists an absolute—not only a relative—distinction between Confederation and Federal State. The 'constitution' of the Federal State now differs in its essence from the 'treaty' of the Confederation as much as the 'treaty' of the Federal State differs from the 'constitution' of the Confederation. For only the constitution or the treaty of the Federal State have the quality of originality in that they derive their validity and legal force from the 'originality hypothesis'—a petitio principii.[90]

This attack on the tautological nature of European federal thought was joined by a second—equally brilliant—critique: the federal theory of Schmitt.[91] Schmitt agreed with Kelsen that the European debate had unduly concentrated on idealized differences between two *species* of the federal principle.[92] It had thereby forgotten to pay attention to the federal *genus* from which both species sprang. What were the *general* characteristics shared by the two *specific* manifestations of the federal principle? What had 'con*federation*' and '*Federal* State' in common? These questions centred on the 'federal' principle as such.

What, then, was federalism? A Federal Union was 'a permanent union based on a *voluntary* agreement whose object is the political preservation of its members'. The normative foundation for such a Federal Union was a

[90] H Kelsen, *Allgemeine Staatslehre*, 197–8 (translation—RS).
[91] C Schmitt, *Verfassungslehre*, Part IV: 'Verfassungslehre des Bundes', 361–91.
[92] Ibid 366.

'federal treaty'. The 'federal treaty' was a *'constitutional* treaty'. It was a treaty that 'changes the overall political status of each federated member in respect of this common aim'. A federal treaty was an international (status) treaty of a constitutional nature.[93] 'Its conclusion is an act of the *pouvoir constituant*. Its content establishes the federal constitution and forms, at the same time, a *part of the constitution of every Member State'*.[94] The dual nature of each federation, standing on the middle ground between international and national order, was thus reflected in the dual nature of its foundational document. The 'federal treaty' stood in between an international treaty and a national constitution. Each federation was thus a creature of international *and* national law.[95]

What, then, distinguished a federation from an ordinary international organization? Unlike an international league, every Federal Union had 'a common will and, thus, its own *political* existence'.[96] What distinguished a federation from an ordinary State? Unlike a unitary State, the federation was characterized by a political *dualism*. 'In each federal union, two kinds of political bodies co-exist: the existence of the whole federation and the individual existence of each federal member. Both kinds of political existence must remain coordinate in order for the federal union to remain alive.' Each Federal Union permanently lives in an 'existential equilibrium'. 'Such an existential limbo will lead to many conflicts calling for decision.' Yet, for the political equilibrium to remain alive, the conflict over the locus of sovereignty must remain 'suspended'. The question of sovereignty may be posed, but it must never be answered. Only constitutional silence over the locus of sovereignty *perpetuates* the federal equilibrium.[97]

Where the sovereignty question is—definitely—answered in favour of the Union, only it has political existence. The 'Union' is transformed into a sovereign State, whose legal structure may be federal but whose substance

[93] Ibid 367 and 368 (translation—RS): 'zwischenstaatlicher Statusvertrag', 'Bundesvertrag' and 'Verfassungsvertrag'.

[94] Ibid.

[95] Ibid 379: 'Jeder Bund ist als solcher sowohl völkerrechtliches wie staatsrechtliches Subjekt'.

[96] Ibid 371 (translation—RS, emphasis added). For Schmitt, the federation and its members are 'political' bodies. On Schmitt's (controversial) definition of the 'political', see: C Schmitt, *Der Begriff des Politischen*.

[97] Ibid 376–8 (translation—RS). For that silence to remain, a homogeneity of interests must be fostered. This had already been pointed out by A de Tocqueville, *Democracy in America*, 175–6: 'Since legislators cannot prevent such dangerous collisions as occur between the two sovereignties which coexist in the Federal system, their first object must be, not only to dissuade the confederate States from warfare, but to encourage such dispositions as lead to peace.' 'A certain uniformity of civilization is not less necessary to the durability of a confederation than a uniformity of interests in the States which compose it'.

is not (*'ohne bündische Grundlage'*). Contrariwise, where the sovereignty question is—definitely—answered in favour of the Member States, the political existence of the federation disappears and the Union dissolves into an international league. The normative ambivalence surrounding the location of sovereignty lay at the core of all—real—federations. Not dual or shared sovereignty, but suspended sovereignty constituted the political heart of the federal principle.[98]

II. The European Union: American and European Perspectives

The various efforts at European cooperation after the Second World War formed part of the general transition from an international law of coexistence to an international law of cooperation. 'Europe was beginning to get organised[.]'[99] Four European organizations emerged in the years 1948 and 1949: the Western European Union, the Organization for European Economic Cooperation, the North Atlantic Treaty Organization, and the Council of Europe. However, a 'new' approach to international cooperation in Europe occurred with a fifth international organization founded in 1951: the European Coal and Steel Community ('ECSC'). The Treaty of Paris had set up the first European Community.[100] Its original members were six European States: Belgium, France, Germany, Italy, Luxembourg, and the Netherlands. The Community had been created to *integrate* an important industrial sector—coal and steel. The very concept of *integration* was to indicate the wish of the contracting States 'to break with the ordinary forms of international treaties and organisations'.[101] Together with the two European Communities to follow in 1957, the evolution of European integration ultimately led to the foundation of the European Union in 1992.

What kind of Union is the European Union? Could it be described as a federal Union? Economic Unions fall, undoubtedly, into the category of

---

[98]   C Schmitt, *Verfassungslehre*, 378.

[99]   AH Robertson, *European Institutions: Co-Operation, Integration, Unification*, 17.

[100]   For a detailed discussion of the negotiations leading up to the signature of the ECSC Treaty, see: H Mosler, *Der Vertrag über die Europäische Gemeinschaft für Kohle und Stahl*.

[101]   Ibid 24 (translation—RS): 'Die Vertragspartner wollten den Boden der zwischenstaatlichen Beziehungen verlassen. Sie erstrebten eine engere Gemeinschaft, die die der Völkerrechtsordnung geläufigen Formen internationaler Verträge und Einrichtungen sprengt'.

Federal Unions.[102] Nonetheless, answers to these questions may depend on the federal perspective one chooses. After a (very) brief overview of the history of European integration, this section will analyse the European Union in the light of the American and European 'federal' traditions. It will employ the inductive approach of the former and examine the European Union alongside three dimensions: a foundational, an institutional, and a functional dimension. The Union will be found to occupy federal ground. This inductive approach contrasts with the deductive method of European federal thought. The European Union is here pressed into a conceptual duality: it is either an *international* organization or a *national* federation. While the European tradition has tried to hide behind the *sui generis* thesis, this view collapses in moments of constitutional crisis.

1. *The 'Supranational' Europe: A (Very) Brief History*

In what ways was the European Coal and Steel Community a novel legal phenomenon? The coal and steel industry had been placed under the auspices of a 'supranational' body—the High Authority.[103] It could carry out its tasks through the adoption of 'decisions', which would be 'binding in

---

[102]　In a brilliant chapter of his 'Unions of States', Forsyth analyses the emergence of economic Unions as a special category. Accordingly (ibid 161): 'Economic confederations begin to crystallize into a distinct form alongside security confederations when relatively small states begin to feel their independence and statehood threatened as much by the commercial and industrial power of larger states as by their military strength'. 'It is no accident that this crystallization first emerges at the time of the industrial revolution, for it is this revolution, by mechanizing, and thus multiplying dramatically the manufacturing power of individual states, and by making it possible for this power to make itself felt on an unprecedented scale across state boundaries, that brings the problems of the economic independence of states to the fore and gives it an urgency alongside that of military independence. It is when this happens that the self-same forms which have been used to secure the military independence of small states become consciously transferred to the economic sphere.'

[103]　On the birth of the term 'supranational', see : P Reuter, *Le Plan Schuman*, 343: 'Au cours des négociations sur le Traité on vit apparaître spontanément comme une chose allant de soi le terme de "supranational". Le succès de cette expression, plutôt nouvelle dans la langue française, fut considérable[.]' We find a reference to the 'supranationality' of the Coal and Steel Community in Article 9 (5) ECSC (emphasis added): 'The members of the High Authority shall, in the general interest of the Community, be completely independent in the performance of their duties. In the performance of these duties, they shall neither seek nor take instructions from any government or from any other body. They shall refrain from any action incompatible with the *supranational character* of their duties.' Article 9 ECSC was repealed by the Merger Treaty and replaced by a new Article 10 ECSC. The latter made no longer reference to the 'supranational' character of the Community. The Merger Treaty also replaced the name 'High Authority' with the 'European Commission'.

their entirety'.[104] The directly effective nature of ECSC law would naturally lead early commentators to presume an 'inherent supremacy of Community law'.[105] The 'new' character of the ECSC—its 'break' with the ordinary forms of international organizations—thus lay in the normative quality of its secondary law.[106] Piercing the dualist veil of classic international law, Community law did not require a 'validating' national transformation before it could become binding on individuals. The Member States were deprived of a 'normative veto' at the borders of their national legal orders. The transfer of decision-making powers to the Community represented a transfer of 'sovereign' powers to the European level.[107] While the Community still lacked *physical* powers,[108] it was the strong *normative* quality of its powers that would be identified with its 'supranational' character.[109]

However, this was only one dimension of the Community's 'supranationalism'. Under the Treaty of Paris, the organ endowed with supranational powers was

---

[104] Article 14 (2) ECSC .

[105] G Bebr, *The Relation of the European Coal and Steel Community Law to the Law of the Member States: A Peculiar Legal Symbiosis*, 788: 'The supremacy of the Community law is sometimes asserted on the traditional ground of the supremacy of international law. Undeniably the European Coal and Steel Community Treaty is an international Treaty concluded among the several member states. However, any attempt to assimilate the Treaty with traditional international treaties beclouds the true nature of the Treaty. *The fact that Community law can be enforced directly demonstrates the inherent supremacy of the Community law better than any analogy to traditional international treaties which do not penetrate so deeply into national legal systems*'.

[106] In addition to binding secondary law, the ECSC Treaty also envisaged directly effective Treaty articles. Article 65 ECSC prohibited anticompetitive agreements, which were—unless authorized by the High Authority—'automatically void' (para 5). In Joined Cases 7 and 9/54 *Groupement des Industries Sidérurgiques Luxembourgeoises v High Authority of the Coal and Steel Community*, the Court also found Article 4 ECSC directly effective. Article 4 ECSC 'recognised as incompatible with the common market for coal and steel' and therefore as 'abolished and prohibited within the Community, as provided in this Treaty', inter alia, discriminatory measures. The Court ruled that '[t]he provisions of Article 4 are sufficient of themselves and are directly applicable when they are not restated in any part of the Treaty' (ibid 195).

[107] P Reuter, *Le Plan Schuman*, 543.

[108] According to Article 86 ECSC, the Member States undertook 'to take all appropriate measures, whether general or particular, to ensure fulfillment of the obligations resulting from decisions or recommendations of the institutions of the Community and to facilitate the performance of the Community's tasks'. For pecuniary decisions adopted by the High Authority, Article 92 (2) ECSC expressly stipulated: 'Enforcement in the territory of Member States shall be carried out by means of the legal procedure in force in each State, after the order for enforcement in the form in use in the State in whose territory the decision is to be enforced has been appended to the decision, without other formality than verification of the authenticity of the decision. This formality shall be carried out at the instance of a Minister designated for this purpose by each of the Governments'. The same was true for judgments of the Court of Justice, cf Article 44 ECSC.

[109] Cf AH Robertson, *Legal Problems of European Integration*, 143–5.

itself 'supranational'—that is: independent of the will of the Member States. The High Authority was composed of independent 'bureaucrats' and could act by a majority of its members.[110] While the High Authority was not the only organ of the European Coal and Steel Community, it was its *central* decision-maker. Indeed, it was the High Authority that was charged with ensuring that the objectives of the Treaty would be attained.[111] To carry out this task, the High Authority would adopt decisions, recommendations, and opinions.[112] The ability of the Community to bind Member States *against their will* departed from the 'international' idea of respecting their sovereign equality through unanimity voting. And indeed, it was *this* decisional dimension that had originally inspired the very notion of supranationalism.[113] Early analysis consequently linked the concept of supranationality to the decision-making mode of the Community. Finer analytical minds even distinguished between 'supranational powers', 'limited supranational powers', and 'state powers preserved', depending on the procedural balance between the High Authority and the Council.[114]

The legal formula behind the European Coal and Steel Community was thus dual: the absence of a normative veto in the national legal orders was complemented by the absence of a decisional veto in the Community legal order. It was this *dual* independence of the European Community from the will of its Member States that would eventually be associated with supranationalism.[115]

---

[110] Article 13 ECSC (repealed by the Merger Treaty and replaced by Article 17 ESCS).

[111] Article 8 ECSC .

[112] Article 14 ECSC. Community acts were thus considered to be acts of the High Authority—even if other Community organs had been involved in the decision-making process. Under the Paris Treaty, the Council's task was primarily that of 'harmonizing the action of the High Authority and that of the governments, which are responsible for the general economic policy of their countries' (Article 26 ECSC). Its involvement was seen as a 'political safeguard' to coordinate activities that fell into the scope of the ECSC with those economic sectors that had not been brought into the Community sphere (cf H Mosler (n 100 above) 41). For an analysis of the powers of the Council under the ECSC, see: G Jaenicke, *Die Europäische Gemeinschaft für Kohle und Stahl (Montan-Union): Struktur und Funktionen ihrer Organe*, 757–61.

[113] That is: the composition of the High Authority, see: n 103 above.

[114] G Bebr, *The European Coal and Steel Community: A Political and Legal Innovation*, defined 'supranational powers' as those 'exercised by the High Authority' alone, 'limited supranational powers' as those acts for which 'the Authority needs the concurrence of the Council of Ministers'—qualified or unanimous. Powers reserved to the States were identified with the Council's exclusive competences, that is, where the Treaty required a unanimous decision of the Council without any involvement of the High Authority (ibid 20–4).

[115] HL Mason, *The European Coal and Steel Community: Experiment in Supranationalism*, 34–5; as well as G Jaenicke, *Der übernationale Charakter der Europäischen Wirtschaftsgemeinschaft*,

It was this legal formula that European federalists soon tried to export into wider fields. The ECSC had been 'a first step in the federation of Europe';[116] and the six Member States soon tried to expand the supranational sphere to the area of defence. The Treaty instituting the European Defence Community ('EDC') provided for a European army under the command of a supranational institution.[117] Yet, this Community would be stillborn as the French rejected its ratification in 1954. The failure equally stopped the embryonic European Political Community ('EPC').[118] With the idea of *political* integration discredited, European integrationists now returned to the 'functionalist' philosophy of economic integration.[119] The fruits of this strategy were the European Atomic Energy Community and the European (Economic) Community. The latter was the broadest attempt at European integration thus far: 'by establishing a common market and progressively approximating the economic policies of Member States', the (Economic) Community was

153: 'Diese Organisationsform unterschied sich von den bisher bei zwischenstaatlichen Zusammenschlüssen verwendeten Organisationsformen dadurch, daß einem von den Mitgliedstaaten unabhängigen, insoweit also "überregionalen" Organ selbständige Entscheidungsbefugnisse gegenüber den Mitgliedstaaten und ihren Staatsangehörigen zur Verfolgung der Zwecke und Ziele des Zusammenschlusses gegeben wurden'.

[116] 'Schuman Declaration' of 9 May 1950.

[117] On the history and structure of the EDC, see: G Bebr, *The European Defence Community and the Western European Union: An Agonizing Dilemma*.

[118] Article 1 of the Draft Treaty establishing the European Political Community characterized the proposal in the following terms: 'The present Treaty sets up a European Community of a supranational character. The Community is founded upon a union of peoples and States, upon respect for their personality and upon equal rights and duties for all. It shall be indissoluble.' The European (Political) Community had been designed to amalgamate the European Coal and Steel Community with the European Defence Community into a new institutional structure (cf Article 5 EPC). This institutional design had been identified with the federal idea (cf Article 38 (1) (c) EPC). The proposed European Parliament would have consisted of two Houses—the House of the Peoples and the Senate—and would have been the principal law-making organ of the European (Political) Community. For an analysis of the European Political Community, see: AH Robertson, *The European Political Community*.

[119] In the words of PH Spaak (*Address to the Assembly*, 21 October 1955—quoted in AH Robertson, *European Institutions: Co-Operation, Integration, Unification*, 26): 'After the [EDC] venture it was not reasonable to repeat exactly the same experiment a few months later. A means must be found of reaching the same goal—that distant goal of an integrated Europe—by other methods and through other channels. We then considered that, having failed on the political plane, we should take up the question on the economic plane and use the so-called functional method, availing ourselves to some extent—although, of course, without drawing any strict parallels—of the admittedly successful experiment already made with the European Coal and Steel Community'.

to 'lay the foundations of an ever closer union among the peoples of Europe'.[120]

The new European Community ('EC') carefully avoided all references to the concept of 'supranationalism'.[121] Had it abandoned the dual formula behind the ECSC Treaty? Early doubts on its supranational nature were not confined to semantics. The enormously enlarged scope for European integration had required a high price: the return to a more international format of decision-making. While the European Community established similar institutions to those of the European Coal and Steel Community, the balance among them had significantly changed. Emblematically, the EC Treaty now charged the Council—and not the Commission—with the task '[t]o ensure that the objectives set out in this Treaty are attained'.[122] Instead of the 'supranational' Commission, it was the 'international' Council that operated as its central decision-maker.[123] The Council was composed of 'a representative of each Member State';[124] and, '[t]his traditional method of international representation is, of course, devoid of supranational character-istics'.[125] However, decisional supranationalism could still be seen at work, when the Council acted by (qualified) majority. But what distinguished the unanimously acting Council from an 'ordinary' international organization?[126]

[120] Article 2 EEC.

[121] R Efron & AS Nanes, *The Common Market and Euratom Treaties: Supranationality and the Integration of Europe*, 682.

[122] Article 202 EC.

[123] AH Robertson, *European Institutions: Co-Operation, Integration, Unification*, 159–60: 'Indeed, it was the reluctance of governments in subsequent years to accept anything in the nature of the supranational which produced the result that powers of the Commission of the EEC were less extensive than those of the High Authority'.

[124] Article 203 EC.

[125] R Efron & AS Nanes (n 121 above) 675.

[126] During the first two stages of the transitional period—stipulated in Article 8 EEC—unanimous decisions would remain the rule (eg Article 43 (2) EEC: 'The Council shall, on a proposal from the Commission and after consulting the Assembly, acting unanimously during the first two stages and by a qualified majority thereafter, make regulations, issue directives, or take decisions, without prejudice to any recommendations it may also make.') The transition from unanimity to (qualified) majority voting was, of course, to take much longer. The (in)famous Luxembourg Compromise would allow States to insist on their veto power within the Council. And even after the demise of the Luxembourg Compromise (cf AL Teasdale, *The Life and Death of the Luxembourg Compromise*), decision-making in the Community is said to be still informed by 'consensus' politics. In the 1990s the Council practice was described in the following terms: 'Let me say it again: the wishes and concerns of delegations in the minority on a given issue will not be brutally overridden, as long as they are willing to negotiate constructively. There is no tyranny of the majority within the Council, because majorities are ephemeral: experienced ministers and officials know it will be their turn before long to rely on colleagues' understanding. The ethos of

The Rome Treaty answered this question by an institutional innovation: it tied the decision-making of the 'international' Council to proposals by a 'supranational' Commission. A 'supranational' element in European law-making would thus be preserved in the prerogative of the Commission to initiate and formulate Community bills. This institutional novelty would soon be identified as the quintessence of the 'Community method'.

While the decline of 'decisional' supranationalism cast a shadow over the supranational quality of the European Community, what about the norma-tive dimension of supranationalism? Like its predecessor, the European Community would enjoy autonomous powers. The EC Treaty acknowledged two 'supranational' instruments in Article 249 EC. The Community could act upon individuals through legislative 'regulations' or executive 'decisions', and these norms would be directly applicable within the national legal orders. Moreover, the supremacy of Community law was also announced as a constitutional principle of the European Community:

> By contrast with ordinary international treaties, the E[]C Treaty has created its own legal system which, on the entry into force of the Treaty, became an integral part of the legal systems of the Member States and which their courts are bound to apply. By creating a Community of unlimited duration, having its own institutions, its own personality, its own legal capacity and capacity of representation on the international plane and, more particularly, real powers stemming from a limitation of sovereignty or a transfer of powers from the States to the Community, the Member States have limited their sovereign rights, albeit within limited fields, and have thus created a body of law which binds both their nationals and themselves.

> The integration into the laws of each Member State of provisions which derive from the Community, and more generally the terms and the spirit of the Treaty, make it impossible for the States, as a corollary, to accord precedence to a unilateral and sub-sequent measure over a legal system accepted by them on a basis of reciprocity. Such a measure cannot therefore be inconsistent with that legal system. The executive force of Community law cannot vary from one State to another in deference to subsequent domestic laws, without jeopardizing the attainment of the objectives of the Treaty . . . *It follows from all these observations that the law stemming from the Treaty, an independent source of law, could not, because of its special and original nature, be overridden by domestic legal provisions, however framed, without being deprived of its character as Community law and without the legal basis of the Community itself being called into question.*[127]

the institution remains consensual' (A Dashwood, *States in the European Union*, 206). However, with qualified majority voting having—formally—become the constitutional norm, the decision-making *context* had—in the brilliant phrase by Weiler—moved from the 'shadow of the veto' to the 'shadow of the vote' (J Weiler, *The Transformation of Europe*, in *The Constitution of Europe*, 72).

[127] Case 6/64 *Flaminio Costa v ENEL* 593–4 (emphasis added).

But if the EC Treaty contrasted with 'ordinary international treaties' because it had set up a government endowed with 'real powers stemming from a limitation of sovereignty or a transfer of powers from the States', what kind of legal object was the European Community? The question has troubled international and national lawyers ever since the early days of European integration.[128] Its importance has increased with the evolution of the European project and its culmination in the European Union. With the spread of majority voting in the Council, the rise of the European Parliament to become co-legislator, and the widening of Europe's powers, the question has become fundamental. From the very beginning, the European Community was said to constitute 'the highest form of international integration'.[129] But would it go *beyond* the frontiers of international law? Was it 'in-between' international and national law? Was the European Union a Federal Union, or even a Federal State in the making?

The following two subsections will contrast two intellectual approaches to these questions. Walking in the footsteps of the American tradition, the first approach operates inductively. It analyses various dimensions of the European legal order in the light of their 'international' or 'national' character. The second approach follows the European federal tradition and operates deductively: the European Union must be either an international or a national legal phenomenon. As the legal and social reality of European integration did not fit this classificatory dichotomy, the European tradition tried to escape into the—misleading and mystical—belief that the European Union was *sui generis*. However, whenever the sovereignty question was posed, Europe would fall back into its old statist tradition.

Let us look at each intellectual approach in turn.

2. *The European Union in the Light of the American Tradition*

The American tradition had identified the middle ground between an international and a national legal structure with the very idea of federalism. Refusing to concentrate on the metaphysics of sovereignty, three analytical dimensions had been singled out: the foundational, the institutional, and the functional dimension. The first relates to the origin and nature of the new legal order; the second concerns the composition of its 'government'; while the third deals with the scope and nature of the federation's powers. In the light of these three

---

[128] For a critical evaluation of the early classificatory attempts, see: P Hay, *Federalism and Supranational Organisations*, 74.

[129] G Schwarzenberger, *The Frontiers of International Law*, 280.

constitutional dimensions, the overall legal structure under the 1787 Constitution was found 'in strictness, neither a national nor a[n] [international]
Constitution, but a composition of both'.[130] Federalism was a legal hybrid: an
(inter)national phenomenon.

Within the classic period of European law, the European Union was indeed
described as a hybrid that was placed 'between international and municipal
law'.[131] 'The Community is a new structure in the marches between internal
and international law'.[132] It 'is neither an international Confederation, nor a
Federal State'. 'It simultaneously combines characteristics from both types of
State relations and thus forms a *mixtum compositum*'.[133] How did this mixed
format express itself? What were its 'international' and 'national' features?[134]
American constitutionalism offered a potent analytical approach to these
questions. This approach may also prove fruitful for a legal analysis of the
European Union.

a. The Foundational Dimension: Europe's 'Constitutional Treaty'

The European Community was conceived as an international organization.
Its birth certificate is an international treaty. Its formation had been 'international'—just like the American Union. However, unlike the latter, the
European treaties have been ratified by the national *legislatures*—not the
national peoples—of its Member States. Genetically, they are 'legislative'—
not constitutional—treaties.[135]

---

[130] A Hamilton et al, *The Federalist*, 187. The original quote uses the term 'federal' for
'international', but as we saw above the federal principle was identified with 'international' (treaty)
relations; cf Section I (1).

[131] C Sasse, *The Common Market: Between International and Municipal Law*; as well as P Hay,
The Contribution of the European Communities to International Law, 199: 'The contribution of
the Communities for legal science is the breaking-up of the rigid dichotomy of national and
international law'.

[132] E Van Raalte, *The Treaty Constituting the European Coal and Steel Community*, 74.

[133] L-J Constantinesco, *Das Recht der Europäischen Gemeinschaften*, 332 (translation—RS).

[134] In the following subsection, the terms 'international' and 'national' will be used as analytical
terms. The former refers to a voluntary and horizontal structure recognizing the sovereign equality
of the States; the latter stands for the hierarchical and vertical structure within a unitary State. Even
if the notion of 'unitary' is less charged with symbolic connotations than 'national', we shall use the
latter term to facilitate a comparison with Madison's discussion of the mixed structure of the
American Union; cf Section I (2).

[135] It is difficult—if not impossible—to accept that 'the founding treaties as well as each
amendment agreed upon by the *governments* appear as the *direct* expression of the common will
of the [national] *peoples* of the Union' (I Pernice, *Multilevel Constitutionalism and the Treaty of
Amsterdam: European Constitution-Making Revisited?*, 717 (emphasis added)). National ratifications
are—with the exception of Ireland—only *indirect* expressions of the common will of the national

Would this (legislative) 'treaty' origin categorically rule out the idea of a European 'constitution'? This is not a matter of logical necessity.[136] And as soon as we accept that the status of a legal norm depends on the function a society gives it, it is hard to deny that the European treaties have been elevated to a constitutional status. They have evolved into a 'Treaty-Constitution'.[137] The Court has insisted on the normative 'autonomy' of the European legal order and this 'originality hypothesis' severed the umbilical cord with the international legal order.[138] This emancipation manifested itself in the following legal facts. First, in contrast to the normative regime governing international treaties, the Court of Justice insisted on the 'unilateral' nature of European law: a Member State could not invoke the breach of Community law by another Member State to justify a derogation from its own obligations under the Treaty.[139]

Secondly, the European Court insisted on the supremacy of Community law over all national law, including national constitutional law.[140] This contrasts with classic international law doctrine of which the supremacy doctrine forms no part.[141] However, the absolute supremacy of European law has

peoples of the Union. National consent is typically expressed through national legislatures. It is equally difficult to agree that these national ratifications should be regarded 'as a *common* exercise of constitution-making power by the peoples of the participating State' (ibid 717 (emphasis added)). This theory does not explain how each *unilateral* national act ultimately transforms itself into a collective act (*Gesamtakt*). On the German legal concept of '*Gesamtakt*', see: HF Köck, *Der Gesamtakt in der deutschen Integrationslehre*.

[136]   On this point, see the analysis by H Kelsen in Section I(3b).

[137]   Stein uses the compound 'Treaty-Constitution' (cf *Toward Supremacy of Treaty-Constitution by judicial Fiat: On the Margin of the Costa Case*).

[138]   Case 6/64 *Flaminio Costa v ENEL*.

[139]   Cf Case 90–91/63 *Commission v Luxemburg and Belgium*; Case 52/75 *Commission v Italy*.

[140]   Cf Case 11/70 *Internationale Handelsgesellschaft mbH v Einfuhr- und Vorratsstelle für Getreide und Futtermittel*.

[141]   Some legal scholars refer to the 'supremacy' of international law vis-à-vis national law (cf F Morgenstern, *Judicial Practice and the Supremacy of International Law*). However, the concept of supremacy is here used in an imprecise way. Legal supremacy stands for the priority of one norm over another. For this, two norms must conflict and, therefore, form part of the same legal order. However, classic international law is based on the sovereignty of States and the latter implied a dualist relation with national law. The dualist veil protected national laws from being overridden by norms adopted by such 'supranational' authorities as the Catholic Church or the Holy Roman Empire. (When a State opens up to international law, this 'monistic' stance is a *national* choice. International law as such has never imposed monism on a State. On the contrary, in clearly distinguishing between international and national law, it is based on a dualist philosophy.) How, then, can one claim that one of the 'foundational principles of international law' is 'the general principle of supremacy of treaties over conflicting domestic law, even domestic constitutional law' (J Weiler, *Federalism without Constitutionalism: Europe's Sonderweg*, 55)? Reference to the international law

not been accepted by all Member States. In parallel with a *European* perspective, there co-exists a *national* perspective on the supremacy issue.[142] The national perspective insists on placing the fundamental structures and values of national legal orders beyond the reach of European supremacy.[143] Where European law trespasses on the very identity of a national constitutional order, the latter would oppose it. But will the existence of a national perspective on the supremacy of European law rule out the 'constitutional' or 'federal' character of the European Union? This is not the case. While the existence of a *dual* perspective on the supremacy issue may be interpreted in the light of a theory of 'constitutional pluralism',[144] the normative ambivalence surrounding supremacy and sovereignty can better be viewed as part and parcel of Europe's *federal* nature. The 'suspension' of the supremacy question in the European Union is the very proof of the *political* co-existence of *two* political bodies and thus evidence of Europe's living federalism. The theory

---

doctrine *pacta sunt servanda* will hardly help. The fact that a State cannot invoke its internal law to *justify* a breach of international obligations is not supremacy. Behind the doctrine of *pacta sunt servanda* stands the concept of legal responsibility: a State cannot—without legal responsibility—escape its international obligations. The duality of internal and international law is thereby maintained: the former cannot affect the latter (as the latter cannot affect the former).

[142] For a brief overview of the jurisprudence of national Supreme Courts, see: P Craig & G de Búrca, *EU Law: Text Cases and Materials*, 353—'The Second Dimension: Supremacy of Community Law from the Perspective of the Member States'. For a longer overview, see: R Oppenheimer, *The Relationship between European Community Law and National Law: The Cases* (vols I & II).

[143] Let us concentrate on the German legal order to illustrate this point. In 1974, the German Constitutional Court conceded the supremacy of Community law over some national constitutional provisions, but denied the legal effect of 'any amendment of the Treaty which would destroy the identity of the valid constitutional structure of the Federal Republic of Germany by encroaching on the structures which go to make it up' (BVerfGE 37, 271, (*Solange I*), para 43). These judicially asserted national constitutional limits have been codified in Article 23 (1) of the German Constitution. The paragraph reads: 'The establishment of the European Union, as well as changes in its treaty foundations and comparable regulations that amend or supplement this Basic Law, or make such amendments or supplements possible, shall be subject to paragraphs (2) and (3) of Article 79.' Article 79 (3) deals with the substantive constitutional limits to any amendment of the German Constitution and states: 'Amendments to this Basic Law affecting the division of the Federation into Länder, their participation on principle in the legislative process, or the principles laid down in Articles 1 and 20 shall be inadmissible'.

[144] The 'pluralist position' claims 'that there is no objective basis—no Archimedean point—from which one claim can be viewed as more authentic than the other, or superior to the other within a single hierarchy of norms'. 'Rather the claims of the Member States and the claims of the EU to ultimate authority within the European legal order are equally plausible in their own terms and in their own perspective.' (Cf N Walker, *Sovereignty and Differentiated Integration in the European Union*, 361–2).

of constitutional pluralism thus speaks federal prose, without—as Molière's Monsieur Jourdain—being aware of it!

Thirdly, in establishing a direct link with individuals, Europe's constitutional order recognized from the very start an incipient form of European citizenship.[145] The latter was to be expressly acknowledged with the official introduction of a 'citizenship of the Union' in the Maastricht Treaty. According to Article 17 EC '[e]very person holding the nationality of a Member State shall be a citizen of the Union'. In accord with federal theory, every European will thus be a citizen of *two* political orders: the '[c]itizenship of the Union shall complement and not replace national citizenship'. Equally in line with federal theory, Union citizenship has a horizontal and a vertical dimension: it forces Member States to horizontally extend *national* rights to citizens of other European States; while it vertically grants *European* political and civil rights in relation to the European Union.[146]

To conclude: in the eyes of the European Court and the majority of European scholars, the normative force of European law derives no longer from the normative foundations of international law. The ultimate normative base within Europe—its 'originality hypothesis' or '*Grundnorm*'—is the Rome Treaty as such. '[T]he E[]C Treaty, albeit concluded in the form of an international agreement, none the less constitutes the constitutional charter of a Community based on a rule of law[.]'[147] While 'international' in formation, the EC Treaty has assumed 'national' characteristics. This 'national' semi-nature is not put into question by the 'international' nature of the amendment process. In contrast to the American Union, the amendment of Europe's constitution is *not* a mixed act. Treaty amendment requires the ratification of all the Member States according to their respective national constitutional requirements.[148] But whereas the Member States—in the collective plural—remain the 'Masters of the Treaties'; *individual* Member

---

[145] For the opposite view, see: HP Ipsen, *Europäisches Gemeinschaftsrecht*, 251: '*Es gibt keine Gemeinschaftsangehörigkeit*. Gleichwohl kann ihre Gemeinschaftsrechts-Berührung ihre Rechtsstellung kennzeichnen, und dies unter ihrer individuellen Benennung als "Marktbürger", ihrer derartigen Rechtsstellung als "Marktbürgerschaft"'.

[146] For a brilliant analysis, see: C Schönberger, *European Citizenship as Federal Citizenship: Some Citizenship Lessons of Comparative Federalism*, 79.

[147] Opinion 1/91 (*EFTA*), para. 21. See also, Case 294/83 *Les Verts v Parliament* para 23: 'basic constitutional charter'.

[148] Cf Article 48 TEU. On the scope and role of the provision in the European legal order, see: Chapter 3—Section I (3) below.

States have lost their 'competence-competence'.[149] Legally, Member States are no longer competent to determine *unilaterally* the limits of their own competences themselves.[150] And: the European legal order has even blocked the avenues to modify *multilaterally* the EC Treaty outside the official amendment procedure by successfully subordinating the legal regime for subsequently concluded agreements between all Member States to the supremacy of European law.[151]

b. The Institutional Dimension: A European Union of States and People(s)

How are we to analyse the institutional dimension of the European Union? The Community's principal law-making organs are the Commission, the Council, and the European Parliament. How should we characterize each of them alongside the international versus national spectrum; and what will it tell us about the nature of the European legislator?

In terms of its composition, the Commission is like a 'national' organ: once appointed, the Commissioners are to act 'in the general interest of the Community' and should be 'completely independent in the performance of their duties'.[152] The Commission is chosen by the Member States and the European Parliament in a procedure that is partly 'international' and partly 'national'.[153] It acts by the majority of its members;[154] and this decision-making mode follows a 'national' formula.

In terms of its composition, the Council is an 'international' organ: 'The Council shall consist of a representative of each Member State at ministerial

---

[149] HP Ipsen, *Europäische Verfassung—Nationale Verfassung*, 202: 'Die staatliche Kompetenz-Kompetenz hat sich durch den Beitritt zur Gemeinschaft selbst beschränkt'.

[150] A von Bogdandy & J Bast, *The European Union's Vertical Order of Competences: The Current Law and Proposals for its Reform*, 237: '[T]he individual Member State has forfeited its right to determine its own competences (*Kompetenz-Kompetenz*) insofar as it is not permitted to extend its powers *unilaterally* to the detriment of the Union. While the Member States acting jointly as the Contracting Parties may amend the Treaties, transferring powers back to the Member States, they are bound by the procedures provided for in Article 48 TEU'.

[151] On this point, see: Chapter 6—Section II (1a).

[152] Article 213 (2) EC.

[153] The Council, meeting in the composition of Heads of State or Government and acting by a qualified majority will nominate a President of the Commission. The nomination has to be approved by the European Parliament. A list of Commissioners will then be suggested 'in accordance with the proposals by each Member State'. But 'the Commission thus nominated shall be subject as a body to a vote of approval by the European Parliament'. Only after this approval by the European Parliament, the Commission 'shall be appointed by the Council, acting by a qualified majority' (Article 214 EC).

[154] Article 219 EC.

level, authorised to commit the government of that Member State'.[155] Each national minister thus represents 'its' State government; and where decision-making is by unanimity, the sovereign equality of the Member States is respected. Yet, the EC Treaty also envisaged procedures that would break with the international idea of sovereign equality. It permits the Community to act by a (qualified) majority of States; and where a qualified majority suffices, the Member States have weighed votes depending—roughly—on the size of their populations.[156] (Strictly speaking, the Council will thus not represent the Member *States*—a notion that implies their *equality*—but the national *peoples*.[157]) To act by qualified majority, the Council needs a 'triple majority': a majority of the *States* must obtain a majority of the votes from the *national peoples*; and the latter must also represent a majority of the *European people*.[158] Formally, then, decision-making within the Council is neither completely international nor completely national, but a combination of both. It stands on federal middle ground.

The composition of the European Parliament has changed over time. Originally, it was an assembly of 'representatives of the *peoples of the States* brought together in the Community'.[159] This designation was adequate as

[155] Article 203 EC.

[156] Article 205 EC.

[157] For a similar conclusion albeit from a different perspective, see: A Peters, *Elemente einer Theorie der Verfassung Europas*, 563 and 566: 'Es ist bedenklich, einen Gegensatz zwischen Staaten und Bürgern zu konstruieren. *Die Staaten sind kein Selbstzweck, sondern vertreten ihrerseits die Bürger.* Die Repräsentation der Staaten als geschlossene Entitäten (etwa im Rat) soll doch eine spezifische Interessenvertretung *der Bürger* dieser kleineren Einheiten (in ihrer Rolle als Staatsbürger) darstellen, so daß diese nicht in der Gesamtvertretung aller EU-Bürger untergehen ... Die Staaten (im Rat oder einer potentiellen Staatenkammer) vertreten die Bürger, in ihrer Rolle als Staatsbürger. Das Europäische Parlament vertritt ebenfalls die Bürger, in ihrer Rolle als EU-Bürger'.

[158] Article 205 EC stipulates that for a qualified majority the Council must have 'at least 255 votes in favour cast by a majority of the members' (para 1). In addition, any member of the Council is allowed to request verification 'that the Member States constituting the qualified majority represent at least 62% of the total population of the Union' (para 3). 'If that condition is shown not to have been met, the decision in question shall not be adopted.' The Lisbon Treaty would replace the triple majority system with a double majority system. Article 16 (4) (reformed) TEU stipulates that 'a qualified majority shall be defined as at least 55% of the members of the Council, comprising at least fifteen of them and representing Member States comprising at least 65% of the population of the Union'. The Lisbon Treaty would thus get rid of the idea of weighted votes (after a transitional period).

[159] Article 137 EEC (emphasis added). France preferred this symbolic formulation. And to safeguard the indivisibility of the French Republic guaranteed under Article 1 of the 1958 Constitution, the idea of a 'representative mandate' was also rejected by the Constitutional Council in its 1977 decision on the 1976 European Parliament Election Act. This has been explained in the following way: 'Sans reprendre l'idée qui consisterait à voir dans les élus français une délégation

long as the Parliament consisted of 'delegates who shall be designated by the respective Parliaments from among their members in accordance with the procedure laid down by each Member State'.[160] However, the composition of the Parliament dramatically changed with the introduction of direct elections.[161] While there remain 'international' elements, its composition steadily evolved towards the 'national' pole. Today, the European Parliament *directly* represents—even if in a distorted way—a European people.[162] The anachronistic

nationale devant rendre compte de non mandat, la conception du Conseil fait d'eux les représentants de la circonscription française au sein du Parlement Européen et non les élus de l'Europe. L'élu représente *sa circonscription*, la France et non la collectivité européenne dans son ensemble, c'est la négation du mandat représentatif . . . Pour la France, le refus du mandat représentatif et la représentation par les élus font du Parlement une chambre plus proche d'une second chambre fédérale que d'une chambre populaire. Il n'exprime pas une volonté générale européenne différente de la volonté des Etats membres, mais permet la rencontre des volontés des représentantes des différents Etats. Beaucoup plus qu'à la formation d'une volonté unique, il contribue à la manifestation d'une volonté commune aux Etats'. (JP Jacqué, *La Souveraineté française et l'élection du Parlement Européen au suffrage universel direct*, 76–7).

[160]   Article 138 EEC.

[161]   Direct elections were introduced by the Decision of 20 September 1976 relating to the Act concerning the election of the representatives of the Assembly by direct universal suffrage (76/787/ECSC, EEC, Euratom). The 'decision' represented an international agreement between all the Member States and required 'adoption in accordance with their respective constitutional requirements'. The Act stated that '[t]he representatives in the Assembly of the peoples of the States brought together in the Community shall be elected by direct universal suffrage' (Article 1). Representatives would be elected for a term of five years (Article 3). Article 4 (1) required independence: 'Representatives shall vote on an individual and personal basis. They shall not be bound by any instructions and shall not receive a binding mandate.' For an overview and a commentary of the provisions of the Act, see: B Paulin & J Forman, *L'élection du Parlement Européen au suffrage universel direct*.

[162]   To this day, the EC Treaty allocates a—neither equal nor proportional—number of parliamentary mandates to the Member States and there is still no uniform European electoral procedure. The aim of establishing a uniform electoral procedure has been as old as the Community itself. Pending such a uniform European election law, the 1976 Direct Election Decision provided in Article 7 (2) that 'the electoral procedure shall be governed in each Member State by its national provisions'. However, Articles 9 and 11–12 of the Act had already established a common core. Moreover, since 1976 a number of developments have taken place. First, the EC Treaty now provides under Article 19 (2) EC that 'every citizen of the Union residing in a Member State of which he is not a national shall have the right to vote and to stand as a candidate in elections to the European Parliament in the Member State in which he resides, under the same conditions as nationals of that State'. Second, since 2004, European Parliamentarians must not be a Member of a national Parliament (the application of this rule is delayed for certain Member States). Most importantly, in 2005, the European Parliament was given a single statute for its members (Decision 2005/684 of the European Parliament of 28 September 2005 adopting the Statute for members of the European Parliament). This will enter into force in 2009. According to its Article 2, European Parliamentarians 'shall be free and independent'. Article 3 insists that '[m]embers shall vote on an individual and personal basis' and 'shall not be bound by any instructions and shall not receive a binding mandate'. Parliamentarians will be paid out of the Community budget (Article 23).

characterization in Article 189 EC of Parliamentarians as 'representatives of the peoples of the States brought together in the Community' is thus misleading.[163] The European Parliament no longer represents the national *peoples* in their collective capacity, but a—constitutionally posited—European people. Its legal existence precedes its political essence.[164] Socially, the European demos will 'constitute itself as a political unit through the very process of representation'.[165] The Parliament's 'national' composition is reflected in its decision-making mode, which is majority voting.[166]

Having analysed the composition and operating mode of each institution, what—then—is the nature of the European legislator? Depending on the legislative procedure applicable, there are a number of European legislators. The Commission will generally be charged with the formulation of a legislative proposal. However, where the Council operates on the basis of unanimity, the legislative procedure will still be predominantly of an 'international' nature: after all each State guards its sovereign equality in the form of a decisional veto power. According to the now dominant co-decision procedure, on the other hand, the Council decides by a qualified majority and the European Parliament acts as 'co-legislator'.[167] The European legislator is here 'bicameral' and this constitutional structure 'reflects a subtle federal balance': 'Legislation comes into being through majority voting in the two houses of the legislature and only after the approval by both of them. One house

---

[163] The ambiguous formulation in Article 189 EC would change under the Lisbon Treaty. Article 10 (reformed) TEU states in its second paragraph: 'Citizens are *directly* represented at Union level in the European Parliament' (emphasis added). And Article 14 (2) states: 'The European Parliament shall be composed of representatives of the Union's citizens'.

[164] In the words of Habermas: 'The ethical-political self-understanding of citizens in a democratic community must not be taken as an historical-cultural *a priori* that makes democratic will-formation possible, but rather as flowing contents of a circulatory progress that is generated through the legal institutionalization of citizens' communication. This is precisely how national identities were formed in modern Europe. Therefore it is to be expected that the political institutions to be created by a European constitution would have an inducing effect.' Cf J Habermas, *Remarks on Dieter Grimm's 'Does Europe need a Constitution?'*, 306.

[165] E Grabitz, *Der Verfassungsstaat in der Gemeinschaft*, 793. And referring to the French intellectual tradition, Peters finds that 'we can already discern a European "demos"', at least *in statu nascendi'* (A Peters, *European Democracy after the 2003 Convention*, 72).

[166] Article 198 EC: 'Save as otherwise provided in this Treaty, the European Parliament shall act by an absolute majority of the votes cast'.

[167] A Dashwood, *Community Legislative Procedures in the Era of the Treaty on European Union*, 362–3. 'The "product" of the procedure is an act adopted jointly by the European Parliament and the Council—in contrast to that of the consultation or co-operation procedures, which is simply an act of the Council . . . [T]he acts in question shall be signed by both the President of the European Parliament and the President of the Council, symbolising in the most concrete way possible the joint character of such acts'.

represents the people in their capacity as citizens of the Union, the other house represents the component entities of the federation, the Member States, and—through them the people in their capacity as citizens of the Member States'.[168] Europe's prevailing legislator is consequently a combination of 'international' and 'national' elements. While the Parliament represents a—constitutionally posited—European people, the Council represents the Member States. This institutional arrangement reflects the *dual* basis of democratic legitimacy in the European Union.

c. The Functional Dimension: The Division of Powers in Europe

What about the allocation of the functions of government? What kind of powers does the European Union enjoy? Within the internal sphere, Europe clearly enjoys significant economic and political powers. This is equally the case in the external sphere.[169] However, the European Union's powers remain enumerated powers. Its scope of government is 'incomplete'. The reach of Europe's powers is *not* 'national'—that is: sovereign—in scope.

But what is the nature of Europe's powers? When the European Community was born, the Treaty of Rome envisaged two instruments with direct effect on individuals. Regulations were to have direct and general application in all Member States.[170] Decisions allowed the Community to adopt directly effective measures addressed to particular persons.[171] In making regulations and decisions directly applicable in domestic legal orders, the EC Treaty thus recognized two 'national' instruments—one legislative, the other executive. The European Community also possessed an 'international' instrument: the directive. In order to operate on individuals, the European command would need to be incorporated by the States. However, through a series of courageous rulings, the European Court of Justice partly transformed the directive's morphology by injecting 'national' elements. Today, directives can have vertical direct effects within national legal orders. However, in refusing to grant them horizontal direct effect, the Court has insisted on an 'international' remnant. Directives thus combine 'international' and

---

[168] K Lenaerts, *Federalism: Essential Concepts in Evolution—the Case of the European Union*, 763.

[169] On the scope of the European Community's internal and external powers, see: Chapter 3—Section I, and Chapter 6—Section I (1) below.

[170] Article 249 (2) EC.

[171] Article 249 (4) EC.

'national' features.[172] They are a form of 'incomplete legislation' and thus symbolically represent Europe's 'federal' middle ground.

What about Europe's *executive* powers? While the Union had established its own enforcement machinery in some sectors,[173] the direct administration of European legislation has remained an exception—even if Europe has enlarged its executive presence in recent years.[174] Indirect Community administration still characterizes the European federation, which continues to largely rely on its Member States to apply and implement Community law.[175] The decentralized application of European law is effected through the supremacy principle: all organs of a Member State's administration— executive *and* judicial—must disapply conflicting national law in every individual case before them. Supremacy and pre-emption, in fact, primarily concern the executive application of European law.[176] Unlike contemporary American federal doctrine,[177] European federalism even imposes an obligation on national administrations to implement European law. Thus, although national administrations are—from an institutional perspective—not integrated into the European administrative machinery; national administrations operate—from a functional perspective—as a decentralized European administration. However, there is an important caveat. The obligation to execute European law is on the Member States as 'corporate' entities. Where a national administration refuses to give effect to European law, the only road open for the European Community to enforce its laws is to bring an action before the European Court of Justice. In the execution of its legislative choices, European law thus still 'largely follows the logic of state responsibility in public international law'.[178]

---

[172] On the instrumental format of directives, see: R Schütze, *The Morphology of Legislative Power in the European Community: Legal Instruments and the Federal Division of Powers*, 118–29.

[173] For EC competition law, see: Regulation 17/62 and Regulation 1/2003.

[174] For the increasing role of European agencies in the direct implementation of European law, see: E Chiti, *The Emergence of a Community Administration*.

[175] Cf K Lenaerts, *Regulating the Regulatory Process: 'delegation of powers' in the European Community*, 27; as well as C Möllers, *Durchführung des Gemeinschaftsrechts*, 496: 'Die praktisch bedeutsamsten Vollzugsorgane des Gemeinschaftsrechts stellen die mitgliedstaatlichen Verwaltungen dar'.

[176] HP Ipsen, *Europäisches Gemeinschaftsrecht*, 288: 'Die Vorrangregel wird allein bei der Recht*sanwendung* wirksam (durch den Prozeßrichter, ebenso durch andere Rechtsanwendungsorgane wie die Verwaltung), also *nicht* bereits in der Stufe der nationalen Recht*setzung*'.

[177] On the 'no-commandeering rule' in US federalism, see: D Halberstam, *Comparative Federalism and the Issue of Commandeering*.

[178] S Kadelbach, *European Administrative Law and the Law of a Europeanized Administration*, 176.

d. Overall Classification: The European Union on Federal 'Middle Ground'

In the light of these three dimensions, how should we classify the European Union? Its formation was clearly international and its amendment still is. However, its international birth should not prejudge against the 'federal' or 'constitutional' status of the EC Treaty. Was not the 1787 American *Federation* the result of an international act? And had not the 1949 German *Constitution* been ratified by the State legislatures?[179] The fact remains that the European legal order has adopted the 'originality hypothesis' and cut the umbilical cord with the international legal order. The Treaty *as such*—not international law—is posited at the origin of European law. Functionally, then, the European Union is based on a 'constitutional treaty' that stands on federal middle ground. The same conclusion was reached when analysing Europe's 'government'. The European Union's dominant legislative procedure strikes a federal balance between 'international' and 'national' elements. And while the scope of its powers is limited, the nature of Europe's powers is predominately 'national'. Overall then, the legal structure of the European Union is also 'in strictness, neither a national nor a[n] international Constitution, *but a composition of both*'.[180]

3. *The European Union in the Light of the European Tradition*

European constitutionalism has historically insisted on the indivisibility of sovereignty. Its federal tradition focuses on the locus of sovereignty. Where States form a union but retain their sovereignty, the object thereby created is an international organization (confederation) regulated by international law. By contrast, where States transfer sovereignty to the centre, a new State emerges. Within this State—a Federal State if powers are territorially divided— all legal relationships are now regulated by national law. Federalism is thus conceived in 'national' or 'statist' terms. The *absolute* idea of sovereignty operates as a prism that blinds out all *relative* nuances within a mixed or dual legal structure. Mixity or duality are irregularities and aberrations.

European federal thought would apply this conceptual apparatus to the legal analysis of the European Union. But as these categories could not explain the social and legal reality of European law, Europe's quest for a new word to describe the middle ground between 'international' and 'national'

---

[179] Article 144(1) of the German Constitution states: 'This Basic Law shall require ratification by the *parliaments* of two thirds of the German *Länder* in which it is initially to apply' (emphasis added).

[180] A Hamilton et al, *The Federalist*, 187.

law would soon be answered by a novel concept—supranationalism. Europe was said to be a *sui generis* legal phenomenon.[181] It was incomparable for 'it cannot be fitted into traditional categories of international or constitutional law'.[182]

Was the European Union really a species without a genus? There are serious problems with the *sui generis* argument. First of all, it lacks explanatory value for it is based on a conceptual tautology.[183] Worse, the *sui generis* theory 'not only fails to analyze but in fact asserts that no analysis is possible or worthwhile, it is in fact an "unsatisfying shrug"'.[184] Secondly, it only views the Union in *negative* terms—it is *neither* international organization *nor* Federal State—and thus indirectly perpetuates the conceptual foundations of the European tradition.[185] Thirdly, in not providing any external standard, the *sui generis* formula cannot detect, let alone measure, the European Union's evolution. Thus, even where the European Community lost some of its 'supranational' features—as occurred in the transition from the ECSC to the E(E)C—*both* would be described as *sui generis*. But worst of all: the *sui generis* 'theory' is historically unfounded. All previously existing Unions of States lay between international and national law.[186] More concretely: the power to adopt legislative norms binding on individuals—this acclaimed *sui generis* feature of Europe—cannot be the basis of its claim to specificity.[187] The same lack of 'uniqueness' holds true for other normative or institutional features of the European Union.[188] And even if one sees Europe's *Sonderweg*— yet another way of celebrating the *sui generis* idea—in 'the combination of

---

[181] Hallstein would use this term, but then add '[a]ber damit ist nicht widerlegt, daß sie der Keim einer Föderation ist. Jede Föderation ist sui generis' (W Hallstein, *Die Europäische Gemeinschaft*, 365).

[182] HL Mason, *The European Coal and Steel Community: Experiment in Supranationalism*, 126.

[183] P Hay, *Federalism and Supranational Organisations*, 37: 'It should be clear, however, that the term has neither analytic value of its own nor does it add in analysis: the characterization of the Communities as supranational and of their law as "supranational law" still says nothing about the nature of that law in relation either to national legal systems or to international law'.

[184] Ibid 44.

[185] For this brilliant point, see: C Schönberger, *Die Europäische Union als Bund*, 83: 'Denn die verbreitete sui-generis-Formel überwindet die Begriffswelt der klassischen Dichotomie von Staatenbund und Bundesstaat nur dem Schein nach. In Wirklichkeit verewigt sie genau dieses Kategoriensystem'.

[186] JB Westerkamp, *Staatenbund und Bundesstaat: Untersuchungen über die Praxis und das Recht der modernen Bünde*.

[187] C Schönberger (n 185 above) 93.

[188] To give but one more illustration: Europe's supremacy principle is, in its structure, not unique. The Canadian doctrine of 'federal paramountcy' also requires only the 'disapplication' and not the 'invalidation' of conflicting provincial laws.

a "confederal" institutional arrangement and a "federal" legal arrangement',[189] this may not be too special after all.[190]

In any event, the *sui generis* 'theory' only provides a tranquilizing *non liquet* in times of constitutional peace. It will not prevent classificatory wars in times of constitutional conflict. Whenever the 'sovereignty question' is posed, Europe's statist tradition still structures the constitutional debate. This subsection will analyse the classificatory war in the wake of the signing of the Treaty on European Union. The Maastricht battle structured the European legal debate for more than a decade.[191] In such times of constitutional conflict, Europe's federal tradition only offers a polarized and idealized alternative: the European Union is either an international organization (confederation) or a Federal State. And because the Union was not a State, it must be an international organization.[192] This would, in turn, lead to three constitutional denials: the European Union could have no people, no constitution, and no constitutionalism.

a. Posing the Sovereignty Question: The 'Maastricht Decision'

Constitutional problems arise when society revels. European society revelled in the wake of the Treaty on European Union. The ratification of the Maastricht Treaty was *the* constitutional moment when the symbolic weight of European integration entered into the collective consciousness of European society. The ensuing legal debate crystallized into national constitutional reviews on the nature of the European Union. The most controversial and celebrated review was the 'Maastricht Decision' of the German Constitutional Court.[193] The German Supreme Court posed the sovereignty question. Its central contestation was this: Europe's present *social* structure would set limits to the *constitutional* structure of the Europe Union. As long as there was no European equivalent to national peoples, there would be an absolute legal limit to European integration. In this moment of constitutional conflict, European federal thought was forced to reveal its deeper intellectual structure.

How did the German Supreme Court derive national limits to European integration? The Court based its reasoning on the democratic principle—*the*

---

[189] J Weiler, *Federalism without Constitutionalism: Europe's Sonderweg*, 58.

[190] On this point, see: P Pescatore, *The Law of Integration: Emergence of a New Phenomenon in International Relations, Based on The Experience of the European Communities*, 58.

[191] J Baquero-Cruz, *The Legacy of the Maastricht-Urteil and the Pluralist Movement*.

[192] For this thesis, see: D Wyatt, *New Legal Order, Or Old*; T Schilling, *The Autonomy of the Community Legal Order*; as well as A Pellet, *Les fondements juridiques internationaux du droit communautaire*.

[193] BVerfGE 89, 155 (*Maastricht Decison*). The following discussion refers to the English translation of the judgment, cf [1994] CMLR 57 (*Maastricht Decision*).

cornerstone of modern constitutional thought. How could European laws be legitimized from a democratic point of view? Two options existed. First, European laws could be regarded as legitimized—directly or indirectly—through national democracy. Secondly, they could be legitimized by the existence of a European democracy. As regards the first option, national democracy could only be *directly* safeguarded through unanimity voting in the Council. However, the rise of majority voting in the Council increasingly allowed the European Union to adopt legislation against the will of the German people.[194] European integration indeed imposed formidable limits on the effectiveness of *national* democracy. Yet, majority voting was necessary for European integration;[195] and this had been recognized by Germany's choice to transfer sovereign powers to Europe. The situation in which a Member State was outvoted in the Council could thus still be *indirectly* legitimized by reference to the national decision to open up to European integration. (That argument works only where the national decision is of a constitutional nature—as in the case of Article 23 of the German Constitution.) But even this decision was subject to the fundamental boundaries set by the national Constitution.[196]

How did the Court assess the second option—legitimation through a European democratic structure? The Court readily admitted that 'with the building-up of the functions and powers of the Community, it becomes increasingly necessary to allow the democratic legitimation and influence provided by way of national parliaments *to be accompanied* by a representation of the peoples of the Member States through a European Parliament as the source of a *supplementary* democratic support for the policies of the European Union'. Formal progress in this direction was made by the establishment of European citizenship. The latter created a legal bond between Europe and its subjects, which 'although it does not have a tightness comparable to the common nationality of a single State, provides a legally binding expression of the degree of *de facto* community already in existence'.[197] But would this *constitutional* structure correspond to Europe's *social* structure? The existing

---

[194] Ibid 78.

[195] Ibid 86: 'Unanimity as a *universal* requirement would inevitably set the wills of the particular States above that of the Community of States itself and would put the very structure of such a community in doubt'.

[196] Article 79(3): 'Amendments to this Basic Law affecting the division of the Federation into *Länder*, their participation on principle in the legislative process, or the principles laid down in Articles 1 and 20 shall be inadmissible'.

[197] *Maastricht Decision* (n 193 above) 86.

democratic structure of the European Community would only work under certain social or '*pre*-legal' conditions. And these social pre-conditions for constitutional democracy did not (yet) exist in Europe.[198]

The very purpose behind the European Union was to realize a 'Union of States' as 'an *ever closer union of the peoples of Europe (organised as States) and not a State based on the people of one European nation*'.[199] The European Union was never to become a (federal) State. And from this negation, the Court drew is dramatic and (in)famous conclusions. First, the Union would need to recognize that the primary source of democratic legitimacy for European laws had remained the *national peoples*. Secondly, all legal authority of the European Union derived thus from the Member States. Thirdly, European laws could consequently 'only have effects within the German sovereign sphere by virtue of the German instruction that its law is applied'. European norms required a national 'bridge' over which to enter into the domestic

---

[198] Let us quote the contested para 41 (ibid 87) in full. 'Democracy, if it is not to remain a merely formal principle of accountability, is dependent on the presence of certain pre-legal conditions, such as a continuous free debate between opposing social forces, interests and ideas, in which political goals also become clarified and change course and out of which comes a public opinion which forms the beginnings of political intentions. That also entails that the decision-making processes of the organs exercising sovereign powers and the various political objectives pursued can be generally perceived and understood, and therefore that the citizen entitled to vote can communicate in his own language with the sovereign authority to which he is subject. Such factual conditions, in so far as they do not yet exist, can develop in the course of time within the institutional framework of the European Union . . . Parties, associations, the press and broadcasting organs are both a medium as well as a factor of this process, out of which a European public opinion may come into being[.]' The idea that no political system can operate without a broad consensus on the purposes of government by members of the polity is generally accepted. Only in passing did the German Constitutional Court seemingly define the substantive preconditions of democracy by a relative 'spiritual[], social[] and political[]' homogeneity of a people (ibid 88). The reference to Heller was designed to express—opposing Schmitt—the Court's belief in the necessity of a common set of civic values (!) as the basis of parliamentarianism (cf HP Ipsen, *Zehn Glossen zum Maastricht Urteil*, 6). There is no trace in the judgment on an insistence on racial or ethnic homogeneity. Suggestions to the contrary, describing the German Court's position as one of 'organic ethnoculturalism' and as a 'worldview which ultimately informs ethnic cleansing' (cf J Weiler, *Does Europe Need a Constitution: Demos, Telos and the German Maastricht Decision*, 251–2) are uninformed and unfair. Ironically, much of what Weiler pronounces to be 'his' civic theory of social and political commitment to shared values (ibid 253) is what we read in the German Constitutional Court's judgment.

[199] *Maastricht Decision*, 89 (emphasis added). The Court continues the theme a little later: 'In any event the establishment of a "United States of Europe", in a way comparable to that in which the United States of America became a State, is not at present intended'. Incidentally, the German Supreme Court did, superficially, acknowledge the *sui generis* characteristics of the European Union by inventing a new term for the European Union—the 'Staaten*ver*bund'.

legal order.[200] Fourthly, where a European law went beyond this national scope, it could have no effects in the national legal order. Fifthly, the ultimate arbiter of that question would be national Supreme Courts.

In conclusion, *each* Member State had remained a master of the treaties. Each of them had preserved 'the quality as a sovereign State in its own right and the status of sovereign equality with other States within the meaning of Article 2(1) of the United Nations Charter'.[201] European law was international law.[202]

b. Europe's Statist Tradition Unearthed: Three Constitutional Denials

The constitutional conflict over the Treaty on European Union had awoken old spirits: Europe's statist tradition. The reactions to the Maastricht challenge were manifold and ranged from the placid and guided to the aggressive and misguided.[203] But underneath superficial differences, much of the ensuing constitutional debate would not escape the conceptual heritage of Europe's federal tradition. The latent presence of the latter manifested itself in a series of three 'constitutional denials': Europe was said to have *no* people, *no* constitution, and *no* constitutionalism. These denials derived from a deep-seated belief in the indivisibility of sovereignty. Because sovereignty could not be divided, it had to be in the possession of *either* the Union *or* the Member States; that is, *either* a European people *or* the national peoples. Depending on the locus of sovereignty, the European Union would be *either* based on a

---

[200] On the bridge metaphor, see: CU Schmid, *From Pont d'Avignon to Ponte Vecchio: The Resolution of Constitutional Conflicts between the European Union and the Member States Through Principles of Public International Law*. But when the German legal order insists on the dualist reading of Community law via the theory of 'advance general incorporation', it uses a device that is 'a manifest absurdity': 'For the notion that one can transform [or incorporate] a rule of international law into municipal law before the rule has been established, and even that such incorporation need refer to no specific rule, but may operate in advance and in an entirely general manner, contradicts the essential and only meaning of the concept of incorporation—that of a free conscious decision of the competent national institutions incorporating international law into municipal law. Seen in this light, incorporation is no longer incorporation at all, but has become a mere word, designed to veil as best it may the inadequacy of incorporation theory and, consequently, of the dualist view of international law'. (Cf C Sasse, *The Common Market: Between International and Municipal Law*, 725).

[201] *Maastricht Decision*, 91.

[202] Cf I Pernice, *Multilevel Constitutionalism and the Treaty of Amsterdam: European Constitution-Making Revisited?*, 711: 'internationalist' view of the Court that 'treats Community law as any other rule of international law'.

[203] For a moderate and informed analysis in English, see: U Everling, *The* Maastricht *Judgment of the German Federal Constitutional Court and its Significance for the Development of the European Union*. For the opposite, see: J Weiler (n 198 above).

(national) constitution *or* an (international) treaty. And even if Europe had a constitutional treaty, the lack of a 'constitutional demos' denied it a constitutionalism of its own.

Let us look at the underlying philosophical rationale for each of these denials, before subjecting each to constructive criticism.

Will a people—the 'constituency' for constitutional politics—precede its polity, or be a product of it? This question has received different philosophical and constitutional answers. To some, the 'people' will emerge only through subjection to a common sovereign.[204] To others, the 'people' will precede the State for it is they who invest the government with its powers.[205] Most early modern European States were 'supra-national' in character in that they housed multiple 'nations' under one governmental roof.[206] However, with the rise of nationalism in the nineteenth century States would come to be identified by their nation.[207] Multiple nations within one State came to be seen as an anomaly. This anomalous status was equally attached to the idea of 'dual citizenship': an individual should only be part of one political body.[208] (National) peoples thus came to be seen as mutually exclusive. Transposed to the context of the European Union, this meant that a European people could not exist alongside national peoples. (And European citizenship could not exist alongside national citizenship.) Both peoples would exclude—not complement—each other; and as long as national peoples exist—as they do—a European people could not.

---

[204] Cf T Hobbes, *Leviathan*, 114 and 120: 'A Multitude of men, are made *One* Person, when they are by one man, or one Person, Represented; so that it be done with the consent of every one of that Multitude in particular. For it is the *Unity* of the Representer, not the *Unity* of the Represented, that Maketh the Person *One* ... This done, the Multitude so united in one Person, is called a COMMON-WEALTH, or in latine CIVITAS. This is the generation of that great LEVIATHAN, or rather (to speake more reverently) of that *Mortall God*, to which wee owe under the *Immortal God*, our peace and defence'. I am grateful to Q Skinner for shedding much light on these passages.

[205] The theory of popular sovereignty will typically distinguish between a 'people' (nation), on the one hand, and a 'subject' (citizen) on the other. The former refers to a *community* characterized by an emotion of solidarity that gives the group consciousness and identity. The latter refers to an *individual's* legal relation to its State. On these issues, see: JW Salmond, *Citizenship and Allegiance*.

[206] Before the 1789 French Revolution, French kings would refer to the 'peoples' of France (cf B Voyenne, *Histoire de l'idée fédéraliste: Les Sources*, 165). The United Kingdom is still a multi-*demoi* State that comprises the English, Scottish, Welsh and a part of the Irish Nation (cf M Keating, *Plurinational Democracy: Stateless Nations in a Post-Sovereign Era*, 123: 'one of the most explicitly plurinational States in the word').

[207] On these issues generally, see: E Gellner, *Nations and Nationalism*; as well as EJ Hobsbawn, *Nations and Nationalism since 1780: Programme, Myth, Reality*.

[208] O Beaud, *The Question of Nationality within a Federation: a Neglected Issue in Nationality Law*, 317.

This brings us to the second denial: the absence of a European constitution. Under the doctrine of popular sovereignty, only a 'people' can formally 'constitute' itself into a legal sovereign. A constitution is regarded as a unilateral act of the *'pouvoir constituant'*.[209] Thus, 'it is inherent in a constitution in the full sense of the term that it goes back to an act taken by or at least attributed to the people, in which they attribute political capacity to themselves'.[210] This normative—or better: democratic—notion of constitutionalism is said to have emerged with the American and French Revolutions and to have, since then, become the *exclusive* meaning of the concept.[211] 'There is no such source for primary Community law. It goes back not to a European people but to the individual Member States, and remains dependent on them even after its entry into force. While nations give themselves a constitution, the European Union is given a constitution by third parties'.[212] And assuming, hypothetically, that a European people would in the future give the Union a constitution? Then, 'the Union would acquire competence to decide about competences (*Kompetenzkompetenz*)'. It would have the power to unilaterally change its constitution and would thus have turned itself from a confederation of States into a Federal State.[213] However, for the time being, the Union is no State.[214] And failing that, the European Union has no constitution.

Let us finally look at a third—milder—denial: 'The condition of Europe is not, as is often implied, that of constitutionalism without a constitution, but of a constitution without constitutionalism'.[215] (Paradoxically, this very same

---

[209] On the theory: E Zweig, *Die Lehre vom Pouvoir Constituant*.

[210] D Grimm, *Does Europe Need a Constitution?*, 290.

[211] Grimm acknowledges the past existence of a 'descriptive' concept of 'constitution' that preceded the 'normative' idea of 'constitution'. However, according to him, only the latter is today accepted since it refers to State power and to the democratic idea of a *pouvoir constituant*. What is perplexing in this context is his reference to the US American Constitutions, especially the Articles of Confederation (cf D Grimm, *Die Verfassung im Prozess der Entstaatlichung*, 146: 'Die normative Verfassung trat 1776 an der Peripherie der damaligen westlichen Welt, in Nordamerika, ins Leben[.]')—none of which was adopted by 'the' American people. In a different publication, he even acknowledges the existence, in the nineteenth (!) century, of treaty-constitutions: 'But in the nineteenth century treaty-based constitutions could be found, both through State mergers or out of revolutionary pressure on kings, who did not necessarily fully abandon their pre-constitutional legitimacy while partially recognizing popular sovereignty' (cf D Grimm, *Treaty or Constitution: The Legal Basis of the European Union after Maastricht*, 74).

[212] D Grimm, *Does Europe Need a Constitution?*, 290.

[213] Ibid 299.

[214] This is universally accepted; see: BVerfGE 22, 293 (*EWG Verordnungen*), 296: 'Die Gemeinschaft ist selbst kein Staat, auch kein Bundesstaat'.

[215] J Weiler, *Does Europe Need a Constitution: Demos, Telos and the German Maastricht Decision*, 220.

denial had been made in relation to the American Union(s) in the eighteenth century.[216]) 'In federations, whether American or Australian, German or Canadian, the institutions of a federal state are situated in a constitutional framework which presupposes the existence of a "constitutional demos", a single *pouvoir constituant* made of the citizens of the federation in whose sovereignty, as a constituent power, and by whose supreme authority the specific constitutional arrangement is rooted.' 'In Europe, that precondition does not exist. Simply put, Europe's constitutional architecture has never been validated by a process of constitutional adoption by a European constitutional *demos*[.]'[217] And in the absence of a unitary constitutional demos, Europe could have no constitutionalism.

What is common to these three denials? Each is rooted in Europe's statist tradition and based on the idea of indivisible sovereignty: a *unitary* people forms a *unitary* State on the basis of a *unitary* constitution. The inability to accept shared or divided sovereignty thus blinds the European tradition to the possibility of *federal* arrangements or a *duplex regimen* between peoples, States, and constitutions. It is unable to envisage *two* peoples living in the same territory—yet, this is generally the case in Federal Unions.[218] It is unable to envisage *two* constitutional orders existing within the same territory—yet, this is generally the case in Federal Unions.[219] It is unable to envisage *two* governments operating in the same territory—yet, this is generally the case in Federal Unions. Finally, it is unable to envisage a compound *pouvoir constituant* of multiple *demoi*—yet, this is generally the case in Federal Unions.[220]

---

[216] C Schmitt, *Verfassungslehre*, 78: 'Den amerikanischen Verfassungen des 18. Jahrhunderts fehlt es an einer eigentlichen Verfassungstheorie'.

[217] J Weiler, *Federalism without Constitutionalism: Europe's Sonderweg*, 56–7.

[218] Cf O Beaud, *The Question of Nationality within a Federation: a Neglected Issue in Nationality Law*, 320: 'Dual citizenship, essential to federations, is then nothing but the duplication of the fundamental law of duality of political entities constituting them. In contrast to the State, the federation here is characterised by a "political dualism".'

[219] American and German constitutionalism accept the idea 'State *Constitutions*'. However, in both cases, the federal Constitution establishes a normative frame around the State Constitutions. Article IV, Section 4 of the US Constitution states: 'The United States shall guarantee to every State in this Union a Republican Form of Government'. And Article 28(1) of the German Constitution states: 'The constitutional order in the *Länder* must conform to the principles of a republican, democratic, and social State governed by the rule of law, within the meaning of this Basic Law. In each Land, county, and municipality the people shall be represented by a body chosen in general, direct, free, equal, and secret elections'.

[220] When Professor Weiler confesses that 'I am unaware of any federal state, old or new, which does not presuppose the supreme authority and sovereignty of its federal demos' (J Weiler, *Federalism without Constitutionalism: Europe's Sonderweg*, 57), we may draw his attention to the United States of America. None of the two Constitutions of the United States was ratified by a 'federal demos' in the form of 'the' American people. The Articles of Confederation were ratified by the State *legislatures*,

The black-or-white logic of unitary constitutionalism is simply unable to capture the federal 'blue' on the international versus national spectrum.

The European Union's constitutionalism must, in the future, be (re)constructed in federal terms. It is half-hearted to—enigmatically—claim that Europe has a constitution, but no constitutionalism. For once we admit that Europe has a constitution, who tells us so? National legal theory? International legal theory? Since none affirms the statement that 'Europe has a constitution', the latter presupposes a system of thought that allows us to 'recognize' or 'verify' that statement as true. Logically, the affirmation of a 'constitution' presumes the existence of a 'constitutionalism'. But more importantly: the misguided insistence on a 'constitutional demos' shows that 'constitutionalism' is still identified with the legitimizing theory underlying a—*unitary*—nation State. But Europe's mixed constitutional system cannot be conceived in purely unitary—or 'national'—terms. Only a *federal* constitutionalism can explain and give meaning to normative problems that arise in compound systems like the European Union.[221] And once we apply a *federal* constitutionalism to the European Union, the above 'denials' are shown for what they are: *false problems*. They are created by a wrong constitutional theory. National constitutionalism simply cannot explain the 'dual nature' of federations as classical physics was unable to explain the dual nature of light.[222] By insisting that the European Union is *either* international *or* national, it denies its status as an (inter)national phenomenon.

Applying a *federal* constitutional theory to the European Union may equally place the European Union's 'deficits' into a new light. The classic illustration

while the 1787 Constitution was ratified by the State *peoples*. And as regards constitutional amendment, Article V of the US Constitution still requires the concurrence of the federal demos—acting indirectly through its representatives—and three fourths of the State *demoi*—acting either through their representatives or in conventions. More generally: in all (democratic) Federal Unions the *pouvoir constituant* should be a compound of the federal and the State *demoi* (cf H Schneider, *Alternativen der Verfassungsfinalität: Föderation, Konföderation—oder was sonst?*, 174: 'So könnte man sagen: in einem genuin föderalen Gemeinwesen kann auch der "pouvoir constituant" sozusagen nicht im Singular gedacht werden, sondern von vorn herein als "kompositorischer" Plural, entsprechend dem föderalistischen Grundgedanken der "Einheit-in-Vielheit", die zugleich "Vielheit in Einheit" ist'). Where the 'constitutional demos' is conceived in unitary terms, the federal Union loses its federal base (cf C Schmitt, *Verfassungslehre*, 389: 'Durch den demokratischen Begriff der verfassungsgebenden Gewalt des *ganzen* Volkes wird die bündische Grundlage und damit der Bundescharakter aufgehoben. Im Bundesstaat ohne bündische Grundlage gibt es nur ein einziges Volk. Der staatliche Charakter der früheren Gliedstaaten ist also beseitigt').

[221] For a remarkable step towards a general theory of federal constitutionalism, see: O Beaud, *Théorie de la Fédération*.

[222] Classical physics insisted that a phenomenon must be *either* a particle *or* a wave; and it could not be both. Following the works of Einstein, modern physics now accepts the dual nature of light. On Einstein's discovery, see: W Isaacson, *Einstein: His Life and Universe*, Chapter 5.

of the distorted constitutional discourse on the European Union is the debate about Europe's 'democratic deficit'. It is not difficult to find such a deficit if one measures decision-making in the European Union against the democratic standard of a unitary State. There, all legislative decisions are, theoretically, legitimized by one source—'the' people represented in the national parliament. But is this—unitary—standard the appropriate yardstick for a compound body politic? In a federal structure there are *two* arenas of democracy: the 'State demos' and the 'federal demos'. Both offer independent sources of democratic legitimacy. Duplex regimen, dual democracy. A *federal* constitutionalism will then need to take account of the *dual* basis of democratic legitimacy in Federal Unions. One *functional* expression of this is the division of legislative powers between the State demos and the federal demos. One *institutional* expression of this dual legitimacy is the compound nature of the central legislator. One *foundational* expression of this dual legitimacy is the—typically—compound nature of a federation's constitutive power.

The latter point has been well made in relation to the United States of America:

Half a century ago J. Allen Smith wrote a book in which he bitterly criticized the undemocratic spirit of the American Scheme of government. In it he argued that a true democracy had to embrace the principle of majority rule . . . His criticism was justified, but only within his own frame of reference. It was phrased in the wrong terms. He was in fact criticising a federal system for serving the ends it was intended to serve . . . What he ignored was that even in 1907 the United States was still composed of States. The amending clause was an excellent spot for his attack and the criticism he made of it would have been equally applicable to any federation. Nearly all governments that are called federal employ some device in the amending process to *prevent* a mere majority from changing the constitution . . . Does this prove federalism i[s] undemocratic? Certainly it does, if democracy be defined in terms of majority rule . . . They argue that the will of the majority is being thwarted and suggest by implication at least that this is ethically wrong; the term 'will of the majority' carries with it certain moral overtones in these days of enlightened democracy. But what the *ad hoc* majoritarians forget is that a federal state is a different thing, that it is not intended to operate according to a majority principle. We cannot apply the standard of unitary government to a federal state. If the opinion of a majority is a sufficient guide for public policy in a community then it is unlikely that a federal system will have been established in that community.[223]

How enlightening *comparative* constitutionalism can be!

[223] WS Livingston, *Federalism and Constitutional Change*, 311–14.

Conclusion: The European Union as a 'Federation of States'

Modern federal thought emerged in the wake of the Westphalian State system. In an attempt to make sense of the 'Unions of States' that existed in the seventeenth century, classic international law conceives them in treaty terms. Federal Unions are based on a *foedus*—an international treaty—that safeguards the sovereignty of its Member States. A Federal Union was a *voluntary* arrangement that contrasted with the *forced* arrangement within an empire.[224] The emergence of the United States of America at the end of the eighteenth century triggered the greatest semantic revolution in the history of the federal principle.[225] Federalism came to be identified with a mixed structure between international and national organization. When this second tradition crossed the Atlantic in the nineteenth century, Europe's obsession with indivisible sovereignty pressed the novel idea into a third format: the national format of federalism. The idea of sovereignty operated as a lens that polarized the federal principle into two—mutually exclusive—species: confederation and federation. The concept of confederation thereby becomes the semantic carrier of the classic tradition of federal thought.[226] A federation, on the other hand, becomes exclusively identified with a Federal State.[227]

In Europe, then, the federal idea came, in the course of 300 years, to signify its very opposite. Had it originally stood for a *treaty* relation *between* States in *international* law, it came to represent a *constitutional* relation *within* a State in *national* law. The conceptual evolution of the federal principle from the

---

[224] O Beaud, *La notion de pacte fédératif*, 248–9.

[225] KC Wheare, *Federal Government*, 11–12: 'since the United States is universally regarded as an example of federal government, it justifies us in describing the principle, which distinguishes it so markedly and so significantly, as the *federal principle*'.

[226] Of course, the idea of confederalism changes also in each federal tradition. Within the international tradition, the notion of confederation and federation are coterminous. Within the American tradition, a confederation is a loose or weak Union of States. Within the European tradition, a confederation is categorically different from a federation: the former falls under international law, the latter is a creature of national law.

[227] Our discussion concentrated on the German history of ideas; yet, the very same semantic identification between federation and federal State can be found in French constitutional thought, cf L Le Fur, *L'etat fédéral et confédération d'etats*; and more recently: B de Witte, '*Fédération*' in O Duhamel & Y Mény (eds), *Dictionaire constitutionnel*, 435: contrasting 'fédération ou État fédéral' with 'confédération'. On the success of the (German) distinction between 'Confederation' and 'Federal State' in France, see: O Beaud, *La notion de pacte federative*, 221–2.

seventeenth to the twentieth century suggested a teleological reduction from an international format over a mixed format to a national format. However, history is not teleology. And more importantly: the American tradition has not been replaced by the European tradition. Both traditions co-exist, for American constitutionalism has never completely endorsed the national format of the federal principle—despite a vocal countercurrent in contemporary American constitutional thought.[228] Today there are, thus, *two* living traditions of federalism. And the battle between the American and the European tradition over the federal principle has come to the fore in the terminological contest to classify the European Union. The emergence of the European Union in the twentieth century has challenged Europe's own 'statist' tradition as the national format of the federal principle fell increasingly out of step with the social and legal reality within Europe.

What, then, is the relation between the federal idea and the European Union? We saw above that the American tradition easily classifies the European Union as a Federal Union. The Union has a mixed or compound structure; and in combining international and national elements, it stands on federal 'middle ground'.

The federal label is, ironically, denied by Europe's own intellectual tradition. In pressing the federal principle into a national (State) format, the concept of federation is reduced to that of a Federal State. And while the creation of a Federal State may have been a long-term aim in the early years of European integration, the failure of the European Political Community in the 1950s caused the demise of federal ideology.[229] The fall of federalism gave rise to (neo-)functionalism.[230] The latter remained agnostic on what kind of

---

[228] The famous spokesman of this countercurrent is Ackerman, who has advanced a purely 'national' format of the federal principle. His 'We, the People' insists on the absolute national supremacy of 'the' American people, which may be occasionally expressed in 'constitutional moments'. The national feeling is enough to make higher law in breach of the positive *federal* constitution. The similarity between Ackerman's theory and the theories developed by German federal scholars at the end of the nineteenth century is striking (cf Section I (3a) above). For an excellent critique of Ackermann's school of thought, see: L Tribe, *Taking Text and Structure Seriously: Reflections on Free-Form Method in Constitutional Interpretation*; as well as S Choudhry, *Ackerman's Higher Lawmaking in Comparative Constitutional Perspective: Constitutional Moments as Constitutional Failures*.

[229] M Forsyth, *The Political Theory of Federalism: The Relevance of Classical Approaches*, 26.

[230] The functionalist classic is D Mitrany, *A Working Peace System: An Argument for the Functional Development of International Organization*. Neofunctionalism discards the belief in the automaticity of the integration process and emphasizes the need to build new loyalties with strategic elites. The classics here are: E Haas, *The Uniting of Europe: Political, Social and Economic Forces, 1950–1957*; and LN Lindberg, *The Political Dynamics of European Economic Integration*.

object the Union was. The Union was celebrated as a *process*—a 'journey to an unknown destination'.[231] But this agnosticism could not forever postpone the fundamental question: 'What is the European Union?' 'Les contraintes de *l'existence publique* ne permettent plus de s'accommoder du flou[!]'[232]

Early commentators were aware that the new European construct had moved on the 'middle ground' between international and national law. Yet, Europe's conceptual tradition blocked the identification of that middle ground with the federal idea. De Tocqueville's quest for a new word was thus answered by a neologism: the idea of supranationalism. Europe was celebrated as *sui generis*. But how common exceptionalisms are![233] The *sui generis* 'theory' was, in any event, but a veneer. In times of constitutional conflict, Europe's old federal tradition returned from the depths and imposed its two polarized ideal-types: Europe was either an international organization or a Federal State. And since it was not the latter, it must be the former.

What is the explanatory power of the international law thesis? Can it satisfactorily explain the legal and social reality within the European Union? In the last 50 years, 'Little Europe' has emancipated herself from her humble birth and has grown into a mature woman: the European Union. The international law thesis thus runs into great many explanatory difficulties. *Unlike* international doctrine predicts, the obligations imposed on the Member States are not interpreted restrictively.[234] *Unlike* international doctrine predicts, the Member States are not allowed a free hand in how to execute their obligations. *Unlike* international doctrine predicts, the Member States cannot modify their obligations *inter se* through the conclusion of subsequent international treaties. In order to defend the international law hypothesis, its adherents must denounce these legal characteristics as non-essential 'marks'

---

[231] A Shonfield, *Journey to an Unknown Destination*. Ironically, the process metaphor itself has been identified with federalism, see: CJ Friedrich, *Trends of Federalism in Theory and Practice—* Chapter 1: 'The Theory of Federalism as Process'.

[232] Editorial: '*Nation, federation: quelle Europe?*', 87 (emphasis added).

[233] Calhoun described the 1787 American legal order as 'new, peculiar, and unprecedented' (cf JC Calhoun, *A Discourse on the Constitution and Government of the United States*, 117). The legal structure of the British Commonwealth has been described as *sui generis*. The Balfour Report (1926) stated: 'The Committee are of opinion that nothing would be gained by attempting to lay down a Constitution for the British Empire. Its widely scattered parts have very different characteristics, very different histories, and are at very different stages of evolution; while, considered as a whole, it defies classification and bears no real resemblance to any other political organization which now exists or has ever yet been tried'.

[234] U Everling, *Sind die Mitgliedstaaten noch Herren der Verträge*, 178: 'Jedenfalls in dieser Hinsicht, also bei der Anwendung und Auslegung des Gemeinschaftsrechts durch den Gerichtshof, sind die Mitgliedstaaten deshalb nicht mehr Herren der Verträge'.

of sovereignty. And in relegating the social reality of European law to a false appearance, European thought refuses comparing the *ideal* with the *real*. *Was nicht sein darf, das nicht sein kann*. But facts are stubborn things!

The *sui generis* thesis and the international law thesis had *both* caused the Community to disappear from the federal map. How did the federal idea return? Its revival in discussions of the structure of the European Union was slow. As a first step, it was accepted that the Community had borrowed the federal principle from the public law of federal States.[235] The European Union was said to be the 'classic case of federalism without federation'.[236] It had 'federal' features, but it was no 'federation'. Federation thus still meant Federal State.[237] The word 'federal', by contrast, attached to a *function* and not to the *essence* of the organization. The adjective was allowed—adjectives refer to *attributes*, not to *essences*—but the noun was not. In order for European constitutionalism to accept the idea of a 'Federation of States' a second step was required. Europe needed to abandon its obsession with the idea of undivided sovereignty. It needed to accept that '[t]he law of integration rests on a premise quite unknown to so-called 'classical' international law: that is the

---

[235] Haas separated the idea of 'federation' from the notion of 'State' (E Haas (n 230 above) 37) and could, consequently, speak of the 'federal attributes' (ibid 42) of the ECSC. The ECSC was, overall, described as a 'hybrid form, short of federation' (ibid 51), for it did not satisfy all the federal attributes believed by the author to be necessary for a federation to exist (ibid 59): 'While almost all the criteria point positively to federation, the remaining limits on the ability to implement decisions and to expand the scope of the system independently still suggest the characteristics of international organisation'.

[236] M Burgess, *Federalism and the European Union: the Building of Europe 1950–2000*, 28–29: '[I]t is not necessarily the case that every 'federalism' will always lead to 'federation' in the sense that Europe will simply be like Germany or Switzerland writ large—a new putative national state. Nor will it replicate the United States of America, although it does already exhibit many of the traits of the American Confederation during 1781–89. The EU of course is not a federation; it does not fit the established criteria by which we conventionally define such a state. Logically, then, we have a classic case of federalism without federation ... Whatever the EU is, it is not yet a state. But it has to be acknowledged that it does have several institutional features and policy-making characteristics of an established federation'.

[237] Cf WG Friedmann, *The Changing Structure of International Law*, 98: 'The Community Treaties stop short of the establishment of a federation. They do not transfer to a federal sphere the general powers usually associated with a federal state[.]'; as well as: Ch Pentland, *International Theory and European Integration*, who also identified federalism with the 'State model'. In fact, his chapter on federalist theory is entitled: 'Power and the Supranational State: Varieties of Federalist Theory' and therein we read 'federalists are concerned to direct the integrative process toward a definitive, well-articulated ideal—a supranational state with specific characteristics' (ibid 148); and P Schmitter, *Imagining the Future of the Euro-Polity with the Help of New Concepts*, 133: federation 'implies the existence of an orthodox sovereign state'.

divisibility of sovereignty'.[238] The Community enjoys 'real powers stemming from a *limitation of sovereignty* or a transfer of powers from the States to the Community' through which, in turn, 'the Member States have *limited their sovereign rights*, albeit within limited fields'.[239] The European Union is indeed based on a conception of divided sovereignty and in strictness neither international nor national, 'but a composition of both'. It represents an (inter) national phenomenon that stands on—federal—middle ground.

In conclusion, the European Union is a Federation of States.[240] The Union may even represent the best manifestation of 'true' federalism that presently exists in positive law.[241] Once this idea is accepted, it is possible—in a third step—to ask what type of federation the European Union is. This is the question this book will try to answer in relation to the federal division of legislative powers. What federal philosophy has the European Union followed? What is the structure of European law? These questions can best be answered with the assistance of comparative constitutional law. To understand the structure of European law, we will compare it with the structure of American law. This comparative excursion will be the task of the second chapter of this book.

---

[238] P Pescatore, *The Law of Integration: Emergence of a New Phenomenon in International Relations, Based on the Experience of the European Communities*, 30. This corresponds to J Fischer's vision: 'The completion of European integration can only be successfully conceived if it is done on the basis of a division of sovereignty between Europe and the nation-state. Precisely this is the idea underlying the concept of "subsidiarity," a subject that is currently being discussed by everyone and understood by virtually no one', cf *From Confederacy to Federation: Thoughts on the Finality of European Integration* (Speech at the Humboldt University in Berlin, 12 May 2000).

[239] Case 6/64 *Flaminio Costa v E.N.E.L.*, 593 (emphasis added).

[240] Cf A Dashwood, *The Relationship between the Member States and the European Union/Community*, 356: 'a federation of sovereign States'; T Börzel & T Risse, *Who is afraid of a European Federation?*; J Delors: 'federation of nation states'.

[241] O Beaud, *Europa als Föderation? Relevanz und Bedeutung einer Bundeslehre für die Europäische Union*, 14 (translation—RS).

2

Federal Philosophies and the Structure of American Law

Introduction: Federal Philosophies and Constitutional Structures

The 1787 Constitution set up a structure under which the federal government could act directly upon the people within those powers 'delegated' to it. The States, by contrast, would enjoy all powers not exclusively delegated to the federation. Within these powers the States could act as 'sovereigns'—unless the Constitution prohibited such action. What was the scope of the federal powers and how did they relate to the powers 'inherent' in the States? The Articles of Confederation had answered this question in its text, whenever they gave 'the United States in Congress assembled' '*the sole and exclusive right and power*' to act.[1] By contrast, the 1787 Constitution contained no verbal reference on the nature and extent of the federation's powers. The question would soon be hotly debated in American constitutionalism—'and will probably continue to arise as long as [the American] system shall exist'.[2]

Two views on the nature of the federal order came to compete. The 'international' view saw the 1787 Constitution as a treaty among 'sovereign' States; and the sovereignty of the States was *the* interpretative principle governing the Constitution. The powers of the federation had, consequently, to be interpreted restrictively. A second view also emerged in the early days of the young federation. It was 'nationalist' and claimed that the federation was sovereign. This view 'rejected the general principle of strict construction in its most insidious special application, that the existence of the states operated as an impalpable limitation upon national powers'.[3]

---

[1] Article IX of the Articles of Confederation.

[2] *McCulloch v Maryland* 17 US 316 (1819), 405: 'This government is acknowledged by all, to be one of enumerated powers. The principle, that it can exercise only the powers granted to it, would seem too apparent, to have required to be enforced by all those arguments, which its enlightened friends, while it was depending before the people, found it necessary to urge; that principle is now universally admitted. But the question respecting the extent of the powers actually granted, is perpetually arising, and will probably continue to arise, so long as our system shall exist'.

[3] F Frankfurter, *Taney and the Commerce Clause*, 1286. In *Gibbons v Ogden* 22 US 1 (1824), Marshall explained this view as follows (ibid 187–8): 'This instrument contains an enumeration of powers expressly granted by the people to their government. It has been said, that these powers ought to be construed strictly. But why ought they to be so construed? Is there one sentence in the constitution which gives countenance to this rule? In the last of the enumerated powers, that which grants, expressly, the means for carrying all others into execution, Congress is authorized "to make all laws which shall be necessary and proper" for the purpose. But this limitation on the means

These two—extreme—views would never completely disappear from American constitutional thought. However, it was a third view that would reign over the better part of the nineteenth century. Accepting that the 1787 Constitution had split the atom of sovereignty,[4] conciliatory voices advanced the idea of *dual* sovereignty. This third view offered an intellectual compromise between the two contenders for 'ultimate' sovereignty: 'The United States are sovereign as to all the powers of Government actually surrendered: Each State in the Union is sovereign as to all the powers reserved'.[5] The federal government and the States were seen as 'equal' and 'coordinate' within their respective spheres. '[T]he powers of the General Government, and of the State, although both exist and are exercised within the same territorial limits, are yet separate and distinct sovereignties, acting separately and independently of each other within their respective spheres'.[6] In contrast to the 'international' position, the philosophy of dual federalism accepted the idea of autonomous federal powers. However, unlike the 'nationalist' interpretation, it also accepted the idea of 'implied limitations'.[7] The central idea behind dual federalism 'was that of *the federal equilibrium*; in other words, the idea that the then existing distribution of powers between the states and the national government should be regarded as something essentially fixed and unchangeable'.[8]

The philosophical key to the idea of dual federalism became the image of two mutually exclusive spheres.[9] 'In America, the powers of sovereignty are

---

which may be used, is not extended to the powers which are conferred; nor is there one sentence in the constitution, which has been pointed out by the gentlemen of the bar, or which we have been able to discern, that prescribes this rule. We do not, therefore, think ourselves justified in adopting it'.

[4] *US Term Limits, Inc v Thornton* 514 US 779 (1995), 838 (Justice Kennedy, concurring).

[5] *Chisholm v State of Georgia* 2 US 419 (1793), 435.

[6] *Ableman v Booth* 62 US 506 (1859), 516.

[7] WF Dodd, *Implied Powers and Implied Limitations in Constitutional Law*.

[8] ES Corwin, *The Twilight of the Supreme Court: A History of Our Constitutional Theory*, 11.

[9] The view contradicted the belief of some founding fathers that the grants of legislative power to the Union were predominantly 'shared' in nature. In 'The Federalist No 32', Hamilton had argued that 'the necessity of a concurrent jurisdiction in certain cases results from the division of the sovereign power; and the rule that all authorities, of which the States are not explicitly divested in favour of the Union, remain with them in full vigor, is not a theoretical consequence of that division, but is clearly admitted by the whole tenor of the instrument which contains the articles of the proposed Constitution'. Where the federation was to have exclusive powers, the framers had taken 'the most pointed care in those cases where it was deemed improper that the like authorities should reside in the States, to insert negative clauses prohibiting the exercise of them by the States'. 'This exclusive delegation, or rather this alienation, of State sovereignty, would only exist in three cases: where the Constitution in express terms granted an exclusive authority to the Union; where it granted in one

divided between the Government of the Union and those of the States. They are each sovereign with respect to the objects committed to it, and neither sovereign with respect to the objects committed to the other'.[10] This image had its consequences: 'there should not be *concurrent* jurisdiction over a particular subject'. For each particular subject, the citizen must 'be accountable to only one sovereign'.[11] The thought that the federal legislator is supreme over the State legislator was absurd to dual federalism.[12] But how could this view be squared with the 'Supremacy Clause'?[13] Dual federalists solve this problem by reducing the supremacy principle to the supremacy of the *Constitution*. The Constitution reigns above both 'sovereign' *governments;* but under dual federalism, there is no *legislative* supremacy.[14] 'The supremacy of

---

instance an authority to the Union, and in another prohibited the States from exercising the like authority; and where it granted an authority to the Union, to which a similar authority in the States would be absolutely and totally contradictory and repugnant'.

[10] *McCulloch v Maryland* 17 US 316 (1819), 410.

[11] W Needham, *The Exclusive Power of Congress over Interstate Commerce*, 255. This point may well be illustrated by quoting Justice Washington in *Houston v Moore* (1820), 21–3 (emphasis added): 'If, in a specified case, the people have thought proper to bestow certain powers on Congress as the safest depository of them, and Congress has legislated within the scope of them, the people have reason to complain that the same powers should be exercised at the same time by the State legislatures. To subject them to the operation of two laws upon the same subject, dictated by distinct wills, particularly in a case inflicting pains and penalties, is, to my apprehension, something very much like oppression, if not worse. *In short, I am altogether incapable of comprehending how two distinct wills can, at the same time, be exercised in relation to the same subject, to be effectual, and at the same time compatible with each other.* If they correspond in every respect, then the latter is idle and inoperative; if they differ, they must, in the nature of things, oppose each other, so far as they do differ. If the one imposes a certain punishment for a certain offence, the presumption is, that this was deemed sufficient, and, under all circumstances, the only proper one. If the other legislature impose a different punishment, in kind or degree, I am at a loss to conceive how they can both consist harmoniously together'.

[12] SR Davis, *The Federal Principle: A Journey through Time in Quest of a Meaning*, 106: 'To be coordinate was to be of equal standing; the national and the state governments were "co-ordinate" or "co-equal" in status because both were equally subject to the Constitution, not each other; as "co-ordinate" governments neither could command, direct, control, dictate, compel, or regulate the other; the relationship of equal status was different from any previous relationship, different from the Articles of Confederation, and different from the relationship of Westminster to the counties of England'.

[13] Article VI, Section 2 US Constitution states: 'This Constitution, and the Laws of the United States which shall be made in pursuance thereof; and all Treaties made, or which shall be made, under the Authority of the United States, shall be the supreme Law of the land'.

[14] The Supreme Court is here regarded 'as standing outside of and over both the National Government and the States, and vested with authority to apportion impartially to each center its proper powers in accordance with the Constitution's intentions' (ES Corwin, *The Passing of Dual Federalism*, 16).

the general government, therefore, so much relied upon by council for the plaintiff in error, in respect to the question before us, cannot be maintained. The two governments are upon equality. In respect to the reserved powers, the state is as sovereign and independent as the general government'.[15] And since '[d]ual federalism cannot possibly be squared logically with the "supremacy" clause',[16] the Supremacy Clause itself was subordinated to the *meta*-constitutional philosophy of dual federalism.[17]

The philosophy of dual federalism offered, for almost a century, a constitutional compromise to the American Union. Yet, 'like the conciliatory medieval formula of *regnum et sacerdotium* which acknowledged the two distinct but equal powers of Pope and Holy Roman Emperor in their separate realms, the language of "co-ordinate" or "co-equal" status in 1787 was no more than a formal symbol of political accommodation'.[18] This accommodation would gradually disappear in the first half of the twentieth century; and by 1950, dual federalism was dead.

To demonstrate the demise of the old and the emergence of the new federalism in the United States of America, this chapter will be divided into three sections. The first section will analyse the decline of constitutionally exclusive spheres of power. The rise of national power led not only to a demise of the idea of exclusive State 'police powers'; it also triggered the gradual abandonment of the exclusive power theory for the federation's own competences. This double change will be analysed through the prism of the Commerce Clause. However, the 'new nationalism' did not *ipso facto* imply a 'new federalism'. The latter would only emerge, once federal powers were exercised in such a way as to allow for legislative 'cooperation' between the two governments. This required a change in the very structure of federal law: only once automatic field pre-emption was left behind, could a new federalism emerge. This transformation will be discussed in the second section. A third section provides an excursion into the constitutional principles governing foreign affairs. This 'field' has remained loyal to dual federalism and warrants special attention.

---

[15] *Collector v Day* 78 US 113 (1870), 126.

[16] ES Corwin (n 8 above) 183.

[17] For a similar meta-constitutional subordination of the 'Supremacy Clause' under German federalism, see: R Schütze, *German Constitutional Federalism: Between* Sein *and* Bewußtsein.

[18] SR Davis (n 12 above) 115.

I. The 'New Nationalism': The Decline of Constitutional Exclusivity

The battlefield on which much of the constitutional controversies over dual and cooperative federalism would be fought was the 'Commerce Clause'. The clause gives Congress the power 'to regulate Commerce with foreign Nations, and among the several States'.[19] In combination with the 'Necessary and Proper Clause',[20] this provision granted the widest legislative power to the American Federation. Nonetheless, the scope of this power had to be limited—even the most 'nationalist' reading of the Constitution would not deny this. Federal powers were enumerated powers; and 'enumeration presupposes something not enumerated'. In the context of the Commerce Clause, 'that something, if we regard the language or the subject of the sentence, must be the exclusively internal commerce of a State'.[21]

But where would interstate commerce begin and internal commerce end? The philosophy of dual federalism was to safeguard 'sovereign' enclaves for the States from the reach of federal power. This did not always mandate a restrictive interpretation of the Commerce Clause. Indeed, dual federalism acknowledged the autonomous character of the federation's power; yet, it protected the States through a strategy of implied limitations to that power.

---

[19] Article I, Section 8, Clause 3 US Constitution.

[20] This is the last clause in Article I, Section 8, Clause 18. It provides Congress with the power '[t]o make all Laws which shall be necessary and proper for carrying into Execution the foregoing Powers, and all other Powers vested by this Constitution in the Government of the United States'. In American constitutional practice, the clause will only be used in combination with one of the 'foregoing powers'. The 'sweeping clause' is thus 'not a self-contained power' as it 'must always be tied to the exercise of some other identifiable constitutional power of the national government' (G Lawson & PB Granger, *The 'Proper' Scope of Federal Power: A Jurisdictional Interpretation of the Sweeping Clause*, 274–5). The Necessary and Proper Clause thus requires the presence of an expressly enumerated power in the Constitution. In this sense: R Beck, *The New Jurisprudence of the Necessary and Proper Clause*, 592: 'The clause merely confirmed the existence of lesser powers, not expressly detailed in the Constitution, which would serve as the means of carrying the enumerated powers into effect'. (This contrasts with the equivalent provision in the EC Treaty—Article 308 EC. On the scope and nature of Article 308 EC, see: Chapter 3—Section I (1).) The 'Necessary and Proper Clause' may then best be identified with a rule of interpretation for the scope of an express power. It allows the—very—wide *exercise* of a 'pre-existing' power, see: *McCulloch v Maryland* 17 US 316 (1819), 421: 'Let the end be legitimate, let it be within the scope of the constitution, and all means which are appropriate, which are plainly adapted to that end, which are not prohibited, but consistent with the letter and spirit of the constitution, are constitutional'.

[21] *Gibbons v Ogden* 22 US 1 (1824).

We find a first illustration of this type of reasoning in *United States v Knight*.[22] There, the Supreme Court held that '[i]t cannot be denied that the power of a state to protect the lives, health, and property of its citizens, and to preserve good order and the public morals, "the power to govern men and things within the limits of its dominion," *is a power originally and always belonging to the states, not surrendered by them to the general government, nor directly restrained by the constitution of the United States, and essentially exclusive*'. 'It is vital that the independence of the commercial power and of the police power, and the delimitation between them, however sometimes perplexing, should always be recognized and observed, for, while the one furnishes the strongest bond of union, the other is essential to the preservation of the autonomy of the states as required by our dual form of government[.]'[23] Thus, since 'Commerce succeeds to manufacture, and is not a part of it',[24] federal power could not extend to the regulation of the latter; for otherwise, Congress may be empowered to regulate 'every branch of human industry'.[25] Production was not commerce; and, as such, identified with a State competence. The mid-nineteenth century Supreme Court thus assumed 'two sharply separated and distinct areas of power'.[26]

A second internal limitation strategy concentrated on the word 'regulate'. Did the Commerce Clause power allow the federal government to 'prohibit' interstate commerce in a product? Was it true that '[t]he right to prohibit was the commerce power at the end of its journey'?[27] There were indeed signals

---

[22] *United States v Knight* 156 US 1 (1895).

[23] Ibid 11 and 13.

[24] Ibid 12.

[25] The well-known passage from *Kidd v Pearson* 128 US 1(1888), 20–2 reads: 'No distinction is more popular to the common mind, or more clearly expressed in economic and political literature, than that between manufactures and commerce. Manufacture is transformation—the fashioning of raw materials into a change of form for use. The functions of commerce are different. The buying and selling and the transportation incidental thereto constitute commerce; and the regulation of commerce in the constitutional sense embraces the regulation at least of such transportation. . . . If it be held that the term [commerce] includes the regulation of all such manufactures as are intended to be the subject of commercial transactions in the future, it is impossible to deny that it would also include all productive industries that contemplate the same thing. The result would be that congress would be invested, to the exclusion of the states, with the power to regulate, not only manufacture, but also agriculture, horticulture, stock-raising, domestic fisheries, mining,—in short, every branch of human industry. For is there one of them that does not contemplate, more or less clearly, an interstate or foreign market?'

[26] F Frankfurter (n 3 above) 1294.

[27] JW Davis, *The Growth of the Commerce Clause*, 214.

in this direction,[28] albeit confined to prohibiting the *interstate* transportation of certain goods or persons or the *instrumentalities* of transport. Still, a dual federalist boundary to these 'nationalist' tendencies was drawn in *Hammer v Dagenhart*.[29] The federal Child Labor Law aimed at standardizing the ages at which children could be employed in mining and manufacture. Congress had prohibited goods that, while in themselves harmless, shared in the 'original sin' of production through child labour. 'Like an illegitimate child, they were made to bear the taint of the evil which brought them into existence[.]'[30] However, the Supreme Court insisted that the Commerce Clause would *not* allow the federal Government to regulate production; and Congress could not get around that boundary by *prohibiting* the interstate commerce of goods that resulted from dislikable production processes. The Court invalidated the federal law as it could not be shown to have any positive effect on interstate commerce. The power to regulate commerce was 'directly the contrary of the assumed right to forbid commerce from moving and thus destroying it as to particular commodities'.[31] The power to regulate commerce is the power to 'regulate' not to 'prohibit'.[32]

---

[28] Cf *Champion v Ames* 188 US 321 (1903), where the Court found that Congress could prohibit the transportation of lottery tickets across State lines as well as *Caminetti v United States* 242 US 470 (1917), where the prohibitory power under the Commerce Clause was extended to the transportation of prostitutes. The justification for this line of cases lay in the fact that Congress regulated the 'transportation or instrumentalities' of commerce (cf *United States v EC Knight* (1895), 13): 'Contracts to buy, sell, or exchange goods to be transported among the several states, the transportation and its instrumentalities, and articles bought, sold, or exchanged for the purposes of such transit among the states, or put in the way of transit, may be regulated; but this is because they form part of interstate trade or commerce. The fact that an article is manufactured for export to another state does not of itself make it an article of interstate commerce, and the intent of the manufacturer does not determine the time when the article or product passes from the control of the state and belongs to commerce.' In the same category fall 'stream of commerce' cases, such as *Houston, East and West Texas Railway Co v United States (Shreveport Rate Case)* 234 US 342 (1914); and *Stafford v Wallace* 258 US 495 (1922), where Chief Justice Taft explained the rationale behind these cases as follows: 'It was the inevitable recognition of the great central fact that such streams of commerce from one part of the country to another, which are ever flowing, are in their very essence the commerce among the states and with foreign nations, which historically it was one of the chief purposes of the Constitution to bring under national protection and control. This court declined to defeat this purpose in respect of such a stream and take it out of complete national regulation by a nice and technical inquiry into the noninterstate character of some of its necessary incidents and facilities, when considered alone and without reference to their association with the movement of which they were an essential but subordinate part' (ibid 518–9).

[29] *Hammer v Dagenhart* 247 US 251 (1918).

[30] RE Cushman, *The National Police Power under the Commerce Clause of the Constitution (II)*, 452.

[31] *Hammer v Dagenhart* 247 US 251 (1918), 270.

[32] See already: *Champion v Ames (Lottery Cases)* 188 US 321 (1903): '[T]he authority given to Congress was not to prohibit, but only to regulate'. In *Hammer v Dagenhart*, the Supreme Court

These implied limitations protected the dual federalist structure.

When was the 'new nationalism' born? Reforms follow crises. The 'reformation' of American federalism followed the Great Depression of 1929. The spirit of the time was this: 'Architecturally we have an antiquated frame of government when we lack nation-wide power to deal with nation-wide conditions that can not be dealt with effectively by the several states. It is abundantly clear that the states could not do much to revive agriculture and industry. If it were clear that the nation by national regulation could do a lot to revive and maintain agriculture and industry, it would then be clear that the nation ought to have the power to do it. An objection to the possession of national power for national planning must come down to a confidence in *laissez faire* as the only worth-while national physician[.]'[33] Amazingly, the 'new nationalism' would not result from constitutional amendment. To reinvigorate the American economy, a series of statutes had been enacted under the *old* constitutional powers.[34] Yet this 'new deal' under the old Constitution was to encounter a dual federalist Supreme Court.[35] The reforms were judicially vetoed at first and only after the Roosevelt administration threatened to 'pack' the Court, the 'switch in time that saved the nine' endorsed the birth of a new era.

The future evolution of the Commerce Clause would reflect, in an emblematic way, the conceptual development of American federalism. In a first

---

also insisted that the Commerce Clause could not be used to simply 'equalize' competitive conditions between States (ibid 273–4, emphasis added): 'There is no power vested in Congress to require the states to exercise their police power so as to prevent possible unfair competition. Many causes may co-operate to give one state, by reason of local laws or conditions, an economic advantage over others. *The commerce clause was not intended to give to Congress a general authority to equalize such conditions.* In some of the states laws have been passed fixing minimum wages for women, in others the local law regulates the hours of labor of women in various employments. Business done in such states may be at an economic disadvantage when compared with states which have no such regulations; surely, this fact does not give Congress the power to deny transportation in interstate commerce to those who carry on business where the hours of labor and the rate of compensation for women have not been fixed by a standard in use in other states and approved by Congress. The grant of power of Congress over the subject of interstate commerce was to enable it to regulate such commerce, and not to give it authority to control the states in their exercise of the police power over local trade and manufacture. *The grant of authority over a purely federal matter was not intended to destroy the local power always existing and carefully reserved to the states in the Tenth Amendment to the Constitution*'.

[33] TR Power, *Some Aspects of Constitutionalism and Federalism*, 26.

[34] For a brief summary, see: RL Stern, *The Commerce Clause and the National Economy, 1933–1946*, 653.

[35] The Supreme Court dealt with the Agricultural Adjustment Act in *United States v Butler et al* 297 US 1 (1936); and the National Recovery Administration Act in *Schechter Poultry Corp v United States* 295 US 495 (1935).

subsection, we will look at the expanding scope of the Commerce Clause. The expanding universe of federal power would gradually absorb the States' police powers. This decline of exclusive State powers would not be the only aspect of the demise of dual federalism. The expansion of the Commerce Clause transformed, in turn, its own nature from an exclusive to a concurrent power. This shall be discussed in a second subsection.

1. *Expanding the Federal Universe: The Decline of State 'Police Powers'*

Historical beginnings are always difficult to locate. This is certainly true for the constitutional start of the 'new nationalism'. However, we can see the new constitutional philosophy at work in *Jones & Laughlin*. This case concerned the constitutionality of the National Labor Relations Act (1935), which had been challenged 'as an attempt to regulate all industry, thus invalidating *the reserved powers of the States over their local concerns*'.[36] In its judgment, the Court abandoned the dual federalist approach that had tried to distinguish between 'commerce' and 'production':

The congressional authority to protect interstate commerce from burdens and obstructions is not limited to transactions which can be deemed to be an essential part of a 'flow' of interstate or foreign commerce. Burdens and obstructions may be due to injurious action springing from other sources. The fundamental principle is that the power to regulate commerce is the power to enact 'all appropriate legislation' for its 'protection or advancement'; to adopt measures 'to promote its growth and insure its safety'; 'to foster, protect, control, and restrain.' That power is plenary and may be exerted to protect interstate commerce 'no matter what the source of the dangers which threaten it.' *Although activities may be intrastate in character when separately considered, if they have such a close and substantial relation to interstate commerce that their control is essential or appropriate to protect that commerce from burdens and obstructions, Congress cannot be denied the power to exercise that control.* Undoubtedly the scope of this power must be considered in the light of our dual system of government and may not be extended so as to embrace effects upon interstate commerce so indirect and remote that to embrace them, in view of our complex society, would effectually obliterate the distinction between what is national and what is local and create a completely centralized government. The question is necessarily one of degree.[37]

---

[36] *National Labor Relations Board v Jones & Laughlin Steel Corp* 301 US 1 (1937), 29 (emphasis added).

[37] Ibid 36–7 (emphasis added).

Instead of concentrating on the categorical distinction between 'interstate' commerce and 'intrastate' production, the Court focused on the effect of the federal legislation. '[I]ndustrial strife would have a most serious effect upon interstate commerce': 'When industries organize themselves on a national scale, making their relation to interstate commerce the dominant factor in their activities, *how can it be maintained that their industrial labor relations constitute a forbidden field into which Congress may not enter when it is necessary to protect interstate commerce from the paralyzing consequences of industrial war?*'[38] The Court's novel effect-centred test would cut across the categories of dual federalism by focusing on the consequences and not the 'nature' of different types of activities. This would even potentially include 'trivial' activities, whose accumulative effect might be 'far from trivial'.[39]

The arrival of a new constitutional era was confirmed in *United States v Darby*: 'The power of Congress over interstate commerce is not confined to the regulation of commerce among the states. It extends to those intrastate activities which so affect interstate commerce or the exercise of the power of Congress over it as to make regulation of them appropriate means to the attainment of a legitimate end, the exercise of the granted power of Congress to regulate interstate commerce'.[40] This new type of reasoning was to culminate in *Garcia v San Antonio Metropolitan Transit Authority*, where the Supreme Court felt the following:

Apart from the limitation on federal authority inherent in the delegated nature of Congress' Article I powers, the principal means chosen by the Framers to ensure the role of the States in the federal system lies in the structure of the Federal Government itself. It is no novelty to observe that the composition of the Federal Government was designed in large part to protect the States from overreaching by Congress. The Framers thus gave the States a role in the selection both of the Executive and the Legislative Branches of the Federal Government. The States were vested with indirect influence over the House of Representatives and the Presidency by their control

---

[38] Ibid 41 (emphasis added).

[39] *Wickard v Filburn* 317 US 111 (1942), 127–8: 'The maintenance by government regulation of a price for wheat undoubtedly can be accomplished as effectively by sustaining or increasing the demand as by limiting the supply. The effect of the statute before us is to restrict the amount which may be produced for the market and the extent as well to which one may forestall resort to the market by producing to meet his own needs. That appellee's own contribution to the demand for wheat may be trivial by itself is not enough to remove him from the scope of federal regulation where, as here, his contribution, taken together with that of many others similarly situated, is far from trivial'.

[40] *United States v Darby* 312 US 100 (1941), 118.

of electoral qualifications and their role in Presidential elections. They were given more direct influence in the Senate, where each State received equal representation and each Senator was to be selected by the legislature of his State. The significance attached to the States' equal representation in the Senate is underscored by the prohibition of any constitutional amendment divesting a State of equal representation without the State's consent... *Of course, we continue to recognize that the States occupy a special and specific position in our constitutional system and that the scope of Congress' authority under the Commerce Clause must reflect that position. But the principal and basic limit on the federal commerce power is that inherent in all congressional action—the built-in restraints that our system provides through State participation in federal governmental action. The political process ensures that laws that unduly burden the States will not be promulgated.*[41]

What the Supreme Court here seemed to deny was the existence of a constitutionally protected nucleus of exclusive State power. The 'political safeguards of federalism' would be sufficient.[42] The consequent denial of *judicial* safeguards of federalism was the strongest expression of the 'new nationalism'. It also informed the Supreme Courts post-1937 jurisprudence on the Tenth Amendment, where the Court would give short shrift to any potential external limits to the Commerce Clause. Under the new spirit, '[t]he amendment state[d] but a truism that all is retained which has not been surrendered'. Instead of constituting an independent limit on the Commerce Clause, the Tenth Amendment must be 'construed as not depriving the national government of authority to resort to all means for the exercise of a granted power which are appropriate and plainly adapted to the permitted end'.[43] The Court thus left the federal balance completely in the hands of the federal legislator. The political process as such would ensure that States' rights were protected.

[41]   *Garcia v San Antonio Metropolitan Transit Authority* 469 US 528 (1985), 550–1 and 556 (emphasis added).

[42]   On the theory of the political safeguards of federalism, see: H Wechsler, *The Political Safeguards of Federalism: The Role of the States in the Composition and Selection of the National Government.*

[43]   *United States v Darby* 312 US 100 (1941), 124. In *National League of Cities v Usery* 426 US 833 (1976), the Supreme Court had still found the 'truism' to be of *some* significance. This 'exception' to the inoperability of the Tenth Amendment as an external limit on the Commerce Clause was explicitly overruled in *Garcia v San Antonio Metropolitan Transit Authority* 469 US 528 (1985), where the Supreme Court held: 'We therefore now reject, as unsound in principle and unworkable in practice, a rule of state immunity from federal regulation that turns on a judicial appraisal of whether a particular governmental function is "integral" or "traditional." . . . We doubt that courts ultimately can identify principled constitutional limitations on the scope of Congress' Commerce Clause powers over the States merely by relying on a priori definitions of state sovereignty' (ibid 446–548).

This theory of the political safeguards of federalism is difficult to defend;[44] unless, States are given a decisional veto within the federal legislative process.[45] The Supreme Court's celebration of absolute judicial passivism was indeed not to last. The Court recently revived the idea of *some* conceptual boundaries around the Commerce Clause. In *United States v Lopez*, it confirmed the existence of constitutional limits and its role in enforcing them.[46] The Commerce Clause could only be of federal avail to regulate an 'economic' activity that would 'substantially affect' interstate commerce.[47] Was this a return to the category thinking of dual federalism? Hardly so.[48] The world of dual federalism had been—irretrievably—lost. While the Court did insist on some limits, these limits were not defined in terms of policy areas reserved to the States. Federal power under the Commerce Clause was only *functionally* limited by an effects-based test. The revival of some degree of judicial intervention equally occurred in relation to the Tenth Amendment. To maintain the 'etiquette of federalism',[49] the federal Government could not 'commandeer' the 'States as States' to implement federal laws.[50] These judicial

---

[44] L Tribe, *American Constitutional Law*, 865–6: 'The political safeguards of federalism cannot *always* be counted on to prevent state-subordinating excesses of federal legislative power. The fact that Congress is made up of (and represents) individuals obviously does not guarantee that that body . . . will always act in accordance with individual rights; so too the fact that Congress is made up of (and reflects) the elected representatives of states does not assure that the nation's legislature will always adequate respect to the rights of states'.

[45] For a discussion of the political safeguards of federalism in the context of the European Union legal order: Chapter 3—Section I, Chapter 5—Section I, and Chapter 6—Section I (2b).

[46] *United States v Lopez* 514 US 549 (1995).

[47] Ibid 560. The Court distinguished three commerce clause strands, namely (1) the regulation of the channels of interstate commerce; (2) the regulation of the instrumentalities of interstate commerce; and (3) all economic activities that substantially affect interstate commerce. *Lopez* thereby recognized the continued validity of two per se rules that escape the effects analysis. These per se rules will also apply to non-economic activities. This was confirmed in *United States v Morrison* 529 US 598 (2000).

[48] In *United States v Lopez* 514 US 549 (1995) as well as in *Gonzales, Attorney General, et al v Angel McClary Raich et al* 545 US 1 (2005), the Supreme Court confirmed *Wickard v Filburn*—a symbol of the nationalist reading of the post-new deal Commerce Clause. 'Our case law firmly establishes Congress' power to regulate purely local activities that are part of an economic "class of activities" that have a substantial effect on interstate commerce . . . *Wickard* thus establishes that Congress can regulate a purely intrastate activity that is not itself "commercial," in that it is not produced for sale, if it concludes that failure to regulate that class of activity would undercut the regulation of the interstate market in that commodity' (ibid 18–19).

[49] MD Adler & SF Kreimer, *The New Etiquette of Federalism: New York, Printz, and Yeskey*.

[50] In *New York v United States* 505 US 144 (1992), petitioners had not contended that the Tenth Amendment limited the power of Congress to act in relation to the *subject-matter* at issue (and the Court would affirm that Congress had power over the issue). They had only contended that the

safeguards did not amount to substantive policy restrictions on the scope of the federal Commerce Clause. They protected federalism *as such* and cannot be seen as a revival of dual federalist philosophy.

2. *Changing Nature: From Exclusive to Concurrent Power*

The expansion of the Commerce Clause gradually reduced the scope of the States' exclusive 'police powers'.[51] But this was not the only sign of the demise of dual federalism. The expansion of the Commerce Clause also triggered a change in the very nature of the competence. Its expanding scope would gradually make the claim to its exclusive nature indefensible. To show this transformation we shall trace the evolution of the Commerce Clause from an exclusive power, to a partially exclusive power, and to a shared power.

In *Gibbons v Ogden*, we encounter the exclusive power theory of dual federalism.[52] Here, Chief Justice Marshall found 'great force' in the argument that the Commerce Clause 'implied in its nature full power over the thing to be regulated' and that the competence thereby 'excludes, necessarily, the action of all others that would perform the same operation on the same thing'.[53] While the States had retained their police powers, these laws—in this case: inspection laws—could not be regulations of commerce:

That inspection laws may have a remote and considerable influence on commerce, will not be denied; but that a power to regulate commerce is the source from which the right to pass them is derived, cannot be admitted. The object of inspection laws, is to improve the quality of articles produced by the labour of a country; to fit them for

manner in which Congress had exercised its power was unconstitutional. The question was, whether 'Congress may use the States as implements of regulation; that is, whether Congress may direct or otherwise motivate the States to regulate in a particular field or a particular way'. The Court found that Congress may not simply 'commandee[r] the legislative processes of the States by directly compelling them to enact and enforce a federal regulatory program' (ibid 161). 'Whatever the outer limits of that sovereignty may be, one thing is clear: the Federal Government may not compel the States to enact or administer a federal regulatory program' (ibid 188). In *Printz v United States* 521 US 898 (1997), this no-commandeering rule was confirmed to apply to the executive branch (ibid 935): 'We held in *New York* that Congress cannot compel the States to enact or enforce a federal regulatory program. Today we hold that Congress cannot circumvent that prohibition by conscripting the State's officers directly'.

[51] 'But what are the police powers of a State? They are nothing more or less than the powers of government inherent in every sovereignty to the extent of its dominions.' (Cf Chief Justice Taney in *Thurlow v Massachusetts; Fletcher v Rhode Island*; and *Peirce v New Hampshire (License Cases)* 46 US 504 (1847). For a discussion of the concept of 'police power', see P Kens, *The Source of a Myth: Police Powers of the States and Laissez Faire Constitutionalism, 1900–1937*.

[52] *Gibbons v Ogden* 22 US 1 (1824).

[53] Ibid 209.

exportation; or, it may be, for domestic use. They act upon the subject before it becomes an article of foreign commerce, or of commerce among the States, and prepare it for that purpose. They form a portion of that immense mass of legislation, which embraces every thing within the territory of a State, not surrendered to the general government: all which can be most advantageously exercised by the States themselves ... No direct general power over these objects is granted to Congress; and, consequently, they remain subject to State legislation. If the legislative power of the Union can reach them, it must be for national purposes; it must be where the power is expressly given for a special purpose, or is clearly incidental to some power which is expressly given ... So, if a State, in passing laws on subjects acknowledged to be within its control, and with a view to those subjects, shall adopt a measure of the same character with one which Congress may adopt, it does not derive its authority from the particular power which has been granted, but from some other, which remains with the State, and may be executed by the same means. All experience shows, that the same measures, or measures scarcely distinguishable from each other, may flow from distinct powers; but this does not prove that the powers themselves are identical. Although the means used in their execution may sometimes approach each other so nearly as to be confounded, there are other situations in which they are sufficiently distinct to establish their individuality.[54]

For Marshall, the power to regulate interstate commerce was an exclusive federal power. The constitutionality of State laws in this area, while not denied, would 'not imply an acknowledgment that a State may rightfully regulate commerce with foreign nations, or among the States; for they do not imply that such laws are an exercise of that power, or enacted with a view to it'. The States did not have a 'concurrent' power over interstate commerce. They would act under the acknowledged 'power of a State to regulate its police, its domestic trade, and to govern its own citizens'.[55] The decision in *Gibbons v Ogden* was thus based on the distinction between an exclusive federal 'commerce' power and an exclusive State 'police' power.[56] (Paradoxically, the latter was not yet seen externally to restrict the former. On the contrary,

---

[54] Ibid 203–4.

[55] Ibid 208.

[56] *Mayor, Aldermen and Commonality of City of New York v Miln* 36 US 102 (1837), 131–2: '[W]e are of the opinion that the act is not a regulation of commerce, but of police; and that being thus considered, it was passed in the exercise of a power which rightfully belonged to the states.' The concept of 'police power' was thus directly linked to the States so 'that if Congress is to exercise a police power at all it must do by a process of something akin to indirection; that is, by using the powers which are definitely confided to it, for the purposes of the police power ... In short, Congress exercises a generous police power not because that power is placed directly in its hands but because it has the power to regulate commerce ... and uses that authority for the bread purposes of the general welfare' (RE Cushman, *The National Police Power under the Commerce Clause of the Constitution* (I), 291).

Marshall argued for a 'nationalist' interpretation of the Commerce Clause and refused to accept implied limitations on its scope. But should the 'exclusive' nature of the Commerce Clause not exclude the States? The Court circumvented the question;[57] and, as a result, the exclusivity thesis remained in a constitutional limbo. One artificial way to 'solve' this—unsolvable paradox—lay in a theory that determined the character of legislation by reference to its purpose.[58] This teleological fallacy would cloud constitutional theory for a century.) Be that as it may, in the constitutional imagination, *Gibbons v Ogden* came to mean that the federation's commerce power was exclusive.[59]

A second stage in the exclusivity theory was *Cooley v Board of Wardens of the Port of Philadelphia*.[60] In that case, a State statute fell into the scope of the Commerce Clause; yet, the Supreme Court was not ready to declare the former, *ipso facto*, void. Instead the Court admitted the diversity of opinion on the subject and proposed an intellectual compromise between the exclusivity camp and the partisans of the concurrent power thesis.[61] The result was the idea of 'partial exclusivity'. In a well-known passage, the Court explained:

The grant of commercial power to Congress does not contain any terms which expressly exclude the States from exercising an authority over its subject-matter. If they are excluded it must be because the nature of the power, thus granted to Congress, requires that a similar authority should not exist in the States . . . But when the nature of a power like this is spoken of, when it is said that the nature of the power requires that it should be exercised exclusively by Congress, it must be intended to refer to the subjects of that power, and to say they are of such a nature as to require exclusive legislation by Congress. Now the power to regulate commerce, embraces a vast field, containing not only many, but exceedingly various subjects, quite unlike in their nature; some imperatively demanding a single uniform rule, operating equally on the commerce of the United States in every port; and some, like the subject now in question, as imperatively demanding that diversity, which alone can meet the local

[57] The 'great expounder' of the Constitution relied on a constitutional shortcut that seemed to 'solve' the case: the Supremacy Clause. It would thus 'be immaterial whether those laws were passed in virtue of a concurrent power "to regulate commerce with foreign nations and among the several States," or, in virtue of a power to regulate their domestic trade and police' (*Gibbons v Ogden*, 210).

[58] HW Biklé, *The Silence of Congress*, 216.

[59] This is the (almost) universally accepted view, which could rely on *Gibbons v Ogden*, 197: 'If, as has always been understood, the sovereignty of Congress, though limited to specific objects, is plenary as to those objects, the power over commerce with foreign nations, and among the several States, is vested in Congress as absolutely as it would be in a single government'.

[60] *Cooley v Board of Wardens of the Port of Philadelphia* 53 US 299 (1851).

[61] An outspoken advocate of the concurrent power thesis was Marshall's successor as Chief Justice: RB Taney. See in particular his separate opinion in the *License Cases* 46 US 504 (1847).

necessities of navigation. Either absolutely to affirm, or deny that the nature of this power requires exclusive legislation by Congress, is to lose sight of the nature of the subjects of this power, and to assert concerning all of them, what is really *applicable but to a part*. Whatever *subjects* of this power are *in their nature national*, or admit only of one uniform system, or plan of regulation, may justifiably be said to be of such a nature as to require exclusive legislation by Congress.[62]

The *Cooley* Court thus introduced 'the new doctrine of selective exclusiveness'.[63] This was done by analytically separating the Commerce Clause *power* from the *subject-matters* over which it operated. While, the Supreme Court—paradoxically—insisted that the Commerce Clause itself was not 'partially' exclusive,[64] it agreed that only subjects that were 'national' in character would require a uniform federal regime. Here, dual federalism meant that the silence of Congress was its 'regulation': 'where the power of Congress to regulate is exclusive the failure of Congress to make express regulations indicates its will that the subject shall be left free from any restrictions or imposition'.[65]

Importantly, 'local' subjects would *not* be exclusively reserved for the States. Congress could act upon them by means of its Commerce Clause.[66] But what did dual federal doctrine make of the zone in which federal and State power seemingly overlapped? The 'twilight zone' between the police power and the Commerce Clause seemed to contradict the philosophy of dual federalism as it represented an encounter of two sovereigns.[67] However, by arguing that the States would not 'regulate' interstate 'commerce' when exercising their police

[62] *Cooley v Board of Wardens of the Port of Philadelphia*, 319 (emphasis added).

[63] F Frankfurter, *Taney and the Commerce Clause*, 1292.

[64] In subsequent jurisprudence, the Supreme Court would confirm that the *entire* Commerce Clause was exclusive; see: *Southern Railway Co v King* 217 US 524, 531 (1910): 'It has been frequently decided in this court that the right to regulate interstate commerce is, by virtue of the Federal Constitution, exclusively vested in the Congress of the United States. The States cannot pass any law directly regulating such commerce'.

[65] *Robbins v Shelby Country Taxing District* 120 US 489 (1887), 493.

[66] In *James Clark Distilling Co v Western Maryland R Co* 242 US 311 (1917), the Supreme Court expressed this in the following words: 'It is settled, says the argument, that interstate commerce is divided into two great classes, one embracing subjects which do not exact uniformity and which, although subject to the regulation of Congress, are in the absence of such regulation subject to the control of the several States (*Cooley v Board of Wardens*, 12 How. 299), and the other embracing subjects which do require uniformity and which in the absence of regulation by Congress remain free from all state control' (ibid 327–8).

[67] KF Burgess, *The Twilight Zone between the Police Power and the Commerce Clause*, 163: 'This twilight zone exists because under our theory of dual sovereignty precisely the same sort of regulation may be exercised by the states, within their sphere, under their police power, as Congress, within its sphere, may exercise under its power to regulate interstate commerce'.

powers,[68] the image of two separate spheres of power was—ingeniously—maintained. The 'either-or-logic' was kept intact: '[t]hat which belongs to commerce is within the jurisdiction of the United States, but that which does not belong to commerce is within the jurisdiction of the police power of the State'.[69] And in those situations where Congress had not acted at all on 'local' subjects, '[i]naction by Congress upon these subjects of a local nature, unlike its inaction upon matters affecting all the States and requiring uniformity of regulation is not to be taken as a declaration that nothing should be done with respect to them, but is rather to be deemed a declaration that, for the time being and until it sees fit to act, they may be regulated by State authority'.[70]

Would the States thus be allowed to frustrate interstate commerce until Congress removed the dangers of economic parochialism through positive action? The post-*Cooley* Supreme Court solved this problem by developing a novel constitutional weapon: the *dormant* Commerce Clause. On its face the Commerce Clause only granted Congress a power positively to regulate interstate commerce. While the drafters may have intended to leave the elimination of State interferences with interstate trade to Congress,[71] the Commerce Clause was now said to also contain a negative side: where Congress' legislative power had remained 'dormant', the Commerce Clause *as such* was to

---

[68] W Needham, *The Exclusive Power of Congress over Interstate Commerce*, 255, 257 and 260: 'What then is the true delimitation of state and Federal powers affecting interstate commerce? This question cannot be answered clearly without a brief reference to our constitutional history. *All of the sovereign powers now possessed by the Federal and state governments* first existed in the original thirteen States. These powers were absolute . . . Wherever, therefore, a power, stated in a general phrase is vested in the Federal Government, that whole power, in all of its particulars, and all of the functions necessary to its exercise, is absolutely withdrawn from the individual State, and is absolutely vested in the Federal Government . . . We must, therefore, conclude that the power to *regulate* the commerce described, is a sovereign power, exclusively vested in the Federal Government.' 'We here have a clear rule of delimitation between Federal and state control. If the commerce is foreign, or interstate or with the Indian tribes, then the absolute and exclusive sovereignty over it is in the Federal Government. If the commerce is intrastate, then the State is the absolute and exclusive sovereign over it. The police power is solely in the State and may be exercised over all commerce within the State . . . Such burdens enforced by the State in the exercise of its exclusive powers will have to be born by interstate commerce until Congress regulates the particular matter'.

[69] *United States v EC Knight Co* 156 US 1 (1895).

[70] *Parkersburg & Ohio River Transportation Co v Parkersburg* 107 US 691(1883), 703–4.

[71] JN Eule, *Laying the Dormant Commerce Clause to Rest*, 430: The American Constitution 'did not attempt to solve economic parochialism by an express prohibition against interference with free trade. Instead, it shifted legislative power over economic matters that affect more than one state to a single national body. The commerce clause does not expressly prohibit states from enacting protectionist economic legislation. It merely gives Congress the power to rectify such excesses by superseding enactments'.

implicitly prohibit certain State laws. The theory of the 'dormant Commerce Clause' provided an *independent constitutional rationale* to exclude the States from passing laws that conflicted with interstate commerce.

With its partially exclusive nature and its dormant side, the Commerce Clause had come to assume a complex constitutional architecture. Yet, conceptual remnants of dual federalism took its slow and winding road into the twentieth century. One milestone on the road was the—interim—ascendancy of the direct–indirect effect test.[72] But once the key rationale for the dormant Commerce Clause was whether a State measure constituted a 'direct' burden on interstate commerce, the idea of classes of 'sovereign' and exclusive police powers of the States was seriously threatened. In *Kansas Southern Railway*,[73] we thus find the Supreme Court declaring that 'a state cannot avoid the operation of [the Commerce Clause] rule by simply invoking the convenient apologetics of the police power', since 'a direct interference with commerce among the States could not be justified in this way'.[74] The States could not, through 'legislation proper in kind, but excessive in degree', invoke the plea of police powers.[75]

The complexities of constitutional doctrine would increasingly lose touch with social reality. And by 1927, an eminent commentator diagnosed the complete analytical breakdown of dual federalist categories. The latter could no longer explain and justify the cases. The only rule of thumb left was 'that the states may regulate interstate commerce, but not too much'.[76] This flew in the face of the dual federalist belief that it was not the degree or effect, but the nature or area of legislation, that determined whether federal or State laws were valid or not.[77] The idea of an exclusive Commerce Clause power was branded as 'an empty form of words, a pseudo-doctrine, a myth, an

---

[72] Eg *Smith v Alabama* 124 US 465 (1888), 474–5: 'In conferring upon Congress the regulation of commerce, it was never intended to cut the states off from legislating upon all subjects relating to the health, life, and safety of their citizens, though the legislation might indirectly affect the commerce of the country. Legislation, in a great variety of ways, may affect commerce and persons engaged in it, without constituting a regulation of it within the meaning of the constitution. ... And it may be said, generally, that the legislation of a state, not directed against commerce or any of its regulations, but relating to the rights, duties, and liabilities of citizens, and only indirectly and remotely affecting the operations of commerce, is of obligatory force upon citizens within its territorial jurisdiction, whether on land or water, or engaged in commerce, foreign or interstate, or in any other pursuit'.

[73] *Kansas Southern Railway v Kaw Valley District* 233 US 75 (1914).

[74] Ibid 79.

[75] DW Brown, *The Exclusive Power of Congress to Regulate Interstate and Foreign Commerce*, 497.

[76] TR Powell, *Current Conflicts between the Commerce Clause and State Police Power, 1922–1927 (II)*, 491.

[77] DW Brown, *The Concurrent Power of the States to Regulate Inter-State and Foreign Commerce*, 307.

illusion, an unreality, a superstition, if you please', since 'from the standpoint of sound constitutional construction, the contrary view, that Congress and the States have general concurrent power in this respect is the true one'.[78] The post-new deal jurisprudence would eventually drop the direct–indirect dichotomy altogether. This development forced the Supreme Court to fully abandon the idea of constitutional exclusivity.[79] The Commerce Clause had become a 'concurrent' power.

II. The 'New Federalism': The Decline of Legislative Exclusivity

Each federal philosophy has its federal structure. In a dual federalist universe, legislative conflicts should never arise as each 'sovereign' enjoys exclusive power within 'its' sphere of jurisdiction. Rival legislative claims will be arbitrated at the competence level. Within the 'watertight compartment' either-or-logic of dual federalism, governments are coordinated and not subordinated. The expansion of federal powers in the first half of the twentieth century had made this vision untenable. The constitutional boundaries around exclusive categories of State power had been dissolved. With federal powers potentially reaching into any policy field, legislative conflicts or legislative cooperation had become inevitable. The new 'concurrent' power paradigm brought the supremacy principle back onto constitutional centre-stage. In its wake, the perhaps most important constitutional principle of modern American federalism emerges: the doctrine of pre-emption. The principle had no legitimate place within a dual federalist structure, where federal law and State law could not, in theory, both validly deal with the same issue.

---

[78] FH Cooke, *The Pseudo-Doctrine of the Exclusiveness of the Power of Congress to Regulate Commerce*, 298.

[79] The current test under the dormant Commerce Clause is two-pronged. The Supreme Court will first ask whether the State regulation discriminates against out-of-State commerce. The measure can theoretically be justified by a valid factor unrelated to economic protectionism, but the Supreme Court applies a strict scrutiny review that approaches per se invalidity. Non-discriminatory measures will only fall foul with the dormant Commerce Clause, where they impose an 'excessive burden' (*Dean Milk Co v City of Madison* 340 US 349 (1951), 353) on interstate commerce. The balancing test for this second class of State measures is spelled out in *Pike v Bruce Church, Inc* 397 US 137 (1970), 142: 'Where the statute regulates even-handedly to effectuate a legitimate local public interest, and its effects on interstate commerce are only incidental, it will be upheld unless the burden imposed on such commerce is clearly excessive in relation to the putative local benefits'.

What was the role of the pre-emption doctrine? The 'new nationalism' had made legislative overlaps between federal and State powers inevitable. Where the federation exercised its power, the Supremacy Clause would guarantee that federal law prevailed over conflicting State law. But when would a conflict arise? Would every exercise of a federal power pre-empt the States from acting within the same field? If this were the case, the 'new nationalism' 'would not really have ended dual federalism, it would simply have drastically altered the relative sizes of the 'spheres' within which the two governments operated'.[80] Why? Because field pre-emption continues to operate within a dual federalist paradigm by maintaining the existence of two mutually exclusive spheres of authority. The only difference to the 'old' static dual federalism is that the federal boundary is no longer considered fixed. The federal boundary is now seen as dynamic. It shifts with time on behalf of the nation into previous domains of State power. The expanding scope of national power after the 'new deal' was thus a necessary but not a sufficient condition for the transition from dual to cooperative federalism. A 'new nationalism' was not, as such, a 'new federalism'.[81] The expansion of federal power will not tell us *how* federal power is *exercised*. Yet, the actual exercise of federal power will be critical in deciding whether a dual or a cooperative federalist philosophy prevails.

What, then, was required for cooperative federalism to emerge? The very structure of American law would have to change if federal law and State law were to cooperate within a policy area. Field pre-emption denies the very possibility of the federation and its States to exercise power *in the same area at the same time*. Field pre-emption thus excludes a *cooperative* federal arrangement. Since the essential hallmark of cooperative federalism lies in the *actual* sharing of power, the transition from dual to cooperative federalism required a departure from field pre-emption. A 'new federalism' would only arrive with the emergence of softer pre-emption types. Federal law will here only pre-empt State law that substantively conflicts with it. And where there was no substantive conflict, federal and State law would complement each other to form a legislative 'whole'. The arrival of a modern pre-emption doctrine ushered in the demise of legislative exclusivity. It opened legislative spaces for the States under federal legislation and, thereby, the possibility of cooperative federalism. The transformation of the 'classic' into the 'modern' pre-emption

---

[80] MJC Vile, *The Structure of American Federalism*, 70.

[81] Dual federalism is agnostic about the actual boundary line between State and federal sovereignty. It only tells us how sovereignty is divided. There could thus be a 'nationalist' dual federalism. On this point, see: *Introduction: Coming to Constitutional Terms*, above.

framework took place in the first half of the twentieth century and will be the subject of this second section.

1. *From Concurrent to Shared Powers: The Decline of 'Classic' Pre-emption*

The 'classic' version of the pre-emption doctrine identified pre-emption with the total exclusion of the States from a field once the federation had legislated. We find typical illustrations of this classic pre-emption format in the pre-new deal jurisprudence. In *Southern Railway Co v Reid*, the Supreme Court quashed a State statute setting price rates for railroads on the ground that a federal act on this issue had 'taken possession of the field'.[82] The exercise of federal power was 'such that when exercised it is exclusive, and *ipso facto*, supersedes existing state legislation on the same subject'.[83] State regulation that would comple-ment the federal scheme had no place in such a constitutional federalism: 'the power of the State over the subject-matter ceased to exist from the moment that Congress exerted its paramount and all embracing authority over the subject' as there can be 'no divided authority over interstate commerce'.[84] Justice Holmes couched classic pre-emption in the following terms: '[w]hen Congress has taken the particular subject-matter in hand coincidence is as ineffective as opposition, and a state law is not to be declared a help because it attempts to go father than Congress has seen fit to go'. Conflict was simply 'immaterial'.[85] Thus, whenever Congress had entered a field, all State law within the same area was automatically pre-empted.[86]

Dual federalism 'refrained from considering whether a particular state regulation could be harmonized with the federal regime or could be viewed

---

[82]   *Southern Railway Co v Reid* 222 US 424 (1912), 442.

[83]   *Southern Railway v Railroad Commission of Indiana* 236 US 439 (1915), 446.

[84]   *Chicago, Rock Island & Pacific Ry Co v Hardwick Farmers Elev Co* 226 US 426 (1913), 435.

[85]   *Charleston & Western Carolina Railway Co v Varnville* 237 US 597 (1915), 604.

[86]   It goes without saying that this dual federalist vision was not lived out in every single case. An exception can be found in *Savage v Jones* 225 US 501 (1912), 533: 'Is, then, a denial to the State of the exercise of its power for the purposes in question necessarily implied in the Federal statute? For when the question is whether a Federal act overrides a State law, the entire scheme of the statute must, of course, be considered, and that which needs must be implied is of no less force than that which is expressed. If the purpose of the act cannot otherwise be accomplished—if its operation within its chosen field else must be frustrated and its provisions be refused their natural effect—the state law must yield to the regulation of Congress within the sphere of its delegated power . . . But the intent to supersede the exercise by the state of its police power as to matters not covered by the Federal legislation is not to be inferred from the mere fact the Congress has seen fit to circumscribe its regulation and to occupy a limited field. In other words, such intent is not to be implied unless the act of Congress, fairly interpreted, is in actual conflict with the law of the state'.

to foster its aims'.[87] In *New York Central Railroad Co v Winfield*,[88] an employee had lost an eye in the service of a railroad company. The injury had not been the result of fault or negligence but was nonetheless granted compensation under the relevant State law. The carrier appealed claiming that the situation was 'exclusively governed' by the federal Employers' Liability Act (1916), which did not require compensation for non-negligence. The Court sided with the business interest:

It is settled that under the commerce clause of the Constitution Congress may regulate the obligation of common carriers and the rights of their employees arising out of injuries sustained by the latter where both are engaged in interstate commerce; and it also is settled that when Congress acts upon the subject all state laws covering the same field are necessarily superseded by reason of the supremacy of the national authority ... '*[I]f Congress have a constitutional power to regulate a particular subject, and they do actually regulate it in a given manner, and in a certain form, it cannot be that the state legislatures have a right to interfere; and, as it were, by way of complement to the legislation of Congress, to prescribe additional regulations, and what they may deem auxiliary provisions for the same purpose. In such a case, the legislation of Congress, in what it does prescribe, manifestly indicates that it does not intend that there shall be any farther legislation to act upon the sub-ject-matter. Its silence as to what it does not do is as expressive of what its intention is as the direct provisions made by it.*' Thus the act is as comprehensive of injuries occurring without negligence, as to which class it impliedly excludes liability, as it is of those as to which it imposes liability. In other words, it is a regulation of the carriers' duty or obligation as to both'.[89]

The identification of the pre-emption phenomenon with automatic 'field' pre-emption was a child of the ailing—but still powerful—philosophy of dual federalism. The Supreme Court continued to labour under a vision that federal and State law operated in mutually exclusive spheres. Legislation 'was a zero-sum game' as two 'sovereigns could not be sovereign within the same field'.[90] While the 'new nationalism' had forced the Court to acknowl-edge the existence of concurrent *powers*, it had not yet accepted the existence of concurrent *legislation*. During this interim phase, dual federalism—while renouncing the idea of two *static* mutually exclusive spheres of power—compromised for a *dynamic* variant of dual federalism.[91] Instead of a fixed

[87] SC Hoke, *Preemption Pathologies and Civic Republican Values*, 738–9.

[88] *New York Central Railroad Co v Winfield* 244 US 147 (1917).

[89] Ibid 148 and 153–4 (emphasis added).

[90] SC Hoke (n 87 above) 739.

[91] Kramer refers to the 'fluid' boundaries of State exclusive power under this variant of dual federalism: cf *Understanding Federalism*, 1499.

boundary, the federal boundary was moving with time. 'Thus, although the notion of exclusive *dormant* federal power was on the wane, the proposition that federal power *when exercised* inherently and inevitably precludes concurrent state power prevailed into the 1930s'.[92] Under concurrent competences, two sovereign wills could still not come into conflict, for once Congress had expressed its will, the States would, *ipso facto*, be completely pre-empted. And in an attempt to explain the 'transformation' of a formally concurrent power into a subsequently exclusive power, the Supreme Court would occasionally have recourse to the idea of 'latent exclusivity' in the field of interstate commerce.[93]

a. The Rise of the Modern Pre-emption Framework

The second life of dual federalism received its death blow when the idea of automatic field pre-emption was abandoned in the transformative years following the new deal.[94] The shift from classic to modern pre-emption analysis may at first seem anachronistic. After all, it took place in the midst of a period of American constitutional history characterized by strong centralizing tendencies. However, a closer look betrays a federal logic that was part and parcel of the new constitutional settlement. A 'new nationalism', coupled with automatic field pre-emption, would have seriously threatened the *raison d'être* of the States: their existence as autonomous legislative centres. The modern pre-emption regime would reintroduce federal elements into the constitutional equation. The new federal equilibrium was achieved by making the question of pre-emption contingent on congressional intent and by protecting State legislation through a number of constitutional presumptions *against* pre-emption.

For the modern pre-emption doctrine, Congressional intent became the touchstone.[95] The intent rationale channelled the development of the modern pre-emption doctrine alongside two dimensions.[96] The first dimension concerns the extent to which the federal government has exercised its powers

---

[92]   DE Engdahl, *Constitutional Federalism in a Nutshell*, 338.

[93]   SA Gardbaum, *The Nature of Preemption*, 801.

[94]   Ibid 806.

[95]   Doubtlessly, from its inception the new intent-centred analysis would contain a speculative element, since 'Congress, embroiled in controversy over policy issues, rarely anticipates the possible ramifications of its acts upon state law' (Note, *Pre-emption as a Preferential Ground: A New Canon of Construction*, 209). In the worst case scenario, it would be 'the court that is doing the intending' (TR Powell, *Supreme Court Decisions on the Commerce Clause and State Police Power*, 1910–1914, 48).

[96]   SC Hoke (n 87 above) 735–6.

to the exclusion of the States. Early on, the Supreme Court recognized Congress' power to choose among different *types* or degrees of pre-emption. The second dimension, by way of contrast, concerns the *mode* of pre-emption, that is, how Congress has spoken its collective mind. Here, modern pre-emption analysis distinguishes between express and implied pre-emption and has, regarding the implied pre-emption mode, developed constitutional 'presumptions' that assist the courts in deciding whether federal law pre-empts State law or not.

Let us look at the first dimension. The intent rationale behind the modern pre-emption phenomenon 'voluntarized' the doctrine. As Congress could express its will *not* to totally pre-empt all State laws in a policy field, a flexible pre-emption doctrine emerged from the ashes of dual federalism at the end of the 1930s. Instead of the single pre-emption type under the classic doctrine, various types would exist under the modern doctrine. The three pre-emption formats subsequently identified by American constitutionalism are, respectively, *field* pre-emption, *rule* pre-emption, and *obstacle* pre-emption.[97] Field pre-emption refers to situations 'where state law is found not to conflict *in its actual operation* with the substantive policies underlying the federal legislation', but where Congress has exercised its 'jurisdictional veto'.[98] The second pre-emption type occurs where federal legislation 'fairly interpreted' is in 'actual conflict' with State law.[99] Rule pre-emption occurs where a State law contradicts a federal rule. The third type of pre-emption has proven much more elusive: State law will be pre-empted wherever it stands 'as an obstacle to the accomplishment and execution of the full purpose and objectives of Congress'.[100] Obstacle pre-emption, so defined, does not represent a very

---

[97] There is no generally recognized pre-emption terminology in US constitutionalism. On the contrary, a plethora of 'pre-emption frameworks' has developed. The Supreme Court's three pre-emption types are well illustrated in *Silkwood v Kerr-McGee Corp* 464 US 238 (1984), 248: 'If Congress evidences an intent to occupy a given field, any state law falling within that field is pre-empted. If Congress has not entirely displaced state regulation over the matter in question, state law is still pre-empted to the extent it actually conflicts with federal law, that is, when it is impossible to comply with both state and federal law or where the state law stands as an obstacle to the accomplishment of the full purposes and objectives of Congress'. For the three pre-emption types enumerated, we shall choose the terms field pre-emption, rule pre-emption and obstacle pre-emption, as they arguably best reflect the ideas behind these conflict thresholds.

[98] L Tribe, *American Constitutional Law*, 1204–5.

[99] *Savage v Jones* 225 US 501, 533 (1912) (dictum).

[100] *Pacific Gas & Electric Co v State Energy Resources Conservation & Development Commission* 461 US 190 (1983), 204.

clear normative threshold,[101] especially if it is taken to displace 'any state legislation which frustrates the *full* effectiveness of federal law'.[102]

Importantly, the constitutional rationale behind all three pre-emption claims is that federal and State legislation *conflict*.[103] It follows that 'every federal law has some pre-emptive effect, and—in the face of ambiguity—the issue is *always* one of scope'.[104] The federal government is free to choose the extent to which the States remain active legislative participants. The determination of the degree of conflict, that is, the extent to which the federal exercise of a shared power excludes the States from exercising theirs, becomes *the* quintessential federal question. The doctrine of pre-emption draws the jurisdictional boundary line and thus settles the federal equilibrium within a policy area.

Let us now turn to the second dimension of the modern pre-emption analysis. What are the modes in which a particular pre-emption type is expressed? The fundamental starting point here is the idea that Congress must speak its mind. It must express its intent to pre-empt State laws when legislating.[105] Express pre-emption represents the most straightforward mode in doctrinal terms. The federal legislation itself defines to what extent State law will be pre-empted.[106] Inversely Congress may explicitly allow for the

---

[101] The jurisprudence of the Supreme Court has given a long commentary to the phrase. It failed, however, in establishing clear boundaries around 'obstacle pre-emption'. In *City of Burbank v Lockheed Air Terminal Inc* 411 US 624 (1973), the Court pre-empted a State ordinance that 'severely' (ibid 639) impeded the functioning of a federal scheme. In *Commonwealth Edison Co v Montana* 453 US 609 (1981), pre-emption was said to require more than creating an obstacle to mere '*general* expressions of national policy' (ibid 634 (emphasis added)). In a number of cases on the pre-emptive effect of the Sherman Act, the Court would find that State legislation would not be invalidated simply because of some anti-competitive effect (cf *Fisher v Berkeley* 475 US 260 (1986)). For a discussion of those cases, see generally: L Tribe (n 98 above) 1179–95.

[102] *Perez v Campbell* 401 US 637 (1971), 652.

[103] Even field pre-emption should be understood as a species of conflict pre-emption: '[F]ield pre-emption may be understood as a species of conflict pre-emption: a state law that falls within a pre-empted field conflicts with Congress' intent (either express or plainly implied) to exclude state regulation' (*English v General Electric Co* 496 US 72 (1990), 79 note 5). See also: *Gade v National Solid Wastes Management Ass'n* 505 US 88 (1992).

[104] L Tribe, *American Constitutional Law*, 1195, fn 74 (emphasis in original).

[105] '[T]he purpose of Congress is the ultimate touchstone of pre-emption analysis' (*Cipollone v Ligett Group* 505 US 514 (1992), 516).

[106] An express pre-emption clause could simply state 'These State laws are prohibited' or 'States are prohibited from adopting stricter rules on environmental protection'. Express pre-emption may not avoid the practical problems of determining the actual scope of the pre-emption clause. Consider, for example the doctrinal argument between Justice Scalia and the majority Court in *Cipollone v Ligett Group* 505 US 514 (1992). The latter had insisted on a *narrow* interpretation of the express pre-emption clause, while Scalia claimed that pre-emption doctrine demanded no more

continued and unaffected application of State measures in certain areas in spite of a potential or actual interference with the federal legislation. This form of 'express saving' constitutes the logical flip side of express pre-emption and has been relatively uncontested constitutional territory.[107] Absent conclusive legislative intent, when will federal legislation pre-empt State laws? The Supreme Court has developed a set of constitutional presumptions that structure the Court's federal vision. It is here that we should observe the transition from dual to cooperative federalism best.

b. Changing Judicial Philosophies: The 'New Federalism'

The move towards cooperative federalism occurred soon after the new deal. The Court made clear that State legislation was not automatically pre-empted simply because national legislation on the subject existed. 'Undoubtedly, every subject that merits congressional legislation is, by definition, a subject of national concern. That cannot mean, however, that every federal statute ousts all related state law . . . Instead, we must look for special features warranting pre-emption'.[108] More than that: the Court would establish a presumption against pre-emption in the areas of traditional police powers of the States. 'Congress legislated here in a field which the States have traditionally occupied. So we start with the assumption that the historic police powers of the States were not to be superseded by the Federal Act unless that was the clear and manifest purpose of Congress.' Where the State and federal legislation did not collide, the former 'regulatory scheme should be allowed to supplement the Federal Act'. Both could form a 'harmonious' entity, where State law would 'strengthen and bolster the federal regulatory scheme and in no way dilute, impair or oppose it'.[109]

than a determination of the 'ordinary meaning' since the anti-pre-emption presumption would only apply to cases of implied intent. Once Congress had spoken its mind on the pre-emption issue, 'normal canons' of interpretation governed the issue.

[107] An express saving clause may state: 'These State laws shall not be affected by the federal legislation' or 'Nothing in this federal law shall prevent the States from adopting stricter standards'. However, the Supreme Court seems to presume that Congress will always intend to oust State law that actually conflicts with the federal rules. This may even operate as against an express savings clause; cf *Geier et al. v American Honda Motor Co Inc* et al 529 US 861 (2000), 872: 'To the extent that such an interpretation of the saving provision reads into a particular federal law toleration of a conflict that those principles would otherwise forbid, it permits that law to defeat its own objectives, or potentially, as the Court has put it before, to "destroy itself." ' Rule pre-emption thus operates as a 'default position' (MJ Davis, *Unmasking the Presumption in favor of Preemption*, 1021).

[108] *Hillsborough County v Automated Medical Laboratories Inc* 471 US 707 (1985), 719.

[109] *Rice v Santa Fe Elevator Corporation* 331 US 218 (1947), 230–2.

Legislative cooperation was the Court's novel commitment: *'reconciliation of the conflicting claims of state and national power is to be attained only by some appraisal and accommodation of the competing demands of the state and national interests involved'*.[110] The interpretation of federal law should then be 'tempered by the conviction that the proper approach is to reconcile "the operation of both statutory schemes with one another rather than holding one completely ousted"'.[111]

This commitment to cooperative federalism involved—in the first place—limiting field pre-emption. The latter would, henceforth, only be inferred, where 'the nature of the regulated subject matter permits no other conclusion' or where 'Congress has unmistakably so ordained'.[112] Federal law should be '[f]loor, not ceiling'.[113] Field pre-emption was to be restricted to two instances only: when the federal law 'touch[ed] a field in which the federal interest is so dominant that the federal system will be assumed to preclude enforcement of state laws on the same subject';[114] or, where '[t]he scheme of federal regulation may be so pervasive as to make reasonable the inference that Congress left no room for the States to supplement it'.[115] The Court pledged that it would 'seldom infer solely from the comprehensiveness of federal regulations, an intent to pre-empt in its entirety a field related to health and safety'.[116] And where such complete harmonization was found, the Court promised to narrowly construct the scope of such a field: only those State laws that 'have some direct and substantial effect' on the federal legislation would be caught.[117]

---

[110]   *Southern Pacific Co v Arizona* 325 US 761 (1945) 768 (emphasis added).

[111]   *Merrill Lynch, Pierce, Fenner & Smith v Ware* 414 US 117 (1973), 127.

[112]   *Florida Lime & Avocado Growers v Paul* 373 US 132 (1963), 142.

[113]   P Wolfson, *Preemption and Federalism: The Missing Link*, 83.

[114]   *Rice v Santa Fe Elevator Corporation* 331 US 218 (1947), 230. An example of such a strong federal interest is foreign affairs, see: *Hines v Davidowitz* 312 US 51 (1941), 67–8. In *Boyle v United Technologies* 487 US 500 (1988), the Supreme Court ruled that field pre-emption is easily inferred where the subject matter concerns a 'uniquely federal interest', but for all other areas the 'clear statement rule' would apply. Advocates of federal pre-emption frequently argue that there is a 'dominant federal interest' in interstate or international activities—an argument based on the dictum in *Rice v Santa Fe Elevator Corp*. In *Hillsborough County Fla v Automated Medical Laboratories* 471 US 707 (1985), the Supreme Court gave a sobering definition by limiting 'dominant federal interests' to matters whose 'special features' would be of such an order as the responsibility of the national government for foreign affairs.

[115]   *Rice v Santa Fe Elevator Corporation* 331 US 218 (1947), 230.

[116]   *Hillsborough County Fla v Automated Medical Laboratories* 471 US 707 (1985), 718.

[117]   *English v General Electric Co* 496 US 72 (1990), 85.

The move towards cooperative federalism would—secondly—also involve a more restrictive concept of obstacle pre-emption. A good illustration of this restrictive approach can be seen in *Head v New Mexico Board*.[118] Head, a newspaper owner, was enjoined from accepting or publishing within the State of New Mexico a Texas optometrist's advertising found to be in violation of New Mexico law. The New Mexican statute regulated sales techniques and prohibited, inter alia, the advertising by quotation or comparison of any prices or terms on eyeglasses. The applicant had done just that and claimed, in addition to a dormant Commerce Clause violation, that the State law had been pre-empted by the federal Communications Act. Having laconically found that 'these facts alone do not add up to an unconstitutional burden on interstate commerce',[119] the Court turned to the pre-emption claim. And here we may cite the Court's new federal philosophy at length:

In dealing with the contention that New Mexico's jurisdiction to regulate radio advertising has been preempted by the Federal Communications Act, we may begin by noting that the validity of this claim cannot be judged by reference to broad statements about the 'comprehensive' nature of federal regulation under the Federal Communications ... In areas of the law not inherently requiring national uniformity, our decisions are clear in requiring that state statutes, otherwise valid, must be upheld unless there is found 'such actual conflict between the two schemes of regulation that both cannot stand in the same area, [or] evidence of a congressional design to preempt the field.' ... [W]e are nevertheless not persuaded that the federal legislation in this field has excluded the application of a state law of the kind here involved. The nature of the regulatory power given to the federal agency convinces us that Congress could not have intended its grant of authority to supplant all the detailed state regulation of professional advertising practices, particularly when the grant of power to the Commission was accompanied by no substantive standard other than the 'public interest, convenience, and necessity.' ... In the absence of positive evidence of legislative intent to the contrary, we cannot believe Congress has ousted the States from an area of such fundamentally local concern.[120]

This new commitment to reconcile federal and State law into a harmonious legislative entity would become the hallmark of cooperative federalism. The new federal philosophy was confirmed in the context of the relationship between federal health and safety legislation and State tort laws. In *Silkwood*,[121] the Court found that 'Congress assumed that traditional principles of state

---

[118] *Head v New Mexico Board*, 374 US 424 (1963).
[119] Ibid 428.
[120] Ibid 429–32.
[121] *Silkwood v Kerr-McGee Corp* 464 US 238 (1984).

tort law would apply with full force unless they were expressly supplanted'.[122] This result was confirmed in *English v General Electric Co*,[123] where the Supreme Court reprimanded a District Court for having 'failed to follow this Court's teaching that "[o]rdinarily, state causes of action are not pre-empted solely because they impose liability over and above that authorized by federal law." Absent some specific suggestion in the text or legislative history . . . we cannot conclude that Congress intended to pre-empt all state actions.' 'The Court has observed repeatedly that pre-emption is ordinarily not to be implied absent an "actual conflict"'.[124]

The new presumption *against* pre-emption was, of course, a presumption in favour of the *complementarity* of federal and State law. This legislative complementarity would become the hallmark and manifestation of cooperative federalism. And, in spite of recent doubts,[125] it is a characteristic that American federalism has never lost. Nonetheless, it is important to note that the presumption against pre-emption and the clear statement rule are only *procedural* hurdles. They would not *constitutionally* guarantee the co-existence of federal and State legislation: 'clear statement rules set no fixed, constitutional limits'.[126] Where Congress speaks clearly in favour of pre-emption, the States' legislative complements must give way. This lack of substantive constitutional safeguards in American federalism contrasts with the presence of such safeguards in the cooperative federalism of the European Union. The latter's most striking constitutional commitment to the idea of legislative complementarity is the emergence of complementary competences in the Community legal order.[127]

---

[122]   Ibid 255.

[123]   *English v General Electric Co* 496 US 72 (1990).

[124]   Ibid 89–90.

[125]   The late Rehnquist Court's pre-emption decisions have placed a shadow over the presumption against federal pre-emption (cf *Geier et al v American Honda Motor Co Inc et al* 529 US 861 (2000)). Did this signal an abandonment of the constitutional premise of cooperative federalism? Two points speak against such a view. First, even if 'recent pre-emption cases evidence a federal law preference very much like those early cases', 'they do not evidence a wholesale return to that expansive pre-emption doctrine which would find pre-emption as a result of the very exercise of federal regulation in a field' (MJ Davis, *Unmasking the Presumption in favor of Preemption*, 1015). Secondly, the very rationale of these cases is not informed by a particular federal or nationalist philosophy, but a substantive pro-business philosophy of the Court. Some even speak of the 'hypocrisy' (E Chemerinsky, *Empowering States: the Need to Limit Federal Preemption*, 69) of the Rehnquist Court in federalist issues.

[126]   Note, *Clear Statement Rules, Federalism, and Congressional Regulation of States*, 1963.

[127]   On this point, see: Chapter 5—Section II below.

2. *Changing Nature: From Constitutional to Legislative Pre-emption*

The pre-emption doctrine is *the* constitutional principle of modern American federalism. Under the modern doctrine, all pre-emption types represent a species of conflict. State law will only be displaced where, and to the extent that, it 'conflicts' with federal law. However, the spectrum of conflict is open-ended and ranges from purely hypothetical frictions to literal contradictions. There is no easy way to measure normative conflicts; and, in an attempt to classify degrees of conflict, pre-emption typologies have been developed. Most pre-emption typologies will, to a great extent, be arbitrary classifications: there simply are no *a priori* boundaries between the various degrees of normative conflict. Pre-emption typologies will, therefore, at best *reflect* the various judicial reasons created to explain why a State norm conflicts with federal legislation.

Where did the pre-emption doctrine come from? The origin and nature of the doctrine are shrouded in constitutional mist. For a long time, the doctrine was the neglected 'stepchild' of American constitutional law. Various constitutional theories have since been suggested to explain the pre-emption phenomenon, the majority of which orbit around the Supremacy Clause. Are supremacy and pre-emption one and the same, fundamentally different, or two sides of the same coin? The Supreme Court sometimes conceptualizes pre-emption as a logical consequence of the Supremacy Clause.[128] However, the conceptual fusion of the two doctrines has attracted criticism. The two doctrines are linked, but ultimately distinct. Supremacy and pre-emption are twin doctrines: whereas the supremacy principle decrees *that* federal law will be supreme over conflicting State law, the doctrine of pre-emption determines *when* such a conflict arises. Supremacy 'serves as a traffic cop, mandating a federal law's survival instead of a state law's',[129] while pre-emption represents the substantive principle that specifies when such conflicts have arisen. In brief, the pre-emption doctrine determines what constitutes a conflict, whereas the Supremacy Clause decides *how*, that is, in *whose favour* this conflict is resolved.

But if the principles of supremacy and pre-emption are indeed different, how has the unwritten constitutional principle been justified? Here, modern pre-emption analysis offers a much better explanation than 'classic'

---

[128] For example: *Philadelphia v New Jersey* 430 US 141 (1977), 142: 'federal preemption of state statutes is, of course, ultimately a question under the Supremacy Clause'.

[129] SC Hoke, *Preemption Pathologies and Civic Republican Values*, 755.

pre-emption doctrine.[130] Instead of locating the pre-emptive effect of federal law in the constitutional principle of supremacy *as such*, it is seen as emanating directly from *each piece of federal legislation*. Pre-emption claims are thus not

---

[130] The 'classic' doctrine is today defended by SA Gardbaum, *The Nature of Preemption*, 768. Gardbaum proposes the Necessary and Proper Clause as constitutional source for the pre-emption doctrine. In order to understand his reasoning, we need first look at his definition of the pre-emption phenomenon. Pre-emption is taken to mean '(a) that states are deprived of their power to act *at all* in a given area, and (b) that this is so *whether or not* state law is in conflict with federal law. When states lose their concurrent lawmaking powers through pre-emption by Congress, the issue of potential substantive conflict between the content of valid state and federal laws is simply not reached, for the state no longer has power to legislate at all in the given area. Preemption is thus a jurisdiction-stripping (or "jurispathic") concept, unlike supremacy which deals with conflict resolution in particular cases . . . Whereas supremacy resolves a conflict resulting from the exercise by two or more entities of their concurrent powers, pre-emption implies that one entity (the federal) has attained exclusive power on the issue' (ibid 771). Pre-emption is here understood as a constitutional phenomenon for it affects the federal division of powers by turning a concurrent competence into an exclusive federal power, thus constitutionally depriving the States of their power to act.

　　Second, Gardbaum now assumes that the power to say 'there shall be no state regulation of field X' is not a power normally included in a legislative grant. ('The difference between pre-emption and supremacy is precisely the difference between the sufficiency of "some" federal regulation and the necessity of "conflicting" regulation of the non-application of state law' (ibid 797).) The power to adopt uniform laws is greater than the power to adopt conflicting laws (presumably because Congress can only positively 'regulate' and not express pure prohibitions?). So he asks: 'why is pre-emption a constitutionally justified form of regulation?' (ibid 778). The answer he gives is as follows: 'Undoubtedly, the basic and most compelling argument in favour of a congressional power of pre-emption is a practical one—the need for uniform national regulation, for one set of rules, in particular areas. . . To see the issue of pre-emption in terms of this need, however, is to point to a more satisfactory constitutional justification of it. Simply put, in certain areas and under certain circumstances, Congress needs to pass uniform national laws in order to exercise its express powers effectively . . . Yet, these are precisely the circumstances under which Congress is authorized to use the power contained in the Constitution's Necessary and Proper Clause located at the end of Section 8, Article I . . . There is thus a straightforward plausibility behind ultimately deriving pre-emption from Congress's enumerated power under the Necessary and Proper Clause . . . In sum, the power of pre-emption derives from the Necessary and Proper Clause; it is authorized as a means of effectuating other congressional powers. It has nothing to do with the Supremacy Clause. The independent principle of supremacy alone is insufficient to guarantee the uniform national regulation that is sometimes required' (ibid 781–2).

　　Gardbaum's analysis is thus premised on a categorical distinction between the doctrines of supremacy and pre-emption: federal supremacy means that federal law overrides conflicting State law; pre-emption implies that the federal legislator gains exclusive power within a policy area regardless of a conflict. Supremacy is reduced to situations of substantive 'conflict', while the pre-emption doctrine is reduced to instances of jurisdictional field pre-emption. Within this analytical framework, 'conflict pre-emption' constitutes necessarily a contradiction in terms (ibid 784). In reducing pre-emption to its 'non-conflict' form of field pre-emption, Gardbaum sees 'confusion and ambivalence' in the Supreme Court's jurisprudence where it arguably exists in the eye of the beholder. A similar conceptual confusion has been made in the Community legal order. For a critique of this view, see: R Schütze, *Supremacy without Pre-emption? The very slowly emergent Doctrine of Community Pre-emption*.

constitutional claims but *legislative* claims.[131] The legislative quality of the pre-emption phenomenon is underscored by the Supreme Court's choice of congressional intent as the 'touchstone' of the pre-emption analysis.[132] In order to understand this, we need to remind ourselves of an important characteristic of federal orders: here statutory interpretation has—simultaneously—a horizontal powers *as well as* a vertical powers dimension. The pre-emption doctrine thereby covers the vertical dimension and may, consequently, be conceived of as a *federal theory of interpretation*. It assembles those federal values and assumptions that will guide a judicial decision in addition to the 'ordinary' canons of statutory interpretation.[133]

But even if we accept that a federal pre-emption framework condenses the historical sensitivities of a federal order in a number of interpretative presumptions, what is the constitutional status of these conventions? 'Ordinary' textual interpretation cannot explain why the Supreme Court recognizes a presumption against pre-emption in policy fields touching on the traditional police powers of the States; nor can it explain the application of vigorous field pre-emption in an area of an important federal interest. Here, the interpretive choices of the Supreme Court enter meta-constitutional ground. If the *traditional* division of responsibilities provides an *argument* in favour of the restrictive construction of federal legislation,[134] American constitutionalism acknowledges that not only textual and purposive elements but constitutional history as such will determine the federation's present. Thus, in the same way as the various modes of constructing the Constitution are 'external' to it,

---

[131] Pre-emption cases 'cannot properly be considered constitutional cases' since the 'federal pre-emption question is an alleged conflict between a federal statutory or regulatory principle and a state law or action' (SC Hoke, *Transcending Conventional Supremacy: A Reconstruction of the Supremacy Clause*, 886).

[132] *Gade v National Solid Wastes Management Ass'n* 505 US 88 (1992), 96.

[133] For an alternative vision, see: SA Gardbaum, *The Nature of Preemption*, 770: 'Pre-emption claims should be resolved through the application of ordinary rules of statutory interpretation, and not through doctrinal categories such as "conflict pre-emption" and "field pre-emption", both of which constitute distorting filters through which the determination of congressional intent is mistakenly required to pass. In short, there should be no such thing as pre-emption doctrine'. This unorthodox view may have a strong centralizing tendency (cf SC Hoke (n 131 above) 888: '[W]ithout some larger principles to guide pre-emption decision making, courts would likely interpret any differences between the state and federal statutes as constituting forbidden "conflict", thus necessitating the displacement of state law. Though the relative ease of application may have appeal, the centralising, nationalistic prospects of this methodology should be deeply troubling').

[134] In *Gregory v Ashcroft* 501 US 452 (1991) 460, the Supreme Court promised that in the absence of a clear statement to the contrary, it would interpret a federal law in such a way that it would not upset the '*usual* constitutional balance of federal and state powers'.

dual and cooperative federalism are *pre*-conceptions of the constitutional division of powers. They are not 'internal' to the Constitution, but externally brought *into* the Constitution.[135]

Excursus—The Foreign Affairs 'Exception'

From the very beginning, foreign affairs were of 'central' concern to the American Republic. In war, a united stance had been necessary to win independence from Great Britain. The 1777 Articles of Confederation had then not only subjected the power to wage war to central control; they had also placed the treaty-making power under the auspices of the confederal Congress.[136] The 1787 reform of the 'imperfect' constitutional arrangements under the Articles led to the further centralization of foreign affairs. And while there was no express provision delegating the power to conclude international treaties to the Union as such, the 1787 Constitution granted this power to its President.[137] Normatively, the 1787 Constitution also strengthened the status of international treaties by providing that 'all treaties made, or which shall be made, under the Authority of the United States, shall be the supreme Law of the Land; and the Judges in every State shall be bound thereby'.[138] International treaties concluded by the federation would be valid within the States as supreme law.[139]

These were formidable external powers for the United States. But what was the scope of its treaty-making power? Would the power follow those

[135] Can the legislative branch limit the Supreme Court's favoured type of federalism? In 1999, three bills had been proposed to achieve just that, namely, the Federalism Act, the Federalism Accountability Act, and the Federalism Preservation Act. According to Section 6 of the Federalism Accountability Act, pre-emption could only be found, where a statute 'expressly states that such pre-emption is intended' or where there was a direct conflict between federal and State law 'so that the two cannot be reconciled or consistently stand together'. For a discussion of the constitutionality of these bills, see: PL Donze, *Legislating Comity: Can Congress enforce Federalism Constraints through Restrictions on Preemption Doctrine?*.

[136] Article IX stated: 'The United States in Congress assembled, shall have the sole and exclusive right and power of determining on peace and war, except in the cases mentioned in the sixth article—of sending and receiving ambassadors—entering into treaties and alliances'.

[137] Article II, Section 2, Clause 2: 'He shall have Power, by and with the Advice and Consent of the Senate, to make Treaties, provided two thirds of the Senators present concur; and he shall nominate, and by and with the Advice and Consent of the Senate, shall appoint Ambassadors'.

[138] Article VI, Section 2.

[139] *Foster v Neilson* 27 US 253 (1829), 314 (per Chief Justice Marshall).

federal lines that structured the internal sphere; or was it plenary? And even if it were plenary, would this mean that the States were generally excluded from foreign affairs? Would the constitutional principles governing foreign affairs follow the federal reform in the domestic sphere; or is it true that American constitutionalism has assumed 'a sharp distinction between what is foreign and what is domestic, between what is external and what is internal'?[140] We shall try to answer these questions in this final section. A first part looks at the treaty-making power in the American federation. American constitutionalism here grants the federation plenary powers. This, in itself, will not mean dual federalism. However, since the States have been prohibited from autonomously concluding international agreements, the treaty-making power is an exclusive power. This dual federalism has also, for a long time, affected the States' power to adopt internal legislation dealing with foreign affairs. However, some recent Supreme Court decisions offer a glimpse of a more cooperative federalism with regard to this second situation.

1. *Foreign Affairs and the Treaty-Making Power: Dual Federalism Constitutionalized*

When the Constitution was drafted, the treaty-making power constituted a small bundle of activities. The traditional treaty of friendship, commerce, and navigation would only have domestic affects with regard to the rights of aliens, that is, nationals of the other party. These treaties hardly ever dealt with the 'internal' choices of a State vis-à-vis its own subjects and State police powers would, thus, not be affected—even if a plenary treaty-making power was conceded to the federal Government. The growth of international cooperation in the twentieth century and the subsequent emergence of an international cooperative law changed this state of affairs dramatically. Today, international agreements may regulate subject-matters that once belonged to the exclusive sphere of internal State 'police powers'. The internationalization of the world had created new foreign affairs occupations and the federal question would become ever more important. Should the treaty-making power be 'conceived as an independent grant of power "delegated" to the national government or as only an alternative mode of exercising the legislative powers granted to Congress in Article I of the

---

[140] CA Bradley, *The Treaty Power and American Federalism*, 391.

Constitution'?[141] American constitutionalism would adopt the first option. It would insist on a dual federal principle in the foreign affairs context and thus cement their 'exceptional' constitutional status.

a. Constitutional Certainties: The Unitary Scope of the Federal Treaty Power

Much ink has flown to describe the history and scope of the American foreign affairs power. Some pens marshal evidence in favour of an 'original' plenipotentiary authority;[142] others consider the 'plenary power' view a twentieth-century invention.[143] Be history as it may, modern American constitutionalism certainly accords the Union full treaty-making powers.

The modern classic in favour of plenary federal treaty-making powers is *Missouri v Holland*.[144] This case concerned the protection of migratory birds that were in danger of extermination. The States had been individually unable to limit hunting and Congress tried to remedy the impasse by adopting the federal Migratory Bird Act (1913). The Act was declared unconstitutional. In an attempt to bypass constitutional troubles, the Senate invoked the idea of an international treaty with Great Britain—acting on behalf of Canada—as an alternative. The Migratory Bird Treaty was duly signed in 1916. But in the face of this constitutional trick, it was hardly surprising that these birds would eventually flow into the offices of the Supreme Court. Could the federation conclude treaties on subject-matters over which it had no internal power? Or was the federal treaty-making power limited by the exclusive competences of the States? Would the treaty power be an independent power or only provide the federal government with an additional instrument to implement its internal competences under the Constitution?

The famous answer by the Supreme Court held that the internal division of powers would *not* structure the external sphere. In the words of Justice Holmes, '[a]cts of Congress are the supreme law of the land only when made

---

[141] DM Golove, *Treaty-Making and the Nation: The Historical Foundations of the Nationalist Conception of the Treaty Power*, 1087–8.

[142] Cf DM Golove (ibid) referring to A Hamilton's *The Defence No XXXVI* (1796): 'It was impossible for words more comprehensive to be used than those which grant the power to make treaties. They are such as would naturally be employed to confer a *plenipotentiary* authority'.

[143] Cf CA Bradley (n 140 above) 410: '[T]he historical record reveals a fairly consistent understanding that the treaty power was limited either by subject matter, states' rights, or both'. Bradley refers to T Jefferson's *A Manual of Parliamentary Practice: For the use of the Senate of the United States*, in Jefferson's *Parliamentary Writings*, 420 (Wilbur S Howell (ed) 1988) in which the treaty power is, inter alia, limited by 'the rights of the states; for surely the President and Senate cannot do by treaty what the whole government is interdicted from doing in any way' (ibid 421).

[144] *State of Missouri v Holland* 252 US 416 (1920).

in pursuance of the Constitution, while treaties are declared to be so when made under the authority of the United States'. 'It is obvious that there may be matters of the sharpest exigency for the national well being that an act of Congress could not deal with but that a treaty followed by such an act could, and it is not lightly to be assumed that, in matters requiring national action, "a power which must belong to and somewhere reside in every civilized government" is not to be found.' 'The only question is whether it is forbidden by some invisible radiation from the general terms of the Tenth Amendment.'[145] The only limit to the federal treaty power seemingly acknowledged was that the federal Government must confine its external powers to situations where a *national* problem required a *national* answer.[146] Was this a sign that the Court accepted inherent limits to the treaty-making power? Should international treaties be confined to inter-*national* concerns? This reading was supported by subsequent jurisprudence, finding the treaty power to 'extend to all *proper subjects of negotiation* between our government and other nations'.[147] However, any invisible radiation from the Tenth Amendment originally intended would soon be withered away by modern treaty-making practice. The modern treaty-making power is a plenary power. The States simply cannot invoke 'sovereign rights' over their—internally—exclusive domains to limit the treaty-making power of the federation.

But how could a plenary power originate in a federal Constitution based on *divided* sovereignty? The idea of the 'exceptional' character of foreign affairs has been a constant theme since the foundational period.[148] It achieved its purest—and most controversial—expression in *United States v Curtiss-Wright Export Corp*.[149] The Supreme Court famously drew a categorical distinction between the external and the internal powers of the federal Government:

The two classes of powers are different, both in respect of their origin and their nature. The broad statement that the federal government can exercise no powers except those specifically enumerated in the Constitution, and such implied powers as are necessary and proper to carry into effect the enumerated powers, is categorically true only in respect of our internal affairs. In that field, the primary purpose of the Constitution was to carve from the general mass of legislative powers then possessed by the states

---

[145] Ibid 433–4.

[146] Ibid 435: 'Here a national interest of very nearly the first magnitude is involved. It can be protected only by national action in concert with that of another power'.

[147] *Asakura v City of Seattle* 265 US 332 (1924), 341 (emphasis added).

[148] Cf PJ Spiro, *Foreign Relations Federalism*.

[149] *United States v Curtiss-Wright Export Corp* 299 US 304 (1936).

such portions as it was thought desirable to vest in the federal government, leaving those not included in the enumeration still in the states. That this doctrine applies only to powers which the states had is self-evident. And since the states severally never possessed international powers, such powers could not have been carved from the mass of state powers but obviously were transmitted to the United States from some other source . . . [T]he investment of the federal government with the powers of external sovereignty did not depend upon the affirmative grants of the Constitution. The powers to declare and wage war, to conclude peace, to make treaties, to maintain diplomatic relations with other sovereignties, if they had never been mentioned in the Constitution, would have vested in the federal government as necessary concomitants of nationality.[150]

The theory that the federation's external powers are of *extra*-constitutional origin was 'historically indefensible' and thus attracted much academic criticism.[151] Even the Supreme Court would subsequently reject the theory: if plenary in scope, the treaty-making power was an enumerated power.[152] Nonetheless, the picture painted by US constitutionalism is one in which legislative powers are internally divided, while the treaty-making powers are externally united.

A constitutional justification for the federation's plenary treaty-making power has pointed to the political safeguards of federalism. Substantive limits

---

[150] Ibid 315–16, 18. Sutherland justified the theory of extra-constitutional foreign affairs powers by another controversial constitutional interpretation of post-Colonial history: 'During the Colonial period, those powers were possessed exclusively by and were entirely under the control of the Crown. By the Declaration of Independence, "the Representatives of the United States of America" declared the United (not the several) Colonies to be free and independent states, and as such to have "full Power to levy War, conclude Peace, contract Alliances, establish Commerce and to do all other Acts and Things which Independent States may of right do." As a result of the separation from Great Britain by the colonies, acting as a unit, the powers of external sovereignty passed from the Crown not to the colonies severally, but to the colonies in their collective and corporate capacity as the United States of America. Even before the Declaration, the colonies were a unit in foreign affairs, acting through a common agency—namely, the Continental Congress, composed of delegates from the thirteen colonies. That agency exercised the powers of war and peace, raised an army, created a navy, and finally adopted the Declaration of Independence. Rulers come and go; governments end and forms of government change; but sovereignty survives. A political society cannot endure without a supreme will somewhere. Sovereignty is never held in suspense. When, therefore, the external sovereignty of Great Britain in respect of the colonies ceased, it immediately passed to the Union' (ibid 316–17).

[151] Cf DM Levitan, *The Foreign Relations Power: An Analysis of Mr. Justice Sutherland's Theory*; and MD Ramsay, *The Myth of Extraconstitutional Foreign Affairs Power*.

[152] *Reid v Covert*, 354 US 1 (1957), 18: 'To the extent that the United States can validly make treaties, the people and the States have delegated their power to the National Government and the Tenth Amendment is no barrier'.

would be unnecessary as the conclusion process itself would guarantee the protection of States' rights. Unlike the ordinary legislative procedure, the President must obtain the consent of two-thirds of the Senate—the organ representing the interests of the States. The qualified majority rule would ensure that States' rights are better protected than within the internal sphere: 'The two-thirds rule was designed as a *special* political protection for state and sectional interests because the Founders felt compelled both to cede the power over treaties and to refrain from limiting it in ways that might ultimately prove detrimental to the national interest'.[153] Still, the unitary nature of the treaty-making power came under heavy attack when the Truman administration pushed for the adoption of the Universal Declaration of Human Rights and even began negotiations for a binding international human rights treaty.[154] States' rightists concentrated their efforts to get the Constitution amended to overrule *Missouri* and to limit the treaty-making power to those subjects over which the federation enjoyed internal powers. However, the 'Bricker Amendment'—named after the Senator chiefly associated with it—would ultimately fail; and, in any event, it would have been a pyrrhic victory after the 'new nationalism' had dramatically expanded the internal sphere of the federation.

b. Constitutional Ambivalences: The Treaty-Making Powers of the States

The 1787 Constitution not only enumerated the external powers of the federation, it equally listed those foreign affairs powers prohibited for the States. 'No State shall enter into any Treaty, Alliance, or Confederation.'[155] 'No State shall, without the Consent of Congress, lay any duty of Tonnage, keep Troops, or Ships of War in time of Peace, enter into any Agreement or Compact with another State, or with a foreign Power, or engage in War, unless actually invaded, or in such imminent Danger as will not admit of delay'.[156] Did these specific prohibitions signal the wish generally to exclude the States from all foreign affairs activities? This idea persistently surfaces in American constitutional thought. The United States Government was said to be 'invested with power over all the foreign relations of the country, war, peace, and negotiations and intercourse with other nations; all which are

---

[153] DM Golove, *Treaty-Making and the Nation: The Historical Foundations of the Nationalist Conception of the Treaty Power*, 1296.

[154] Ibid 1274.

[155] Article I, Section 10, Clause 1.

[156] Article I, Section 10, Clause 3.

forbidden to the State governments'.[157] 'For local interests the several states of the Union exist, but for national purposes, embracing our relations with foreign nations, we are but one people, one nation, one power'.[158] But how would these judicial pronouncements combine with the wording of the Constitution? Did the Constitution's text not allow the States—with the consent of Congress—to 'enter into any Agreement or Compact with another State, *or with a foreign Power*'?

From the beginning, there existed an 'ambiguity of the constitutional language';[159] and the Compact Clause would remain a source of constitutional ambivalence for 200 years.[160] What distinguished 'treaties'—from which the States were absolutely barred—from 'agreements' or 'compacts' that would be constitutional if consented to by the Federal Union? The textual differentiation between a 'treaty' and an 'agreement or compact' under the 1787 Constitution reflected a common distinction in eighteenth-century international law. The classic text that influenced the drafters of the American Constitution was de Vattel's 'Law of Nations'.[161]

While the distinctions would be effaced by international practice in the nineteenth century,[162] what did the Supreme Court make of them in the last 200 years? In *Holmes v Jennison*,[163] Chief Justice Taney redefined treaty to 'mean an instrument written and executed with the formalities customary among nations'. The reference to 'agreements' or 'compacts' only proved 'the intention of the framers of the Constitution to use the broadest and most comprehensive terms; and that they anxiously desired to *cut off all connection*

---

[157] *Knox v Lee & Parker v Davis (Legal Tender Cases)* 79 US 457 (1870), 555.

[158] *Chae Chan Ping v United States* 130 US 581 (1889), 606.

[159] DE Engdahl, *Characterization of Interstate Arrangements: When a Compact is not a Compact?*, 65 (referring to J Story, *Commentaries on the Constitution of the United States*, § 1397 (1st edn 1833)).

[160] This ambivalence is reflected in the slightly schizophrenic position of traditional doctrine. Thus, even the great ES Corwin 'is able, within the confines of a single volume, to state on one page that 'so far as International Law is concerned the States do not exist' and, on another, that the States 'retain only a very limited capacity at International Law" (RS Rodgers, *The Capacity of States of the Union to conclude International Agreements: The Background and some recent Developments*, 1022).

[161] E de Vattel, *The Law of Nations*, 1883, Book II, § 152-4. Here, a treaty was defined as 'a compact made with a view to the public welfare by the superior power, either for perpetuity, or for a considerable time'. By contrast, '[t]he compacts which have temporary matters for their object are called agreements, conventions, and pactions'. 'They are accomplished by one single act, and not by repeated acts.' Public treaties were viewed as equivalents to 'laws'—lasting forever or a considerable time. Agreements or compacts were executive in nature as they settled a specific situation. On the influence of Vattel on the founding fathers, see: AC Weinfeld, *What did the Framers of the Federal Constitution mean by 'Agreements or Compacts'?*, 458.

[162] DE Engdahl (n 159 above) 82.

[163] *Holmes v Jennison* 39 US 540 (1840).

or communication between a state and a foreign power'.[164] 'The framers of the Constitution manifestly believed that any intercourse between a state and a foreign nation was dangerous to the Union; that it would *open a door of which foreign powers would avail themselves to obtain influence in separate states*'. Every part of the Constitution 'shows that our whole foreign intercourse was intended to be committed to the hands of the general government: and nothing shows it more strongly than the treaty-making power, and the power of appointing and receiving ambassadors; both of which are immediately connected with the question before us, and undoubtedly belong exclusively to the federal government'. '*It was one of the main objects of the Constitution to make us, so far as regards our foreign relations, one people, and one nation; and to cut off all communications between foreign governments, and the several state authorities*'.[165]

But: how to square this solution with the textual authorization in Article I, Section 10, Clause 3? One way out of the textual dilemma potentially lies in the constitutional role given to Congressional consent.[166] Would the consent of Congress transform the *State* agreement into a *federal* agreement? The thesis has gained strength with *Cuyler v Adams*,[167] albeit in the context of *inter se* agreements between sister States.[168] The Supreme Court held that 'where Congress has authorized the States to enter into a cooperative agreement,

---

[164] Ibid 571–2 (emphasis added).

[165] Ibid 573–6 (emphasis added).

[166] The literal reading of the Compact Clause subjects all agreements to consent. However, in *Virginia v Tennessee*, 148 US 503 (1893), the Supreme Court nuanced this position. 'There are many matters upon which different states may agree that can in no respect concern the United States.' The consent requirement applied only to 'those [agreements] which may tend to increase and build up the political influence of the contracting states, so as to encroach upon or impair the supremacy of the United States, or interfere with their rightful management of particular subjects placed under their entire control' (ibid 518). However, it seems that the suspension of the constitutional requirement of consent is confined to *inter se* agreements between sister States—to cater for the rise of horizontal cooperation within the United States (cf F Frankfurter & J Landis, *The Compact Clause of the Constitution—A Study in Interstate Adjustments*).

[167] *Cuyler v Adams* 449 US 433 (1981).

[168] There had been earlier signs for the proposition that Congressional consent transforms 'state compacts' into federal law: cf *State of Pa v Wheeling & Belmont Bridge Co* 54 US 518 (1851), 566: 'This compact, by the sanction of Congress, has become a law of the Union'. However, this line of cases had been overruled by *Hinderlider v La Plate River & Cherry Creek Ditch Co* 304 US 92 (1938), 109: 'The assent of Congress to the compact between Colorado and New Mexico does not make it a "treaty or statute of the United States"'. Prior to *Cuyler v Adams*, the 'law of the Union' doctrine had already been heavily criticized by academics, such as DE Engdahl, *Construction of Interstate Compacts: A Questionable Federal Question*, 1013 *et seq*. In the light of these judicial and academic opinions, *Cuyler v Adams* 'revolutionized the interpretation of the Compact Clause' (LM Eichorn, *Cuyler v Adams and the Characterization of Compact Law*, 1387).

and where the subject matter of that agreement is an appropriate subject for congressional legislation, the consent of Congress transforms the States' agreement into federal law under the Compact Clause'.[169] The transformation doctrine has been criticized as 'a remarkable feat of judicial alchemy'.[170] However, it could reconcile the text of Article I, Section 10 with the unitary external posture established for the United States in past jurisprudence. In concluding an international agreement with the consent of Congress, a Member State could be seen as acting as the 'agent' or 'organ' of the federation. (An alternative interpretation has viewed these agreements as 'mixed' legal phenomena.[171] Considering their 'hybrid status' as derived from State and federal sources,[172] this interpretation brings 'agreements or compacts' between a State and a foreign power close to the idea of mixed agreements. Federal consent would not transform the State agreement into a pure federal agreement, but make the United States an additional contracting partner to the agreement.) Yet, in the light of these constitutional uncertainties, '[t]he safest conclusion' still is 'that the states of the American Union are not presently subjects of international law'.[173] This seems to be the dominant view within the international community.

2. *Foreign Affairs and Internal Legislation: Dual Federalism De-Constitutionalized?*

'Governmental power over internal affairs is distributed between the national government and the several states. Governmental power over external affairs is not distributed, but is vested exclusively in the national government'.[174] This judicial statement was true for the treaty-making power; but would it also hold true for internal legislation touching on foreign affairs? The legal problem of treaty *transformation* will not arise as American constitutionalism accepts a monistic relation to international treaties. International treaties are valid laws of the land—even for those parts of the treaty that fall within the exclusive competences of the States. And where a federal treaty was not self-executing and required legislative implementation, federal legislation

---

[169] *Cuyler v Adams* 449 US 433 (1981), 440.

[170] Ibid 455 (Justice Rehnquist—dissent).

[171] DE Engdahl (n 168 above) 1039.

[172] LM Eichorn (n 168 above) 1410.

[173] I Bernier, *International Legal Aspects of Federalism*, 51.

[174] *United States v Belmont* 301 US 324 (1937), 330.

could be constitutionally based on the Necessary and Proper Clause.[175] The legislative powers of the federation to implement an international treaty matched its power to conclude them: both were plenary in scope. The federation will thus enjoy a legislative power to implement an international treaty even in areas in which the States enjoy an—internally—exclusive power.

But what will happen to State legislation touching on foreign affairs? Will State legislation interfering with foreign relations be automatically void as unconstitutional interference in a national exclusive domain? Various American constitutional scholars have acknowledged the general 'exclusivity' of foreign affairs: 'Foreign relations are national relations. The language, the spirit and the history of the Constitution deny the States authority to participate in foreign affairs[.]'[176] However, constitutional practice following the new deal shows a nuanced picture. The Supreme Court would not decisively commit itself to the constitutional exclusivity theory. A good illustration of this judicial ambivalence can be found in *Hines v Davidowitz*.[177] In the year of the commencement of the Second World War, Pennsylvania had adopted State legislation that required the registration of all aliens residing in the State's borders. In 1940, Congress followed suit and enacted a federal registration act. In this case, the Supreme Court was asked to determine the relationship between the two acts. Emphasizing that the federal government had been 'entrusted with full and exclusive responsibility for the conduct of affairs with foreign sovereignties' and admitting that '[e]xperience has shown that international controversies of the gravest moment, sometimes even leading to war, may arise from real or imagined wrongs to another's subjects', the Court nonetheless did *not* strike down the State law as an illegitimate trespasser on an exclusive federal fief. The Court was agnostically content to note that 'whatever power a state may have is subordinate to supreme national law'.[178] It then moved on to a modern pre-emption analysis:

[W]here the federal government, in the exercise of its superior authority in this field, has enacted a complete scheme of regulation and has therein provided a standard for

---

[175] In *State of Missouri v Holland* 252 US 416 (1920), Justice Holmes clarified that the legal foundation of the internal implementing legislation depended solely on the validity of the international treaty. 'If the treaty is valid there can be no dispute about the validity of the statute under Article I, Section 8, as a necessary and proper means to execute the powers of the Government' (ibid 432). For a critical analysis of this claim, see: NQ Rosenkrantz, *Executing the Treaty Power*, 1918.

[176] L Henkin, *Foreign Affairs and the Constitution*, 228.

[177] *Hines v Davidowitz*, 312 US 52 (1941).

[178] Ibid 68.

the registration of aliens, states cannot, inconsistently with the purpose of Congress, conflict or interfere with, curtail or complement, the federal law, or enforce additional or auxiliary regulations. There is not—and from the very nature of the problem there cannot be—any rigid formula or rule which can be used as a universal pattern to determine the meaning and purpose of every act of Congress. This Court, in considering the validity of state laws in the light of treaties or federal laws touching the same subject, has made use of the following expressions: conflicting; contrary to; occupying the field; repugnance; difference; irreconcilability; inconsistency; violation; curtailment; and interference. But none of these expressions provides an infallible constitutional test or an exclusive constitutional yardstick. In the final analysis, there can be no one crystal clear distinctly marked formula . . . [However] it is of importance that this legislation is in a field which affects international relations, the one aspect of our government that from the first has been most generally conceded imperatively to demand broad national authority. Any concurrent state power that may exist is restricted to the narrowest of limits; the state's power here is not bottomed on the same broad base as is its power to tax [.][179]

In light of the dominant federal interest in foreign relations, the Court chose to field pre-empt the State legislation.[180] Its reasoning suggested that in foreign affairs contexts, the Court will start from a presumption *in favour* of federal pre-emption. Nonetheless, the judicial agnosticism as to the nature of the foreign affairs power indirectly recognized that shared powers over alien registration was theoretically conceivable and not necessarily a 'foolish' thing.[181]

---

[179] Ibid 66–8.

[180] Ibid 73–7: 'The legislative history of the Act indicates that Congress was trying to steer a middle path, realizing that any registration requirement was a departure from our traditional policy of not treating aliens as a thing apart, but also feeling that the Nation was in need of the type of information to be secured. Having the constitutional authority so to do, it has provided a standard for alien registration in a single integrated and all-embracing system in order to obtain the information deemed to be desirable in connection with aliens. When it made this addition to its uniform naturalization and immigration laws, it plainly manifested a purpose to do so in such a way as to protect the personal liberties of law-abiding aliens through one uniform national registration system, and to leave them free from the possibility of inquisitorial practices and police surveillance that might not only affect our international relations but might also generate the very disloyalty which the law has intended guarding against. Under these circumstances, the Pennsylvania Act cannot be enforced'.

[181] For the opposite view, see: *Chy Lung v Freeman* 92 US 275 (1875), 280: 'If that government has forbidden the States to hold negotiations with any foreign nations, or to declare war, and has taken the whole subject of these relations upon herself, has the Constitution, which provides for this, done so foolish a thing as to leave it in the power of the States to pass laws whose enforcement renders the general government liable to just reclamations which it must answer, while it does not prohibit to the States the acts for which it is held responsible?'.

Be that as it may, foreign affairs were to receive their judicial baptism as a constitutionally exclusive sphere in 1968. In *Zschernig v Miller*,[182] an East German national had been deprived of an inheritance on the basis of an Oregon law that denied such a right to nationals of States that would not recognize the reciprocal right of a United States citizen to take property on the same terms as the citizen of that nation. There was no federal law in existence that would vaguely govern the situation. If the Supreme Court were to prohibit the State law as an improper 'cold war' tool that upset relations with the German Democratic Republic, it would have to look to the Constitution as such. That was what the Court did. In categorical language, it declared that foreign affairs and international relations were 'matters which the Constitution entrusts solely to the Federal Government'.[183] While the States have 'traditionally regulated the descent and distribution of estates', the Oregon law 'affects international relations in a persistent and subtle way' and 'must give way if they impair the effective exercise of the Nation's foreign policy'. 'Where those laws conflict with a treaty, they must bow to the superior federal policy. Yet, even in absence of a treaty, a State's policy may disturb foreign relations.' Any State law was constitutionally excluded that had 'a direct impact upon foreign relations and may well adversely affect the power of the central government to deal with those problems'.[184]

To some this was a 'new constitutional doctrine';[185] and in parallel to the Commerce Clause terminology, it has been called the 'dormant foreign affairs power'.[186] Yet, unfortunately, for more than 30 years, the dormant foreign affairs power thesis itself lay 'dormant'. *Zschernig* remained unconfirmed. Today, contemporary Supreme Court decisions on the Foreign Commerce Clause have cast doubt over the constitutional exclusivity thesis. These decisions, while recognizing a dominant federal interest in foreign commerce cases, operate within a *legislative* pre-emption paradigm.[187] *Crosby* is a case

---

[182]　*Zschernig v Miller* 389 US 429 (1968).

[183]　Ibid 436.

[184]　Ibid 440–1.

[185]　L Henkin, *Foreign Affairs and the Constitution*, 239.

[186]　EA Young, *Dual Federalism, Concurrent Jurisdiction, and the Foreign Affairs Exception*, 169.

[187]　Cf *Barclays Bank plc v Franchise Tax Bd* 512 US 298 (1994), where the Supreme Court spoke of 'the unique context of foreign commerce'. A State's power is here especially constrained because of 'the special need for federal uniformity', which would require 'additional scrutiny' (ibid 311, 317). However, in actual fact, the Court allowed a State law that interfered with foreign commerce in the light of 'indicia of Congress' willingness to tolerate States' worldwide combined reporting mandates, even when those mandates are applied to foreign corporations and domestic corporations with foreign parents' (ibid 327). The Court pointed to the US–UK Convention for Avoidance of

in point.[188] Here, a Massachusetts statute barred State entities from buying goods or services from companies doing business with Burma. A few months after the Massachusetts law had been enacted Congress itself passed a statute on economic sanctions against Burma. The federal law called upon the President to develop 'a comprehensive, multilateral strategy to bring democracy to and improve human rights practices and the quality of life in Burma'.[189]

The National Foreign Trade Council, representing the interests of companies blacklisted under the Massachusetts legislation, brought proceedings arguing that the State law was unconstitutional on three independent grounds: it infringed the federal foreign affairs power, it violated the foreign Commerce Clause, and it was preempted by the federal act. From these three alternative grounds, the Court chose the last one as the sole focal point of its analysis. Invoking the principle that federal legislation can pre-empt State laws, the Court found that the Massachusetts law constituted 'an obstacle to the accomplishment of Congress's full objectives under the federal Act'. The State law would undermine the purpose and effect of the federal statute. The stricter State standard conflicted with 'the federal choice about the right degree of pressure to employ' against Burma and as such distorted the federal legislative scheme.[190]

In *Crosby*, the Supreme Court firmly operated within a legislative pre-emption framework; and thus, indirectly, distanced itself from the exclusive competence thesis. 'W(h)ither *Zschernig*?'[191] This reading has gained ground with *American Insurance Association v Garamendi*.[192] President Clinton had concluded executive agreements, inter alia, with Germany in which the latter had agreed to set up a foundation to compensate all those who suffered at the hands of German companies during the National Socialist era. This voluntary compensation mechanism had been established on the expectation of immunity from lawsuits in American courts though the US Government

---

Double Taxation, a previous version of which had contained a provision prohibiting the State law in question. Since the Senate had rejected this version and since the agreement specifically excluded political subdivisions or local authorities from its application, the Court did not find the State law pre-empted.

[188] *Crosby v National Foreign Trade Council* 530 US 363 (2000).

[189] § 570 (c) of the Foreign Operations, Export Financing, and Related Programs Appropriations Act, 1997, § 570, 110 Stat. 3009–166 to 3009–167.

[190] Ibid 373 and 380.

[191] CM Vázquez, *W(h)ither Zschernig?*

[192] *American Insurance Association et al v Garamendi, Insurance Commissioner, State of California* 539 US 396 (2003).

had given no legal commitment to that effect.[193] Simultaneous to these international efforts, California had adopted its own Holocaust Victim Insurance Relief Act. The State law allowed State residents to sue in State courts on insurance claims based on acts perpetrated in the Holocaust and required foreign insurance companies to disclose details of their activities in Europe between 1920 and 1945. While the California law had the same objective as the international agreement, the federal Government claimed that the State law 'would possibly derail the German Foundation Agreement'. The Court agreed:

> The exercise of the federal executive authority means that state law must give way where, as here, there is evidence of clear conflict between the policies adopted by the two . . . The basic fact is that California seeks to use an iron fist where the President has consistently chosen kid gloves. We have heard powerful arguments that the iron fist would work better, and it may be that if the matter of compensation were considered in isolation from all other issues involving the European allies, the iron fist would be the preferable policy. But our thoughts on the efficacy of the one approach versus the other are beside the point, since our business is not to judge the wisdom of the National Government's policy; dissatisfaction should be addressed to the President or, perhaps, Congress. The question relevant to preemption in this case is conflict, and the evidence here is 'more than sufficient to demonstrate that the state Act stands in the way of [the President's] diplomatic objectives'.[194]

The finding of a 'clear conflict' between the Agreement and the State law allowed the Court to avoid a principled choice between constitutional exclusivity à la *Zschernig* and legislative pre-emption à la *Hines*.[195] Yet

---

[193] Ibid 406: '[T]he Government agreed that whenever a German company was sued on a Holocaust-era claim in an American court, the Government of the United States would submit a statement that "it would be in the foreign policy interests of the United States for the Foundation to be the exclusive forum and remedy for the resolution of all asserted claims against German companies arising from their involvement in the National Socialist era and World War II." Though unwilling to guarantee that its foreign policy interests would "in themselves provide an independent legal basis for dismissal," that being an issue for the courts, the Government agreed to tell courts "that U. S. policy interests favor dismissal on any valid legal ground"'.

[194] Ibid 421 and 427.

[195] In fact, *Zschernig* was translated into pre-emption terms (ibid 419): 'It is a fair question whether respect for the executive foreign relations power requires a categorical choice between the contrasting theories of field and conflict preemption evident in the *Zschernig* opinions, but the question requires no answer here. For even on Justice Harlan's view, the likelihood that state legislation will produce something more than incidental effect in conflict with express foreign policy of the National Government would require preemption of the state law'. And in footnote 11, the Court further explained: 'The two positions can be seen as complementary. If a State were simply to take a position on a matter of foreign policy with no serious claim to be addressing a traditional state responsibility, field preemption might be the appropriate doctrine, whether

again, the Supreme Court relied on the pre-emptive effect of the concrete federal law rather than on the general exclusivity of foreign affairs. Was this evidence of an (un)conscious shift from dual to cooperative federalism? Not necessarily so. The particularly aggressive presumption in favour of federal pre-emption still makes foreign affairs *special affairs*.[196] Yet, *even if* the presumption in favour of federal pre-emption is much stronger in the external sphere than in the internal sphere, this milder version of foreign affairs exceptionalism can—ultimately—be integrated into a cooperative federal picture.[197]

Conclusion: The Changing Structure of American Law

The constitutional battle over the nature of sovereignty and federalism in America had produced a compromise in the nineteenth century: dual federalism. The philosophy of dual federalism suggested a particular constitutional structure for the idea of *duplex regimen*: the tasks of government would be divided between two—mutually exclusive—spheres. 'In America, the powers of sovereignty are divided between the Government of the Union and those of the States. They are each sovereign with respect to the objects committed to it, and neither sovereign with respect to the objects committed to the other'.[198] The federal Government and the States were seen as 'equal' and

the National Government had acted and, if it had, without reference to the degree of any conflict, the principle having been established that the Constitution entrusts foreign policy exclusively to the National Government. Where, however, a State has acted within what Justice Harlan called its "traditional competence," but in a way that affects foreign relations, it might make good sense to require a conflict, of a clarity or substantiality that would vary with the strength or the traditional importance of the state concern asserted'.

[196] The Court's approach to pre-emption in *Crosby* 'was far from ordinary', cf CM Vázquez, *W(h)ither Zschernig?*, 1287. However, the existence of a special pre-emption standard in Crosby has been contested: '*Crosby* both decides the case on pre-emption grounds and cites *Hines's* "obstacle" test as guiding the inquiry. Yet from reading the Court's opinion in *Crosby*, we would not know that *Hines* strongly emphasized the foreign affairs context of its pre-emption inquiry. Indeed, *Crosby* studiously avoids citing or quoting any portion of *Hines* that discusses general considerations of the federal/state balance in foreign affairs. And *Crosby* refrains from quoting the *Hines* proviso about the specific foreign affairs context in which federal power is broad and state power is at a minimum. Instead, *Crosby* simply quotes *Hines's* general 'obstacle' formula and approaches the question as one of pre-emption without presumption' (D Halberstam, *The Foreign Affairs of Federal Systems: A National Perspective on the Benefits of State Participation*, 1026–7).

[197] EA Young, *Dual Federalism, Concurrent Jurisdiction, and the Foreign Affairs Exception*, 175.

[198] *McCulloch v Maryland* 17 US 316 (1819), 410.

'coordinate' within their respective spheres. This imagery would appease moderate 'Nationalists' and 'Statists' for more than a century 'like the conciliatory medieval formula of *regnum et sacerdotium* which acknowledged the two distinct but equal powers of Pope and Holy Roman Emperor in their separate realms'.[199]

The constitutional theory of dual federalism collapsed when the economic reality of the United States needed national solutions for problems previously thought to fall within the exclusive domain of the States. The shift away from dual federalism took place in the 1930s and is linked to the 'new deal'. Federalist theory succumbed to emotional facts.[200] '[N]ational problems required national responses'.[201] The Supreme Court would articulate the newly arrived federal philosophy in 1937 in the following words: 'The United States and the State of Alabama are not alien governments. They co-exist within the same territory. Unemployment is their common concern. Together the two statutes now before us embody a cooperative legislative effort by state and national governments, for carrying out a public purpose common to both, which neither could fully achieve without the cooperation of the other. The Constitution does not prohibit such cooperation'.[202] The new federalism was soon baptized 'cooperative federalism'. Its credo was that 'the National Government and the States are mutually complementary parts of a *single* governmental mechanism all of whose powers are intended to realize the current purposes of government according to their applicability to the problem at hand'.[203]

The passing of dual federalism took place on a number of levels. Modern 'new deal' jurisprudence would gradually abandon the conceptual duality between commerce versus police power; that is: national versus local power. This abandonment signalled a decline of constitutional exclusivity. With time, federal powers became—almost—unlimited.[204] '[T]he Constitution

---

[199] SR Davis, *The Federal Principle: A Journey through Time in Quest of a Meaning*, 115.

[200] RL Stern, *The Commerce Clause and the National Economy: 1933–1946*, 645: '[P]hilosophy and economic theory succumb to facts in so far as the public is concerned. When the people began to suffer as a result of the unrestrained freedom of enterprise, they called for help from the only peaceful protective organization at their command, their Government. Their call was addressed to the national government rather than to the states, since the problems of an integrated nationwide economy were obviously not remediable by state action'.

[201] RE Epstein, *The Proper Scope of the Commerce Power*, 1143.

[202] *Carmichael v Southern Coal & Coke Co* 301 US 495 (1937), 526.

[203] ES Corwin, *The Passing of Dual Federalism*, 19.

[204] L Kramer, *Understanding Federalism*, 1496: 'There were, however, supposed to be boundaries—areas outside the reach of federal law. Those boundaries have almost disappeared today. True, one

does not carve out express elements of state sovereignty that Congress may not employ its delegated powers to displace'.[205] Congress thus enjoyed a—bounded—*Kompetenz-Kompetenz*.[206] However, the expansion of federal power not only minimized enclaves of exclusive State power; it would also eventually transform the very nature of federal power. Importantly, the demise of exclusive legal spheres took place equally at the legislative level. The Supreme Court moved away from automatic field pre-emption and developed a modern pre-emption typology. Modern pre-emption doctrine was a doctrine of shared power, since it acknowledges the 'possibility that both federal and state governments may have regulatory jurisdiction over a particular subject at any given time and seek to moderate actual and potential conflicts between the two authorities'.[207] Today, the zone of power shared between the federation and its States is nearly all-embracing. The passing of dual federalism has given rise to a world of shared powers. Instead of a competence typology as developed by European federalism,[208] American federalism has developed a pre-emption typology. The rise of cooperative federalism would limit the actual exercise of federal legislative powers. It ensured the co-existence of federal and State legislation by means of presumptions against the total exclusion of State law.

The obituary of dual federalism occurred in 1950. 'This entire system of constitutional interpretation touching the Federal System is today in ruins.' 'Today neither the State Police Power not the concept of Federal Equilibrium is any "ingredient of national legislative power"[.]'[209] The departure was hardly bemoaned. Dual federalism had 'died for a reason'.[210] The impossibility of maintaining two mutually exclusive spheres of federal and State 'sovereignty' had become all too obvious. With goods, persons, and capital moving across

still hears the occasional judicial murmur about how federal powers are limited by the enumeration in Article I. But as a practical matter, the enumeration ceased to do any real work long ago.'

[205] Cf *Garcia v San Antonio Metropolitan Transit Authority* 469 US 528 (1985), 550. Subsequent Supreme Court decisions have signalled a symbolic retraction from the absolutes principles of process federalism, cf *New York v United States*, 505 US 144 (1992); *Lopez v United States* 514 US 549 (1995); and *Printz v United States* 521 US 898 (1997).

[206] This was already feared in 1907 by JW Davis, *The Growth of the Commerce Clause*, 216: 'If Congress may declare what articles shall be the subject of commerce and then regulate commerce as so defined, what is this in the last resolve but the fixing, by the legislative branch of the limits for its own power under the guise of definition'.

[207] EA Young, *Dual Federalism, Concurrent Jurisdiction, and the Foreign Affairs Exception*, 151.

[208] On the various competence types developed in the European legal order, see: R Schütze, *The European Community's Federal Order of Competences: A Retrospective Analysis*.

[209] ES Corwin, *The Passing of Dual Federalism*, 17.

[210] EA Young (n 207 above) 139.

State frontiers, national solutions became necessary. This did not usher in the unitary American State. Under the 'new federalism', national legislation would allow States to complement the federal standard and thus to adjust it to local circumstances. The federal and the State governments were partners—even if reluctant partners—in the business of government.[211]

Since the middle of the twentieth century, the constitutional theory of cooperative federalism better *reflects* and *explains* the modern constitutional *practice* of American federalism. The principal exception to the rise of cooperative federalism is foreign affairs. The exclusion of the States from international treaty-making preserves an enclave of dual federalism. Was this 'suspended' federalism mandated by the 1787 Constitution? Doubts have been voiced: the 'most natural inference' from the text and structure of the Constitution 'is that all foreign matters not excluded by Article I, Section 10 fall within the concurrent power of the state and federal governments'.[212] If that view ever became dominant in American constitutionalism, foreign affairs would, at least to some extent, lose their 'exceptional' status and come to reflect the federal structure of the internal sphere.[213] A tendency in this direction may already be seen in relation to foreign affairs legislation (*Crosby*).

This concludes the General Part of this book. Its Special Part hopes to show that Europe follows, *mutatis mutandis*, the American evolution from dual to cooperative federalism. The transition is reflected in the structure of Europe's law. The latter has moved away from exclusive legal blocks of European or State law towards legislative complementation. This will be

---

[211] D Elazar, *Cooperative Federalism*, 69: '[T]he adjective cooperative in cooperative federalism does not imply that intergovernmental relations are always peaceful and friendly. . . Cooperative refers to the fact that governments must cooperate, that is, work and function together. It is not a statement of how they work and function together. There can also be coercive cooperation, which is the antithesis of a normative view of cooperation as a matter of mutuality among partners'.

[212] JA Goldsmith, *Federal Courts, Foreign Affairs, and Federalism*, 1642.

[213] Such a conceptual switch may be desirable for the following reason: '"[F]oreign affairs" is no more sustainable a category than "intrastate commerce" or "state police powers" was in 1937. Whether or not "foreign affairs" was *ever* a coherent category, entirely separate from domestic concerns, globalization has brought a wave of situations in which the two categories overlap. Unless we are prepared to exclude states entirely from regulating criminal law, family law, or pollution and product safety requirements—to name just a few areas—then state governments are going to regulate in ways that affect foreign relations. Concurrent power over foreign affairs is already with us. It is time the Court and the academy turned their energies from trying to police an elusive boundary between "foreign" and "domestic" to developing doctrines to manage a reality, where these concerns are almost always intertwined' (EA Young, *Dual Federalism, Concurrent Jurisdiction, and the Foreign Affairs Exception*, 188).

shown by adopting the structure of this chapter. We shall first investigate the decline of constitutional exclusivity (Chapter 3). We then move to the decline of legislative exclusivity as the hallmark of cooperative federalism (Chapter 4). European federalism has—unlike its American counterpart—even decided to 'constitutionalize' the philosophy of cooperative federalism in the form of the principle of subsidiarity and the recognition of complementary competences (Chapter 5). However, like American federalism, Europe has retained a—more—dual federalist philosophy in its external sphere (Chapter 6).

SPECIAL PART

The Changing Structure of European Law

The Decline of Constitutional Exclusivity

Introduction: Federalism and Exclusive Powers

Exclusive competences are the hallmark of dual federalism. They are constitutionally guaranteed monopolies, since only one government is entitled to act. Exclusive competences are thus double-edged provisions: their positive side entitles one authority to act, while their negative side excludes any other public body from legislating within their scope.

Would the European legal order acknowledge exclusive powers of the Member States or the Union? The existence of the former appeared certain. After all, the Member States had, by creating the European Union, limited their sovereign rights only 'within limited fields'.[1] And Article 5 EC—the European equivalent of the Tenth Amendment to the American Constitution—confirmed: 'The Community shall act within the limits of the powers conferred upon it by this Treaty and of the objectives assigned to it therein'. Europe's powers were delegated and enumerated powers. But what were their limits? Would the Union adopt an 'international' vision and accept that its 'constitution' was a compact among sovereign States—a view that invited a restrictive interpretation of its powers? Or would the Union insist on the autonomous character of its powers and adopt a 'national' interpretation of their scope? And even if the latter view was chosen, would certain State 'police powers' be deemed beyond the scope of European law? What, if any, were the implied limitations to the Union's powers?

The EC Treaty did not specify the relationship between European competences and national competences.[2] Two competing conceptions therefore

---

[1] Case 6/64 *Flaminio Costa v ENEL*, 593.

[2] J-V Louis, *Quelques Réflexions sur la répartition des compétences entre la communauté européenne et ses états membres*, 357.

emerged in the early years of the European legal order.[3] According to a first view, all Community competences were exclusive competences. The Member States had forfeited their powers by means of a 'transfer' to the European Union.[4] The division of sovereign powers between the Community and the Member States was said to be based on a strict separation of competences. 'The answer to the question how the Community legal order and the national legal orders relate is simple: the Member States and the European Community stand, their respective jurisdiction delimited by policy areas, side by side. . . The Community is sovereign over those areas that have been transferred to it; the Member States are sovereign over those areas that they have retained'. 'Legislative power can either exclusively belong to the States (as part of their original sovereignty) or exclusively belong to the Community (when transferred)'.[5] The view was buttressed by early pronouncements of the European Court of Justice.[6]

A second view also emerged in those early days: the Community's powers were shared powers.[7] In attributing powers to Europe, the Member States had not completely renounced their powers within the scope of the Community's competences. They had only given up their *exclusive* right to act by permitting an international organization to share in the exercise of certain powers. Through the act of creation, the Member States had *attributed*—not transferred—legislative powers to the European Union.

---

[3] For an early discussion of these two conceptions, see: A Tizzano, *The Powers of the Community*, 63–7.

[4] This term is used in *Costa v ENEL*.

[5] CF Ophüls, *Die Geltungsnormen des Europäischen Gemeinschaftsrechts*, 22 (translation—RS); and CF Ophüls, *Staatshoheit und Gemeinschaftshoheit: Wandlungen des Souveränitätsbegriffs*, 569–70 (translation—RS). The view was informed by German federalism, but the idea that the concept of 'transfer' signified an exclusive Community competence had also been suggested by P Reuter, *Organisations Européennes*, 231 as well as AG Toth, *A Legal Analysis of Subsidiarity*, 39: 'in all matters transferred to the Community from the Member States, the Community's competence is, in principle exclusive and leaves no room for any concurrent competence on the part of the Member States'. Consequently, 'where the competence of the Community begins, that of the Member States ends'.

[6] Cf Case 30/59 *De Gezamenlijke Steenkolenmijnen in Limburg v High Authority of the European Coal and Steel Community*, 22: 'In the Community field, namely in respect of everything that pertains to the pursuit of the common objectives within the Common Market, the institutions of the Community have been endowed with exclusive authority'.

[7] Eg HP Ipsen, *Europäisches Gemeinschaftsrecht*, 432: 'Im übrigen verwendet die Abgrenzung zwischen ihnen und den Aufgaben der Mitgliedstaaten—anders als etwa das Grundgesetz—nicht das Mittel der Kompetenz*ausscheidung* nach *Sachgebieten* mit der Folge, daß diese jeweils ausschließlich oder alternativ-konkurrierend entweder nur der Gemeinschaft oder aber nur den Mitgliedstaaten zur Regelung zustünden. Die Verträge folgen vielmehr einem System kumulativ-konkurrierender Zuständigkeit'.

The constitutional development of the Community legal order was to take place between these two extreme views. Different types of competences were 'discovered' in the course of the Community's development and, thence, Community constitutionalism moved from abstract speculation on 'the' nature of Europe's powers to the credo of the new era: 'il n'y a pas *une* notion de la compétence communautaire mais *plusieurs* acceptations possibles'.[8] Exclusive European powers were discovered in the 1970s.

While there exist, thus, dual federalist structures in the form of exclusive competences, have they declined in past decades? This depends on their relative size and status in the European legal order. We shall investigate this question with regard to *national* exclusive powers in the first section of this chapter. It argues that the European Community has dramatically expanded its legal sphere into areas that were originally thought to fall within the exclusive 'police powers' of the Member States. The second section of this chapter changes perspective: after an account of the emergence of exclusive *European* powers, it looks at two judicial strategies that would restrict and relativize the dual federalist logic within the exclusive competences of the European Community.

I. Europe's Expanding Sphere: The Decline of State 'Police Powers'

Having enumerated the 'tasks', 'activities', and 'institutions' of the Community,[9] the Treaty of Rome did *not* enumerate the Community's 'competences'. The Treaty had pursued a different legal technique: it attributed power for each and every Community activity in the respective Treaty title. Each policy area would contain a provision—sometimes more than one—on which Community action could be based.[10] The quantum of legal power for a policy area was thus determined by the specific competence(s) within *that* policy. The general aims of the Treaty mentioned in Article 2 EC and the Preamble were

---

[8] V Constantinesco, *Compétences et pouvoirs dans les communautés européennes: contribution à l'étude de la nature juridique des communautés*, 248. On the various competence types that have crystallized in the EC legal order in the past 50 years, see: R Schütze, *The European Community's Federal Order of Competences: A Retrospective Analysis*.

[9] These were enumerated in Articles 2, 3 and 4 EEC respectively.

[10] The only exception to that logic is Article 3(u) EC. However, as we shall see below, Article 308 EC will be an available competence.

no general competences;[11] and Article 3 EC made clear that the activities of the Community should be pursued only 'as provided in this Treaty'.[12] Every legal action on the part of the Community required a competence, which was to be found in the specific provisions set out in the Treaty's subsequent chapters.

What were the constitutional boundaries around Europe's legal universe? We shall explore this question through the prism of the two broadest European powers: Article 308 and Articles 94/95 EC. The former was the European Union's 'Necessary and Proper Clause'. It allowed the Community to 'take the appropriate measures' '[i]f action by the Community should prove necessary to attain, in the course of the operation of the common market, one of the objectives of the Community and this Treaty has not provided the necessary powers'. Article 94, on the other hand, represented Europe's 'Commerce Clause'. It originally permitted the European Union to 'issue directives for the approximation of such provisions laid down by law, regulation or administrative action in Member States as directly affect the establishment or functioning of the common market'. Following the Single European Act, Article 94 was given a 'brilliant assistant'.[13] This constitutional neighbour strengthened the Community's Commerce Clause. Article 95 EC would *not* contain the threshold of a 'direct effect'; and the new legal basis would not require the unanimous decision of all Member States.[14]

Let us look at Europe's 'Necessary and Proper Clause' and Europe's 'Commerce Clause(s)' in turn.

1. *Europe's 'Necessary and Proper Clause': The Scope of Article 308 EC*

From the beginning, the interpretation of Article 308 EC lay in the eye of the beholder.[15] Those viewing the Community as the offspring of an international treaty, and therefore governed by the 'normal' doctrines of international law,

---

[11] The opening 'principles' of the EC Treaty, especially Articles 2 and 3 EC, cannot be the direct source of rights and obligations (cf Case 126/86 *Gimenez Zaera v Institut Nacional de la Seguridad Social and Tesoreria General de la Seguridad Social*, para 11).

[12] Article 3 EC.

[13] D Vignes, *The Harmonisation of National Legislation and the EEC*, 367.

[14] The reinforcement of the Community's harmonization power had a price. The provision would 'not apply to fiscal provisions, to those relating to the free movement of persons nor to those relating to the rights and interests of employed persons'. Obstacles to trade arising from regulatory barriers within these areas had to be eliminated by recourse to Article 94 or one of the special legal basis provided for in the Treaty (eg Article 93 for the harmonization of indirect taxation).

[15] DW Dorn, *Art. 235 EWGV—Prinzipien der Auslegung—Die Generalermächtigung zur Rechtsetzung im Verfassungssystem der Gemeinschaften*, 19.

would construct Article 308 restrictively in order to maximize national sovereignty. These authors would emphasize the *exceptional* nature of the provision and argue for a restrictive—international—interpretation of the clause. The Article should be limited to those few instances in which additional powers were strictly 'indispensable' for the operation of Community affairs.[16]

By contrast, the 'national' vision among European commentators would make a case for the use of the clause as an independent competence in its own right. Their view was born out by constitutional practice. For while recourse to Article 308 EC had remained limited in the foundational period,[17] this was to dramatically change after 1972. Article 308 EC rose to one of the most popular powers in the Community's system of competences. This popularity placed it into the spotlight of critics of European integration.[18] For if Article 308 EC was used extensively, the Community legal order ran the risk of subverting the very system of enumerated powers on which it was—supposedly—based. This tension between the Community's general power under Article 308 and the principle of attributed powers has long fascinated European constitutionalism.[19]

---

[16] H von Meibom, *Lückenfüllung bei den Europäischen Gemeinschaftsverträgen*, 2168.

[17] With the central and fundamental tasks still at the top of the legislative agenda, there was yet no time, nor need, for controversial appendages to the Community project. Specific legal bases still proved sufficient to authorize the early steps along the road to economic integration. Against this background, it comes as no surprise that Article 308 remained half-dormant. A normatively stronger claim has argued that this restrictive use reflected a 'mentality' of the young Community in which 'strict enumerated powers and the concept of limited Community were fairly strongly enshrined in the political culture of the time', cf JHH Weiler, *Supranational Law and Supranational System: Legal Structure and Political Process in the European Community*, 368–9.

[18] Article 308 was a protagonist in the greatest challenge to the European Union's legal autonomy: the *Maastricht Decision* of the German Constitutional Court. Here, Europe was reminded that it was based on the principle of enumerated powers prohibiting the 'inference from the existence of a [task] to the existence of a power' (cf BVerfGE 89, 155 (*Maastricht*) as translated in [1994] 1 CMLR 57, 92). This is—as we shall see below—precisely the function that Article 308 has assumed in the Community legal order. On the *Maastricht Decision* in general, see: Chapter 1—Section II (3a) above.

[19] For the relevant literature, see: E Wohlfarth, *Artikel 235*; H von Meibom, *Lückenfüllung bei den Europäischen Gemeinschaftsverträgen*; HP Gericke, *Allgemeine Rechtsetzungsbefugnisse nach Artikel 235 EWG-Vertrag*; G Marenco, *Les conditions d'application de l'article 235 du traité CEE*; G von Donnersmarck, *Planimmanente Krisensteuerung in der Europäischen Wirtschaftsgemeinschaft*; A Giardina, *The Rule of Law and Implied Powers in the European Communities*; U Everling, IE Schwartz, and C Tomuschat, *Rechtsetzungsbefugnisse der EWG in Generalermächtigungen, insbesondere in Artikel 235 EWG-Vertrag*; L-J Constantinesco, *Das Recht der Europäischen Gemeinschaften: Das institutionelle Recht*, 272–81; A Tizzano, *The Powers of the Community*, 43–67; P Lachmann, *Some Danish Reflections on the use of Article 235 of the Rome Treaty*; JHH Weiler (n 17 above),

What were, if any, the internal or external limits to the Community's 'Necessary and Proper Clause'?

a. Internal Limits: Legislation Necessary in the Course of the Common Market

Article 308 grants the Community a power to legislate, where it is 'necessary' 'in the course of the operation of the common market' to attain 'one of the objectives of the Community'. Would Article 308 EC be limited by 'strict textual requirements'?[20] The express reference to the necessity of Community action was a unique reminder of the 'special' character of Article 308 in the Community's system of competences. While the necessity of Community action was normally presumed by the very *existence* of an express legal power, the Treaty appeared to make legislation under Article 308 conditional upon a *case-by-case* assessment. However, early jurisprudence soon showed that even if the 'necessity' criterion was justiciable, the actual standard of review was to be extremely light.[21] The requirement that action be adopted 'in the course of the common market' would equally pose no serious conceptual limit. The Community had decided to cultivate the so-called 'flanking policies' on the foundations of Article 308—despite the obvious linguistic contradiction this would entail.[22] In the absence of any clear conceptual limits imposed by these two criteria, the boundaries around Article 308 would thus principally depend on the identity and extent of the Community objectives.[23]

---

and by the same author, *The Transformation of Europe*, 2443–53; R Böhm, *Kompetenzauslegung und Kompetenzlücken im Gemeinschaftsrecht*; DW Dorn, *Art. 235 EWGV—Prinzipien der Auslegung— Die Generalermächtigung zur Rechtsetzung im Verfassungssystem der Gemeinschaften*; E Grabitz, *Artikel 235*, in E Grabitz and M Hilf (eds), *Das Recht der Europäischen Union*; JA Usher, *The Gradual Widening of European Community Policy on the Basis of Articles 100 and 235 of the EEC Treaty*; E Steindorff, *Grenzen der EG-Kompetenzen*, 121–2; F Tschofen, *Article 235 of the Treaty Establishing the European Economic Community: Potential Conflicts between the Dynamics of Lawmaking in the Community and National Constitutional Principles*; A Dashwood, *The Limits of European Community Powers*, 113–28; IE Schwartz, *Artikel 235*, in H von der Groeben, J Tiesing, and C-D Ehlermann (eds), *Kommentar zum EU-/EG-Vertrag*.

[20] In this sense: L-J Constantinesco, *Das Recht der Europäischen Gemeinschaften*, 273.

[21] Cf Case 38/69 *Commission v Italy*; and Case 8/73 *Hauptzollamt Bremerhaven v Massey-Ferguson GmbH*.

[22] The notion of 'flanking policy' provided a handy label for such diverse policy areas as regional policy, research and development, and environmental policy, which at that time were seen as only 'flanking' the establishment of a common market.

[23] L-J Constantinesco, *Das Recht der Europäischen Gemeinschaften*, 274. Discussing Article 308 EC's teleological relation to the objectives of the Treaty, G Marenco, *Les conditions d'application de l'article 235 du traité CEE*, 148 claims that those have '*l'effect d'étendre de façon indéterminée les*

What are the objectives of the European Community? The Treaty did not clearly define what its 'objectives' are. Its opening provisions refer to the—similar but not identical—concepts of 'tasks' and 'activities'. One influential current in the European law literature during the 1970s suggested that Article 308 could only be used to fill gaps inside those areas in which the Community had already been given a *specific* competence.[24] Outside the expressly enumerated fields, it was impossible to assume the existence of an 'objective' since the Community legislator was not meant to regulate those areas in the first place. According to this view, Article 308's scope was to find a limit in the jurisdictional boundaries set by the 'activities' of the Community—a position which linked the notion of 'objective' in Article 308 to the areas listed in Article 3 EC. A gap in the Treaty could be identified only by comparing the extent of the specific legal entitlements *within* a policy field and the *specific* aims of the Community policy within that area.[25]

A second academic camp favoured a much wider application of Article 308. This position was premised on a two-layered understanding of the enumeration principle, which draws on a conceptual distinction between *jurisdiction* and *competence*.[26] Article 308 could be used to fill any gap between the Treaty's *aims* and its *powers*. The perhaps most comprehensive manifesto of this expansionist rationale argued that Article 308 was 'designed to bridge the discrepancy between the Community's jurisdiction—as defined by its objectives—and a partial *or complete absence of powers for their realisation*'. The provision would create a 'gap-less system of competences for achieving all Community objectives'.[27] The Community's jurisdiction and its competence would, thus, coincide.

---

compétences communautaires et en même temps d'en fixer les bornes. Ces bornes sont celles des "objets de la Communauté"'.

[24] E Wohlfarth, *Artikel 235*, fn 6. See also: H von Meibom, *Lückenfüllung bei den Europäischen Gemeinschaftsverträgen*, 2166–7 (emphasis added): 'Eine deutliche Grenze, die hierbei nicht in der Anwendung des [Artikel 308] überschritten werden darf, zeigt sich dann, wenn es sich in Wirklichkeit um die Einbeziehung *neuer Sachbereiche* handelt.' The same restrictive view was voiced by DW Dorn, *Art. 235 EWGV—Prinzipien der Auslegung—Die Generalermächtigung zur Rechtsetzung im Verfassungssystem der Gemeinschaften*, 19.

[25] PJG Kapteyn & P VerLoren van Themaat, *Introduction to the Law of the European Communities*, 236 tersely state that 'the lacuna must be in the powers granted, not in the sum of the objectives of the Community'.

[26] This conception of the enumeration principle is now mirrored *expressis verbis* in Article 5 EC. Article 5(1) EC reads: 'The Community shall act within the limits of the powers conferred upon it by this Treaty and of the objectives assigned to it therein'.

[27] IE Schwartz, *Artikel 235*, in H von der Groeben, J Tiesing, and C-D Ehlermann (eds), *Kommentar zum EU-/EG-Vertrag*, rn 4–7 (translation—RS; emphasis added).

Wherever a matter fell into the scope of the Treaty, the Community would have a legislative competence—at least a subsidiary one under Article 308 EC. The Community's competence was the sum of its objectives.[28]

Which of the two views would the European Court prefer? What were the 'objectives' and what was the jurisdictional frame around the European Community? Ever since *Massey-Ferguson*,[29] there has been no doubt that the European Court would qualify the 'activities' of the Community in Article 3 EC as objectives for the purposes of Article 308. But would Article 308 stop there? The constitutional practice of the European legal order soon disappointed such minimalist hopes.[30] By the end of the 1970s, Article 308 had been allowed to tap into the global objectives of the Community set out in Article 2 EC. Ever since, conceptual limits to the Community's competence became hard to identify. If the Community could act to promote—for example—closer relations between the States, such a competence would be devoid of internal boundaries as all *common* legislation will, by definition, diminish legislative disparities and thereby increase the legal proximity between the Member States.[31]

The textbook illustration for the dramatic expansion of Europe's competence sphere on the basis of Article 308 EC is provided by the Community's environmental policy.[32] Stimulated by the political enthusiasm of the

[28] E Grabitz speaks of the '*Verbands*kompetenz *als Summe der* Aufgaben' (E Grabitz, *Artikel 235*, in E Grabitz and M Hilf (eds), *Das Recht der Europäischen Union*, rn 21 (emphasis added)). For the identification of the Community's 'jurisdiction' with its 'objectives', see also: Opinion of Advocate General Lenz in Case 45/86 *Commission of the European Communities v Council of the European Communities (Generalized tariff preferences)*: 'I have grave doubts whether such a method of interpretation—extensive interpretation of the objectives *and hence of the jurisdiction* of the Community and restrictive interpretation of its means of action and thus hindering those means—can be reconciled with the system of the Community treaties, which are designed to attain limited objectives using effective means' (ibid 1512 (emphasis added)).

[29] Case 8/73 *Hauptzollamt Bremerhaven v Massey-Ferguson GmbH*.

[30] A Tizzano, *Lo Sviluppo Delle Competenze Materiali Delle Communita' Europee*, 167: 'Non mancano invece riferimenti all'art. 3 o ad obiettivi specifici indicate nei singoli Capi del Trattato. Ma nella grande maggioranza dei casi gli atti in discorso si richiamano agli obiettivi enunciate dall' art. 2'.

[31] Thus Weiler claims that 'it became virtually impossible to find any activity which could not be brought within the "objectives of the Treaty". This constituted the climax of the process of mutation and is the basis of my claim not merely that no core activity of state function could be seen any longer as still constitutionally immune from Community action . . . but also that no sphere of the material competence could be excluded from the Community acting under [Article 308]' (cf JHH Weiler, *The Transformation of Europe*, 2445–6).

[32] Prior to the entry into force of the SEA, a significant number of environment-related measures were adopted on the basis of Articles 94 and 308, thus 'laying the foundation for the formation of a very specific Community environmental policy' (cf F Tschofen, *Article 235 of the Treaty*

Member States after the Paris Summit, the Commission and the Council faced the legal problem that environmental policy was not an official Community activity. There was therefore no specific legal title offered by the Treaty. The way out of this dilemma had been suggested in the 1972 Paris Communiqué. It called on the Community institutions to make the widest possible use of all provisions of the Treaties, including Article 308.[33] The Member States had thus themselves proposed an extensive interpretation of the Treaties' objectives to cause a 'small revision' of the Treaty by means of Article 308.[34] This 'constitutional' spirit would overcome the Treaty's textual boundaries. It can be gauged by the following commentary, in which Usher neatly captured the interpretative climate of legislative free style that would replace the missing Treaty amendment:

[T]hose responsible for drafting Community environmental legislation appear to have found their own route for solving this dilemma. By about 1980, as exemplified in Council Directive 80/68 on the protection of ground water against pollution by certain dangerous substances, the recitals justify making use of [Article 308] on the grounds of the necessity for Community action in the sphere of the environmental protection and improvement of the 'quality of life', a phrase which is found neither in the recitals to the Treaty nor in its general introductory provisions . . . Nevertheless, over the years, the phrase the 'raising of the standard of living' was linked to improving the 'quality of life' and by the time this Directive was adopted it could be stated that legislation was justified in terms of [Article 308] on the basis that it improved the quality of life, *as if that were a Treaty objective*.[35]

There was, in the words of another commentator, 'no doubt that practice confirmed the trend outlined, towards a widening of the Community's powers *and even objectives*'.[36] Express recognition of environmental protection as an independent 'objective' only occurred a decade after the 'environment' had

---

Establishing the European Economic Community: Potential Conflicts between the Dynamics of Lawmaking in the Community and National Constitutional Principles, 477).

[33] The Declaration read: 'They [Heads of State or Government] agreed that in order to accomplish the tasks laid out in the different action programmes, it was advisable to use as widely as possible all the provisions of the Treaties *including [Article 308 EC]*' (European Council, *First Summit Conference of the Enlarged Community*, 23 (emphasis added)).

[34] Eg Declaration of the Council of the European Communities and of the Representatives of the Governments of the Member States meeting in the Council of 22 November 1973 on the Programme of Action of the European Communities on the Environment.

[35] JA Usher, *The Gradual Widening of European Community Policy on the Basis of Articles 100 and 235 of the EEC Treaty*, 32–3 (emphasis added).

[36] A Tizzano, *The Powers of the Community*, 53.

entered Community law; yet still before the Treaty officially acknowledged it as a flanking policy.[37]

The birth and growth of the Community's environmental policy prior to the Single European Act serves as a powerful illustration for the degree of *de facto* constitutional amendment on the basis of Article 308 EC. The Court left smaller constitutional adaptations to the political safeguards of federalism. And the policy of judicial *laissez-faire* gave rise to the slippery slope character of Article 308 EC.[38] The inventiveness of the Community legislator paralleled Jefferson's brilliant satire on the federal 'reasoning' under the Necessary and Proper Clause.[39]

b. External Limits: The 'Constitutional Identity' of the European Community

In the absence of clear internal borders around Article 308, were there nonetheless external limits to its reach? From the very beginning, the existence of the 'big revision' clause in (now) Article 48 TEU could have erected an *external* barrier to the provision's internal growth.[40] And while constitutional

---

[37] In 1985, the Court finally came to acknowledge environmental protection as 'one of the Community's essential objectives', cf Case 240/83 *Procureur de la Republique v Association de defense des bruleurs d'huiles usagees (ADBHU)*, para 13. The SEA would expressly recognize the de facto expansion of the Community's legislative competence through the insertion of a specific title on the environment. For an analysis of this title, see: Chapter 5—Section II (1).

[38] The need to base the Community's environmental policy on the economic functioning of the common market could, at times, render the legislative discourse fairly absurd; as, for example, when the Community legislator explained the necessity for a Directive on wild birds—based on Article 308 EC—in terms of the economic functioning of the common market: 'Whereas the conservation of the species of wild birds naturally occurring in the European territory of the Member States is necessary to attain, within the operation of the common market, the Community's objectives regarding the improvement of living conditions, a harmonious development of economic activities throughout the Community and a continuous and balanced expansion but the necessary powers to act have not been provided for in this Treaty' (Preamble, Directive 79/409). This justification 'simply begs the question and, in fact, reveals the institutional problems facing an economic Community that wishe[d] to legislate in non-economic areas' (cf D Vandermeersch, *The Single European Act and the Environmental Policy of the European Economic Community*, 411).

[39] 'The H. of R. sent us yesterday a bill for incorporating a company to work Roosevelt's copper mines in New Jersey. I do not know whether it is understood that the Legislature of Jersey was incompetent to this, or merely that we have concurrent legislation under the sweeping clause. Congress are authorized to defend the nation. Ships are necessary for defence; copper is necessary for ships; mines, necessary for copper; a company necessary to work the mines; and who can doubt this reasoning who has ever played at 'This is the House that Jack Built'. Under such a process of filiation of necessities the sweeping clause makes clean work' (T Jefferson in a letter on 30 April 1800 to E Livingston as quoted in C Warren, *The Supreme Court in United States History*, 501).

[40] U Häde and A Puttler, *Zur Abgrenzung des Art. 235 EGV von der Vertragsänderung*, 13–17.

practice had created 'a large measure of overlap between the spheres where [Article 308 EC and Article 48 TEU] apply in matters covered by the Treaty's vast socio-economic objectives', the existence of the 'big revision' clause provided a textual reminder that 'qualitative leaps' that changed the identity of the European Community ought not be brought about through the back door.[41] However, the few judicial pronouncements on the scope of Article 48 TEU seemed to erect no external barrier to the internal evolution of the 'small revision' under Article 308 EC.

A first external limit on the scope of the residual power emerged with the Single European Act ('SEA'). The SEA officially incorporated the sensitive field of economic and monetary policy into the Treaty framework; and with it, a first constitutional safeguard *against* the use of Article 308 to effect major institutional changes. Article 102a(2) EEC stated that where and insofar as 'further development in the field of economic and monetary policy necessitated *institutional changes*, the provision of [Article 48 TEU] shall be applicable'.[42] This constitutional safeguard thus prohibited any covert 'communitarization' of the area through an extensive reading of Article 308.

A second limit emerged with the Treaty on European Union. The new constitutional architecture of Europe now clearly separated Community objectives from second or third pillar objectives. This demarcation sealed off certain objectives from Article 308 EC. The 'very wording of Article 308 EC' prohibited 'the adoption of Community measures concerning not one of the objectives of the Community but one of the objectives under the EU Treaty in the sphere of external relations, including the CFSP'.[43] The pillar

---

[41] A Tizzano, *The Powers of the Community*, 58–9: 'To be more specific [Article 308] cannot go beyond the bounds, described below, set by what has become known as the Community constitution'. The author then lists three criteria, namely the 'observance of the principles essential to the organization's structure', the 'observance of substantial principles of the Community constitution', and the 'observance of the general principles of law laid down by the Court of Justice', thereby anticipating the ECJ's stance in Opinion 2/94.

[42] Emphasis added. The wording was replaced by a new version under the Maastricht Treaty.

[43] Case C-402/05P *Kadi v Council and Commission*, paras 198–9. The *Kadi* Court nevertheless found that the contested Regulation could be based on Articles 60, 301 and 308 EC as the first two provisions provided 'a foundation for that measure from the point of view of its material scope' (ibid para 216). Thus, '[t]he objective pursued by the contested regulation may be made to refer to one of the objectives of the Community for the purpose of Article 308 EC', since 'Articles 60 EC and 301 EC are the expression of an implicit underlying objective, namely, that of making it possible to adopt such measures through the efficient use of a Community instrument'; and '[t]*hat* objective may be regarded as constituting an objective of the Community for the purpose of Article 308 EC' (ibid paras 225–7 (emphasis added)).

architecture established at Maastricht thus created an indirect external limit to the jurisdiction—not the powers (!)—of the European Community.[44]

A third external limits was delivered in Opinion 2/94.[45] The ECJ had been requested to preview the Community's power to accede the European Convention on Human Rights ('ECHR') *without* Treaty amendment. There was of course no express power to accede to the ECHR in the Treaty; nor could a parallel external competence easily be implied. In the absence of an express or implied specific power, Europe's competence had to be assessed in light of the Community's residual power. In its opinion the Court would—for the first time—characterize the function and outer limits of Article 308 EC. The Community's residual power was:

designed to fill the gap where no specific provisions of the Treaty confer on the Community institutions express or implied powers to act, if such powers appear none the less to be necessary to enable the Community to carry out its functions with a view to attaining one of the objectives laid down by the Treaty. That provision, being an integral part of an institutional system based on the principle of conferred powers, cannot serve as a basis for widening the scope of Community powers *beyond the general framework* created by the provisions of the Treaty as a whole and, in particular, by those that define the *tasks* and the *activities* of the Community. On any view, [Article 308] cannot be used as a basis for the adoption of provisions whose effect would, in substance, be to amend the Treaty without following the procedure which it provides for that purpose.[46]

The framework of the Treaty was defined by the Community's tasks and activities as set out in Articles 2 and 3 EC. These programmatic provisions would form the outer jurisdictional circle within which any legislative activity of the Community had to take place.[47] However, instead of clarifying whether the protection of human rights constituted an 'objective' of

---

[44] The competences of the European Community under the first pillar were protected by Article 47 TEU. The provision states: 'Subject to the provisions amending the Treaty establishing the European Economic Community with a view to establishing the European Community, the Treaty establishing the European Coal and Steel Community and the Treaty establishing the European Atomic Energy Community, and to these final provisions, nothing in this Treaty shall affect the Treaties establishing the European Communities or the subsequent Treaties and Acts modifying or supplementing them'.

[45] Opinion 2/94 (*Accession by the European Community to the European Convention of Human Rights*).

[46] Ibid paras 29–30 (emphasis added).

[47] Whether the Court consciously mentioned the notions 'tasks' and 'activities' in a careful attempt to limit Article 308 to areas directly linked to Articles 2 and 3 EC must be determined in future jurisprudence. If it were so, the Preamble to the Treaty could not be a source of 'autonomous' objectives of the Community. The opinion has indeed been considered as a first clarification of the

the European Community,[48] the Court—prudently to some, cowardly to others—concentrated on the *external* constitutional limits any interpretation of Article 308 would encounter. The judicial reasoning in this second part of the judgment was as follows: the accession of the Community to the ECHR would not constitute a small change of the Community system, but one with '*fundamental institutional implications* for the Community and for the Member States, [which] would be of *constitutional significance* and would therefore be such as to go beyond the scope of [Article 308]'. 'It could be brought about only by way of Treaty amendment. It must therefore be held that, as Community law now stands, the Community has no competence to accede the Convention'.[49]

Article 308 would thus encounter an external border in the constitutional identity of the Community system. But what was the 'identity' of the Community? Which changes would have 'fundamental institutional implications' or a 'constitutional significance'? These criteria hardly promised to ensure a better demarcation of the European legal universe. The circularity of the Court's reasoning—the use of Article 308 will be unconstitutional where it goes beyond the constitution—was but an expression of the dialectic nature of all constitutional interpretation: the meaning of a single provision is informed by, and itself informs, the meaning of the constitution.[50] Article 308 is not limited by the scope of the Treaty but to some extent *represents* and *defines* it. Instead of clear criteria, we are left with a paradox as old as the interpretation of foundational texts. Nonetheless, the ECHR opinion might be viewed as evidence of a renewed judicial interest in recognizing *some* constitutional limits to the Community's Necessary and Proper Clause. Whether this has marginalized

notion of 'objective' in Article 308 EC, cf U Häde and A Puttler, *Zur Abgrenzung des Art. 235 EGV von der Vertragsänderung*, 17.

[48] According to the ECJ, human rights would only constitute a *condition* for the lawfulness of Community acts. The laconic reasoning on the part of the Court might be taken to mean that it did not exclude the possibility of considering a human rights policy as an autonomous objective or task of the Community (consider paras 32–4 of Opinion 2/94). Alston and Weiler assert that '[a]t no point in that Opinion did the Court suggest that the protection of human rights was not an objective of the Community, nor did it say that the Community lacked competence to legislate in the field of human rights', cf P Alston and JHH Weiler, *An 'Ever Closer Union' in Need of a Human Rights Policy: The European Union and Human Rights*, 24–5.

[49] Opinion 2/94, paras 35–6.

[50] The hermeneutic circle of constitutional theory is nicely captured by J Weiler, *Supranational Law and Supranational System: Legal Structure and Political Process in the European Community*, 356.

Article 308 EC may be doubted in the light of Europe's recent constitutional practice.[51]

2. Europe's 'Commerce Clause(s)': The Scope of Articles 94 and 95 EC

The principal idea behind the European (Economic) Community had been the creation of a 'common market'. The gradual unification of national markets was to be achieved by two complementary mechanisms. In the first place, the Treaty itself would 'negate' certain national barriers to intra-Community trade.[52] These trade barriers were illegal, unless they could be justified by reference to traditional 'police powers' of the States.[53] A second constitutional instrument for the creation of a common European market was 'positive integration'. Europe was competent to adopt measures for the 'approximation of the laws of Member States to the extent required for the proper functioning of the common market'.[54] Harmonization was 'deregulation through re-regulation': differences in national laws would be abolished through the adoption of a European norm. The most general competences for the harmonization of laws are contained in Articles 94 and 95 EC.[55]

The Community's competence to harmonize applies where national measures affected the establishment *or* functioning of the internal market.

---

[51] Cf Council Regulation 168/2007 establishing a European Union Agency for Human Rights, which is based on Article 308 EC; as well as Case C-402/05P *Kadi v Council and Commission*.

[52] Article 3(a)–(c) of the original EEC Treaty. In its subsequent titles, the treaty would lay down specific provisions on the free movement of goods, persons, services, and capital. The most well-known of these 'dormant Commerce Clauses' is Article 28 EC. The provision reads: 'Quantitative restrictions on imports and all measures having equivalent effect shall be prohibited between Member States'.

[53] According to Article 30 EC, restriction to intra-Community trade can be justified 'on grounds of public morality, public policy or public security; the protection of health and life of humans, animals or plants; the protection of national treasures possessing artistic, historic or archaeological value; or the protection of industrial and commercial property'.

[54] Article 3(h) of the EEC Treaty.

[55] The Community's harmonization competences were scattered across the Treaty. Examples at the time of the adoption of the EC Treaty were: ex-Article 27 for the harmonization of *customs legislation*; ex-Article 54(3)(g) in the field of *company law*; ex-Article 56(2) in the area of justified *restrictions* on the *freedom of establishment* and *free provision of services*; ex-Article 57(2) & (3) concerning access and exercise of *professional activities*; ex-Article 70 gave a specific harmonization competence as regards *free movement of capital*; ex-Article 99 was confined to *indirect taxation*; and ex-Article 117 was to permit the harmonization of *social systems*.

The former alternative concerns obstacles to intra-Community trade; the latter alternative captures distortions of competition resulting from disparities between national laws. From the very beginning, the scope of Article 94 appeared, to some, 'quite simply unlimited'.[56] The constitutional practice after 1972 seemed to confirm that: Article 94 and Article 308 EC were regarded as 'twins, if not "terrible twins"'.[57] Would this change after the introduction of Article 95 EC—a power that allowed the European Community to act *without* the consent of every single Member State? Would the decline in the political safeguards of federalism induce the Court to strengthen the judicial safeguards of federalism? What were the internal and external limits to the Community's 'Commerce Clause(s)'?

a. *Internal Limits: Harmonization of National Laws for the Internal Market*

The European Community is entitled to pass measures for the 'approximation' of national laws under Article 95 EC, 'which have as their object the establishment and functioning of the internal market'. Would the idea of 'approximation' or 'harmonization' conceptually require the prior or subsequent existence of national laws? Would the European law have to serve the free movement of trade; or would it also provide the Community with a competence to totally prohibit certain trading activities? Similar questions had already been answered by American federalism and would soon trouble the European Court of Justice. The jurisprudence of the Court, up to the end of the twentieth century, unequivocally confirmed the widest possible reading of the European Commerce Clause. This 'European' interpretation has only recently been qualified by a Court insisting on some judicial safeguards of federalism.

The potentially unlimited scope of Europe's harmonization power is illustrated in *Spain v Council*.[58] The European legislator had regarded the national protection period for medicinal products as insufficient, and this insufficiency was seen to penalize European pharmaceutical research. It had therefore created a supplementary protection certificate, which could be granted under

---

[56] P Leleux, *Le rapprochement des législations dans la communauté economique européenne*, 138.

[57] J Usher, *The Gradual Widening of European Community Policy on the Basis of Articles 100 and 235 of the EEC Treaty*, 26. On the function and scope of Article 94 EC in the Community legal order, see: F Marx, *Funktion und Grenzen der Rechtsangleichung nach Art.100 EWG-Vertrag*; and C Eiden, *Die Rechtsangleichung gemäß Art.100 des EWG-Vertrages*.

[58] Case C-350/92 *Spain v Council*.

the same conditions as national patents by each of the Member States.[59] Three major constitutional hurdles seemed to oppose the legality of this European law. First, Article 95 EC could theoretically not be used to create *new* rights as it could only harmonize *existing* rights.[60] Secondly, the European law should theoretically further the creation of a single European market; yet, the supplementary certificate extended the duration of national patents and thus prolonged the compartmentalization of the common market into distinct national markets. Finally, at the time of its adoption only *two* Member States had legislation concerning a supplementary certificate. Was this enough to trigger the Community's *harmonization* power?

The Court took the first hurdle by force. It simply rejected the claim that the European law created a new right.[61] The same blind force would be applied to the second argument. The Court did not discuss whether the European law hindered the free circulation of pharmaceutical goods between States. Instead, the Court concentrated on the third hurdle in the form of the question, whether Article 95 required the *pre*-existence of diverse national laws. In the eyes of the Court, this was not the case. The Court accepted that the contested law aimed 'to prevent the heterogeneous development of national laws leading to further disparities which would be likely to create obstacles to the free movement of medicinal products within the Community and thus directly affect the establishment and the functioning of the internal market'.[62] The European legislator was thus entitled to use its harmonization power to prevent *future* obstacles to trade or a *potential* fragmentation of the internal market.[63] Would all future obstacles or disparities in national laws be sufficient to trigger Articles 94/95? If so, the scope of Europe's 'Commerce Clause(s)' seemed devoid of conceptual boundaries.

The Court did finally confirm the existence of inner limits to the scope of Article 95 in *Germany v Parliament and Council (Tobacco Advertising)*.[64] The bone of contention had been a European law that banned the advertising and

---

[59] Regulation 1768/92 concerning the creation of a supplementary protection certificate for medicinal products.

[60] Legislation for the creation of new rights will have to be based on Article 308 EC, cf Case C-350/92 *Spain v Council*, para 23 (with reference to Opinion 1/94, para 59).

[61] Case C-350/92 *Spain v Council*, para 27.

[62] Ibid para 35 (with reference to the 6th Recital of Regulation 1768/92).

[63] On the idea of 'preventive' harmonization in the internal market, see: M Seidel, *Präventive Rechtsangleichung im Bereich des Gemeinsamen Marktes*.

[64] Case C-376/98 *Germany v Parliament and Council (Tobacco Advertising)*.

sponsorship of tobacco products.[65] Could a prohibition or ban be based on the Community's *Commerce* Clause? Germany objected to the idea. It argued that the Community's harmonization power could only be used to promote the internal market; and this was not so in the event, where the federal legislation constituted, in practice, a total prohibition of tobacco advertising.[66] And even if total bans could legitimately be based on Article 95 on the ground of removing distortions of competition,[67] this second alternative would have to be limited to cases where the distortion was 'considerable'.[68] The requirement of an 'appreciable' effect—developed to set a jurisdictional frame around EC competition law—should equally apply to the Community's harmonization competence.[69]

The Court accepted—to the surprise of many—these invitations and annulled, for the first time in its history, a European law on the ground that it went beyond the Community's 'Commerce Clause'. Emphatically, the Court pointed out that the latter could not grant the Community a general power to regulate the internal market:

To construe that article as meaning that it vests in the Community legislature a general power to regulate the internal market would not only be contrary to the express wording of the provisions cited above but would also be incompatible with the principle embodied in [Article 5] of the EC Treaty that the powers of the Community are limited to those specifically conferred on it. Moreover, a measure adopted on the basis of [Article 95] of the Treaty must genuinely have as its object the improvement of the conditions for the establishment and functioning of the internal market. If a mere finding of disparities between national rules and of the abstract risk of obstacles to the exercise of fundamental freedoms or of distortions of competition liable to result therefrom were sufficient to justify the choice of [Article 95] as a legal basis, judicial review of compliance with the proper legal basis might be rendered nugatory. The Court would then be prevented from discharging the function entrusted to it by

---

[65] Directive 98/43/EC on the approximation of the laws, regulations and administrative provisions of the Member States relating to the advertising and sponsorship of tobacco products.

[66] Germany had pointed out that the sole form of advertising allowed under the Directive was advertising at the point of sale, which only accounted for 2% of the tobacco industry's advertising expenditure (*Tobacco Advertising*, para 24).

[67] Cf Directive 92/41/EEC amending Directive 89/622/EEC on the approximation of the laws, regulations and administrative provisions of the Member States concerning the labelling of tobacco products; as well as, Directive 92/28/EEC on the advertising of medicinal products for human use.

[68] *Tobacco Advertising*, para 29. There was case law to support this claim, eg Case 91/79 *Commission v Italy*, para 8; as well as Case C-300/89 *Commission v Council (Titanium Dioxide)*, para 23.

[69] The Council strongly opposed this argument in para 50.

[Article 220] of the EC Treaty of ensuring that the law is observed in the interpretation and application of the Treaty.[70]

What consequences did the Court draw from this general conclusion? The Court split its analysis into two parts and analysed, in turn, the two alternative applications of the Community's harmonization power.

Regarding the elimination of obstacles to free movement, the Court qualified its generous ruling in *Spain v Council*. While accepting that 'recourse to [Article 95] as a legal basis is possible if the aim is to prevent the emergence of future obstacles to trade resulting from multifarious development of national laws', the Court nonetheless insisted that 'the emergence of such obstacles must be *likely* and the measure in question must be designed to prevent them'.[71] Were future obstacles to intra-Community trade in tobacco advertising likely? The Court accepted this for press products. 'However, for numerous types of advertising of tobacco products, the prohibition under Article 3(1) of the Directive cannot be justified by the need to eliminate obstacles to the free movement of advertising media or the freedom to provide services in the field of advertising'.[72] Worse: the Directive did not contain a 'free movement clause' guaranteeing free circulation within the internal market. The Member States could thus potentially extend stricter national health standards to imports from other Member States.[73] In the light of this, the European legislature had not been entitled to rely on its harmonization powers on the ground that the measure would eliminate obstacles to free movement.

But recourse to the competence could still have been justified by means of the second alternative in Article 95: the elimination of distortions of competition. But here, the Court accepted Germany's invitation and introduced the internal limitation of 'appreciable' distortions of competition. 'In the absence of such a requirement, the powers of the Community legislature would be practically unlimited. National laws often differ regarding the

---

[70] Ibid paras 83–4.

[71] Ibid para 86 (emphasis added).

[72] Ibid paras 97 and 99.

[73] Article 5 of Directive 98/43/EC stated: 'This Directive shall not preclude Member States from laying down, in accordance with the Treaty, such stricter requirements concerning the advertising or sponsorship of tobacco products as they deem necessary to guarantee the health protection of individuals'. The provision was, however, subject to the EC Treaty's free movement regime. The fear of the Court that in the absence of an express free movement clause stricter national measures could, *ipso facto*, be applied to imports from other Member States was thus only partly justified. The case law on whether Article 30 EC can be used in such circumstances is mildly chaotic, cf M Dougan, *Minimum Harmonization and the Internal Market*.

conditions under which the activities they regulate may be carried on, and this impacts directly or indirectly on the conditions of competition for the undertakings concerned.' Constitutionally, the federal legislator could not pass laws under Article 95 'with a view to eliminating the smallest distortions of competition'. The opposite view would be incompatible with the principle of enumerated powers on which the Community's federal structure was based.[74] In the case of the Tobacco Advertising Directive, the national laws had only a 'remote and indirect' effect on competition. Disparities between national laws could here not lead to distortions that were appreciable.[75] The Directive could thus not have been legitimately based on the second prong of the harmonization power and the Court consequently annulled the European law.

With *Tobacco Advertising*, the Court appears to accept *some* constitutional limits on the Community's Commerce Clause. First, the European law has to harmonize national laws; it cannot be used to create 'new' legal phenomena. A Community law 'which leaves unchanged the different national laws already in existence, cannot be regarded as aiming to approximate the laws of the Member States'.[76] Secondly, a simple disparity in national laws will not be enough to trigger the Community's Commerce Clause. The disparity must give rise to obstacles in trade or appreciable distortions in competition. Thus, while Article 95 EC can be used to 'harmonize' *future* disparities in national laws, it must be 'likely' that the divergent development of national laws leads to obstacles in trade. (The Court seems to verbalize this requirement by extending the constitutional criterion of a 'direct effect'—textually mandated only in Article 94 EC—to Article 95 EC.[77]) Thirdly, the Community measure must actually contribute to the elimination of obstacles to free movement or distortions of competition.[78] These three constitutional limits to the Community's 'Commerce Clause' were confirmed *in abstracto* by subsequent jurisprudence;[79] yet, their concrete application has led to renewed accusations

---

[74] Ibid paras 106–7.

[75] Ibid para 109.

[76] Case C-436/03 *Parliament & Council*, para 44 (emphasis added). The Court here confirmed and extended the point made in relation to intellectual property law (cf Case C-350/92 *Spain v Council*; as well as Case C-377/98 *Netherlands v Council and Parliament*) to 'new' legal forms in addition to the national forms of cooperative societies' (ibid para 40).

[77] Cf Case C-210/03 Swedish Match, para 29; as well as Case 380/03 *Germany v Parliament and Council (Tobacco Advertising II)*, para 37.

[78] Case C-491/01 *British American Tobacco*, para 60.

[79] Cf nn 76 and 77 above; and Case C-66/04 *United Kingdom v Parliament and Council*.

that Article 95 grants the Community a general competence for the internal market.[80]

b. External Limits: Constitutional 'Saving Clauses' for State 'Police Powers'?

From the beginning of the European Community, certain provisions within the Treaty could be read as constitutional guarantees for national exclusive powers. Apart from the mysterious Article 295 EC,[81] one of the prominent candidates was Article 30 EC. The provision allows States to justify a violation of the free movement of goods on grounds of, inter alia, public morality, public policy, and public security. Had these policy fields remained within the exclusive powers of the States? The European Court gave short shrift to that argument in *Simmenthal*.[82] Pointing out that Article 30 EC was 'not designed to reserve certain matters to the exclusive jurisdiction of Member States',[83] the Member States could not insist on their stricter national laws where Community harmonization legislation provided for the necessary protection of the interests in Article 30 EC. Reacting to this early defeat, the Member States have used subsequent Treaty amendments to increasingly insert provisions designed to protect national exclusive powers within the Treaty. The most important species of these clauses excludes the Community from harmonizing national laws within a policy area.[84]

---

[80] Cf *Tobacco Advertising II*, para 80: 'Recourse to Article 95 EC as a legal basis does not presuppose the existence of an actual link with free movement between the Member States in every situation covered by the measure founded on that basis. As the Court has previously pointed out, to justify recourse to Article 95 EC as the legal basis what matters is that the measure adopted on that basis must actually be intended to improve the conditions for the establishment and functioning of the internal market'. This statement explains why a total ban on the marketing of a product may still be justified under Article 95 EC (cf *Swedish Match*). This has led D Wyatt, *Community Competence to Regulate the Internal Market*, to query whether *Tobacco Advertising* was a 'false dawn' (ibid 23).

[81] The provision reads: 'This Treaty shall in no way prejudice the rules in Member States governing the system of property ownership'.

[82] Case 35/76 *Simmenthal v Italian Minister of Finance*.

[83] Ibid para 14. However, for a judicial 'slip of tongue', see Case 265/95 *Commission v France* paras 32–3: '[Article 28] therefore requires the Member States not merely themselves to abstain from adopting measures or engaging in conduct liable to constitute an obstacle to trade but also, when read with [Article 10] of the Treaty, to take all necessary and appropriate measures to ensure that that fundamental freedom is respected on their territory. In the latter context, the Member States, which retain exclusive competence as regards the maintenance of public order and the safeguarding of internal security, unquestionably enjoy a margin of discretion in determining what measures are most appropriate to eliminate barriers to the importation of products in a given situation'.

[84] For an overview of the various types of constitutional 'saving clauses' in the Community legal order, see: R Schütze, *The European Community's Federal Order of Competences: A Retrospective Analysis*, 87–90.

Would these 'saving clauses' protect exclusive national 'police powers'? The European Court has expressed a negative inclination in *Germany v Parliament and Council (Tobacco Advertising)*.[85] The case involved the 'express saving' clause of Article 152(4)(c) EC. The provision allows the Community to adopt health incentive measures 'excluding any harmonisation of the laws and regulations of the Member States'. However, the Community had not acted on the basis of this competence. Instead, it had chosen its general harmonization competence under Article 95 EC; yet, as the Court admitted, '[t]he national measures *affected* [were] to a large extent inspired by public health policy objectives'.[86] Could the European legislator harmonize 'health'-related national laws? Or, would Article 152(4)(c) EC be an external limit to Article 95 EC? Was there, in other words, an exclusive national competence for laws that protect and improve human health? The Court disagreed. Article 152(4)(c) EC did 'not mean that harmonising measures adopted on the basis of other provisions of the Treaty cannot have any impact on the protection of human health'.[87] '[T]he Community legislature cannot be prevented from relying on that legal basis on the ground that public health protection is a decisive factor in the choices to be made'.[88] The express saving clause would thus *not* operate as a constitutional *Querschnittsklausel*. Where Community legislation serves an internal market objective, the Community legislator can enter into health-related fields. Article 152(4) did not represent an absolute constitutional border protecting a nucleus of exclusive national powers.[89]

However, the Court conceded that these saving clauses did have some constitutional significance: the Community must not use its general harmonizing powers 'to circumvent the express exclusion of harmonisation laid down in [Article 152(4)(c)] of the Treaty'.[90] Where the centre of gravity of a Community law fell on the side of the public health competence under Article 152 EC, intervention that harmonizes national laws must be excluded. (In this case Community action may still be possible under Article 308 EC. However, this remains controversial.[91]) The EC Treaty will thus only provide

[85] Case C-376/98 *Germany v Council (Tobacco Advertising)*.
[86] Ibid para 76 (emphasis added).
[87] Ibid para 78.
[88] Ibid para 88.
[89] Contra, H Hablitzel, *Harmonisierungsverbot und Subsidiaritätsprinzip im europäischen Bildungsrecht*, 409. The concept of 'negative competence' (cf FC Mayer, *Die drei Dimensionen der Europäischen Kompetenzdebatte*, 583) will thus not perfectly fit these 'constitutional saving clauses'.
[90] *Germany v Council (Tobacco Advertising)*, para 79.
[91] For the two opposing views, see: K Lenaerts, *Education in European Community Law after 'Maastricht'*; and M Niedobitek, *Die kulturelle Dimension im Vertrag über die Europäische Union*.

a *relative* constitutional guarantee for national police powers falling within the scope of the Treaty. However, saving clauses are no absolute constitutional recognition of exclusive national powers. They do not completely 'negate' the competence of the European Community as their limiting effects will not go beyond the scope of the legal base of which they form part. The Community legal order has thus still not committed itself to constitutionally safeguard a 'nucleus of sovereignty that the Member States can invoke, as such, against the Community'.[92]

3. *The European Union and the Problem of Competence-Competence*

A government 'without the means of some change is without the means of its conservation'.[93] In order to pave the way towards an 'ever closer union',[94] the Treaty contained two provisions for 'organized' change. Within their respective spheres of application, Articles 235 and 236 EEC offered two distinct methods for constitutional adaptation.[95]

Article 236 EEC—today: Article 48 TEU—set out the requirements for formal Treaty amendment. The government of any Member State or the Commission could submit proposals to the Council for the amendment of the Treaty. The Council could then call for an intergovernmental conference to discuss these proposals. Amendments needed to be decided by 'common accord' and be ratified by all the Member States 'in accordance with their respective constitutional requirements'.[96] The provision thus recognized the

The Lisbon Treaty would settle the issue, for Article 352 TFEU—the equivalent of Article 308 EC—clarifies in its third paragraph that '[m]easures based on this Article shall not entail harmonisation of Member States' laws or regulations in cases where the Treaties excludes such harmonisation'.

[92] K Lenaerts, *Constitutionalism and the Many Faces of Federalism*, 220.

[93] E Burke, *Reflections on the Revolution in France*, 16.

[94] The symbolic phrase was already part of the 1957 Treaty whose Preamble committed the European Community 'to lay[ing] the foundations of an ever closer union among the peoples of Europe'.

[95] Some saw a third form of Treaty amendment ('*autonome Vertragsveränderung*') in such a provision as Article 14(7) EEC and Article 165(4) EEC, cf HP Ipsen, *Europäisches Gemeinschaftsrecht*, 103. The Lisbon Treaty would distinguish between an 'ordinary' and various 'simplified' revision procedures.

[96] Article 48 TEU reads: 'The government of any Member State or the Commission may submit to the Council proposals for the amendment of the Treaties on which the Union is founded. If the Council, after consulting the European Parliament and, where appropriate, the Commission, delivers an opinion in favour of calling a conference of representatives of the governments of the Member States, the conference shall be convened by the President of the Council for the purpose of determining by common accord the amendments to be made to those Treaties. The European

Member States as '*Herren der Verträge*', while simultaneously ensuring some procedural involvement of the Community organs in the Treaty revision process.

In addition to possible 'big revisions', the Treaty also provided for 'small revisions' by means of Article 235 EEC—today: Article 308 EC.[97] The disparity between the complexity of the 'international' procedure under Article 48 TEU and the simplicity of the 'legislative' procedure set out in Article 308 EC remains striking: the European Commission would propose and the Council of Ministers could dispose the measure with unanimity. The constitutional adaptation process was thus entirely left to *Community* organs. They had the final say on the direction and extent of the European Community progressing into new fields.[98] The existence of a 'small revision' clause had been justified by reference to its restrictive scope and auxiliary nature. Its function was to fill the gaps *within* the sphere of powers already ceded to the Community.[99] But where lay the limits to Europe's legal universe? The answer given by the European Court had been the following: the limits of the European Community's powers are determined by its constitutional identity. Within these constitutional boundaries, it is for the Community itself to determine the scope of its powers.

How should we characterize Europe's 'Necessary and Proper Clause'? Does Article 308 EC represent an ordinary competence and, if not, what sort of competence is it? Article 308 is a borderline provision. Its twilight character is symbolized in the geographic position it occupies at the edges of the Treaty. The Article itself would come to define the boundaries of Europe's legislative sphere—standing somewhere between the presence and the future of the European Community.[100] Many a label have been given to the

Central Bank shall also be consulted in the case of institutional changes in the monetary area. The amendments shall enter into force after being ratified by all the Member States in accordance with their respective constitutional requirements'.

[97] The notion of '*la petite révision*' was originally reserved for the specific amendment procedures under Article 95(3) and (4) ECSC. However, the phrase usefully indicates that Article 308 allows for *de facto* Treaty amendment. The ECJ itself seemed to subscribe to this idea in Case 38/69 *Commission v Italy*, para 10, where it described Article 308 as 'in some respects to supplement the Treaty'.

[98] Doubts about the *Community* nature of legislation adopted under Article 308 EC were dispersed by the European Court at a very early stage in Case 38/69 *Commission v Italy*, ibid: 'The power to take measures envisaged by this article is conferred, not on the Member States acting together, but on the Council in its capacity as a Community institution'.

[99] HP Ipsen, *Europäisches Gemeinschaftsrecht*, 103.

[100] Already the wording of the provision is perplexing as it speaks of giving the Community a power 'where *this Treaty* has not provided the necessary powers'—suggesting that the Article would

provision.[101] But can we identify Article 308 with the concept of 'competence-competence'? In federal theory, the notion of competence-competence designates the power to grant itself 'new' competences autonomously.[102] Did Article 308 EC come close to this idea? The European federal tradition's answer to this question is 'no', since the European Union is not a Federal State. However, if we abandon the 'statist' format of federalism and adopt the American federal tradition would this answer change? 'It is, after all, the very purpose of [Article 308] to bridge the divide between the Community's objectives and powers through an *expansion* of the competences of the Community'.[103]

Three legal arguments have been advanced against the identification of Article 308 as Europe's competence-competence. First, the very possibility of the latter was denied out of hand, since a competence-competence would contradict the system of enumerated powers on which the Community legal order is built. A second argument puts forward that Article 308 could not function as a competence-competence as it does not entitle the Community to create or expand 'attributed powers *as such*'. The effect of Article 308 is not to create new competences, but simply to create new Community *law*. While every exercise of Article 308 leads to an extension of the reach of Community *law*, it will not extend the Community's *competence*.[104]

---

somehow be 'outside' the Treaty framework, (cf DW Dorn, *Art. 235 EWGV—Prinzipien der Auslegung—Die Generalermächtigung zur Rechtsetzung im Verfassungssystem der Gemeinschaften*, 40–41).

[101] The provision has been described as a 'provision to expand competences' (cf BVerfGE 89, 155—*Maastricht*, 196: 'Kompetenzerweiterungsvorschrift'; as well as L-J Constantinesco, *Das Recht der Europäischen Gemeinschaften*, 272: 'Ermächtigung zur sog. Kompetenzausdehnung'; and A Tizzano, *The Powers of the Community*, 50: 'instrument for extending Community powers'); a 'competence reservoir' (cf IE Schwartz, *Artikel 235*, in H von der Groeben, J Tiesing, and C-D Ehlermann (eds), *Kommentar zum EU-/EG-Vertrag*, rn 2); or finally, a 'competence-competence' (cf H von Meibom, *Lückenfüllung bei den Europäischen Gemeinschaftsverträgen*, 2166: 'Art. 235 gibt dem Rat eine Kompetenz, sich selbst durch Rechtsakte neue zusätzliche Kompetenzen zu hoheitlichem Handeln bewilligen zu können'; HP Ipsen, *Europäisches Gemeinschaftsrecht*, 476: 'einstimmige Ratsentscheidung . . . durch die Befugnisse begründet werden'; A Giardina, *The Rule of Law and Implied Powers in the European Communities*, 102: 'ad hoc procedure for granting new powers to the Community'; E Steindorff, *Grenzen der EG Kompetenzen*, 114: 'Kompetenz-Kompetenz der Gemeinschaft').

[102] On the emergence of the concept in German federal doctrine, see: Chapter 1—Section I (3a) above.

[103] L-J Constantinesco, *Das Recht der Europäischen Gemeinschaften*, 278 (translation—RS).

[104] The separation between *primary competence* and *secondary law* has clouded the issue of Article 308's characterization from the very beginning. When the German discussion invokes that Article 308 only offers 'potential competences' (eg R Böhm, *Kompetenzauslegung und Kompetenzlücken im Gemeinschaftsrecht*, 115 (translation—RS), it commits a metaphysical transgression. If we define

Finally, a third argument denies Article 308's family resemblance to a competence-competence by insisting that the provision will not entitle the Community to create new objectives or to modify the scope of existing objectives of the Community.[105] Article 308 encounters a definite limit in the objectives presently 'enumerated' in the Treaty.

Let us look at each argument in turn. The first argument transgresses, of course, the philosophical boundaries between 'is' and 'ought'.[106] It is based on a normative circularity as it 'derives' the *in*existence of a competence-competence from the *existence* of the enumeration principle in the Community legal order. But could one not equally 'derive' the inexistence of the enumeration principle from the existence of a competence-competence in the Community legal order? This line of thinking represents a logical dead end. Secondly, to object that Article 308 does not create legal competences *as such*, but only the legal base for Community secondary law has aptly been described as a 'scholastic pseudo-problem'.[107] The Community's decision to enact a European law will always tacitly recognize the Community's competence for this *particular piece* of legislation. The *exercise* of Article 308 in border areas of its conceptual scope—and this is true for any legislative competence—will always clarify and *define* the scope of the competence for future legislation. The objection that the Community simply exercises an 'existing' competence seems to be the civil law expression of the common law's old-fashioned declaration theory. It artificially deposits the existence of a static and permanent law 'out there'.

a competence as a *potential* entitlement to legislate, a potential competence is a paradoxical pleonasm.

[105] In unison with the tenor of the *Maastricht* decision (cf [1994] CMLR 57, para 78): 'The Member States have given the European Union objectives in [Article 2] of the Union Treaty, and laid down that these may only be achieved as provided in the Treaty. In addition they have defined the tasks and powers of the three European Communities in detail . . . Any alterations and extensions of those definitions of tasks and powers are subject to their prior formal agreement, which restricts the possibilities for further legal developments on the basis of the existing Treaty'.

[106] Contra, E Grabitz, 'Artikel 235', in E Grabitz and M Hilf (eds), *Das Recht der Europäischen Union*: 'Aus dem Prinzip der begrenzten Ermächtigung folgt, daß [Artikel. 308] keine Kompetenz-Kompetenz darstellt' (ibid rn 2). Compare this with the subtler syllogism in the BVerfG's *Maastricht* decision, where the German Supreme Court argued that a wide expansive teleological interpretation of Article 6 (3) TEU would turn this provision into a *Kompetenz-Kompetenz*—a result that clearly contradicted the expressed will of the High Contracting Parties to codify the principle of attributed powers (ibid para 68).

[107] C Tomuschat, *Die Rechtsetzungsbefugnisse der EWG in Generalermächtigungen, insbesondere in Artikel 235 EWG-Vertrag*, in U Everling, I E Schwartz, and C Tomuschat (eds), *Rechtsetzungsbefugnisse der EWG in Generalermächtigungen, insbesondere in Artikel 235 EWG-Vertrag*, rn 50.

What about the third argument? While it is true that Article 308 is deline-
ated by the objectives of the Community, this boundary is rather fluid; and,
within limits, determined by the Community itself. A legal order that allows
its federal legislator to justify action by reference to a desire to 'increase
the standard of living' (Article 2) grants it a competence to base virtually *all*
activities on its 'Necessary and Proper Clause'. Each exercise of the residual
power in areas in *'which the Treaty has not provided the necessary powers'* thus
represents an expansion of European law beyond the Community's ordinary
powers. The history of the Community's legislative engagement in the
area of environmental policy demonstrated how a continued constitutional
praxis may even create—or: more softly, discover—one of the Community's
objectives. Exegesis and genesis are sometimes inseparable.[108]

In conclusion, to label Article 308 a normal competence misses the point
about its 'special' character in the Community legal order.[109] It is true that
Article 308 EC *appears* like an ordinary competence. However, the fact that
Article 308 has an almost unlimited scope cannot be downplayed as a
quantitative difference. A competence to act where the Treaty has 'not
provided the necessary powers' simply functions like a competence *reservoir*
and thus exhibits *some* characteristics of a competence-competence. This
legislative competence-competence follows from and complements the
Community's *judicial* competence-competence.[110] However, the Community

---

[108] This has given rise to a complex *ex post facto* categorization of the various objectives 'discovered' in the last 50 years. The interested reader is referred to the extensive discussion of the
subject by IE Schwartz, *Artikel 235*, in H von der Groeben, J Tiesing, and C-D Ehlermann (eds),
Kommentar zum EU-/EG-Vertrag. The author distinguishes at least five categories of objectives
(express and implicit special objectives, immediate and mediate general objectives, and (implied)
horizontal objectives). The imaginative invention of objectives for Community legislation did
not stop with the teleological interpretation of express objectives—nor did the ink of academic
glossaries to explain the 'logic' of this development. Some commentators were even referring to the
possibility of 'implied objectives' to justify the use of Article 308 in such 'tenuous' cases.

[109] HP Ipsen, *Europäisches Gemeinschaftsrecht*, 434–5 characterized Article 308 EC as a 'special
competence' (*Sonderermächtigung*). See also: G Gaja, P Hay, and RD Rotunda, *Instruments for Legal
Integration in the European Community—A Review*, 117–18 (emphasis added): in Article 308 'a *different concept* of Community competence emerges, one that encompasses the area in which the
Community may act, although the institutions may not yet have acquired the necessary powers'.

[110] Contra, J Weiler, 'The Autonomy of the Community legal order: through the Looking
Glass', in J Weiler, *The Constitution of Europe*. Weiler's analysis is inconsistent in a number of ways.
First, it is already hard to accept that 'the ECJ, in adopting its position on judicial *Kompetenz-
Kompetenz*, was not following any constitutional foundation but rather an *orthodox* international law
rationale' (ibid 290–1, emphasis added). But how can we square this statement with the following
assertion—only a few pages later—that within an 'orthodox' international organization 'should
there be a disagreement over the interpretation of a clause within a treaty, an agreement of all
parties will normally be the final word as either an authentic interpretation or a de facto amendment'

itself has accepted the existence of some limits to the scope of its legislative sphere.[111] It lacks the *unlimited* power of self-organization and still depends on the Member States to determine the fundamental structure of its institutions: its constitutional identity.[112] The best label for Article 308 may thus be *bounded* competence-competence or 'partial competence-competence'.[113] This characterization aligns itself with the idea of divided or partial sovereignty and thus captures the federal nature of the Community legal order best.

II. Europe's Contracting Sphere: The Decline of Federal Exclusive Powers

The EC Treaty originally contained no verbal reference to the concept of exclusivity. Did this mean that the idea was 'foreign' to the Community legal

---

(ibid 293–4)? If *that* is the orthodox international law doctrine, then the Court's judgment in Case 43/75 *Defrenne v Sabena*—analysed in Chapter 6—Section II (1a) below—followed a constitutional foundation in that it opted against the 'ordinary' international law doctrine that permitted States to interpret 'their' Treaty. Be that as it may, a serious inconsistency arises with Weiler's second claim (ibid 312): 'The assumption that a Community without a legislative *Kompetenz-Kompetenz* cannot contain a court without judicial *Kompetenz-Kompetenz* . . . is false'. How can that be? How can one grant judicial *Kompetenz-Kompetenz* as 'the competence to declare or to determine the limits of the competences of the Community' (ibid 288); and yet, deny that if there is no other legal authority to set limits to the scope of its legislative powers, the Community can determine the limits of its legislative competences? In the words of T Schilling, *Rejoinder*: 'The jurisdiction of a court to decide on the "constitutionality" of a norm is at the borderline between judicial and legislative competences. Indeed, decisions of a court to quash a norm as unconstitutional have repeatedly been deemed to be "negative legislation". Whilst this point is not relevant to the present discussion, the following question is: whether a court decision wrongly "maintaining" in force a legislative act issued outwith the competence of the issuing body is a (purely) judicial, or (also) a legislative act. As the original legislative act was, in the period between its enactment and the decision of the court, by definition either void or at least voidable, it is only the decision of the court which makes it valid. It follows that a decision of a court by which a void or voidable legislative act is (wrongly) declared to be valid must be considered to be an act of legislation. If one accepts this reasoning, the assumption that a Community without legislative *Kompetenz-Kompetenz* cannot contain a court with such *Kompetenz-Kompetenz* certainly gains in force'.

[111]   See the discussion of external limits above.

[112]   U Di Fabio, *Some Remarks on the Allocation of Competences between the European Union and its Member States*, 1292–3.

[113]   For the latter concept, see: J Kaiser, *Grenzen der EG-Zuständigkeit*, 115; and A Bleckmann, in A Bleckmann and G Ress (eds), *Souveränitätsverständnis in den Europäischen Gemeinschaften*, 46: 'Auch hier wird man darauf abstellen müssen, ob die EG die Kompetenz-Kompetenz besitzt. Das ist jedenfalls in begrenztem Maße zu bejahen'.

order?[114] It is true that the Community legal order had, after an initial period of doubt, adopted the shared power thesis. However, this did not prevent the development of *some* exclusive powers belonging to the European Community. These powers were 'discovered' by the European Court of Justice in the 1970s. Today, the existence of a European sphere of exclusive powers is acknowledged in Article 5 EC and through that provision the concept of 'exclusive competence' has become a part of the official constitutional vocabulary of the European legal order.[115]

What are the European Community's exclusive powers? Having analysed the scope of exclusive national power in the first part of this chapter, this second section will investigate the extent to which European constitutionalism has adopted a dual federal philosophy through a sphere of exclusive power *for the Community*. In order to locate the Community's commitment to dual federalism, we shall proceed in the following way. We will first look at the genesis of constitutionally exclusive powers and see that the Court's jurisprudence has been rather 'pointillist'. Having identified the areas that European constitutionalism considers to fall into the exclusive domain of the Community, we will then look at two strategies that were subsequently developed to minimize the dual federalist consequences. The first strategy limits the dispossessing effect of exclusive competences by restrictively constructing their scope. This has led to 'ontological deformations' and would, ultimately, give rise to partial exclusivity. The second strategy goes to the very substance of the concept of exclusivity. By relaxing the constitutional regime governing the delegation doctrine, the 'exclusive' effect of Europe's exclusive powers has been dramatically softened. This evolution makes the Community's exclusive powers less exclusive—if at all—than in other federal constitutional orders.

1. *Dual Federalism Constitutionalized: The Genesis of Exclusive Powers*

How has the concept of exclusive powers been translated into the European legal order? 'Exclusive competence comprises powers which have been definitely and irreversibly forfeited by the Member State by reason of their straightforward transfer to the Community.' 'Where the Community has exclusive competence, this means that any action by a Member State in the same field is *a priori* in conflict with the Treaty'.[116] 'An exclusive competence

---

[114] C Stewing, *Subsidiarität und Föderalismus in der Europäischen Union*, 104.
[115] Article 5(2) EC.
[116] K Lenaerts & P van Nuffel, *Constitutional Law of the European Union*, 5-022 and 5-026.

of the Union means that *the mere existence of such a norm* prohibits the Member States from acting in this area'.[117] The negative effect of exclusive competences originates thus in the Constitution. But what were these exclusive competences? The Community legal order has accepted two exclusive powers.[118] This subsection will reconstruct their constitutional birth (conditions).

a. Judicial Genesis no 1: The Common Commercial Policy

The Rome Treaty had given the Community the central task of 'establishing a common market and [of] progressively approximating the economic policies of Member States'.[119] This involved 'the elimination, as between Member States, of customs duties', 'the establishment of a common customs tariff and of a common commercial policy towards third countries'.[120] The provisions on the customs union had been placed inside the title on the free movement of goods.[121] The chapter on 'commercial policy' was to be found in the title of the Treaty dealing with economic policy.[122] Despite heavy amendment, the textual bones of the Common Commercial Policy ('CCP') have proved remarkably solid.[123] According to Article 131 EC, the Member States aim, by establishing a customs union between themselves, to contribute to the harmonious development of world trade and the progressive abolition of restrictions on international trade. Article 132 commits the Member States to progressively harmonize their national systems of aid for export to third countries so as to ensure that competition between undertakings in the Community is not distorted. The central provision of the CCP, however,

---

[117] A von Bogdandy & J Bast, *The European Union's Vertical Order of Competences: The Current Law and Proposals for its Reform*, 241. An even 'purer' definition of exclusive power has been suggested by R Bieber, *On the Mutual Completion of Overlapping Legal Systems: The Case of the European Communities and the National Legal Orders*, 152. By way of contrast, a moderate notion of exclusivity had entered the 1984 Draft Constitutional Treaty of the European Parliament. Article 12 of the Draft Treaty, simply entitled 'competences', distinguished between exclusive and concurrent competences. Regarding the former the first paragraph of the article determined: 'Where this Treaty confers exclusive competence on the Union, the institutions of the Union shall have sole power to act; national authorities may legislate only to the extent laid down by the law of the Union. Until the Union has legislated, national legislation shall remain in force'.

[118] On the candidature of other competences, see: R Schütze, *The European Community's Federal Order of Competences: A Retrospective Analysis*, 72–4.

[119] Article 2 EEC.

[120] Article 3(a) and (b) EEC.

[121] Articles 12–29 EEC.

[122] Articles 110–16 EEC.

[123] But see: ex-Article 116 EEC.

is Article 133(1) EC: 'The common commercial policy shall be based on uniform principles, particularly in regard to changes in tariff rates, the conclusion of tariff and trade agreements, the achievement of uniformity in measures of liberalisation, export policy and measures to protect trade such as those to be taken in the event of dumping or subsidies'.

From the point of view of a systematic or textual interpretation methodology, Article 133 EC did not appear to be destined for exclusivity. Placed in an area of the Treaty more characterized by coordination than by integration,[124] the CCP may well have been interpreted in tandem with the provisions on conjunctural policy and the balance of payments. Moreover, the 'achievement of uniformity' was to take place through the establishment of 'uniform *principles*'—arguably leaving a degree of external commercial powers to the Member States.[125] From a teleological perspective, on the other hand, the commercial policy of the Community had strong credentials for constitutional exclusivity. First, in order to benefit from the special regime for customs unions under GATT,[126] the European Community would not only be required to substantially eliminate customs duties and restrictive regulations as between its Member States. As a customs union, it also needed to ensure that 'substantially the same duties and other regulations of commerce are applied by each of the members of the union to the trade of territories not included in the union'.[127] (This, certainly, begged the question how much uniformity was required by the phrase 'substantially the same'.) Secondly, ex-Article 116 EEC smacked of the idea of exclusivity when stipulating that '[f]rom the end of the transitional period onwards, Member States shall, in respect of all matters of particular interest to the common market, proceed within the framework of international organisations of an economic character only by common action'. From a teleological perspective, then, the candidature of the CCP as an *a priori* exclusive Community competence was, consequently,

---

[124] For the distinction between the spheres of 'integration' and 'coordination', see: L-J Constantinesco, *Das Recht der Europäischen Gemeinschaften*, 246–60.

[125] 'What is puzzling about this wording is why one should speak of "uniformly established principles" in the context of a "common policy" considering that a common policy could by its very nature be nothing but uniform' (U Everling, *Legal Problems of the Common Commercial Policy in the European Economic Community*, 150). For the opposite position, see: C Calliess, *Der Schlüsselbegriff der 'ausschließlichen Zuständigkeit' im Subsidiaritätsprinzip des Art.3 b II EGV*, 696: 'Diese Formulierung überläßt den Mitgliedstaaten in klarer und bestimmter Weise keinerlei Befugnisse mehr'.

[126] Cf Article XXIV(8)(a) GATT.

[127] Ibid. For a discussion of the point, see: JH Jackson, *World Trade and the Law of GATT*, 607–10.

strong from the beginning. In the words of one eminent commentator at the time: '[t]he common commercial policy of the European Economic Community is generally regarded as a typical example of a Community policy, i.e., a policy on which jurisdiction is withdrawn from the member states and committed to the Community'.[128]

The European Court of Justice would, indeed, transform the CCP into the Community's exclusive competence par excellence. The crystallization process began in relation to the European customs union with *Sociaal Fonds voor de Diamantarbeiders*.[129] A national charge had been levied on the import of rough diamonds coming from third countries. The Community's common customs tariff had been introduced by Regulation 950/68 and had entered into force on July 1, 1968. Could Member States maintain or introduce charges having an effect equivalent to customs duties thereafter? Having clarified that the national charge fell into the scope of the CCP, the Court found that the Member States had lost all power to act. 'According to [Article 133 (1)] of the Treaty, the common commercial policy shall be based on uniform principles . . . It is for the Commission or the Council to evaluate these requirements in each case both as regards the establishment of the common customs tariff and the adoption of the commercial policy. It follows therefore that *subsequent to the introduction of the common customs tariff all Member States are prohibited from introducing, on a unilateral basis, any new charges or from raising the level of those already in force*'.[130] The judicial reasoning had remained slightly ambivalent. Was the exclusion of national action a direct result of Article 133 EC or a consequence of the pre-emptive effect of Regulation 950/68? The Court gradually moved to accept the former option.

The first signs of a choice in favour of a constitutionally exclusive power rationale began to take shape in the form of the 'succession' doctrine

---

[128] U Everling (n 125 above) 141. Yet, the same author adds a nuance to this (ibid 151): 'The external relations of a customs union require by their very nature collective action in cases like tariff agreements. On the other hand, this need does not go beyond a certain point. The unusual wording of [Article 133] may well have been chosen to express a limitation in this sense: the common commercial policy must in any case bring about uniform principles in the specified fields. Whether these principles are, however, to be carried into effect by truly collective proceedings or rather by the concerted action of Member States remains open and is left to the discretion of the Council to decide from case to case'.

[129] Joined Cases 37 and 38/73 *Sociaal Fonds voor de Diamantarbeiders v NV Indiamex et Association de fait De Belder*.

[130] Ibid paras 15–18.

established by the Court in *International Fruit*.[131]   Yet, the constitutional exclusivity thesis only fully emerged in Opinion 1/75.[132] In that advisory opinion, the European Court had been asked to clarify the scope and nature of Article 133 EC in the context of an OECD agreement on export credits. The Court started by confirming that a Community commercial policy envisaged internal as well as external measures.[133] While recognizing that the development of a common commercial policy was a matter of a gradually evolving body of rules, the Court characterized the Community competence as an exclusive power:

Such a policy is conceived in that Article in the context of the operation of the common market, for the defence of the common interest of the Community, within which the particular interests of the Member States must endeavour to adapt to each other. Quite clearly, however, *this conception is incompatible with the freedom to which the Member States could lay claim by invoking a concurrent power,* so as to ensure that their own interests were separately satisfied in external relations, at the risk of compromising the effective defence of the common interests of the Community. In fact any unilateral action on the part of the Member States would lead to disparities in the conditions for the grant of export credits, calculated to distort competition between undertakings of the various Member States in external markets. Such distortion can be eliminated only by means of a *strict uniformity* of credit conditions granted to undertakings in the Community, whatever their nationality. . . To accept that the contrary were true would amount to recognizing that, *in relations with third countries, Member States may adopt positions which differ from those which the Community intends to adopt, and would thereby distort the institutional framework, call into question the mutual trust within the Community and prevent the latter from fulfilling its tasks in the defence of the common interest.*[134]

The harmonious operation of the institutional framework of the Community and the solidarity among its members would be called into question if the States retained a competence to engage autonomously in external commercial activities. In the defence of the European interest, any national law adopted in the hope that a Member State's 'own interests were

---

[131] Joined Cases 21–24/72 *International Fruit Company NV v Produktschap voor Groenten en Fruit.* For a discussion of the European succession doctrine, see: R Schütze, *EC Law and International Agreements of the Member States—An Ambivalent Relationship?*, 394–406.

[132] Opinion 1/75 (*Draft understanding on a local cost standard*).

[133] Ibid 11: 'A commercial policy is in fact made up by the combination and interaction of internal and external measures, without priority being taken by one over the others. Sometimes agreements are concluded in execution of a policy fixed in advance, sometimes that policy is defined by the agreements themselves'.

[134] Ibid 13 (emphasis added).

separately satisfied in external relations' was to be prohibited. Only 'strict uniformity' in relations with third countries would eliminate the distortions of competition in the common market. This was heavy armoury to justify the exclusion of any 'concurrent' power on the part of the Member States both in the internal and the external sphere.[135] Opinion 1/75 had announced the arrival of constitutional exclusivity in the EU legal order: exclusivity was unconnected with the presence of European legislation and originated in the Treaty provisions themselves.[136]

The announcement was confirmed a year later in *Donckerwolcke*.[137] The *Donckerwolcke* Court painted a colourful picture claiming that 'full responsibility in the matter of commercial policy was transferred to the Community by means of [Article 133(1)]' with the consequence that 'measures of commercial policy of a national character are only permissible after the end of the transitional period by virtue of specific authorization by the Community'.[138] Member States, therefore, no longer enjoyed autonomous legislative powers as the legality of all national action derived from a Community mandate. Since then, the constitutionally exclusive nature of the CCP could no longer be questioned.[139] And the exclusive nature of the CCP has today become commonplace in European constitutionalism.[140]

b. *Judicial Genesis no 2: The Conservation of Biological Resources of the Sea*

If the first judicial dot resulted from constitutional design, the second point of exclusivity emerged by constitutional accident. The Community's powers in relation to the conservation of biological resources of the sea would, in 1958, hardly have appeared as a candidate for constitutional exclusivity. Article 38 of the Treaty of Rome had declared the common market to extend to agriculture and trade in agricultural products, *including fisheries*. A 'Common Market Organization' for fishing products emerged in 1970,

---

[135] The original symmetry in scope and content of the competence in the internal and the external sphere was expressed more clearly in Case 45/86 *Commission of the European Communities v Council of the European Communities (Generalised tariff preferences)*.

[136] For a sceptical assessment, see: HH Maas, *The External Powers of the EEC with Regard to Commercial Policy: Comment on Opinion 1/75*, 386.

[137] Case 41/76 *Suzanne Criel, née Donckerwolcke and Henri Schou v Procureur de la République au tribunal de grande instance de Lille and Director General of Customs*.

[138] Ibid para 32.

[139] Eg Opinion 1/78 (*International Agreement on natural rubber*).

[140] The decline of full exclusivity and the rise of partial exclusivity within the CCP will be discussed below.

together with a proposal for a common structural policy for this area.[141] Fisheries seemed 'an agricultural activity just like any other'.[142]

Matters began to change with the accession of Denmark, Ireland, and the United Kingdom. For the three accession countries, fishing was of major importance—they had greater fish stocks and better conservation policies[143]— and to accommodate their geopolitical interests, the 1972 Act of Accession permitted derogations from the existing Community regime. Moreover, because the Community had not yet developed a structural fishing policy, Article 102 of the Act of Accession provided: 'From the sixth year after accession at the latest, the Council, acting on a proposal from the Commission, shall determine conditions for fishing with a view to ensuring protection of the fishing grounds and conservation of the biological resources of the sea'. The character of Article 102 of the Act was a little odd. The article 'confirm[ed] existing competences of the Community—a confirmation that may have been deemed necessary in view of the fact that the preceding two articles (Article 100 and Article 101) allow derogations from the most basic principle of the common fisheries policy—*i.e.*, the principle of equal access—for a period of ten years'. 'However, Article 102 added one new element: it obliged the institutions of the Community to exercise their competences in respect of marine fisheries before a specific deadline'.[144] The Article was thus of a transitory nature.[145] Once the time-limit had expired, it could no longer be used as a legal basis for the Community fisheries policy.[146] Apart from the special transitional regime, fishing conservation measures continued to be firmly rooted

---

[141] The Council had adopted two Regulations. Regulation 2141/70 laid down a common structural policy and Regulation 2142/70 established the common organization of fishing products. The former Regulation spelled out in its Article 1 that 'common rules shall be laid down for fishing in maritime waters' in order 'to encourage rational use of the biological resources of the sea and inland waters'. In Article 5 it empowered the Council to 'adopt the necessary conservation measures' if a stock of fish in the waters subject to the sovereignty or jurisdiction of a Member State is in danger of being over-fished. Following the first enlargement of the Community, the provisions of the two Regulations were repeated in, respectively, Regulations 100/76 on the common organization of the market in fishery products and Regulation 101/76 on a common structural policy for the fishing industry. Today, the common fisheries policy is structured by Regulation 104/2000 on the common organization of the markets in fishery and aquaculture products and Regulation 2371/2002 on the conservation and sustainable exploitation of fisheries resources under the Common Fisheries Policy.

[142] '*La pêche: une activité "agricole" comme les autres*', in D Yandais, *La communauté et la pêche*, 165.

[143] R Churchill, *Revision of the EEC's Common Fisheries Policy—Part I*, 6.

[144] AW Koers, *The External Authority of the EEC in Regard to Marine Fisheries*, 279.

[145] It was placed in the forth part of the 1972 Act entitled 'Transitory measures'.

[146] R Churchill (n 143 above) 14.

in the Common Agricultural Policy ('CAP') and thus seemed to fall within the sphere of shared powers.

Surprisingly, this changed rather dramatically. The transformation from shared to exclusive competence began with *Kramer*.[147] Let us revisit the scene. Criminal prosecutions had been brought against Dutch fishermen for having violated national fishing quotas. The Netherlands had implemented a recommendation from the North-East Atlantic Fisheries Commission—an international body that had been set up by the North-East Atlantic Fisheries Convention—to which all the Member States, except Italy and Luxembourg, and seven non-Member countries, belonged. In the course of a preliminary ruling, the national criminal court raised a number of questions relating to the division of competences in the external and the internal sphere of the European legal universe. In relation to the external sphere, the Court developed the doctrine of parallel external powers and found an implied external power of the Community to accede to the international Convention.[148] In the next step, the Court then asked 'whether the Community institutions in fact assumed the functions and obligations arising from the Convention and from the decisions taken thereunder'.[149] Finding that the Community had legislative power in relation to conservation measures, the Court conceded that the Community had not actually exercised them. From there, the Court reasoned as follows:

This being so, and the Community not yet having fully exercised its functions in the matter, the answer which should be given to the questions asked is that at the time when the matters before the national courts arose, the Member States had the powers to assume commitments, within the framework of the North-East Atlantic Fisheries Convention, in respect of the conservation of the biological resources of the sea, and that consequently they had the right to ensure the application of those commitments within the area of their jurisdiction.

However, it should be stated first, that this authority which the Member States have is only of a transitional nature and secondly that the Member States concerned are now bound by Community obligations in their negotiations within the framework of the Convention and of other comparable agreements. *As to the transitional nature of the abovementioned authority, it follows from the foregoing considerations that this authority will come to an end 'from the sixth year after accession at the latest', since the Council must by then*

---

[147] Joined Cases 3, 4 and 6/76 *Cornelis Kramer*.

[148] On the various theories and constitutional readings of the implied power doctrine in the external sphere, see: Chapter 6—Section I (1b) below.

[149] *Kramer*, para 34.

*have adopted, in accordance with the obligation imposed on it by Article 102 of the Act of
Accession, measures for the conservation of the resources of the sea.*[150]

The Court did not once refer to 'exclusive powers'—neither in the external
nor in the internal sphere.[151] The Court *did*, however, speak of the 'transitional
nature' of the 'authority' of the Member States to engage in international
agreements and that this authority will come to an end 'from the sixth year
after accession at the latest'. However, the anticipated reason for the exclusion
was the *future* legislative pre-emption of the Member States 'since the Council
must by then have adopted, in accordance with the obligation imposed on it
by Article 102 of the Act of Accession, measures for the conservation of the
resources of the sea'.[152] The partial exercise of the Community's powers would
thereby not be sufficient. Only once the Community had '*fully* exercised its
power in the matter' would the Member States have to disappear from the
legislative scene.[153] The mere existence of the Community power was thus not
sufficient to deprive the Member States of their power.[154]

[150]   Ibid paras 39–41 (emphasis added).

[151]   As regards the division of powers between the Community and the Member States in the
internal sphere, the Court employed a traditional pre-emption analysis. The Court was asked
to investigate whether the national fishing quotas conflicted with the Community legislation
on fishing policy. The two pieces of legislation would only conflict, according to the Court, if
the national quota 'jeopardized the objectives or the functioning of the system' established by the
Community legislation. The Court found that there was no interference with the objectives of the
common policy. The relevant Community legislation itself provided for comparable measures and
even authorized the Member States to limit the catches of their fishing fleet.

[152]   *Kramer*, para 41.

[153]   Case 61/77 *Commission v Ireland*, paras 63–5 (emphasis added): '[S]o long as the transitional
period laid down in Article 102 of the Act of Accession has not expired and the Community has
not yet *fully exercised* its power in the matter, the Member States are entitled, within their own
jurisdiction, to take appropriate conservation measures without prejudice, however, to the obligation to co-operate imposed upon them by the Treaty, in particular [Article 10] thereof'. At the time,
the case received the following commentary: 'In the *Irish Fisheries* case the Court suggested that
the power to establish permanent rules for fishing belongs to the Community as such and that
this power is an exclusive one. Given, first, that the Court is referring here to *permanent* rules and,
secondly that it tends to view the question of exclusivity in terms of measures actually adopted
rather than the competence as such to adopt measures, it would seem that, in theory at least,
Member States are not totally precluded from taking national measures. Clearly if any such
measures conflict directly with Community fishery provisions, they will be set aside as a result of
the operations of the normal rules relating to the supremacy of Community law over conflicting
law' (R Churchill (n 143 above) 18).

[154]   Consider the Opinion of Advocate General Trabucchi in *Kramer*: '[T]he mere existence of a
Community legislative power in a particular field does not suffice to deprive the States of power to
negotiate internationally in that field . . . there must have been an exercise of this power and to that
end Community rules have actually been applied in this field: only in this way can the international
jurisdiction of the States be fully replaced by that of the Community . . . [T]he incompatibility of

But what would happen once the six years had passed *without any European legislation?* Would the competence of the Member States automatically vanish? The Court answered this question in another judgment. The 1978 deadline had indeed elapsed and the Community legislature had been inoperative as a result of British obstinacy. The United Kingdom had vetoed every single legislative proposal,[155] justifying its unilateralism by invoking the Luxembourg Accord. It had, moreover, stubbornly adopted its own preferred *national* conservation model in 1979. This proved too much for the European Community. The Commission brought the State before the Court.[156] Pitilessly, Britain argued that 'as long as the Council has not exercised the powers conferred upon it by Article 102 of the Act of Accession, even after the expiration of the period laid down in that article, the Member States retain residual powers and duties until the Community has fully exercised its powers'.[157]

The Court was not impressed and decided to help the 'deficient Community legislator'.[158] It was in *Commission v United Kingdom* that the European Court formally declared the constitutional exclusivity of this policy area. The Court pointed to the expiry of the deadline and held that 'Member States are therefore no longer entitled to exercise any power of their own in the matter of conservation measures in the waters under their jurisdiction. The adoption of such measures, with the restrictions which they imply as regards fishing activities, is a matter, as from that date, of Community law'.[159] The Council's failure to exercise the legislative power could not 'restore to the Member States the power and freedom to act unilaterally in this field'. The transfer of powers in the area of biological resources was 'total and definitive'.[160] Therefore, national legislators wishing to act could only do so with a 'specific authorization' issued from the Commission. In a word, the Community

a State's power in a particular field must not be determined in theory but by an actual comparison with the Community legislation'. The Advocate General then referred to the case law on the effect of Community legislation in the internal sphere and concluded that since the existence of Community competence did not automatically rule out the legislative powers of the Member States with respect to domestic legislation this must 'by the same token also apply to the external powers of the states' (ibid 1320).

[155] The almost heart-breaking story can be found in D Yandais, *La communauté et la pêche*, 241–2.

[156] Case 804/79 *Commission v United Kingdom*.

[157] Ibid para 14.

[158] P Pescatore, *La carence du législateur communautaire et le devoir du juge*, 559–80.

[159] Case 804/79 *Commission v United Kingdom*, para 18.

[160] Ibid para 20.

had, from 1 January 1979, assumed 'exclusive powers' on the subject of conservation measures as set out by Article 102 of the Act of Accession.[161] And since the exclusivity was independent of prior legislative action on the part of the Community, it had to be 'original' and of a constitutional nature.

2. *Ontological Deformations: Restrictive Interpretation and 'Partial Exclusivity'*

Having created exclusive powers for the European Union, how would European constitutionalism deal with them? Would it expand the philosophy of dual federalism by interpreting these powers widely; or would it limit their scope? The answer has changed with the course of time. While the Court seemed, at first, to favour a wide teleological interpretation of the Community's exclusive powers, it would later interpret these competences restrictively. The restrictive interpretation was, this second subsection argues, a direct result of the exclusive *nature* of the competences. These 'ontological' deformations in Europe's exclusive competences would ultimately lead to their partial exclusivity. Let us illustrate these symptoms of the decline—or at least: relativization—of constitutional exclusivity in relation to the CCP.

There were few textual criteria establishing a conceptual fence around the scope of the CCP. The formulation in the opening article seemed to tie this Community policy to the establishment of a customs union between the Member States.[162] Ex-Article 3(b) EEC seemed to confirm that by treating the common customs tariff and the CCP as Siamese twins. However, there also existed a broader teleological reading of Articles 131 *et seq*. The latter saw the CCP as 'une projection sur le plan externe de la notion de marché commun'.[163] In which direction would the European legal order tilt? Would the scope of the external commercial policy embrace all aspects that fell into the internal market?

---

[161] Ibid para 27.

[162] Article 110 EEC read: 'By establishing a customs union between themselves, Member States aim to contribute, in the common interest, to the harmonious development of world trade, the progressive abolition of restrictions on international trade and the lowering of customs barriers'.

[163] Cf P Demaret, *La politique commerciale: perspectives d'évolution et faiblesses présente*, 75. However, Demaret argued that certain aspects appear to be *a priori* excluded from the scope of Article 133 EC. This would be the case for the free movement of persons 'pour une raison d'ordre moral' (ibid). Yet, apart from this exception '[l]e rattachement d'autres matières économiques au domaine de la politique commercial est plus facile à justifier du moins en ce qui concerne leurs aspects externes. Il s'agit en particulier des services, de la propriété industrielle, des investissements, ce qui devrait retenir sur le régime des accords de coopération' (ibid 76).

We find two conflicting institutional views on this point in Opinion 1/78.[164] The Court had to analyse the Draft Agreement on Natural Rubber, subject to negotiations in the United Nations Conference on Trade and Development ('UNCTAD'). Predictably, the Commission had argued that the subject-matter of the agreement fully fell within the exclusive power of the Community. The Council, on the other hand, submitted that the agreement covered an area of general economic policy that the Treaty had expressly left to the disposition of the Member States.[165] The Court sided with the Commission. 'Although it may be thought that at the time when the treaty was drafted liberalization of trade was the dominant idea, the treaty nevertheless does not form a barrier to the possibility of the Community's developing a commercial policy aiming at a regulation of the world market for certain products rather than at mere liberalization of trade'.[166] An interpretation that froze the scope of the CCP in historic time, the Court held, would be disastrous for the Community. '[A]n interpretation the effect of which would be to restrict the common commercial policy to the use of instruments intended to have effect only on the traditional aspects of external trade' would render the concept of commercial policy 'nugatory in the course of time'.[167]

The Court thus favoured a dynamic and evolutionary scope for the Community's external commercial policy. Holding that the enumeration of subjects covered in Article 133 was a non-exhaustive one, it acknowledged

---

[164] Opinion 1/78 (*International Agreement on Natural Rubber*).

[165] The Council's position was summarized in the following way: 'The Council, after recalling that the exclusive nature of Community powers in the matter of commercial policy is not in question and that it does not reject the idea of a gradual evolution in this sphere, emphasizes that the common commercial policy nevertheless fulfils a function of its own in the context of the structure of the Treaty inasmuch as it applies to "any measure the aim of which is to influence the volume or flow of trade". Thus [Article 133] should be interpreted so as not to render meaningless other provisions of the Treaty, in particular those dealing with general economic policy, including the supply policy for raw materials which remains within the powers of Member States and for which the Council has only, under [Article 202], a power of co-ordination. According to the Council there is here a close interrelation between the powers of the Community and those of the Member States, since it is difficult to distinguish between international economic relations and international political relations. In this connexion the Council once again draws attention to the fact that rubber is a 'strategic product' so that the agreement in question impinges also on the defence policy of Member States. In these circumstances the Council takes the view that the negotiation of the agreement envisaged comes not only under [Article 133] of the Treaty but also under [ex-] Article 116 [EEC, now repealed] relating to common action by Member States within the framework of international organizations of an economic character to which they belong' (Opinion 1/78, para 39).

[166] Ibid para 44.

[167] Ibid.

that the agreement in question did not belong to the 'classic commercial agreements';[168] yet, it still found that 'it would no longer be possible to carry on any worthwhile common commercial policy if the Community were not in a position to avail itself also of more elaborate means devised with a view to further-ing the development of international trade'.[169] A restrictive interpretation of the concept of commercial policy, the Court underlined, 'would risk causing distur-bances in intra-Community trade by reason of the disparities which would then exist in certain sectors of economic relations with non-member countries'.[170]

Having rid itself of the vestiges of historical interpretation, the Court equally disabled systematic considerations that could have restricted the scope of the exclusive competence. The Council had invoked the 'structure of the Treaty'. Arguing that the agreement dealt primarily with general 'economic policy', it should have been concluded under the powers granted in this chapter of the Treaty. And since the latter only imposed a duty upon the Member States to ensure coordination,[171] this mandated mixed external action. The Court, again, disagreed with the Council. Finding that the rubber agreement came 'at least in part' under the broad scope of the CCP, the Court insisted that the specific nature of the commercial policy provisions required that 'their scope cannot be restricted in the light of more general provisions relating to economic policy and based on the idea of mere co-ordination'.[172] The Community's competences in other parts of the Treaty would 'not constitute a reason for excluding such objects from the field of application of the rules relating to the common commercial policy'.[173] The Community's *other* competences, in other words, would not operate as an external limit to the scope of the Community's exclusive power under Article 133 EC.[174]

---

[168] Ibid para 41.

[169] Ibid para 43.

[170] Ibid para 45.

[171] Ibid para 47.

[172] Ibid para 49. The Court had also pointed out that the agreement 'could not, in the name of general economic policy, be withdrawn from the competence of the Community' (ibid para 48).

[173] Ibid. In relation to the demarcation of the sphere of application between Articles 133 EC and 116 EEC (now repealed), the Court referred to Opinion 1/75, stressing that 'what counts with regard to the application of the Treaty is the question whether negotiations undertaken within the framework of an international organization are intended to lead to an "undertaking entered into by entities subject to international law which has binding force". In such a case it is the provisions of the Treaty relating to the negotiation and conclusion of agreements, in other words [Article 133 EC, Article 114 EEC (now repealed) and Article 300 EC], which apply and not Article 116 [EEC, now repealed]' (ibid para 51).

[174] The Court thus held the agreement to fall within the scope of the CCP from which the Community's exclusive competence should have followed. Yet, as is well known, the last part of the

The open and dynamic character of the CCP provisions was confirmed in *Generalized Tariff Preferences*.[175] This case concerned two tariff Regulations that had been adopted with the assistance of Article 308 EC. The Commission had wanted them to be based on the CCP competence alone. The Council, however, had added Article 308 EC, insisting that development policy was one of the 'major policy aims' of the two legislative measures.[176] Giving a wide teleological reading to the Community's exclusive competence, the Court again declared the Commission the winner of the institutional contest. It first pointed out that the interaction between trade and development had become 'progressively stronger in modern international relations' and that the Community's commercial policy will have to be adjusted to take account of those changes.[177] The Community had absorbed the 'new concept of international trade relations in which development aims play a major role'.[178] The Community legislature was consequently entitled to base both regulations on Article 133 EC alone.

Originally then, the Community legal order embraced an expansive and evolutionary concept of the CCP.[179] Changes in the mode of international economic relations—such as the transition from the *liberalization* of trade to

---

Opinion leads to a 'negation of the Community's exclusive competence' (as the Court itself puts it in para 52). Finding the issue of financing to be an essential feature of the agreement, the Court fell back on a mixed agreement. This was indeed a murky constitutional back door. It will be remembered that the Commission had originally suggested that the costs be covered by the Community budget and that the Council, ie the Member States themselves, had insisted upon assuming financial responsibility. The reasoning of the Court indeed seemed to 'put the cart before the horse' (JHH Weiler, *The External Legal Relations of Non-Unitary Actors: Mixity and the Federal Principle*, 174). (In this respect, the Opinion was a strange departure from Opinion 1/75, where the Court had maintained that it was 'of little importance that the obligations and financial burdens inherent in the execution of the agreement envisaged are borne directly by the Member States' (Opinion 1/75, 15).) The scope of the doctrine's application has been clarified in Opinion 1/94, where the Court stated that the fact that the Member States would bear 'some' of the expenses of the WTO could not, in itself, negate the assumption of an exclusive external competence on the part of the Community (Opinion 1/94, para 21).

[175]   Case 45/86 *Commission v Council (Generalized tariff preferences)*.

[176]   The Council maintained that 'it departed from the Commission's proposal to base the Regulations on [Article 133] alone because it was convinced that the contested Regulations had not only commercial policy aims, but also major development policy aims. The implementation of development policy goes beyond the scope of [Article 133] of the Treaty and necessitates recourse to [Article 308]' (ibid para 10).

[177]   Ibid paras 17–9.

[178]   Ibid para 18.

[179]   P Demaret, *La politique commerciale: perspectives d'évolution et faiblesses présente*, 70: 'En effet, le concept de politique commercial est par essence de nature évolutive'.

the *regulation* of international trade—were reflected in the expanding scope of the CCP. It seemed likely that this teleological approach would soon also bring a second international development within the scope of the CCP: the rise of service economies. Services had become an important item on the GATT agenda in the last quarter of the twentieth century. It appeared natural that if *national* trade and commercial policies had so drastically changed, the *Community* commercial policy would have to follow suit—or else become nugatory. Had Opinion 1/75 not expressly linked both notions together?[180] Surprisingly, the European Court refused to extend the scope of the CCP to services. The reason for this refusal lay in the *nature* of Europe's commercial policy competence. Had the CCP been a shared competence, the Court may have shown less resistance towards the changing structure of international law. However, *because* the CCP was 'exclusive', its scope became 'deformed' to accommodate the Member States' wishes to remain independent players with regard to services in the WTO.

The famous pronouncement of this 'ontological deformation' of the CCP appeared in Opinion 1/94. What was the division of external powers for the conclusion of the WTO agreement and its annexes? The Commission—relying on a wide interpretation of the CCP—argued, among other things, that all aspects of the international agreement fell within the ambit of Europe's exclusive competence. As for the power to regulate services on the international plane, the Commission appealed to the dynamic and open character of the CCP provisions established in previous jurisprudence.[181]

The Court, though at first inclined to accept the evolutionary expansion of the commercial policy concept,[182] refused to validate the 'update' of the Community concept by international practice. Instead, the Court reverted to systemic considerations. Asking 'whether the overall scheme of the Treaty is not such as to limit the extent to which trade in services can be included within [Article 133]', the Court invoked structural external limits to the Community's exclusive competence. Suddenly, the Court found that it

---

[180] The Opinion stated that the concept of 'commercial policy' would have 'the same content whether it is applied in the context of the international action of a State or to that of the Community' (Opinion 1/75, 11).

[181] The Commission referred to Opinion 1/75 and Opinion 1/78.

[182] The Court, in seeking to establish a general principle, employed an inclusive tenor before entering the details of the exceptions. Having regard to the trend in international relations increasingly characterized by a service economy, the Court asserted that 'it follows from the open nature of the common commercial policy, within the meaning of the Treaty, that trade in services cannot immediately, and as a matter of principle, be excluded from the scope of [Article 133]' (Opinion 1/94, para 41).

followed from the distinction made in Article 3 between 'a common commercial policy' in paragraph (b) and 'measures concerning the entry and movement of persons' in paragraph (d) that the legal aspects covered by the latter could not be simultaneously covered by the former.[183] 'More generally', the Court extrapolated, 'the existence in the Treaty of specific chapters on the free movement of natural and legal persons shows that those measures do not fall within the common commercial policy'.[184] This was a strong statement. Did it imply that all those sectors covered elsewhere in the Treaty were excluded from the scope of the CCP? This—strange—idea would have transformed Article 133 into a 'subsidiary power' like Article 308 EC; and in later jurisprudence,[185] the Court corrected the unfortunate wording. However, services remained excluded from the scope of the CCP; and the reason behind this restrictive interpretation was the exclusive nature of the CCP.[186] The deformation of its scope was the direct result of its exclusivity.[187]

---

[183] The Community was, however, given exclusive competence as regards 'cross-frontier supplies'. Since neither the supplier nor the consumer moves in this scenario, this mode of services was seen as 'not unlike trade in goods' and thus 'unquestionably covered by the common commercial policy within the meaning of the Treaty' (ibid para 44).

[184] According to some scholars, the Court applied two separate standards in determining the relationship between the common commercial policy and the two sectoral policies of agriculture and transport (cf T Tridimas and P Eeckhout, *The External Competence of the Community and the Case-Law of the Court of Justice: Principles versus Pragmatism*, 163).

[185] Cf Opinion 2/00 (*Cartagena Protocol*) as well as Case 281/01 *Commission v Council*. In deciding whether a measure fell into the scope of the CCP or another policy sector, a 'centre of gravity' test would apply. Those international agreements or European legislation that principally concerned international trade policy could be based on Article 133 EC (ibid para 25).

[186] The sharpest critique of Opinion 1/94 has come from Pescatore. Pescatore viewed Opinion 1/94 as a 'vast sham construction, put up to make us believe that the major part of the Agreement on "*trade* in services" and almost the entire Agreement on "*trade aspects*" of intellectual property rights" are not "*trade* agreements" in the sense of [Article 133 EC] and, to that extent, remain outside the EC's competence' (P Pescatore, *Opinion 1/94 on 'conclusion' of the WTO Agreement: Is There an Escape from a Programmed Disaster?*, 393). Interestingly, the former judge and eminent scholar nevertheless arrived at a mixed agreement by means of an argument that should have deserved more attention from the Court. Instead of adopting an inward-looking perspective in interpreting the scope of Article 133 EC, the Court should have focused on the 'constitutional innovation' brought by the WTO agreement: 'Had this been done, it would then have appeared that, while it was possible to lodge, the economic substance of the whole WTO complex in the categories of "commercial policy" and "trade agreements" of [Article 133], *there was no appropriate basis in the EC Treaty for the creation of an organizational framework of the amplitude provided for in the central WTO Agreement including in this new system of dispute settlement*' (ibid 400–1). Rather than internal limits stemming from the substance of the CCP, the external limit of a constitutional dimension à la Opinion 2/94 would thus have provided a better justification for bringing the Member States into the WTO agreement.

[187] CWA Timmermans, *La libre circulation des marchandises et la politique commerciale commune*, 95: 'En tant que telle, je considère cette exclusivité, comme je l'ai déjà dit, entièrement justifiée, mais, elle complique, c'est le moins que l'on puisse dire, une interprétation extensive de [l'article 133]'.

This ontologically deformed scope was—partly—remedied by the Nice Treaty, which broadened Article 133 EC to include trade in services.[188] However, this expansion had the price of introducing cooperative federalist arrangements into the CCP. The Community's *new* commercial policy powers are *shared* powers.[189] Paragraph 5 extends the treaty-making power of the Community into the previously unchartered fields of trade in services and commercial aspects of intellectual property, but stipulates that this inclusion 'shall not affect the right of the Member States to maintain and conclude agreements with third countries or international organizations in so far as such agreements comply with Community law and other relevant international agreements'. In these fields, *both* the Community and the Member States will be entitled to act at the same time. The CCP was, henceforth, only partially exclusive. The integrity of the CCP is thereby ensured through the twin principles of supremacy and pre-emption.[190] To protect the autonomy of the Member States even further, Article 133(6) even constitutionalized a political safeguard of federalism in the external sphere: mixed agreements. The reason behind this federal arrangement was the wish by some Member States to protect their cultural specificity.[191] The Nice reforms thus represented a step away from the philosophy of dual federalism under the CCP.[192]

3. *The Delegation Doctrine: How Exclusive are Europe's 'Exclusive' Powers?*

In parallel to limiting the scope of Europe's exclusive powers, there was a second strategy that the Community developed to mitigate the constitutional

---

[188] The competences under Article 133 (5)–(7) are treaty-making powers. They do not grant competence to the Community to adopt internal legislation. Herein lies a difference to the older powers listed under Article 133 (1)–(4) EC.

[189] Contra, M Krajewski, *External Trade Law and the Constitution Treaty: Towards a Federal and More Democratic Common Commercial Policy*, 96 and 99.

[190] M Cremona, *A Policy of Bits and Pieces? The Common Commercial Policy after Nice*, 86.

[191] The second subparagraph of Article 133(6) reads: '[A]greements relating to trade in cultural and audiovisual services, educational services, and social and human health services, shall fall within the shared competence of the Community and its Member States. Consequently, in addition to a Community decision taken in accordance with the relevant provision of Article 300, the negotiation of such agreements shall require the common accord of the Member States. Agreements thus negotiated shall be concluded jointly by the Community and the Member States'.

[192] The Lisbon Treaty, by contrast, would again move towards dual federalism. The new Article 207 TFEU contains no sign of a 'partial exclusivity' of the competence. The provision acknowledges the broadened scope of the CCP to cover trade in services, commercial aspects of intellectual property rights as well as foreign direct investment. Article 207(5) will exempt transport agreements from the scope of the CCP competence.

consequences of dual federalism. This alternative strategy focuses on the very idea of 'exclusivity'. How exclusive are exclusive powers in the Community legal order? The strongest version of exclusivity implies the automatic invalidity of *all* national measures—present and future—that fall within the Community's exclusive sphere. From the very beginning, the Court opted out of the retrospective invalidation thesis.[193] Within the ambit of an exclusive Community power, the Member States would only be constitutionally prevented from adopting measures that fell within its scope *after* the competence had been declared exclusive. National legislative powers were frozen in time; for as long as the Community had not harmonized national commercial policies exhaustively, existing national legislation would remain valid. Paradoxically, this dependency on the *legislative* elimination of national disparities would make the commercial policy of the EC, over time, look less integrated than some legislative regimes adopted under its shared powers.[194]

But what about *future* laws on the part of the Member States? The concept of exclusive power, looked up in the lexicon of constitutional federalism, implies that only one level is entitled to *autonomous* action. Yet, the possibility of *delegating* the exercise of federal exclusive powers to States

---

[193]   In Joined Cases 2 and 3/69 *Sociaal Fonds voor de Diamantarbeiders*, a national charge on the import of rough diamonds from third countries was to be assessed. The common customs tariff had been introduced by Regulation 950/68 which entered into force on 1 July 1968. While the Court clarified in its ruling that the Member States had lost all power to unilaterally adopt future national charges, Member States were permitted to maintain their existing differential charges even after the coming into force of the common customs tariff. These national tariff measures were not automatically and retrospectively unconstitutional: 'As regards charges already in existence, prior evaluation by the Community authorities is necessary in order to establish their incompatibility with the Treaty and the obligation to eliminate them. It follows that such charges may only be considered to be incompatible with Community law *pursuant to provisions adopted by the Community*' (ibid paras19–20). And later on: 'Since the adoption of this common commercial policy falls within the exclusive jurisdiction of the Community, the equalization of charges other than customs duties as such for all the Member States or their elimination is *dependent upon an intervention by the Community*' (ibid para 24). The equalization or abolition of national charges, even after the end of the transitional period, thus depended on subsequent Community legislation and was not the result of an automatic invalidation inherent in the notion of exclusive power.

[194]   While the Court increasingly attacked the legislative fragmentation of the common market in goods through the application of negative integration principles (it will be recalled that *Cassis de Dijon* underlined that these principles would apply '[i]n the absence of Community harmonization'), the Court did not similarly restrict the legislative powers of the Member States in their economic relations with third countries. The disparity of legislative powers in the internal and external sphere is illustrated in relation to goods in Case 270/80 *Polydor Ltd and RSO Records Inc v Harlequin Records Shops Ltd and Simons Records Ltd*. This led to the ironic result that, in the absence of Community legislation, Member States retained greater legislative liberty within the scope of the CCP than under the shared competence of Article 95 EC!

is generally recognized. However, the States only act as representatives of the federation. Within Europe's exclusive powers, then, all future State legislation must theoretically be based on delegated *Community* powers. Despite controversy,[195] European constitutionalism has accepted the possibility of delegating legislative powers back to the Member States. However, in order to assess the rigour of the Community concept of exclusivity, we must investigate the constitutional principles that govern the delegation doctrine. The more generous the delegation is, the less exclusive the Community powers are. The fewer and stricter the authorizations given, the more exclusive the Community competence.

a. Delegation within the CCP: From Specific Authorization to Carte Blanche

The constitutional legality of delegating legislative powers back to the Member States had been announced in *Donckerwolke*.[196] In the exclusive sphere of the CCP, 'measures of commercial policy of a national character are only permissible after the end of the transitional period by virtue of specific authorization by the Community'.[197] What was meant by the requirement of a 'specific' authorization? Would the Member States have to obtain permission for each and every legislative act adopted within the area? This would seem to be mandated by a robust format of exclusivity. However, the terms of

[195] For a negative attitude towards the delegation doctrine, see: HP Ipsen, *Europäisches Gemeinschaftsrecht*, 443–4: 'Soweit die Verträge Gemeinschaftsorganen einen Regelungsauftrag im Wege allgemein verbindlicher Normsetzung (Verordnung, allgemeine Entscheidung) erteilen und ihnen das mildere Mittel der nur zielverbindlichen Richtlinie (EGKS-Empfehlung) nicht anheimgeben (so im EWGV Art. 94 für den Rat, Art. 48 III für die Kommission), besteht gemeinschaftsrechtliche Regelungs*verpflichtung*. Insoweit ist etwaige Delegation an die Mitgliedstaaten ausgeschlossen'.

[196] This section will not engage with the specific type of authorization under Article 134 EC. The provision reads: 'In order to ensure that the execution of measures of commercial policy taken in accordance with this Treaty by any Member State is not obstructed by deflection of trade, or where differences between such measures lead to economic difficulties in one or more Member States, the Commission shall recommend the methods for the requisite cooperation between Member States. Failing this, the Commission may authorise Member States to take the necessary protective measures, the conditions and details of which it shall determine. In case of urgency, Member States shall request authorisation to take the necessary measures themselves from the Commission, which shall take a decision as soon as possible; the Member States concerned shall then notify the measures to the other Member States. The Commission may decide at any time that the Member States concerned shall amend or abolish the measures in question. In the selection of such measures, priority shall be given to those which cause the least disturbance of the functioning of the common market'. On this provision, see: P Eeckhout, *The European Internal Market and International Trade: A Legal Analysis*, 170–85.

[197] Case 47/76 *Suzanne Criel, née Donckerwolcke and Henri Schou v Procureur de la République au tribunal de grande instance de Lille and Director General of Customs*, para 32.

the delegation mandate have come to be very generously interpreted in the Community legal order. Through subsequent jurisprudence, the concept of 'exclusivity' would thus lose much of its constitutional substance.

The epitome of this development is *Bulk Oil*.[198] Under its CCP power, the Community had adopted Regulation 2603/69 outlawing quantitative restrictions on exports from the Community to third countries.[199] According to Article 10 of the Regulation, certain products were not covered by the liberalizing measure until such time as the Council had introduced common rules. A Community policy for the export of these products, among them crude oil, would thus only be established by *subsequent* Community legislation. In 1981, the United Kingdom had imposed *new* quantitative restrictions on the export of crude oil to certain non-Member countries, in particular Israel. In a tricky commercial dispute between two companies, Bulk Oil had raised the objection that the British Government policy violated the exclusive nature of the CCP.[200] The British measure would be void as no specific authorization for the national law had been given by the Community. According to Bulk Oil, Article 10 of the Regulation could not be regarded as such an authorization. The provision only 'legalized' the existing disparities in national commercial policy measures before the end of the transitional period. The United Kingdom, on the other hand, argued that Article 10 of the Regulation not only permitted Member States to keep their 1969 export policies in place, but also authorized States to autonomously decide on the trade policy for goods excluded from the Regulation 'until such time as the Council should adopt common rules for those products'.[201] While thus fully accepting the exclusivity of the CCP, the United Kingdom argued that Article 10 represented a 'specific authorization' in the meaning of the *Donckerwolke* ruling.

In a baffling and curt judgment, the Court accepted the British view. With the same schizophrenic tendency that had marked its *ERTA* jurisprudence,

---

[198]   Case 174/84 *Bulk Oil (Zug) AG v Sun International Limited and Sun Oil Trading Co.*

[199]   The Regulation had been adopted on the basis of Articles 131, 133 and 308 EC. Article 1 of the Regulation provided: 'The exportation of products from the European Economic Community to third countries shall be free, that is to say, they shall not be subject to any quantitative restrictions, with the exception of those restrictions which are applied in conformity with the provisions of this Regulation'.

[200]   *Bulk Oil*, para 23. In an earlier part of the judgment the argument was strongly shaped by pre-emption thinking. For example: in para 13, Bulk Oil seemed to argue that it was the *exercise* of the CCP competence in this area that triggered the need for specific authorization of the national measures. Related to this contention was an alternative argument submitted by Bulk Oil that claimed that the Community had occupied the field of trade relations between the EC and Israel through exhaustive regulation.

[201]   Ibid para 27.

the Court first dutifully recited the dual federalist philosophy of Opinion 1/75. Accordingly 'it cannot be accepted that in a field covered by export policy and more generally by the common commercial policy the Member States should exercise a power concurrent to that of the Community, in the Community sphere and in the international sphere'. Consequently, 'measures of commercial policy of a national character are only permissible after the end of the transitional period by virtue of specific authorization by the Community'.[202] Yet, the Court generously accepted the Council Regulation as satisfying the requirements of a 'specific authorization'. Article 10 would indeed 'constitute a specific authorization permitting the Member States to impose quantitative restrictions on exports of oil to non-member countries, *and there is no need to distinguish in that regard between previously existing quantitative restrictions and those which are subsequently introduced*'.[203]

The legality of national commercial policy measures, old and new, was simply reviewed by *reference to the terms of existing Community legislation*. Thus, despite the lip service paid to the exclusive nature of the CCP provisions, the constitutional principles governing the supposedly 'exclusive' competence were identical to the legal principles governing shared competences.[204] Not the exclusive competence as such, but the concrete Community legislation determined the legality of the national measure. The idea of a 'specific authorization' for each national measure within the scope of an exclusive competence was dismissed. Bulk Oil's intelligent argument that an uncontrolled re-delegation of European competences to the national level would violate the exclusive nature of the CCP was rebuked with a simple reference to the discretion the Council enjoyed in this matter.[205] This view paid little heed to the constitutional philosophy behind exclusive competences.

The reasoning has been confirmed in *Fritz Werner Industrie-Ausrüstungen GmbH v Germany*.[206] The case arose over the question, whether Article 133 EC also covered commercial measures motivated by foreign policy objectives. After an affirmative answer, the Court moved to an analysis of Regulation 2603/69—the same Regulation that had featured in *Bulk Oil*. On this occasion, it was Article 11 of the Regulation, which provided an exception from the

---

[202] Ibid paras 30–1.

[203] Ibid paras 32–3 (emphasis added).

[204] K Lenaerts, *Les répercussion des compétences de la communauté européenne sur les compétences externes des états membres et la question de 'preemption'*, 48.

[205] *Bulk Oil*, para 36.

[206] Case C-70/94 *Fritz Werner Industrie-Ausrüstungen GmbH v Federal Republic of Germany*.

general rule of free exportation. According to this provision, 'this Regulation shall not preclude the adoption or application by a Member State of quantitative restrictions on exports on grounds of public morality, public policy or public security; the protection of health and life of humans, animals or plants; the protection of national treasures possessing artistic, historic or archaeological value, or the protection of industrial and commercial property'. Did this legislative recognition of the States' police powers constitute a 'specific authorization'? The Court response was this:

[T]he concept of public security within the meaning of [Article 30] of the Treaty covers both a Member State's internal security and its external security. To interpret the concept more restrictively when it is used in Article 11 of the Export Regulation would be tantamount to authorizing the Member States to restrict the movement of goods within the internal market more than movement between themselves and non-member countries. . . So, the risk of a serious disturbance to foreign relations or to peaceful coexistence of nations may affect the security of a Member State. . .

The answer to the question submitted by the national court must therefore be that [Article 133] of the Treaty, and in particular Article 11 of the Export Regulation, do not preclude national provisions applicable to trade with non-member countries under which the export of a product capable of being used for military purposes is subject to the issue of a licence on the ground that this is necessary in order to avoid the risk of a serious disturbance to its foreign relations which may affect the public security of a Member State within the meaning of Article 11 of the Export Regulation.[207]

This type of reasoning did not reflect the logic of exclusive competences. On the contrary, the Court based its analysis on the parallelism between the internal and the external sphere. The justifications found in Article 30 EC for restrictions on intra-Community trade were simply projected to the external sphere. There was no mention of the need for a 'specific authorization' to exceptionally allow national measures within the scope of an exclusive Community competence. Absent Community harmonizing legislation, the Member States would enjoy the same degree of freedom to exercise their powers in areas covered by Article 30 EC (and mandatory requirements) in the external as in the internal sphere. This represented a *de facto* recognition of autonomous national power in the commercial policy field *even in relation to goods*.

In conclusion, in both CCP cases, the Court operated within a legislative pre-emption framework. Instead of asking whether the act fell within an exclusive Community competence and, if so, whether national action was

---

[207] Ibid paras 25, 27 and 29.

covered by a *specific* Community authorization, the Court asked whether national measures were in conformity with a general legislative act.[208] If that solution is extrapolated to all commercial policy fields, the constitutional practice under the CCP would come close to that of a shared competence. Some have tried to justify this emasculation of the concept of exclusivity: in the absence of a politico-constitutional yardstick, the European judiciary rightly defers to the legislative assessment of the Community decision-making organs.[209] Be that as it may, the carte blanche for national commercial policy choices goes well beyond any ordinary constitutional doctrine of delegated powers. And so long as the Court refuses to 'tie' national powers to a strict Community control, the national powers within the CCP will be closer to *autonomous* than to *delegated* powers.

b. Delegation within the Conservation Policy: Cooperative Federalism at Sea?

We find *two* delegation doctrines in the area of the Community's maritime biological conservation policy.

The first situation occurs where the Member States exercise emergency powers as trustees of the Community interest. In *Commission v United Kingdom*,[210] the Court had started from the idea of prospective exclusivity: the transfer of powers as from the 1 January 1979 was 'total and definitive' and the Community legislator's failure to act could not restore to Member States the power to act unilaterally in this field. '[T]his is a field reserved to the powers of the Community, within which the Member States may henceforth act only as trustees of the common interest[.]'[211] The Member States could thus only temporarily fill a legislative gap left open by a dysfunctional Community legislator.[212] However, the national measures were subject to *ex ante* and *ex post* control. The European Court formulated the terms of the delegation doctrine in the following conditioned manner: '[T]he requirements inherent in the

---

[208] In the words of an early commentator of the *Bulk Oil* judgment: 'the court has muddied external relations waters by its reiteration of the Community's exclusive competence for the common commercial policy while, at the same time, introducing what seems to be an incompatible notion of delegated powers, *i.e.* "special authorization". Better, perhaps, that the Court had more clearly said that the Community has not yet occupied the field of trade with Israel completely, be it for strategic or other reasons or that it had acknowledged in more straightforward fashion the emergence of a more flexible pre-emption doctrine' (MF Dominick, *Bulk Oil Case Note*, 470).

[209] P Demaret, *La politique commerciale: perspectives d'évolution et faiblesses présente*, 100.

[210] Case 804/79 *Commission v United Kingdom*.

[211] Ibid para 30.

[212] Ibid.

safeguard by the Community of the common interest and the integrity of its powers, imposed upon the Member States not only an obligation to undertake detailed consultation with the Commission and to seek its approval in good faith, but also a *duty not to lay down national conservation measures in spite of objections, reservations, conditions which might be formulated by the Commission*.[213] Finding the consultation by the British authorities unsatisfactory, the British conservation measures conflicted with the Treaty.

What is the relevance of the trustee's doctrine? The doctrine has been rightly characterized as nothing but an expression of emergency legislation.[214] The Community opted for a decentralized emergency system. It is not the Commission but the Member States that are called upon to act. However, these national measures are subject to *ex ante* control and can ultimately be vetoed by the Community.[215] Considering the degree of European control, one can hardly speak of autonomous powers of the Member States. The powers are here indeed best characterized as delegated European powers.[216] The 'trustee' doctrine spelled out in *Commission v United Kingdom* is, therefore, fully in line with the concept of exclusive competences. It did not 'relativize' the Community's exclusive competences.

However, in the course of the last two decades, a second delegation doctrine emerged in the context of the conservation of biological resources of the sea. This second doctrine mirrored the relativization of exclusivity in the context of the CCP. If one takes a closer look at the recent constitutional history in the competence's biography, one cannot escape the conclusion that the Community institutions—at least partly—no longer consider the conservation of marine biological resources as an exclusive competence. The legislative regime in place rather reflects the constitutional philosophy of cooperative federalism.

Since 1983, the Community legislator has been fairly active in the field of conservation measures for the sea.[217] In 1998, the Community adopted a new

---

[213]   Ibid para 31.

[214]   Emergency powers exist in every legal order. For the EC Treaty, they have always been expressly recognized in relation to the free movement of capital in what is today Article 60 EC.

[215]   In the words of the title of the 1981 editorial in the Common Market Law Review: 'Inactivity of the Council: Implied power for the Commission' (ibid 267).

[216]   M Pechstein, *Die Mitgliedstaaten der EG als 'Sachwalter des gemeinsamen Interesses'*, 224.

[217]   Cf Regulation 170/83 establishing a Community system for the conservation and management of fishery resources. Regulation 170/83 was amended by Regulation 171/83 laying down certain technical measures for the conservation of fishery resources. Regulation 170/83 was repealed by Regulation 3760/92 establishing a Community system for fisheries and aquaculture. The rules introduced by Regulation 171/83 have been amended on several occasions. That regulation was repealed by Regulation 3094/86 laying down certain technical measures for the conservation of fishery resources. According to the first recital of Regulation 894/97 laying down certain technical measures for the conservation of fishery resources, the regulation codified, for reasons of clarity and

legislative regime in the form of Regulation 850/98 EC, whose Article 46 (1) read as follows:

Member States may take measures for the conservation and management of stocks:
   (a) in the case of strictly local stocks which are of interest solely to the Member State concerned; or
   (b) in the form of conditions or detailed arrangements designed to limit catches by technical measures:
      (i) supplementing those laid down in the Community legislation on fisheries; or
      (ii) going beyond the minimum requirements laid down in the said legislation;
provided that such measures apply solely to fishing vessels flying the flag of the Member State concerned and registered in the Community or, in the case of fishing activities which are not conducted by a fishing vessel, to persons established in the Member State concerned.[218]

The article acknowledged in clear terms the power of the Member States to take measures for the conservation and management of stocks, while at the same time limiting their legislative involvement to matters that are of interest solely to them. In clarifying the exact mode of cooperation between the Community and the national level, the provision specifically referred to the idea of complementing national legislation that could go beyond the Community minimum standard. On its face, Article 46 (1) of Regulation 850/98 seemed to be a model of cooperative federalism. What about the provision's constitutional context? Did the European Court, perhaps, construct the provision as a 'specific authorization' as it had done in relation to the CCP?

The Court was indeed offered an occasion to spell out its constitutional vision. In *Annie Pansard*,[219] the French transport minister had adopted an order that prohibited the catching and landing of scallops in the French costal waters between Belgium and Spain between 15 May and 30 September 1980. Madame Pansard had fished in the territorial waters of the Channel Island of Jersey, from a vessel registered in France, and landed on the 24 May on the French coast at Saint-Cast Le Guildo. She was prosecuted for having infringed the French conservation measures. The national trial court, uncertain as to the legality of the national order, referred a number of questions to the Court of Justice. The central question was 'whether Community fisheries law precludes national legislation such as that at issue in the main proceedings

rationality, Regulation 3094/86, which was therefore repealed by Article 19 of Regulation 894/97. The provisions and annexes of that last regulation, with the exception of Articles 11 and 18 to 20, were repealed by Regulation 850/98 for the conservation of fishery resources through technical measures for the protection of juveniles of marine organisms.

   [218] The provision has been amended by Regulation 1298/2000.
   [219] Case C-265/01 *Annie Pansard and Others*.

which prohibits, during a given period, the landing, on part of the coastline of the Member State concerned, of scallops caught within the territorial waters of another Member State'.[220]

So what did the Court say? How did it conceptualize the national action? The Court started by reciting Article 34 EC on the common agricultural policy, yet immediately referred to Article 102 of the 1972 Act of Accession to state that, since 1 January 1979, the power to adopt measures for the protection of biological resources of the sea was 'vested exclusively in the Council'.[221] But the Court zigzagged back: the next paragraph returned to the pre-emption logic typically found in the CAP: '[T]he Court has already held that once the Community has, pursuant to [Article 34] of the EC Treaty, adopted legislation establishing an organization of the market in a given sector, the Member States are under an obligation to refrain from taking any measure which might undermine or create exceptions to it . . . Admittedly, the existence of a common organization of the market does not prevent the competent authorities of a Member State from adopting national measures on the terms provided for by Community legislation forming part of that organization'.[222] The Court admitted that there was no specific Community rule on scallop stocks. In light of the existing Community legislation, the Court therefore concluded:

Thus, it follows from the above that the competence of the Member States to take measures for the conservation and management of fishery stocks is part of a specific framework. The measures which Member States are empowered to adopt in that regard must concern strictly local stocks or only the fishermen of the Member State concerned or fishing vessels flying the flag of that State and may apply only to waters coming under its sovereignty or jurisdiction.

The national provision at issue in the main proceedings exceeds the competence of the Member State concerned since, first, it concerns neither strictly local stocks nor is it in the form of conditions or detailed arrangements designed to limit catches by technical measures, and, second, it prohibits the landing of fish caught in waters which do not come under the sovereignty or jurisdiction of the Member State concerned.[223]

The Court consequently found that 'Community fisheries law precludes national legislation'.[224] On the basis of the Court's reasoning, 'Community law' should be understood as Community *secondary* law. There was no further

---

[220] Ibid para 21.
[221] Ibid para 28.
[222] Ibid paras 29, 31.
[223] Ibid paras 36–7.
[224] Ibid para 38 (emphasis added).

rhetorical return to the constitutionally exclusive nature of the Community's powers in this field flowing from Article 102 of the Act of Accession. The entire judicial analysis was conducted through the optic of shared powers. The Court analysed the extent to which the relevant legislative frame pre-empted national powers to co-legislate. The French measure had violated the Community framework which limited the State's supplementary powers to set stricter national conservation measures for its domestic jurisdiction. France was simply prevented from 'exporting' its higher national standard beyond its territorial jurisdiction.

With *Annie Pansard*, it is hard to present the conservation of biological resources of the sea as an island of exclusivity in an ocean of shared powers. Fish conservation measures now seem to be merely a specific aspect of the Community's common agricultural policy. This is confirmed by the new Community legislation structuring the field. According to Article 1 of Regulation 2371/2002 EC, the scope of the common fisheries policies 'shall cover conservation, management and exploitation of living aquatic resources, aquaculture, and the processing and marketing of fishery and aquaculture products'. The new Regulation codifies the 'trustee of the common interest' doctrine by expressly acknowledging the 'emergency powers' of the Member States.[225] The greatest innovation, viewed from the old legislative status quo of Regulation 850/98, appears to be Article 9. It reads as follows:

Member State measures within the 12 nautical mile zone
   1. A Member State may take non-discriminatory measures for the conservation
       and management of fisheries resources and to minimise the effect of fishing on
       the conservation of marine eco-systems within 12 nautical miles of its baselines

---

[225] Article 8 of Regulation 2371/2002: 'Member State emergency measures' states: '1. If there is evidence of a serious and unforeseen threat to the conservation of living aquatic resources, or to the marine ecosystem resulting from fishing activities, in waters falling under the sovereignty or jurisdiction of a Member State where any undue delay would result in damage that would be difficult to repair, that Member State may take emergency measures, the duration of which shall not exceed three months. 2. Member States intending to take emergency measures shall notify their intention to the Commission, the other Member States and the Regional Advisory Councils concerned by sending a draft of those measures, together with an explanatory memoran-dum, before adopting them. 3. The Member States and Regional Advisory Councils concerned may submit their written comments to the Commission within five working days of the date of notification. The Commission shall confirm, cancel or amend the measure within 15 working days of the date of notification. 4. The Commission decision shall be notified to the Member States concerned. It shall be published in the Official Journal of the European Communities. 5. The Member States concerned may refer the Commission decision to the Council within 10 working days of notification of the decision. 6. The Council, acting by qualified majority, may take a different decision within one month of the date of receipt of the referral'.

provided that the Community has not adopted measures addressing conservation and management specifically for this area. The Member State measures shall be compatible with the objectives set out in Article 2 and no less stringent than existing Community legislation.

Where measures to be adopted by a Member State are liable to affect the vessels of another Member State, such measures shall be adopted only after the Commission, the Member State and the Regional Advisory Councils concerned have been consulted on a draft of the measures accompanied by an explanatory memorandum.

2. Measures applying to fishing vessels from other Member States shall be subject to the procedures laid down in Article 8(3) to (6).

This provision has been described as a '*(re)nationalisation rampante*'.[226] Unlike the previous regulatory frame, the operative criterion for delimiting the residual national competences is not the local stocks but a territorial zone. Within the twelve-zone territorial strip, the Member States are entitled to adopt *national* conservation measures if they are non-discriminatory and above the mandatory Community minimum standard. Only where the national measures are liable to affect vessels from another Member State will the Community organs be involved in monitoring the adoption of appropriate national measures. Within this twelve mile zone, Member States therefore enjoy an *autonomous* legislative competence for biological conservation measures of the sea.

Conclusion: European Federalism and Exclusive Powers

Exclusive competences are the trademark of dual federalism. In federal orders, they grant a legal monopoly to one legislator to the exclusion of the other. To what extent has European constitutionalism recognized mutually exclusive legal spheres? The question has two dimensions and this chapter has analysed them in two sections.

In Section I, we investigated the extent to which the Community legal order recognizes exclusive State powers. The extent of these powers depends on the reach of Europe's legal universe (or the extent to which it recognizes implied limitations). In the last half-century, European law has been expanding into ever more policy areas through two mechanisms of organized change. 'Big revisions' were brought about by means of formal treaty amendments, while

---

[226] A Cudennec, *Compétence communautaire exclusive et mesures nationales d'application*, 676.

'small revisions' were effected by means of Article 308 EC. Article 308 allowed the Community to act even though the Treaty had not expressly provided it with the necessary powers. What was the scope and nature of this strange competence? Unlike American constitutionalism, this European 'Necessary and Proper Clause' could be used as an independent legal competence—even if a 'subsidiary' one.[227] But like its American counterpart, European constitutionalism did not set clear internal limits by restrictively interpreting the 'necessity' criterion or the jurisdictional frame to which the provision would apply. The only implied limitation the Court would eventually settle upon was that the 'small revision' could not be used to circumvent the 'big revision' procedure. The only general external limit around Article 308 was the 'constitutional identity' of the European Community. But within this amorphous scope, Article 308 operated as a 'bounded' or 'partial' competence-competence.

The ability of the European institutions—the legislative and judicial organs—to set boundaries for themselves followed from the autonomy of the European legal order. We could see this also in relation to the European 'Commerce Clause(s)': Articles 94 and 95 EC. The power to harmonize national laws in order to further the establishment or functioning of the common market constitutes the Community's second widest competence. Would the Court of Justice here insist on stricter judicial safeguards of federalism? After all, this competence—unlike Article 308—allowed for majority voting and thus seriously reduced the effectiveness of the political safeguards of federalism within Europe. In *Tobacco Advertising*, the Court outlawed a European law on the ground that it represented a (near) total ban and consequently did not enhance intra-Community trade. In the absence of a liberalizing effect on trade or an equalizing effect on (appreciable) distortions of competition within the common market, Article 95 was not available. However, these internal limits would not be matched by external ones. Despite the introduction of constitutional saving clauses in a number of flanking policies, these clauses are no absolute constitutional recognition of exclusive national powers.

In sum, the Community legal order has still not committed itself to constitutionally safeguard a 'nucleus of sovereignty that the Member States can invoke, as such, against the Community'.[228]

---

[227] On the 'subsidiary' nature of Article 308 in the Community's order of competences, see: R Schütze, *Organized Change Towards an 'Ever Closer Union': Article 308 EC and the Limits to the Community's Legislative Competence*, 95–101.

[228] K Lenaerts, *Constitutionalism and the Many Faces of Federalism*, 220.

But what about Europe's own sphere of exclusivity? The idea of exclusive Community powers was undecided in the 1957 Treaty. While eventually opting for the shared power thesis, a number of exclusive Community competences have nonetheless emerged '*sous la plume de la Cour*'.[229] The judicial creation of constitutional exclusivity has remained pointillist: only two exclusive points were added to the canvas of shared power. The idea of exclusive Community powers has remained very exclusive indeed. Why did the Court never use a broader brush to widen Europe's sphere of exclusive power? Was the discovery of exclusive competences perhaps 'the child of a particular period in the Court's case law'?[230] In order to answer this question, we need to again take a closer look at the constitutional period during which exclusive competences first emerged in the Community legal order.

Three factors characterized the Community's federalism in the 1970s: the first being 'cultural', the second 'institutional' and the third 'normative' in nature. On a cultural level, the 1970s saw the Community working under the premise that 'strict uniformity' was a constitutional end in itself.[231] On the institutional level, decision-making until the Single European Act was dominated by unanimity. The infamous Luxembourg Compromise allowed each Member State to veto Community legislation by invoking its national interest. The 'deficiency of the Community legislator'—diagnosed during this time[232]—was surely the result of a decline in decisional supranationalism. The question the Court had to answer during this period was: should States that had vetoed Community legislation against the will of all other Member States—as the United Kingdom had done in relation to maritime conservation measures—be allowed to enjoy autonomous competence within that policy area? The 'discovery' of exclusive Community competences provided a useful constitutional means to defend the common interest of the Community by foreclosing national 'exit' strategies.

---

[229] V Michel, *Recherches sur les compétences de la communauté européenne*, 169.

[230] P Eeckhout, *External Relations of the European Union*, 15 (with reference to D Waelbroeck, *The Emergent Doctrine of Community Pre-emption—Consent and Re-delegation*).

[231] C-D Ehlermann, *The Modernization of EC Antitrust Policy: A Legal and Cultural Revolution*, 540: '[T]he dominant legal and administrative culture of the EC of the "Six" was still rather centralist. France was clearly the politically dominant Member State. French views heavily influenced EC legislation and administration. French preoccupations about "uniformity" (and not only "coherence" or "consistency") of the EC's legal order were pervasive'.

[232] P Pescatore, *La carence du législateur communautaire et le devoir du juge*, 559–80.

Could the emergence of constitutional exclusivity thus be explained as a normative reaction to the decline in decisional supranationalism?[233] While arguably providing a necessary condition, the threat posed by the Luxembourg Compromise for the functioning of the Community cannot convincingly furnish a *sufficient* condition for the emergence of exclusive Community competences. The institutional reading fails to explain why exclusivity appeared in *some* policy fields, but not in others. Why did constitutional exclusivity—original as well as subsequent exclusivity[234]—emerge predominantly in the *external* and not in the internal sphere of the Community legal order? There is no single and simple answer to this question. However, one influential factor explaining the emergence of exclusivity in the external sphere might—surprisingly—be found in the structure of the Community's *normative* supranationalism in the 1970s. While the supremacy of Community law vis-à-vis unilateral national measures had been firmly established by that time,[235] the relationship between Community law and international agreements concluded by the Member States was

---

[233] In an affirmative sense: P Koutrakos, *EU International Relations Law*, 21: 'In theoretical terms, if examined against the antithesis between normative and decisional supranationalism articulated early on by Weiler, the approach adopted in Opinion 1/75 is easily explained'. But, is it? And if so, which facet of supranationalism influenced the other? Did the rise of normative supranationalism—of which the doctrine of exclusivity forms part—influence the decline in decisional supranationalism, or the other way around? Weiler himself seems to have changed opinion on this point over the years. Writing in 1981, he claimed that the European Court had shown political acumen in that 'in evolving its doctrine of pre-emption the Court will have been cognizant of decisional difficulties in the Communities' policy- and rule-making structure. To insist on pure pre-emption and expect it to work necessitates efficient central organs; the absence of these in the Community gives one explanation to the pragmatic, less pure, approach adopted by the Court'. 'Looking at the relationship the other way round we have already suggested the possible negative effect to which ERTA may have contributed' (JHH Weiler, *The Community System: the Dual Character of Supranationalism*, 295). The above passage clearly shows a preferential explanatory direction: the rise of normative supranationalism—of which ERTA forms part—contributed to the decline in decisional supranationalism, therefore, the Court showed political acumen in abandoning pure pre-emption/exclusivity in favour of a pragmatic approach. (In 1981, this negative correlation appeared indeed more visible with Case 804/79 *Commission v United Kingdom*, not yet having been decided). Ten years later, however, Weiler preferred a positive correlation. In his well-known *The Transformation of Europe*, the eminent scholar now concluded: 'Exclusivity and preemption not only constitute an additional constitutional layer on those already mentioned but also have had a profound effect on Community decision-making. *Where a field has been preempted or is exclusive and action is needed, the Member States are pushed to act jointly*' (JHH Weiler, *The Transformation of Europe*, 2417 (emphasis added)).

[234] On the nature and extent of the Community's subsequently exclusive powers, see: Chapter 6—Section I (2a) and II (2) below.

[235] Case 11/70 *Internationale Handelsgesellschaft mbH v Einfuhr- und Vorratsstelle für Getreide und Futtermittel*.

much less settled. With the supremacy issue still in suspense, the Court moved down the more aggressive road of constitutional exclusivity. The Court's 'flight into dual federalism' blocked the Member States' 'flight into international law'.[236]

Today, all of these three reasons for the emergence of exclusive Community power have largely disappeared. First, with the rise of cooperative federalism as the dominant constitutional philosophy, the Community's constitutional culture has changed. Secondly, the need to force the Member States into common action by declaring a competence exclusive at the constitutional level is less vital with the rise of qualified majority voting. Legislative pre-emption and not constitutional pre-emption should be the order of the day. Finally, the normative ambivalence that originally characterized the relationship between European law and the international legal powers of the Member States has also disappeared. The supremacy of European law over international agreements concluded by the Member States has firmly been established. In sum, the constitutional conditions that spurred the emergence of exclusive competences within the Community legal order have today largely disappeared.

But more than that: Section II of this chapter has analysed two constitutional devices that were developed to restrict or relativize the Community's existing exclusive powers. Not only would the European Court go against its own interpretive methodology and deform the scope of exclusive competences for fear of an unacceptable political outcome; it has also accepted the emasculation of the Community concept of exclusive competence through the medium of the delegation doctrine. The latter has been so liberally constructed that it seems as if the Member States act under autonomous powers instead of delegated powers. In the area of maritime conservation measures, the Community even ceased to refer to the delegation doctrine at all. Europe's sphere of exclusive powers has thus—in terms of scope—remained frozen and—in terms of its nature—declined.

---

[236] On this point see: Chapter 6—Section II (1) below.

4

The Decline of Legislative Exclusivity

Introduction: European Federalism and Shared Powers

Shared competences permit two legislators to adopt their laws within the same area and at the same time.[1] Since competences are potentialities—entitlements for future legislation—shared competences within a federal legal order will only provide abstract guidelines about the legislative responsibilities of either government. And since two legislative wills may come into conflict, each federal legal order opting for shared competences will have to determine *when* conflicts arise and *how* these conflicts are to be resolved. For the Community's shared powers, these two dimensions have indeed been developed and structure the relationship between European and national legislation. In Europe's constitutionalism they have been described as, respectively, the principle of pre-emption and the principle of supremacy: 'The problem of pre-emption consists in determining whether there exists a conflict between a national measure and a rule of Community law. The problem of primacy concerns the manner in which such a conflict, if it is found to exist, will be resolved'.[2] Pre-emption and supremacy represent 'two sides of the same coin'.[3] They are like Siamese twins: different though inseparable.

In the EC legal order, the supremacy of European law has long been established. In the event of a conflict between Community and national law, the former will prevail. But when do such legislative conflicts between a Community and a national norm arise? The contrast between the prodigious literary presence of the supremacy doctrine and the shadowy existence of the doctrine of pre-emption in the Community law literature is arresting. Libraries have been filled with doctrinal treatments of the supremacy principle, whereas a contoured doctrine of Community pre-emption has still not materialized. The very concept of pre-emption—let alone a *doctrine* of pre-emption—has remained foreign to the Community legal order. The concept forms no element in the constitutional vocabulary of the European Court of Justice and the student of Community law will have to search hard for general treatments of the pre-emption doctrine in the majority of today's

---

[1] In this temporal aspect, shared powers differ from 'concurrent competences'. On the (German) concept of concurrent competence, see: R Schütze, *German Constitutional Federalism: Between* Sein *and* Bewußtsein.

[2] M Waelbroeck, *The Emergent Doctrine of Community Pre-emption—Consent and Redelegation*, 551.

[3] S Krislov, C-D Ehlermann and J Weiler, *The Political Organs and the Decision-Making Process in the United States and the European Community*, 90.

European law textbooks.[4] The constitutional terrain of pre-emption remains 'one of the most obscure areas of Community law'.[5]

Which federal philosophy informs the Community's shared competences? Has the Community legal order insisted on dual federalism, whereby 'il n'y a jamais concours ou concurrence mais seulement exercice par l'un ou par l'autre des titulaires d'une seul et même compétence'?[6] Or, would the Community exercise its shared competences in a cooperative way, allowing for complementary national legislation? The key to answering these questions lies in the doctrine of pre-emption. The doctrine of pre-emption is a federal theory of normative conflict. The use of a particular pre-emption type reveals the federal philosophy underlying the Community legislator, for it reflects the *actual exercise* of shared powers within a policy field.

Has European constitutionalism endorsed a modern pre-emption framework for the Community legal order? Unfortunately, the European Court has not (yet) committed itself to a principled pre-emption statement à la *Pacific Gas & Electric Co v State Energy Resources Conservation & Development Commission*.[7] In linguistic alliance with US American constitutionalism, we shall therefore analyse the exercise of the Community's shared competences through the lens of the pre-emption categories developed in that federal order.

Field pre-emption, thereby, represents the 'either-or-logic' of dual federalism. It is based on the idea of two mutually exclusive legal spheres. Field pre-emption refers to those situations, where the Member States are excluded on

---

[4] The word 'pre-emption' hardly occurs in the judicial discourse of the ECJ. In the rare event that the Court refers to 'pre-emption', it uses the concept in the specific context of European company law to refer to the 'right of pre-emption' of a shareholder (cf Case C-42/95, *Siemens AG v Henry Noll*). Perhaps it is this lack of judicial recognition that has caused the relative marginalization of the doctrine of pre-emption in the major Community law textbooks.

[5] Cf M Cappelletti, M Seccombe & J Weiler, *Integration through Law: Europe and the American Federal Experience—A General Introduction*, 32.

[6] V Constantinesco, *Compétences et pouvoirs dans les communautés européennes: Contribution à l'étude de la nature juridique des communautés*, 280.

[7] Cross—wrongly—mentions Case 218/85, *Association comite économique agricole régional fruits et légumes de Bretagne v A Le Campion (CERAFEL)* as a potential candidate (cf ED Cross, *Pre-emption of Member State Law in the European Economic Community: A Framework for Analysis*). There the Court stated that 'to ascertain whether and to what extent Regulation 1035/72 precludes the extension of rules established by producers' organizations to producers who are not members, either because the extension of those rules affects a matter with which the common organization has dealt exhaustively or because the rules so extended are contrary to the provisions of Community law or interfere with the proper functioning of the common organization of the market' (ibid para 13). The Court has, however, never extrapolated this pre-emption statement from its specific CAP context. Moreover, not even in the agricultural context has *CERAFEL* become a standard point of reference in subsequent cases.

the ground that the Community legislator has exhaustively legislated for the field. Underlying the idea of field pre-emption is a 'jurisdictional' conflict criterion. This is the most powerful format of pre-emption: *any* national legislation within the occupied field is prohibited. The strict uniformity under field pre-emption thus reproduces, albeit at the legistative level, the effects of a 'real' exclusive competence within the scope occupied by European law. The most concrete form of conflict will occur where national legislation literally contradicts a *specific Community rule*. Compliance with both sets of rules is (physically) impossible. This scenario can be described as rule pre-emption. In between these two extremes lies obstacle pre-emption. This third preemption type requires some *material* conflict between European and national law. Unlike rule pre-emption, however, it does not base the exclusionary effect of Community law on the normative friction between a national law and a *particular Community rule*. The Court will not go into the details of the Community scheme, but will be content in finding that the national law somehow interferes with the proper functioning or impedes the objectives behind the Community legislation.

What, then, is the structure of European law under the Community's shared competences? Has it changed? Can we detect a move from dual to cooperative federalism? The following two sections will look at the exercise and changing legislative regimes for the Community's Commerce Clause(s) and Europe's Common Agricultural Policy ('CAP'). The demise of field pre-emption and the emergence of softer forms of conflict pre-emption will be our constitutional compass. Since softer pre-emption formats will outlaw only parts of national legislation within a policy field, they ratify the peaceful co-existence of European and national legislation and, as such, signal a cooperative federal arrangement.

I. The Commerce Clause(s): Harmonization in the Internal Market

When the European Community was founded, its principal objective was the creation of a European 'common market'. 'The purpose of a common market must be the creation of a vast area with a common economic policy that forms a powerful unit of production and allows a continuous expansion, an increased stability, an accelerated increase of the standard of living, and the development of harmonious relations between the Member States.

To attain these objectives, a fusion of the separate markets is an absolute necessity'.[8]

Common markets are areas offering the free movement of factors of production. This elevates them from customs unions, which merely prohibit tariffs between Member States. In Europe, the elimination of customs duties had been a painless task. The original six Member States had agreed on a schedule of twelve years. The successful removal of all customs barriers was announced on 1 July 1968—even before the constitutional deadline. This brought to the fore the next category of trade barriers fragmenting the common market: non-tariff barriers. These were regulatory barriers that would also hinder the free movement of goods, persons, services, and capital. In relation to goods, the most obstructive species of these regulatory barriers were technical barriers to trade. Technical barriers are 'obstacles to international trade resulting from differences between national legislative and administrative provisions concerning the marketing or the use of products, which necessitates the adoption of export products during the production process'.[9] Product requirements were a creature of the twentieth century. They ordinarily pursue a social aim, such as public security, public health, or public morality. Unlike customs duties, it is thus not product requirements as such, but the *differences* in these national standards that erect barriers to trade.

The elimination of technical barriers formed an integral part of the Community's strategy to create a common market. This strategy was two-fold. On the one hand, the Treaty provided for the elimination of all unlawful barriers to trade through the free movement provisions. In relation to goods, Article 28 EC prohibited all '[q]uantitative restrictions on imports and all measures having equivalent effect' between the Member States. The provision—the equivalent of the dormant Commerce Clause in American constitutional law—would unify national markets by 'negating' unjustified national trade restrictions. Where a national law escaped the scope of 'negative integration',[10] the Community would still be able to remove barriers to trade

---

[8]   Report of the Heads of Delegation to the Ministers of Foreign Affairs (*Spaak Report*), 13.

[9]   PJ Slot, *Technical and Administrative Obstacles to Trade in the EEC*, 4. In its 1985 *White Paper*, the Commission extended this definition beyond goods, especially to services; see: *White Paper*, point 13. The concept of 'technical regulation' is also defined in Article 1(9) of Directive 83/198.

[10]   The Treaty accepted from the start that certain national laws within the scope of Article 28 EC could be justified. Article 30 EC thus exempted 'prohibitions or restrictions on imports, exports or goods in transit justified on grounds of public morality, public policy or public security; the protection of health and life of humans, animals or plants; the protection of national treasures possessing artistic, historic or archaeological value; or the protection of industrial and commercial property'.

or distortions of competition by means of positive integration. Here, European laws would replace divergent national laws and create a European market governed by common laws. The principal harmonization competences were Articles 94 and 95 EC. These two provisions form the heart of Europe's Commerce Clause(s).[11]

How and to what extent has the federal legislator used this power? Inroads into national autonomy are determined by two dimensions: the scope and intensity of harmonizing legislation. These two dimensions correspond, at the legislative level, to the distinction between the scope and nature of a Community competence. The jurisdictional dimension of *whether* Community legislation has harmonized an issue will typically precede discussions as to *how* the Community has harmonized it. Has Europe's exercise of its Commerce Clause(s) changed over time? The present section will investigate this question in relation to the harmonization of technical barriers to trade. Technical barriers have been said to represent the 'paradigm case for harmonization' that 'provide[s] the yardstick by which the harmonization programme as a whole has to be judged'.[12] To clarify the terminological ground, this section begins by revisiting the distinction between the scope and intensity of European law. We shall then analyse the 'old approach' to harmonization against these two dimensions. A third subsection will search for changes brought by the 'new approach' to harmonization and investigate whether these changes can be identified with a move from dual to cooperative federalism.

1. *The Two Dimensions of European Legislation: Scope and Intensity*

The pre-emptive capacity of European law is determined by two dimensions: the scope and intensity of a legislative act. The *scope* of a legislative act sets jurisdictional limits to the Community rules. It determines the legislative 'field'. The determination of the jurisdictional limits of a particular European law thereby raises similar federal questions to those which characterize the determination of the scope of a Community competence.[13] Matters found to lie outside the legislative field of a harmonization measure remain

[11] The American Commerce Clause gives Congress the power 'to regulate Commerce with foreign Nations, and among the several States'. On the scope and nature of the clause, see: Chapter 2—Section I above. On the scope and nature of the European Commerce Clause(s), see: Chapter 3—Section I (2) above.

[12] A Dashwood, *Hastening Slowly: The Community's Path Towards Harmonization*, 183–4.

[13] The *locus classicus* here is Case 9/74 *Donato Casagrande v Landeshauptstadt München*. For a detailed discussion of the ruling, see: JHH Weiler, *The Transformation of Europe*, 2438–41.

non-harmonized and thus within the residual powers of the Member States. Where European law does not harmonize all aspects within a policy area, Community terminology speaks of *partial harmonization*.[14] Here, the scope of a Community measure is viewed against the harmonization effort in the entire economic policy field.[15] Partial harmonization, as non-harmonization, may even be expressed *within* a single Community law.[16]

[14] The term 'partial harmonization' is contested. Confusion has arisen because the term is used in—at least—three ways. In addition to defining the concept by reference to the scope of the legislative act, the concept of partial harmonization has also been used to refer to the situation where the Community rule only applies to cross-border transactions (PJ Slot, *Harmonisation*, 384). And the concept has equally been employed with regard to Community legislation that establishes optional or minimum standards while allowing national legislators to supplement the Community standard (cf R Streinz, *Mindestharmonisierung im Binnenmarkt*).

The Court bears its share of the confused and confusing terminology. For example, in Case 227/82 *Criminal Proceedings against Leendert van Bennekom*, the Court introduced a dichotomy between complete/full harmonization and partial harmonization. The Court linked the concept of 'full harmonization' to 'all the measures needed to ensure the protection of human and animal life' (ibid para 35). Viewed in this manner, full harmonization did not relate to the intensity of harmonization within the scope of a particular harmonization measure, but to a social aim as an external yardstick. In Joined Cases C-426/00 and C-16/01 *Paul Dieter Haug*, the Court uses the concept of exhaustive harmonization in relation to the scope of a harmonization measure and not to its intensity. Finding that a particular Community rule 'carried out exhaustive harmonization', the Court nevertheless inferred from the preamble of the directive that the Community measure was 'general and applicable horizontally' and as such 'allows Member States to lay down rules in addition to those of the directive' (para 24).

[15] See, for example: first and eighth recital of Directive 79/112.

[16] The most well-known example is the development risk defence in the Product Liability Directive, ie Directive 85/374. The Directive purports to harmonize the different liability regimes within the Member States, while at the same time leaving it to the Member States whether to allow for a development risk defence for manufacturers. The defence represents a non-harmonized provision that was consciously placed *outside* the scope of the Community measure. Another example of a *non*-harmonized element within a Directive can be found in Case C-313/94 *F.lli Graffione SNC v Ditta Fransa*, in which the European Court was called upon to interpret Article 12(2)(b) of the Trade Mark Directive in the light of an Italian law prohibiting the use of a trade mark on the ground that it was liable to mislead consumers, yet it had been lawfully marketed in its home State. The Court said: 'The Trade Mark Directive, which, as its title indicates, is the first directive in that field, does not aim to bring about complete harmonization of the Member States' trade mark laws, and Article 12 of that directive merely lists the grounds on which a trade mark is liable to revocation. Moreover, according to the fifth recital in the preamble to that directive, the Member States remain free to determine the effects of revocation or invalidity of trade marks. Furthermore, according to its sixth recital, the Trade Mark Directive does not exclude the application to trade marks of provisions of Member State law other than trade mark law, such as provisions relating to unfair competition, civil liability or consumer protection. Consequently, as the Advocate General has observed in paragraphs 19 and 20 of his Opinion, Article 12(2) of the Trade Mark Directive leaves it to national law to determine whether and to what extent the use of a revoked trade mark must be prohibited' (paras 29–31). For further illustrations, see: Section II on agricultural policy below.

The second dimension—the intensity of harmonizing legislation—investigates the relationship between European and national rules within the scope of the particular Community law. Where an area is governed by European and national law, it will be necessary to determine whether the Community legislation is meant to be 'exclusive' or not. The intensity of the European law depends on the method of harmonization employed. Europe's Commerce Clause(s) did not prescribe any specific method of harmonization. The use of a particular method was consequently within the legislative discretion of the Community. In some situations, the Community legislator may exhaustively regulate an issue and thereby totally preclude national action within the harmonized field. Member States are excluded because the European legislation 'occupies the field'. At other times, harmonizing legislation may accept the continued presence of national law within the scope of European law. European and national law thereby either peacefully exist in parallel universes or they unite to form 'co-legislation'.

What harmonization techniques have been developed by the Community legislator in the past fifty years? Three principal methods have crystallized in the European legal order.[17] *Total harmonization* exists where the Community exhaustively regulates a matter to the exclusion of national legislators. The Community assumes exclusive responsibility to deal with all regulatory issues within the scope of a legislative act. Three elements characterize total harmonization: the relevant act lays down rules that define a 'European' product standard. It, secondly, contains a clause obliging the Member States to permit the free circulation of products conforming to the common standard (the free movement clause). Finally, it contains a clause that prohibits the marketing of all non-conforming products (the exclusivity clause).[18] European products would thus *replace* national products. Total harmonization leads to field pre-emption and *legislative* exclusivity.[19] It embodies the idea of legislative

[17] Some go so far as to list five distinct methods of harmonization (cf PJ Slot, *Harmonisation*). These different methods are sometimes combined in a single piece of Community legislation, see: Directive 80/778.

[18] Cf Article 3 of Directive 76/768 on the approximation of cosmetic products: 'Member States shall take all necessary measures to ensure that only cosmetic products which conform to the provisions of this Directive and its Annexes may be put on the market'.

[19] The field for this exclusivity may span over the entire scope of the piece of Community legislation. However, the Court has also employed the language of exhaustive legislation with regard to single provisions. See, for example, Case 52/92 *Commission of the European Communities v Portuguese Republic*, para 19: 'Article 10 of Directive 90/425, which establishes a new system of precautionary measures implemented very rapidly in order to combat effectively the spread of diseases likely to constitute a serious hazard to animals or to human health, brings about the complete harmonization of the precautionary measures against such diseases and defines precisely the

uniformity and the ideal of creating a 'level playing field' on which all economic actors within the Community would operate under equally competitive conditions.

Optional harmonization represents the second principal harmonization method. Here, the EC lays down a Community standard, compliance with which will constitutionally guarantee free movement within the common market.[20] While the legislation is binding on the Member State, the optional nature of this harmonization technique derives from the choice left to manufacturers: they can adopt the European standard or stick to their national standards. Unlike total harmonization, optional harmonization will not

respective obligations and tasks of the Member States and of the Commission in this field. The Member States thus have no power, in the area covered by that article and by Decision 91/237, adopted in implementation of that article, to take measures other than those expressly provided for therein'.

In light of this development, is becomes difficult to distinguish between 'exhaustion (preemption) versus harmonization methods' as suggested by Slot: 'The various harmonization methods discussed in the previous section should be clearly distinguished from the question of whether a directive exhaustively occupies a certain field. . . The issue of exhaustion concerns the question of whether a directive or another piece of Community legislation occupies the relevant area so as to pre-empt national action. . . Once it is determined that Community legislation occupies a field exhaustively, such legislation then forms the relevant framework for assessing the compatibility of national legislation with Community law. . . If Community action is exhaustive, the next question will be which harmonization method is embodied in the directive. When the total harmonization method is used, no derogation by national rules is permitted, except for safeguard measures provided for in the directive. In cases of partial, alternative and minimum harmonization, national rules may derogate from the norms prescribed in the directive within the permitted boundaries' (PJ Slot, *Harmonisation*, 388–9). On the contrary, it is advisable to identify exhaustive regulation with total harmonization and occupation of the field. (See in this regard, with respect to the Toy Safety Directive: A McGee & S Weatherill, *The Evolution of the Single Market— Harmonisation or Liberalisation*, 584.)

The Court's terminology on this issue is not 'harmonized' at all. It has cast exhaustive regulation and minimum regulation as conceptual antipodes in Case 278/85 *Commission of the European Communities v Kingdom of Denmark*, para 22: '[T]he rules of the Directive relating to notification are not meant to be rules providing a minimum degree of protection which leave the Member States free to widen the obligations provided for therein, but are intended to be exhaustive'. In Case C-1/96 *The Queen v Minister of Agriculture, Fisheries and Food, ex parte Compassion in World Farming Ltd*, however, the Court has spoken of 'exhaustively common minimum standards' and found that 'the fact that the Member States are authorised to adopt within their own territory protective measures stricter than those laid down in a directive does not mean that the Directive has not exhaustively regulated the powers of the Member States in the area of the protection of veal calves' (paras 56 and 63).

[20] Cf Directive 70/220 on the approximation of the laws of the Member States relating to measures to be taken against air pollution by gases from positive-ingestion engines of motor vehicles; and Directive 70/157 on permissible sound level and exhaust system of motor vehicles.

prohibit the marketing of non-conforming goods.[21] European law and national law exist in parallel universes. Optional harmonization thus creates *two* markets that exist alongside each other. In addition to a national market for traditional goods there exists a European market in 'Euro' goods. Compliance with the uniform Community standard permits exports to *all* national markets inside the Community. The Community standard will thus tend to be stricter than the national standards; and the national legislators remain free to introduce *less* stringent national requirements for their own national production.[22] Under optional harmonization, the Community standard thus functions 'more as a ceiling than a floor'.[23]

The third harmonization method is *minimum harmonization*. The idea behind minimum harmonization is that Member States remain entitled to adopt *stricter* national standards.[24] The presence of a Community standard on a certain issue will not prevent Member States from retaining or adopting complementary national laws. Minimum harmonization will set a mandatory floor and allow for *upward* legislative differentiation. This harmonization technique is thus also conducive to the conservation of national diversities. Not all national rules falling within the ambit of the Community measure will be replaced by a uniform European solution. Under minimum harmonization the Community and the national level act as co-legislators. Member States are, to some extent, allowed to preserve their traditional 'ways of life'. The upward legislative space offered to the national level is only limited by

---

[21] J Currall, *Some Aspects of the Relation between Articles 30–36 and Article 100 of the EEC Treaty, with a Closer Look at Optional Harmonisation*, 179.

[22] E Rehbinder & R Stewart, *Environmental Protection Policy*, 209. This has been contested: 'Die optionelle Harmonisierung beläßt den Mitgliedstaaten hierbei jedoch nicht die Befugnis, beispielsweise für die inländische Produktion von Waren und Dienstleistungen Regelungen mit einem geringeren Standard als von dem Harmonisierungsakt vorgesehenen festzulegen. Ein solches Vorgehen würde importierte Waren oder Dienstleistungen, für die der Gemeinschaftsstandard maßgeblich ist, benachteiligen und verstieße gegen Gemeinschaftsrecht. Die Methode der optionellen Harmonisierung beläßt daher dem Mitgliedstaat nur die Befugnis, für die inländische Produktion von Waren oder Dienstleistungen abhängig von der Richtlinienbestimmung gleichwertige andere oder auch strengere Standards für die Vermarktung festzulegen' (M Wagner, *Das Konzept der Mindestharmonisierung*, 51).

[23] D Geradin, *Trade and Environmental Protection: Community Harmonization and National Environmental Standards*, 180.

[24] Minimum harmonization co-existed since the early days with total harmonization and was particularly used in the emerging Community environmental and consumer protection policies. For a discussion of the former, together with a number of examples of minimum harmonization, see: Chapter 5—Section II (1) below.

the general free movement principles enshrined in the Treaty.[25] Community harmonization sets the floor and the Treaty draws the ceiling.[26] The concept of minimum harmonization will, thereby, not imply a European commitment to a 'minimal' standard in the form of the lowest denominator amongst the national legal orders.[27]

2. Harmonization under the 'Old Approach': Shared Powers and Dual Federalism

The original harmonization programme of the Community was 'epic'. Its scope can be identified by means of Directive 70/50 which had been adopted as an interpretive guide for the concept of 'measures having an equivalent effect to a quantitative restriction' under Article 28 EC. The Commission's institutional conviction at that time was that national 'measures governing the marketing of products which deal, in particular, with shape, size, weight, composition, presentation, identification or putting up' would normally apply equally to domestic and imported products.[28] Restrictions on intra-Community trade that were 'inherent in the disparities between rules applied by Member States' would, thus, generally fall outside the scope of the negative integration provisions.[29] To eliminate trade restrictions or distortions of competition, harmonization under Article 94 EC constituted the central constitutional option. The extensive harmonization programme was reflected in the Council's 'General Programme for the Elimination of Technical Barriers to Trade arising from disparate National Regulations'. The Programme was adopted in 1969 and envisaged a three-stage package of measures to be completed by 1970.[30] However, only a third

---

[25]   The question of how far Member States can also impose stricter national standards on imports remains very controversial. See the excellent analyses by M Dougan, *Minimum Harmonization and the Internal Market*; and S Weatherill, *Pre-emption, Harmonisation and the Distribution of Competence to Regulate the Internal Market*.

[26]   S Weatherill, *Beyond Preemption? Shared Competence and Constitutional Change in the European Community*, 25.

[27]   The European Court has been explicit about this point in Case C-84/94 *United Kingdom of Great Britain and Northern Ireland v Council of the European Union*, paras 17 and 56.

[28]   Article 3(1) of Directive 70/50.

[29]   Ibid Recital 9. The presumption of legality for national product requirements would be neutralized where the restrictive effect on the free movement of goods exceeded the effects intrinsic to trade rules.

[30]   Council Resolution of 28 May 1969 drawing up a Programme for the Elimination of Technical Barriers to Trade.

of the envisaged Directives were adopted by 1973.[31] The original deadline
had been far too ambitious and a supplementary programme approved a
new timetable.[32] The deadline slipped again and not many barriers had been
eliminated.[33]

Two reasons for the failure of the 'old approach' to harmonization can be
identified. First, low legislative output was inherent in the Commission's
chosen methodology. In these 'heroic days', total harmonization constituted
the preferred legislative method of the Community. Optional harmonization
became a serious alternative in the 1970s.[34] By contrast, minimum harmonization, while gradually emerging in the flanking areas of environmental and
consumer protection, hardly played a role in the harmonization of product
requirements. Here, almost all European laws were based on total or optional
harmonization.[35] The vertical approach to harmonization represented a
second fatal choice. Instead of harmonizing the social values and policy
objectives *behind* product requirements, the Community tried to harmonize
'products' themselves. A single Community standard should replace the different national product specifications and, thereby, ensure the free circulation of
goods. Total harmonization combined with a vertical approach to harmonization inevitably diminished the delivery rate of the federal legislator, as it
required negotiating the smallest of details for each product.

The 'old approach' under Europe's Commerce Clause had direct consequences for the role of the State legislators. For what would happen to national
legislation once Europe had passed Community legislation? A brief look
at the jurisprudence of the European Court will be revealing. In *Ratti*, criminal proceedings had been brought in 1978 against the head of an Italian
undertaking manufacturing solvents and varnishes.[36] Italian legislation
obliged manufacturers of those products to affix labels indicating the total
percentage of particular substances. The Italian law appeared to conflict with

---

[31] KA Armstrong & S Bulmer, *The Governance of the Single European Market*, esp Chapter 6.

[32] Resolution of the Council of 21 May 1973 concerning the Elimination of Technical Obstacles to Trade in Industrial Products.

[33] According to one survey, only 159 Council directives on the removal of technical obstacles—discounting certain amending and implementing directives—were adopted in the period 1962–84 (RH Lauwaars, *The 'Model Directive' on Technical Harmonization*, 154–5).

[34] A Dashwood, *Hastening Slowly: The Community's Path Towards Harmonization*, 195. The sta-
tistics during the early days of the Community harmonization programme are revealing. Out of 70 legislative acts, 30 embodied total harmonization, while around 39 were based on the optional harmonization method (PJ Slot, *Harmonisation*, 383).

[35] RH Lauwaars, *The 'Model Directive' on Technical Harmonization*, 156.

[36] Case 148/78 *Criminal Proceedings against Tullio Ratti*.

Directive 73/173 on the classification, packaging, and labelling of dangerous preparations (solvents). The Community act, based on Article 94 EC, had been adopted in light of 'considerable differences' in the national legal orders that created barriers to trade and thus 'directly affected the establishment and functioning of the market in dangerous preparations such as solvents'.[37] To eliminate these differences, the Directive prohibited Member States to 'restrict or impede on the grounds of classification, packaging or labelling the placing on the market of dangerous preparations which satisfy the requirements of the Directive'.[38]

A loyal national court referred a number of preliminary questions to the European Court. And while the first part of the judgment shall not interest us here,[39] the second and third questions concerned the material 'incompatibility' of the Community law and national legislation.[40] The central issue was 'whether, in incorporating the provisions of the Directive on solvents into its national legal order, the State to which it is addressed may prescribe "*obligations and limitations which are more precise and detailed than, or at least different from, those set out in the Directive*"'.[41] Granted that a directive could be directly effective in the national legal orders, the national court was concerned with the pre-emptive effect of the Community law vis-à-vis stricter national laws. The Court found that it pre-empted the stricter Italian legislation. Looking at the combined effect of Articles 3 to 8 of the Directive, any solvents that complied with provisions of the Directive should be allowed on the common market. Member States were:

not entitled to maintain, parallel with the rules laid down by the Directive for imports, different rules for the domestic market. Thus it is a consequence of the system introduced by Directive No 73/173 that a Member State may not introduce into its national legislation conditions which are more restrictive than those laid down in the Directive in question, or which are even more detailed or in any event different, as regards the classification, packaging and labelling of solvents and that this prohibition on the imposition of restrictions not provided for applies both to the direct marketing of the products on the home market and to imported products.[42]

---

[37] Ibid paras 10–11.

[38] Article 8 of the Directive.

[39] The national court had raised 'the general problem of the legal nature of the provisions of a directive adopted under [Article 249] of the Treaty' (*Ratti* para 18).

[40] Ibid para 29.

[41] Ibid para 25.

[42] Ibid paras 26–7.

Stricter national provisions were consequently not permitted as they went beyond the terms laid down in the Directive.[43] Moreover, in addition to enquiring about a possible conflict between national and European legislation, the prudent national court had also asked whether the national law 'nevertheless' constituted an obstacle to the free movement of goods— a question the European Court chose to understand as an 'allusion' to the justified exercise of national police powers under Article 30 EC.[44] Consistent with its earlier ruling in *Simmenthal*,[45] the Court clarified the premises of the total harmonization regime in clear dual federalist terms: '[W]hen, pursuant to [Article 94] of the Treaty, Community directives provide for the harmonization of measures necessary to ensure the protection of the health of humans and animals and establish Community procedures to supervise compliance therewith, recourse to [Article 30] ceases to be justified'.[46] Unilateral national measures within the scope of the Directive could no longer be excused by reference to Article 30. Within its field of application, the Community legislation would provide *all* the answers and pre-empt *all* national laws.

The constitutional principles structuring the relationship between European and national legislation were developed in subsequent jurisprudence. The enduring validity of dual federalism might be gauged by the degree of similarity with which the Court continued to analyse legislative conflicts in a case

[43] Ibid para 33.

[44] Ibid para 34.

[45] According to the famous phrase of the first *Simmenthal* ruling: '[Article 30] is not designed to reserve certain matters to the exclusive jurisdiction of Member States but permits national laws to derogate from the principle of the free movement of goods to the extent to which such derogation is and continues to be justified for the attainment of the objectives referred to in that article' (Case 35/76 *Simmenthal SpA v Ministere des finances italien*, para 14). Subsequent jurisprudence on the meaning of the *Simmenthal* ruling clarified that not all types of harmonization measures would block Article 30. Only in cases of complete harmonization would the Member States cease to be entitled to justify national measures hindering trade by recourse to that article, cf Case C-39/90 *Denkavit Futtermittel GmbH v Land Baden-Württemberg*, para 19: 'Finally, as the Court has explained, in particular in its judgment in *Carlo Tedeschi v Denkavit Commerciale s.r.l.*, Case 5/77, recourse to [Article 30] ceases to be justified only if, pursuant to [Articles 94/95], Community directives provide for the complete harmonization of national laws. It must therefore be accepted that where the approximation of the laws of the Member States has not yet been achieved in a given field the corresponding national laws may place obstacles in the way of the principle of free movement in so far as the obstacles in question are justified by one of the grounds set out in [Article 30] of the Treaty or by imperative requirements'. This point has recently been confirmed in Case 121/00 *Criminal proceedings against Walter Hahn*, para 34: 'However, although, in the absence of complete harmonization in the field, the Member States may prescribe the standards which products intended for human consumption must satisfy in their own territories, the national provisions in question cannot be exempt from the application of Articles 28 EC and 30 EC'.

[46] Case 148/78 *Criminal Proceedings against Tullio Ratti*, para 36.

decided a decade after the Court had pronounced the basic parameters of this relationship. In *Commission v Kingdom of Denmark*,[47] the Court scrutinized the relationship between Directive 79/831 on the classification, packaging, and labelling of dangerous substances and preparations, and the Danish implementing legislation. The Directive had been adopted to strengthen the protection of human health and the environment against potential risks which could arise from the placing on the market of new substances.[48] The core of the European law was a notification requirement imposed on the manufacturer or importer of those substances. The Danish Government had extended this mechanism and imposed *stricter* national standards. The Commission brought proceedings for wrongful implementation. The Danes defended themselves by denying that the provision was contrary to the Directive because the national rule was only '*wider than that provided for in the Directive*'.[49] Stricter national health and environmental standards, the Danish Government held, could not be in conflict with the European legislation since the former pursued the same objective as the latter.

The Court disagreed. It noted that Directive 79/831 was designed to pursue two objectives: the protection of humans and the environment *as well as* the elimination of obstacles to intra-Community trade in dangerous substances.[50] To cater for the second aim, the Directive contained a free movement clause.[51] The Court found that 'the Community legislature has laid down an exhaustive set of rules governing the notification, classification, packaging and labelling of substances, both old and new, and that it has not left to the Member States any scope to introduce other measures in their national legislation'. '[T]he protection of man and the environment is only one of the objectives of the Directive; the other objective is to eliminate obstacles to trade in the substances in question within the Community. Consequently, the rules of the Directive relating to notification are not meant to be rules providing a minimum degree of protection which leaves the Member States free to widen the obligation provided for therein, but are intended to be exhaustive'.[52] A 'widening of the exception provided for by the Directive', the

---

[47] Case 278/85 *Commission of the European Communities v Kingdom of Denmark*.
[48] First Recital of the Directive.
[49] Case 278/85 *Commission of the European Communities v Kingdom of Denmark*, para 15.
[50] Ibid para 16.
[51] Article 22 of the Directive expressly prohibited Member States to restrict or impede the placing on the market of products which complied with the Directive, on grounds relating to notification, classification, or labelling.
[52] Case 278/85 *Commission of the European Communities v Kingdom of Denmark*, paras 12 and 22.

Court later explained, 'was not *intended* by the Community legislature'.[53] Stricter national standards on the issue of notification would thus fall foul, because they departed from the uniform Community standard. The stricter national measure was consequently contrary to the Community legislation.[54]

The ideal behind total harmonization was total uniformity within the internal market. Once the Community legislator had adopted common rules, they should provide the *exclusive* standard within the field. The pre-emptive effect of Community legislation could thereby go beyond the constitutional limits imposed by negative integration. The ability of European legislation to penetrate purely internal situations—constitutionally untouchable under free movement law—followed from the distinctive characteristic of total harmonization: the ideal of total equality among all European citizens. In fact, since the terms of the Community legislation exclusively determined the rights and obligations of all citizens, leaving no discretion to national authorities to establish stricter measures, the problem of reverse discrimination did not occur. Once total harmonization was in place, no reverse discrimination through stricter national rules was allowed.[55]

---

[53] Ibid para 44.

[54] In this respect, see: Case 815/79 *Criminal Proceedings against Gaetano Cremonini and Maria Luisa Vrankovich*, para 6: 'The Directive was adopted on the basis of [Article 94] of the Treaty and aims to secure the approximation of the provisions laid down by law, regulation or administrative action of the Member States to the extent to which such provisions are likely to form technical obstacles to trade in such equipment. The purpose of such a directive would be frustrated if the competent national authorities in the exercise of the powers reserved to them relating to the form and method of implementing the Directive did not keep within the limits of the discretion outlined by this Directive, because any overstepping of these limits might create new disparities and therefore fresh barriers to trade and as a result prevent the free movement of goods in a field in which the Community legislature had adopted provisions in order to ensure such freedom'.

[55] The conceptual connection between harmonization, free movement, and equality changes with the rise of minimum harmonization. Here, the Community legislator sets common mandatory standards, but allows additional national legislation on the issue. Reverse discrimination is thus an inbuilt possibility of upward flexibility applied to domestic situations. Under the free movement provisions of Article 28 *et seq.*, the Court has indeed accepted the possibility of reverse discrimination and thus a certain degree of distorted competition. This was confirmed in Case C-241/89 *SARPP & SARL v Chambre syndicale des raffineurs et conditionneurs de sucre de France and others*, para 16: 'if the provisions of the directive preclude the application of certain national rules on the labelling of foodstuffs, such rules may not be applied either to imported foodstuffs or to national foodstuffs . However, when national rules on advertising are contrary to [Articles 28 and 30] of the Treaty, the application of those rules is prohibited only in respect of imported products and not national products'.

3. *Harmonization under the 'New Approach': The Rise of Cooperative Federalism*

The relatively low legislative output in the early 1970s was to be given a *regressive* momentum by the neo-protectionist tendencies of Member States at the end of that decade. Two economic recessions had lowered the solidarity, morale, and political will of the Member States to loosen 'boundary control'. The adoption of new technical standards was seen as a way of protecting national economies from competitive imports. This exogenous factor sealed the fate of the 'old' approach to harmonization. A new solution had to be found to reinvigorate the idea of a European common market It was the European judiciary that would lead the way to a constitutional solution. The judicial suggestion to reduce the scope of Europe's legislative involvement would—happily—be taken up by the Community legislator. The European legislative branch would even go further than the Court had suggested and eventually reduce the intensity of European harmonization. *Both* strategies—the reduced scope and the reduced intensity of European law—signalled a move from dual to cooperative federalism under Europe's Commerce Clause.

a. *Reducing Europe's Scope:* Cassis de Dijon *and the Commission's 'New Strategy'*

New constitutional momentum arrived in the form of a judgment on a French liqueur: *Cassis de Dijon*.[56] The judgment elevated the principle of mutual recognition—and the underlying idea of home State control—to a general constitutional principle of the internal market.[57] The idea behind *Cassis de Dijon* was that—absent or pending Community legislation—mutual recognition of national legislation would provide a second best solution.[58] Under the

---

[56] Case 120/78 *Rewe-Zentral AG v Bundesmonopolverwaltung für Branntwein (Cassis de Dijon)*.

[57] The idea of mutual recognition as a regulatory technique was already known under the original EC Treaty, whose Article 47 (1) provided for 'directives for the mutual recognition of diplomas, certificates and other evidence of formal qualifications' in order to make it easier for persons to take up and pursue activities as self-employed persons.

[58] The Court's (sad) reminder of the absence of common rules on the production and marketing of alcohol at the time of *Cassis de Dijon* points at the *auxiliary* character of the solution found. Only as long as the Community was unable to act would the national legislation of the home State enjoy a presumption of validity throughout the common market. Once the Community had adopted common rules harmonizing the disparate national technical standards, the Community regime would prevail. According to this reading, the principle of mutual recognition had a temporary status. It was the 'second best' option pending harmonization of the relevant field.

constitutional regime of mutual recognition, a Member State is entitled to keep technical regulations for its own products. However, it must—as a *quid pro quo*—principally accept imports produced according to the national standard of the country of origin. Importantly, *Cassis* was no cry for absolute mutual recognition. The presumption of a functional equivalence among national laws had limits. Member States could invoke mandatory requirements to justify host State control in certain circumstances. Nevertheless, the Court showed its intent to break the harmonization deadlock and to judicially remove national technical barriers. It was a broadside against recalcitrant States: if positive European legislation was not forthcoming, the Court would push market unification through the process of negative integration. *Cassis de Dijon* thus put political pressure on those governments in the Council that had a vital interest in high standards of protection.

However, there was a more direct political consequence of the judicial revolution: the Commission reduced the scope of Europe's harmonization programme by aligning its legislative progamme to the *Cassis* approach.[59] This adaptation progressed in stages. The emergence of the principle of mutual recognition had enlarged the scope of negative integration by means of a more extensive definition of what may constitute an unlawful technical trade barrier. The scope of Europe's harmonization programme could consequently be diminished, since *unlawful* trade barriers needed not be harmonized. The Commission spelled out its new harmonization strategy in a Communication on the consequences of *Cassis de Dijon*.[60] The text of the Communication was sent to the Member States and was notified to the European Parliament and the Council. It represents an invaluable insight into the institutional thinking of the Commission at the time. Acknowledging the interpretive guidance of the European judiciary, the Commission accepted that the application of national product requirements to imports would constitute an unlawful obstacle to intra-Community trade since '[a]ny product imported from another Member State must in principle be admitted to the territory of the importing Member State if it has been lawfully produced . . . in the exporting country, and is marketed in the territory of the latter'.[61] 'The Commission's work of harmonization will henceforth have to be directed mainly at national laws having an impact on the functioning of the common

---

[59] For a detailed account, see: K Alter & S Meunier-Aitsahalia, *Judicial Politics in the European Community*.

[60] (Commission) Communication concerning the consequences of the judgment given by the Court of Justice on 20 February 1979 in Case 120/78 (*Cassis de Dijon*).

[61] Ibid 2.

market where barriers to trade to be removed arise from national provisions which are admissible under the criteria set by the Court'.[62]

Two conclusions imposed themselves. First, the scope of the harmonization programme would be reduced. The Commission would limit its legislative proposals to measures that aimed to harmonize those national product requirements that could be *justified* under mandatory requirements. The harmonization of these national laws would be the 'finishing touch' of the internal market.[63] Harmonization would thus only occur where mutual recognition of national standards was inadequate in the light of the significant policy differences between Member States. Wherever the functional equivalence of national traditions had been shown *not* to work—a State had successfully invoked a police power to protect a legitimate interest—harmonization would step in to remedy this 'defect' in the logic of mutual recognition. The reduced scope of the harmonization programme thus led to a *de facto* recognition of the Member States' responsibility to define product requirements. It acknowledged a degree of 'constitutional' immunity from the pre-emptive effect of European law. Secondly—and this is an important point—the Commission's new strategy was not yet inspired by a 'new approach' to the intensity of European law. The Community's harmonization effort, albeit reduced, remained relative to *product requirements*; and this implied a continued preference for the old-fashioned methods of total and optional harmonization. The reduction in the *scope* of the harmonization programme was consequently not automatically coupled with a change from dual to cooperative federalism. The latter would only come in the wake of another innovation.

b. The 'New Approach' to Harmonization: From Vertical to Horizontal Legislation

Two decades of Community harmonization policy had yielded some success, but a true common market was far from being established. In relation to technical obstacles, the results had been shamefully poor. Those early decades had demonstrated the inherent shortcomings of the 'old approach' to harmonization. Excessive uniformity in matters of technical detail would block agreement in the Council. If matters were to continue in the same way, a legislative rhythm of ten to fifteen directives per year was the likely prospect by the end of the 1980s.[64] This modest output would not deliver the common

---

[62] Ibid.

[63] PJ Slot, *Harmonisation*, 378.

[64] A Dashwood, *Hastening Slowly: The Community's Path Towards Harmonization*, 206.

market in decades.[65] Luckily, this pessimistic projection never materialized. Two reforms revolutionized the Community's harmonization policy after 1985. The first was the Commission's change of harmonization methodology. It was embodied in the White Paper on the completion of the internal market, whose radically ambitious hope was to pass more than 300 legislative measures.[66] The legislative project could certainly not have been completed without a second reform: the introduction of (qualified) majority voting by the Single European Act. These two changes were the necessary ingredients for the success of the greatest legislative project in the history of the European Community.

What were the policy changes brought by the White Paper? The White Paper 'Completing the Internal Market' would be the centrepiece of the newly invested Delors Commission. The political and personal blood transfusion had given a new vitality to the Community. The White Paper had been written in seven weeks. Bold language reflected its bold purpose: 'The time for talk has now passed. The time for action has come' declared its introduction.[67] Leaving the legislative failures of the past behind, it sought to revamp the idea of the common market. A fresh term—the internal market—reflected the desire to break with the past. The structure of the paper corresponded to three types of trade barriers: physical, technical, and fiscal.

Two innovations lay at the heart of the White Paper: a new strategy and a new method of harmonization. The new strategy was not that new after all. However, the White Paper would consolidate the constitutional value of the principle of mutual recognition: '[T]he general principle should be approved that, if a product is lawfully manufactured and marketed in one Member State, there is no reason why it should not be sold freely throughout the Community'. National product laws that protect public interests 'essentially come down to the same thing, and so should normally be accorded recognition in all

---

[65] By 1980, much of the Commission's time was apparently spent in adjusting existing directives to technical change and pursuing some 250 infringement cases against Member States for non-implementation of the existing directives (KA Armstrong & S Bulmer, *The Governance of the Single European Market*, 153).

[66] European Commision, *Completing the Internal Market: White Paper from the Commision to the European Council*. The Annex of the *White Paper* listed more than 300 Commission proposals and a concrete timetable for their adoption. However, as an astute observer remarked: 'The merit of the White Paper is not the assiduous compilation of 300 topics for harmonization directives, but the renunciation of more than 1000 directives which would have been necessary according to the traditional internal market strategies' (H Schmitt von Sydow, *The Basic Strategies of the Commission's White Paper*, 91–2).

[67] *White Paper*, point 7.

Member States'.[68] However, this did not mean that there was no place for European harmonization. The Commission proposed a combined strategy that would employ both mutual recognition and harmonization. Its harmonization approach confirmed and avowed that 'a clear distinction needs to be drawn in future internal market initiatives between what it is essential to harmonize, and what may be left to mutual recognition of national regulations and standards'.[69] No harmonization was necessary where the principle of mutual recognition applied.

The real innovation of the White Paper lay in the conception of a 'new approach to technical harmonization'.[70] Legislative harmonization would—henceforth—be restricted to essential health and safety requirements. The Community would thus drop any attempt at defining *binding* product requirements. In those 'sectors where barriers to trade are created by *justified* divergent national regulations concerning the health and safety of citizens and consumer and environmental protection, legislative harmonization will be confined to laying down the *essential requirements*, conformity to which will entitle a product to free movement within the Community'.[71] The task of setting—voluntary—European product norms would be left to private standard-setting bodies.[72] The new legislative technique of European intervention was to be based on the 'new approach directive'. The latter provided a standard model designed to set the framework for the new approach.[73] Product standards would be set by European standardization bodies and

---

[68] Ibid point 58.

[69] Ibid points 64–5.

[70] The new approach had been predefined by Council Resolution of 7 May 1985: 'A New Approach to Technical Harmonization and Standards'.

[71] *White Paper*, point 68.

[72] Under the 'reference to standards' approach, these private organizations would flesh out product standards around the essential Community health and safety requirements. A manufacturer could adopt the voluntary European standard or could continue to use the national standard of the home State. The new approach thus catered for the co-existence of a European standard and national standards, whereby the latter had to comply with the essential safety requirements set by Community harmonization. As regards product requirements, the new approach therefore shares to some extent a family resemblance with optional harmonization. The Community would privilege compliance with the (voluntary) technical standards by guaranteeing free market access across the Community.

[73] Council Resolution of 7 May 1985 on a New Approach to Technical Harmonization and Standards (Annex II), 2. The Directive is discussed by RH Lauwaars, *The 'Model Directive' on Technical Harmonization*.

were voluntary.[74] New national laws had to be notified to the Commission.[75] This new information procedure promised to be a major step 'in pre-empting a number of potential obstacles to the free movement of goods between Member States'.[76]

Surprisingly, the White Paper did not mention minimum harmonization. On the contrary, the model directive appeared to endorse total harmonization. New approach directives should, while horizontal in nature, exhaustively regulate their field.[77] The new approach thus did not rule out total harmonization. However, due to the changed 'object' of harmonization, the new approach was ultimately more *susceptible* to minimum harmonization. After all, horizontal legislation would apply to a number of products and—when viewed against these products—only represented partial harmonization *of these products.*[78] Fundamentally, the rise of mutual recognition to become

---

[74] Council Resolution of 7 May 1985 on a New Approach to Technical Harmonization and Standards (Annex II), 3: '[A]t the same time national authorities are obliged to recognize that products manufactured in conformity with harmonized standards (or, provisionally, with national standards) are presumed to conform to the "essential requirements" established by the Directive. (This signifies that the producer has the choice of not manufacturing in conformity with the standards but that in this event he has an obligation to probe that his product conforms to the essential requirements of the Directive.)'

[75] Directive 83/189. The Directive was repealed and replaced by Directive 98/34/EC laying down a procedure for the provision of information in the field of technical standards and regulations. Article 8(1) of the Directive reads as follows: 'Subject to Article 10, Member Sates shall immediately communicate to the Commission any draft technical regulation, except where it merely transposes the full text of an international or European standard, in which case information regarding the relevant standards shall suffice; they shall also let the Commission have a statement of the grounds which make the enactment of such a technical regulation necessary, where these have not already been made clear in the draft'. The Court of Justice has ruled that the notification obligation of Article 8 of the Directive is directly effective. New national technical measures that have not been notified in accordance with the Community procedure will be pre-empted (cf Case C-194/94 *CIA Security International SA v Signalson SA and Securitel SPRL*, para 44).

[76] *White Paper*, point 76.

[77] Council Resolution of 7 May 1985 on a New Approach to Technical Harmonization and Standards (Annex II), 4: 'The Directive would provide for total harmonization as a general rule. Consequently, any product placed on the market falling within the scope of the Directive must be in conformity with the requirements of the Directive. In certain specific conditions, optional harmonization for certain products may prove to be opportune. The outline Directive, however, is drawn up with a view to total harmonization'.

[78] This idea would be endorsed in Case C-241/89 *SARPP & SARL v Chambre syndicale des raffineurs et conditionneurs de sucre de France and others*, where the Court found that *'because* the directive is general and applicable horizontally, it allows the Member States to maintain or adopt rules in addition to those laid down by the directive' (ibid para 15 (emphasis added)).

a 'first' best solution in the internal market eventually triggered the constitutional rise of minimum harmonization.[79]

An excellent illustration of the use of minimum harmonization under the new approach is provided by *Gallaher*.[80] Imperial Tobacco and Rothmans International Tobacco had brought proceedings before the High Court of England to obtain a declaration that certain provisions of the British Tobacco Products Labelling (Safety) Regulations 1991 infringed Directive 89/622 concerning the labelling of tobacco products. Article 3(3) of Directive 89/622 stipulated that the 'indications concerned shall be printed on the side of cigarette packets, in the official language or languages of the country of final marketing in clearly legible print on a contrasting background so that at least 4% of the corresponding surface is covered'. Article 8 of the Directive provided that 'Member States may not, for reasons of labelling, prohibit or restrict the sale of products which comply with this Directive' while they retained the right 'to lay down, in compliance with the Treaty, requirements concerning the import, sale and consumption of tobacco products which they deem necessary in order to protect public health, provided such requirements do not imply any changes to labelling as laid down in this Directive'. Reading the 'at least' formula as allowing for stricter national standards, the British Government had tightened the obligation on manufacturers. The British law required that the specific warning ought to at least cover 6% of the surfaces on which they were printed.

The applicants in the main proceedings contended this reading and argued that the European law left no discretion to national legislators to adopt stricter national standards. The provisions of the Directive had to be applied uniformly to both domestic goods and imports; stricter conditions applicable to domestic products would result in discrimination against British manufacturers and thus distort competition within the internal market. The Court was therefore asked to rule on the compatibility of the stricter national requirements with the Community harmonization.

---

[79] There is no logical link between the two regulatory techniques, but the existence of a Community minimum standard will normally be the precondition for the operation of mutual recognition of national standards (P Behrens, *Kommentar zu R. Streinz*, in U Everling & W-H Roth (eds), *Mindestharmonisierung im Europäischen Binnenmarkt: Referate des 7. Bonner Europa-Symposions vom 27. April 1996*, 46).

[80] Case C-11/92 *The Queen v Secretary of State for Health, ex parte Gallaher Ltd, Imperial Tobacco Ltd and Rothmans International Tobacco (UK) Ltd*.

The European Court's answer contrasts strikingly with its earlier ruling in *Ratti*. The Court read Article 8 of the Directive as relating only to imports and acknowledged the existence of an implied power to establish stricter standards for national products. The Court confined itself to pointing out that 'common rules are not always identical in nature'. 'Some of them give Member States no discretion to impose stricter requirements than those provided for in the directive', while other provisions would 'allow the Member States a degree of discretion'.[81] Interpreting Articles 3 and 8 of the Directive, the European Court found that:

It should be borne in mind that the directive, which was adopted pursuant to [Article 95], is designed to eliminate barriers to trade which might arise as a result of differences in national provisions on the labelling of tobacco products and thereby impede the establishment and operation of the internal market. With that end in view, the directive contains common rules concerning the health warnings to appear on the unit packet of tobacco products and the indications of the tar and nicotine yields to appear on cigarette packets...

The expression 'at least' contained in both articles must be interpreted as meaning that, if they consider it necessary, Member States are at liberty to decide that the indications and warnings are to cover a greater surface area in view of the level of public awareness of the health risks associated with tobacco consumption... [T]his interpretation of the provisions may imply less favourable treatment for national products in comparison with imported products and leaves in existence some inequalities in conditions of competition. However, those consequences are attributable to the degree of harmonization sought by the provisions in question, which lay down *minimum* requirements.[82]

The Court—following the European legislator—thus allowed for stricter national measures. Such measures should, nonetheless, not restrict intra-Community trade, and could consequently not be applied to imported goods. This followed from the aim of the Directive to eliminate barriers to trade and from Article 8 thereof. 'Member States which have made use of the powers conferred by the provisions containing minimum requirements cannot, according to Article 8 of the directive, prohibit or restrict the sale within their territory of products imported from other Member States which comply with the Directive'.[83] The constitutional regime for minimum harmonization

---

[81] Ibid paras 12 and 14.
[82] Ibid paras 10, 20 and 22.
[83] Ibid para 16.

would thus accept the possibility of reverse discrimination. A Member State could go beyond the European standard, but could only enforce its national legislative choice against its own citizens. Minimum harmonization thus abandoned the idea of a totally unified common market. A degree of legislative fragmentation was the price to pay for allowing national legislators to express their normative choices in addition to that of the European legislator.

Can we identify the change in the Community's harmonization policy with a move from dual to cooperative federalism? Total harmonization was the Community's preferred harmonization method in the early years. Once the Community had acted, national laws would be excluded by a unified European standard. The latter provided for exhaustive regulation and occupied the field. The Community thus started its legislative activities within the 'Commerce Clause' under the premise of dual federalism. Optional harmonization too was, in its own way, informed by a philosophy of dual federalism. While allowing national legislators the power to regulate their national production, optional harmonization would nonetheless provide an 'exhaustive' European standard. Admittedly, this optional standard was voluntary and thus allowed for the continued existence of national laws. However, the (exhaustive) optional Community standard and the (exhaustive) national standard would not cooperate; the latter would not complement the former. European law and national law would live in two distinct legal worlds—a logic that invoked the image of dual federalism.

Total harmonization and its regulatory ideal of European *uniformity* proved unsustainable—practically and politically. The first step in the direction of cooperative federalism was taken in *Cassis de Dijon*. The emergence and subsequent rise of the principle of mutual recognition significantly reduced the *scope* of the European harmonization programme. Legislative labours in the field of product requirements would in the future be left to national legislators or (European) private standardization bodies. It is therefore misleading to identify the system of mutual recognition as *de facto* harmonization.[84] The principle of mutual recognition—especially after its elevation in the Commission White Paper—legitimized *national* differentiation; and this brings it close to the idea of subsidiarity.[85] However, the

---

[84] This is the intriguing term used by P Oliver, *Measures of Equivalent Effect: A Reappraisal*, 214.

[85] In the Commission Communication to the European Parliament and the Council, *Mutual Recognition in the context of the follow-up to the action plan for the Single Market (16 June 1999)*, mutual recognition is viewed as an expression of subsidiarity. As it avoids the need for the systematic

diversity of national product standards as such was not cooperative federalism. For this, a second change in the structure of European law would have to take place. This was to happen with the rise of the 'new approach' to harmonization. The transition from the vertical harmonization of each product to the horizontal harmonization of essential health and safety requirements opened the way for allowing stricter national standards. The balance struck in minimum harmonization is to allow for free movement, while permitting the Member States to supplement the European standard with regard to their own territory.

The new approach was not designed to fully replace the traditional approach to harmonization.[86] However, as an alternative to total harmonization, it represented a move away from field pre-emption. Softer forms of pre-emption could, henceforth, determine the relationship between European law and national legislation. The rise of minimum harmonization stood for legislative cooperation between the two levels of government. Minimum harmonization permits legislative differentiation within the internal market *after* the Community had established common European standards. It acknowledged a legislative space for Member States within a legislative framework established by the Community. European law and national law could form a legislative whole that would balance uniformity with diversity. The spread of minimum harmonization as a *general harmonization method* therefore represented a step towards cooperative federalism. Its subsidiarity overtones have given it a special status within the Community legal order. In the words of the Presidency of the Edinburgh Council: 'Where it is necessary to set standards at Community level, consideration should be given to setting minimum standards, with freedom for Member States to set higher national standards, not only in the areas where the Treaty so requires ([Articles 137(4), 176]) but also in other areas where this would not conflict with the objectives of the proposed measure or with the Treaty'.[87] One such 'other area' could—potentially—even be the Community's common agricultural policy.

---

creation of rules at the Community level, it would allow greater respect for the local, regional and national traditions.

[86] KA Armstrong & S Bulmer, *The Governance of the Single European Market*, 152.

[87] (Edinburgh) European Council, *Conclusions: Overall Approach to the Application by the Council of the Subsidiarity Principle and Article 3b of the Treaty on European Union*, 15. For an analysis of this document, see: Chapter 5—Section I (1) below.

II. The Common Agricultural Policy: A Policy Unlike Any Other?

When the European Community was founded, agricultural production was characterized by insufficiency. In most European States, agriculture was subject to national intervention policies to ensure a degree of national autonomy. Two options therefore existed in 1957. The EC Treaty could exclude agricultural products from the liberal principles of the common market. Alternatively, the Treaty could include agriculture, but replace *national* agricultural policies with a *Common* Agricultural Policy ('CAP').[88] The first option proved unacceptable to the 'agricultural' countries in Europe. Freedom of movement for industrial but not for agricultural goods would have tilted the balance in favour of German industrial export trade.[89] The Treaty thus did include agriculture within the scope of the common market, but—in the light of its special status—established a special regime for it. A separate title would be dedicated to agricultural goods—following the title on industrial goods. Its opening article confirmed that '[t]he common market shall extend to agriculture and trade in agricultural products'.[90] Yet, while agricultural products were part of the common market, the normal constitutional principles of that market would only apply 'save as otherwise provided in 33-38 EC'.[91] The agricultural regime would constitute a *lex specialis* in the law of the internal market.

The reason behind the special status of agricultural policy was the strong nexus between the common *market* and a common *policy*. This constitutional link was clarified in the very first provision: 'The operation and development

[88] Less integrated economic unions—such as free trade areas or customs unions—typically leave agriculture outside their scope. For an excellent introduction into the 'historical' conditions of the birth of the common agricultural policy, see: M Melchior, *The Common Agricultural Policy*, 437–8.

[89] For an analysis of the geo-political situation, see: A Moravcik, *The Choice for Europe: Social Purpose and State Power from Messina to Maastricht*, Chapter 2.

[90] Article 32(1) EC. The Treaty generally defined agricultural products as follows: '"Agricultural products" means the products of the soil, of stockfarming and of fisheries and products of first-stage processing directly related to these products'. Article 32(3) specifically clarified the products to which the agricultural title was to apply: 'The products subject to the provisions of Articles 33 to 38 are listed in Annex I to this Treaty'. The Annex expressly included 'fish, crustaceans and molluscs' in the definition of agricultural products. The Common Fisheries Policy would thus be part of the CAP. The common market organization for fishery and aquaculture products can today be found in Regulation 104/2000, Article 1 of which states: 'A common organization of markets is hereby established, comprising a price and trading system and common rules on competition'.

[91] Article 32(2) EC.

of the common *market* for agricultural products *must be accompanied* by the establishment of a common agricultural *policy*.[92] The objectives of this Common Agricultural Policy would include the increase of agricultural productivity, the guarantee of a fair standard of living for farmers, and the stabilization of markets.[93] In order to attain these objectives, the Treaty had anticipated the establishment of 'common organization of agricultural markets'. Common market organizations should be established by the end of the transitional period. (This was in fact achieved for most products.[94]) Each Common Market Organization ('CMO') could thereby follow one of three regulatory mechanisms: (a) common rules on competition; (b) the coordination of national market organizations; or (c) a European market organization.[95] The distinction was to be of 'little importance' as the European legislator would 'invariably' favour the third option.[96] These European market organizations would—ideally—'replace the national market organisations'.[97]

The close connection between negative and positive integration—that is: the extent to which market unity required a uniform policy—predestined the CAP to become the 'most developed and coherent field of Community law'.[98] Agricultural policy would hold a unique position in European constitutional law: while it had not been declared an exclusive Community competence, it was the *de facto* most centralized Community policy. This gave rise to the common belief that once the Community had intervened through the setting up of a CMO, the Community's competence would become 'exclusive'

---

[92] Article 32(4) EC (emphasis added).

[93] Article 33(1) a–c.

[94] Common market organizations should have been brought into force by the end of the transitional period 'at the latest' (Article 40(1) EEC (repealed)). The notable exceptions were, *inter alia*, potatoes and sheepmeat. Originally, it was thought that by virtue of Articles 37 and 38 EC and ex-Article 45 EEC (repealed) national market organizations could be maintained until they had been replaced by CMOs. This view was even taken by the Commission. However, in Case 48/74 *M Charmasson v Minister for Economic Affairs and Finance*, the Court disagreed in relation to the free movement of goods provisions. The protected position of national market organizations would only last until the end of the transitional period. This doctrine was reaffirmed in Case 288/83 *Commission of the European Communities v Ireland*, in which the Court stated that 'agricultural products in respect of which a common organization of the market has not been established are subject to the general rules of the common market with regard to importation, exportation and movement within the Community' (ibid para 23).

[95] Article 34(1).

[96] FG Snyder, *Law of the Common Agricultural Policy*, 71. The distinction between these three intervention methods has not been consistently maintained by the Community legislator in the past. Constitutional practice has instead extended the expression *common market organization* to situations that combine elements from each method (M Melchior, *The Common Agricultural Policy*, 443).

[97] Article 37(3) EC. Article 37 EC provided the legal basis for Community measures in the title.

[98] R Barents, *The Agricultural Law of the EC*, 366.

through an 'occupation of the field'.[99] Was the CAP therefore a fiefdom of dual federalism—albeit in the more moderate form of legislative exclusivity? While there is truth in the statement, it will be seen that European constitutionalism has not been purist. Instead of purely relying on the jurisdictional criterion of field pre-emption, it has also had recourse to obstacle pre-emption in this area of European law. However, even this second pre-emption standard was extremely aggressive towards national measures. The CAP thus came *very* close to a dual federalism under which the Community would—almost completely—replace the Member States.

This picture is changing. The MacSharry Reforms started a shift in European agricultural law from vertical to horizontal legislation. How have the subsequent reforms affected the division of responsibility between the European Community and its Member States? Have they injected elements of cooperative federalism into the 'sacred cow' of European law?[100] Has the CAP moved from a—predominantly—dual to a—predominantly— cooperative federal philosophy? The (future) emergence of softer pre-emption types will be our heuristic compass. We shall proceed in two steps. We shall first investigate the constitutional principles governing the 'old' CAP regime. What follows is an analysis of the regulatory architecture under the 'new' CAP and its—prospective—impact on the structure of European agricultural law.

1. *The 'Old' CAP: Common Market Organizations as Vertical Legislation*

From the outset, the Community legal order preferred a 'vertical' approach to the regulation of agricultural markets. The original structure of Community

---

[99] Various academic commentators referred to the 'exclusive powers' of the EC under agriculture. See: G Olmi, *Politique agricole commune*, 291, 298; as well as M Blumental, *Implementing the Common Agricultural Policy: Aspects of the Limitations on the Powers of the Member States*, 32: 'In relation to agriculture, however, Community rules seek not only to control but actively to manage the markets. It is an area where the exclusive competence of the Community as against that of individual Member States stretches furthest'. The Court itself has—occasionally—referred to the 'exclusive powers' under the agricultural title, cf Case 216/86 *Antonini & Prefetto di Milano*, para 10: '[A]s regards wholesale prices for pigmeat and beef and veal, the Community has the exclusive legislative power which precludes any action on the matter by a Member State, it is not necessary to examine the question whether such national rules do or do not jeopardize the objectives or the functioning of the common organizations in the sectors under consideration'.

[100] We must not forget how 'sacred' the CAP was! It was the CAP that led the French Government to adopt its cripplingly successful 'empty chair policy' that culminated in the Luxembourg Accords. For an analysis of the Accord in the agricultural context, see: M Vasey, *Decision-making in the Agriculture Council and the 'Luxembourg Compromise'*.

agricultural policy would be characterized by *product* support as opposed to *producer* support. Each 'product' was to be regulated by a common market organization.[101] Each common market organization would form a comprehensive regulatory regime for the product(s) to which it applied. The Treaty thereby provided the Community legislator with a wide spectrum of regulatory methods. To establish European CMOs, the Community would be entitled to adopt 'all measures required to attain the objectives of the CAP', 'in particular regulation of prices, aids for the production and marketing of the various products, storage and carryover arrangements and common machinery for stabilising imports or exports'.[102] In order to encourage production, the Community had chosen to influence supply and demand of a product by regulating its price. The Community's price policy was principally designed to ensure an adequate level of agricultural income and a coherent and stable production policy.[103]

The 'typical' CMO would contain three essential components.[104] It would first define the scope of the CMO by specifying the products falling under it. The heart of the CMO would be formed by provisions establishing the 'common price' system for production within the internal market. The internal market would—thirdly—be protected by a special section that filtered external trade through a system of import quotas and levies. In the event of a Community surplus, the CMO could provide for the eventuality of export subsidies.[105]

---

[101]   However, instances of 'horizontal' legislation existed since the 1970s: cf Regulation 645/75 (export levies) and Directive 79/112 on the approximation of the laws of the Member States relating to the labelling, presentation, and advertising of foodstuffs. Some of these horizontal measures even follow a minimum harmonization approach. In Case 4/75 *Rewe-Zentralfinanz GmbH v Landwirtschaftskammer*, the Court identified Directive 69/466—based on Articles 39 and 94 EC—as allowing for additional national measures. For an exemplary list of minimum harmonization in the field of agriculture, see: M Wagner, *Das Konzept der Mindestharmonisierung*, 179–83.

[102]   Article 34(2) EC.

[103]   Case 26/69 *Commission v France*.

[104]   The prototype CMO has been that in cereals. After a transitional regime established by Regulation 19/62, it was put in place by Regulation 120/67. The CMO was much amended and subsequently consolidated by Regulation 2727/75. The latter Regulation was repealed in 1992 by Regulation 1766/92 and again reformed in 2003 by Regulation 1784/2003. Today, the sectoral approach has been abandoned and the CMO has been brought into Regulation 1234/2007 establishing a common organization of agricultural markets and on specific provisions for certain agricultural products (Single CMO Regulation).

[105]   Snyder distinguished three groups of common market organizations: those that provide for complete, partial, or no price guarantee (FG Snyder, *Law of the Common Agricultural Policy*, 73). A complete price guarantee was established for products that constitute an important component

The establishment and regulation of common prices developed into *the* policy instrument of the CAP. Common prices were so essential that 'the common agricultural policy and the common price policy were almost identical concepts'. 'It is thus not surprising that the common price instrument has exercised a profound effect on the structure and nature of Community agricultural law'.[106] The central idea behind price regulation was the 'market principle'.[107] According to that principle agricultural producers had to obtain their income from the market and not—at least not directly—from Community funds.[108] To secure the survival of the European agricultural sector and to stabilize the product markets, a sophisticated intervention system was established to keep Community prices at a constant level. The 'socialist' complexity of the regulatory structure had important consequences for the division of legislative responsibilities between the Community and the Member States.

To what extent could national legislators tinker with a CMO? This was the burning legal issue in the 1970s. The question was 'whether the compatibility of national legislation with the rules of the common organization should be

of farm income (eg cereal, sugar, and milk products). For products that are of less economic importance for farm income, the price mechanism would either be conditional (pigmeat, wine), or the Community policy was limited to a frontier mechanism (poultry, eggs). G Olmi, *Politique agricole commune*, 158–229 distinguished between CMOs that provide price guarantees (cereals, rice, sugar, diary products, etc), CMOs that provide for production aids (olive oil, tobacco, etc), and those CMOs that provide no guarantee (trees, flowers).

[106] R Barents, *The Agricultural Law of the EC*, 89. In Case 2/77 *Hoffmann's Starkefabriken AG v Hauptzollamt Bielefeld*, para 16 the European Court stated that 'the annual fixing of agricultural prices indeed constitutes a basic economic feature of the common agricultural policy as it is at present implemented'. The classical price model comprised three common price concepts: the target price, the intervention price, and the threshold price. The intervention price was the price at which the producer would be able to sell his produce to a public agency if no higher price could be obtained on the market. The target price represented the price at which imports from third countries may be purchased. The threshold price was a reflection of the target price for imports. The Treaty did not lay down criteria for determining prices. Prices could be freely negotiated on a 'contractual' basis, thus leaving them to intergovernmental bargaining. This 'free price formation' was a feature of most market organizations. The annual setting of these prices pursuant to the procedure set out in Article 37(2) EC has been a melodramatic ritual ever since the establishment of the CAP.

[107] M Melchior, *The Common Agricultural Policy*, 439. The principle has been defined as guaranteeing a 'market to which every producer has free access and whose operation is regulated only by the measures provided for by the common organization' (Case 218/85 *Association comite economique agricole regional fruits et legumes de Bretagne v A Le Campion (CERAFEL)*, para 20).

[108] In the words of F Snyder, the reference to the market principle is 'at best confusing' as it— misleadingly—'implies that CAP prices are determined by supply and demand, whereas in fact they are determined by negotiation and then administered' (FG Snyder (n 105 above) 73). Public authorities would be authorized to intervene in the common market to adjust the balance between supply and demand so as to keep prices at the desired level.

tested in relation to the *scope of the regulations forming the common organization as a whole*, or simply in relation to the *specific provisions in those regulations*.[109]

In order to identify the constitutional principles underlying the exercise of legislative powers in the agricultural fields, we need to dive into some agricultural case law. Two specific issues shall be addressed in particular. First, which type of legislative pre-emption would the Community legal order adopt within a CMO? Secondly, in what circumstances were the Member States still allowed to adopt national laws for a product governed by a CMO?

a. The Exclusionary Effect of CMOs: Between 'Field' and 'Obstacle' Pre-emption

Two approaches resurfaced in the early jurisprudence of the European Court. They have been referred to as the 'conceptualist-federalist' and the 'pragmatic' approach. The former involved automatic field pre-emption: the very existence of a CMO for a given product seemed to preclude all national law within its scope.[110] By contrast, under the latter approach the Court would search for a substantial conflict between the CMO and the relevant national legislation. By the end of the 1970s, the ECJ definitely preferred the pragmatic approach.[111] Since then, it was settled 'that the mere existence of a common organization does not *per se* exclude national legislation relating to its subject-matter, but care must be taken to ensure that the national legislation does not conflict with the specific provisions of that common organization, with the aims and objectives which may be deduced from those provisions or with general provisions of Community law which may apply within

---

[109] JA Usher, *The Effects of Common Organizations and Policies on the Powers of a Member State*, 430.

[110] There are, admittedly, scattered rhetorical pieces that use a purely dual federalist approach. The—perhaps—most emblematic expression of this 'conceptualist-federalist' rhetoric is Case 407/85 *3 Glocken GmbH and Gertraud Kritzinger v USL Centro-Sud and Provincia autonoma di Bolzano*, para 26: '[O]nce the Community has established a common market organization in a particular sector, the Member States must refrain from taking any unilateral measure even if that measure is likely to support the common policy of the Community. It is for the Community and not for a Member State to seek a solution to the problem described above in the context of the common agricultural policy'. See also: Case 177/78 *Pigs and Bacon Commission v McCarren & Co Ltd*; and Case 222/82 *Apple and Pear Development Council v KJ Lewis Ltd*. According to M Waelbroeck, *The Emergent Doctrine of Community Pre-emption—Consent and Re-delegation*, 559, '[t]he *Galli* judgement is the clearest and the most extreme expression of the conceptualist-federalist theory'. However, a close reading of the case will not support that conclusion.

[111] Waelbroeck's fine and meticulous analysis of the case law in the agricultural field revealed that '[s]ince 1976, the pragmatic approach appears to have prevailed' (ibid 555).

their scope'.[112] But if the Court had not insisted on automatic field pre-emption, what type of pre-emption would generally apply for the CAP? Labelling the lion's share of the case law 'pragmatic' at best evades the question *which* conflict criterion is employed.

The constitutional principles governing the doctrine of pre-emption inside CMOs come to the fore in *Galli*.[113] An Italian decree controlled the prices of goods produced or distributed by large firms. The national measure was reviewed in the light of two CMOs. In relation to cereals, the Community legislator had established a common price system which intended to create a 'single market' in cereals subject to a common administration. The European legislator had thereby intended to establish a system that comprised a set of rules 'to meet all foreseeable situations'. The 'central place' within that system was held by a price mechanism.[114] The importance and objective of the price system was explained as follows:

The purpose of this price system is to make possible *complete freedom* of trade within the Community and to regulate external trade accordingly, all in accordance with the objectives pursued by the common agricultural policy. *So as to ensure the freedom of internal trade the Regulation comprises a set of rules intended to eliminate both the obstacles to free movement of goods and all distortions in intra-Community trade due to market intervention by Member States other than that authorized by the Regulation itself. . . Such a system excludes any national system of regulation if impeding directly or indirectly, actually or potentially, trade within the Community.* Consequently, as concerns more particularly the price system, any national provisions, the effect of which is to distort the formation of prices as brought about within the framework of the Community provisions applicable, are incompatible with the Regulation. Apart from the substantive provisions relating to the functioning of the common organization of the market in the sector under consideration, Regulation No 120/67 comprises a framework of organization designed in such a way as to enable the Community and Member States to meet all manner of disturbances.[115]

The Court thus concluded that '*in sectors covered by a common organization of the market*—even more so when this organization is based on a common price system—Member States can no longer interfere through national

---

[112] JA Usher, *The Effects of Common Organizations and Policies on the Powers of a Member State*, 443. For the opposite view, see: JA McMahon, *EU Agricultural Law*, 61: 'So, the existence of a common organization of the market precluded national legislation on matters covered by the common organization'.

[113] Case 31/74 *Filippo Galli*.

[114] Ibid paras 8–10.

[115] Ibid paras 11–16.

provisions taken unilaterally in the machinery of price formation established under the common organization'. National legislation falling within this field would conflict with the Community legislation as well as with the 'general provision of the second paragraph of [Article 10] of the Treaty according to which Member States must abstain from "any measure which could jeopardize" the attainment of the objectives of the Treaty'.[116] The reason given by the Court for this enormously wide pre-emptive effect was that the Community legislator had intended to create a single market characterized by 'complete freedom of trade' in which 'all distortions' of competition due to national legislation were eliminated.

The nexus between the intention to create a true 'single market' in a product and the strength of the pre-emptive effect of European legislation re-emerged in *Pigs Marketing Board v Redmond*.[117] Here, the Court had to deal with the CMO in pigmeat and found that the market in that product was 'regulated solely by the instruments provided for by that organization'. 'Hence any provision or national practices which might alter the patterns of imports or exports or influence the formation of market prices by preventing producers from buying and selling freely within the State in which they are established, or in any other Member State, in conditions laid down by Community rules and from taking advantage directly of intervention measures or any other measures for regulating the market laid down by the common organization are incompatible with the principles of such organization of the market'.[118] Thus, the Court concluded, 'any intervention by a Member State or its regional or subordinate authorities in the market machinery apart from such intervention as may be specifically laid down by the Community Regulation *runs the risk of obstructing the functioning of the common organization of the market*'.[119]

This was not quite field pre-emption, but a very aggressive format of obstacle pre-emption. The latter would lead to the near-total exclusion of any national legislation within the scope of a CMO. Thus, within a CMO, the silence of the Community legislator would not necessarily signify a gap that national legislation could close. This constitutional consequence was spelt out in *van den Hazel*.[120] The Court had been asked to rule on the legality of a national measure that restricted the slaughtering of poultry in the light

[116] Ibid paras 29–30.
[117] Case 83/78 *Pigs Marketing Board v Raymond Redmond*.
[118] Ibid paras 57–8.
[119] Ibid para 60.
[120] Case 111/76 *Officier van Justitie v Beert van den Hazel*.

of the CMO in poultrymeat. Noting that there was no concrete conflict between the national measure and any specific provision in the CMO, the Court still found the silence of the Community legislator to be significant: '[T]he absence', stated the Court, 'does not stem from an omission or from an intention to leave measures of this nature to the appraisal of the Member States but is rather the consequence of a considered choice of economic policy of relying essentially on market forces to attain the desired balance'.[121] The CMO was based on 'freedom of commercial transactions under conditions of genuine competition'.[122] It would exclude all national laws since 'uncoordinated action is of such a nature as to cause discrimination between producers' and 'distort trade between Member States'.[123] There was thus a presumption of exhaustive regulation and the legislative exclusivity of the Community regime.

The jurisprudence cited above showed that the Court did *not* employ the general topos of field pre-emption. National legislation was not found to violate European law *because* the Community had established a CMO. CMOs did not—as such—induce automatic field pre-emption within their scope as not every CMO constituted a complete system that would exhaustively regulate all aspects falling within its scope.[124] Instead, the Court employed an aggressive format of obstacle pre-emption to oust supplementary national legislation. The—perhaps—clearest expression of this pre-emption standard emerges in *Compassion*.[125] 'Rules which interfere with the proper functioning of a common organization of the market are also incompatible with such common organization, *even if the matter in question has not been exhaustively regulated by it*[.]'[126] Emphasizing the unity of the common market, the Court has traditionally insisted that a CMO would try to recreate the 'conditions for

---

[121] Ibid para 16.

[122] Ibid para 18.

[123] Ibid para 22.

[124] See however: Case 16/83 *Criminal proceedings against Karl Prantl*, para 13: '[O]nce rules on the common organization of the market may be regarded as forming a complete system, the *Member States no longer have competence in that field* unless the Community provides otherwise'.

[125] Case C-1/96 *The Queen v Minister of Agriculture, Fisheries and Food, ex parte Compassion in World Farming Ltd*.

[126] Ibid para 41 (emphasis added). A similar pronouncement had already been made in Case 218/85 *Association comite economique agricole regional fruits et legumes de Bretagne v A Le Campion (CERAFEL)*, para 13: 'In order to reply to the question raised by the national court it is therefore necessary to ascertain whether and to what extent Regulation 1035/72 precluded the extension of rules established by producers' organizations to producers who are not members, either because the extension of those rules affects a matter with which the common organization of the market has dealt exhaustively or because the rules so extended are contrary to

trade within the Community similar to those existing in a national market'.[127] Those national measures that impeded the proper functioning of the CMO or jeopardized its aims would be pre-empted by the Community legislation. While not as potent as field pre-emption, the virility of this obstacle conflict criterion was nevertheless remarkable. The pre-emption format came close to a dual federal philosophy.

This strong pre-emption standard would hold sway over the CAP for over three decades.[128] The golden rule behind European agricultural cases seemed as follows: the closer the national measure was to the production or price formation of agricultural products, the more likely would it be pre-empted. National legislation dealing with prices at the production level was presumed to be incompatible with European law. By contrast, consumer price regulations would only be pre-empted, where they jeopardized the objectives or functioning of a CMO.[129] The Court thus created a distinction between

the provisions of Community law or interfere with the proper functioning of the common organization of the market'.

[127] Case 4/79 *Société coopérative 'Providence agricole de la Champagne' v Office national interprofessionnel des céréales (ONIC)*, para 25.

[128] In Case 117/78 *Pigs and Bacon Commission v McCarren and Co Ltd*, the Court had to decide on the compatibility of a levy intended to subsidize export marketing with, *inter alia*, Regulation 2759/75 on the common organization of the market in pigmeat. Having repeated that 'once the Community has, pursuant to [Article 34] of the Treaty, legislated for the establishment of the common organization of the market in a given sector, Member States are under an obligation to refrain from taking any measure which might undermine or create exceptions to it' (para 14), the Court considered the Community marketing system as '*intended* to ensure the freedom of trade within the Community by the abolition both of barriers to trade *and of all distortions in intra-Community trade* and hence precludes *any intervention by Member States in the market otherwise than as expressly laid down by the Regulation itself*' (ibid, emphasis added). The Court consequently found the national levy 'incompatible with the rules' on the free movement of goods '*and more particularly* under the provisions of Regulation 2759/75' (para 17, emphasis added). Similarly strong formulations are used in Case 222/82 *Apple and Pear Development Council v KJ Lewis Ltd and others*, where the Court inspected the common organization of the market in fruit and vegetables (Regulation 1035/72). The Court found that 'an exhaustive system of quality standards applicable to the products in question' existed, therefore preventing national authorities from imposing national quality requirements unless the Community legislation itself provided for such a power (para 25). For a more recent case, see also: Case 22/99 *Cristoforo Bertinetto and Biraghi SpA*.

[129] This reading is supported by Case 65/75 *Ricardo Tasca*. The case concerned an Italian law that fixed maximum *consumer* prices for sugar in the context of the common market organization for that product. Cautioning that 'a strict distinction between maximum consumer prices and maximum prices applicable at previous marketing stages is difficult' 'due to the fact that on the one hand price rules at the stage of the sale to the ultimate consumer may well have repercussions on the price formation at the previous states', the Court affirmed that national legislation dealing with the same marketing stages as the Community system will 'run a greater risk of conflicting with the

'product' related measures and 'marketing' measures, which we now find in other areas of European law.[130] This distinction between 'price' measures and all other national laws would also influence the way in which the Court constructed national caveats within a CMO.

b. National Caveats: Delegated Community Powers or Autonomous State Powers?

How would the Court conceive Community rules that referred to national action within a CMO? Theoretically, two answers were possible: the Court could either conceive of these 'authorizations' as Community delegations, or it could conceive of them as simple acknowledgments of autonomous national powers. The Court has often preferred the first solution when 'essential' elements of a CMO are concerned. Here, the powers 'left' to the Member States are constructed as federal authorizations. Where, on the other hand, non-essential aspects were at issue, the Court has had few qualms in acknowledging the autonomous powers of the Member States.

Let us investigate the first scenario. In *Cucchi*,[131] the Court had to deal with an Italian surcharge on sugar imports. Italy contended that the measure was allowed under the CMO. The Court rejected this, clarifying that derogations from the general provisions of Community agricultural legislation 'must arise from an express provision or, at least, a form of words which make clear

said system' (ibid para 6). Having looked at the sugar market, the Court held that a Member State would jeopardize the objectives of the organization, where it regulated prices in such a way as to directly or indirectly make it more difficult for sugar manufacturers to obtain the intervention price. The Court added that an indirect obstruction would exist where a national measure—without regulating the price at the production stage—fixed maximum selling prices for the wholesale or retail stages at such a low level that the producer found it actually impossible to sell at the intervention price (ibid para 11).

The clearest manifestation of this result can be found in Case 216/86 *Antonini & Prefetto di Milano*, where the Court dealt with the CMO in pigmeat, beef, and veal. Here, the Court held that 'as regards wholesale prices for pigmeat and beef and veal, the Community has the exclusive legislative power which precludes any action on the matter by a Member State, it is not necessary to examine the question whether such national rules do or do not jeopardize the objectives or the functioning of the common organizations in the sectors under consideration; such an examination is necessary, however, when national measures are adopted in respect of retail or consumer prices and are thus in a field which does not fall within the exclusive powers of the Community' (para 10).

[130] Case C-267/91 *Criminal Proceedings against Keck and Mithouard*.
[131] Case 77/76 *Entreprise F.lli Cucchi v Avez SpA*.

the Council's intentions in this respect'.[132] Referring to its *Rey Soda* ruling,[133] the Court extrapolated from it the following conclusion: 'the functioning of a common organization of the markets and in particular the formation of producer prices must in principle be governed by the general Community provisions as laid down in general rules amended annually with the result that any specific interference with this functioning is strictly limited to the cases expressly provided for'. The Community was, therefore, 'in the absence of express derogation, alone competent to adopt specific measures involving intervention in the machinery of price formation'.[134] For matters affecting the price mechanism, the Member States would only be allowed to act where the CMO expressly provided so.

But where the CMO did so expressly provide, how would these 'residual powers' be construed? In *Plimveeslachterij Midden-Nederland BV*,[135] the Court gave an answer to that question.[136] The CMO in poultrymeat had been established by Regulation 2777/75. In Article 2, the Community legislator had left the issue of European marketing standards to subsequent legislation.[137] This power had not been used. Would Dutch legislation on quality standards for the slaughtering of poultry nevertheless be pre-empted? The Commission argued this, claiming that 'the Community legislature expressed its intention to "occupy the ground" regarding matters governed by the organization of the market and the Member States may therefore no longer legislate on those matters'.[138] The Court agreed about the occupation of the field, but allowed

[132] Ibid para 9.

[133] Case 23/75 *Rey Soda v Cassa Conguaglio Zucchero*. The case confirmed that essential policy choices had to be made by the Community legislator and could not be delegated to national authorities via express legislative caveats or a discretionary margin left under an implementation scheme. The delegation of essential legislative powers from the Commission to the Member States violated the inter-institutional balance between the Commission and the Council.

[134] Ibid paras 31 and 35.

[135] Joined Cases 47/83 and 48/83 *Pluimveeslachterij Midden-Nederland BV*.

[136] This CMO was weaker than a normal CMO (ibid para 17): 'In order to answer the question raised by the College van Beroep it should first be recalled that the common organization of the market in poultrymeat, as at present laid down in Regulation 2777/75, is based on a set of measures designed to stabilize the market and ensure fair process without resort to intervention measures of the kind provided for in other agricultural markets. According to Article 2, supply is to be adjusted to market requirements by means of a set of measures designed to promote better organization of production, processing and marketing, to improve quality and to facilitate the establishment of market forecasts and the recording of price trends'.

[137] Article 2(2) of Regulation 2777/75 stated that '[s]tandards, their scope and the general rules for their application shall be adopted by the Council, acting by a qualified majority on a proposal from the Commission'.

[138] Joined Cases 47/83 and 48/83 *Pluimveeslachterij Midden-Nederland BV*, para 12.

the national action. How? Pointing to 'the Council's almost total failure to act', this CMO was still not able to function normally.[139] The Court, referring to its 'trustee of the common interest' doctrine, added that the exercise of national powers *'must not be regarded as involving the exercise of the Member State's own powers, but as the fulfilment of the duty to cooperate in achieving the aims of the common organization of the market which, in a situation characterized by the inaction of the Community legislature, [Article 10] of the Treaty imposes on them'*. 'Consequently, the measures adopted by the Member States may only be temporary and provisional in nature and they must cease to be applied as soon as Community measures are introduced'.[140] The Court thus projected the idea of the Member States acting as trustees of the common interest— established in its jurisprudence on the conservation of biological resources of the sea[141]—to the agricultural field. The Court thereby extended a dog-matic construction developed in the context of an *exclusive competence* to the phenomenon of *legislative exclusivity*.

Let us now look at the second scenario. Where an issue would not affect the price mechanism—and thus be of only secondary importance for the CMO— the Court adopted a more generous approach. Member States would not have to point to an express authorization in the Community scheme. This was clarified in *Jongeneel Kaas*.[142] The case concerned the common organization of the market in milk and milk products. Dutch legislation had laid down rules on the quality and types of cheeses which could be produced in the Netherlands. The national regime was contested by Dutch cheese dealers. They claimed it constituted a violation of the Community organization of the market. The Court disagreed. Unlike other CMOs, having as their purpose the support of the market by maintaining either a given price level or minimum quality standards, the present market organization did not (yet) contain any provi-sions on the quality of cheese. Thus, even though Member States were obliged to refrain from taking any measures to undermine the CMO, 'the fact that the legislation in question makes no mention of the designation and quality of cheese does not mean that the Community consciously and of necessity decided to impose on the Member States in that sector an obligation to adhere to a system of absolute freedom of protection. In the absence of any rule of Community law on the quality of cheese products the Court considers that

---

[139] Ibid para 21.
[140] Ibid paras 22–3 (emphasis added).
[141] On this point, see: Chapter 3—Section II (3b) above.
[142] Case 237/82 *Jongeneel Kaas BV and others v State of the Netherlands and Stichting Centraal Orgaan Zuivelcontrole*.

the Member States retain the power to apply rules of that kind to cheese producers established within their territory'.[143]

The Court confirmed the existence of *autonomous* national powers within the scope of a CMO in *Prantl*.[144] German legislation had limited the use of the *Bocksbeutel* bottle to quality wine produced in certain German regions, thus prohibiting the marketing of Italian wine in similarly-shaped bottles. The Court started by repeating that 'once rules on the common organization of the market may be regarded as forming a complete system, the Member States no longer have competence in that field unless Community law expressly provides otherwise' and even agreed that the common organization in wine 'could be regarded as forming a complete system, especially as regards prices and intervention, trade with non-member countries, rules on production and oenological practices and as regards requirements relating to the designation of wines and labelling'. However, as regards rules on the presentation of products, the CMO had left the adoption of common rules to the discretion of a future Community legislator.[145] And while the European legislator had indeed acted to protect the use of a bottle known as the 'Flute d'Alsace', the Court rejected the contention that the Community had thereby exhaustively harmonized the issue of bottle shapes.[146] In light of the 'secondary importance' of the question of bottle shapes for the fundamental elements of the CMO, the possibility of adopting national legislation on the issue had *not* been totally pre-empted by the European legislation.

In conclusion, traditional agricultural case law followed two lines of jurisprudence. For measures that concerned the price system, the Court requires specific authorization in the Community measure before a Member State can act within a CMO. The national action was—in the most extreme dual federalist version—conceived as a delegated Community power that was exercised by the Member States acting as 'trustee' of the Community interest. This view brought the essential aspects of a CMO close to exclusive Community competences. However, for non-essential matters of a CMO, the Member States could continue to act autonomously.[147] Here, legislative

---

[143]   Ibid para 13.

[144]   Case 16/83 *Criminal proceedings against Karl Prantl*.

[145]   Ibid paras 13–15.

[146]   Ibid para 16.

[147]   Subsequent case law has confirmed *Prantl*: cf Case C-312/98 *Schutzverband gegen Unwesen in der Wirtschaft eV v Warsteiner Brauerei Haus Cramer GmbH & Co KG*, para 49; Case C-121/00 *Criminal proceedings against v Walter Hahn*, para 34; and Case C-409/03 *Société d'exportation de produits agricoles SA (SEPA) v Hauptzollamt Hamburg-Jonas*, paras 24–5.

caveats would only 'recognize' or 'declare' the existence of autonomous powers of the Member States, which a CMO has left untouched. (However, national action would be subject to Community review.[148]) The Court thus seemed to acknowledge a laxer pre-emption standard in relation to agricultural 'flanking' measures. (The three principal flanking policies here follow three objectives: the health of persons and animals, consumer protection, and the quality of the products.[149] These 'horizontal' measures were often adopted under the dual legal basis of Articles 37 and 94 EC.[150]) Stricter national standards would often be allowed in these 'flanking' areas.[151] This laxer pre-emption standard towards horizontal measures is likely to be

---

[148] Case C-313/99 *Gerard Mulligan and Others v Minister for Agriculture and Food, Ireland and Attorney General*. In that case, a legislative caveat allowed Member States a national choice under the common organization of the market in milk and milk products. While admitting that the Member States were in principle free to introduce certain national measures, the Court qualified this freedom by stating that 'this finding cannot lead to the conclusion that the Member States are authorised to introduce any type of . . . measure in any circumstances whatsoever. It must be observed, first, that, having regard to the fact that the adoption of a national measure such as that at issue in the main proceedings falls within the scope of the common agricultural policy, such a measure cannot be established or applied in such a way as to compromise the objectives of that policy and, more particularly, those of the common organization of the markets in the milk sector' (para 33).

[149] C Blumann, *Politique agricole commune*, 213–38.

[150] From the mid-1980s, Article 37 could also be chosen as the sole legal basis for these measures. See, in particular: Case 131/86 *United Kingdom of Great Britain and Northern Ireland v Council of the European Communities*, in which the Court clarified that consumer protection, protection of health and life of humans and animals were also objectives of Article 37. This was confirmed in Case C-269/97 *Commission of the European Communities v Council of the European Union*.

[151] In relation to animal welfare, for example, the approach of the Community legislator has been to lay down minimum standards, see: Directive 91/629 relating to the protection of calves, Directive 91/630 relating to the protection of pigs, Directive 98/58 relating to the protection of animals kept for farming purposes, and Directive 1999/74 relating to the protection of laying hens. More generally on minimum flanking measures, see also: Case C-108/01 *Consorzio del Prosciutto di Parma and Salumificio S Rita SpA v Asda Stores Ltd and Hygrade Foods Ltd*, esp. para 50.

We should expect similar constitutional principles in this area to those applying to industrial products. A cautioning note has, however, been voiced by Blumann. According to this author, the transition provoked by the new approach to harmonization in relation to industrial products could not necessarily be extended to agricultural products. Speaking about the 1985 White Book, the author notes: 'Le volet agricole et agro-alimentaire du Livre blanc s'avère des plus consistants. En effet, sur les 300 mesures annoncées, une centaine concerne ces produits. Leur importance n'est pas seulement quantitative, mais qualitative, car les produits agro-alimentaires cadrent mal avec la nouvelle approche de la Commission. D'abord, les normes techniques relatives à ces produits sont quasiment inexactes, d'autre part, le secteur agro-alimentaire entrant de plain-pied parmi ceux relevant des exigences essentielles, en matières de santé, de sécurité des produits et de protection des consommateurs, le principe de reconnaissance mutuelle s'y avère quasi inapplicable et il importe d'opter en faveur d'une harmonisation législative de type classique' (C Blumann, *Politique agricole commune*, 208).

generalized, and become dominant, once the Community abandons the vertical approach to agricultural law and the price mechanism it entails.

2. The 'New' CAP: From Vertical to Horizontal Legislation

Why was there such a demand for legislative uniformity under the old CAP? The insistence on uniformity in agricultural law was a direct consequence of its intervention method. The powerful pre-emption standard in this area of European law must be understood against this background. The complexity of the price mechanism required that any national law that could affect it had to be banned as a potentially conflicting interference with the Community regime. Uniformity followed the price mechanism. In the Court's own words: 'in a sector covered by a common organisation, *a fortiori where that organisation is based on a common pricing system*, Member States can no longer take action, through national provisions taken unilaterally, affecting the machinery of price formation at the production and marketing stages established under the common organisation'. It followed that 'the functioning of a common organisation of the markets and *in particular the formation of producer prices* must in principle be governed by the general Community provisions as laid down in general rules amended annually, with the result that any specific interference with this functioning is strictly limited to the cases for which express provision has been made'.[152]

This connection between the regulatory architecture of the old CAP and the insistence on legislative uniformity has also been emphasized in academic analysis:

[I]n principle, every element of the intervention mechanism has to be regulated by the Community. As a result, common market organizations are characterized by a multitude of explicit and implicit prohibitions for the Member States. The Court's doctrine on the division of powers between the Community and Member States in the field of price intervention and the near-absolute prohibition of any unilateral action can largely be explained in terms of the uniformity requirement. It is standing case law that any unilateral intervention in the common mechanism of price formation is excluded. . .This explains why under a common system of price intervention the role of the Member States is limited to a strict application to individual cases of the Community rules concerned. . . By its very nature price intervention cannot take the form of framework legislation which has to be worked out by Member States according to their own situations and administrative structures.[153]

---

[152] Case C-283/03 *AH Kuipers v Productschap Zuivel*, paras 42, 49.
[153] R Barents, *The Agricultural Law of the EC*, 227–8, 235–7.

European federalism was in a stranglehold of the price mechanism. The ever greater 'centrifugal influence of the price intervention system on the agricultural legislation' had already emerged in the 1970s.[154] Shaken by monetary fluctuations in exchange rates, an ever more sophisticated intervention system had been put in place to stabilize the common market and bridge price differences between national agricultural markets. Beginning with monetary compensatory amounts and moving to export refunds, new subsidy mechanisms and non-marketing premiums as well as conversation premiums, the Community system became increasingly complex and averse to outside national 'interferences'. The impact of such a regulatory architecture on the division of legislative power between the Community and the Member States was decisive.[155] The vertical approach, combined with the price support system, aligned the CAP to a dual federal philosophy.

Has this changed? The reform efforts of the last decade will indeed substantially alter the structure of European agricultural law. The shift from product to producer support is 'likely to have a substantial effect on the structure and features of Community agricultural law' with 'consequences for the tasks of the Community legislator, the division of powers between the Community and the Member States'.[156] The gradual abandonment of the price mechanism will potentially lead to a breaking up of (largely) occupied fields and, thereby, free legislative space for the national legislators. 'As a consequence, Community agricultural law will lose to an increasing extent its rather uniform character resulting from the formal equality brought about by price intervention'.[157] What were these fundamental reforms? Will they cause a shift from a (predominantly) dual to a (predominantly) cooperative federalism in the structure of European agricultural law?

a. Restructuring the CAP: From Product to Producer Support

The 'old' CAP had been designed in a situation of agricultural insufficiency in Europe. This situation had dramatically changed after only two decades.

---

[154] Ibid 377.

[155] Ibid 367: 'The uniformity principle has decisively influenced the structure of Community agricultural law. It explains, *inter alia*, why the position of the operator under the market and price policy is almost exclusively a matter of Community law and why, in general, the role of the Member States is limited to the strict application of the Community legislation. Moreover, this feature has significantly contributed to the legalistic structure of this field of law, as any divergent practice on the level may undermine its effectiveness and thus has to be prevented by the laying down of Community rules. The result is a strong centralization of agricultural legislation'.

[156] Ibid 365.

[157] Ibid 371.

Modern agricultural production methods have led to an impressive agricultural surplus in the Community. Yet, due to the price mechanism within the Community, this surplus could not be automatically sold off on the world market as Community prices were above the world market level. By the end of the 1980s, internal and external pressure on the CAP had increased to such an extent that reform seemed inevitable.[158] First attempts to change the structure of European agricultural law started in 1992. The MacSharry reforms reduced the price support for cereals (and beef) and started the process of 'decoupling' the CAP from product support. This was not (yet) a comprehensive reform. The latter was finally suggested in the 'Agenda 2000'.[159] The Commission felt it was 'now time to formulate concrete proposals to reshape the common agricultural policy and prepare it for the next century'. There was 'an urgent need' for 'a greater decentralisation of policy implementation, with more margin being left to Member States and regions'. The Commission thus proposed 'deepening and extending the 1992 reform through further shifts from price support to direct payments, and developing a coherent rural policy to accompany this process'.[160] The Agenda 2000 proposals would structure the CAP into two 'pillars': income support and rural development.[161]

Reforms in both pillars would be continued and reviewed in 2002, when the Commission undertook a 'mid-term review'.[162] The review acknowledged the need to enhance the competitiveness of European agriculture by 'completing the shift from product to producer support with the introduction of a decoupled system of payments per farm'. It equally recognized the need to '[s]trengthen rural development by transferring funds from the first to the second pillar of the CAP via the introduction of an EU-wide system of compulsory dynamic modulation and expanding the scope of currently available instruments for rural development to promote food quality, meet higher

---

[158] LA Patterson, *Agricultural Policy Reform in the European Community: a Three-level Game Analysis*, 135.

[159] Commission, *Agenda 2000 for a stronger and wider Union*.

[160] Ibid 26–9.

[161] The major legislative fruit of the second pillar was Regulation 1257/1999 on support for rural development from the European Agricultural Guidance and Guarantee Fund ('EAGGF'), whose Article 1 states: '(1) This Regulation establishes the framework for Community support for sustainable rural development. (2) Rural development measures shall accompany and complement other instruments of the common agricultural policy and thus contribute to the achievement of the objectives laid down in Article 33 of the Treaty'.

[162] Commission, *Communication: Mid-Term Review of the Common Agricultural Policy*.

standards and foster animal welfare'.[163] To ensure a fair standard of living for farmers, the loss of farm income through cuts in agricultural prices would be 'cushioned' by compensating farmers through direct payments.[164] This did not necessarily mean total 'decoupling'. However, '[i]n order to achieve the proper balance in maximising the benefits of decoupling, the Commission propose[d] to accomplish the final step in the shift of support from product to producer by introducing a system of a single income payment per farm'. 'Such a system would integrate all existing direct payments a producer receives from various schemes into this single payment, determined on the basis of historical references'.[165] As regards rural development, the Commission proposed 'to consolidate and strengthen the second pillar by increasing the scope of the accompanying measures and widening and clarifying the scope and level of certain measures'. This reinforcement of the Second Pillar was believed to lead to greater decentralization.[166]

In 2005, the Community adopted a new central legislative act for rural development.[167] More importantly still, the Community introduced the single farm payment. The central legislative act here was Regulation 1782/2003 establishing common rules for direct support for farmers. The Regulation introduced a Single Payment Scheme that was horizontal to, and independent of, production.[168] Full receipt of the direct payment would be conditional on complying with statutory management requirements as defined in—horizontal—Community legislation in the areas of public, animal, and plant health; the environment; and animal welfare.[169] This 'cross-compliance' mechanism was the second facet of the new system of horizontal harmonization.

From 2003 onwards, the Community also started to reform each European CMO by inserting the single payment scheme. Substantive reform would—at this stage—be confined to some sectors in the first pillar.[170] However, the move towards horizontal legislation would lead to proposals to bring all

---

[163] Ibid 3.

[164] Ibid 7.

[165] Ibid 19.

[166] Ibid 24 and 10.

[167] Regulation 1698/2005 on support for rural development by the European Agricultural Fund for Rural Development ('EAFRD').

[168] However, the Community legislator did not favour total decoupling; see: Chapter 5 of the Regulation.

[169] Article 4 of Regulation 1782/2003; and now: Article 5 of Regulation 73/2009.

[170] Cf Regulation 318/2006 (Sugar), Regulation 1182/2007 (Fruit and Vegetables), and Regulation 479/2008 (Wine).

existing sectoral market organizations under the umbrella of a single CMO. This feat of technical simplification was achieved by Regulation 1234/2007—the 'Single CMO Regulation'. The new horizontal Regulation establishes a common structure for CMOs;[171] yet, it did not represent a major substantive reform as it still paid partial homage to price control through public intervention in the internal and external market.[172] However, by the end of 2007, the Commission conducted another review of the reform process in the form of a 'health check'.[173] These reform impulses translated, in May 2008, into a new package for agricultural legislation.[174] And an explanatory memorandum from the Commission now insisted that 'any remaining supply controls of the CAP (namely diary quotas and set aside) should be removed'.[175] This commitment was translated into three agricultural Regulations in January 2009.[176] The first Regulation thereby expressly continued the past reform effort: 'As was the case with the CAP reform of 2003, with a view to enhancing the competitiveness of Community agriculture and promoting market-oriented and sustainable agriculture, it is necessary to continue the shift from production support to producer support by abolishing the existing aids

---

[171] The Regulation would not cover all CMOs as Recital 8 clarified: 'Against this background, this Regulation should not include those parts of CMOs which are subject to policy reforms. This is the case with regard to most parts of the fruit and vegetables, processed fruit and vegetables and the wine sectors. The provisions contained in the respective Regulations (EC) 2200/96, (EC) 2201/96 and (EC) 1493/1999 should, therefore, be incorporated into this Regulation only to the extent that they are not themselves subject to any policy reforms. The substantive provisions of these CMOs should only be incorporated once the respective reforms have been enacted'.

[172] Parts II and III of Regulation 1782/2003.

[173] Commission, *Communication: Preparing for the 'Health Check' of the CAP Reform*.

[174] COM (2008) 306 final: Proposal for a Council Regulation establishing common rules for direct support schemes for farmers under the common agricultural policy and establishing certain support schemes for farmers; Proposal for a Council Regulation on modifications to the common agricultural policy by amending Regulations (EC) 320/2006, (EC) 1234/2007, (EC) 3/2008 and (EC) [. . .]/2008, Proposal for a Council Regulation amending Regulation (EC) 1698/2005 on support for rural development by the European Agricultural Fund for Rural Development ('EAFRD') and Proposal for a Council Regulation amending Decision 2006/144/EC on the Community strategic guidelines for rural development (programming period 2007 to 2013).

[175] Ibid 3. However, according to the Commission, these proposals, while making a contribution to the overall reform effort, would not constitute a new fundamental reform (ibid 4).

[176] Regulation 72/2009 on modifications to the Common Agricultural Policy by amending Regulations 247/2006, 320/2006, 1405/2006, 3/2008 and 479/2008 and repealing Regulations 1883/78, 1254/89, 2247/89, 2055/93, 1868/94, 2596/97, 1182/2005 and 315/2007; Regulation 73/2009 establishing common rules for direct support schemes for farmers under the Common Agricultural Policy and establishing certain support schemes for farmers, amending Regulations 1290/2005, 247/2006, 378/2007 and repealing Regulation 1782/2003; and, finally, Regulation 74/2009 amending Regulation 1698/2005 on support for rural development by the European Agricultural Fund for Rural Development ('EAFRD').

in the Single CMO Regulation for dried fodder, flax, hemp and potato starch and integrating support for these products into the system of decoupled income support for each farm'.[177]

b. The Rise of Cooperative Federalism: 'Breaking up' Occupied Fields?

Today's CAP is based on two pillars. In relation to the first pillar, the 2003 reforms had introduced a gradual shift from product to producer support. This was the heart of the changing structure of the CAP. 'La pierre angulaire de cette nouvelle étape du processus de réforme agricole lancé en 1992 est le principe de découpage : couper le lien entre soutien au revenu agricole et la production'.[178] Decoupling will eventually restructure all CMOs. Under the new regulatory system, farmers will be eligible to receive direct income support. Payment would not only come from Community sources, but so-called 'national envelopes' may exist. '[A] Community-wide scheme with uniform payments to all producers would be too rigid to respond adequately to the structural and natural disparities and the diverse needs resulting therefrom'.[179] In the light of this new regulatory architecture, can we identify a move towards greater decentralization and cooperative federalism? Would the 'new approach' under the CAP lead to a breaking up of (largely) 'occupied fields' through a revival of shared national regulatory responsibilities?

There is an element of speculation involved in attempting to answer these questions. However, even if we have to wait until the European Courts give us authoritative guidance, the very structure of the new agricultural legislation already proves insightful. Let us concentrate on the recently reformed CMO in wine.[180] Are there structural elements indicative of cooperative federalism? The new Community regime envisages the existence of *national*

---

[177] Regulation 72/2009, Recital 12.

[178] V Adam, *Les droits à paiement, une création juridique innovante de la réforme de la politique agricole commune*, 96.

[179] Regulation 1254/1999, Recital 15 (and Articles 14–20). The discretion left to the Member States in the context of environmental protection has also been regarded as 'considerable' under the 1999 'horizontal regulation' (M Cardwell, *The European Model of Agriculture*, 259): 'What is clear is that Agenda 2000 reforms have offered sufficient latitude for Member States to implement very different programs on grounds which may be objectively justified, but which may have very different financial impacts on participants... [I]n the context of environmental measures, it is also clear that Member States enjoy the ability both to retain and introduce higher national standards' (ibid 261–2).

[180] Regulation 479/2008 on the common organization of the market in wine amending Regulations 1493/1999, 1782/2003, 1290/2005, 3/2008 and repealing Regulations 2392/86 and 1493/1999.

support programmes to finance support measures in the wine sector.[181] Each Member States is free to choose the geographical level at which it wishes to implement these measures and may accommodate regional particularities, but must submit a draft five-year support programme to the Commission.[182] In the context of the Community's grubbing-up scheme, 'complementary national aid' is expressly provided for in Article 106 of the Regulation.

Apart from these cooperative administrative structures, can we even find instances where Member States are expressly granted legislative freedom under the Regulation? One instance is offered by Article 28 allowing Member States to 'provide for more stringent restrictions for wines author-ised under Community law produced in their territory with a view to rein-forcing the preservation of the essential characteristics of wines with a protected designation of origin or protected geographical indication and of sparkling wines and liqueur wines'. Another cooperative federal sign can be seen in the title on production potential and dealing with planting rights. Article 96 states: 'Member States may adopt stricter national rules in respect of the award of new planting rights or replanting rights'. While these instances may be regarded as signs of a more cooperative legislative arrangement in a specific—vertical—market organization, the real break with the CAP's dual federalist past will need to be 'ratified' by the Court. For the reasons referred to above, the decline of the price mechanism and the rise of direct income support is likely to introduce a less aggressive pre-emption standard into this field.

Can we also see concrete evidence for a move towards cooperative federal-ism in the CAP's second pillar? The new Regulation on rural development expressly states that '[a]ction by the Community should be complementary to that carried out by the Member States or seek to contribute to it'. Complementary European action was deemed necessary as the objectives of rural development 'cannot be achieved sufficiently by the Member States given the links between it and other instruments of the common agricultural policy, the context of the disparities between the various rural areas and the limits in the financial resources of the Member States in an enlarged Union'.[183] Article 4 of the Regulation defines the three objectives of the Community's rural development policy as improving the competitiveness of the agricul-tural sector, improving the environment and the countryside, and improving

---

[181] Article 2 of Regulation 479/2008.
[182] Article 5 of Regulation 479/2008.
[183] Recitals 4 and 5 of Regulation 1698/2005.

the quality of life in rural areas as well as diversification of the rural economy. And Article 5 obliges the Community to 'complement national, regional and local actions contributing to the Community's priorities'. Article 7—entitled 'Subsidiarity'—charges the Member States with the responsibility for implementing the rural development programmes at the appropriate territorial level, according to their own institutional arrangements. The commitment to the principle of subsidiarity is translated into the mechanism of national strategy plans.[184] Under the Regulation, the European Agricultural Fund for Rural Development will refund costs incurred in the pursuit of rural development. In accordance with the principle of subsidiarity,[185] '[t]he rules on eligibility of expenditure shall be set at national level, subject to the special conditions laid down by this Regulation for certain rural development measures'.[186]

Europe's agricultural law, it seems, is opening up to the principle of subsidiarity.

Conclusion: European Federalism and Shared Powers

The great majority of the European Union's powers are shared competences. Here, two governments—the European and the national ones—may co-legislate in the same area at the same time. The presence of shared competences within a federal order will not in itself signify a choice in favour of cooperative federalism. The constitutional experience of the American—and German—federation proves that a dual federalist rationale may equally structure non-exclusive competences.[187]

Various types of legislative conflict have been recognized in the jurisprudence of the European Court of Justice and—borrowing the terminology of American federalism—we have termed them 'field', 'obstacle', and 'rule' pre-emption. The use of field pre-emption reflects a dual federalist philosophy: the total exclusion of national legislators maintains the idea of two mutually exclusive legislative spheres. Softer pre-emption types, by way of

---

[184] Ibid Articles 10–14.
[185] Ibid Recital 61.
[186] Ibid Article 71(3).
[187] For the American legal order, see: Chapter 2 above; and for the German legal order, see: R Schütze, *German Constitutional Federalism: Between* Sein *and* Bewußtsein.

contrast, will represent a cooperative federalist paradigm. Here, the national legislator can legislate within the same field with the European legislator.

In search of the European Community's federal philosophy, this chapter has analysed two substantive policy areas that represent the regulatory core of the European Union: the Community's harmonization policy in relation to the free movement of goods, and the common agricultural policy. As regards the former, the transition from the 'old' to the 'new' approach to harmonization could be identified with a move from dual to cooperative federalism. While not eliminating field pre-emption from the scope of the harmonization programme altogether, the new approach's focus on the satisfaction of essential health and safety requirements was more conducive to legislative cooperation. Instead of pre-empting all national laws within an occupied field, softer types of pre-emption would be allowed to emerge. Minimum harmonization thereby represents the emblem of legislative cooperation: European legislation would set a mandatory legislative frame which the Member States could fill in if they wanted to. The rise of minimum harmonization therefore represents a constitutional milestone on the road towards cooperative federalism.

The transition towards a more cooperative federal model could equally be seen in the CAP. Here the Community legal order has traditionally employed an aggressive pre-emption criterion, which almost approached the pre-emptive power of field pre-emption. The CAP thus tended towards a dual federal philosophy. Yet, it was argued that there are signs that the Community legal order is here too in the process of creating cooperative European law. The gradual decline of the price mechanism and the shift from product to producer support constitutes the most radical reform of the CAP ever since the inception of the Community. This reform will cause a fundamental change in the structure of European agricultural law with important 'consequences for the tasks of the Community legislator, the division of powers between the Community and the Member States'.[188] We speculated that the reform of the regulatory architecture governing the CAP has and will necessarily involve the repeal of old Community agricultural legislation. Vertical—that is: product-specific—Community legislation will increasingly be replaced by horizontal legislation. This evolution will thus parallel the shift caused by the 1985 White Paper and the 'new approach' to harmonization. If this is the case, national governments will regain legislative space to adopt stricter national measures within hitherto (largely) occupied agricultural fields.

[188] R Barents, *The Agricultural Law of the EC*, 365.

This re-opening of national legislative spaces would bring the CAP closer to the philosophy of cooperative federalism.

Let us raise an afterthought. Is the European legislator constitutionally entitled to decentralize? A negative answer would condemn the re-nationalization reforms in the areas of harmonizaton, agriculture (and competition law) to the constitutional gallows. The argument has indeed been made that the *acquis communautaire* constitutionally prevents the Community legislator from breaking up occupied fields in order to create legislative spaces for national legislators.[189] The reasoning goes as follows: where the Community had established complete harmonization, the repealing Community legislator would have to demonstrate that the deregulatory measure would equally well achieve the integration of national markets.[190] The integrationist bias of the Community legal order would thus have a blocking effect. It permanently solidifies legislative exclusivity. Where the Community legislator deregulates, this deregulation would not mean decentralization. The field remains totally occupied by the Community legislator; only now it reflects its intention to leave the field totally unregulated.[191] Such a view brings legislative exclusivity close to constitutional exclusivity.[192]

Adherents of this—wrong—view have referred to *Ramel* to support the idea of the protected status of the achieved level of integration.[193] There, the Court had found that the Community's legislative powers must 'be exercised from the perspective of the unity of the market'. 'Any prejudice to what the Community has achieved in relation to the unity of the market moreover risks opening the way to mechanisms which would lead to disintegration contrary to the objectives of progressive approximation of the economic policies of the Member States set out in Article 2 of the Treaty'.[194] However, these passages only superficially lend themselves to prohibiting

---

[189] On the concept of the *acquis communautaire*, see: C Delcourt, *The Acquis Communautaire: Has the Concept had its Day?*.

[190] On this point, see: D Dittert, *Die ausschließlichen Kompetenzen der Europäischen Gemeinschaft im System des EG-Vertrags*, 131.

[191] Ibid 132–3.

[192] K Lenaerts & P van Yersele, *Le principe de subsidiarité et son contexte: étude de l'article 3B du traité CE*, 22–3 : 'Par conséquent, les exercices de pouvoir ne sont réversibles que si la restitution de leur compétence aux Etats membres permet de réaliser aussi bien ou mieux les objectifs du traité… Ces considérations montrent que, quant à leurs effets concrets, les compétences exclusives par exercice ont tendance à se rapprocher des compétences exclusives par nature'.

[193] Joined Cases 80 and 81/77 *Societé Les Commissionnaires Réunis SARL v Receveur des douanes ; SARL Les fils de Henri Ramel v Receveur des douanes*.

[194] Ibid paras 35–6.

re-nationalization.[195] Indeed, we can easily find a case illustrating the constitutionality of revoking the exhaustive nature of EC legislation in *Cidrerie Ruwet*.[196] Revocability is not only constitutionally possible; it has been applied in the past to mean decentralization.[197] (This 'empirical' result would be confirmed by the Lisbon Treaty. The latter expressly refers to the possibility of legislative re-nationalization.[198]) Shared competences are indeed no one way road. They permit centralization as well as decentralization; and thus allow the European legislator to periodically change the federal structure of European law.

---

[195] These statements must be seen in the context of the special constitutional regime set up for the free movement of agricultural goods: according to Article 32(2) EC, the general principles for the free movement of goods would apply save as otherwise provided in Articles 33 to 38 EC. A Community regulation had allowed Member States to limit intra-Community trade in wine by introducing charges (cf Regulation 816/70 laying down additional provisions for the common organization of the market in wine), and it therefore became 'necessary to find in [Articles 33 to 38] a provision which either expressly or by necessary implication provides for or authorizes the introduction of such charges' (para 26). The Court found no such provision in the Treaty. The Community measure's authorization to reintroduce import charges created an obstacle to trade that was therefore contrary to the Treaty. The judgment in no way implies that the Community legislator would be bound by the entire *acquis communautaire*. It was the fundamental free movement provisions—and not past legislative acts—that posed a limit to the discretion of the Community legislator. The absolute protection of the *acquis communautaire* cannot be derived from this ruling.

[196] Case C-3/99 *Cidrerie Ruwet SA v Cidre Stassen SA and HP Bulmer Ltd*. Directive 75/106 on the harmonization of pre-packaged liquids had originally undertaken 'full harmonization' to overcome all obstacles to the free movement of certain liquid foodstuffs. To that effect, Article 4(2) excluded the marketing of pre-packages of volumes that differed from those exhaustively listed in Annex III of the Directive—this was the so-called exclusivity clause—while Article 5 guaranteed the free movement of products complying with the Community standard. The exclusivity of the uniform Community standard had been repealed by amending legislation. Henceforth, the Community regime represented only 'partial harmonization'. Member States were again entitled to permit the marketing of pre-packages that differed from those indicated in Annex III (ibid para 43). While many Member States had reintroduced diverse national standards, in the present case, Belgium had not repealed the previously exclusive uniform Community standard within its territory. The question thus arose as to how the by now partial harmonization would interact with the free movement principles, in particular, the principle of moderated mutual recognition under *Cassis de Dijon*.

[197] Cf K Lenarts & D Geradin, *Decentralisation of EC competition law enforcement: judges in the frontline*.

[198] According to Declaration 18, the European Union may decide to 'cease exercising its competence'. This re-opening of legislative space arises 'when the relevant EU institutions decide to repeal a legislative act, in particular better to ensure constant respect for the principles of subsidiarity and proportionality'.

5

Cooperative Federalism Constitutionalized

Introduction: The Constitutional Safeguards of Cooperative Federalism

Within shared competences, the acceptance of complementary national legislation had been a *political* choice for the European legislator. Legislative discretion determined the degree to which national legislators would be pre-empted by European legislation. Where the Community legislator intended to field pre-empt the States, no constitutional device could stop it. The Single European Act would restrict this constitutional liberty. It elevated the philosophy of cooperative federalism from a *legislative* to a *constitutional* phenomenon through two novel constitutional ideas: the principle of subsidiarity, and complementary competences. The Treaty on European Union broadened these two constitutional devices to *general* safeguards of European federalism. Both safeguards were designed to provide a 'way of reconciling what for many appears to be irreconcilable: the emergence of a united Europe and loyalty to one's homeland; the need for a European power capable of tackling the problems of our age and the absolute necessity to preserve our roots in the shape of our nations and regions; and decentralization of responsibilities, so that we never entrust to a bigger unit anything that is best done by a smaller one'.[1]

The origin of the principle of subsidiarity in the European legal order has remained mysterious. (Nor are there any clear evolutionary lines for its development.) The principle has even been decried as 'totally alien' to the European legal order.[2] Yet celebrated as the principle that 'save[d] Maastricht',[3] subsidiarity has not left the European constitutional imagination ever since. The principle was designed—in a constitutional moment of immense centralization—to provide a safeguard for decentralized federalism. With the scope of the European legal universe expanding and the institutional arrangements

---

[1] J Delors, *Address at the College of Europe in Bruges*, 110.

[2] The subsidiarity principle would be 'totally alien to' the European Union, since it 'contradicts the logic, structure and wording of the founding treaties and the jurisprudence of the European Court of Justice' (AG Toth, *The Principle of Subsidiarity in the Maastricht Treaty*, 1079). This—radical—misunderstanding derives from a dual federalist reading of the European Union: 'In all matters transferred to the Community, the Community's competence is in principle exclusive and leaves no room for any concurrent competence on the part of the Member States. On the other hand, over matters not brought within Community competence or which have been expressly allocated to the Member States, the latter exercise exclusive competence'. 'Therefore, where the competence of the Community begins, that of the Member States ends' (ibid 1080–1).

[3] DZ Cass, *The Word that Saves Maastricht? The Principle of Subsidiarity and the Division of Powers within the European Community.*

deepening, the Member States placed their hopes in a principle that should limit the exercise of the European Union's powers. Would their hopes be redeemed? The evolution and meaning of the Community principle of subsidiarity will be discussed in the first section of this chapter. We shall see that European constitutionalism has favoured the procedural dimension of the subsidiarity principle. The principle of subsidiarity is—predominantly—viewed as a *political* safeguard of federalism in the European legal order.

This contrasts with the second constitutional devise: complementary competences. While the division of legislative powers between a federation and its members is a central task of every federal constitution, a typology of competences is *not* an essential element of federalism.[4] Where such a typology exists, different types of competences constitutionally pitch the degree of legislative responsibility of each level in relation to the other. Each competence category represents a calibrated quantum of legislative power. The existence of complementary competences in the Community legal order expresses a *substantive* commitment towards cooperative federalism. The federal balance is not left to the vagaries of the political process. Under complementary competences, the primary legislative responsibility of the States is constitutionally acknowledged as these competences only entitle the federal legislator to *complement* State legislation. These competences thus constitutionalize the philosophy of cooperative federalism: the Union and the States 'are mutually complementary parts of a *single* governmental mechanism all of whose powers are intended to realize the current purposes of government according to their applicability to the problem at hand'.[5] We shall discuss the emergence and structure of complementary competences as judicial safeguards of federalism in the second section of this chapter.

I. The Principle of Subsidiarity: A Political Safeguard of Federalism

'[T]hree correcting words of the legislator and entire libraries are turned into maculature'.[6] Worse still: three additional words and entire libraries may be

---

[4] American federalism relies—with the exception of foreign affairs—on a pre-emption typology and has not generated a competence typology like European or German federalism, cf Chapter 2 above.

[5] ES Corwin, *The Passing of Dual Federalism*, 19.

[6] JH von Kirchmann, *Die Wertlosigkeit der Jurisprudenz als Wissenschaft*, 23 (translation—RS).

filled again with learned commentaries. Libraries have indeed been filled since the introduction of three magic words into the Community legal order: the 'principle of subsidiarity'.[7]

Where did the principle come from and how would it change the structure of European law? Subsidiarity—the quality of being 'subsidiary'—derives from *subsidium*. The Latin concept evolved in the military context. It represented an 'assistance' or 'aid' that stayed in the background. An entity is subsidiary where it provides a 'subsidy'—an assistance of subordinate or secondary importance. In political philosophy, the principle of subsidiarity came to represent the idea 'that a central authority should have a subsidiary function, performing only those tasks which cannot be performed effectively at a more immediate or local level'.[8] The principle was invoked in 1891 by the Catholic Church in its attempt to find the middle ground between capitalism

---

[7] From the—abundant—literature, see only: G Barrett, *'The King is dead, long live the king': the Recasting by the Treaty of Lisbon of the Provisions of the Constitutional Treaty concerning National Parliaments*; G Berman, *Taking Subsidiarity Seriously: Federalism in the European Community and the United States*; N Bernard, *The Future of European Economic Law in the Light of the Principle of Subsidiarity*; R von Borries, *Das Subsidiaritätsprinzip im Recht der Europäischen Union*; G de Búrca, *Reappraising Subsidiarity Significance after Amsterdam*; C Calliess, *Subsidiaritäts- und Solidaritätsprinzip in der Europäischen Union*; DZ Cass, *The Word that Saves Maastricht? The Principle of Subsidiarity and the Division of Powers within the European Community*; V Constantinesco, *Who's Afraid of Subsidiarity?*; I Cooper, *The Watchdogs of Subsidiarity: National Parliaments and the Logic of Arguing in the EU*; G Cross, *Subsidiarity and the Environment*; G Davies, *Subsidiarity: The Wrong Idea, in the Wrong Place, at the Wrong Time*; N Emiliou, *Subsidiarity: An Effective Barrier Against 'the Enterprises of Ambition'?*; K Endo, *Subsidiarity and its Enemies: To what Extent is Sovereignty contested in the Mixed Commonwealth of Europe*; A Estella, *The EU Principle of Subsidiarity and its Critique*; JP Gonzalez, *The Principle of Subsidiarity: (a Guide for Lawyers with a Particular Community Orientation)*; AG Soares, *Pre-emption, Conflicts of Powers and Subsidiarity*; P Häberle, *Das Prinzip der Subsidiarität aus der Sicht der vergleichenden Verfassungslehre*; K Lenaerts & P van Ypersele, *Le principe de subsidiarité et son contexte: étude de l'article 3B du traité CE*; K Lenaerts, *Subsidiarity and Community Competence in the Field of Education*; K Lenaerts, *The Principle of Subsidiarity and the Environment in the European Union: Keeping the Balance of Federalism*; Lord Mackenzie-Stuart, *Subsidiarity—A Busted Flush?*; W Moersch, *Leistungsfähigkeit und Grenzen des Subsidiaritätsprinzips*; P-C Müller-Graf, *Binnenmarktauftrag und Subsidiaritätsprinzip*; P Pescatore, *Mit der Subsidiarität leben*; T Schilling, *A New Dimension of Subsidiarity: Subsidiarity as a Rule and a Principle*; B Schima, *Das Subsidiaritätsprinzip im Europäischen Gemeinschaftsrecht*; J Steiner, *Subsidiarity under the Maastricht Treaty*; C Stewing, *Subsidiarität und Föderalismus in der Europäischen Union*; ET Swaine, *Subsidiarity and Self-Interest: Federalism at the European Court of Justice*; AG Toth, *The Principle of Subsidiarity in the Maastricht Treaty*; AG Toth, *Is Subsidiarity Justiciable?*; M Wilke & H Wallace, *Subsidiarity: Approaches to Power-sharing in the European Community*; D Wilkinson, *Maastricht and the Environment: The Implications for the EC's Environment Policy of the Treaty on European Union*; G Winter, *Subsidiarität und Deregulierung im Gemeinschaftsrecht*; D Wyatt, *Subsidiarity and Judicial Review*.

[8] Oxford English Dictionary: 'subsidiary' and 'subsidiarity'.

(individualism) and communism (collectivism).[9] It received its celebrated form forty years later in the Encyclical Quadragesimo Anno:

As history abundantly proves, it is true that on account of changed conditions many things which were done by small associations in former times cannot be done now save by large associations. Still, that most weighty principle, which cannot be set aside or changed, remains fixed and unshaken in social philosophy: Just as it is gravely wrong to take from individuals what they can accomplish by their own initiative and industry and give it to the community, so also it is an injustice and at the same time a grave evil and disturbance of right order to assign to a greater and higher association what lesser and subordinate organizations can do. For every social activity ought of its very nature to furnish help [subsidium] to the members of the body social, and never destroy and absorb them.

The supreme authority of the State ought, therefore, to let subordinate groups handle matters and concerns of lesser importance, which would otherwise dissipate its efforts greatly. Thereby the State will more freely, powerfully, and effectively do all those things that belong to it alone because it alone can do them: directing, watching, urging, restraining, as occasion requires and necessity demands. Therefore, those in power should be sure that the more perfectly a graduated order is kept among the various associations, in observance of the principle of 'subsidiary function,' the stronger social authority and effectiveness will be the happier and more prosperous the condition of the State.[10]

Subsidiarity was to achieve 'unity arising from the harmonious arrangement of many objects';[11] and in attempting to reconcile unity with diversity, subsidiarity could become a topos for centralizers and decentralizers alike.

---

[9] The idea that responsibility should be divided between smaller and larger social groupings had not been invented by the Catholic Church (cf K Endo, *Subsidiarity and its Enemies: To what Extent is Sovereignty contested in the Mixed Commonwealth of Europe*, 9). However, the idea of subsidiary social organizations re-emerged in the Encyclical 'Rerum Novarum' (*Of New Things*, 1891). In para 14 we read: 'The contention, then, that the civil government should at its option intrude into and exercise intimate control over the family and the household is a great and pernicious error. True, if a family finds itself in exceeding distress, utterly deprived of the counsel of friends, and without any prospect of extricating itself, it is right that extreme necessity be met by public aid, since each family is a part of the commonwealth. In like manner, if within the precincts of the household there occur grave disturbance of mutual rights, public authority should intervene to force each party to yield to the other its proper due; for this is not to deprive citizens of their rights, but justly and properly to safeguard and strengthen them. But the rulers of the commonwealth must go no further; here, nature bids them stop'. For an analysis of the application of the subsidiarity principle *inside* the Church, see: JA Komonchak, *Subsidiarity in the Church: The State of the Question*.

[10] Pope Pius XI, *Quadragesimo Anno: Encyclical on Reconstruction of the Social Order*, paras 79–80.

[11] Ibid para 84.

Indeed, the principle has a positive and a negative aspect.[12] It positively encourages 'large associations' to assist smaller ones, where they needed help; and it negatively discourages 'to assign to a greater and higher association what lesser and subordinate organizations can do'. It is this dual character that has given the principle of subsidiarity its 'Janus-like' character.[13] But there was a second ambivalence surrounding subsidiarity. '[S]ubsidiarity can be applied in two different situations: on the one hand, the dividing line between the private sphere and that of the State, in the broad meaning of the term; on the other hand, the repartition of tasks between the different levels of political power'.[14] In the former situation, subsidiarity operates as a *liberal* principle in defending *private* freedom against public intervention. In the latter scenario, it functions as a *federal* principle in defending smaller *public* communities against larger ones. We shall concentrate on the *federal* dimension of the subsidiarity principle and ignore its liberal connotations.[15]

When did the subsidiarity principle become a *constitutional* principle? The legal principle of subsidiarity emerged as a—contested—principle of German constitutional law.[16] Indeed, it is through the medium of German constitutionalism that the principle of subsidiarity enters into the European legal order.[17] This section will—first—discuss the textual evolution of the federal principle of subsidiarity. We shall see that—originally—there were two potential meanings of the principle of subsidiarity in the European legal order. The principle was invoked as a *meta*-constitutional guide for the division of competences as well as a *constitutional* restraint on the exercise of those competences granted to the centre.[18] The constitutional codification

---

[12] C Calliess, *Subsidiaritäts- und Solidaritätsprinzip in der Europäischen Union*, 26.

[13] V Constantinesco, *Who's Afraid of Subsidiarity?*, 35.

[14] J Delors, *The Principle of Subsidiarity: Contribution to the Debate*, 7.

[15] This is not to forget that it was the liberal dimension that had been propagated in the papal encyclicals. In dealing with the relation between public and private power, the liberal principle of subsidiarity is broader. In the Community legal order, we encounter both dimensions of the subsidiarity principle. We see the restrictive—federal—dimension of subsidiarity in Article 5(2) EC and discover the broader—liberal—dimension of subsidiarity in the Preamble of the TEU. While the former is a constitutional principle, the latter is of a *meta*-constitutional nature. It urges the European Union 'to continue the process of creating an ever closer union among the peoples of Europe, in which decisions are taken as closely as possible to the citizen in accordance with the principle of subsidiarity'. On the liberal principle of subsidiarity, see: C Millon-Delsol, *L' État Subsidiare*.

[16] On the German *constitutional* principle of subsidiarity, see: J Issensee, *Subsidiaritätsprinzip und Verfassungsrecht*.

[17] Ibid 333.

[18] Both dimensions of the principle can be found in the European Parliament's 1990 Resolution on the Principle of Subsidiarity: '[T]he principle of subsidiarity is important not only as a means of

of subsidiarity in Article 5(2) EC would limit the principle to the second meaning. Subsidiarity was to function as a constitutional safeguard of federalism that should limit the *exercise* of powers granted to the European Union. A textual genealogy of the principle will be offered in a first subsection. In the last decade, various reform proposals have been made to strengthen subsidiarity. These *de lege ferenda* suggestions will be discussed in a second subsection.

1. *Subsidiarity* De Lege Lata: *A Textual Genealogy*

Since when has the principle of subsidiarity been a *Community* principle? We find an early textual reference in the 'Report on European Union' in 1975. The Commission had responded to the invitation to reflect upon 'the major objective of transforming, before the end of the present decade and with the fullest respect for the Treaties already signed, the whole complex of the relations of the Member States into a European Union'.[19] Dealing with the '[d]ivision of fields of competence between Union and Member States', the Report argued the following. 'No more than the existing Communities have done so, the European Union is not to give birth to a centralizing superstate. Consequently, and in accordance with the *principe de subsidiarité*, the Union will be given responsibility only for those matters which the Member States are no longer capable of dealing with efficiently.' '[I]n deciding on the Union's competence, application of the *principe de subsidiarité* is restricted by the fact that the Union must be given extensive enough competency for its cohesion to be ensured'.[20] Subsidiarity was thus—primarily—defined as a principle governing the *meta-constitutional* allocation of competences.[21]

---

clearly defining the respective competences of the Community and the Member States, but also in respect of the way those competences are exercised' (ibid para 11). On the metaconstitutional and constitutional dimension of the principle of subsidiarity, see: K Lenaerts & P van Ypersele, *Le principe de subsidiarité et son contexte: étude de l'article 3B du traité CE*, 8–13.

[19] Conference of Heads of Government (Paris, 9–10 December 1974), *Final Communiqé*, point 13.

[20] Commission, *Report on European Union*, 10–11.

[21] However, in a subsequent passage, the Report also contained traces of a second meaning of the principle (ibid 16): 'Intervention by the Union in those fields should always be consonant with the *principe de subsidiarité* already mentioned. The Union's aim, therefore, would be to assume direct responsibility for problems for the solution of which the range of efficient action available to the Member States is insufficient. At the same time, it would endeavour to avoid divergent responses from the Member States which would threaten the cohesion of the Union. To this end, it is necessary: (a) to provide an overall framework for national policies by introducing common rules; and

This idea of subsidiarity was taken up by the European Parliament's 1984 'Draft Treaty establishing the European Union'.[22] Its preamble declared the intention 'to entrust common institutions, *in accordance with the principle of subsidiarity*, only with the powers required to complete successfully the tasks they may carry out more satisfactorily than the States acting independently'.[23] However, the Draft Treaty also contained an idea that was—in the future—to become the dominant version of the subsidiarity principle. Its article on competences stated: 'Where this Treaty confers concurrent competence on the Union, the Member States shall continue to act so long as the Union has not legislated. *The Union shall only act to carry out those tasks which may be undertaken more effectively in common than by the Member States acting separately, in particular those whose execution requires action by the Union because their dimension or effects extend beyond national frontiers*'.[24]

It was this second idea that would be translated into the first *de lege lata* expression of the principle of subsidiarity in the Community legal order. This was achieved by the Single European Act, albeit within the limited sphere of environmental policy. Having recognized the environment as an express competence, Article 130r(4) EEC stated: 'The Community shall take action relating to the environment to the extent to which the objectives referred to in paragraph 1 can be attained better at Community level than at the level of the individual Member States'. The Fifth Environmental Programme would subsequently provide a lengthy gloss on the subsidiarity principle in that context.[25] The Commission here expressly combined the principle of subsidiarity with the idea of 'shared responsibility'.[26] 'Since the objectives and targets put forward in the Programme and the ultimate goal of sustainable development can only be achieved by *concerted action* on the part of all the relevant actors working together in *partnership*, the Programme combines the principle of subsidiarity with the wider concept of *shared responsibility*. This latter concept involves not so much a choice of action at one level to the exclusion of others but, rather, *a mixing of actors*

(b) to give the institutions of the Union their own instruments and facilities for exerting direct influence on certain structures or certain factors of economic development'.

[22] On this point, see: V Constantinesco, *Division of Fields of Competence between the Union and the Member States in the Draft Treaty establishing the European Union*.

[23] Draft Treaty, Last Recital (emphasis added).

[24] Article 12(2) Draft Treaty (emphasis added).

[25] Commission, *Towards Sustainability: A European Community Programme of Policy and Action in Relation to the Environment and Sustainable Development*.

[26] Ibid Chapter 8.

and instruments at the appropriate levels, without any calling into question of the division of competences between the Community, the Member States, regional and local authorities.' Important was the '*complementarity of actions at different levels within an overall framework of subsidiarity and shared responsibility*'.[27]

The Treaty on European Union lifted the subsidiarity principle out of its environmental confines and broadened it to a general constitutional principle. This elevation of subsidiarity came at a time when the Community resolutely continued its path away from decisional intergovernmentalism. With the political safeguards of federalism in the Council loosened, a new constitutional principle was searched for to protect the Member States from the dangers of *over*-centralization. Placed into the part of the Treaty dealing with 'Principles', the Maastricht Treaty cut with the tradition that identified subsidiarity with the allocation of competences. In distinguishing the enumeration principle from the subsidiarity principle, the latter was confined to restrict the *exercise*—not the existence—of the Union's competences. Subsidiarity would set limits *intra vires*.[28] This constitutional function was codified in Article 5(2) EC: 'In areas that do not fall within its exclusive competence, the Community shall take action, in accordance with the principle of subsidiarity, only if and in so far as the objectives of the proposed action cannot be sufficiently achieved by the Member States and can therefore, by reason of the scale or effects of the proposed action, be better achieved by the Community'.[29]

The new definition clarified that subsidiarity was only to apply within the sphere of powers *shared* by the Union and the Member States. Where a matter fell within the exclusive sphere of the Member States, subsidiarity could not apply. Nor could it apply in the sphere of Europe's exclusive powers. The definition in Article 5(2) EC confirmed that the Community principle of subsidiarity was a principle of *cooperative* federalism. It was a federal safeguard in overlapping spheres of competences; and, as such, had no place under dual federalism.[30]

---

[27] Ibid 73 (emphasis added).

[28] K Lenaerts, *The Principle of Subsidiarity and the Environment in the European Union: Keeping the Balance of Federalism*, 849.

[29] On the second—wider—formulation in the Preamble of the TEU, see n 15 above.

[30] From this perspective, it is misleading to claim that the principle of subsidiarity 'is the cornerstone of all federalisms, old and new' (JP Jacqué & JHH Weiler, *On the Road to European Union—A New Judicial Architecture: An Agenda for the Intergovernmental Conference*, 202); and the statement has therefore been subject to severe criticism (cf P Pescatore, *Mit der Subsidiarität leben*, 1074).

The Maastricht definition of subsidiarity restricted the principle known under the Single European Act.[31] Its formulation now included *two* tests. The first may be called the *national insufficiency test*. The Community could only act where the objectives of the proposed action could not be sufficiently achieved by the Member States. This appeared to be an absolute standard. But how could this test be squared with the second test in Article 5(2) EC? That test was a *comparative efficiency test*.[32] The Community should not act unless it could *better* achieve the objectives of the proposed action. Did the combination of these two tests mean that the Community would not be entitled to act where it was—in relative terms—better able to tackle a social problem, but where the Member States could—in absolute terms—achieve the desired result? The wording of Article 5(2) EC was a textual failure.[33] Too many political cooks had spoiled the legal broth.

Worse: Article 5(2) EC contained two more textual ambivalences. The Maastricht subsidiarity formula left open whether the national insufficiency and the comparative efficiency test would cover *collective* national action.[34] Could the Member States avoid the argument that the Community was better placed to solve a transnational problem by having recourse to international cooperation *inter se*? Finally, the formulation 'if and in so far' potentially offered *two* versions of the subsidiarity principle. The first version concentrates on the 'if' question by asking *whether* the Community should act. This has been defined as the principle of subsidiarity *sensu stricto*. The second version concentrates on the 'in-so-far' question by asking *how* the Community should act. This has been referred to as the principle of subsidiarity *sensu lato*.[35]

In the light of these three textual ambivalences, constitutional and judicial clarifications were more than welcome.

---

[31]   D Wikinson, *Maastricht and the Environment: The Implications for the EC's Environment Policy of the Treaty on European Union*, 225.

[32]   This is the name given by the Commission, see: *Commission Communication on the Subsidiarity Principle*, 122.

[33]   On the unreflective combination of the two tests, see: Lord Mackenzie-Stuart, *Subsidiarity—A Busted Flush*, 22; as well as R Dehousse, *The Legacy of Maastricht: Emerging Institutional Issues*, 207–8. The original Luxembourg draft had only referred to the comparative efficiency test as laid down in Article 130r (4) EEC. It read: 'In areas which do not fall within its exclusive jurisdiction, the Community shall only take action, in accordance with the principle of subsidiarity, if and insofar as those objectives can be better achieved by the Community than by the Member States acting separately because of the scale or effects of the proposed action'.

[34]   The 1984 Draft Treaty as well as the TEU Luxemburg Draft had expressly excluded *inter se* cooperation by referring to the 'Member States acting *separately*'.

[35]   K Lenaerts, *The Principle of Subsidiarity and the Environment in the European Union*, 875.

a. *Constitutional Clarifications: From Edinburgh to Amsterdam*

A first clarification came from the European Council.[36] It was followed by a Commission communication on subsidiarity.[37] A common institutional vision was, thirdly, ratified by an inter-institutional agreement on the matter.[38]

In its Edinburgh Conclusions, the Council insisted that 'both aspects of the subsidiarity criterion are met: the objectives of the proposed action cannot be sufficiency achieved by Member States' action *and* they can therefore be better achieved by action on the part of the Community'. In assessing the insufficiency test, the transnational aspects of a problem as well as the Union's commitment to creating an internal market should be taken into account. As regards the comparative efficiency test, the Edinburgh Guidelines insist that Community action would need to 'produce *clear* benefits by reason of its scale or effects compared with action at the level of the Member States'. This should be substantiated by qualitative or, wherever possible, quantitative indicators.[39] The Council's approach thereby betrayed a preference for a categorical distinction between the 'whether' and 'how' of subsidiarity. The former was subsidiarity *sensu stricto* and was dealt with under Article 5(2) EC. The latter was addressed by the principle of proportionality under paragraph 3 of that provision.[40] It was thus proportionality—not subsidiarity—that dictated that 'Community measures should leave as much scope for national decisions as possible' by setting 'minimum standards, with freedom to member states to set higher national standards'. It was the proportionality principle that stipulated that Community action should be aiming at 'coordinating national action or to complementing, supplementing or supporting such action'.[41]

This institutional vision would become 'constitutional' with the Amsterdam Treaty. The Edinburgh Guidelines were confirmed by a special 'Protocol on the Application of the Principles of Subsidiarity and Proportionality'.[42]

---

[36] (Edinburgh) European Council, *Conclusions, Annex 1: Overall Approach to the Application by the Council of the Subsidiarity Principle and Article 3b of the Treaty on European Union*.

[37] Commission, *Communication on the Subsidiary Principle*.

[38] Interinstitutional Declaration, *Democracy, Transparency and Subsidiarity*.

[39] Edinburgh Guidelines (n 36 above) 14–15 (emphasis added).

[40] Insistence on the conceptual distinction will also be found in the Commission Communication (n 37 above) 119. Under the heading 'The two dimensions of the subsidiarity principle', the Commission explains that 'the notion of subsidiarity covers two distinct legal concepts which are often confused: the need for action (second paragraph); the intensity (proportionality) of the action taken (third paragraph)'.

[41] Edinburgh Guidelines (n 36 above) 15.

[42] Protocol 30 on the Application of the Principles of Subsidiarity and Proportionality.

The Amsterdam Protocol repeated the Edinburgh Council's substantive conditions on the subsidiarity principle:

For Community action to be justified, both aspects of the subsidiarity principle shall be met: the objectives of the proposed action cannot be sufficiently achieved by Member States' action in the framework of their national constitutional system and can therefore be better achieved by action on the part of the Community. The following guidelines should be used in examining whether the abovementioned condition is fulfilled:

 — the issue under consideration has transnational aspects which cannot be satis-factorily regulated by action by Member States;
 — actions by Member States alone or lack of Community action would conflict with the requirements of the Treaty (such as the need to correct distortion of competition or avoid disguised restrictions on trade or strengthen economic and social cohesion) or would otherwise significantly damage Member States' interests;
 — action at Community level would produce clear benefits by reason of its scale or effects compared with action at the level of the Member States.[43]

The Protocol also confirmed the—predominantly—*procedural* nature of the subsidiarity enquiry. Each institution was called upon to ensure that it complies with the principles of subsidiarity and proportionality.[44] 'For any proposed Community legislation, the reasons on which it is based shall be stated with a view to justifying its compliance with the principles of subsidiarity and proportionality; the reasons for concluding that a Community objective can be better achieved by the Community must be substantiated by qualitative or, wherever possible, quantitative indicators'.[45] These procedural obligations are then subsequently specified for each institution. The Commission must 'justify the relevance of its proposals with regard to the principle of subsidiarity; whenever necessary, the explanatory memorandum accompanying a proposal will give details in this respect'.[46] The Council and the Parliament 'shall, as an integral part of the overall examination of Commission proposals, consider their consistency with Article 5 of the Treaty'.[47]

The Protocol was indeed infused, through and through, with the philosophy of process federalism. However, its final provision acknowledged the

[43] Ibid Article 5.
[44] Ibid Article 1.
[45] Ibid Article 4.
[46] Ibid Article 9.
[47] Ibid Article 11.

possibility of *judicial* review of the subsidiarity principle: 'Compliance with the principle of subsidiarity shall be reviewed in accordance with the rules laid down by the Treaty'.[48] This called on the European Court of Justice.

b. *Judicial Clarifications: Subsidiarity and Proportionality*

Any substantive meaning of subsidiarity was thus in the hands of the European Court of Justice. How would the Court define the relationship between the national insufficiency test and the comparative efficiency test? Would both tests focus on the unilateral capacity of Member States; or, would they take *inter se* cooperation into account? Would the Court favour the restrictive meaning of subsidiarity; or would the Court incorporate a proportionality analysis into subsidiarity *sensu lato*?

There are surprisingly few judgments that address the principle of subsidiarity.[49] In *United Kingdom v Council (Working Time)*,[50] the United Kingdom had applied for the annulment of the Working Time Directive.[51] The Directive had been adopted on the basis of Article 137 EC entitling the Community to adopt legislation that improves the health and safety of workers in their working environment. The applicant claimed 'that the Community legislature neither fully considered nor adequately demonstrated whether there were transnational aspects which could not be satisfactorily regulated by national measures, whether such measures would conflict with the requirements of the EC Treaty or significantly damage the interests of Member States or, finally, whether action at Community level would provide clear benefits compared with action at national level'. The principle of subsidiarity would 'not allow the adoption of a directive in such wide and prescriptive terms as the contested directive, given that the extent and the nature of legislative regulation of working time vary very widely between Member States'.[52] How did the Court respond? It first conceded the complementary character of the Community competence under Article 137, which had left the health

---

[48] Ibid Article 13. See also: Edinburgh Guidelines (n 36 above) 14: 'The principle of subsidiarity cannot be regarded as having direct effect: however, interpretation of this principle, as well as review of compliance with it by the Community institutions are subject to control by the Court of Justice, as far as matters falling within the Treaty establishing the European Community are concerned'.

[49] There was not a single environmental case on the principle of subsidiarity prior to the TEU.

[50] Case C-84/94 *United Kingdom v Council (Working Time Directive)*.

[51] Directive 93/104 concerning certain Aspects of the Organization of Working Time.

[52] Case C-84/94 *United Kingdom v Council (Working Time Directive)*, para 46.

and safety of workers 'primarily in the responsibility of the Member States'.[53]
In two sentences, the Court then offered an interpretation of subsidiarity that
has structured the judicial vision of the principle ever since:

Once the Council has found that it is necessary to improve the existing level of protection as regards the health and safety of workers and to harmonize the conditions in this
area while maintaining the improvements made, achievement of that objective through
the imposition of minimum requirements necessarily presupposes Community-wide
action, which otherwise, as in this case, leaves the enactment of the detailed implementing provisions required largely to the Member States. The argument that the
Council could not properly adopt measures as general and mandatory as those forming the subject-matter of the directive will be examined below in the context of the
plea alleging infringement of the principle of proportionality.[54]

This judicial definition indicated two fundamental choices. First, the Court
assumed that where the Community had decided to 'harmonize' national laws,
that objective was 'necessarily presuppos[ing] Community-wide action'. This
view not only disregards *inter se* cooperation as an alternative method for the
(international) harmonization of national laws, but more importantly it uses
an ontological tautology—only the Community can harmonize laws in the
Community—to justify a positive result in the national insufficiency test.
And because the Member States failed the first test already, the Community
must—'therefore'—be better placed to achieve the desired objective. But
assuming the 'whether' of European action had been affirmatively established,
could the European law go 'as far' as it had? This was the second crucial choice
in the above passage. The Court decided against the idea of subsidiarity *sensu
lato*. Instead of analysing the intensity of the European law under Article 5(2)
EC, it chose to review it under the auspices of the principle of proportionality.

It is there that the Court made a third important choice. In analysing the
proportionality of the European law, it ruled: '[T]he Council must be allowed
a wide discretion in an area which, as here, involves the legislature in making
social policy choices and requires it to carry out complex assessments'.
'Judicial review of the exercise of that discretion must therefore be limited to
examining whether it has been vitiated by manifest error or misuse of powers,
or whether the institution concerned has manifestly exceeded the limits of its
discretion'.[55] The Court would thus apply the same *low* degree of judicial

---

[53] Ibid para 47.
[54] Ibid.
[55] Ibid para 58.

scrutiny that it had developed for the liberal dimension of the proportionality principle.[56]

In subsequent jurisprudence, the Court drew a fourth—procedural— conclusion from choices one and three. In *Germany v Parliament & Council* (*Deposit Guarantee Scheme*),[57] the German Government had claimed that the Community measure violated the *procedural* obligation to state reasons set out in Article 253 EC.[58] The European law had not explained how it was compatible with the principle of subsidiarity; and Germany insisted that it was necessary that 'the Community institutions must give detailed reasons to explain why only the Community, to the exclusion of the Member States is empowered to act in the area in question'. 'In the present case, the Directive does not indicate in what respects its objectives could not have been sufficiently attained by action at Member State level or the grounds which militated in favour of Community action'.[59] The Court gave short shrift to that accusation. Looking at the recitals of the European law, the Court found that the Community legislator had given 'consideration' to the principle of subsidiarity. Having found previous actions by the Member States insufficient, the European legislator had found it indispensible to ensure a harmonized minimum level. This was enough to satisfy the procedural obligations under the subsidiarity enquiry.[60] It was a low explanatory threshold indeed.

Choices one, three, and four have been confirmed in subsequent jurisprudence. The Court has concentrated on an ontological argument and thereby short-circuited the comparative efficiency test.[61] It has not searched for 'clear'

---

[56] On the development of the judicial review standard for Community measures in this context, see: G de Búrca, *The Principle of Proportionality and its Application in EC Law*.

[57] Case C-233/94 *Germany v Parliament and Council* (*Deposit Guarantee Scheme*).

[58] Article 253 EC reads: 'Regulations, directives and decisions adopted jointly by the European Parliament and the Council, and such acts adopted by the Council or the Commission, shall state the reasons on which they are based and shall refer to any proposals or opinions which were required to be obtained pursuant to this Treaty'. Germany made it an express point that it was this provision—and not the principle of subsidiarity as such—that it claimed to be violated (ibid para 24).

[59] Ibid para 23.

[60] Ibid paras 26–8.

[61] Cf Case C-491/01 *The Queen v Secretary of State for Health, ex parte: British American Tobacco (Investments) Ltd and Imperial Tobacco Ltd*, paras 181–3: '[T]he Directive's objective is to eliminate the barriers raised by the differences which still exist between the Member States' laws, regulations and administrative provisions on the manufacture, presentation and sale of tobacco products, while ensuring a high level of health protection, in accordance with Article 95(3) EC. Such an objective cannot be sufficiently achieved by the Member States individually and calls for action at Community level, as demonstrated by the multifarious development of national laws in this case'; as well as: Case C-377/98 *The Netherlands v Parliament & Council*, para 32; Case C-103/01

qualitative or quantitative benefits of European laws, but confirmed its manifest error test—thus leaving subsidiarity to the political safeguards of federalism.[62] This is reflected in the low justificatory standard imposed on the Community legislator.[63] By contrast, as regards the second choice, the Court has remained ambivalent. While in some cases it has incorporated the intensity question into its subsidiarity analysis,[64] other jurisprudence has kept the subsidiarity and the proportionality principles at arm's length.[65]

2. *Subsidiarity* De Lege Ferenda: *Strengthening the Safeguards of Federalism*

Despite its literary presence, the principle of subsidiarity has remained a subsidiary principle of European constitutionalism. The reason for its shadowy existence is its lack of conceptual contours. While its ambiguity may well have 'save[d] Maastricht',[66] its protean character defied concrete application as Europe's new safeguard of federalism. If subsidiarity was everything to everyone, how should the Commission or the Court of Justice apply it? To limit this semantic uncertainty, subsequent constitutional and judicial clarifications had confined subsidiarity to 'whether' the Community should act, and concentrated on the procedural dimension of that question. The assessment of subsidiarity had thus been—largely—left to the *Community legislator*.

Commission v Germany, paras 46–7; as well as Joined Cases C-154 & 155/04 *The Queen, ex parte: National Association of Health Stores and others et al v Secretary of State for Health*, paras 104–8.

[62] Cf Case C-233/94 *Germany v Parliament & Council (Deposit Guarantee Scheme)*, para 56; as well as: Case C-110/03 *Belgium v Commission*, para 68.

[63] Cf Case C-377/98 *The Netherlands v Parliament & Council*, para 33: 'Compliance with the principle of subsidiarity is necessarily implicit in the fifth, sixth and seventh recitals of the preamble to the Directive, which state that, in the absence of action at Community level, the development of the laws and practices of the different Member States impedes the proper functioning of the internal market. It thus appears that the Directive states sufficient reasons on that point'.

[64] In Case C-491/01 *The Queen v Secretary of State for Health, ex parte: British American Tobacco (Investments) Ltd and Imperial Tobacco Ltd*, the Court identified the 'intensity of the action undertaken by the Community' with the principle of subsidiarity and not the principle of proportionality (ibid para 184). This acceptance of subsidiarity *sensu lato* can also be seen at work in Case C-55/06 *Arcor v Germany*, where the Court identified the principle of subsidiarity with the idea that 'the Member States retain the possibility to establish specific rules on the field in question' (ibid para 144).

[65] Cf Case C-84/94 *United Kingdom v Council (Working Time Directive)*; as well as: Case C-103/01 *Commission v Germany*, para 48.

[66] DZ Cass, *The Word that Saves Maastricht? The Principle of Subsidiarity and the Division of Powers within the European Community*, 1107.

It was hardly surprising that this voluntarist arrangement meant that subsidiarity was not taken very seriously by the political process.[67]

In the light of this failure, various constitutional projects have tried to strengthen the subsidiarity principle as a safeguard of European federalism. Two reform options have crystallized in the last decade. The first option builds on the procedural aspect of the principle and attempts to reinforce subsidiarity as a *political* safeguard of federalism. The second option tries to 'substantiate' the principle by strengthening subsidiarity as a *judicial* safeguard of federalism.

a. Strengthening the Political Safeguards of Federalism

Believing in the 'political' nature of the subsidiarity enquiry, the first option concentrates on the procedural dimension.[68] How could this dimension be reinforced? The beloved proposal in the last decade has tried to integrate national parliaments into the decision-making process of the European Union.[69] It was hoped that this idea would kill two birds with one stone. The procedural involvement of national parliaments promised to strengthen the federal *and* the democratic safeguards within Europe. This could be done in two ways. First, one could create a new European institution—a Senate—that would assemble national parliamentarians. Secondly, national parliaments *as such* could be integrated in the European legislative process.

In the past, the idea to create a European Senate as a second European parliamentary chamber had high political support.[70] 'At the root of all of the proposals for a second chamber there seems to lie a perception that there is a problem with the democratic legitimacy of the EU and its institutions'.[71] National parliaments are not directly involved in the European legislative process and they lack control over national ministers voting in the Council.

---

[67] G Berman, *Proportionality and Subsidiarity*, 86.

[68] This view has had wide support from the academic community, see: G Berman, *Taking Subsidiarity Seriously: Federalism in the European Community and the United States*, 336: 'My basic view is that the Community should respond to this challenge by recasting subsidiarity from a jurisdictional principle (that is, a principle describing the allocation of substantive authority between the Community and the Member States) into an essentially procedural one (that is, a principle directing the legislative institutions of the Community to engage in a particular inquiry before concluding that action at the Community rather than Member State level is warranted)'.

[69] Cf (Amsterdam) Protocol No 9 on the Role of National Parliaments in the EU.

[70] It had been suggested by various French political luminaries, but also by former Prime Minister Tony Blair and the former President of the Czech Republic, Vaclav Havel. For an overview of the various proposals for a second chamber, see: House of Lords, Select Committee on European Union, *Seventh Report* (2001–02), paras 7–21.

[71] Ibid para 26.

But is the creation of a European Senate the best constitutional medicine for the alleged democratic malaise? Would it add a *third* source of democratic legitimacy to the European Union?[72] Serious doubts are in order. The Senate idea would not solve the practical problems which it seeks to address.[73] And from a theoretical point of view, it makes little sense. '[I]f the Council makes the law, and if Ministers in the Council represent their national parliaments, how can their parliaments be given a separate, valid legislative role?'[74] Why should there be *two* European institutions representing the national peoples? If the reason for this functional doubling is the increased independence of *national* governments from their *national* parliaments, why not strengthen the *national* safeguards of democracy? A European Senate would not add much democratic legitimacy to the European Union. The better view has therefore concentrated on its potential function as a political safeguard of *federalism*.[75] Yet, the idea of a European Senate was soon discarded on the road to reform.[76]

The idea of involving national parliaments in the European legislative procedure was—not unsurprisingly—celebrated as the best solution by the European Convention.[77] 'Such a mechanism would enable national parliaments to ensure the correct application of the principle of subsidiarity by the institutions taking part in the legislative process through a direct relationship

---

[72] For an affirmative answer, see: G van der Schyff & G-J Leenknegt, *The Case for a European Senate: A Model for the Representation of National Parliaments in the European Union*, 243 and 251.

[73] For an analysis of this point, see: House of Lords (n 70 above) paras 40 *et seq*. The Lords suggested that the Council should operate in a more transparent way. 'Achieving greater accountability would significantly help reconnection of citizens with the institutions of Europe and provide important reassurance to the public about the working of their institutions.' 'Our recommendation is accordingly that member States' governments should make every effort to ensure that they are fully accountable to their national parliaments both in being scrutinized on Council meetings in advance, and in reporting the outcome of Council meetings after the event' (ibid para 62).

[74] Andrew Duff (MEP) as quoted in ibid para 59.

[75] This has been the theme of reform proposals by the French Senate, cf *Rapport d'information au nom de la délégation du Sénat pour l'Union européenne sur une deuxieme chambre européenne*, No 381.

[76] The European Convention ruled out the creation of a new institution to monitor the application of the principle of subsidiarity; cf Conclusions of the Working Group IV on the Role of National Parliaments, 11: 'The majority of the members of the Group recommended a "process based approach" for monitoring subsidiarity and proportionality by national parliaments and rejected the idea of creating new permanent or ad hoc bodies or institutions for this purpose'.

[77] 'That a consensus in favour of empowering national parliaments emerged in the Convention is not altogether surprising given that a majority of its full members, 56 out of 105, were representatives of national parliaments.' Cf I Cooper, *The Watchdogs of Subsidiarity: National Parliaments and the Logic of Arguing in the EU*, 288.

with the Community institutions'.[78] This procedural vision of subsidiarity would find its way into the (failed) Constitutional Treaty and the (suspended) Lisbon Treaty. National parliaments are to be accorded an active role in the federal functioning of the European Union 'by seeing to it that the principle of subsidiary is respected in accordance with the procedures provided for in the Protocol on the application of the principles of subsidiarity and proportionality'.[79]

What would the Lisbon Protocol change?[80] Did it offer the national parliaments a veto right (hard constitutional solution) or only a monitoring right (soft constitutional solution)? In addition to reaffirming the procedural hurdles of the Amsterdam Protocol,[81] the new Protocol will strengthen the political safeguards of federalism by involving the national parliaments as 'watchdogs of subsidiarity'.[82] According to Article 6, each national parliament may within eight weeks produce a reasoned opinion stating why it considers that a European legislative draft does not comply with the principle of subsidiarity. Each national parliament will thereby have two votes;[83] and where the negative votes amount to one third of all the votes, the European Union

---

[78] European Convention, *Conclusions of the Working Group I on the Principle of Subsidiarity*, 5. For a critical commentary on the report, see the excellent analysis by S Weatherill, *Using National Parliaments to Improve Scrutiny of the Limits of EU Action*, 909–10: 'The Working Group Report largely promoted an impression that the proper corrective to perceived problems in today's European Union is enhanced national "control" over the European institutions. This is troublingly backward-looking. "Nationalising" the context in which EU decisions are taken may produce selfish State-centric outcomes which fail to pay heed to the need to adjust political decision-making in line with the growth of economic and social activities undertaken in the transnational domain. So greater involvement of national parliaments is not necessarily a virtue'.

[79] Article 12(b) of the (Lisbon) TEU.

[80] Lisbon Protocol No 2 on the Application of the Principles of Subsidiarity and Proportionality.

[81] Article 5 of the new Protocol states: 'Draft legislative acts shall be justified with regard to the principles of subsidiarity and proportionality. Any draft legislative act should contain a detailed statement making it possible to appraise compliance with the principles of subsidiarity and proportionality. This statement should contain some assessment of the proposal's financial impact and, in the case of a directive, of its implications for the rules to be put in place by Member States, including, where necessary, the regional legislation. The reasons for concluding that a Union objective can be better achieved at Union level shall be substantiated by qualitative and, wherever possible, quantitative indicators. Draft legislative acts shall take account of the need for any burden, whether financial or administrative, falling upon the Union, national governments, regional or local authorities, economic operators and citizens, to be minimised and commensurate with the objective to be achieved'.

[82] I Cooper (n 77 above).

[83] Article 7(1) of the Lisbon Protocol on the Application of the Principles of Subsidiarity and Proportionality.

draft 'must be reviewed'. This is called the 'yellow card' mechanism, since the Union legislator 'may decide to maintain, amend or withdraw the draft'.[84] The mechanism is strengthened in relation to legislative proposals under the co-decision procedure (although, here, only a majority of the votes allocated to the national parliaments will trigger it).[85] Under the 'orange card' mechanism, the Commission's justification for maintaining the proposal as well as the reasoned opinions of the national parliaments will be submitted to the Union legislator. The latter will then have to decide whether the proposal is compatible with the principle of subsidiarity. Where *one* of its chambers—the Council or the Parliament—finds that the proposal violates the principle subsidiarity, the proposal is rejected.[86] While this arrangement makes it—slightly—easier for the European Parliament to reject a legislative proposal on subsidiarity grounds, it makes it—ironically—more *difficult* for the Council to block a proposal on the basis of subsidiarity than on the basis of a proposal's lack of substantive merit.[87]

The Lisbon Protocol rejects the idea of a 'red card' mechanism. The rejection of the hard subsidiarity solution is bemoaned by some as the proposed procedural safeguards would 'add very little' to the federal control of the Union legislator.[88] Others have—rightly—greeted the fact that the envisaged mechanism will leave the political decision on subsidiarity ultimately to the *European* legislator. '[T]o give national parliaments what would amount to a veto over proposals would be incompatible with the Commission's constitutionally protected independence'.[89] Indeed, 'a veto power vested in national Parliaments would distort the proper distribution of power and responsibility in the EU's complex but remarkably successful system of transnational governance by conceding too much to State control'.[90] To have turned

---

[84] Ibid Article 7(2). The 'yellow card' threshold is lowered to a quarter of votes for European laws in the area of freedom, security and justice.

[85] Ibid Article 7(3).

[86] Ibid Article 7(3)(b): 'if, by a majority of 55% of the members of the Council or a majority of the votes cast in the European Parliament, the legislator is of the opinion that the proposal is not compatible with the principle of subsidiarity, the legislative proposal shall not be given further consideration'.

[87] For an analysis of this point, see: G Barrett, '*The King is dead, long live the king*': the Recasting by the Treaty of Lisbon of the Provisions of the Constitutional Treaty concerning National Parliaments, 80–1. In the light of the voting threshold, 'it seems fair to predict that blockade of legislative proposals under Article 7(3) is likely to be a highly exceptional and unusual situation'.

[88] House of Commons, *Thirty-third Report of the Commons European Scrutiny Committee: Subsidiarity, National Parliaments and the Lisbon Treaty*, para 35.

[89] A Dashwood, *The Relationship between the Member States and the European Union/Community*, 369.

[90] S Weatherill, *Using National Parliaments to Improve Scrutiny of the Limits of EU Action*, 912.

national parliaments into 'co-legislators' in the making of European law would have aggravated the 'political interweaving' of the European and the national level and thereby deepened joint-decision traps.[91] Lisbon will thus continue to 'proceduralize' subsidiarity without turning the principle into a hard and fatally efficient political safeguard of federalism. The soft constitutional solution will also allow national parliaments to channel their scrutiny to where it can be most useful and effective: on their respective national governments.

b. Strengthening the Judicial Safeguards of Federalism

The past decade of constitutional reform predominantly concentrated on the procedural aspect of the subsidiarity principle. Has European constitutionalism thus rejected the substantive dimension of the principle and fully embraced the philosophy of 'process federalism'?

This is not the place to arbitrate between 'process-based' and 'value-based' constitutional or federal theories.[92] It is uncontested that States can be protected by a procedural duty on the federal legislator to 'think hard' about subsidiarity.[93] However, procedural obligations only provide *some* protection of State autonomy. And, more importantly, the democracy-centred rationale behind process constitutionalism is hard to apply to a federal context. Here the question is *not* whether a non-democratic court or a democratic majority should decide, but whether the democratic majority of the *federation* or the democratic majority of a *State* should decide on the matter.[94] In federal contexts, the principal question should therefore not be whether judicial review

---

[91] On the concept and shortfalls of 'political interweaving' (*Politikverflechtung*), see: FW Scharpf, *The Joint-Decision Trap: Lessons from German Federalism and European Integration*.

[92] For two remarkable contributions to the American debate, see: L Tribe, *The Puzzling Persistence of Process-Based Constitutional Theories*; as well as EA Young, *Two Cheers for Process Federalism*.

[93] Let us remember the amusing anecdote of Agassiz as told by E Pound, *ABC of Reading*, 17–8: 'A post-graduate student equipped with honors and diplomas went to Agassiz to receive the final and finishing touches. The great man offered him a small fish and told him to describe it. Post-Graduate Student: "That's only a sunfish." Agassiz: "I know that. Write a description of it." After a few minutes the student returned with the description of the Ichthus Heliodiplodokus, or whatever term is used to conceal the common sunfish from vulgar knowledge, family of Heliichtherinkus, etc., as found in textbooks of the subject. Agassiz again told the student to describe the fish. The student produced a four-page essay. Agassiz then told him to look at the fish. At the end of three weeks the fish was in an advanced state of decomposition, but the student knew something about it'.

[94] On the conceptual distortions of a unitary constitutionalism in analysing democracy in a federal Union, see Chapter 1—Section II (3b) above; and, more extensively: R Schütze, *On 'Federal' Ground: The European Union as an (Inter)national Phenomenon*.

is necessary to maintain the political safeguards of federalism, but whether it should go beyond that.[95]

The parallel application of political and judicial safeguards of federalism is generally accepted in the European legal order.[96] This will be confirmed by the Lisbon Protocol.[97] But more than that: the European Convention advanced the argument that 'judicial review carried out by the Court of Justice concerning compliance with the principle of subsidiarity *could be reinforced*'.[98]

How could the *judicial* safeguards of federalism be reinforced? One idea has proposed an *ex ante* judicial review on subsidiarity grounds.[99] Modelled on the *ex ante* jurisdiction of the Court for international agreements,[100] this would allow the Court to subject a European bill to a subsidiarity review prior to its entry into force. A second proposal reified this idea by suggesting an independent Court specialized in questions of competence and subsidiarity.[101] The Convention discarded both suggestions on the ground 'that the introduction of a judicial review in the legislative phase would be tantamount to the monitoring of subsidiarity losing its primarily political nature'.[102] But if *ex ante* review was not an option, how can *ex post* judicial review of subsidiarity be reinforced? In order to answer this question, we need to take a step back and ask—again—what the subsidiarity principle *is* and what we want it to *do*.

We saw above that the Court, and much of the academic literature, makes a distinction between 'whether' the Community should exercise its

---

[95] On this point, see: LA Baker, *Putting the Safeguards back into the Political Safeguards of Federalism*, 972: 'Substantive judicial review of federalism is necessary both to remind Congress of its own obligation to restrain itself, and to catch any particularly egregious examples of federal overreaching—vertical or horizontal—that slip through the system's political and procedural checks'.

[96] For an exception to the consensus that subsidiarity is also a judicial question, see: N Emiliou, *Subsidiarity: An Effective Barrier Against 'the Enterprises of Ambition'?*, 406: 'not amenable to judicial review'.

[97] Article 8 of the Lisbon Protocol on Subsidiarity and Proportionality: 'The Court of Justice shall have jurisdiction in actions on grounds of infringement of the principle of subsidiarity by a legislative act, brought in accordance with the rules laid down in Article 163 of the Treaty on the Functioning of the European Union by Member States, or notified by them in accordance with their legal order on behalf of their national Parliaments or a chamber thereof'.

[98] European Convention, *Conclusions of the Working Group I on the Principle of Subsidiarity*, 7 (emphasis added).

[99] JP Jacqué & JHH Weiler, *On the Road to European Union—A New Judicial Architecture: An Agenda for the Intergovernmental Conference*, 204–6.

[100] Article 300(6) EC: 'The European Parliament, the Council, the Commission or a Member State may obtain the opinion of the Court of Justice as to whether an agreement envisaged is compatible with the provisions of this Treaty. Where the opinion of the Court of Justice is adverse, the agreement may enter into force only in accordance with Article 48 of the Treaty on European Union'.

[101] JHH Weiler, *The Constitution of Europe*, 322.

[102] European Convention, *Conclusions of the Working Group I on the Principle of Subsidiarity*, 9.

competence and 'how' it does it. The former is conceptualized as subsidiarity proper, the latter is viewed as proportionality. This distinction is misleading. Subsidiarity must be understood in terms of federal proportionality. Why? There are two reasons—one theoretical and one conceptual. Theoretically, a subsidiarity principle that concentrates on the 'whether' of Community action operates within a philosophy of dual federalism. It is based on an either-or-logic in which certain objectives should not involve the European Community or the Member States at all. By excluding the Community from the scene, subsidiarity *sensu stricto* protects a sphere in which the Member States can *exclusively* exercise their competences. And by insisting that certain objectives are 'Community objectives' as they can only be achieved by the Community, the principle equally constructs a sphere in which *only* the European Union can exercise its competences.

But more importantly: on a conceptual level, it is impossible to reduce subsidiarity to 'whether' the Community should exercise one of its competences. This follows from the constitutional structure of Article 5 EC, which distinguishes three constitutional principles: enumeration, subsidiarity, and proportionality. Where the Union enjoys a competence it is entitled to generally act within an area. The general 'whether' of Union action is here already answered for that policy area. The distinction between 'competence' and 'subsidiarity'—between Article 5(1) and 5(2) EC—will thus only make sense if the subsidiarity principle concentrates on the 'whether' of *the specific act at issue*. But the 'whether' and the 'how' of the specific action are inherently tied together. The principle of subsidiarity will thus ask *whether* the European legislator has *unnecessarily* restricted national autonomy. A subsidiarity analysis that will not question the *federal* proportionality of a European law is bound to remain an empty formalism. Subsidiarity properly understood *is* federal proportionality.

What, then, is the difference between subsidiarity in Article 5(2) and proportionality in Article 5(3) EC? The answer is that both principles share a family resemblance.[103] The proportionality principle was historically designed to safeguard *liberal* values. Proportionality would protect *private* rights against excessive public interference.[104] The idea of excessive government interference can be extended into a federal context. But here it is not the individual autonomy of a person, but the *collective* autonomy of a group that is protected.

---

[103] On the concept of 'family resemblance', see: L Wittgenstein, *Philosophical Investigations*, §§65–71.

[104] On the origin of the concept, see: J Schwarze, *European Administrative Law*, 678–9.

In addition to its liberal dimension, the principle of proportionality may thus receive a federal dimension.[105] But this federal proportionality *is* the principle of subsidiarity; and to draw a line between proportionality and subsidiarity, the best solution would be to restrict the principle of proportionality in Article 5(3) EC to its liberal dimension. The constitutional triumvirate of Article 5 EC could thus be explained as follows: the enumeration principle will tell us whether the Community *can* act within a policy field. The subsidiarity principle would examine whether a European law *disproportionally restricts national autonomy*; and the principle of proportionality would, finally, tell us whether a European law *unnecessarily interfered with liberal values*.

But even if the Court comes to embrace subsidiarity as federal proportionality, what principles could assist it in *reinforcing* judicial review of subsidiarity? American federalism has never recognized the existence of a principle of subsidiarity in theory or practice.[106] However, two *indirect* inspirations may be distilled from the jurisprudence of the American Supreme Court. They are: the 'clear statement rule' and the 'presumption against pre-emption'. The former is a judicial principle to maintain the political safeguards of federalism. Congress must state its intention to pre-empt State law clearly; for 'to give the state-displacing weight of federal law to mere congressional *ambiguity* would evade the very procedure for lawmaking'.[107] The presumption against pre-emption goes slightly further than this.[108] It adds a substantive value in favour of State legislation and forms part of a 'normative canon designed to protect federalism values'. 'As such, the presumption against preemption is much like a number of other rules of construction derived from constitutional values, such as the rule of lenity in criminal law[.]'[109]

These two American judicial devices can, without much effort, be translated into European safeguards of federalism. The Court could insist on

---

[105] The principle of subsidiarity, as we saw above, also has a liberal dimension in the sense of protecting individuals or *private* groups from unnecessary public intervention. However, this liberal dimension of subsidiarity is *not* codified in Article 5(2) EC, cf n 15 above.

[106] G Berman, *Taking Subsidiarity Seriously: Federalism in the European Community and the United States*, 403: 'not only would the European not have found subsidiarity in the lexicon of U.S. constitutional law, but they would not have found it to be a central feature of U.S. constitutional practice'.

[107] *Gregory v Ashcroft*, 501 US 452 (1991), 464 (quoting LH Tribe).

[108] The Supreme Court has found a presumption against pre-emption in areas of traditional State police powers. For an analysis of the American case law, see above: Chapter 2—Section II (1).

[109] EA Young, *Two Cheers for Process Federalism*, 1387–8.

express pre-emption before concluding that a European law occupied the field. It could equally develop a *judicial* presumption against pre-emption in sensitive policy areas. (Indeed, it has been argued that the subsidiarity principle as such constitutes the textual foundation for a presumption in favour of national responsibility.[110]) Yet, these two devices would only provide for a *soft* constitutional solution: the subsidiarity-inspired *interpretation* of European legislation. What about situations in which the European legislator spoke clearly and expressly overturned a presumption against field-pre-emption? Then, the European Court would face a choice. It could conceive the judicial safeguards of federalism as mere 'resistance norms', that is 'constitutional rules that make governmental action more difficult, but do not categorically exclude it'.[111] This is the present American solution.[112] Alternatively, it could—and indeed should—outlaw disproportionate interferences into national legislative autonomy. This *hard* constitutional solution will require that the Court abandons its manifest-error standard in relation to the question of subsidiarity. The Court would need to develop a stricter standard in its *federal* proportionality review. The fact that the latter may depart from the laxer standard for the liberal dimension of proportionality is no constitutional anomaly.[113] However, the hard constitutional solution will mean that the Court of Justice gets involved in fundamental political and social questions. But this is—after all—what *constitutional* courts do.

II. Complementary Competences: A Judicial Safeguard of Federalism

Outside the core areas of European integration, the dominant federal philosophy had long been that of legislative cooperation.[114] For those 'flanking

[110] EA Young, *Protecting Member State Autonomy in the European Union: Some Cautionary Tales from American Federalism*, 1717: '[T]he introduction of the principle of subsidiarity into the EU treaties at Maastricht provides substantial support for a shift in interpretive principles. If anything, the underlying legal texts offer firmer support for an interpretative "presumption against preemption" in the EU than exists in the United States'.

[111] Ibid 1652.

[112] On this point, see: Chapter 2—Section II.

[113] The co-existence of *two* or more judicial review standards is well-established in American constitutional law, see: *United States v Caroline Products*, 304 US 144 (1938), 152 fn.4.

[114] For environmental legislation, see: n 140 below.

policies', Community legislation would not, *ipso facto*, exclude stricter national measures that harmoniously complemented the Community standard. Minimum harmonization would set a mandatory floor and permit upward legislative differentiation. National measures that conformed to European legislation would not be pre-empted. However, recourse to minimum harmonization under Articles 95 and 308 EC had always been a *legislative* choice. Political feasibility and legislative discretion determined the intention of the Community legislator to allow for complementary national legislation. Cooperative federalism was a *legislative* technique.

Since the Single European Act ('SEA'), the phenomenon of cooperative federalism has increasingly been 'constitutionalized'. In addition to the principle of subsidiarity, newly introduced competences have set *constitutional* limits to the powers of the European legislator in two ways.[115] For a number of policy fields, the Treaty mandated the federal legislator to set minimum standards only. The method of constitutionally fixing minimum harmonization emerged for the first time in relation to environmental and social policy. Subsequent amendments have extended this technique to other areas. The constitutional relationship between the European and the national legislator is here relatively straightforward: the Treaty guarantees the ability of the national legislator to adopt higher standards. The legislative cooperation is thus a result of the constitutional structure of the competence as such. This particularity sets them apart from 'normal' shared competences.

A second variant of constitutionally enshrined cooperative federalism appears with the Maastricht Treaty. Instead of referring to 'minimum' standards, the Treaty characterizes the power of the Community legislator as 'complementing' or 'supplementing' national action. The contours of this type of competence are still largely unexplored, especially as some of these competences introduce the concept of 'incentive measures' that may exclude all harmonization within the field.[116] Europe's federalism has come to describe *both* variants as 'complementary competences', especially since a number of 'minimum harmonization' competences expressly refer

---

[115] The two methods are not mutually exclusive and might be combined within a single competence, see the Community power for public health under Article 152 EC discussed below.

[116] The exclusion of harmonization can be found in (a), (c), (e), (f) and (g) below.

to making a contribution or supplementing national action. Today, the following complementary competences can be found in the European Union:

(a) Community action to combat discrimination: Article 13(2) allows the Council to adopt Community 'incentive measures, excluding any harmonization of the laws and regulations of the Member States', to support action taken by the Member States in order to contribute to the achievement of the objectives referred to in this particular competence.

(b) Visa, asylum, and immigration: the Council was called upon to establish, until 1 May 2004, 'minimum standards' for asylum seekers and refugees.[117] The Community was equally entitled to adopt measures on immigration, which 'shall not prevent any Member State from maintaining or introducing in the areas concerned national provisions which are compatible with this Treaty and with international agreements'.[118]

(c) Employment policy: the Community 'shall contribute to a high level of employment by encouraging cooperation between Member States and by supporting and, if necessary, complementing their action. In doing so, the competences of the Member States shall be respected'.[119] For this purpose, the Community shall adopt 'incentive measures designed to encourage cooperation between Member States and to support their action in the field of employment'. Those measures shall not include harmonization of the laws and regulations of the Member States.[120]

(d) Social policy: the Community 'shall support and complement the activities of the Member States' in certain fields by adopting measures 'designed to encourage cooperation between Member States' as well as 'minimum requirements'. Community legislation will thereby in no way 'prevent any Member State from maintaining or introducing more stringent protective measures compatible with this Treaty'.[121]

(e) Education and vocational training: the Community is entitled to 'contribute to the development of quality education by encouraging cooperation between Member States and, if necessary, by supporting and supplementing their action, while fully respecting the responsibility of the Member States for the content of teaching and the organization of education systems and their cultural and linguistic diversity'. To that effect, the Council 'shall adopt incentive measures,

---

[117] Article 63(1), (2) EC.
[118] Article 63(3), (4) EC—both paragraphs make no reference to 'stricter' national measures and might therefore constitutionally guarantee upward and downward flexibility for national legislators.
[119] Article 127 EC.
[120] Article 129 EC.
[121] Article 137(1), (2) and (4) EC.

excluding any harmonization of the laws and regulations of the Member States'.[122] The same applies, *mutatis mutandis*, to vocational training.[123]

(f) Culture: the Community's cultural involvement 'shall be aimed at encouraging cooperation between Member States and, if necessary, support and supplementing their action' through 'incentive measures, excluding any harmonization of the laws and regulations of the Member States'.[124]

(g) Public health: Community action shall complement national policies through legislative measures in certain fields (paragraph 4a, b); and may adopt 'incentive measures designed to protect and improve human health, excluding any harmonization of the laws and regulations of the Member States'.[125]

(h) Consumer protection: the Community shall 'contribute to protecting the health, safety and economic interests of consumers' through measures which 'support, supplement, and monitor the policy pursued by the Member States', whereby Member States would not lose their legislative power to maintain or introduce more stringent measures.[126]

(i) Trans-European Networks: to build trans-European networks, the Community shall contribute to their establishment and the development of trans-European networks in the areas of transport, telecommunications, and energy infrastructures.[127]

(j) Industrial policy: the Community shall 'contribute' to enhancing the competitiveness of the European industry by means of 'specific measures in support of action taken in the Member States'.[128]

(k) Research and technological development: the Community shall complement the activities of the Member States with regard to research and technological development. The Community and the Member States shall thereby coordinate their research and technological development activities so as to ensure that national policies and Community policy are mutually consistent.[129]

(l) Environment: the Community is permitted to contribute to a policy on the environment, while not preventing Member States from maintaining or introducing more stringent protective measures.[130]

---

[122] Article 149 (1) and (4).

[123] Article 150 EC also limits Community policy to measures that 'support and supplement the action of Member States, while fully respecting the responsibility of the Member States for the content and organization of vocational training', 'excluding any harmonization of the laws and regulation of the Member States' (Article 150(1), (4) EC).

[124] Article 151(2), (5) EC.

[125] Article 152(1), (4) EC.

[126] Article 153(1), 3(b), (5) EC.

[127] Article 154 EC.

[128] Article 157 EC.

[129] Articles 164, 165 EC.

[130] Articles 175, 176 EC.

(m) Development cooperation: the Community policy in the sphere of development cooperation 'shall be complementary to the policies pursued by the Member States'.[131]

(n) Economic, financial and technical cooperation with third countries: Community measures 'shall be complementary to those carried out by the Member States and consistent with the development policy of the Community'.[132]

The existence of complementary competences in a federal legal order represents, in itself, a constitutional choice in favour of cooperative federalism. But if the essence of complementary competences appears to be their constitutionally limited 'legislative' capacity, the central question for this competence type will be how much legislative space the European legislator must leave to the national level. What is the frame of reference by which the 'complementary' nature of European laws will be evaluated? Do complementary competences prevent the Community legislator from ever laying down exhaustive standards with regard to a specific legislative *measure*? Or, will the Community legislator be allowed to—occasionally—fully pre-empt the Member States within the *scope of a piece of legislation*, while it can never fully exclude the national legislator from all action within the *scope of the competence*?

We shall attempt to answer these questions in a first subsection through an overview of the jurisprudence of the European Court in relation to environmental policy. A second subsection will analyse the Community's emerging public health policy in order to distil the constitutional principles that govern this relatively young competence. The Community's public health competence exhibits (nearly) all the novel constitutional strategies for limiting the legislative powers of the Community. The primary focus of this section is on the constitutional structure behind complementary competences, that is: the division of *powers* ordained by the European treaty-constitution as such.[133]

---

[131] Article 177 EC.

[132] Article 181a EC.

[133] It is still worth mentioning that the trend towards cooperative federalism for environmental *legislation* has been said to have increased in recent years. While minimum harmonization has here always been one of the principal legislative methods, Krämer has pointed to the growing number of horizontal Directives in this area. These horizontal Directives do not concern specific sectors of the environment and would leave a considerable degree of differentiation to the national, regional, and local level (cf L Krämer, *Differentiation in EU Environmental Policy*, 136). The trend has also been noted by P Davies, *European Union Environmental Law*, 23: 'The trend away from the early style of environmental legislation (which often set highly detailed rules such as specific emission limit values) to the adoption of measures establishing only frameworks for action can be said to be reflective of this requirement [proportionality]. Framework measures typically set narrowly defined

1. *Environmental Policy: A Constitutional Commitment to Minimum Harmonization*

There was no mention of a European environmental policy in 1958. The original Treaty of Rome wished to create an economic union that committed itself to 'promote throughout the Community a harmonious development of economic activities', a 'balanced expansion' and 'an accelerated raising of the standard of living'.[134] Environmental policy was not regarded as a Community policy. Yet, national environmental policies could impede the proper functioning of the common market and potentially create obstacles to trade and distortions of competition.[135]

The birth of a Community environmental *policy* occurred in 1972 with the Paris Summit.[136] That political impulse was translated into the first environmental action programme, which admitted that 'a harmonious development of economic activities and a continuous and balanced expansion cannot now be imagined in the absence of an effective campaign to combat pollution and nuisances or of an improvement in the quality of life and the protection of the environment'.[137] However, in the absence of a clear *constitutional* mandate on environmental matters, the Community legislator had to base its environmental legislation on Articles 94 and 308 EC or, sometimes, both. Environmental legislation had therefore to be necessary in the course of the operation of the common market.[138] In the period leading up to the Single

objectives but provide Member States with as much flexibility as possible in the implementation taking into account regional and local conditions'.

[134] Article 2 EEC.

[135] Article 30 EC recognized this possibility for it permitted restrictions on imports or exports to be justified on the ground of 'the protection of health and life of humans, animals and *plants*'(emphasis added).

[136] Between 1958 and 1972, only a small number of Community measures fell into the 'environmental field'. Illustrations of early Community environmental measures are: Directive 70/157 on the permissible sound levels and exhaust systems in motor vehicles and Directive 72/306 regulating the emission of pollutants from vehicles with diesel engines. The 1972 Declaration of the Heads of States and Government stated: 'Economic expansion, which is not an end in itself, must as a priority help to attenuate the disparities in living conditions. . . In the European spirit special attention will be paid to non-material values and wealth and to protection of the environmental so that progress shall serve mankind' (European Council, *First Summit Conference of the Enlarged Community*, 15–16).

[137] Council, *Declaration of the Council of the European Communities, and of the Representatives of the Governments of the Member States meeting in the Council of 22 November 1973 on the Programme of Action of the European Communities on the Environment*, 1–2.

[138] For a discussion of the birth of environmental policy out of the lap of Articles 94 and 308 EC, see: Chapter 3—Section I (1a) above.

European Act, some 200 environmentally-related measures were thus adopted that would create 'the foundation for the formation of a very specific Community environmental policy'.[139] Most of these environmental acts were designed as 'minimum harmonization'.[140]

Formal constitutional foundations for a European environmental law were laid by the SEA. Thence, the EC Treaty provided a specific legislative competence for environmental policy.[141] Emblematically, the subsidiarity principle emerged for the first time in relation to environmental matters.[142] The Maastricht Treaty reinforced the constitutional status of environmental policy by amending Articles 2 and 3 EC, which now commit the Community to 'a high level of protection and improvement of the quality of the environment'.[143] In the present constitutional arrangement, environmental policy finds its place in Title XIX comprising Articles 174–176 EC.

The constitutional regime for environmental policy is in many respects paradigmatic for the Community's complementary competences. First, the conceptual contours of this competence are much more precise than in older policy areas. Secondly, the Community's role is characterized as a 'contribution'—thus acknowledging the continued legitimacy of national legislation in the field.[144] The cooperative federal structure of the environmental power is specified in Article 176 EC: European legislation 'shall not prevent any Member State from maintaining or introducing more stringent protective measures'. Community legislation only lays down minimum

---

[139] DH Scheuing, *Umweltschutz auf der Grundlage der Einheitlichen Europäischen Akte*, 157. More modest statistics attribute about 100 legislative measures to the period between 1973 and 1988—still 'no mean feat' given the lack of an express competence (cf SP Johnson and G Corcelle, *The Environmental Policy of the European Communities*, 5).

[140] Eg Article 7(2) of Directive 76/160 (quality of bathing water), Article 6 of Directive 75/440 (quality of surface water) or Article 10 of Directive 76/464 (pollution caused by dangerous substances discharged into the aquatic environment). In the words of Krämer (n 133 above): 'Community policy makers were aware from the very beginnings of environmental policy that the Community space between the south of Italy and the north of Scotland, between the Alps and the plains in northern Germany/Denmark, is very diversified, that environmental pressures differ and that the degree of awareness of environmental degradation varies considerably from one region to the other, provoking different answers to the environmental challenges. . . Environmental directives were drafted as minimum directives, which allowed Member States to maintain or introduce more protective environmental measures at national level'.

[141] Title VII of the EEC Treaty comprised three Articles: Articles 130r, 130s, and 130t.

[142] On this point, see: Section I (1) above.

[143] Article 2 EC.

[144] Article 174(1) EC.

standards and permits national 'opt-ups'.[145] These stricter national standards will not be subject to the—European—proportionality principle. '[I]nasmuch as other provisions of the Treaty are not involved, that principle is no longer applicable so far as concerns more stringent protective measures of domestic law adopted by virtue of Article 176 EC and going beyond the minimum requirements laid down by [European legislation]'.[146]

The Community has committed itself to a 'high level of protection'.[147] (A European minimum standard would thus not mean minimal.) However, this constitutional commitment will *not* require a high level of protection in every single legislative piece. It constitutes a general and abstract constitutional orientation for the development of the Community's environmental policy.[148] And this leads us—indirectly—into the conceptual heart of complementary competences: does the same 'abstract approach' also apply to the constitutional mandate to only adopt 'minimum standards'? Or, does Article 176 EC prevent the Community legislator from ever adopting any environmental measure that 'exhaustively harmonizes' all matters within its scope?

a. Article 175 EC: Soft or Hard Constitutional Frame?

Are all measures adopted under Article 175 minimum harmonization measures; or, does Article 176 only 'softly' require the Community legislator to leave some—abstractly defined—legislative space to the national legislators? Surprisingly, after nearly two decades of constitutional practice, the issue has not been definitely resolved. Two views are possible. According to a first view, Article 176 will not constitutionally prevent the Community legislator from

---

[145] This is the difference to the 'opt-out' mechanism in Article 95(4)—(9) EC, which allows for a *derogation* from Community legislation.

[146] Case C-6/03 *Deponiezweckverband Eiterköpfe*, para 63.

[147] Article 174(2) EC. Similar commitments to a 'high' level of protection are found in the following complementary competences: Article 61(2)(e) (measures in the field of police and judicial co-operation); Article 95(3) EC (harmonization measures concerning health, safety, environmental protection, and consumer protection); Article 127(1) EC (high level of employment); Article 152 (high level of human health); Article 153 (high level of consumer protection); and, finally, Article 163 (research and technological development activities of high quality). In Case C-341/95 *Gianni Bettati v Safety Hi-Tech Srl*, the Court clarified that, in the environmental policy of the Community, a high level of protection 'does not necessarily have to be the highest that is technically possible' (ibid para 47).

[148] This point has been made by Krämer who argued that 'sich das Ziel "hohes Schutzniveau" in Artikel 175 auf die gemeinschaftliche Umweltpolitik insgesamt, nicht auf eine einzelne Regelung oder gar eine einzelne Vorschrift bezieht. Deswegen steht dieses Ziel dem Absinken des geltenden Schutzniveaus im Einzelfall auch nicht entgegen' (L Krämer, *Artikel 174*, rn.18, in H von der Groeben & J Schwarze (eds), *Kommentar zum Vertrag über die Europäische Union*).

adopting single legislative measures that totally harmonize all matters within their scope. The SEA, it is claimed, only codified a legislative practice in which minimum harmonization was the predominant—not the exclusive—method of environmental harmonization. Article 176 was inserted into the Treaty:

without thereby implicitly making total harmonization impossible. . .This view implies that the inclusion of Article 176 in the Treaty was not really intended to have legal consequences. According to this interpretation Article 176 merely expresses the principle that *in general* decision-making under Article 175 takes the form of minimum harmonisation, but does not limit the Council's power, by way of 'self-binding', of setting total harmonisation standards. In other words it is up to the Council to decide to what extent Member States are allowed to adopt more stringent standards than those set in the Directive.[149]

The first view thus accepts a strong *presumption* against field pre-emption—codified in Article 176. However, the Community legislator faces no absolute *constitutional limitation* to exhaustively harmonize an environmental issue through a European law adopted under Article 175. Consequently, 'when a Member State, based on Article 176 of the Treaty, wants to take more protective measures, its legislative discretion is reduced in proportion to the concretisation which Community secondary law has given to the balance between environmental and economic interests in a specific situation'.[150]

Pointing to the insufficiency of this *soft* constitutional frame, a second view argues that Article 176 refers to every single piece of European legislation adopted under Article 175. The Community legislator will never be able to occupy a field. Each Community measure will need to leave a degree of legislative space to the national legislators. There are heavy legal arguments in favour of this *hard* constitutional solution for Article 175. First, the very wording of Article 176 points in that direction: the frame of reference for the higher national standard is not the Community environmental *policy*, but the specific Community *measure(s)*. Secondly, from a teleological perspective, the aim of achieving a high level of protection within the Community would be better served by always allowing Member States to go beyond the federal compromise represented in the European legislation.[151] Thirdly, it

---

[149] JH Jans, *European Environmental Law*, 118.

[150] L Krämer, *EC Environmental Law*, 121.

[151] G Winter, *Die Sperrwirkung von Gemeinschaftssekundärrecht für einzelstaatliche Regelungen des Binnenmarkts mit besonderer Berücksichtigung von Article 130 t EGV*, 380.

seems dubious, if not wrong, to reduce the SEA to having codified previous legislative practice.[152] Lastly, recent legislative practice has shown that environmental directives are no longer likely to contain a 'minimum harmonization clause'; and it is, furthermore, not unknown for such clauses to be removed from European environmental legislation in the course of a subsequent amendment.[153] It could therefore be argued that today's legislative practice recognizes Article 176 as a *direct* constitutional limit for *every* single environmental Community measure.

A hard constitutional frame around Article 175 would have a number of advantages.[154] First, the 'complementary' quality of the Community's activities could be enforced for every single piece of legislation. Instead of an abstract standard—presumably measured against the totality of existing Community environmental legislation—the frame of reference would be set by the scope of the specific piece(s) of legislation. Requiring the Community legislator to leave legislative space *within the scope of the Community measure*, would provide a more concrete 'jurisdictional' standard that would better safeguard the Member States' legislative autonomy. Following this second view, the Community's complementary competences à la Article 176 EC would come close to the constitutional regime developed under German federalism with regard to framework competences.[155]

What are the judicial guidelines from the European Court of Justice? The question about the nature of Community legislation adopted under Articles 175 and 176 had not been raised before *Dusseldorp*,[156] and it would, for that reason alone, 'have been desirable to interpret in some detail the purpose, meaning and relevance of Article 176 in the system of the Treaty'.[157] In this case, Dutch legislation had made the export of waste for recovery subject to an additional condition that was not mentioned in the relevant European environmental legislation. In a preliminary reference, the European

---

[152] DH Scheuing (n 139 above) 192: 'Entgegen erstem Anschein hat die Einheitliche Europäische Akte für die Umweltpolitik der Gemeinschaft doch einige wichtige Neuerungen gebracht'.

[153] JH Jans *European Environmental Law*, 114 (quoting Directive 97/11 amending Directive 85/337 on the assessment of the effect of certain public and private projects on the environment that deleted the minimum harmonization clause in Article 13 of the latter Directive).

[154] However, the constitutional limitation should only take effect *after* the introduction of Article 176 EC. For the opposite view, see: E Epiney, *Umweltrecht in der EU*, 126.

[155] For a discussion of the German constitutional concept of 'framework law', see: R. Schütze, *German Constitutional Federalism: Between* Sein *and* Bewußtsein.

[156] Case C-203/96 *Chemische Afvalstoffen Dusseldorp BV v Minister van Volkshuisvesting, Ruimtelijke Ordening en Milieubeheer*.

[157] L Krämer, *Casebook on EU Environmental Law*, 28.

Court was expressly asked whether Article 176 could provide a basis for the legality of stricter national laws. The Court avoided the question of the constitutional relationship between national legislation and Article 176 by focusing on the free movement aspect of the case. Indeed, if the national rules were found to violate the Treaty, then the complex discussion of the division of legislative powers in the area of environmental policy was unnecessary.[158] Analysing the obstacles to export trade created by the stricter national environmental rules, the Court found that Article 176 would not allow national legislators to extend the application of those stricter rules 'when it is clear that they create a barrier to exports which is not justified either by an imperative measure relating to protection of the environment or by one of the derogations provided for by [Article 30] of the Treaty'.[159] A later case was a little more forthcoming. In *Fornasar*,[160] the Court had to interpret the exhaustiveness of European legislation on hazardous waste, in particular Directive 91/689. Article 1(4) of the Directive provided:

For the purpose of this Directive 'hazardous waste' means:
— wastes featuring on a list to be drawn up in accordance with the procedure laid down in Article 18 of Directive 75/442/EC on the basis of Annexes I and II to this Directive, not later than six months before the date of implementation of this Directive. These wastes must have one or more of the properties listed in Annex III. The list shall take into account the origin and composition of the waste and, where necessary, limit values of concentration. This list shall be periodically reviewed and if necessary revised by the same procedure,
— any other waste which is considered by a Member State to display any of the properties listed in Annex III. Such cases shall be notified to the Commission and reviewed in accordance with the procedure laid down in Article 18 of Directive 75/442/EC with a view to adaptation of the list.

---

[158] This elegant, albeit evasive, solution had been suggested by Advocate General F Jacobs: 'In my view, however, none of the issues which might arise under [Article 176] need to be resolved in the present case. [Article 176] provides that the measures permissible by virtue of that article must in any event be compatible with the other provisions of the Treaty. For the reasons given below, I consider that the contested rule is contrary to [Article 29] of the Treaty' (Opinion of AG Jacobs, Case C-203/96 *Chemische Afvalstoffen Dusseldorp BV v Minister van Volkshuisvesting, Ruimtelijke Ordening en Milieubeheer*, para 74).

[159] Ibid para 50.

[160] Case C-318/98 *Criminal proceedings against Giancarlo Fornasar, Andrea Strizzolo, Giancarlo Toso, Lucio Mucchino, Enzo Peressutti and Sante Chiarcosso*.

A Council Decision had established a list of hazardous waste pursuant to Article 1(4) of Directive 91/689.[161] In national proceedings, the issue arose whether the list drawn up was exhaustive or not. The Commission maintained that the list could not be supplemented for waste falling within the scope of the annexes of the Community legislation.[162] The German and Austrian Governments, on the other hand, argued that the list could not be exhaustive because the second indent of Article 1(4) indicated that other waste may also be classified as hazardous by the Member States.[163] While the Court pointed to the need for a precise and uniform definition of hazardous waste,[164] it did not find the Community list to be exhaustive. The passage of interest here read as follows:

> *In that connection, it must be observed that the Community rules do not seek to effect complete harmonization in the area of the environment. Even though [Article 174] of the Treaty refers to certain Community objectives to be attained, both [Article 176] of the EC Treaty . . . and Directive 91/689 allow the Member States to introduce more stringent protective measures.* Under [Article 174] of the Treaty, Community policy on the environment is to aim at a high level of protection, taking into account the diversity of situations in the various regions of the Community. . .

It follows from the foregoing that, pursuant to Article 1(4) of Directive 91/689, the list provided for by that directive entitles the Member States to classify any other waste which a Member State considers to display one of the properties listed in Annex III to that directive as hazardous. Thus, such waste is considered hazardous only in the territory of the Member States which have adopted such a classification. In that event, the Member States are bound to notify such cases to the Commission for review in accordance with the procedure laid down in Article 18 of Directive 75/442, with a view to adaptation of the list of hazardous waste. Accordingly, on the basis of experience, the Commission is called upon to examine the extent to which it is appropriate to supplement the general list of hazardous waste applicable to all Member States of the Community by adding to it waste considered hazardous by one or more Member States pursuant to the second indent of Article 1(4) of Directive 91/689.[165]

The first part of the ruling signalled the Court's support for the hard constitutional solution outlined above. Indeed, the general tenor of the opening statement appears to endorse a hard frame around Article 175 EC:

---

[161] Council Decision 94/904 establishing a list of hazardous waste pursuant to Article 1(4) of Directive 91/689.

[162] Case C-318/98 *Fornasar*, para 35.

[163] Ibid para 36.

[164] Ibid para 43.

[165] Ibid paras 47–9.

'Community rules do not seek to effect complete harmonization in the area of the environment'. Isolated from the specific legislative measure on the judicial table, Article 176 would then always entitle national legislators to complement the common European standard. Had the Court stopped here, few doubts would have remained. However, the Court continued and the second part of the ruling represented a specific analysis of the legislative regime established for hazardous waste under the Directive. The second indent of Article 1(4) expressly entitled Member States to supplement the Community list. It could consequently be construed as a 'minimum harmonization clause'. A narrow reading of the ruling could therefore characterize the complementary quality of the Community intervention as a *legislative* choice embedded in the specific Community measure. The evasive ambivalence of *Fornasar* showed that the Court had still to make up its mind on whether to choose a 'soft' or a 'hard' constitutional solution for Article 175.[166]

b. The Scope of Article 176 EC: Cutting Across the Treaty?

Will Article 176 EC only entitle national legislators to adopt stricter national standards in relation to Community legislation adopted under Article 175 EC; or will Article 176 EC—either as a soft presumption or a hard constitutional limit—also apply to European legislation adopted under another legislative competence?

This question has been hotly debated in German academic circles under the banner of 'the principle of optimal environmental protection'.[167] According to this hypothesized general principle, Member States would always be entitled to adopt more stringent national environmental laws regardless of the

---

[166] The Court did not dissolve this ambivalence in Case C-6/03 *Deponiezweckverband Eiterköpfe*. The Court, again, started out by a broad constitutional statement (ibid para 27): 'The first point to be noted is that the Community rules do not seek to effect complete harmonisation in the area of the environment'. However, in a second step, the Court found—again—that the specific Directive only set minimum standards (ibid para 31): 'The wording and broad logic of those provisions make it clearly apparent that they set a minimum reduction to be achieved by the Member States and they do not preclude the adopting by the latter of more stringent measures'. And—again—it found that 'Article 176 EC *and the Directive* allow the Member States to introduce more stringent protection measures that go beyond the minimum requirements fixed by the Directive' (ibid para 32 (emphasis added)).

[167] '*Grundsatz des bestmöglichen Umweltschutzes*'. The principle was 'discovered' by Zuleeg in a path-breaking article in 1987, cf M Zuleeg, *Vorbehaltene Kompetenzen der Mitgliedstaaten der Europäischen Gemeinschaft auf dem Gebiete des Umweltschutzes*, 280. Since then, the principle has conquered German academia to such an extent that it is almost universally accepted. See the monograph on the principle by W Kahl, *Umweltprinzip und Gemeinschaftsrecht: Eine Untersuchung zur Rechtsidee des 'bestmöglichen Umweltschutzes' im EWG-Vertrag*.

underlying legislative competence on which the Community law is based. This view has arguably gained ground with the Amsterdam Treaty and the transposition of the environmental *Querschnittsklausel* (cross-section clause) into the first part of the Treaty dealing with the fundamental principles of the Community legal order. Article 6 EC states: 'Environmental protection requirements must be integrated into the definition and implementation of the Community policies and activities referred to in Article 3, in particular with a view to promoting sustainable development'. However, does this *Community* commitment to incorporating environmental sensibilities into the operation of other Community policies also imply Article 176 EC's general application to all Community legislation? Will Article 176 apply to legislation based on Articles 37, 95, 133 or 308?

Some serious doubts are in order. Article 6 EC is addressed to the Community legislator. Literal and systematic interpretations of Article 176, moreover, suggest that its scope of application is to be confined to Community measures adopted under Article 175 only. Finally, the horizontal application of Article 176 would—at least for environmental legislation—undermine the specific 'opt-out' regime established under Article 95(4)–(9).[168]

The debate is still open with the Court not having yet decided the issue. The closest the Court got to this point was in the judicial constellation in *Nederhoff*.[169] There, a national water protection measure went beyond the Community environmental legislation embodied in Directive 76/464. Article 10 of the Directive expressly authorized Member States to take more stringent measures than those provided for in the Directive. However, the stricter national environmental standard collided with Directive 76/769 on the approximation of the laws, regulations, and administrative provisions of the Member States relating to restrictions on the marketing and use of certain dangerous substances and preparations—based on Article 94 EC— as amended by Directive 94/60 that was based on Article 95 EC. How would

---

[168] L Krämer, *EC Environmental Law*, 132. Krämer argues that both Article 176 and Article 95(4)—(9) EC are exceptions from the general principles of the Community legal order and, therefore, have to be interpreted restrictively: 'As none of the Treaty provisions on which an environmental action can be based contain provisions similar to those of Arts 176 and 95, the conclusion must be that these provisions are exceptions to the general rule that Community measures cannot be derogated from by Member Sates, unless Community law expressly so provides. Their application to measures which had been adopted by virtue of Arts 37, 71, 93 or 133 of the EC Treaty is therefore not possible; all the more so since it would not be clear whether Arts 176 or 95 should apply in a specific case'.

[169] Case C-232/97 *Nederhoff & Zn v Dijkgraaf en hoogheemraden van het Hoogheemraadschap Rijnland*.

the Court conceptualize the relation between the higher national *environmental* standard and Community *harmonization* under Europe's Commerce Clause(s)?

The Court obviously recognized the tension: 'That raises the question whether Directive 76/769, as amended, which merely introduces restrictions on the marketing and use of wood treated with creosote, precludes a national water protection measure which has the effect of prohibiting or permitting only in exceptional cases the use of that substance for treating wood to be introduced into surface water. Even if the effects of a national measure such as that at issue in the main proceedings may be regarded as an obstacle to the free movement of products containing creosote, as regulated by Directive 76/769, it is sufficient to note that, in accordance with Article 1 thereof, that directive applies without prejudice to the application of other relevant Community provisions'.[170] However, the express saving clause found in Article 1(1) of Directive 76/769 'saved' the Court from entering a difficult pre-emption analysis.

2. *Public Health: Novel Constitutional Techniques*

The official recognition of a European policy regarding 'public health' occurred only with the second, and not with the first major Treaty amendment. The Maastricht Treaty granted the Community a competence for public health. This competence had been a compromise between those Member States that did not wish to endow the European level with an express mandate and those who wanted to 'centralize' health issues even further.[171] The introduction of the new competence was certainly no clear victory for a comprehensive European health policy. On the contrary, the competence offered a prime illustration of the constitutional corset increasingly placed around Community competences. Its sharp textual edges created a tight constitutional frame, which could harness Community action that might hitherto have been based on Article 95 EC. The Amsterdam Treaty loosened the corset a little—after the Bovine Spongiform Encephalopathy ('BSE') and the Creutzfeldt-Jakob disease ('CJD') crises had demonstrated the European dimension of certain health threats even to the staunchest defenders of State police powers in this field. Today, we find the Community's competence for public health codified in a single Article that by itself forms

---

[170] Ibid paras 63–64.
[171] TK Hervey and JV McHale, *Health Law and the European Union*, 74.

Title XIII of the EC Treaty. Article 152 is the prototype of the new complementary competences and assembles (almost) all the novel constitutional techniques. It reads:

Public Health—Article 152

1. A high level of human health protection shall be ensured in the definition and implementation of all Community policies and activities.

    Community action, which shall complement national policies, shall be directed towards improving public health, preventing human illness and diseases, and obviating sources of danger to human health. Such action shall cover the fight against the major health scourges, by promoting research into their causes, their transmission and their prevention, as well as health information and education.

    The Community shall complement the Member States' action in reducing drugs-related health damage, including information and prevention.

2. The Community shall encourage cooperation between the Member States in the areas referred to in this Article and, if necessary, lend support to their action. Member States shall, in liaison with the Commission, coordinate among themselves their policies and programmes in the areas referred to in paragraph 1. The Commission may, in close contact with the Member States, take any useful initiative to promote such coordination.

3. The Community and the Member States shall foster cooperation with third countries and the competent international organizations in the sphere of public health.

4. The Council, acting in accordance with the procedure referred to in Article 251 and after consulting the Economic and Social Committee and the Committee of the Regions, shall contribute to the achievement of the objectives referred to in this article through adopting:

    (a) measures setting high standards of quality and safety of organs and substances of human origin, blood and blood derivatives; these measures shall not prevent any Member State from maintaining or introducing more stringent protective measures;

    (b) by way of derogation from Article 37, measures in the veterinary and phytosanitary fields which have as their direct objective the protection of public health;

    (c) incentive measures designed to protect and improve human health, excluding any harmonization of the laws and regulations of the Member States.

5. Community action in the field of public health shall fully respect the responsibilities of the Member States for the organization and delivery of health services and medical care. In particular, measures referred to in paragraph 4(a) shall not affect national provisions on the donation or medical use of organs and blood.

What are the constitutional characteristics of this complementary competence? First of all, its length: Article 152 numbers 390 words. Quantity is not everything, but it counts for something. Compared to the humble 50 words that make up Article 94 and the 57 words that built Article 308, the careful wording shows that the amenders of the EC Treaty did not want to grant an abstractly phrased competence that would work as a formidable teleological platform for further centralization. More words, more precision. This linguistic strategy is as old as the desire to codify itself.[172]

Let us turn to the substance of the competence. Paragraph 1 defines the specific objectives of the Community's public health policy and specifies that Community action shall *complement* national policies in the pursuit of these aims. A special part of the Community's efforts should thereby be channelled into encouraging *cooperation among the Member States* (paragraph 2) as well as cooperation with third countries (paragraph 3).

The legal base for Community action is embedded in paragraph 4 which distinguishes three situations: regarding organs and substances of human origin, blood and blood derivatives, the Community may only lay down minimum standards. Here, we thus find the type of 'minimum harmonization' competence that was discussed above in the context of environmental policy. Article 152(4)(b) expressly creates a specific legal base for measures in the veterinary and phytosanitary fields that were previously adopted within the Common Agricultural Policy. Measures 'which have as their direct objective the protection of public health' can now be based on Article 152 EC to the pleasure of the European Parliament and the people of Europe.[173] In addition to these specific fields, paragraph 4(c) finally grants a 'general' public health competence to the Community. However, this competence is limited to the adoption of 'incentive measures' 'excluding any harmonization of the laws and regulations of the Member States'. Whatever the concept of 'incentive measure' is supposed to mean, one has to assume that it was designed as a constitutional limitation to those 'normal measures' that can be adopted under paragraph 4(a) and (b). Literally, the concept suggests the desire to have the Community primarily encourage the coordination of national policies.

---

[172] The *Allgemeine Landrecht für die preußischen Staaten* (Prussian General Law 1794) counted more than 19,000 paragraphs in order to regulate every single imaginable situation and thereby to limit judicial activism.

[173] Article 37(2) EC only entitles the European Parliament to be consulted for measures adopted under the CAP. Among the 'agricultural' health measures adopted under Article 152 EC are Regulation 999/2001 and Regulation 1829/2003.

But what exactly is the prohibition of 'harmonization' supposed to mean? Two views can be put forward. According to the first, the exclusion of harmonization means that European legislation must not modify *existing* national public health legislation. However, considering the wide definition given to the concept of 'harmonization' by the Court of Justice in *Spain v Council*, any legislative intervention on the part of the Community will unfold a *de facto* harmonizing effect within the national legal orders.[174] From this strict reading, the exclusion of harmonization under paragraph 4(c) would consequently deny all pre-emptive effect to Community legislation.[175] A second—less restrictive—view argues that the Community's legislative powers are only trimmed so as to prevent the *de jure* harmonization of national legislation.[176]

Both views appear problematic from a cooperative federalist perspective. Let us imagine a new public health threat that affects Europe. Let us also imagine that national legislators are—still—much quicker in adopting measures than the Community legislator. Will the Community therefore ever be able to adopt Community-wide standards for the problem? Will Community action be confined to coordinating national policies without setting common European standards? If so, it would be difficult to speak of a truly independent Community *policy* as the Community legislator simply cannot make its own *policy* choices for public health. The Community would have no *competence* to legislate. The principle of subsidiarity would then not even come into play—even for those situations where it is clear that common European rules would be more effective! The national 'pre-emption' of Community action would only be lifted, where the diverse national laws create genuine obstacles to intra-Community trade and/or distortions of competition. The Community would then be entitled to have recourse to Article 95 EC.[177]

---

[174] Case C-350/92 *Spain v Council*, where the Court found the adoption of a Regulation not beyond the scope of Article 95 as it aimed 'to prevent the heterogeneous development of national laws leading to further disparities' in the internal market (ibid para 35).

[175] A Bardenhewer-Rating and F Niggermeier, *Artikel 152*, rn.20 in H von der Groeben and J Schwarze, *Kommentar zum Vertrag über die EU*, who argue that the pre-Amsterdam version of Article 152 EC was not a legislative competence at all.

[176] For Lenaerts, 'incentive measures can be adopted in the form of Regulations, Directives, Decisions or atypical legal acts and are thus normal legislative acts of the Community'. '[T]he fact that a Community incentive measure may have the indirect effect of harmonizing . . . does not necessarily mean that it conflicts with the prohibition on harmonization' (K Lenaerts, *Subsidiarity and Community Competence in the Field of Education*, 13 and 15).

[177] However, in Case C-376/98 *Federal Republic of Germany v European Parliament and Council of the European Union (Tobacco Advertising)*, the Court clarified that Article 95 EC could not be used for a legislative measure whose principal aim was the protection of public health. Article 95 EC must not be used to circumvent the express exclusion of harmonization found in Article 152(4)(c) EC. A 'health' measure adopted under Article 95 EC must therefore 'genuinely have as its object the

This constitutional regime may again give rise to a benign degree of 'cynical reasoning',[178] for the Community legislator may need to justify politically desired European 'health measures' by means of the economic vocabulary of the internal market.

Finally, we find a last characteristic feature of the novel type of competence in paragraph 5. Here, the Treaty constitutionally recognizes the 'responsibility' of the Member States for the organization and delivery of health services and medical care. Moreover, measures adopted under paragraph 4a shall 'not affect' national provisions on the donation or medical use of organs and blood. Either formulation sounds like an 'express saving clause' at the constitutional level and would, if the Court decides to go down this road, mean that Community health measures cannot 'pre-empt' any national legislation within the areas enumerated. These constitutional exemptions—some have called them 'negative competences'—must nonetheless not be confused with a constitutional recognition of exclusive national police powers. Unlike the operation of a *Querschnittsklausel*, these provisions will not have any effect beyond the scope of Article 152 EC. Where harmonization under Article 95 EC or Community intervention in the course of the common market under Article 308 EC is necessary, the Community legislator can well enter into these pseudo-exclusive fields.[179]

In conclusion, the federal division of power in the field of public health demonstrates the European constitution's intent to leave legislative space for these matters to the national legislator. It goes too far to describe the Member States as the '*Herren der Gesundheitspolitik*'.[180] However, the invention of novel constitutional techniques—such as 'incentive measures' and the exclusion of harmonization—has been designed to constitutionally limit the competence of the Community to act and to preserve the legislative predominance of the national legislators. Complementary competences have therefore been associated with the principle of subsidiarity. However, it is important to underline that this *structural* expression of subsidiarity undermines to some extent the flexible federalism that is part and parcel of that very same constitutional principle. The exclusion of harmonization in some complementary

---

improvement of the conditions for the establishment and functioning of the internal market'. A 'mere finding of disparities between national rules and of the abstract risk of obstacles to the exercise of fundamental freedoms or of distortions of competition' would not be sufficient (ibid paras 79 and 84). For a discussion of the case, see: Chapter 3—Section I (2a) above.

[178] DH Scheuing (n 139 above) 162.

[179] On this point, see: Chapter 3—Section I (2b) above.

[180] JC Wichard, *Artikel 152* rn.8, in C Calliess and M Ruffert (eds), *Kommentar des Vertrages über die Europäische Union und des Vertrages zur Gründung der Europäischen Gemeinschaft: EUV/EGV*.

competences appears to limit the *very competence* of the Community to act.[181] Complementary competences of this kind breathe, but do thus not '*fully* breathe the air of "subsidiarity"'.[182]

Conclusion: The Constitutional Safeguards of Cooperative Federalism

In the last twenty years, the European Union has not only moved from a dual to a cooperative structure of European law. It has even constitutionalized the philosophy of cooperative federalism by means of two constitutional devises: the principle of subsidiarity and complementary competences.

The principle of subsidiarity operates within the sphere of powers shared by the Union and its Member States. As a principle of cooperative federalism, subsidiarity was designed to safeguard legislative space for the Member States by restricting European legislation to situations, where 'the objectives of the proposed action cannot be sufficiently achieved by the Member States and can therefore, by reason of the scale or effects of the proposed action, be better achieved by the Community'.[183] The Maastricht formulation was ambivalent in a number of ways. However, subsequent constitutional practice would refine the *Community* principle of subsidiarity in two ways. First, the constitutional and judicial clarifications would reduce subsidiarity *proper* to the question *whether* the Community should *exercise* its shared competence in a given situation. In reserving the federal intensity of a European law to the principle of proportionality in Article 5(3) EC, the Court forced itself to concentrate on the abstract question whether the *objectives* of the proposed action can be sufficiently achieved by the Member States. And in falling victim to an ontological fallacy, the Court short-circuited the judicial review of subsidiarity. Secondly, the Court has deferred to the political safeguards of

---

[181]   These are those complementary competences listed under (a), (c), (e), (f) and (g) above.

[182]   For a slightly different view, see K Lenaerts (n 176 above) 28, who claims in the context of the Community's complementary competence in the field of education and vocational training, that: 'Articles 126 and 127 thus fully breathe the air of "subsidiarity". Subsidiarity has plainly been taken into account in the very definition of the Community's competence within these fields. Because the drafters took special pains to incorporate the principles of subsidiarity and proportionality into the definition of Community power, these two principles may not require separate application in order to shield the Member States from too zealous an exercise by the Community of its constitutionally limited powers'.

[183]   Article 5(2) EC.

federalism by granting a wide margin of discretion to the European legislator. Subsidiarity was a *principle*—not a rule.[184]

This procedural dimension of subsidiarity has also been the dominant perspective in recent reform proposals that aim to strengthen the principle of subsidiarity. The beloved option has thereby been to involve national parliaments as watchdogs of subsidiarity. The Lisbon Protocol on the application of the principle of subsidiary and proportionality would create a 'yellow' and an 'orange' card mechanism. The rejection of the 'red card' option is to be welcomed. The hard constitutional solution would *not* have offered a third source of democratic legitimacy and the soft constitutional solution will channel the energy of national parliaments to where it primarily belongs: the control of their national governments. Lisbon would add an additional monitoring task to them, but this European task should only supplement their *national* responsibility. The Lisbon arrangements may equally call upon the Court to reinforce the judicial control of subsidiarity. The Court too would have a choice between a soft and a hard constitutional solution. The European Court could—like the American Supreme Court— essentially view the subsidiarity principle as a *presumption* against pre-emption. However, presumptions can be overturned; and for that reason this chapter has argued in favour of a hard constitutional solution. In federal context, exclusively process-based theories of judicial review are misplaced as there are *two* democratic processes that claim authority.

Strengthening the judicial review of subsidiarity will not mean revolutionary change. European constitutionalism has already made a substantive commitment towards cooperative federalism. Instead of leaving the federal philosophy to the *political* safeguards of federalism alone, the European legal order has accepted *substantive* limits to the European legislator in the form of complementary competences. Today, fourteen Community policies fall into this category. The European legislator is thereby either confined to establishing minimum standards and/or restricted to complementing the national legislator. Legislative cooperation here is not the result of a *legislative* choice but is a *constitutional* choice. The Treaty guarantees the ability of the Member States to legislate in concert with the Community legislator. The pre-emptive effect of European legislation is constitutionally limited. This should theoretically mean that Member States are *always* entitled to

---

[184] *Contra* T Schilling, *A New Dimension of Subsidiarity: Subsidiarity as a Rule and a Principle*, 214: '[T]he subsidiarity principle as laid down in [Article 5 (2)] must be considered, in spite of its name, as a rule (the subsidiarity rule). It is not a very well-defined or clear-cut rule, but a rule it is'.

adopt higher national standards on top of a Community measure—provided, of course, these national measures conform to primary and secondary Community law.

The constitutional regime governing complementary competences has not yet been fully spelled out by the European Court of Justice. We saw above that the Court has so far eschewed the question whether complementary competences will constitutionally prevent the Community legislator from ever adopting legislative measures that totally harmonize all matters within their scope. The 'hard' constitutional solution appears preferable when compared to the 'soft' constitutional option of only allowing the national level some abstract degree of legislative autonomy. The more concrete, the more operational—this wisdom also applies to constitutional safeguards. If the European Court of Justice affirms the hard constitutional frame around 'minimum harmonization' competences, the latter would approach the idea of 'framework competences' known in German constitutional thought. Unfortunately, we must also wait for solidified constitutional principles in relation to the second type of complementary competence represented by the Community's public health policy. There is not yet any authoritative judicial commentary on what an 'incentive measure' is, or what the exclusion of harmonization is supposed to mean.

However, even if the exact degree of legislative space guaranteed to the Member States under the principle of subsidiarity and Europe's complementary competences is still unclear, the very existence of both safeguards represents, in and of itself, a constitutional choice in favour of cooperative federalism. Europe's constitutional commitment to this federal philosophy thus contrasts with the *laissez-faire* approach in the American federal order.

6

Excursus: A Foreign Affairs 'Exception'?

Introduction: The European Union and Foreign Affairs

The rise of international organizations in the twentieth century embodied the philosophy of cooperative international law.[1] *Within* these international structures, States could prepare international conventions or supranational legislation to harmonize their national laws. But could these organizations themselves conclude international treaties with foreign States? Classic international law had remained hostile to this idea. 'Even when the autonomy of the organisation vis-à-vis the member states at the institutional level was conceded', 'this autonomy for a long time had no external dimension: organisations did not yet conduct "external relations", and where they did, it was interpreted in terms of agency on behalf of the member states'.[2] The denial of autonomous external relations of international organizations had been hinted at by the Permanent Court of International Justice in the first half of the twentieth century.[3] Yet, the rise of cooperative international law eventually generated new responses to the foreign affairs powers of international organizations.

The capacity of international organizations to engage in international treaty-making was—if indirectly—recognized in 1949 and is today universally accepted.[4] Nonetheless, international law has remained for a long time ambivalent towards the source and scope of the external powers of international organizations.[5] The foreign affairs of international organizations raised

---

[1] WG Friedmann, *The Changing Structure of International Law*.

[2] C Brölmann, *The Institutional Veil in Public International Law*, 95.

[3] Cf *SS Wimbledon*, (1923) Series A No 1, 15: 'the right of entering into international engagements is an attribute of *State* sovereignty' (ibid 25, emphasis added).

[4] Cf *Reparation for Injuries suffered in the Service of the United Nations*, (1949) ICJ Reports 174: 'Accordingly, the Court has come to the conclusion that the Organization is an international person. That is not the same thing as saying that it is a State, which it certainly is not, or that its legal personality and rights and duties are the same as those of a State. Still less is it the same thing as saying that it is "a super-State", whatever that expression may mean. It does not even imply that all its rights and duties must be upon the international plane, any more than all the rights and duties of a State must be upon that plane. What it does mean is that it is a subject of international law and capable of possessing international rights and duties, and that it has capacity to maintain its rights by bringing international claims' (ibid 179).

[5] Would the power to conclude international treaties originate directly from international law or derive from the will of the Member States of the organization? The idea that international organizations enjoy an 'inherent capacity'—derived not from its Member States, but directly from international law—has been advocated (cf I Pernice, *Völkerrechtliche Verträge Internationaler Organisationen*, 233–6). According to J Klabbers, *An Introduction to International Institutional Law*, the 1986 Vienna Convention opted for the first solution when its preamble states that 'international organizations possess the capacity to conclude treaties which is necessary for the exercise of their functions and

fundamental challenges to the traditional law of treaties. The latter was, after all, based on the sovereign equality of its participants and '[i]nternational organizations are neither sovereign nor equal'.[6] Would international organizations thus remain 'open structures', in the sense that 'member states remain visible behind the corporate veil'?[7] The treaty powers of international organizations would, indeed, be 'continuously challenged from two sides': 'from the outside world, where historically only states have held "full powers", and also from within, where member states are constantly on guard against both loss of sovereignty and against any consequences the activities of the organization might bring for them'.[8]

What would be the outcome of this dual challenge for the foreign affairs powers of the European Union? The Treaty of Rome did acknowledge the legal personality of the European Community.[9] The international *capacity* of the Community would stretch 'over the whole field of objectives defined in Part One of the Treaty'.[10] What about the Community's treaty-making *powers*? Under the original 1957 Treaty, the Community's treaty-making powers were confined to international agreements under the Common Commercial

---

the fulfilment of their purposes'. By contrast, a second view holds that 'the power of an international organization to enter legal relationships is always limited by the organization's constitution and other internal instruments because the separate legal personality of the organization is based on these provisions' (N Sybesma-Knol, *The New Law of Treaties: The Codification of the Law of Treaties concluded between States and International Organizations or between two or more International Organizations*, 427).

[6] P Reuter, *Question of Treaties Concluded between States and International Organizations or Between Two or More International Organizations*, 120.

[7] C Brölmann, *A Flat Earth? International Organizations in the System of International Law*, 322.

[8] N Sybesma-Knol (n 5 above) 428.

[9] Article 281 EC: 'The Community shall have legal personality'. The legal personality of the European Union under the Second and Third Pillar has long been disputed, but seems now, *a posteriori*, accepted. The following chapter will exclusively deal with the foreign affairs of the European Community.

[10] Case 22/70 *Commission v Council* (*ERTA*), para 14. Part One of the 1957 Rome Treaty was entitled 'Principles' and contained the first eight articles. In *ERTA*, the Court extends the legal position under the ECSC to the EC Treaty (cf Article 6 ECSC: 'In international relations, the Community shall enjoy the legal capacity it requires to perform its functions and attain its objectives'). Despite *ERTA's* clarification, the distinction between the Community's 'capacity' and 'power' would be clouded in later analysis. For example, Professor Weiler's 1983 essay on mixed agreements misleadingly asserted that 'the Community cannot have capacity where it does not have treaty power' as '[t]his capacity from the Community point of view would seem to depend on the treaty-making power' (JHH Weiler, *The External Legal Relations of Non-Unitary Actors: Mixity and the Federal Principle*, in: *The Constitution of Europe*, 179 and fn 142, emphasis added). This view was, after *ERTA*, no longer tenable as the ruling clarified the Community point of view that the Community's capacity was wider than the Community's treaty-making powers.

Policy and Association Agreements with third countries or international organizations.[11] This picture changed dramatically through the doctrine of implied external powers. Would these implied powers be exclusive, concurrent, or shared? What was the Community's federal philosophy in the context of foreign affairs? The first section of this chapter deals with these questions. It argues that despite the dramatic growth of European treaty-making power through the doctrine of parallelism, European constitutionalism has traditionally cultivated a dual federal philosophy. The second section searches for possible reasons as to why the European legal order has favoured a dual federalist rationale in the external sphere. Europe's foreign affairs 'exceptionalism', it will be argued, rooted in the uncertainty over the legal status of international treaties concluded by Member States in the Community legal order. This original ambivalence has been resolved today; and Europe's foreign affairs have gradually moved—in constitutional theory and constitutional practice—towards a cooperative federalism.

I. Europe's International Powers: Dual Federalism in the External Sphere

The European Union's powers are enumerated powers; and under the original 1957 Rome Treaty, the Community's treaty-making powers were confined to two instances only.[12] The restrictive attribution of external powers to the Community protected a status quo in which the Member States were the protagonists on the international relations scene. Unhappy with the asymmetry between the richness of the Community's internal powers and the scarcity of its external powers, the European Court has led—and won—a remarkable campaign to expand Europe's treaty-making powers.

The invention of 'parallel powers' added an extra layer of complexity and 'exceptionalism' to this corner of Community law. In order to understand the federal structure of the Community's external regime, we need to respect the fundamental distinction between the existence or scope and the essence or nature of federal powers. Unfortunately, many rulings in the external sphere—even today—only deal with one or the other, or worse: merge the

---

[11] Cf Articles 113 and 238 of the original EEC Treaty.
[12] Ibid.

two layers into one. This has been the source of much confusion in the past. The absence of constitutional rigour created various ambivalences in the foreign affairs federalism of the European Union. The judicial picture offers a 'cubist-like perspective',[13] as even recent jurisprudence has not entirely succeeded in creating a unified single perspective from which to conceptualize the Community's external powers.

This section will analyse this cubist painting. We need to understand its 'building blocks' before we can attempt to identify the federal philosophy structuring the legal canvass. First, we shall look at the invention of parallel external powers in the Community legal order. Having explored the conditions for their existence, we proceed to discuss their—still—enigmatic nature. We will see that European constitutionalism subscribes to the theory of subsequent exclusivity and, thereby, to a dual federal philosophy.

1. *Parallel External Powers: Existence and Scope*

A doctrine of parallelism was not foreign to the Community legal order. The Euratom Treaty provided that '[t]he Community may within the limits of its powers and jurisdiction, enter into obligations by concluding agreements or contracts with a third State, an international organisation or a national of a third State'.[14] No express provision of this sort could be found in the Treaty establishing the European Community—an omission that constituted a strong legal argument against parallel external powers in the EC legal order.[15] However, according to an early commentator '[t]he question remained open whether the Community might conclude agreements also on other matters falling within its jurisdiction, but for which the Treaty has not expressly authorized it to enter into agreements with third States'.[16] The rigorous contours of strict enumeration would indeed soon be softened—if not dissolved—with the assistance of the powerful doctrine of implied external powers invented in *ERTA*.[17]

---

[13] E Stein, *External Relations of the European Community: Structure and Process*, 127.

[14] Article 101(1) Euratom Treaty. As regards the ECSC, its founding treaty did not expressly confer a general treaty-making power; yet academic opinion assumed such a power (I Macleod, ID Hendry and S Hyett, *The External Relations of the European Communities*, 42).

[15] D McGoldrick, *International Relations Law of the European Union*, 48.

[16] P Pescatore, *External Relations in the Case-Law of the Court of Justice of the European Communities*, 618.

[17] Case 22/70 *Commission v Council (ERTA)*.

a. From ERTA to the 'Triumph of Parallelism'

The legal background to the *ERTA* dispute is complex and warrants a brief recapitulation: the European Road Transport Agreement ('ERTA', or under its French acronym: '*AETR*') had been designed to harmonize certain social aspects of international road transport and involved a number of Member States as potential signatories. The negotiations had (re-)started in 1967 and were conducted without formal involvement of the Community. Before their conclusion, the Council enacted in 1969 a regulation dealing with road safety. Since an international treaty was still seen to be an important step in the same direction on the international plane, the Member States agreed to coordinate their positions within the Council. The preceding Member State would act as spokesman and a resolution had been adopted to give legal effect to this gentlemen's agreement. The Commission felt excluded from its role as Europe's external broker. It unsuccessfully insisted on being implicated in the negotiations and eventually brought the matter before the European Court. There, the Commission argued that the Community's powers under its transport policy included treaty-making and that this power had become exclusive after the adoption of Community legislation in the form of the 1969 Council Regulation. This innovative and combative legal reasoning was thus two-layered: the first layer concerned the *existence* of the Community's treaty-making powers, while the second centred on the *essence* or *nature* of this power.

In relation to the existence question, the Commission had argued that Article 71 EC 'conferred on the Community powers defined in wide terms with a view to implementing the common transport policy [which] must apply to external relations just as much as to domestic measures'.[18] This wide teleological interpretation of the wording of Article 71 EC was justified for

---

[18] *ERTA*, para 6. The original EEC provision read as follows: '(1) For the purpose of implementing [Article 70], and taking into account the distinctive features of transport, the Council shall, acting unanimously until the end of the second stage and by qualified majority thereafter, lay down, on a proposal from the Commission and after consulting the Economic and Social Committee and the Assembly: (a) common rules applicable to international transport to or from the territory of a Member State or passing across the territory of one or more Member States; (b) the conditions under which non-resident carriers may operate transport services within a Member State; (c) any other appropriate provisions. (2) The provisions referred to in (a) and (b) of paragraph 1 shall be laid down during the transitional period. (3) By way of derogation from the procedure provided for in paragraph 1, where the application of provisions concerning the principles of the regulatory systems for transport would be liable to have serious effect on the standard of living and on employment in certain areas and on the operation of transport facilities, they shall be laid down by the Council acting unanimously. In so doing, the Council shall take into account the need for adaptation to the economic development which will result from establishing the common market'.

'the full effect of this provision would be jeopardized if the powers which it confers, particularly that of laying down "any appropriate provisions", within the meaning of subparagraph (1) (c) of the article cited, did not extend to the conclusion of agreements with third countries'.[19] The Commission's argument thus emphasized the need for an international legal instrument to implement the objectives under the Community's internal transport competence. The Council opposed this *effet utile* interpretation contending that '[Article 71] relates only to measures *internal* to the Community, and cannot be interpreted as authorizing the conclusion of international agreements'. The power to enter into agreements with third countries 'cannot be assumed in the absence of an express provision in the Treaty'.[20] In its judgment, the European Court famously sided with the Commission's extensive stance:

To determine in a particular case the Community's authority to enter into international agreements, regard must be had to the whole scheme of the Treaty no less than to its substantive provisions. Such authority arises not only from an express conferment by the Treaty—as is the case with [Article 133] and [ex-] Article 114 for tariff and trade agreements and with [Article 310] for association agreements—but may equally flow from other provisions of the Treaty and from measures adopted, within the framework of those provisions, by the Community institutions. . .

According to [Article 70], the objectives of the Treaty in matters of transport are to be pursued within the framework of a common policy. With this in view, [Article 71(1)] directs the Council to lay down common rules and, in addition, 'any other appropriate provisions'. By the terms of subparagraph (a) of the same provision, those common rules are applicable 'to international transport to or from the territory of a Member State or passing across the territory of one or more Member States'. This provision is equally concerned with transport from or to third countries, as regards that part of the journey which takes place on Community territory. It thus assumes that the powers of the Community extend to relationships arising from international law, and hence involve the need in the sphere in question for agreements with the third countries concerned.[21]

The passage spoke the language of teleological interpretation: in the light of the general scheme of the Treaty, the Community's power to adopt 'any other appropriate provision' to give effect to the Community's transport policy objectives must be interpreted as including the legal power to enter

---

[19] *ERTA*, para 7.
[20] Ibid paras 9–10 (emphasis added).
[21] Ibid paras 15–16 and 23–27.

international agreements.[22] According to the tenor of the passage, Europe's treaty-making power seemed implied as an alternative and additional legal instrument, which formed part and parcel of the Community's 'internal' competence.

Matters were, sadly enough, not so 'naturalistic' as this—isolated—component of the judgment suggests. The *ERTA* Court had been 'cubist' in its collage of various lines of reasoning. The resulting judgment appears, at times, more as an edited work than as a monographic entity. The ruling remained ambivalent in relation to the role played by internal legislation in the *creation* of the implied external power of the Community. While the above passage seemed to firmly separate the existence of parallel external powers from the presence of Community legislation, other parts of the judgment suggested that the Community's implied treaty-making power would only come into being when and to the extent that internal legislation had been adopted.[23] And if this was the case, what conditions had to be met before those implied powers would come into being?

Two 1970s rulings cleared the way for a doctrine of parallelism, which gradually separated the existence of implied external powers from the presence of Community legislation. In *Kramer* the Court dealt with the North-East Atlantic Fisheries Convention, which was concluded to ensure the conservation of fish stocks through rational exploitation.[24] The Dutch authorities had implemented their international obligations by creating criminal offences, on the basis of which proceedings had been launched against two Dutch fishermen. The national measure's validity was challenged in three respects, one of which was the claim that the Member States had lost their competence to conclude the international convention in the face of the

---

[22]   In the words of the *ERTA* Court: 'With regard to the implementation of the Treaty the system of internal Community measures may not therefore be separated from that of external relations' (ibid para 19).

[23]   Consider the following parts of the ruling: 'Although it is true that [Articles 70 and 71] do not expressly confer on the Community authority to enter into international agreements, nevertheless the bringing into force, on 25 March 1969, of Regulation No. 543/69 of the Council on the harmonization of certain social legislation relating to road transport necessarily vested in the Community power to enter into any agreement with third counties relating to the subject-matter governed by that regulation. This grant of power is moreover expressly recognized by Article 3 of the said Regulation which prescribes that: "The Community shall enter into any negotiations with third countries which may prove necessary for the purpose of implementing this regulation." Since the subject-matter of the AETR falls within the scope of Regulation No. 543/69, the Community has been empowered to negotiate and conclude the agreement in question since the entry into force of the said Regulation' (ibid paras 28–30).

[24]   Cases 3, 4 and 7/76 *Kramer*.

Community's exclusive treaty-making power in this area.[25] In a preliminary ruling on the issue the Court drew again inspiration from the 'general system of Community law in the sphere of external relations',[26] looking at 'the whole scheme of Community law no less than to its substantive provisions',[27] and concluded that the Community's external powers 'arise not only from an express conferment by the Treaty, but may equally flow *implicitly from other provisions of the Treaty*, from the act of accession and from measures adopted, within the framework of those provisions, by the Community institutions'.[28]

However, the precise constitutional source from which those external powers were to be implied was not yet absolutely clear. Looking at *all* the relevant legal provisions in primary *and* secondary law, the Court found that 'the Community has at its disposal, on the internal level, the power to take any measure for the conservation of the biological resources of the sea'.[29] 'In these circumstances', continued the Court, 'it follows from the very duties and powers which Community law has established and assigned to the institutions of the Community on the internal level that the Community has authority to enter into international commitments for the conservation of the resources of the sea'.[30] The 'authority' to conclude the international convention was thus treated as a reflex to the 'duties and powers' within the Community's internal sphere.[31] The relationship between the creation of those external powers and Community legislation had, thereby, remained unresolved. Parallel external powers had emerged from an amorphous amalgam of primary and secondary law.[32]

---

[25] On this aspect of the ruling, see: Chapter 3—Section II (1b) above. Apart from the claim that the national authorities had not been entitled to conclude the international convention for lack of treaty-making power, a second argument questioned the legality of the national measures in the light of the principle of preemption, while the free movement provisions provided the third ground of review.

[26] *Kramer*, para 16.

[27] Ibid paras 19–20.

[28] Ibid (emphasis added).

[29] Ibid paras 30–3.

[30] Ibid.

[31] Only in a second step did the Court proceed to look at the nature of the competence, ie 'whether the Community institutions in fact assumed the functions and obligations arising from the Convention and from the decisions taken thereunder' (ibid para 34).

[32] 'While the *Kramer* case represented an advance from, or at least a clarification of, the *AETR* decision in so far as the Court recognised the implied treaty-making capacity of the Community even where the powers, though conferred, had not been used, the possibility remained that the Court might not have acknowledged the Community's capacity in the absence of the measures adopted (in particular Regulation No. 2141/70) and Article 102 of the Act of Accession.' (M Hardy, *Opinion 1/76 of the Court of Justice: The Rhine Case and the Treaty—Making Powers of the Community*, 587.)

The heart of the doctrine of parallelism would finally be addressed in Opinion 1/76.[33] There the Court returned to the existence of implied external powers under the Community's transport title. The Commission had claimed that it followed from the case law that the Community possessed the power to conclude international agreements 'once the Treaty provides for an internal power even if the latter has not yet been the subject of developments of secondary [sic] legislation'.[34] The proposed international agreement would, as such, 'introduce at one and the same time common rules into the Community and identical rules into those [third] countries'.[35] Accepting that it was impossible to implement the objectives pursued by Article 71 EC without the participation of Switzerland, the Court famously declared that '*whenever Community law has created for the institutions of the Community powers within its internal system for the purpose of attaining a specific objective, the Community has authority to enter into the international commitments necessary for the attainment of that objective even in the absence of an express provision in that connexion*'.[36]

While the constitutional source for the Community's implied external powers had remained an amorphous mixture of primary and secondary law in *Kramer*, no Community legislation existed in the present case. The external powers simply flowed '*by implication from the provisions of the Treaty creating the internal power*'.[37] The implied external power would not depend on whether or not 'common rules' existed.[38] Opinion 1/76 thus confirmed the independence of implied external powers from the presence of secondary law.[39] As a brilliant commentary prophesied in 1977, the ruling meant that 'it will not now be possible for a Member State to contend that Community participation is legally impossible or *ultra vires* unless it also argues either that the

---

[33] Opinion 1/76 (*Draft Agreement for the Laying-up Fund for Inland Waterway Vessels*).

[34] Commission Submissions to Opinion 1/76, 749.

[35] Ibid 759.

[36] Opinion 1/76, para 3.

[37] Ibid para 4.

[38] The existence of Community legislation would only reinforce their assumption without, however, being constitutive or necessary for the existence of implied external powers. In the words of the Court: 'This is *particularly* so in all cases in which internal power has already been used in order to adopt measures which come within the attainment of common policies. It is, however, not limited to that eventuality' (ibid para 4—emphasis added).

[39] Commenting on Opinion 1/76, Pescatore captured the breakthrough of the doctrine of parallelism in the following words: 'This puts an end to the uncertainty inherent in the *ERTA* judgement as to whether an external competence may be recognized also in cases where the Community, though having jurisdiction, has not yet covered the field by internal measures. *Opinion 1/76* makes it clear that the existence of a virtual capacity is sufficient in this respect, even if it has not yet been exercised for internal purposes' (P Pescatore (n 16 above) 621).

agreement falls entirely outside the scope of the E[]C Treaty, or that, though it comes within that scope, Community participation is not needed'.[40]

Yet, doubts remained. The triumph of parallelism could only be celebrated in Opinion 2/91.[41] The European Court had been requested to give an opinion on the federal division of treaty-making powers in respect of Convention No 170 of the International Labour Organization ensuring safety in the use of chemicals at work. The Court's brief syllogistic reasoning in relation to the existence of implied external powers encapsulates the doctrine of parallelism in its purest form. The Court simply held that the field covered by the relevant Convention fell within the Community's internal competence; and '[*c*]*onsequently*', the adoption of Convention No 170 '*falls within the Community's area of [external] competence*'.[42] From the very fact that the Community possessed an internal power—in this case the competence to adopt social provisions—the Court acknowledged an external power for all matters falling within the scope of this internal competence. (While Community legislation exited on the matter, the latter was deemed to be constitutionally insignificant.) The reasoning of the Court reflected the idea of a *parallel* treaty-making power running alongside Europe's internal legislative powers. This reading was recently confirmed.[43] The European Court has thus established a European doctrine according to which 'Community treaty power is co-extensive with its internal domestic powers', and which thus 'cuts across all areas of its internal domestic competence listed in the Article 3 of the E[]C Treaty'.[44]

b. *Towards a Theory of Implied External Powers: Three Conceptions*

The language of 'parallel powers' is academically engineered. The doctrine of parallelism is a term of art that is not (yet) used by the European Court.[45]

---

[40] M Hardy (n 32 above) 595.

[41] Opinion 2/91 (*Convention No 170 of the International Labour Organization concerning Safety in the Use of Chemicals at Work*).

[42] Ibid paras 15–17 (emphasis added).

[43] C-459/03 *Commission v Ireland (MOX Plant)*.

[44] E Stein, *External Relations of the European Community: Structure and Process*, 146.

[45] None of the cases analysed above refers to 'parallel powers' or the doctrine of 'parallelism' as the constitutional rationale for the assumption of implied external powers. This might be in the process of changing. See, for example, the pronouncement of Advocate General Tizzano in his opinion to the *Open Skies* cases: 'More specifically, it is my view that the necessity for an agreement must be determined in accordance with the procedure laid down for the exercise of the *parallel internal competence*, where such competence is already provided for, or, if that is not the case, in accordance with the procedure laid down in [Article 308] of the Treaty' (Opinion of AG Tizzano in Case 476/98 *Commission v Germany (Open Skies)*, para 52, emphasis added). And in summarizing the

The invention of the doctrine of implied external powers has led to a number of academic theories, three of which shall be discussed here.

The classic version of the doctrine of parallel powers argues that 'the *competence* of the EC to enter into international agreements should run in "parallel" with the development of its internal competence—*in* [foro] *interno in foro externo*'.[46] According to this reading, parallel powers are parallel *competences*.[47] This first theory of implied external powers introduced the idea of two distinct spheres of competences into the Community legal order. Beyond the realm of the Community's internal competences exists a parallel legal universe of external relations competences. This competence dualism has found support in the European Court's ruling in Opinion 2/94, dealing with the EC's competence to accede the ECHR Convention.[48] There the Court declared that 'in the field of international relations, at issue in this request for an Opinion, it is settled case-law that the *competence* of the Community to enter into international commitments may not only flow from express provisions of the Treaty but also be implied from those provisions'.[49] The implication of a 'new' external competence would not, according to the Court, conflict with the enumeration principle.[50]

A second conceptualization of the implied external powers doctrine starts from the distinction between 'competence' and 'power'—a useful theoretical distinction. While the former concept refers to the material policy field in which the Community can act, the latter concept includes the legal

---

ERTA line of cases, the Advocate General stated that according to 'that principle, particularly in view of the need to safeguard the unity of the common market and the uniform application of Community law, the Court also stated that once the Community has actually exercised its internal power by adopting common rules, its *parallel external competence* becomes exclusive, with the result that the Member States lose their freedom to undertake obligations with third countries which affect those rules' (ibid para 64, emphasis added).

[46] D McGoldrick, *International Relations Law of the European Union*, 48.

[47] Cf D Wyatt, *Competence of the Community Internal and External*, 47.

[48] Opinion 2/94 (*Accession by the Community to the European Convention for the Protection of Human Rights and Fundamental Freedoms*). For a longer discussion of this case, see: Chapter 3—Section I (1b) above.

[49] Ibid paras 25–6 (emphasis added).

[50] After having quoted Article 5 EC—whose first paragraph codifies the enumeration principle—the Court found that the 'principle of conferred powers must be respected in both the internal action and the international action of the Community' (ibid para 24). In the opinion of Stein, the Court 'in effect rejected the principle of enumerated powers in favour of the doctrine that Community treaty power is co-extensive with the internal domestic powers and that it cuts across all areas of its internal domestic competence listed in Article 3 of the EEC Treaty' (E Stein, *External Relations of the European Community: Structure and Process*, 146).

instruments available to implement the policy objective.[51] Implied powers in the external sphere are not parallel *competences*, but parallel *instruments*. The 'competence'—in the sense of the legal entitlement to act in a policy field—is thereby located in the 'internal' competence. This perspective finds strong support in the *ERTA* ruling, discussed at length above. There the Court treated the implied treaty-making power not as an independent competence but rather as an additional policy *measure*—a legal instrument to implement its common transport policy.[52]

A third theory argues that the very notion of 'parallel powers' is misleading. It therefore suggests the 'doctrine of complementarity' to conceptualize the case law on implied external powers. 'The Community will be competent under the complementarity principle to conclude an agreement judged *necessary for the attainment of one or more of the objectives specified by the legal basis*'.[53] This doctrine denies that the Community enjoys an external competence that is the mirror image of an internal competence. There is no symmetry or parallelism according to which the Community's external powers are co-extensive to its internal powers. The existence of the former is controlled by a 'necessity requirement' which deforms the logic of parallelism in the Community legal order.[54] This theory can also marshal a number of judicial

---

[51] Cf T Tridimas and P Eeckhout, *The External Competence of the Community and the Case-Law of the Court of Justice: Principles versus Pragmatism*, 144; as well as R Schütze, *The Morphology of Legislative Power in the European Community: Legal Instruments and the Federal Division of Power*, 131–44.

[52] See in particular para 19 of the *ERTA* ruling: 'With regard to the implementation of the provisions of the Treaty the system of internal Community measures may not therefore be separated from that of external relations'. The instrument thesis equally gained strength from Opinion 1/75 in the context of the Community's express treaty-making powers. In exploring the Community's powers under the common commercial policy provisions, the Court found the Community entitled 'pursuant to the powers which it possesses, *not only to adopt internal rules of Community law, but also to conclude agreements with third countries*' since a commercial policy was 'made up by the combination and interaction of *internal and external measures*' (Opinion 1/75, 11 (emphasis added)). Consider also the Court's remarks in Opinion 1/76, where it pointed out that 'an agreement concluded by the Community with a third State is, as far as concerns the Community, an *act of one of the institutions* within the meaning of [Article 234] of the Treaty' (cf Opinion 1/76, para 18, emphasis added).

[53] A Dashwood, *The Attribution of External Relations Competence*, 132 (emphasis added).

[54] Dashwood defines the 'principle of complementarity' in the context of his discussion of Opinion 1/76 in the following way: 'The Court is not saying, as it seemed to be in *AETR*, that Article 71 EC authorizes the use of all appropriate means, including acceptance of international commitments, in pursuing the action that is contemplated. The external competence implicitly conferred by the legal basis in question is here treated as being in a real sense *ancillary to the expressly conferred internal competence*: it is recognised only in so far as the latter may appear insufficient to achieve the specified objective in an optimal way. To call this, as most commentators do, the principle of "parallelism" or of "parallel competence" seems misleading. Things which are parallel,

pronouncements in its favour. In Opinion 1/76, the Community was granted implied external powers only 'in so far as the participation of the Community in the international agreement is . . . *necessary for the attainment of one of the objectives of the Community*'.[55] Even Opinion 1/94 has been invoked to confirm the logic of complementarity.[56]

it has been pointed out, run alongside each other, without ever meeting: manifestly that does not convey the relationship between express internal and implied external competence, as explained in the quoted passage. The logic of that relationship is more accurately indicated by the name, "principle of complementarity", suggested in our discussion of the *Kramer* judgement' (A Dashwood and J Heliskoski, *The Classic Authorities Revisited*, 12–13). Dashwood himself, however, favours what he calls 'the true construction principle', inviting the Court 'to abandon the logic of complementarity in favour of the straightforward principle that the existence of external relations competence in a given case depends on the true construction of the relevant power-conferring provision. The Court should not, as it did in *Kramer*, for instance, first consider whether competence exists to adopt internal legislation on the matters that are the subject of a contemplated agreement . . . It should go straight to the question: is the external action which is envisaged a natural and expected way of attaining any of the objectives authorised by the proposed legal basis? This is here referred to as "the true construction principle". Underlying the true construction principle is . . . that a legal basis in the Treaty which is silent as to the possibility of concluding international agreements, should not, therefore, be understood as conferring internal legislative power only' (A Dashwood, *The Attribution of External Relations Competence*, 136). This characterization comes indeed very close to the instrument version of the parallelism doctrine discussed above. However, Dashwood goes further than that theory in denying the 'implied' character of the Community's external competence/instrument altogether: 'I am not sure whether, after all, it is right to treat this as the recognition of implied Community powers, although this is how the Court itself seems to regard the matter. To my mind, the logic of implied powers is that they relate to matters which, it is assumed, would have been specifically mentioned in the text, if draftsmen were infinitely wise and prescient. Here, I suggest, the logic is different. The failure to mention external powers in the Treaty provisions on agriculture or transport, say, is not because the matter slipped the draftman's mind: it is because to confer powers in these policy areas that stopped short at the Community's frontiers would simply not have made any sense. In other words, a text that is silent on its external application should not be interpreted as one that expressly confers internal powers only: *the natural way of interpreting an express grant of powers is that they are to apply as needed, internally or externally, in furtherance of the objectives specified in the relevant Treaty Articles*' (A Dashwood, *The Limits of European Community Powers*, 125 (emphasis added)).

[55] Opinion 1/76, para 4 (emphasis added). The same principle is repeated in Opinion 2/91: '[W]henever Community law created for the institutions of the Community powers within its internal system for the purpose of attaining a specific objective, the Community had authority to enter into the international commitments *necessary for the attainment of that objective* even in the absence of an express provision in that connection' (ibid para 7, emphasis added).

[56] Commenting on the last sentence of para 81 of Opinion 1/94 Dashwood claims that it 'should *not* be taken as implying that there might be non-exclusive competence to do so. The plain drift of the passage is that no competence of any kind to conclude an agreement designed to facilitate the international provision of services can be derived by implication from legal bases wholly focused on liberalisation within the internal market'. From this, Dashwood draws the conclusion that 'the logic of parallelism contended for by the Commission cannot be right, otherwise the Community would have been competent to conclude the GATS' (A Dashwood, *The Attribution of External*

What is striking about these three conceptualizations of the European Court's jurisprudence is that each theory manages to better explain certain regions of the judicial picture than its competitors. And the ongoing vivid search for a unifying explanatory rationale for the Community's implied external powers in academic circles shows that none of the three dogmatic competitors (yet) represents *the* privileged viewpoint from which to interpret the 'cubist' judicial picture. The multiplicity of—regionally—valid theoretical perspectives has been the result of the stratified character of the case law. In the last thirty years, the Court itself seems to have struggled to define *its* constitutional perspective—a fact that might explain the theoretical draw reached by the three competing conceptualizations.

Can we nevertheless identify a judicial preference for one of the three rationales discussed above? Or, are there constitutional reasons why the Court *should* prefer one of the theories over the two others? It is respectfully submitted that the 'doctrine of complementarity' overvalues the normative function of the 'necessity' criterion. The determination of the latter has been left to the political organs of the Community with the Court employing a submissive 'facilitative effects' test, whose deforming impact on otherwise co-extensive parallel powers has been virtually nonexistent.[57] From a dogmatic perspective,

Relations Competence, 130, emphasis added). This interpretation of para 81 faces one challenge: the Court did not seem to deny a shared competence of the Community for the conclusion of GATS flowing implicitly from the existence of an internal competence in the service sector (or the Community's general legislative competences under Articles 95 or 308 EC). The Court, arguably, simply refused to imply an *exclusive* competence to conclude the agreement.

[57] From the beginning, the necessity requirement has remained ambivalent: 'The issue which is inevitably raised by the Rhine case [ie Opinion 1/76] is: how is it to be determined whether the conclusion of an agreement by the Community is indeed necessary? How much choice is there and how is it to be exercised? ... [Where] although the Commission favours Community participation, the Council does not, a difficult situation may arise. As in the AETR case, it will be open to the Commission, if it considers that the Council (or the Member States) have acted illegally as regards what it or they propose to do, to bring the matter before the Court. Much will depend on the particular facts involved and the reasons advanced; if the Council, by a considered decision taken in conformity, with the Treaty, concluded that Community participation was not "necessary", though it might in certain respects be desirable, then it seems improbable that the Commission would seek to contest such a finding. ... Under the Community system as set out in the Treaty the Council is given the major determining role with respect to external relations, including the final decision as to whether international agreements are to be concluded' (cf M Hardy, *Opinion 1/76 of the Court of Justice: The Rhine Case and the Treaty-Making Powers of the Community*, 594, 596, and 599). The essentially political nature of the necessity test is admitted by Dashwood himself. Revisiting some passages of *Opinion 1/76*, *Kramer*, and *Opinion 2/92*, the author finds that 'in practice, the Court employs a test as to whether Treaty-making power is needed by the Community *to ensure the external use, over time, of its expressly conferred internal competence*. Such a test would be one of facilitation rather than of indispensability' (A Dashwood, *The Attribution of External Relations Competence*, 133).

there is a more serious objection. What is the added value of introducing a necessity test at the *existence* level, when the *exercise* of all Community powers—whether internal or external—is already subjected to a proportionality check under Article 5(3) EC? When Article 5(3) EC stipulates that '[a]ny action of the Community shall not go beyond what is necessary to achieve the objectives of this Treaty', one should assume that this general principle of Community law will function as a sufficient constitutional safeguard to limit external Community action to what is strictly necessary. Why then duplicate the necessity test at the existence level for implied external powers?

This brings us to discussing the respective advantages of the two versions of the doctrine of parallelism. Earlier jurisprudence gave strong support to the view that the Court considered implied external powers as an additional legal instrument for the implementation of an 'internal' competence.[58] However, the Court has now come to speak of the Community's shared or exclusive 'external competences' to conclude international agreements.[59] This betrays an inclination in favour of the theory of parallel *competences* as opposed to parallel *instruments*. The judicial preference for the classic version of the parallelism doctrine is rooted in the way the Court conceptualizes the exclusion of the Member States in the external field. As will be seen below,[60] the Court has chosen to go down the 'exclusive *competence*' road instead of explaining the loss of treaty-making power of the Member States through a doctrine of legislative pre-emption. In doing so, it has foreclosed the instrument thesis of parallel external powers. A theory that views parallel external powers as parallel instruments is, after all, hard to bring into line with a jurisprudence that speaks of shared and exclusive powers.[61] The very language of shared or exclusive powers suggests a *competence* reading of the doctrine of parallelism.

The author concludes: 'In the answer to the existence question which the Court has provided in the form of the principle of complementarity, the word [ie 'necessary'] has the broader meaning of 'tending to facilitate': implied external competence arises, where this will help ensure the optimal exercise of the expressly conferred internal competence.' (Ibid 134). A decision to leave the necessity criterion to the political safeguards of federalism has also been championed by Advocate General Tizzano in the *Open Skies* cases.

[58] Case 22/70 *Commission v Council (ERTA)*.

[59] Eg Opinion 1/94 paras 77 and 95.

[60] For this point see: Section I (2a) below.

[61] This critique can be extended to Dashwood's 'true construction principle': Viewing the Community's 'external' powers simply as part of the internal competence makes it difficult to conceptualize exclusive external powers within an otherwise shared internal competence—unless one accepts the idea of a 'partial exclusivity' of a legislative competence.

2. *Parallel External Powers: Essence and Exercise*

From an international law perspective, the Member States of the European Union enjoy full treaty-making powers as equal and sovereign subjects. This perspective is not shared by the European legal order, in which Member States enjoy only *limited* treaty-making powers. These *Community* limits are set in two ways. First, the EC Treaty may grant the Community a constitutionally exclusive competence.[62] Within these exclusive areas, the Member States will be totally prevented from acting autonomously—internally as well as externally. Yet, the great majority of the Community's powers are non-exclusive powers. This means that the Member States remain entitled to act, unless the Community has adopted legislation that pre-empts them. This second limit on the treaty-making powers of the Member States has been expressed by three constitutional principles that structure Europe's foreign affairs federalism: the '*ERTA* Principle', the '*Opinion 1/76* Principle', and the '*WTO* Principle'.[63]

According to the first principle, the Member States will be deprived of their treaty-making power to the extent that the exercise of the latter affects internal Community law. The limit became famous as the '*ERTA* Principle': each time the Community 'adopts provisions laying down *common rules, whatever form these may take*, the Member States no longer have the right, acting individually or even collectively, to undertake obligations with third countries *which affect those rules*'.[64] The original *ERTA* ruling had left in suspense *when* the exercise of external powers by the Member States would be incompatible with Community law. This was the central ambivalence of the *ERTA* doctrine. Did *ERTA* imply automatic field pre-emption in the external sphere over all matters falling into the scope of the internal European law—regardless of the degree of harmonization achieved? It was up to subsequent jurisprudence to clarify the extent to which the Member States would lose their treaty-making power.[65]

Secondly, the '*Opinion 1/76* Principle' extends the exclusionary effect to situations where the 'external powers may be exercised, and thus become

---

[62] On this point, see: Chapter 3—Section II above.

[63] This tripartite distinction is of an analytic nature. It had been taken up by the (failed) Constitutional Treaty and is now reflected in the Lisbon Treaty, cf Article 3(2) TFEU. The distinction should not be taken to mean that the three principles are categorically unrelated. On the contrary, as will be seen below, the '*WTO* Principle' can be integrated into a '*ERTA*' pre-emption framework.

[64] Case 22/70 *Commission v Council (ERTA)*, para 18 (emphasis added).

[65] This question will be addressed in Chapter 6—Section II (2) below.

exclusive, *without any internal legislation having first been adopted*'.[66] An external Community power could become exclusive *on exercising* that very power through the conclusion of an international agreement. Acknowledging an 'anticipated ERTA effect',[67] the Court insists that only the future exercise of the external power would render it exclusive. The exclusivity is neither purely legislative, since the Member States are prevented from autonomous international action at a time when no Community legislation exists; nor is the exclusivity purely constitutional, for it is *through its exercise* that the external competence becomes exclusive. The Court, thus, positioned the *Opinion 1/76* doctrine somewhere between both forms of exclusivity. The scope of this hybrid exclusivity is very restricted.[68]

Finally, in Opinion 1/94, the Court added a third principle limiting the treaty-making powers of the Member States: the '*WTO* Principle'. It states that '[w]henever the Community has concluded in its internal legislative acts provisions relating to the treatment of nationals of non-member countries or expressly conferred on the institutions powers to negotiate with non-member countries, it acquires *exclusive external competence in the spheres covered by those acts*'.[69]

What is striking about the constitutional vocabulary in the external sphere is that the Court has chosen *not* to employ the language of supremacy and pre-emption. Instead, it conceptualizes the exclusion of the Member States on the international level though the lens of—subsequently—exclusive competences. This vision implies a dual federalist philosophy of mutually exclusive spheres and contrasts with the cooperative federalist structure of the Community's internal sphere. What is the European theory of subsequent exclusivity? Are there constitutional arguments against it? We shall address these questions by focusing on the most prominent external relations doctrine—the '*ERTA* Principle'. Thereafter, we will look at the phenomenon

---

[66] Opinion 1/94 (*Competence of the Community to conclude International Agreements concerning Services and the Protection of Intellectual Property*), para 85 (emphasis added). On the changing *ratio decidendi* of Opinion 1/76, see: R Schütze, *Parallel External Powers in the European Community: From 'Cubist' Perspectives Towards 'Naturalist' Constitutional Principles?*, 250–9.

[67] I am grateful to A Dashwood for this attractive phrase.

[68] The '*Opinion 1/76* Principle' is now confined to 'the situation where the conclusion of an international agreement is necessary in order to achieve Treaty objectives which cannot be attained by the adoption of autonomous rules' (Opinion 2/92 (*OECD*), Section V, para 4). The Community will only enjoy an exclusive external power, where the achievement of an internal objective is 'inextricably linked' with the external sphere (Case 476/98 *Commission v Germany* (*Open Skies*), para 87). Exclusivity will be restricted to a 'situation in which internal competence could effectively be *exercised only at the same time as external competence*' (ibid para 88 (emphasis added)).

[69] Opinion 1/94, para 95 (emphasis added).

of mixed agreements and wonder how this—seemingly—cooperative constitutional arrangement fits into the dual federalist world of Europe's foreign affairs.

a. The Theory of Subsequent Exclusivity: The ERTA Doctrine

While the language of exclusive external powers had been part of the Commission and Council's vocabulary ever since *ERTA*,[70] the European Court would only 'officially' adopt the exclusive power thesis twenty years later in its WTO Opinion. And in Opinion 2/91 the exclusive competence perspective celebrated its triumph: 'The exclusive or non-exclusive nature of the Community's competence', the Court held, 'does not flow solely from the provisions of the Treaty but may also depend on the scope of the measures which have been adopted by the Community institutions for the application of those provisions and which are of such a kind as to deprive the Member States of an area of competence which they were able to exercise previously on a transitional basis'.[71] But even if the European Court now embraces the theory of subsequently exclusive powers, should we accept this conceptualization? Might there be alternative ways to theoretically explain the exclusion of national treaty-making powers in situations governed by the *ERTA* doctrine?

A number of theoretical objections may indeed be advanced against identifying the exclusive effect of internal Community legislation with exclusive external competences. First, to identify the area occupied by secondary law as an exclusive *competence* wrongly suggests that the policy field covered by internal legislation itself could be used as an independent legal base. This is, of course, not the case. Secondly, the idea of subsequently exclusive competences wrongly reduces the *ERTA* doctrine to automatic field-pre-emption. To speak of an exclusive *competence* invokes the image of a policy *field*. However, the reduction of the *ERTA* doctrine to policy fields—an image of dual federalism—no longer corresponds to the constitutional reality in the European Union.[72] Today, the Community and the Member States may act—on the international plane— *in the same field at the same time.*

Thirdly, and most importantly: the assimilation of the *ERTA* doctrine to exclusive powers raises serious objections from the perspective of the

---

[70] Compare the respective submissions of the Commission and the Council in Case 22/70 *Commission of the European Communities v Council of the European Communities (ERTA)*, paras 8 and 11.

[71] Opinion 2/91, para 9.

[72] For this point, see: Section II (2) below.

hierarchy of norms. The extension of the idea of exclusive *competences* to the *ERTA* phenomenon is based on a dynamic understanding of Europe's order of competences. Yet, the scope of a federation's exclusive competences is a *constitutional* question; and, as such, it should—at least theoretically—only be extended by means of *constitutional* amendment. It seems a feat of legal alchemy to permit the Community to modify its order of competences, especially because this would allow Europe's legislator to escape the reach of the subsidiarity principle.[73] Fourthly, the exclusionary effect of the *ERTA* doctrine stems from the effect of internal legislation; and this legislative 'exclusivity' is more fragile and temporal than constitutionally exclusive powers. Unlike the latter, the former can be repealed by a legislative act.[74]

In the light of these theoretical considerations, the two phenomena of constitutional and legislative exclusivity should be kept apart. The *ERTA* doctrine should not be couched in terms of exclusive *competences*, but may be better expressed in the more nuanced vocabulary of the doctrine of legislative pre-emption.[75] The *ERTA* doctrine simply represents the constitutional principle that Community legislation will not only pre-empt national laws in the internal sphere, but will also restrict the international powers of the Member States. The *ERTA* doctrine thus projects the pre-emptive effect of internal legislation into the external sphere.

The legislative pre-emption interpretation of the *ERTA* doctrine would have a number of advantages. First, it reflects the fact that the exclusion of national treaty-making powers is generated by European *legislation* and not constitutionally enshrined. The external competence of the Member States will therefore revive to the extent that European laws have been revoked.[76]

---

[73] C Calliess, *Subsidiaritäts- und Solidaritätsprinzip in der Europäischen Union*, 95. Some authors solve this constitutional problem by only excluding originally exclusive competences from the scope of the subsidiarity principle. Lenaerts and van Nuffel, discussing Opinion 2/91 of the Court, argue as follows: 'Depending upon the extent to which the Community exercises its power, it may confer upon it an "exclusive nature", even though exclusive competence has not been transferred to the Community within the second paragraph of Article 5 (*ex Article 3b*) of the E.C. Treaty' (K Lenaerts and P van Nuffel, *Constitutional Law of the European Union*, 5-023).

[74] On this point, see: Chapter 4—*Conclusion*.

[75] The strange analytical divergence in the constitutional principles applied in the internal and external hemispheres of the Community legal order has been captured as follows: 'Where internal Community rules completely or exhaustively regulate a particular area, the Member States are therefore precluded from legislating in the area. At the internal level, this is described as pre-emption; on the external level, the Community measures give rise to exclusive Community competence externally for that area' (D O'Keeffe, *Exclusive, Concurrent and Shared Competence*, 183).

[76] I Macleod, ID Hendry and S Hyett, *The External Relations of the European Communities*, 62: '[N]on-existent rules can hardly be "affected" by a Member State's acts or by conclusion of an agreement'.

Secondly, the WTO principle—now a third and independent constitutional principle of Europe's external relations law—could henceforth be explained by reference to a mode of pre-emption known as 'express pre-emption'.[77] (By the same token, 'disconnection clauses' could be explained by reference to 'express saving clauses'.[78]) Thirdly, the pre-emption reading would allow the Court to embrace the more elegant and easier doctrine of implied parallel *instruments*. The power of the Community to act by means of internal and/or external action could then be rooted in the same—internal— legal competence. An extension of the doctrine of pre-emption would thus make the fictitious invention of a set of parallel 'competences' superfluous. Lastly, the doctrine of pre-emption— in tandem with the doctrine of parallel instruments—could better account for the pre-emptive effect of directly effective international agreements on national powers.[79] This would, in turn, allow us to integrate the Opinion 1/76 doctrine into the *ERTA* framework.

In conclusion, the *ERTA* line of jurisprudence could well be (re-)interpreted as the 'logical extension' of the principle of pre-emption.[80] Transposing the pre-emption analysis from the internal to the external sphere would arguably provide a clearer dogmatic justification for the restriction of national foreign affairs powers than the complex conceptual mouthful of 'subsequently exclusive implied external competences'. Instead of having recourse to the dual federalist vocabulary of exclusive powers, the Court could base its jurisprudence on the— cooperative—federal language of supremacy and pre-emption.[81]

[77] On the distinction between 'express' and 'implied' pre-emption in the American constitutional context, see Chapter 2—Section II (1a) above.

[78] Disconnection clauses are designed to guarantee the full application of (internal) European law in situations where it may come into conflict with an international treaty. On the—present— status of disconnection clauses in the European legal order, see my discussion of *Opinion 1/2003* in Section II (2) below. Once the legislative exclusivity reading is accepted, the use of a 'disconnection clause' in an international agreement could *not* be irrelevant to the question whether the Community had pre-empted the Member States.

[79] R Schütze, *The Morphology of Legislative Power in the European Community: Legal Instruments and the Federal Division of Power*, 131–44.

[80] D McGoldrick, *International Relations Law of the European Union*, 72–4.

[81] The carefully worded concluding remarks of the European Court in the *Open Skies* cases may represent a small step in the right direction. The Court concluded the part dealing with the implied external powers in the following way: 'It follows from the foregoing considerations that, by entering into international commitments concerning air fares and rates charged by carriers designated by the United States of America on intra-Community routes and concerning CRSs offered for use or used in German territory, the Federal Republic of Germany has *failed to fulfil its obligations under [Article 10] of the Treaty* and under Regulations Nos 2409/92 and 2299/89' (ibid para 137 (emphasis added)). This might be seen as a cautious move away from the language of exclusive external competences towards conceptualizing the issue through the lens of the pre-emption doctrine.

b. Political Safeguards: Mixed Agreements as a Federal Technique

Under Community law neither the European Community nor its Member States enjoy plenary treaty-making powers. Who, then, can conclude international agreements that do not entirely fall into one sphere of external competence? What constitutional mechanisms would the European legal order develop to coordinate the external actions of two governments in these situations? European constitutionalism has concentrated on the mechanism of mixed agreements—that is, agreements to which both the EC and some or all of its Member States appear as contracting parties. This technique had originally been designed for a specific sector of European law.[82] However, it would soon spread to become *the* hallmark of European foreign affairs federalism.[83]

It originally seemed that the European Court would demand specific *constitutional* justification for mixed external action in place of a pure Community agreement.[84] The use of mixed agreements in Europe's foreign affairs federalism could be justified by two principal reasons—one internal and one external to the Community legal order. First, mixed agreements would allow the Community and its Member States to complement their competences into a unitary whole that matched the external sovereignty of a third State. International agreements that cut across the European and national (exclusive) spheres would simply be concluded by each of the two governments. The division of treaty-making powers between them could then be reduced

---

[82] Article 102 Euratom Treaty: 'Agreements or contracts concluded with a third State, an international organization or a national of a third State to which, in addition to the Community, one or more Member States are parties, shall not enter into force until the Commission has been notified by all the Member States concerned that those agreements or contracts have become applicable in accordance with the provisions of their respective national laws'.

[83] The first mixed agreement concluded by the EC was the 1961 Agreement establishing an association between the European Economic Community and Greece. An early survey of mixed agreements up to 1982 can be found in JJ Feenstra, *A Survey of the Mixed Agreements and their Participation Clauses*, 207. For a more up to date registry, see: J Heliskoski, *Mixed Agreements as a Technique for Organizing the International Relations of the European Community and its Member States*, 252–77 listing 154 mixed agreements concluded between 1961 and 2000. Quantitatively, mixed agreements are said to only represent about one-fifth of all agreements concluded by the Community (cf A von Bogdandy, F Arndt & J Bast, *Legal Instruments in European Union Law and their Reform*, 107).

[84] Opinion 1/76 (*Laying Up Fund*), paras 6–8. The Opinion recognized that 'the danger of mixed agreements (and their attraction for Member States) lies in their tendency to over-emphasize at the expense of the Community the participation of the Member States as traditional international legal persons' (M Cremona, *The Doctrine of Exclusivity and the Position of Mixed Agreements in the External Relations of the European Community*, 414).

to a 'domestic' Community affair.[85] Secondly, the uncertainty surrounding the treaty-making powers of non-State actors under international law originally provided an external reason.[86] As long as it remained uncertain whether or how the Community could fulfil its international obligations, mixed agreements offered legal security for third States by involving the Member States as international 'guarantors' of the Community obligation.[87]

The constitutional developments within the Community legal order in the last three decades have weakened both rationales. Not only have the external powers of the Community been significantly expanded through the development of the doctrine of parallelism, its powers have been sharpened to guarantee the enforcement of Community agreements within the Community legal order.[88] Today, the dominant reason behind mixed agreements appears to be of a purely political nature: Member States insist upon participating in their own name so as to remain 'visible' on the international scene.[89] Even for matters that fall squarely into Community competence, the Member States dislike being (en)closed behind a supranational veil.

Surprisingly, the Court of Justice has given its judicial blessing to this third rationale by tolerating the uncontrolled use of mixed agreements in areas of shared competences.[90] What does this tell us about the non-exclusive external

[85] 'It is sufficient to state to the other Contracting Parties that the matter gives rise to a division of powers within the Community, it being understood that the exact nature of that division is a domestic question in which Third States have no need to intervene' (Ruling 1/78 (*IAEA Convention*), para 35). However, third States or international organizations may insist on a declaration of competence (cf UN Convention on the Law of the Sea, Annex XI).

[86] P Pescatore, *Les relations extérieures des communautés européennes: contribution à la doctrine de la personnalité des organisations internationales*, 105.

[87] MJ Dolmans, *Problems of Mixed Agreements: Division of Powers within the EEC and the Rights of Third States*, 95.

[88] International agreements concluded by the European Community will typically have—vertical and horizontal—direct effect and will thus be judicially enforceable in the European and national legal orders, cf R Schütze (n 79 above).

[89] CD Ehlermann, *Mixed Agreements: A List of Problems*, 6: 'Member States wish to continue to appear as contracting parties in order to remain visible and identifiable actors on the international scene. Individual participation is therefore seen as a way of defending and enhancing the prestige and influence of individual Member States'.

[90] In the last thirty years, these 'facultative' mixed agreements—ie agreements in which the Community has competence to conclude the entire agreement—have become the prominent category of mixed agreements: 'Indeed, there is no decision from the Court under the EC Treaty where the explicit justification for recourse to the mixed procedure would have been the limited scope of Community competence—commonly regarded as the principal legal explanation for the practice of mixed agreements' (cf J Heliskoski (n 83 above) 68). It is consequently misleading to claim that '[t]he essence of a mixed agreement is that, to a greater or lesser extent, some of its provisions fall within the competence of the Community, while others fall within the competence of the

competences of the Community? Shared powers do not constitutionally require mixed action. Within shared competences, the Community or the Member States can either act autonomously and conclude independent agreements; or, if they so wish, they may act jointly. The widespread use of joint external action thus evinces a remarkable tolerance towards the Member States' international powers.

How are we to make sense of the phenomenon of mixity in terms of our federal debate? Which federal philosophy aligns itself with mixed external action? Theoretically, mixity may arise under a dual *as well as* a cooperative internal federal structure; and thus aligns itself—partly—with *both* federal philosophies. With dual federalism mixity shares the idea of dual sovereignty and the coordinated equality of two governments. In international negotiations, the European Community and its Member States are coordinated— not hierarchically subordinated—international personalities. Mixity is here a facet of dual federalism, since both levels are independent and 'equal' signatories to an international agreement. With cooperative federalism, mixed external action shares the idea of 'cooperation'. In fact, European constitutionalism has emphasized a 'duty of cooperation' between the Community and the Member States that follows 'from the requirement of unity in the international representation of the Community'.[91]

The best way to conceptualize mixity is to view it as a special manifestation of the idea of political safeguards of federalism. Indeed, according to a European 'constitutional convention', the Council concludes mixed agreements on behalf of the Community only once *all* the Member States have themselves ratified the agreement in accordance with their constitutional traditions.[92] The convention boils down to requiring 'unanimous' consent before the Community can exercise its competence. The arrangement thus prolongs the (in)famous Luxembourg Accord in the external sphere and constitutes the most powerful institutional protection of national autonomy in the external sphere: the decisional veto. Since the Community and the Member States will typically engage in the joint negotiation and conclusion of an international agreement, each Member State may veto the agreement. The constitutionally uncontrolled use of mixed agreements under the

Member States' (I MacLeod, ID Hendry & S Hyett, *The External Relations of the European Communities*, 145).

   [91] Opinion 1/94, para 108.
   [92] The inspiration for this constitutional convention appears to lie in Article 102 of the Euratom Treaty (n 82 above). On the convention, see also: P Eeckhout, *External Relations of the European Union*, 218–19.

Community's shared powers has, consequently, been criticized as 'a way of whittling down systematically the personality and capacity of the Community as a representative of the collective interest'.[93]

II. Theory and Practice: Towards Cooperative Federalism?

The European Community was established in 1957 on the basis of an international treaty. The Treaty of Rome formed part of international law, though the Court of Justice was soon eager to emphasize that '[*b*]*y contrast with ordinary international treaties*, the [EC] Treaty has created its own legal system'.[94] The Community legal order had been declared autonomous in order to establish the supremacy of Community law over national law. But *how* autonomous was the 'new legal order' vis-à-vis the old legal order of international law? The relationship between European law and the international powers of the Member States had remained a 'neglected problem' during the foundational period of the Community legal order.[95] Was this normative ambivalence the reason behind Europe's dual federalism in foreign affairs? What were the—real or imagined—constitutional or international reasons for choosing dual federalism in the external sphere? Has European constitutional theory solved these problems? And, what will constitutional practice tell us about its foreign affairs federalism? This second section tries to give tentative answers to these questions.

---

[93] P Pescatore, *Opinion 1/94 on 'Conclusion' of the WTO Agreement: Is there an Escape from a Programmed Disaster*, fn 6. The criticism on mixed agreements has been rich from the very beginning, see: A Barav, *General Discussion*, in CWA Timmermans et al (eds), *Division of Powers between the European Communities and their Member States in the Field of External Relations*, 144: '[M]ixed agreements are probably a necessary evil, part of the integration process, but nobody would like to see any more of them'; as well as CD Ehlermann (n 89 above) 2: 'Apparently an easy and handy formula, [mixity] creates problems and risks for all sides: the Community, its Member States and the other contracting parties'. For a more recent criticism from the hand of an international lawyer, see: J Klabbers, *An Introduction to International Institutional Law*, 294: '[Mixed agreements] rupture the unity, or would-be-unity, of an organization's external actions, and even place question marks around the very idea of unity to begin with. In particular where mixity is inspired not so much by legal necessity but rather by demands arising from concerns relating to the legitimacy of agreements among those who have to implement them (i.e. the member-states), one may well regard them as a sign of defeatism on the part of the organization concerned: it sends the message that its ambitions cannot be realized without the separate involvement of its member-states'.

[94] Case 6/64 *Flaminio Costa v ENEL*, 593 (emphasis added).

[95] KM Meessen, *The Application of Rules of Public International Law within Community Law*, 485.

1. *Constitutional Theory: The Slowly Emergent Doctrine of Community Supremacy*

The *internal* division of competences between the Community and the Member States does not correspond to the international law perspective that accords *external* sovereignty to the Member States.[96] The 'complex and ambiguous'[97] relationship between the European and the international legal order in the early days of the Community was particularly troubled with regard to the international powers of the Member States. 'If Community law were merely regional international law, the question of status and effect of international law within the Community legal order would have to be answered by international rules on the conflict of treaties and by principles governing the internal law of international organisations'.[98]

From the perspective of international law, subsequent agreements of the Member States would follow the ordinary international law method for 'successive treaties relating to the same subject-matter' as set out in Article 30 of the Vienna Convention on the Law of Treaties.[99] From the outset, it seemed unlikely that this rule was to apply fully within the European legal order. However, in order to protect the integrity of the latter, a simple modification of the international law principles would not be sufficient. While the supremacy of the Community legal order vis-à-vis the national legal orders could still be explained from *within* an international law paradigm,[100] an international law 'theory' could not justify the supremacy of European law over subsequent international treaties of the Member States. A 'new paradigm' was needed to explain and legitimize the supremacy of Community law over all forms of international law *within the Community legal order*. The EC needed to distinguish itself *from* international law in the same way as '[c]hildren too,

---

[96] H Krück, *Die auswärtige Gewalt der Mitgliedstaaten und die auswärtigen Befugnisse der Europäischen Gemeinschaften als Problem des Souveränitätsverständnisses*, 163.

[97] J-P Puissochet, *La place du droit international dans la jurisprudence de la cour de justice des communautés européennes*, 780.

[98] A Peters, *The Position of International Law within the European Community Legal Order*, 11. For the view that considers Community law as part of traditional international law see: D Wyatt, *New Legal Order, or Old?*, 147—arguing that the Community legal order is 'quite explicable in terms of traditional international legal theory and practice' (ibid 148).

[99] Article 5 of the Vienna Convention on the Law of Treaties (1969) clarified that the Convention would also apply to 'Treaties constituting international organisations and treaties adopted within an international organisation'. The provision states: 'The present Convention applies to any treaty which is the constituent instrument of an international organisation and to any treaty adopted within an international organisation without prejudice to any relevant rules of the organisation'.

[100] Cf H Kelsen, *Das Problem der Souveränität und die Theorie des Völkerrechts*.

in order to grow independent and adult, must occasionally dissociate themselves from their parents and mark their independence'.[101]

This subsection offers an explanation for Europe's foreign affairs 'exceptionalism'. The originally ambivalent status of the international powers of
the Member States in the Community legal order induced European constitutionalism to prefer dual federalism in the external sphere. The Community's
flight into dual federalism prevented the Member States' flight into international law. To evaluate this argument, we shall investigate two aspects of the
treaty-making powers of the Member States. The first concerns the normative status of *inter se* agreements concluded by all Member States. The second
aspect looks outwards and analyses the relationship between European law
and international agreements concluded by Member States with third States.
Within both scenarios, the doctrine of Community supremacy was slow to
emerge; and with the supremacy issue in suspense, the Community moved
down the dual federalist road. This normative ambivalence has today been
resolved; and this evolution has opened the way for a cooperative federal
theory in foreign affairs.

a. Normative Ambivalences: International Agreements between (all) Member States

Whereas *inter se* agreements concluded prior to the coming into force of the
EC Treaty had posed virtually no constitutional problems,[102] the normative
ambivalence between Community law and *subsequent* international agreements
of the Member States was diagnosed early on:

In the first place, it is necessary to define the relationship between these [subsequent
inter se] agreements with the Community Treaties. In fact, regulations or decisions
adopted by the Council, by means of the fact that they implement the Treaties,
will always remain subordinate to the Treaties that form their base and justification.
An international agreement, on the other hand, even if styled as an implementing
measure, is concluded by the same parties as the Treaties. Could one, therefore,
not consider such an agreement as equivalent to the Community Treaties? These
so-called 'complementary' or 'executive' agreements could, in this way, become
the instrument of a 'cold revision', that is, a revision outside the formal amendment
procedure set out in the Treaty. This process is, thus, not without danger to the
Communities.[103]

---

[101] C Timmermans, *The EU and Public International Law*, 183.
[102] They would remain effective to the extent that they were compatible with EC law—the
solution suggested by Article 30 Vienna Convention on the Law of Treaties.
[103] P Pescatore, *L'ordre juridique des communautés européennes*, 143–4 (translation—RS).

Apart from Article 293 EC—asking the Member States to engage in the negotiation of *inter se* conventions in certain areas—and the specific permission for the two regional economic unions in Article 306 EC,[104] there was no express provision for *inter se* cooperation. Did this mean that the States' ability to engage in international cooperation *inter se* was generally allowed, or had the Treaty exhaustively enumerated the subject matters for such cooperation in Article 293 EC? What was the nature of these *inter se* agreements—were they Community law or international law? If the latter, would they follow the 'ordinary' international law route, that is, allow *inter se* modifications, except for those matters that interfered with the rights of *other* Member States or with an 'integral norm' of EC law? And, most importantly, could *inter se* agreements amend or modify EC law?[105] In answering these questions, we shall concentrate on agreements between *all* Member States.

Within the category of *inter se* agreements *erga omnes*, 'decisions of the representatives of the Governments of the Member States meeting in the Council' represent the most common and controversial category. The unwieldy name is a misnomer: they are not unilateral acts, as the concept of 'decision' would indicate, but executive international agreements of the Member States.[106] These 'decisions *sui generis*' had become an established constitutional practice by the early 1970s. Despite their popularity, the constitutional nature of these 'decisions' remained obscure. Some commentators thought of them as a special form of Community law.[107] Others viewed them

---

[104] Article 306 reads: 'The provisions of this Treaty shall not preclude the existence or completion of regional unions between Belgium and Luxembourg, or between Belgium, Luxembourg and the Netherlands, to the extent that the objectives of these regional unions are not attained by application of this Treaty'.

[105] In an affirmative sense see: JHF van Panhuys, *Conflicts between the Law of the European Communities and Other Rules of International Law*, 440.

[106] P Pescatore, *L'ordre juridique des communautés européennes*, 140: 'Il s'agit, somme toute, d'accords internationaux "en forme simplifiée", conclus dans le cadre offert par le Conseil des Communautés'. A (slightly) different characterization is given by HP Ipsen, *Europäisches Gemeinschaftsrecht*, 468, considering these decisions as unilateral acts of an international organ set up by the collectivity of the Member States: 'Insgesamt handelt es sich um Beschlüsse eines vertraglich nicht instituierten Kollegialorgans, dessen Mitglieder mit dem kollegialen Rat der Gemeinschaften identisch sind. Deshalb ist weniger seine Erscheinung als Institution, als vielmehr seine Funktion der Beschlussfassung von rechtlicher Bedeutung'.

[107] In favour of a classification as Community law: TC Hartley, *The Foundations of European Community Law*, 92: 'In addition to the constitutive Treaties, there are certain other international agreements between the Member States. Where these deal with matters within the scope of the Community and were drawn up within the Community context, they may be regarded as part of Community law'. See also: J Wuermeling, *Kooperatives Gemeinschaftsrecht*, 199.

as a form of ordinary international law.[108] A third position sat on the fence and declared the international agreements to be legal hybrids between the two.[109] This ambivalence mystified their status and relationship to the Community legal order: were these decisions *sui generis* 'almost omnipotent',[110] or, 'by their very nature', subordinate to EC law?[111]

The legality of decisions *sui generis* had traditionally been justified by reference to their falling *outside* the scope of the Treaty.[112] Where the EC Treaty had given no competence to the Community to pursue its objectives, the Member States were entitled to use their international treaty-making powers to 'complement' Community law.[113] The recourse to *inter se* agreements would elegantly overcome the constitutional limitations flowing from the enumeration principle on which the Community legal order was based.

---

[108] In favour of the international law status: LJ Constantinesco, *Das Recht der Europäischen Gemeinschaften*, 543: 'Die Rechtsangleichung durch völkerrechtliche Abkommen ist ein klassisches Instrument . . . Die Abkommen sind Ausdruck einer rein intergouvernementalen Prozedur, auch wenn sie der EWG dienen'. The ECJ now sides with this position: see Joined Cases C-181 and 248/91 *Parliament v Council (Emergency Aid)*.

[109] A Limpens-Meinertzhagen, *La coordination ou l'unification du droit par voie de convention entre les etats membres*, 158: 'La convention CEE se situe à mi-chemin entre la convention internationale classique et le droit communautaire *stricto sensu*'.

[110] The position was taken by H Wagner, *Grundbegriffe des Beschlussrechts der Europäischen Gemeinschaften*, 242: 'Der "uneigentliche Ratsbeschluß" ist nahezu omnipotent. Er unterliegt keinen Bindungen des Gemeinschaftsrechts'. See also: M Deliege-Sequaris, *Révision des traités européens en dehors des procédures prévus*, 538.

[111] This view was expressed by Hartley (n 107 above) 94–5 (emphasis added) in the context of Community Conventions: 'If a convention is adopted after the Treaty, it could be argued that the convention impliedly amends the Treaty and should therefore prevail. This, however, fails to take account of the fact that both Treaty and convention are part of the Community legal system and in that system the constitutive Treaties are by their very nature of superior status: they *create* the legal system of which the conventions are a part. Moreover, the Treaties contain provisions laying down specific procedures for their amendment . . . [T]here can be little doubt that the existence of these procedures creates a presumption: if the Member States adopt subsequent agreements without going through the procedures, they may be presumed, *in the absence of an express provision to the contrary*, not to have intended to amend the constitutive Treaties . . . If the subsidiary convention does not override the Treaties, it cannot affect the legislative powers conferred by them; consequently, acts adopted under those powers also cannot be affected. It follows from this that, *in the absence of an express provision in the convention*, the Community act will prevail'. (However, did this mean that an *inter se* agreement could make provision that it wished to prevail over the EC Treaty or secondary Community law?)

[112] HP Ibsen (n 106 above) 469 and 471.

[113] The 'decisions of the Member States meeting in the Council' were therefore classified as 'complementary law' by Pescatore, for 'il s'agit d'actes à caractère diplomatique (ou international), complémentaires à la fois des traités eux-mêmes et du système d'actes institutionnels que ceux-ci ont mis en place': P Pescatore, *Remarques sur la nature juridique des 'décisions des représentants des etats membres réunis au sein du conseil'*, 579.

But, what about *inter se* agreements that fell *within* the competence of the Community? Could the cooperating Member States freely choose between the Community channels and the international channels?

In *ERTA*,[114] the Member States—unhappy with the Commission's proposed solutions for a negotiating mandate—had simply adopted 'proceedings' in order to coordinate their position for the negotiation and conclusion of an international agreement. The Member States had settled on a negotiating position that would try to extend the internal Community system to relations with third States, except for 'certain derogations from that system which would have to be accepted by the Community'.[115] The Member States had invited the Commission to make the necessary proposals for amending the internal Community legislation. The Commission disliked the proceedings and went to Court.

The European Court acknowledged that the legal effect of the 'proceedings' would differ 'according to whether they are regarded as constituting the exercise of powers conferred on the Community, or as acknowledging the coordination by the Member States of the exercise of powers which remained vested in them'.[116] So were these proceedings an act of the Council? In Byzantine circular reasoning, the Court simply evaded the question of authorship and equated the 'Council' with the 'Member States acting within the Council'.[117] This would have an important consequence. The Member States, wishing to act in their international capacities, had not played by the procedural rules set out in the EC Treaty. Thus, once the Court decided that the proceedings were to be attributed to the Council, the derogation from the envisaged 'legislative procedure' would become easy prey for judicial scorn. The right to propose and negotiate—these essential institutional roles of the Commission—would then have been violated. Although it was for the Council to 'decide in each case whether it is expedient to enter into an agreement with third countries, it does not enjoy a discretion to decide whether to proceed through inter-governmental or Community channels'.[118] (Let us pause here for a second. Can the Council—a Community institution—act through intergovernmental channels and would

---

[114] Case 22/70 *Commission v Council (ERTA)*. For the facts of the case, see: Section I (1) above.
[115] Ibid para 46.
[116] Ibid para 4.
[117] *ERTA* showed that the concept of 'Community legislation' had not yet been clearly defined. For a fuller discussion of the Court's Byzantine reasoning as regards the Community authorship of the 'proceedings', see: R Schütze, *The Morphology of Legislative Power in the European Community: Legal Instruments and the Federal Division of Powers*, 101–3.
[118] *ERTA*, para 70.

this act still be part of the European legal order? What the Court meant to say was that the *Member States* could not freely choose whether to pursue a given project through international or Community channels.)

Hidden behind the famous '*ERTA* doctrine',[119] thus lay another important constitutional message: the EC Treaty could constitutionally 'pre-empt' international cooperation between *all* Member States within its scope. Did this imply that wherever the Member States wished to act *erga omnes* within the scope of the Treaty, they were forced onto the Community track? Was it true that for this special form of cooperation the Community channels were 'exclusive'?[120]

The thesis of the 'exclusivity' of the Community channels for *inter se* cooperation involving *all* Member States within the scope of the Treaty was indeed accepted for the Community's amendment procedure. Article 48 TEU (previously Article 236 EEC) constitutes the Community's amendment clause. In addition to requiring common accord and ratification by all Member States in accordance with their respective constitutional requirements, the clause also imposed a variety of procedural hurdles.[121] 'This may seem

---

[119] The Court structured *ERTA* into three parts. The *ERTA* doctrine has traditionally been identified with the first part of the judgment (ibid paras 6–32) dealing with the scope and nature of the Community's implied external power, see: Chapter 6—Section I above. The second part of the ruling (paras 33–67) dealt with the legal nature of the proceedings (cf R Schütze (n 117 above)), while the third part (paras 68–96) concerned the horizontal division of powers between the 'Council' and the Commission. In this third part, paras 70–7 could be seen indirectly to support the thesis of the constitutional exclusivity of the Community channels for *erga omnes* cooperation, whereas paras 81–84 appear informed by a legislative pre-emption rationale. According to the latter view, the Member States would be prevented to undertake, acting individually or even collectively, obligations with third countries which affect existing Community legislation.

[120] The constitutional solution proposed in *ERTA* was soon translated into the language of exclusive competences: 'Die Frage lautet: ist es rechtlich zulässig, nicht im EWG-Vertrag vorgesehene Übereinkommen unter den Regierungen der Mitgliedstaaten auszuhandeln und abzuschließen, wenn die Organe der Gemeinschaft eine Befugnis zur Rechtsetzung nach dem EWG-Vertrag besitzen, insbesondere nach [Artikel 94 oder 308]? Meine These ist: sobald hinsichtlich einer bestimmten Frage die Merkmale einer im EWG-Vertrag enthaltenen Ermächtigung der Organe der Gemeinschaft zur Rechtsetzung vorliegen, fehlt den Regierungen der Mitgliedstaaten die Befugnis, die betreffende Frage im Wege der völkerrechtlichen Vereinbarung untereinander zu regeln. Die Organe der Gemeinschaft besitzen von da an die *ausschließliche Zuständigkeit*, über den fraglichen Gegenstand zu legiferieren. Es besteht daher keine Wahl zwischen dem gemeinschaftlichen und dem zwischenstaatlichen Verfahren, und zwar auch nicht so lange, als die Organe von der Rechtsetzungsbefugnis noch nicht Gebrauch gemacht haben': IE Schwartz, *EG-Rechtsetzungsbefugnisse, insbesondere nach Artikel 235—ausschließlich oder konkurrierend?*, 28 (emphasis added).

[121] Article 48 TEU reads: 'The government of any Member State or the Commission may submit to the Council proposals for the amendment of the Treaties on which the Union is founded. If the Council, after consulting the European Parliament and, where appropriate, the Commission, delivers an opinion in favour of calling a conference of representatives of the governments of the

strange', as, '[g]enerally speaking, the reason for the special clause is the contracting parties' willingness to relax the general rule in order to facilitate adaptation of the treaty to changing circumstances'. The amendment clause of the Community legal order seemed to 'serve the wholly different purpose of protecting the treaty regime against its own creators, by putting obstacles in the way of over-hasty revision plans by the contracting parties'.[122]

Would the Member States still be able to rely on their general international treaty-making powers to amend the EC Treaty outside the Community channels of Article 48 TEU? Positive judicial responses were not unknown in the first decade of the European project.[123] However, the Court ultimately rejected this option. In *Defrenne*,[124] the Member States had tried to modify the temporal application of the EC Treaty and the Court was unimpressed: 'apart from the specific provisions, *the Treaty can only be modified by means of the amendment procedure carried out in accordance with [Article 48 TEU]*'.[125] With regard to the *form* of amendment, the Member States were no longer '*Herren der Verträge*'. Within the Community legal order, '[t]he amendment of the European Treaties is not, therefore, within the "*domaine réservé*" of the States'.[126] Whereas informal amendments of the Community legal order may

Member States, the conference shall be convened by the President of the Council for the purpose of determining by common accord the amendments to be made to those Treaties. The European Central Bank shall also be consulted in the case of institutional changes in the monetary area. The amendments shall enter into force after being ratified by all the Member States in accordance with their respective constitutional requirements'.

[122] B de Witte, *Rules of Change in International Law: How Special is the European Community?*, 307 and 309. However, the author ultimately attributes a facilitating function to these procedural conditions (ibid 313): 'Yet, what is facilitated is not the adoption of the amendments itself (the 'common accord' of all States is required as well as ratification by them all), but only the initiative for an amendment: the Council of the European Communities can decide to convene a revision conference'.

[123] These resulted from the constitutional practice under the ECSC Treaty. The ECSC Treaty had been amended twice during the transitional period (although this was prohibited under the Treaty). These amendments were nonetheless regarded as legal, and the Council, the ECSC High Authority, and the European Parliament accepted them, 'allowing the conclusion to be drawn that the Community itself agreed to set aside the provisions prohibiting amendment of its constitution': HG Schermers & N Blokker, *International Institutional Law*, 736. See also: K Carstens, *Die kleine Revision des Vertrages über die Europäische Gemeinschaft für Kohle und Stahl*.

[124] Case 43/75 *Defrenne v Société anonyme belge de navigation aérienne Sabena*.

[125] Ibid para 58 (emphasis added).

[126] B de Witte (n 122 above) 315–16. On the possible substantive limits to the competence of the Member States with regard to Treaty amendment, see also the author's excellent discussion at ibid 318–22 as well as U Everling, *Sind die Mitgliedstaaten der Europäischen Gemeinschaft noch Herren der Verträge?*; and R Bieber, *Les limites matérielles et formelles à la révision des traités établissant la communtauté européenne*. The academic discussion on the possible material limits to the *pouvoir*

be legal *in international law*, they would be illegal in European law—a 'dualist' solution that would safeguard the autonomy and integrity of the Community legal order.

Has the Court confirmed this solution for other forms of *inter se* cooperation *erga omnes*? A judicial cloud for the theory of the exclusivity of the Community channels emerged in *Parliament v Council (Emergency Aid)*.[127] An annulment action was brought by the Parliament against a decision taken 'at a working lunch attended by the Ministers and by a Member of the Commission' to provide ad hoc aid to Bangladesh.[128] The 'decision' had been taken without parliamentary involvement and—just as the Commission had done in *ERTA*—the European Parliament claimed that its institutional prerogatives as set out in Article 272 EC had been violated.

The subject matter of emergency aid fell within the scope of the Treaty: Article 177 EC provided a complementary competence for development cooperation. The Council argued that 'the jurisdiction of the Community to grant humanitarian aid is not exclusive, the Member States remaining free to act, collectively or individually, alongside the Community'. The non-exclusive nature of the competence had been acknowledged by the Parliament; yet, it insisted that 'when the Member States wish to give aid within the framework of the Community, *they can act only through the Council and only in accordance with the Community budget procedure*'.[129]

This time, the Court sided with the Council. Recalling that 'acts adopted by representatives of the Member States acting, not in their capacity as members of the Council, but as representatives of their governments, and thus collectively exercising the powers of the Member States, are not subject to judicial review', the Court simply found that 'the Community does not have exclusive competence in the field of humanitarian aid, and that consequently the Member States are not precluded from exercising their competence in that regard collectively in the Council or outside it'.[130]

---

constituant of the Member States was a reaction to the Court's ruling in Opinion 1/91 (*EFTA*). There, the Court had found that Article 310 EC would not provide the necessary power to conclude the EFTA agreement as the latter would conflict 'with the very foundations of the Community'. However, most importantly the Court added: 'For the same reasons, *an amendment of [Article 310] could not cure the incompatibility with Community law*' (ibid para 6, emphasis added).

[127] Joined Cases C-181 and 248/91 *Parliament v Council (Emergency Aid)*.
[128] Opinion of AG Jacobs, ibid para 2.
[129] Ibid para 15 (emphasis added).
[130] *Parliament v Council (Emergency Aid)* (n 127 above) paras 12, 16.

This answer is, with due respect, not logically conclusive: the non-exclusive nature of the Community competence does not constitutionally imply that the Member States must be entitled to exercise their competence through an *inter se* agreement *erga omnes* outside the Community channels. The prohibition of this mode of cooperation—and this is an important point—will not turn a shared or complementary competence into an exclusive Community competence. The constitutional limitation simply precludes the Member States from *exercising* one aspect of their *shared* competence. (The Court may thus wish to reconsider its choice in the future and outlaw the 'chameleonic' behaviour of Member States.[131]) However, the judicial ruling positively confirmed that European constitutionalism had now subjected international agreements concluded by the Member States to the normative authority of the European legal order. The Member States could conclude international agreements *erga omnes*, but these agreements would be as hierarchically subordinate as unilateral national law. The original normative ambivalence had been resolved in favour of the supremacy of—primary or secondary—European law.

b. A Flight into Dual Federalism: Member States' Agreements with Third States

International law still suffers from its nineteenth-century obsession with sovereign subjects.[132] 'The law of treaties is thus geared to equal subjects; it follows that these are also closed or "impermeable" subjects, like states, since their—divergent—internal features cannot play a role'.[133] In a federation, there are potentially two levels that can engage in international relations with third States. In legal orders that accept the supremacy of federal law, the

---

[131]   A beautiful image by B de Witte, *Chameleonic Member States: Differentiation by Means of Partial and Parallel International Agreements*, 232–3. The exclusivity of the Community channels, triggering the involvement of the Community institutions, would indeed seem justified for this form of *inter se* cooperation: where all Member States get involved, the matter will doubtlessly have a 'Community' dimension and therefore should bring the European Commission and/or the European Parliament onto the scene. For matters falling within the scope of the Treaty, the Community's general legislative power under Article 308 EC could then be used to channel all *inter se* cooperation *erga omnes* into Community waters. The relationship between *inter se* cooperation *erga omnes* and Article 308 EC had already been addressed in *ERTA* (n 114 above), where the Court simply held that '[a]lthough [Article 308] empowers the Council to take any 'appropriate measures' equally within the sphere of external relations, it does not create an obligation, but confers on the Council an option, failure to exercise which cannot affect the validity of proceedings' (ibid para 95). Arguably, this passage did already betray a judicial preference against the thesis of the exclusivity of the Community channels for *inter se* agreements *erga omnes*.

[132]   M Koskenniemi, *From Apology to Utopia*, especially Chapter 4.

[133]   C Brölmann, *The Legal Nature of International Organisations and the Law of Treaties*, 111.

external relations of Member States will, by definition, become problematic under international law.[134]

Imagine the following scenario: a State within a federation enjoys international personality and is allowed to retain certain treaty-making powers under the federal constitution. Having concluded a valid international treaty with a third State for a matter coming within its power, the federation subsequently decides to adopt a federal law that conflicts with these treaty obligations. Being constitutionally prevented from implementing its treaty obligations, the Member State cannot plead this legislative development to justify a breach of contract under international law and will, therefore, incur international liability. To avoid this unenviable normative dilemma, some federations reserve foreign affairs exclusively to the federal level.[135] Others have permitted a degree of foreign affairs federalism, but have made the conclusion of international agreements by a Member State dependent on the consent of the federal level.[136]

The EC Treaty did not eliminate the treaty-making powers of the Member States under international law. The Member States continued to be entitled to conclude international agreements within the scope of the Community legal order. The ensuing doctrinal complexities in the normative relationship between EC law and the treaty-making powers of the Member States were marked. The normative tensions between the autonomous treaty-making powers of the Member States and the integrity of the Community legal order reached a climax in relation to subsequent international agreements concluded with third States. What would happen where a Member State had concluded an agreement with a third State that violated EC law?

How has EC federalism addressed this problem? The European legal order has employed three main techniques.[137] The first technique is based on *ex ante* control by means of an authorization procedure. It could be seen in Article 75

---

[134] R Schütze, *Federalism and Foreign Affairs: Mixity as a (Inter)national Phenomenon.*

[135] This has traditionally been the position in the United States: see Chapter 2—*Excursus.*

[136] This has been the solution adopted in Germany. Dealing with foreign relations, Article 32(3) of the German Constitution states: 'Insofar as the Länder have power to legislate, they may, with the consent of the Federal Government, conclude treaties with foreign states'. For a discussion of German foreign affairs federalism, see: R Schütze (n 134 above).

[137] The—fourth—technique of 'Community clauses' will not be discussed here. These clauses were developed in the context of the Common Commercial Policy and would approximately read as follows: 'Lorsque les obligations découlant du traité instituant la Communauté économique européenne et relatives à l'instauration progressive d'une politique commerciale commune le rendront nécessaire, des négociations seront ouvertes dans le plus bref délai possible afin d'apporter au présent accord toutes modifications utiles': Council Decision of 20 July 1960, quoted in P Pescatore, *Les relations extérieures des communautés européennes*, 168. The Community could only require its

ECSC. The provision recognized the treaty-making powers of the Member States in the area of the Common Commercial Policy, but required them to inform the Community of proposed commercial agreements. Where a proposed agreement contained clauses which would conflict with or 'hinder the future implementation of this Treaty', the Community would require the necessary corrections from the State concerned.[138] Similarly, the external relations chapter in the Euratom Treaty provided:

Member States shall communicate to the Commission draft agreements or contracts with a third State, an international organisation or a national of a third State to the extent that such agreements or contracts concern matters within the purview of this Treaty. If a draft agreement or contract contains clauses which impede the application of this Treaty, the Commission shall, within one month of receipt of such communication, make its comments known to the State concerned. *The State shall not conclude the proposed agreement or contract until it has satisfied the objections of the Commission or complied with a ruling by the Court of Justice, adjudicating urgently upon an application from the State, on the compatibility of the proposed clauses with the provisions of this Treaty.* An application may be made to the Court of Justice at any time after the State has received the comments of the Commission.[139]

The EC Treaty contained no provision that would require Member States to submit their draft agreements for Community consent. It has been claimed that the insertion of this *ex ante* technique into the EC Treaty 'would have been politically unviable if it intended to give the Commission a right of veto or the right to request a binding ruling from the Court'.[140] However, in certain fields, a version of this *ex ante* mechanism has been embedded in EC legislation.[141] As a general constitutional mechanism, however, this technique

Member States to negotiate the inclusion of such a 'disconnection clause'. Where the third State refused to insert such a clause into the international agreement, this *ex ante* mechanism would fail.

[138] Article 75(2) ECSC.

[139] Article 103 Euratom (emphasis added).

[140] G Gaja, P Hay and RD Rotunda, *Instruments for Legal Integration in the European Community— A Review*, 148.

[141] Cf Regulation 847/2007 on the Negotiation and Implementation of Air Service Agreements between Member States and Third Countries. Article 1 lays down a notification requirement for Member States' air service agreements, while Article 4 deals with the conclusion of Member States' agreements. The provision reads: '(1) Upon signature of an agreement, the Member State concerned shall notify the Commission of the outcome of the negotiations together with any relevant documentation. (2) Where the negotiations have resulted in an agreement which incorporates the relevant standard clauses referred to in Article 1(1), the Member State shall be authorised to conclude the agreement. (3) Where the negotiations have resulted in an agreement which does not incorporate the relevant standard clauses referred to in Article 1(1), the Member State shall be authorised, in accordance with the procedure referred to in Article 7(2), to conclude the agreement,

would still seem to be politically 'off limits'—even if the Council (and not the Commission) were given the veto power. Finally, the analogous application of Article 300(6) EC to international agreements to be concluded by Member States has never been accepted.[142]

A second *ex ante* technique was inspired by the philosophy of dual federalism. Normative conflicts between European law and international agreements of the Member States are avoided by means of a strategy of exclusive powers. The Member States lose their very competence to conclude those international agreements that could potentially conflict with present or future Community legislation.[143] Traditionally, the European Court has extensively cultivated this technique through the concept of *a priori* and subsequently exclusive treaty-making powers. This 'flight into dual federalism' avoided the complex supremacy questions within the external relations sphere. It elegantly cut the Gordian knot of the relationship between EC law and international agreements of the Member States as a conflict between Community legislation and international agreements of the Member States could simply never arise. Exclusivity equally promised to avoid another complex issue: the question of Member States responsibility for a breach of a treaty with a third country that had come into conflict with subsequent Community legislation. Gratuitously, the philosophy of dual federalism also maintained—at least symbolically—the myth of the 'sovereign' nature of either international person within its respective sphere of competence.

By contrast, the Court subsequently developed the supremacy doctrine as a third technique to control international agreements of Member States with third States. Under this *ex post* mechanism, Member States remain competent to conclude international agreements even in areas in which European

provided that this does not harm the object and purpose of the Community common transport policy. The Member State may provisionally apply the agreement pending the outcome of this procedure'.

[142] However, this solution has been suggested by Timmermans. See his intervention in A Bleckmann and G Ress (eds), *Souveränitätsverständnis in den Europäischen Gemeinschaften*, 210: 'Ich glaube, das ist eine richtige Interpretation, die es ermöglicht, [Artikel 300 (6)] für eine Lösung solcher Kompetenzkonflikte heranzuziehen'.

[143] The perhaps most explicit exponent of this technique has been CW Vedder, *Die auswärtige Gewalt des Europa der Neun*, 123 (emphasis added): '*Da jeder Vertragsschluß durch die Mitgliedstaaten auf Gebieten innergemeinschaftlicher Rechtsetzungsbefugnisse der EWG den Bestand des Gemeinschaftsrechts gefährden bzw. dessen weitere Entwicklung behindern würde*, führt eine konsequente Anwendung des Art. 5 Abs. 2 EWGV dazu, daß Mitgliedstaaten verpflichtet sind, solche Verträge nicht mehr zu schließen'. To fill the gap created by the total loss of all treaty-making powers of the Member States for matters within the competence of the Community, the Community's implied external powers should be correspondingly extended (ibid 125).

legislation exists. However, international agreements concluded by Member States will be treated—*within the Community legal order*—like unilateral acts of the Member States. In order to protect the integrity of the Community legal order, a distinction is thus drawn between the *Community's* international agreements and *Member States'* international agreements. The former enjoy a hierarchical rank above Community legislation,[144] while the latter would be hierarchically subordinate to Community legislation. This *ex post* control of Member States' international agreements could cause intricate legal problems. What would happen to the international responsibility of Member States, where the supremacy of European law prevented them from implementing their international obligations? After the decline of the Luxembourg compromise—which had allowed a *political* solution to this normative problem[145]—a *constitutional* solution was required.

Which technique has been predominant in the EC legal order? In the last decade, the Community legal order has shifted its attention from the second to the third technique. And in developing the supremacy of EC law over international agreements concluded by the Member States, the Community had two polarized options: it could either impose the absolute supremacy of Community law, or it could 'suspend' it. But if the latter approach were to be followed, the Court would have to apply Article 307 EC *analogously*, for the wording of the provision precluded its direct application to subsequent international agreements of the Member States.[146]

---

[144] This hierarchical position between primary and secondary European law follows from the fact that the European Court uses (directly effective) international agreements as a standard of review for the legality of Community legislation. In Case C–61/94 *Commission of the European Communities v Federal Republic of Germany*, para 52 the Court spoke expressly of the 'primacy of international agreements concluded by the Community over provisions of secondary [sic] Community legislation'.

[145] '[A] Member State bound by an agreement with a third State will reasonably refrain from voting in favour of a Council act which may lead to an infringement of any obligation under the agreement and will also insist on a vote being taken only unanimously' (G Gaja, P Hay, RD Rotunda (n 140 above) 147).

[146] Article 307 EC deals with international agreements of the Member States concluded before 1 January 1958 or prior to their accession. It states: '(1) The rights and obligations arising from agreements concluded before 1 January 1958 or, for acceding States, before the date of their accession, between one or more Member States on the one hand, and one or more third countries on the other, shall not be affected by the provisions of this Treaty. (2) To the extent that such agreements are not compatible with this Treaty, the Member States or States concerned shall take all appropriate steps to eliminate the incompatibilities established. Member States shall, where necessary, assist each other to this end and shall, where appropriate, adopt a common attitude'. On the meaning of this provision in the Community legal order, see: R Schütze, *EC Law and International Agreements of the Member States—An Ambivalent Relationship?*, 390–4.

How did the Community legal order deal with the normative tensions inherent in the supremacy technique? In *Kramer*,[147] the Dutch measure at issue had been adopted in the performance of the international commitments of The Netherlands within the framework of the North-East Atlantic Fisheries Convention. The international treaty had been signed on 24 January 1959, ie *after* the coming into force of the EC Treaty. The Convention bound all Member States—except Italy and Luxembourg—and seven third States. How would the Court treat a national measure that implemented international obligations assumed after 1958? Finding that the Member States (still) had the power to assume commitments within the framework of the North-East Atlantic Fisheries Convention, the Court attested them 'the right to ensure the application of these commitments within the area of their jurisdiction'.[148] Did this mean that they were protected under Article 307 EC, applied *analogously*? No. Referring to the duties stemming from Article 10 EC, the Member States were 'not to enter into any commitment within the framework of these conventions which could hinder the Community in carrying out the tasks entrusted to it'.[149] From there, the Court proceeded to a normal pre-emption analysis under EC law.

The Court also reviewed the compatibility of a post-1958 international treaty with Community legislation in *Arbelaiz-Emazabel*.[150] France had concluded a fisheries agreement with Spain in 1967 as a *voisinage* agreement under the London Fisheries Convention of 1964.[151] Under the terms of the agreement, Spanish fishermen 'enjoyed a permanent right to fish' for all species in the area between six and twelve miles off the Atlantic coast of France. In a preliminary ruling, a French court had to consider the impact of interim Community legislation for Spanish fishermen—at that time still third country nationals—in particular, a Community licensing system.[152] Criminal charges had been brought against the master of a Spanish vessel that had fished without the required licence.

In the first two instances, the French judiciary had acquitted the accused on the ground that French fishing relations with Spain were more lenient than

---

[147] Joined Cases 3, 4 and 6/76, *Cornelis Kramer and others*.
[148] Ibid para 39.
[149] Ibid paras 44–5.
[150] Case 181/80 *Procureur général près la Cour d'Appel de Pau and others v Arbelaiz-Emazabel*.
[151] General Agreement on Fishing concluded between France and Spain by exchange of Notes on 20 March 1967 [1967] JORF 7807.
[152] See, in particular: Regulation 2160/77 laying down interim measures for the conservation and management of fishery resources applicable to vessels flying the flag of Spain.

the Community regime and did not require any licence. The *Cour d'Appel* had found that the Community legislation contravened the Franco-Spanish Agreement on the basis that, contrary to the provisions of the London Fisheries Convention, Spain had not been notified of the Community rules. The case was referred to the European Court of Justice, which was asked to determine whether France could insist on complying with its international obligations as the Community had only *subsequently* developed a legislative system that happened to conflict with France's international treaty.

The Court referred to its *Kramer* ruling and held that, at the time of conclusion, in the absence of any Community regulation on fishing, France had been entitled to sign both the London Fisheries Convention and the bilateral agreement with Spain. The Court then moved to Article 10 of the London Fisheries Convention, permitting the establishment of a specific *inter se* regime for Community Member States, from which it deduced that the parties to the Convention '[m]ust have known that as from a particular time the power to adopt conservation measures under Article 5 of the Convention would, as far as the Member States of the Community are concerned, be exercised by the Community institutions'.[153]

By means of a detour, the Court then described the negotiation history of a draft Community agreement with Spain which was to be signed in 1980 (and would finally enter into force in 1981), as well as the laborious invention of an interim Community regime in which Spain had been actively involved. From that 'legislative context', the Court concluded:

The interim regime which the Community set up under its own rules falls within the framework of the relations established between the Community and Spain in order to resolve the problems inherent in conservation measures and the extension of fishery limits and in order to ensure reciprocal access by fishermen to the waters subject to such measures. Those relations, which were confirmed by the agreement on fisheries concluded by the Community and Spain . . . replaced the prior international obligations existing between certain Member States, such as France, and Spain. *Accordingly, Spanish fishermen may not rely on prior international agreements between France and Spain in order to prevent the application of the interim regulation adopted by the Community in the event of any incompatibility between the two categories of provisions.*[154]

This was not too clear a constitutional message. However, it seemed that the French bilateral agreement could not affect the Community legislation. The case has consequently been seen as a manifestation of the supremacy

---

[153] *Arbelaiz-Emazabel* (n 150 above) para 13.
[154] Ibid paras 29–31 (emphasis added).

of Community legislation over a Member State's international agreements concluded with third States after 1958.[155] This was confirmed in *Commission v Belgium & Luxembourg*,[156] where a normative conflict arose between an agreement concluded by the Belgo-Luxembourg Economic Union and Malaysia on maritime transport and the Community Regulation on services in maritime transport.[157] The Community act had entered into force on 1 January 1987, the international agreement on 29 June 1987. The Court simply found that in concluding the agreement, the two Member States had violated the relevant Community legislation.[158]

While the supremacy of Community law vis-à-vis an international treaty concluded by a State has—slowly—been established, this solution has been described as 'not entirely satisfactory':

The dissatisfaction arises out of what is a general—and still not satisfactorily resolved—problem of the relationship between Community law and treaties concluded by individual member States *after* they have become members of the EC (so that [Article 307] is not relevant) but *before* the Community has developed a comprehensive policy and obtained (exclusive) treaty-making powers in relation to the subject matter of such a policy . . .

While the European Court is entitled to ignore such treaties as not being part of the Community legal order, things are not so straightforward for member States. A member State may well be faced with a conflict between its [EC] obligations and its obligations under the treaty with a third State . . . Here Community law at present does little to help a member State avoid such a conflict. Often the member State concerned will not really be to blame for such a conflict arising. *Because of the evolutionary nature of the Community, the state of Community law in the future is not easy to predict. A member State may conclude a treaty relating to a particular subject matter years before the Community develops a comprehensive policy in the same subject area and before the development of such a policy could be foreseen.*[159]

In the light of the danger of international responsibility of Member States towards third countries, various early commentators in the literature had therefore championed the *analogous* application of Article 307 EC to this type

---

[155] RR Churchill and NG Foster, *European Community Law and Prior Treaty Obligations of Member States: The Spanish Fishermen's Cases*, 519.

[156] Joined Cases C-176 and 177/97 *Commission v Kingdom of Belgium and Grand Duchy of Luxembourg*.

[157] Regulation 4055/86 applying the principle of freedom to provide services to maritime transport between Member States and between Member States and third countries.

[158] Joined Cases C-176 and 177/97 (n 156 above) para 37.

[159] RR Churchill and NG Foster (n 155 above) 519 and 523 (emphasis added).

of situation.'[T]here would be every reason to apply [Article 307] of the [EC] Treaty by extension or analogy, *e.g.* in the case of conflicts between an agreement entered into by a member State and a non-member State after the entry into force of the [EC] Treaty on the one hand, and rules of "secondary law", such as a "Regulation", enacted subsequently to such an agreement, on the other (provided always that the agreement is not *per se* incompatible with the Treaty)'.[160] The supremacy of Community legislation should thus be suspended to allow a Member State to fulfil its international obligations agreed *after 1958.*

The main constitutional thrust behind this argument is that it protects the effective exercise of the treaty-making powers of the Member States— 'otherwise the Member States could not conclude any international treaty without running the risk of a subsequent conflict with Community law'.[161] This has been contested: there would simply be no reason why the normal constitutional principles characterizing the relationship between European law and national law should not also apply to this class of international agreements.[162] A middle position has proposed limiting the analogous application of Article 307 EC to situations where the conflict between post-1958 international treaties of Member States and subsequently adopted Community legislation was 'objectively unforeseeable' and could therefore not be expected.[163]

None of these proposals, as we saw above, have yet been mirrored in the jurisprudence of the European Court of Justice. The Court has come to unconditionally uphold the supremacy of European law against international agreements concluded by the Member States after 1958. In the light of the potential international responsibility of the Member States, is this a fair constitutional solution? Should it make a difference whether a rule is adopted by means of a unilateral national measure or by means of an international

---

[160] JHF van Panhuys, *Conflicts between the Law of the European Communities and Other Rules of International Law*, 434. The same solution has been proposed by Daillier advocating 'comme date critique pour "l'antériorité" de l'établissement de la politique commune des pêches, soit 1979. Deux arguments peuvent être invoqués au bénéfice de la deuxième solution: le principe de bonne foi exige que les tiers aient été alertés par une affirmation concrète de la compétence communautaire; et la jurisprudence Kramer, 1976, admet la compétence des Etats membres pour négocier des accords de pêche avec les Etats tiers au moins jusqu'à cette date, et même jusqu'en 1976' (P Daillier, *Le régime de la pêche maritime des ressortissants espagnols sous juridiction des états membres de la C.E.E.* (1977–1980)*, 190).

[161] E Pache and J Bielitz, *Das Verhältnis der EG zu den völkerrechtlichen Verträgen ihrer Mitgliedstaaten*, 327 (translation—RS).

[162] E Bülow, *Die Anwendung des Gemeinschaftsrechts im Verhältnis zu Drittländern*, 54.

[163] EU Petersmann, *Artikel 234*, rn 6.

agreement with a third State? Instead of 'suspending' the supremacy of European law in the latter scenario, better solutions need to be found to solve the Member States' dilemma of having to choose between the Scylla of liability under the EC Treaty and the Charybdis of responsibility under international law. Should the EC legal order, therefore, be given an *ex ante* authorization mechanism for Member States' international agreements? Should the Community share financial responsibility for breach of contract with the Member State concerned?[164] Perhaps, faced with the alternative of exclusive treaty-making powers being transferred to the Community, the Member States will—more or less happily—accept the risk of international liability as a price worth paying for their presence on the international scene? These are difficult constitutional questions. They await future constitutional answers.

2. *Constitutional Practice: The ERTA Doctrine and Cooperative Federalism*

Despite tectonic changes in its underlying constitutional theory, Europe's foreign affairs paradigm continues to adhere to a dual federalist interpretation of the *ERTA* doctrine: once the Community exercises its internal competences, its parallel external competences become exclusive. Theoretical objections aside, how successful is this reading in explaining current constitutional practice in the external sphere?

What the *ERTA* ruling had left in suspense was *when* the exercise of international powers by the Member States would be incompatible with European law. To what extent would European legislation exclude the Member States? This central ambivalence of the *ERTA* doctrine has been aptly translated into a series of sharp questions: 'If the Council, in the exercise of its internal competence, adopts a regulation (as it did in the *ERTA* case) are the Member States precluded from concluding international agreements on the entire subject which is thus "pre-empted"—and if so, how does one define the "subject", or "the field" that is so pre-empted? Or, and this is an alternative interpretation, are the Member States only forbidden to act intentionally in violation of the specific Community rules set forth in the regulation?'.[165]

---

[164] This solution has been tentatively suggested by Daillier (n 160 above) in the form of the following questions: 'Comment concilier les obligations internationals des Etats members et leurs obligations en vertu du droit communautaire? Dans la mesure où l'incompatibilité des textes successifs résulte d'initiatives tant communautaires que nationales, faut-il envisager un partage de responsabilités internationales entre la CEE et les Etats membres, et si oui, sur la base de quels critères?'.

[165] E Stein, *External Relations of the European Community: Structure and Process*, 157.

The first alternative—corresponding to dual federalism and field pre-emption—gained strength from one part of the *ERTA* judgment: '*Since the subject-matter of the AETR falls within the scope of Regulation No. 543/69*, the Community has been empowered to negotiate and conclude the agreement in question since the entry into force of the said regulation. *These Community powers exclude the possibility of concurrent powers on the part of the Member States*, since any steps taken outside the framework of the Community institutions would be incompatible with the unity of the common market and the uniform application of Community law'.[166] By way of contrast, another part of the judgment suggested a cooperative federal philosophy: '[E]ach time the Community, with a view to implementing a common policy envisaged by the Treaty, adopts provisions laying down *common rules, whatever form these may take*, the Member States no longer have the right, acting individually or even collectively, to undertake obligations with third countries *which affect those rules*'.[167] The Court seemed here to insist on a substantive conflict between the Member States' international agreement and European legislation, but again did not say *when* the autonomous exercise of national external powers would conflict with the uniform application of Community law. Neither the term 'common rules' nor the verb 'affect' were constitutionally pre-defined concepts.[168]

It was up to subsequent jurisprudence to clarify which one of the two versions of the *ERTA* doctrine was to apply. Answers to this constitutional

---

[166] Case 22/70 *Commission v Council (ERTA)*, paras 30–1 (emphasis added). Lenaerts has argued that the *ERTA* Court opted for the dual federalist alternative. Relying on the strong language of para 31, he identified a '*preemption* très englobante' (K Lenaerts, *Les répercussion des compétences de la communauté européenne sur les compétences externes des états membres et la question de 'preemption'*, 60). The author drew two conclusions from this wide notion of pre-emption: 'Par conséquent, face à une action interne de la part de la Communauté, la compétence étatique externe se perd plus facilement que la compétence étatique interne ayant le même objet matériel'. Secondly, 'les limites précises d'une réglementation communautaire interne indiquent le point à partir duquel les Etats membres peuvent agir, à titre concurrent, tant sur le plan interne qu'internationale' (ibid 59).

[167] *ERTA*, para 18 (emphasis added). The Court continued as follows (emphasis added): 'As and when such common rules come into being, the Community *alone* is in a position to assume and carry out contractual obligations towards third countries affecting the whole sphere of application of the Community legal system'.

[168] The expression 'common rules' appears in Article 71(1)(a) of the Treaty. Originally, the phrase seemed to have no specific constitutional significance beyond the formal sense of rules that apply to all the Member States. In the aftermath of the *ERTA* ruling, the view was widely held that the Court had given a substantive meaning to the term (cf D McGoldrick, *International Relations Law of the European Union*, 72–3). The concept of 'common rules' has thereby either been restricted to rules adopted under a common policy—such as transport policy—or has been constructed to refer to exhaustive Community legislation. Both attempts to give a substantive content to the concept have failed in the light of subsequent jurisprudence.

question took more than twenty years to emerge. The last decade finally tilted
the balance in favour of the cooperative federal reading. Judicial cracks in the
dual federal paradigm first surfaced in two legal opinions in the 1990s delivered under Article 300(6) EC. In Opinion 2/91,[169] the Commission had argued
that, through a number of legislative measures, 'common rules' had come
into existence and that they would be affected by international obligations
undertaken autonomously by the Member States under ILO Convention
No 170. The Convention was designed to protect workers against the harm-
ful effects of using chemicals in the workplace. Some of the relevant
Community legislation had been adopted under Article 137 EC. The provision provided the Community with a complementary competence to encourage improvements of the health and safety of workers. However, the
introduction of European rules under this power 'shall not prevent any
Member State from maintaining or introducing more stringent measures for
the protection of working conditions compatible with this Treaty'. Because of
the cooperative federal structure in the internal sphere, the Council (and the
Member States) argued, 'the rules adopted on the basis of Article 137 cannot
be affected, within the meaning of the AETR judgment, by an ILO convention
concluded by Member States in the area covered by those rules'.[170]

The Court's response was enlightening in a number of ways. It began by
clarifying that the *ERTA* doctrine would potentially apply to all legal bases
within the Treaty as it 'cannot be restricted to instances where the Community
has adopted Community rules within the framework of a common policy'.[171]
But would European law adopted under a complementary competence be
automatically affected if the Member States exercised their international
powers to conclude the ILO Convention? Would the Community enjoy an
exclusive external competence through internal minimum harmonization?
The answer to this second question was the following:

> For the purpose of determining whether this competence is exclusive in nature,
> it should be pointed out that the provisions of Convention No 170 are not of such
> a kind as to affect rules adopted pursuant to [Article 137]. If, on the one hand, the
> Community decides to adopt rules which are less stringent than those set out in an
> ILO convention, Member States may, in accordance with [Article 137 (4)], adopt

---

[169] Opinion 2/91 (*ILO Convention No 170*).
[170] Ibid 1073.
[171] Ibid para 10. The justification of the Court is: 'In all the areas corresponding to the objectives
of the Treaty, [Article 10] requires Member States to facilitate the achievement of the Community's
tasks and to abstain from any measure which could jeopardize the attainment of the objectives of
the Treaty'.

more stringent measures for the protection of working conditions or apply for that purpose the provisions of the relevant ILO convention. If, on the other hand, the Community decides to adopt more stringent measures than those provided for under an ILO convention, there is nothing to prevent the full application of Community law by the Member States under Article 19(8) of the ILO Constitution, which allows members to adopt more stringent measures than those provided for in conventions or recommendations adopted by that organization.[172]

There was thus no substantive conflict between the Community legislation and the international agreement. Since the Community legislation and the international convention only established minimum standards and mutually permitted the introduction of stricter standards, the conflict-less co-existence of the two sets of norms was guaranteed. European legislation would consequently not be 'affected' by the international Convention and vice versa.

The smooth parallel existence of European law and the international convention could, on the other hand, not be guaranteed for harmonization measures adopted under Articles 94 and 95 EC. These European laws had exhaustively regulated a large area of the field covered by the Convention.[173] And while admitting that 'there is no contradiction between these provisions of the Convention and those of the directives mentioned', the fact that the international agreement was 'concerned with an area which is already covered to a large extent by Community rules' meant that the international commitments 'are of such a kind as to affect the Community rules laid down in those directives and that consequently Member States cannot undertake such commitments outside the framework of the Community institutions'.[174] The *ERTA* effect was thus applied to situations, where the subject-matter of the agreement was, at least largely, occupied by exhaustive Community legislation. Minimum harmonization, by contrast, would not only permit the Member States to act internally; it would equally allow them to act externally. Opinion 2/91 was thus informed by the idea of symmetry between Europe's internal and external federal structure.

---

[172] Ibid para 18.

[173] The Court mentioned, in particular, Directive 67/548/EC on the approximation of laws, regulations and administrative practices relating to the classification, packaging, and labelling of dangerous substances, adopted pursuant to Article 94 of the Treaty and Directive 88/379/EC on the approximation of the laws, regulations, and administrative provisions of the Member States relating to the classification, packaging, and labelling of dangerous preparations adopted pursuant to Article 95 EC. Both Directives were examples of complete harmonization.

[174] Ibid paras 25–6.

This idea of constitutional symmetry was reinforced by a second opinion: Opinion 1/94.[175] The European Court had been requested to assess the federal division of external powers in relation to the WTO Agreement and its Annexes. Having found those parts of GATT dealing with goods to fall within the ambit of the Community's common commercial policy and thus within the scope of its exclusive competence, the question arose whether the Community would also enjoy an *exclusive* treaty-making power in relation to trade in services and the intellectual property aspects regulated by GATS and TRIPs respectively.[176] In its advisory opinion, the Court reviewed three possible sources for such an exclusive external competence on the part of the Community with regard to GATS.[177] Only one source—*ERTA* exclusivity— shall interest us here.

According to the Court, the Member States would lose their right to assume obligations with non-Member countries 'as and when common rules which could be affected by those obligations come into being'. 'Only in so far as common rules have been established at internal level does the external competence of the Community become exclusive'.[178] Without giving any general definition of when common rules would be affected, the Court found that this would definitively be the case 'where the Community has achieved *complete* harmonization'.[179] The Court thus accepted that not every exercise of an internal power would render the parallel external power exclusive. Only where the Community totally occupied the internal field through exhaustive legislation,

---

[175] Opinion 1/94 (*WTO Agreement*). The ruling has been very controversial. Because of 'the fact that the Court does not sufficiently distinguish between mere competence and exclusive competence, the legality of the Community's concluding the entire GATS becomes clouded' (NA Neuwahl, *The WTO Opinion and Implied External Powers of the Community: A Hidden Agenda*, 145).

[176] The subsequent analysis of the ruling is confined to the GATS aspects of the opinion.

[177] Opinion 1/94, para 73. The Commission had claimed firstly 'that the Community's exclusive competence to conclude GATS and TRIPs flows implicitly from the provisions of the Treaty establishing its internal competence'; or, secondly, 'from the exercise of legislative acts of the institutions giving effect to that internal competence'; or, thirdly, from the 'need to enter into international commitments with a view to achieving an internal Community objective' (ibid para 72). In relation to the Community's internal powers regarding freedom of establishment and services, the Court would enigmatically state that those provisions 'do not contain any provision expressly extending the competence of the Community to 'relationships arising from international law' and that the 'sole objective of those chapters is to secure the right of establishment and freedom to provide services for nationals of Member States'. Those rules did not grant rights to third country nationals and for that reason '[o]ne cannot therefore infer from those chapters that the Community has *exclusive competence* to conclude an agreement with non-member countries to liberalize first establishment and access to service markets' (ibid para 81, emphasis added).

[178] Ibid para 77.

[179] Ibid paras 95–6 (emphasis added).

would Europe's parallel external power become exclusive. The reasoning of the Court—while minimalist in definitional terms—demonstrated a guarded hostility towards a dual federalist reading of the *ERTA* doctrine. The Court's restrictive reading of the *ERTA* doctrine tied its exclusionary effect to complete harmonization in the internal sphere. The federal structure in Europe's external relations sphere should—by and large—reflect the federal structure of its internal sphere.

These two rulings—Opinion 2/91 and Opinion 1/94—constituted first cracks in the dominant dualist federal theory in the external sphere. They were confirmed in 2002. A set of bilateral agreements with the United States, known as 'open skies agreements', was at the centre of a series of cases.[180] Internally, the Community had adopted three legislative packages to ensure freedom to provide services in the air-transport sector. Would these internal rules provide the Community with an exclusive external competence to negotiate an open skies agreement with the United States?

The part of the judgment dealing with the *ERTA* doctrine confirmed the rising judicial preference for symmetry between the internal and the external sphere. The 'recognition of an exclusive external competence for the Community in consequence of the adoption of internal measures' would only occur in situations where the freedom of Member States to enter into international commitments was 'affecting' internal legislation because it would 'jeopardize the attainment of the objective pursued by those rules'.[181] Yet, the fundamental question was: *when* and 'under what circumstances the scope of the common rules may be affected or distorted by the international commitments at issue'?[182] While paying symbolic heed to the dual federalist alternative in *ERTA*,[183] the Court confirmed the propositions made in Opinion 2/91 and Opinion 1/94. And in the light of these, the Court examined the Commission's claim that Regulation 2407/92 and Regulation 2408/92 were affected by national bilateral open skies agreements. It quickly rejected this contention. In the absence of complete harmonization,[184] the Court seemed

---

[180]   The *Open Skies* cases include: C-466/98 *Commission v United Kingdom*; C-467/98 *Commission v Denmark*; C-468/98 *Commission v Sweden*; Case C-469/69 *Commission v Finland* ; C-471/98 *Commission v Belgium*; C-472/98 *Commission v Luxembourg*; C-475/98 *Commission v Austria*; and Case 476/98 *Commission v Germany*. The following analysis will exclusively draw on the *Commission v Germany* judgment when generically referring to the '*Open Skies* cases'.

[181]   Case 476/98 *Commission v Germany*, paras 104–5.

[182]   Ibid para 107.

[183]   Ibid para 108: 'where the international commitments fall within the scope of the common rules' (with reference to para 30 of the *ERTA* judgment).

[184]   Ibid paras 118–19.

to be searching for *some* substantive conflict between the bilateral agreements and the Community legislation before it would admit that the former 'affected' the latter. The strict scrutiny applied by the Court even came close to a search for rule pre-emption.[185]

The transition towards a cooperative federal practice in Europe's foreign affairs may equally be felt in Opinion 1/2003.[186] The Opinion analysed the nature of the Community's treaty-making competence for the conclusion of

---

[185] In his opinion to the *Open Skies* cases, Advocate General Tizzano argued in favour of a strict semantic distinction between 'in conflict' and 'merely affect': 'For my part, I concur with the Commission that the *AETR* judgement is not confined to precluding the Member States from undertaking international obligations that are in conflict with common rules, especially as such conduct would in itself constitute a separate breach of Community law, which could be held unlawful even without regard to *AETR*. What the *AETR* judgment requires of Member States, and in clear terms, is not to assume obligations which may even merely "affect" the common rules. And there are other important precedents to the same effect, and in even more unequivocal terms, if that were possible' (Opinion of the AG Tizzano, para 67). Revisiting briefly Opinions 1/91, 1/92, and 1/94, the Advocate General found that '[i]n these precedents, as may readily be observed, the Court did not stop to examine whether there were specific reasons for which the assumption of the international obligations could in fact impinge in some form on the Community provisions. For the Member States to be precluded from undertaking obligations of this kind, the Court deemed it sufficient, to use its own expressions, that the obligations "[fall] within the scope of" the Community rules, that they are "concerned with an area which is already covered to a large extent by Community rules", that they are "in the spheres covered by those acts" or that "the matters covered by the [agreements] are already the subject of internal legislation". All this is so, I would repeat, simply "because the common rules thus adopted could be affected within the meaning of the *AETR* judgement"' (ibid para 70). 'It must therefore be concluded that, in principle, in matters covered by common rules, the Member States may not under any circumstances conclude international agreements, *even if these are entirely consistent with the common rules, since "any steps taken outside the framework of the Community institutions" would be "incompatible with the unity of the common market and the uniform application of Community law"*. I appreciate that some may find—and have found—this conclusion unduly rigid and even over-formalistic; but I am unable to see any way to limit its implications, in any reasonable and credible manner, without undermining the coherence of the principles and of the system and, in particular, the fundamental requirement of the unity and uniformity of the common action which, as we have seen, the Court has made the cornerstone of its case-law on the matter' (ibid para 71, emphasis added). However, a little later, the Advocate General admits that 'the question whether or not the agreement "affects" the common rules must be assessed in the light of the particular circumstances of each case; in other words, a specific assessment is required in each case to determine if the agreement *conflicts in some respect with the common rules or if it could otherwise in any way impinge on their correct application or alter their scope*' (ibid para 75, emphasis added). Later still, he writes that 'in order to establish that the common rules are "affected" it is not enough to cite general effects of an economic nature which the agreements could have on the functioning of the internal market; *what is required instead is to specify in detail the aspects of the Community legislation which could be prejudiced by the agreements*' (ibid para 77, emphasis added). Paras 78–108 of his opinion represent a concrete and substantive pre-emption analysis of whether the disputed agreements affect the relevant Community legislation.

[186] Opinion 1/2003 (*Competence of the Community to conclude the new Lugano Convention on jurisdiction and the recognition and enforcement of judgments in civil and commercial matters*).

a new Lugano Convention. The 'old' Lugano Convention on jurisdiction and the enforcement of judgments in civil and commercial matters had sprung from the desire to extend—to the greatest possible extent—the *intra-*Community effects of the Brussels Convention to members of the European Free Trade Association ('EFTA').[187] At a time when the Community enjoyed no competence within the area, it had been concluded *without* the participation of Community. This constitutional situation had changed with the introduction of Article 65 EC in the Community legal order. And with the 'communitarization' of the Brussels Convention in the shape of Regulation 44/2001,[188] there even existed European legislation on the subject. Would the Community now possess an exclusive competence for renegotiating the Lugano Convention? Would the *ERTA* effect of the Brussels Regulation lead to the total exclusion of the Member States from the negotiating table?

The Council and most of the intervening Member States were opposed to such a dual federalist reasoning.[189] The exhaustive character of the harmonization achieved by Regulation 44/2001 was doubtful, in particular in relation to its Article 4(1) conceding a residual power to the Member States.[190] The Regulation thus seemed to only *incompletely* harmonize matters falling within its scope. The Council, therefore, entertained doubts whether the Community had exclusive competence with regard to the Convention as a whole.[191] The Commission, on the other hand, had none. It argued that 'the simple objective of transposing common rules into the new Lugano Convention precludes any competence on the part of the Member States, as that would be incompatible with the unity of the common market and the

---

[187] The Convention was signed 16 September 1988 at Lugano. For an early analysis of the Convention, see: J Minor, *The Lugano Convention: Some Problems of Interpretation*. On the relationship between the Brussels Convention and EC law, see: R Schütze, *EC Law and International Agreements of the Member States—An Ambivalent Relationship?*, 416–20.

[188] On the 'Brussels Regulation', see: A Stadler, *From the Brussels Convention to Regulation 44/2001: Cornerstones of a European Law of Civil Procedure*.

[189] Opinion 1/2003, para 59.

[190] Article 4(1) states: 'If the defendant is not domiciled in a Member State, the jurisdiction of the courts of each Member State shall, subject to Articles 22 and 23, be determined by the law of that Member State'. Article 22 deals with cases of exclusive jurisdiction, while Article 23 deals with prorogation of jurisdiction. The French and the Finnish governments argued that Article 4 was 'declaratory' of an autonomous national competence; it did not, in other words, represent a delegation of Community power back to the Member States. Consequently, Article 4(1) could not amount to the adoption of common rules within the meaning of the *ERTA* judgment (Opinion 1/2003, paras 65–6).

[191] Ibid para 87.

uniform application of Community law'. Only the Community would be 'in a position to ensure the consistency of its own common rules if they are elevated to the international sphere'.[192] This was a novel argument and, in the light of the uncertainties still surrounding the *ERTA* doctrine, the Member States had requested a judicial clarification of the constitutional principles governing Europe's external sphere.

What was the constitutional principle *behind ERTA* exclusivity? The Court showed a helpless confusion over its past jurisprudence and zigzagged from illustration to general statement.[193] We may, nonetheless, distil two general ideas from the Court's unsystematic ruling. The first is a methodological principle; the second is of a substantive nature. Methodologically, the Court inferred from the enumeration principle that a finding of exclusive external powers required 'a comprehensive and detailed analysis' of the relationship between European legislation and the international treaty. It must be shown that 'it is *clear* that the conclusion of such an agreement is capable of *affecting the Community rules*'.[194] It would not be enough solely to look at the 'policy areas' concerned; instead, the Court would look at the 'nature and content' of

---

[192] Ibid para 93.

[193] The Court, referring to its previous jurisprudence, distinguished three situations in which exclusive power had been recognized. However, these three situations were 'only examples, formulated in the light of the particular contexts with which the Court was concerned' (para 121). To exemplify these three situations, the Court referred to paras 81–4 of Case C–467/98 *Commission v Denmark*. However, arguably, these paragraphs only mention two situations: the '*WTO* Principle' and the '*ERTA* Principle'. (Admittedly, the latter is expressed in three different ways; namely, where the Community has totally pre-empted the internal field, where international commitments fall within the scope of common rules, or where the Community had largely covered the area of the agreement.) The Court then reformulated the three situations in para 122. 'Ruling in much more general terms', the Court asserted, the three situations of exclusivity arose '*in particular* where the conclusion of an agreement by the Member States is incompatible with the unity of the common market and the uniform application of Community law (*ERTA*, para 31), or where, given the nature of the existing Community provisions, such as legislative measures containing clauses relating to the treatment of nationals of non-member countries or to the complete harmonisation of a particular issue, any agreement in that area would necessarily affect the Community rules within the meaning of the *ERTA* judgment'. In this passage, the Court thus reformulates para 82 of *Commission v Denmark* into more general terms. Strangely, 'the unity of the common market and the uniform application of Community law' seemed to be viewed as a concrete example of exclusivity ('in particular') and not as the underlying principle behind the *ERTA* line of exclusivity. In para 123, the Court then referred to two situations, where the *ERTA* doctrine would not apply; namely, where Community legislation only laid down minimum requirements (Opinion 2/91), or where the adoption of internal rules was possible to remove distortions or restriction in the internal market (Opinion 1/94).

[194] Opinion 1/2003, para 124 (emphasis added).

internal Community rules.[195] This methodological principle was a clear rejection of dual federalism, that is, the idea that spheres of responsibility are divided in terms of 'policy areas'. The Court insisted on a concrete analysis of and comparison between the rules within the relevant Community legislation and those within the (envisaged) international agreement. The second principle was to give substance to the *ERTA* doctrine. *When* would an international treaty 'affect' Community legislation? The Court here clarified that the purpose behind exclusive external Community competences was to prevent an international agreement concluded by the Member States to undermine 'the uniform and consistent application of the Community rules and the proper functioning of the system which they establish'.[196]

How would the Court apply these two general principles in the context of the Lugano Convention? What was the result of the Court's 'comprehensive and detailed analysis' of the 'nature and content' of the Brussels Regulation? The Court noted that the Regulation established 'a particularly complex system which, to be consistent, must be as comprehensive as possible'. The intent of the Community legislator had been 'to unify the rules on jurisdiction in civil and commercial matters'.[197] In the light of the 'uniform and coherent nature of the system of rules', Article 4(1) of the Regulation 'must be interpreted as meaning that it forms part of the system implemented by that regulation, since it resolves the situation envisaged by reference to the legislation of the Member State before whose court the matter is brought'. Did this mean that the Court rejected the idea that Article 4(1) acknowledged an autonomous Member State power and instead regarded it as a delegated Community competence? The Court remained ambivalent on the issue and only admitted that the Member States could use Article 4(1) as a valid legal basis for an international treaty. However, 'the agreement envisaged could still conflict with other provisions of that regulation', because 'any international agreement *also establishing a unified system of rules on conflict of jurisdiction* such as that established by that regulation *is capable of affecting those rules of jurisdiction*'.[198] And since the new Lugano Convention was just such a comprehensive agreement that tried to establish a unified system of rules on

---

[195] Ibid para 126. In its assessment of the 'nature and content' of the rules, the Court would, however, not only look at the current state of Community law, but would also take into account future harmonization efforts within the area.

[196] Ibid para 133. See also para 128.

[197] Ibid paras 141 and 143; and in para 144, the Court confirms: 'That regulation contains a set of rules forming a unified system'.

[198] Ibid paras 148–51 (emphasis added).

conflict of jurisdiction,[199] it followed that its provisions 'affect the uniform and consistent application of the Community rules on jurisdiction and the proper functioning of the system established by those rules'.[200]

This reasoning was a departure from the formulaic Opinion 1/94 jurisprudence. The Court did not ask whether the internal European law covered fully, or at least largely, the scope of the international agreement. Instead, it asked, whether an agreement concluded by the Member States would pose an obstacle to the uniform application or proper functioning of the Community legislation—irrespective of whether or not the area had been fully or largely harmonized. The Court searched for a substantive normative conflict. The Lugano Opinion thus tries to liberate the *ERTA* doctrine from the last

---

[199] Ibid para 152: 'The purpose of the new Lugano Convention is the same as that of Regulation 44/2001, but it has a wider territorial scope'.

[200] Ibid para 161. The Lugano Convention did contain a disconnection clause, yet the Court discarded its effectiveness by reference to three arguments (Opinion 1/2003, paras 154–6). First, a disconnection clause—a legislative tool—could not prejudice the—constitutional (!)—question whether the Community had an exclusive *competence*. 'On the contrary, such a clause may provide an indication that that agreement may affect the Community rules.' This reasoning is hard to swallow. Even if the proposed use of a disconnection clause may show the danger of a normative conflict *in its absence; its presence* prevents the international agreement from ever 'affecting' the application of Community legislation as between the Member States. But more importantly: how can the Court accept that European legislation may—through the '*ERTA* Principle'—change the order of exclusive competences; yet a 'disconnection clause' in European legislation cannot? The *ERTA* effect is, after all, caused by internal legislation and thus much closer to a legislative than a constitutional phenomenon. (The same sense of contradiction results from juxtaposing the Court's reasoning with the '*WTO* Principle'. If the insertion of an express provision in Community legislation leads to an exclusive external competence, why would it be impossible to achieve the opposite result through the inclusion of a disconnection clause in the international agreement?) Secondly, the Court followed the Commission's suggestion that a disconnection clause in an international agreement of private international law differs from a classic disconnection clause. Thirdly, there were exceptions to the disconnection clause that would mean that the Convention would in these areas 'affect' the relevant Community legislation. Only the third argument appears convincing. But why was the Commission so hostile towards the use of a disconnection clause—a clause, after all, that favours the Community over third States (cf CP Economides & AG Kolliopoulos, *La clause de déconnexion en faveur du droit communautaire: une practique critiquable*)? The answer may lie in para 83 of the Opinion: 'Noting that a disconnection clause appears, most often, in a "mixed" agreement, the Commission submits that the Council's intention, expressed in the negotiating directives, to include such a clause in the agreement envisaged may be regarded as a misguided attempt to prejudge whether or not such an agreement is mixed. It considers that the exclusivity of the external competence of the Community, like the legal basis for Community legislation, must be founded on objective criteria which are verifiable by the Court and not on the mere presence of a disconnection clause inserted in the relevant international agreement. If such a requirement is not satisfied, whether or not the Community's competence is exclusive could be subject to manipulation'. The Commission's dislike of these clauses thus lies in their offering an opportunity for mixed agreements.

linguistic vestiges of dual federalism. Opinion 1/2003 (re)centres the *ERTA* doctrine on an 'adverse effect' test.[201] This has a number of analytic advantages. The logic of dual federalism with its insistence on mutually exclusive policy areas fails, where an agreement falls into an area that is *not* (largely) covered by internal rules, but nonetheless poses an obstacle to the existing (minimum) Community legislation. The analytical toolbox of cooperative federalism is here much better able to explain why Member States would be pre-empted in such a situation.

Conclusion: The European Union and Foreign Affairs

The various ambivalences and *Leerstellen* encountered in the early judgments on the Community's implied external powers—reinforced by a pronounced gap between constitutional theory and practice—have been the source of learnt disputes on Europe's foreign affairs federalism. In the absence of a privileged visual perspective, a multiplicity of competing interpretations emerged in the past. This chapter has tried to systematize academic and judicial views and tried to present its own constitutional vision in terms of the book's federal debate. Is Europe's foreign affairs constitutionalism 'exceptional' when compared to the federal philosophy governing its internal sphere? The answer suggested was in the affirmative. Europe has indeed had 'its' reasons—reasons that are diametrically opposed to those underlying the American foreign affairs exception—to follow a dual federal philosophy in the external sphere.

What, then, are the parameters of Europe's dual federalism in the external sphere? Early on, Europe's external powers were tied to its internal powers through the doctrine of parallelism. The Community therefore enjoys the authority to conclude international treaties for all matters falling within its internal sphere. What is the nature of the Community's implied external competences: exclusive, concurrent, or shared? Three jurisprudential lines granting exclusivity were identified: the *ERTA* doctrine, the Opinion 1/76 doctrine, and the WTO doctrine. Each of these doctrines transforms a parallel external competence into an exclusive power. In contrast to the constitutional principles governing the internal sphere, the adoption of Community legislation here deprives Member States of their very competence to conclude

---

[201] In this sense also: N Lavranos, *Opinion 1/2003 Comment*, 1096.

international treaties. The theory of subsequently exclusive powers constituted a signal in favour of the theory of dual federalism in the external sphere. This preference for constitutional—as opposed to legislative—exclusivity encounters serious constitutional objections, especially as it leaves the application of the *constitutional* principle of subsidiarity to a *legislative* decision by the Community.

Why did the Community legal order originally favour a dual federalist rationale in the external sphere? What explains Europe's foreign affairs 'exceptionalism'? The second part of this chapter proposed that the answer may lie in the originally ambivalent normative relationship between European law and the international powers retained by the Member States. What was the hierarchical value of *inter se* agreements concluded by all Member States? What was the status of international agreements concluded by Member States with third parties? In the early years of the Community, these were unresolved constitutional questions. In striking contrast to the rapidly emerging doctrine of Community supremacy in relation to unilateral national measures, the supremacy of EC law over international agreements concluded by the Member States took much longer to emerge. With the supremacy issue still in suspense, the Court moved down the more aggressive route of constitutional exclusivity. The Court's 'flight into dual federalism' blocked the Member States' 'flight into international law'. Moreover, the demarcation of mutually exclusive spheres—in which either the Community or the Member States were 'sovereign'—elegantly avoided the assumption of a normative hierarchy of the Community over the Member States in the context of international relations. Dual federalism in the external sphere suggested the idea of coordination and 'sovereign' equality between the two levels of government.

Today, the originally ambivalent relationship between Europe's legal powers and the international powers of the Member States has been largely resolved. European law has imposed its authority onto the international powers of its Member States. This chapter has, therefore, championed the doctrine of pre-emption as the most suitable constitutional device to understand the essence of the *ERTA* doctrine. The open introduction into the Community's external sphere of the doctrine of pre-emption would remove the extra layer of complexity and legal cubism involved in dogmatically justifying the existence of 'implied subsequently exclusive external competences'. A courageous advance by the Court could enhance the clarity of legal argumentation and speed up the transition from a cubist past to an era of constitutional 'naturalism' in the external sphere. It would be so much more coherent and beautiful if the *same* constitutional principles applied in the internal and external hemisphere of the Community legal order.[202]

Be that as it may, dual federalist theory has increasingly lost touch with Europe's cooperative federal practice. We analysed these 'cracks' in the dual federal paradigm in the context of the *ERTA* line of exclusivity. Here, we witnessed a judicial transition from a dual federalist to a cooperative federalist reading. Briefly, the Court has come to reject field-pre-emptive 'strikes' against Member States' external powers within the scope of internal legislation. Under the *reformed ERTA* doctrine, the Member States will only be prevented from exercising their shared external powers, where such an exercise would create substantive normative conflicts with Community legislation. In the post-*WTO* Opinion jurisprudence, the enigmatic 'affect' formula has indeed been restrictedly interpreted. In the words of an eminent scholar: '[t]he period from 1970 to the late 1980s saw the development of the "classic" form of pre-emption theory', whereby Community competence 'meant distinct, discrete compartments for EC and Member States' competences and did not include the concept of complementary action by both EC and Member States in the same field'; today, a different picture has emerged—one based on 'shared and even complementary competences'.[203]

This move from dual to cooperative federalism is not confined to the context of the *ERTA* doctrine. Ever since the Single European Act,[204] Europe's express foreign affairs powers ushered in an 'era of shared competences'.[205]

---

[202] This should not be taken to be an argument in favour of perfect symmetry between the federal structure of the internal and the external sphere. After all, there *are* constitutional and international considerations *peculiar in the external sphere*. Thus, the pre-emptive effect of internal legislation may be wider in the external than in the internal sphere (cf Opinion 1/2003); while the pre-emptive effect of international agreements may be narrower than an identically worded piece of internal legislation (cf R Schütze, *The Morphology of Legislative Power in the European Community: Legal Instruments and the Federal Division of Powers*, 141–4).

[203] M Cremona, *External Relations and External Competence: The Emergence of an Integrated Policy*, 153 and 158.

[204] See in particular: Article 111(3) (agreements concerning monetary and foreign exchange regime matters), Article 170 (cooperation in Community research with third countries or international organizations), Article 174(4) (cooperation with third countries and international organizations in environmental matters), Article 181 (development cooperation agreements), Article 181a(3) (economic, financial and technical cooperation with third countries). The Treaty now also contains a variety of legal bases that encourage the Community 'to foster co-operation with third countries and the competent international organisations', for example in: Articles 149(3), 150(3) (education, vocational training, and youth), Article 151(3) (culture), Article 152(3) (public health), and Article 155 (3) (trans-European networks) of the Treaty.

[205] D de la Rochère, *L'ère des compétences partagées de l'étendue des compétences extérieures de la Communauté européenne*.

The Community's external powers in these areas 'shall be without prejudice to Member States' competence to negotiate in international bodies and to conclude international agreements'.[206] These shared powers—most of them are complementary competences—confirm the silent arrival of a cooperative federalism in the external sphere. Despite its dual federal form, European foreign affairs therefore already show a significant cooperative federal substance. They have, thus, lost some of their 'exceptional' constitutional status.

---

[206] Article 174 (4); Article 181, Article 181a (3). See also Article 111 (5): 'Without prejudice to Community competence and Community agreements as regards economic and monetary union, Member States may negotiate in international bodies and conclude international agreements'.

CONCLUSION

Europe's Gemeinweg *towards Cooperative Federalism*

'Problems can never be solved by the way of thinking that first created them.'[1] The nature of the European Union has been a legal problem for the last half-a-century. It will never be solved by the way of thinking that reduces the world into sovereign States. European constitutionalism still insists on the indivisibility of (State) sovereignty. This belief reduces out-of-State law to a voluntary sphere of international coordination and provides the intellectual background for the classic tradition of federalism. The *foedus* was conceived as an international treaty that—unlike mere pacts—bound States into a permanent Union. In the last 300 years, this international format of the federal idea was inverted. Had the federal idea originally stood for a *treaty* relation *between* sovereign States in *international* law, it came to represent a *constitutional* relation *within* a sovereign State in *national* law. How had this happened? European thought had learnt about the 'new' American idea of federalism, but its obsession with indivisible sovereignty operated as a lens that polarized all State Unions into two idealized federal species: confederation and federation. The concept of confederation became the semantic carrier of the classic tradition of the federal idea. It designated an international organization in which the Member States have remained sovereign. The concept of federation, on the other hand, became exclusively identified with a Federal State. As a State, the Federal State is solely sovereign and (potentially) omnicompetent. While 'Confederation' and 'Federal State' were 'regular', 'typical', and 'normal', mixed forms were—by definition—'irregular', 'sui generis', and 'anomalous'. European federal thought was a black-or-white theory; it could not explain the federal blue.

---

[1] A Einstein: 'Probleme kann man niemals mit derselben Denkweise lösen, durch die sie entstanden sind' (translation – RS).

This book has tried to bring—forgotten or foreign—ways of thinking about the federal idea to the analysis of the European Union in general and the structure of its law in particular. We saw in Chapter 1 that the American tradition identified the federal idea with a mixed structure between international and national organization. Federations, like light, have a dual nature: they are (inter)national phenomena. The European Union has a mixed or compound structure; and in combining 'international' and 'national' characteristics, it stands on federal 'middle ground'. But since there exist many possible federalisms, what federal philosophy informs the European Union's legal structure? In the history of the United States of America, two philosophies of federalism became prominent in the constitutional imagination: dual and cooperative federalism. Dual federalism is based on the idea of dual sovereignty: the federal government and the State governments are 'sovereign' co-equals and each is operating independently in a separate sphere. Cooperative federalism, on the other hand, stands for the idea that both governments work together: they are complementary parts in a shared legal sphere. Which of the two federal philosophies has informed the European Union? The 'thesis' of this book has been that the European Union—and in particular the structure of its law— has evolved from dual to cooperative federalism.

What were the signs or manifestations of the changing structure of European law? Part II of this book investigated three phenomena to show the transition towards a more cooperative legal reality within Europe. The first concerned the decline of the spheres of constitutional exclusivity on the part of the Member States and the European Union. The States' exclusive sphere of power has been constantly reduced in the past five decades as Europe's competences have expanded either through formal treaty amendment or by means of the Community's general powers. The ability of auto-interpreting Article 308 EC—Europe's 'Necessary and Proper Clause'—even gives the Community a bounded competence-competence. A decline of constitutional exclusivity could equally be traced in the context of the Union's own exclusive competences. Beyond the judicial pointillism of the 1970s, the Court has never broadened the sphere of the Community's exclusive powers. On the contrary, it has interpreted these competences restrictively and, to a great extent, emasculated the very concept of exclusivity through a generous delegation doctrine. The exception to this constitutional rule has been foreign affairs: here, the Community still follows a dual federal theory— despite the fact that constitutional practice increasingly reflects a cooperative federal structure.

The second line of argument extended our investigation to the decline of legislative exclusivity. Comparative constitutionalism teaches us that the existence of non-exclusive powers in a federal order can still be explained by means of a dual federal philosophy.[2] When federal law always field pre-empts State law, the idea of two mutually exclusive legal spheres is maintained. The federation and its States still never legislate in the same area and at the same time. A cooperative federal structure will only emerge where the two governments cooperate by establishing complementary legal rules within a policy area. Looking at the changing regimes within the Community's harmonization powers and its common agricultural policy, we did identify a tendency that signalled a move away from dual federalism. The new approach to harmonization allowed for complementary national laws as the Community standard was no longer seen as always excluding the Member States within its scope of application. The recent reforms of the CAP and the decline of the price mechanism, it was argued, will equally open up new legislative space for the Member States by means of a methodological innovation that parallels the shift from vertical to horizontal harmonization.

However, the most remarkable testimony to the spirit of cooperative federalism in the European legal order has been its elevation to a constitutional commitment. This was first expressed in the principle of subsidiarity. While the constitutional heart of dual federalism is the enumeration principle, the constitutional essence of cooperative federalism is the subsidiarity principle. According to this principle, social problems cannot be boxed into neat competence categories, but should be allocated according to the problem-solving capacity of the two levels of government. European problems need a European solution, while national problems require a national solution. However, the greatest commitment towards a 'new' European federalism is today symbolized in the many legislative competences that 'constitutionalize' the spirit of cooperative federalism. These 'complementary competences' either expressly permit the co-existence of stricter national laws or limit the Community's legislative action to 'supplement' or 'complement' the national legislator. The presence of complementary competences in a federal order represents, in and of itself, a *substantive* constitutional choice in favour of cooperative federalism.

In sum, the European Union has, overall, moved from a dual federal to a—predominantly—cooperative federal philosophy. The following pictogram

---

[2] For the story of American federalism, see: Chapter 2 – Section II; and for the German federal order, see: R Schütze, *German Constitutional Federalism: Between* Sein *and* Bewußtsein.

graphically expresses the corresponding evolution of the structure of European law:

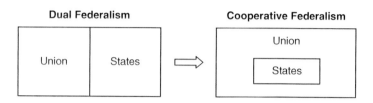

Should European constitutionalism embrace this 'new' federalism? What values and (dis)advantages stand behind cooperative federalism? The dualist reading of the federal principle refers to 'the method of dividing powers so that the general and regional governments are each, within a sphere, coordinate and independent'.[3] And in his classic study on 'Federal Government', Wheare advocated the virtues of dual federalism in the following way:

> The simplest way to organize a federal government, it might seem, is either to decide what matters are to be regulated by the general government and to place them under its actual exclusive control, leaving the rest to the actual exclusive control of the regional governments, or vice versa. There is then one list of subjects only and disputes can be confined to the meaning of the words in that list. If a concurrent list is added, there are not only disputes about the meaning of the words in the new list, but about the extent to which these words overlap or conflict with words in the exclusive list, and about the extent to which laws passed by the general and regional legislatures on concurrent subjects, conflict with each other and are void. Not merely lists but statutes also must be compared and in the result there may be piecemeal legislation and considerable uncertainty over a wide area.[4]

There is little doubt that the idea of two mutually exclusive spheres *theoretically* appears the simplest way to divide legislative powers between two governments. This constitutional structure also avoids the need for a hierarchical ranking between the two governments. In dual federal orders, the idea of federal supremacy leads a shadowy existence.[5] The idea of mutually exclusive legal spheres thus comforts the sensitivities of State rightists, who oppose the subordination of the States under a superior federal government.

---

[3] KC Wheare, *Federal Government*, 79.
[4] Ibid 82.
[5] On the 'shadowy' existence of the principle of supremacy in American dual federalism, see: Chapter 2 – *Introduction*; and for the German federal order, see: R Schütze (n 2 above).

The State governments are 'sovereign' 'equals' to the federal government.[6] In theory, the activities of the federal and the State governments never overlap or conflict. This theoretical reading of the federal principle has the advantage of simplicity and intellectual elegance. But would a constitutional order that is committed to the idea of mutually exclusive spheres necessarily enjoy a more transparent constitutional *practice* than one that accepted cooperative federalism? And more importantly: can we divide an ever more interconnected social reality into neat competence categories that mutually exclude each other? In short, are the promises of dual federalism redeemable?[7]

Let us turn to the first question. Is there more constitutional clarity and less constitutional conflict in a world of exclusive powers? American federalism thought so and German federalism still does.[8] Instead of allowing parallel legislation, dual federal orders prefer the 'conflict-avoiding' technique of—static or shifting—mutually exclusive legal spheres. Once the federation has expressed its will, the Member States lose their competence to enter the field. The advantage of exclusive competences—be they original or subsequent—lies in allocating responsibility exclusively to one level. The question of 'who is responsible for what' will be answered simply by looking at policy fields. There is no need to ask tricky questions about legislative pre-emption according to a functional criterion. However, where should the line be drawn between, say, exclusive trade in services and non-exclusive trade in services? What are the 'essential rules of competition law'? Interpretative problems abound and no constitutional compensation is in sight! The boxing of a complex legislative project into clearly delimited competence categories is indeed a formidable task. Where a complex social problem cuts across a number of policy areas—some belonging to the exclusive federal sphere, others to the States—the decision which government is ultimately responsible to pass the legislative package may involve a complex balancing mechanism. Behind the—seemingly—easy task of policing the constitutional boundary between the two spheres, hide devilishly unpredictable federal questions.[9] The promise of greater constitutional clarity is, then, not an automatic guarantee of dual federalism.

[6] For Elazar, federalism as such is inherently anti-hierarchical: 'Federalism, however, is anti-hierarchical, based on covenant-based principles that see the proper political organization as a matrix with larger and smaller arenas but not higher and lower: a virtually important distinction since larger and smaller do not imply any ranking of degree of importance—for some purposes a larger arena is the most important and for others a smaller arena is' (DJ Elazar, *The United States and the European Union: Models for their Epochs*, 42).

[7] For an affirmative answer favouring the renaissance of dual federalism in the European Union, see: F Scharpf, *Kann es in Europa eine stabile föderale Balance geben?*, 422–6.

[8] R Schütze (n 2 above).

[9] Ibid.

But more importantly: what about the social foundations for a dual federalist constitutionalism? *Can* a federal order that has accepted a degree of interaction between its States clinically cut out tasks that exclusively belong to them? A negative response to this question can be found in what represents the still most influential account of the federal principle in the Federal Republic of Germany. 'The Unitary Federal State' highlighted the homogenizing social tendencies in 'open' federal societies:

The *distribution of public tasks* in a federation presupposes that the tasks that are allocated to the States are, according to their nature, so geographically limited that they can be achieved within the State territory. The scope of these tasks was still relatively great in the Imperial Federation, but has since declined. The history of the Empire already shows a constant growth of federal tasks, and the Weimar Republic would continue this trend forcefully. Today, the scope of the tasks that can, according to their nature, be best fulfilled within each State territory has dwindled. Within the welfare State based on the rule of law, the increasing significance of technology, commerce and transport, the growth of economic and social interpenetrations and interdependencies as well as the increased need to plan, steer and distribute that these developments generate lead to a demand of unity and equality . . . Even traditional State tasks, such as the promotion of scientific research, can today only partially be accomplished within the separate States. The welfare State will, thereby, not necessarily be the 'pacemaker for a unitary Sate'; yet, it demands a broad factual unitarisation.[10]

The point made is quite simple: the increasing social interdependencies within a federation constantly reduce the tasks that *exclusively* concern and can be *exclusively* achieved by the States. Homogenizing forces will be natural in a society that inhabits the same economic space. The European Union has an internal market that permits free movement and that has itself moved towards ever closer economic and political union. If, due to territorial externalities, ever fewer governmental tasks can be exclusively achieved at the national level, what ought to be the constitutional response? Should we allow State A that is affected by the political choices of State B to influence—at least to a certain degree—the latter's political decisions? And if so, can we *nonetheless* guarantee a degree of legislative freedom to *both* States? These are constitutional demands dual federalism cannot fulfill, since it bars a 'functional' allocation of legislative power according to the size of the social problem involved. Dual federalism thus reduces governmental capacities: '[T]he theory that the state is deprived by the Constitution of power to pass legislation, which in the field

---

[10] K Hesse, *Der unitarische Bundesstaat*, 13 (translation – RS).

of its operation deals with interstate commerce in matters of national concern, would render it impossible for the country to utilize state authority as an additional agency of control, even though such course might be in the public interest and in accord with the public will. It seems that it is of advantage to the public to have choice of methods in dealing with specific problems'.[11]

'But if there is to be federalism, one condition must be fulfilled. There must be some matter, even if only one matter, which comes under the exclusive control, actual or potential, of the general government and something likewise under the regional governments. If there were not, that would be the end of federalism.'[12] Cooperative *federalism*—if we follow this line of thought— also requires that the Member States retain matters in which they enjoy total legislative independence. Can we find places where the federal government is *constitutionally* prevented from entering? Under dual federalism, this was the task of the enumeration principle. But how will cooperative federalism *constitutionally* guarantee matters that exclusively belong to the States? Ironically, it is not American but the younger European federalism that provides an answer to this question. Europe has constitutionalized the philosophy of cooperative federalism through the subsidiarity principle and the idea of complementary competences. How do these constitutional mechanisms protect an exclusive power reserved to the States of the European Union? Unlike its dual federalist cousin, cooperative federalism will not protect exclusivity according to policy areas. It will safeguard exclusivity by reserving *functional* tasks *within* policy areas to the States.

This leads us to the heart of our normative evaluation: if the federal principle searches for unity in diversity, is the philosophy of cooperative federalism the 'better' federal arrangement? The idea of allocating governmental tasks according to the problem at hand provides a more flexible and efficient problem solving technique. This is why cooperative federalism should be championed as an end in itself. The mechanism of common federal standards supplemented by territorially differentiated State solutions better expresses the idea of unity in diversity.[13] Cooperative federalism offers—admittedly—a less

---

[11]   HW Biklé, *The Silence of Congress*, 222. Listen also again to the American Supreme Court: 'The United States and the state of Alabama are not alien governments. They co-exist within the same territory. Unemployment is their common concern. Together the two statutes now before us embody a cooperative legislative effort by state and national governments, for carrying out a public purpose common to both, which neither could fully achieve without the cooperation of the other'. Cf *Carmichael v Southern Coal & Coke Co* 301 US 495 (1937), 526.

[12]   KC Wheare, *Federal Government*, 79.

[13]   In this sense also: K Hesse, *Aspekte des kooperativen Föderalismus in der Bundesrepublik*, fn 32.

symbolic and simple way of structuring governmental tasks in compound societies. And in the history of constitutional federalism, the absence of clear competence spheres has—more often than not—worked in favour of a centralizing federation. However, this is not an inherent characteristic of cooperative federalism. The distinction between dual and cooperative federalism is a *structural* one. It is concerned with a constitutional *method* of dividing powers; and, as such, contains no commitment in favour of—respectively— decentralization or centralization.[14]

With this in mind, we may conclude the book. The philosophy of dual federalism has lost touch with a legislative reality within Europe that is increasingly characterized by mutual penetration and interlocking laws. The European Union and its Member States cooperate in an ever wider range of public tasks. The structure of European law has changed from a dual to a cooperative texture. Much European law sets a uniform normative frame that allows for national diversities. Sadly, Europe's constitutionalism has still not become fully conscious of its 'new' federalism.[15] Yet, dual federalism— '[t]his entire system of constitutional interpretation'—lies 'in ruins'.[16] Dual federalism is unable to theoretically explain the *co*-existence of a European standard and a 'higher' State standard within the same policy area, for dual federalism is based on a two-dimensional conception of legislative space. It cannot ask how *deeply* or *intensely* the federal level has legislated. This reductionist vision has created a range of constitutional questions. They will not be solved as long as European constitutionalism limps behind the constitutional reality of European law. European constitutionalism must abandon the very language of dual federalism. Only this linguistic liberation will avoid the raising of—false—constitutional and philosophical problems.

---

[14] On this point, see: *Introduction: Coming to Constitutional Terms.*

[15] The competence provisions of the Lisbon Treaty were—partly—conceived in dual federalist language, see: R Schütze, *Lisbon and the Federal Order of Competences: A Prospective Analysis.*

[16] With reference to the American federal system, ES Corwin, *The Passing of Dual Federalism*, 17.

BIBLIOGRAPHY

Ackermann, B, *We The People: Foundations* (Harvard University Press, 1993)

Adam, R, *Tipologia degli atti comunitari in materia agricola* (1992) 32 Rivista di Diritto Europeo 285

Adam, V & Winter, G, *The framework law in German federalism* in G Winter, *Sources and Categories of EC Law: A Comparative and Reform Perspective* (Nomos, 1996), 273

—— & Bianchi, D, *La PAC à l'heure du découplage: une 'dernière' réforme du soutien à l'agriculture européenne* (2004) 475 Revue du Marché commun et de l'Union européenne 89

—— *Les droits à paiement, une création juridique innovante de la réforme de la politique agricole commune* (2004) 475 Revue du Marché commun et de l'Union européenne 96

Adler, MD & Kreimer, SF, *The New Etiquette of Federalism: New York, Printz, and Yeskey* (1998) Supreme Court Review 71

Alston, P & Weiler, JHH, *An 'Ever Closer Union' in Need of a Human Rights Policy: The European Union and Human Rights* in P Alston, M Bustelo, and J Heenan (eds), *The EU and Human Rights* (Oxford University Press, 1999), 3

Alter, K & Meunier-Aitsahalia, S, *Judicial Politics in the European Community* (1994–95) 26 Comparative Political Studies 535

Amar, VD, *Indirect Effects of Direct Elections: A Structural Explanation of the Seventeenth Amendment* (1996) 47 Vanderbilt Law Review 1347

Armstrong, KA & Bulmer, S, *The Governance of the Single European Market* (Manchester University Press, 1997)

Austin, JL, *How to do Things with Words* (Harvard University Press, 1975)

Baker, LA, *Putting the Safeguards back into the Political Safeguards of Federalism* (2001) 46 Villanova Law Review 951

Baquero-Cruz, J, *The Legacy of the Maastricht-Urteil and the Pluralist Movement* (2008) 14 European Law Journal 389

Barav, A, *Les effets du droit communautaire directement applicable* (1978) 14 Cahiers de Droit Européen 265

Barents, R, *The Agricultural Law of the EC* (Kluwer, 1994)

Barrett, G, '*The King is dead, long live the king': the Recasting by the Treaty of Lisbon of the Provisions of the Constitutional Treaty concerning National Parliaments* (2008) 33 European Law Review 66

Baumann, P, *Common Organizations of the Market and National Law* (1977) 14 Common Market Law Review 303

Beaud, O, *La notion de pacte fédératif: Contribution à une théorie constitutionnelle de la Fédération* in J-F Kervégan & H Mohnhaupt (eds), *Liberté sociale et lien contractual dans l'histoire du droit et de la philosophie* (Klostermann, 1999), 197

—— *The Question of Nationality within a Federation: a Neglected Issue in Nationality Law* in R Hansen & P Weil (eds), *Dual Nationality, Social Rights, and Federal Citizenship in the U.S. and Europe* (Berghahn Books, 2002), 314

—— *Théorie de la Fédération* (Presses Universitaires de France, 2007)

—— *Europa als Föderation? Relevanz und Bedeutung einer Bundeslehre für die Europäische Union*, Forum Constitutionis Europae 5/2008

Bebr, G, *The European Coal and Steel Community: A Political and Legal Innovation* (1953–4) 63 Yale Law Journal 1

—— *The European Defence Community and the Western European Union: An Agonizing Dilemma* (1954–5) 7 Stanford Law Review 169

—— *The Relation of the European Coal and Steel Community Law to the Law of the Member States: A Peculiar Legal Symbiosis* (1958) 58 Columbia Law Review 767

—— *How Supreme is Community Law in the National Courts?* (1974) 11 Common Market Law Review 3

Beck, R, *The New Jurisprudence of the Necessary and Proper Clause* (2002) University of Illinois Law Review 581

Berardis, G, *The Common Organization of Agricultural Markets and National Price Regulations* (1980) 17 Common Market Law Review 539

Berman, G, *Taking Subsidiarity Seriously: Federalism in the European Community and the United States* (1994) 94 Columbia Law Review 331

—— *Proportionality and Subsidiarity* in C Barnard & J Scott (eds), *The Law of the Single European Market: Unpacking the Premises* (Hart, 2002), 75

Bernard, N, *The Future of European Economic Law in the Light of the Principle of Subsidiarity* (1996) 33 Common Market Law Review 633

—— *Multilevel Governance in the European Union* (Kluwer, 2002)

Bernier, I, *International Legal Aspects of Federalism* (Longman, 1973)

Bianchi, D, *La Conditionnalité des paiements directs ou de la responsabilité de l'agriculteur bénéficiant des paiements directs dans le cadre de la politique agricole commune (PAC)* (2004) 475 Revue du Marché commun et de l'Union européenne 91

Bieber, R, *Zur Rolle der Mitgliedstaaten bei der Ausfüllung von Lücken im EG-Recht*, in R Bieber & G Ress, *Die Dynamik des EG-Rechts* (Nomos, 1987), 283

—— *On the Mutual Completion of Overlapping Legal Systems: The Case of the European Communities and the National Legal Orders* (1988) 13 European Law Review 147

—— *Les Limites Matérielles et Formelles à la Révision des Traités établissant la Communauté Européenne* (1993) 367 Revue du Marché Commun et de l'Union européenne 343

Biklé, HW, *The Silence of Congress* (1927–1928) 41 Harvard Law Review 200

Bleckmann, A & Ress, G, (eds), *Souveränitätsverständnis in den Europäischen Gemeinschaften* (Nomos, 1980)

—— *Europarecht: Das Recht der Europäischen Union und der Europäischen Gemeinschaften* (Heymanns, 1997)

Blumann, C, *La fonction législative communautaire* (L.G.D.J., 1995)

—— *Politique agricole commune* (Litec, 1996)

—— *Compétence communautaire et compétence nationale* in J-C Masclet (ed), *La communauté européenne et l'environnement* (La Documentation française, 1997), 63

Blumental, M, *Implementing the Common Agricultural Policy: Aspects of the Limitations on the Powers of the Member States* (1984) 35 Northern Ireland Legal Quarterly 28

Bodin, J, *Method for the Easy Comprehension of History* (ed: B Reynolds) (Octagon Books, 1966)

Bogdandy, A von, *The European Union as a Supranational Federation: A Conceptual Attempt in the Light of the Amsterdam Treaty* (2000) 6 Columbia Journal of European Law 27

—— & Bast, J, *The European Union's Vertical Order of Competences: The Current Law and Proposals for its Reform* (2002) 39 Common Market Law Review 227

—— Arndt, F & Bast, J, *Legal Instruments in European Union Law and their Reform* (2004) 23 Yearbook of European Law 91

—— & Bast, J, (eds), *Principles of European Constitutional Law* (Hart, 2006)

Böhm, R, *Kompetenzauslegung und Kompetenzlücken im Gemeinschaftsrecht* (Lang, 1985)

Boorstin, DJ, *The Americans: The National Experience* (Weidenfeld & Nicolson, 1966)

Borges, JL, *Collected Fictions* (Penguin, 1998)

Borries, R von, *Das Subsidiaritätsprinzip im Recht der Europäischen Union* (1994) 29 Europarecht 263

Börzel, T & Risse, T, *Who is afraid of a European Federation?*, Jean Monnet Working Paper No 7/00

—— *What Can Federalism Teach Us About the European Union? The German Experience* (2005) 15 Regional and Federal Studies 245

Bothe, M, *Die Kompetenzstruktur des modernen Bundesstaates in rechtsvergleichender Sicht* (Springer, 1977)

Bourgeois, JHJ, *Artikel 132, 133, 134* in H von der Groeben & J Schwarze, *Kommentar zum Vertrag über die Europäische Union und zur Gründung der Europäischen Gemeinschaft* (Nomos, 2003), 672

Bradley, CA , *The Treaty Power and American Federalism* (1998–99) 97 Michigan Law Review 390

—— *The Treaty Power and American Federalism – Part II* (2000–2001) 99 Michigan Law Review 98

Brölmann, C, *The Legal Nature of International Organisations and the Law of Treaties* (1999) 4 Austrian Review of International and European Law 85

—— *A Flat Earth? International Organizations in the System of International Law* (2001) 70 Nordic Journal of International Law 319

—— *The Institutional Veil in Public International Law* (Hart, 2007)

Brown, DW, *The Exclusive Power of Congress to Regulate Interstate and Foreign Commerce* (1904) 4 Columbia Law Review 490

—— *The Concurrent Power of the States to Regulate Inter-state and Foreign Commerce* (1905) 5 Columbia Law Review 298

Brown, RA, *Due Process of Law, Police Power and the Supreme Court* (1926–1927) 40 Harvard Law Review 943

Bülck, H, *Föderalismus als internationales Ordnungsprinzip* (1964) 21 Veröffentlichungen der Vereinigung der Deutschen Staatsrechtslehrer 1

Bülow, E, *Die Anwendung des Gemeinschaftsrechts im Verhältnis zu Drittländern* in A Clauder (ed), *Einführung in die Rechtsfragen der europäischen Integration* (Europea Union Verlag, 1972), 52

Bungenberg, M, *Artikel 235 nach Maastricht—Die Auswirkungen der Einheitlichen Europäischen Akte und des Vertrages über die Europäische Union auf die Handlungsbefugnis des Art. 235 EGV* (Nomos, 1999)

—— *Dynamische Integration, Art. 308 und die Forderung nach dem Kompetenzkatalog* (2000) 35 Europarecht 879

Búrca, G de, *The Principle of Proportionality and its Application in EC Law* (1993) 13 Yearbook of European Law 105

—— *Reappraising Subsidiarity's Significance after Amsterdam*, Harvard Jean Monnet Working Paper 1999/07

—— & Witte, B de, *The Delimitation of Powers between the EU and its Member States*, EUI RSCAS Policy Paper 2001/03

Burgess, KF, *The Twilight Zone between the Police Power and the Commerce Clause*, (1929–30) 15 Iowa Law Review 162

Burgess, M, *Federalism and European Union: The Building of Europe 1950–2000* (Routledge, 2000)

Burke, E, *Reflections on the Revolution in France* (London, 1793)

Calliess, C, *Der Schlüsselbegriff der 'ausschließlichen Zuständigkeit' im Subsidiaritätsprinzip des Art. 3 b II EGV* (1995) 6 Europäische Zeitschrift für Wirtschaftsrecht 693

—— *Subsidiaritäts- und Solidaritätsprinzip in der Europäischen Union* (Nomos, 1999)

—— & Ruffert, M, (eds), *Kommentar des Vertrages über die Europäische Union und des Vertrages zur Gründung der Europäischen Gemeinschaft: EUV/EGV* (Luchterhand, 2002)

Cappelletti, M, Seccombe, M & Weiler, J, *Integration Through Law: Europe and the American Federal Experience – A General Introduction* in M Cappelletti, M Seccombe & J Weiler (eds), *Integration through Law* (Volume 1) (de Gruyter, 1986), 3

Cardwell, M, *The European Model of Agriculture* (Oxford University Press, 2004)

Carré de Malberg, R, *Contribution à la Théorie Générale de l'État* (ed: E Maulin) (Dalloz, 2003)

Carstens, K, *Die kleine Revision des Vertrages über die Europäische Gemeinschaft für Kohle und Stahl* (1961) 21 Zeitschrift für ausländisches öffentliches Recht und Völkerrecht 1

Cass, DZ, *The Word that Saves Maastricht? The Principle of Subsidiarity and the Division of Powers within the European Community* (1992) 29 Common Market Law Review 1107

Chemerinsky, E, *Empowering States: the Need to Limit Federal Preemption* (2005–2006) 33 Pepperdine Law Review 69

Chiti, E, *The Emergence of a Community Administration* (2000) 37 Common Market Law Review 309

Choudhry, S, *Ackerman's Higher Lawmaking in Comparative Constitutional Perspective: Constitutional Moments as Constitutional Failures* (2008) 6 International Journal of Constitutional Law 193

Churchill, RR, *Revision of the EEC's Common Fisheries Policy – Part I* (1980) 5 European Law Review 3

—— & Foster, NG, *European Community Law and Prior Treaty Obligations of Member States: The Spanish Fishermen's Cases* (1987) 36 International and Comparative Law Quarterly 504

Close, G, *Harmonisation of Laws: Use or Abuse of the Powers under the EEC Treaty?* (1980) 6 European Law Review 461

Cohen, W, *Congressional Power to Define State Power to Regulate Commerce: Consent and Pre-emption* in T Sandalow & E Stein (eds), *Courts and Free Markets: Perspectives from the United States and Europe* (Volume 2) (Oxford University Press, 1982), 523

Constantinesco, L-J, *Das Recht der Europäischen Gemeinschaften: Das institutionelle Recht* (Nomos, 1977)

Constantinesco, V, *Compétences et pouvoirs dans les Communautés européennes: Contribution à l'étude de la nature juridique des Communautés* (Pichon & Durand-Auzias, 1974)

—— *Division of Fields of Competence between the Union and the Member States in the Draft Treaty establishing the European Union* in R Bieber, J-P Jacqué & JHH Weiler (eds), *An ever closer Union: A critical analysis of the Draft Treaty establishing the European Union* (EC Commission, 1985), 41

—— *Who's afraid of Subsidiarity?* (1991) 11 Yearbook of European Law 33

—— Jacqué, J-P, Kovar, R & Simon, D, *Traité instituant la CEE* (Economica, 1992)

Cooke, FH, *The Pseudo-Doctrine of the Exclusiveness of the Power of Congress to Regulate Commerce* (1910–1) 20 Yale Law Journal 297

Cooper, J, *The Watchdogs of Subsidiarity: National Parliaments and the Logic of Arguing in the EU* (2006) 44 Journal of Common Market Studies 281

Corwin, ES, *The Twilight of the Supreme Court: A History of Our Constitutional Theory* (Yale University Press, 1934)

—— *The Passing of Dual Federalism* (1950) 36 Virginia Law Review 1

Craig, P & Búrca, G de, *EU Law: Text, Cases and Materials* (Oxford University Press, 2008)

Cremona, M, *The Doctrine of Exclusivity and the Position of Mixed Agreements in the External Relations of the European Community* (1982) 2 Oxford Journal of Legal Studies 393

—— *External Relations and External Competence: The Emergence of an Integrated Policy* in P Craig and G de Búrca, *The Evolution of EU Law* (Oxford University Press, 1999), 137

—— *A Policy of Bits and Pieces? The Common Commercial Policy after Nice* (2002) 4 Cambridge Yearbook of European Legal Studies 61

Cross, ED, *Pre-emption of Member State Law in the European Economic Community: A Framework for Analysis* (1992) 29 Common Market Law Review 447

Cross, G, *Subsidiarity and the Environment* (1995) 15 Yearbook of European Law 107

Cudennec, A, *Compétence communautaire exclusive et mesures nationales d'application* (2003) 473 Revue du Marché Commun et de l'Union européenne 670

Currall, J, *Some Aspects of the Relation between Articles 30–36 and Article 100 of the EEC Treaty, with a Closer Look at Optional Harmonisation* (1984) 4 Yearbook of European Law 169

Cushman, RE, *The National Police Power under the Commerce Clause of the Constitution (I)* (1918–9) 3 Minnesota Law Review 298

—— *The National Police Power under the Commerce Clause of the Constitution (II)* (1918–9) 3 Minnesota Law Review 452

Daillier, P, *Le régime de la pêche maritime des ressortissants espagnols sous juridiction des états membres de la C.E.E. (1977–1980)* (1982) 256 Revue du Marché Commun 187

Dashwood, A, *Hastening Slowly: The Community's Path Towards Harmonization* in H Wallace, W Wallace and C Webb (eds), *Policy-Making in the European Community* (Wiley & Sons Ltd, 1983), 177

—— *Community Legislative Procedures in the Era of the Treaty on European Union* (1994) 19 European Law Review 343

—— *The Limits of European Community Powers* (1996) 21 European Law Review 113

—— *Why continue to have Mixed Agreements at all?*, in JHJ Bourgeois et al (eds), *La Communauté euopéenne et les accords mixtes* (Presses interuniversitaires européennes, 1997), 93

—— *States in the European Union* (1998) 23 European Law Review 201

—— *The Attribution of External Relations Competence* in A Dashwood and C Hillion (eds), *The General Law of E.C. External Relations* (Sweet & Maxwell, 2000), 115

—— & Heliskoski, J, *The Classic Authorities Revisited* in A Dashwood and C Hillion (eds), *The General Law of E.C. External Relations* (Sweet & Maxwell, 2000), 3

—— *The Relationship between the Member States and the European Union/Community* (2004) 41 Common Market Law Review 355

Davies, G, *Subsidiarity: the Wrong Idea, in the Wrong Place, at the Wrong Time* (2006) 43 Common Market Law Review 63

Davies, PGG, *European Union Environmental Law* (Ashgate, 2004)

Davis, JW, *The Growth of the Commerce Clause* (1907) 15 Amercian Laywer 213

Davis, MJ, *Unmasking the Presumption in Favor of Preemption* (2001–2) 53 Southern Carolina Law Review 967

Davis, SR, *The Federal Principle: A Journey through Time in Quest of a Meaning* (University of California Press, 1978)

Dehousse, R, *The Legacy of Maastricht: Emerging Institutional Issues* (1994) 3 Collected Courses of the Academy of European Law 181

Delcourt, C, *The Acquis Communautaire: Has the Concept had its Day?* (2001) 38 Common Market Law Review 829

Deliege-Sequaris, M, *Révision des Traités Européens En Dehors des Procédures Prévus* (1980) 16 Cahiers de Droit Européen 539

Delors, J, *Address at the College of Europe in Bruges* (1989) 10 Bulletin of the European Communities 110

—— *The Principle of Subsidiarity: Contribution to the Debate* in European Institute of Public Administration (ed), *Subsidiarity: the Challenge of Change* (EIPA, 1991), 7

Demaret, P, *La politique commerciale: perspectives d'évolution et faiblesses présente* in J Schwarze & H Schermers (eds), *Structure and Dimensions of European Community Policy* (Nomos, 1988), 69

Deuerlein, E, *Föderalismus: Die historischen und philosophischen Grundlagen des föderativen Prinzips* (List, 1972)

Dhondt, N, *Integration of Environmental Protection into other EC Policies* (Europa Law Publishing, 2003)

Diamond, M, *The Federalist's View of Federalism* in GCS Benson (ed), *Essays in Federalism* (Claremont College Press, 1962), 21

Dicey, AV, *Introduction to the Study of the Law of the Constitution* (Liberty Fund, 1982)

Di Fabio, U, *Some Remarks on the Allocation of Competences between the European Union and its Member States* (2002) 39 Common Market Law Review 1289

Dittert, D, *Die ausschließlichen Kompetenzen der Europäischen Gemeinschaft im System des EG-Vertrags* (Peter Lang, 2001)

Dodd, WF, *Implied Powers and Implied Limitations in Constitutional Law* (1919) 29 Yale Law Journal 137

Dolmans, MJ, *Problems of Mixed Agreements: Division of Powers within the EEC and the Rights of Third States* (Asser, 1985)

Dominick, MF, *Bulk Oil Case Note* (1986) 11 European Law Review 466

Donnersmarck, G von, *Planimmanente Krisensteuerung in der Europäischen Wirtschaftsgemeinschaft* (Metzner, 1971)

Donze, PL, *Legislating Comity: Can Congress enforce Federalism Constraints through Restrictions on Preemption Doctrine?* (2000–1) 4 New York University Journal of Legislation and Public Policy 239

Dorn, DW, *Art. 235 EWGV—Prinzipien der Auslegung—Die Generalermächtigung zur Rechtsetzung im Verfassungssystem der Gemeinschaften* (Engel, 1986)

Dougan, M, *Minimum Harmonization and the Internal Market* (2000) 37 Common Market Law Review 853

Dowling, NT, *Interstate Commerce and State Power – Revised Version* (1947) 47 Columbia Law Review 547

Dowrick, FE, *Overlapping European Laws* (1978) 27 International and Comparative Law Quarterly 629

Duhamel, O & Mény Y, (eds), *Dictionaire constitutionnel* (Presses Universitaires de France, 2000)

Economides, CP & Kolliopoulos, AG, *La clause de déconnexion en faveur du droit communautaire: une practique criticable* (2006) 110 Revue Générale de Droit International Public 273

Editorial, *Nation, federation: quelle Europe?* (1995) 87 Le Débat 25

Eeckhout, P, *The European Internal Market and International Trade: A legal Analysis* (Clarendon, 1994)

—— *External Relations of the European Union* (Oxford University Press, 2004)

Efron, R & Nanes, AS, *The Common Market and Euratom Treaties: Supranationality and the Integration of Europe* (1957) 6 International and Comparative Law Quarterly 670

Ehlermann, CD, *Editorial Comments: Harmonisation for Harmonisation's Sake?* (1977) 15 Common Market Law Review 4

—— *Mixed Agreements: A List of Problems* in D O'Keeffe and HG Schermers (eds), *Mixed Agreements* (Kluwer, 1983), 3

—— *L'acte unique et les compétences externes de la Communauté: un progrès?* in P Demaret (ed), *Relations extérieures de la Communauté européenne et marché intérieur: aspects juridiques et fonctionnels* (Collège d'Europe No. 45, 1986), 79

—— *The Internal Market following the Single European Act* (1987) 24 Common Market Law Review 361

—— *The Modernization of EC Antitrust Policy: A Legal and Cultural Revolution* (2000) 37 Common Market Law Review 537

Eichorn, LM, *Cuyler v Adams and the Characterization of Compact Law* (1991) 77 Virginia Law Review 1387

Eiden, C, *Die Rechtsangleichung gemäß Art.100 des EWG-Vertrages* (Duncker & Humblot, 1984)

Elazar, DJ, *Cooperative Federalism* in DA Kenyon & J Kincaid (eds), *Competition among States and Local Governments* (Urban Institute Press, 1991), 65

—— *Constitutionalizing Globalization: The Postmodern Revival of Confederal Arrangements* (Rowman & Littlefield, 1998)

—— *The United States and the European Union: Models for their Epochs* in K Nicolaidis & R Howse (eds), *The Federal Vision: Legitimacy and Levels of Governance in the United States and the European Union* (Oxford University Press, 2001), 31

Ellis, E (ed), *The Principle of Proportionality in the Laws of Europe* (Hart, 1999)

Emiliou, N, *Subsidiarity: An Effective Barrier Against 'the Enterprises of Ambition'?* (1992) 17 European Law Review 383

—— *The Death of Exclusive Competence?* (1996) 21 European Law Review 294

Endo, K, *Subsidiarity and its Enemies: To what Extent is Sovereignty contested in the Mixed Commonwealth of Europe*, EUI RCS Working Paper 2001/24

Engdahl, DE, *Construction of Interstate Compacts: A Questionable Federal Question* (1965) 51 Virginia Law Review 987

—— *Characterization of Interstate Arrangements: When a Compact is not a Compact?* (1965–6) 64 Michigan Law Review 63

—— *Constitutional Federalism in a Nutshell* (West Publishing, 1987)

—— *The Necessary and Proper Clause as an Intrinsic Restraint on Federal Lawmaking Power* (1998–99) 22 Harvard Journal of Law and Public Policy 107

Epiney, A, *Umweltrecht in der Europäischen Union* (Heymanns, 1997)

Epstein, RE, *The Proper Scope of the Commerce Power* (1987) 73 Virginia Law Review 1387

Estella, A, *The EU Principle of Subsidiarity and its Critique* (Oxford University Press, 2002)

Eule, JN, *Laying the Dormant Commerce Clause to Rest* (1982) 91 Yale Law Journal 425

Everling, U, *Legal Problems of the Common Commercial Policy in the European Economic Community* (1966–7) 4 Common Market Law Review 141

—— Schwartz, IE & Tomuschat, C, *Rechtsetzungsbefugnisse der EWG in Generalermächtigungen, insbesondere in Artikel 235 EWG-Vertrag* (1976) 11 Europarecht (Sonderheft 1)

—— *Sind die Mitgliedstaaten der Europäischen Gemeinschaft noch Herren der Verträge?*, in R Bernhardt (ed), *Völkerrecht als Rechtsordnung, international Gerichtsbarkeit, Menschenrechte* (Springer, 1993), 173

—— *The Maastricht Judgment of the German Federal Constitutional Court and its Significance for the Development of the European Union* (1994) 14 Yearbook of European Law 1

—— & Roth W-H, (eds), *Mindestharmonisierung im Europäischen Binnenmarkt: Referate des 7. Bonner Europa-Symposions vom 27. April 1996* (Nomos, 1997)

Farrand, M, *The Framing of the Constitution of the United States* (Yale University Press, 1913)

Favoreu, L, Gaïa, P, Chevontian, R, Mestre, J-L, Pfersmann, O, Roux, A & Scaffoni, G, *Droit constituionnel* (Dolloz, 2002)

Feenstra, JJ, *A Survey of the Mixed Agreements and their Participation Clauses* in D O'Keeffe and HG Schermers (eds), *Mixed Agreements* (Kluwer, 1983), 207

Ferraiuolo, P, *Le pouvoir normatif de la communauté européenne en vertu de l'article 235: possibilités et limites* (Université d'Aix-Marseille III, 1999)

Fleiner, F, *Bundesstaatliche und gliedstaatliche Rechtsordnung in ihrem gegenseitigen Verhältnis im Rechte Deutschlands, Österreichs und der Schweiz* (1929) 6 Veröffentlichungen der Vereinigung deutscher Staatsrechtslehrer 2

Forester, S, *Artikel 235 EGV und das Subsidiaritätsprinzip des Art 3b Abs.2 EGV* (Verwaltungsakademie des Bundes, 1996)

Forsyth, M, *Unions of States: The Theory and Practice of Confederations* (Leicester University Press, 1981)

—— *The Political Theory of Federalism: The Relevance of Classical Approaches* in JJ Hesse and V Wright, *Federalizing Europe?: The Costs, Benefits, and Preconditions of Federal Political Systems* (Oxford University Press, 1996), 25

Foucault, M, *The Order of Things: An Archaeology of the Human Sciences* (Vintage Books, 1994)

Frankfurter, F & Landis, J, *The Compact Clause of the Constitution – A Study in Interstate Adjustments* (1925) 34 Yale Law Journal 685

—— *Taney and the Commerce Clause* (1935–6) 49 Harvard Law Journal 1286

French Senate, *Rapport d'information au nom de la délégation du Sénat pour l'Union européenne sur une deuxieme chambre européenne*, No 381: http://www.senat.fr/rap/r00-381/r00-381.html

Frenz, W, *Europäisches Umweltrecht* (Beck, 1997)

Friedrich, CJ, *Trends of Federalism in Theory and Practice* (Pall Mall, 1969)

Friedmann, WG, *The Changing Structure of International Law* (Stevens, 1964)

Le Fur, L, *L'État fédéral et confédération d'États* (Panthéon-Assas, 2000)

Furrer, A, *The Principle of Pre-emption in European Union Law* in G Winter (ed), *Sources and Categories of European Union Law* (Nomos, 1996), 521

—— *Die Sperrwirkung des sekundären Gemeinschaftsrechts auf die nationalen Rechtsordnungen: Die Grenzen des nationalen Gestaltungsspielraums durch sekundärrechtliche Vorgaben unter besonderer Berücksichtigung des, 'nationalen Alleingangs'* (Nomos, 1994)

Gaja, G, Hay, P & Rotunda, RD, *Instruments for Legal Integration in the European Community – A Review* in M Cappelletti, M Seccombe, & J Weiler (eds), *Integration through Law: Europe and the American Federal Experience* (Volume 1) (de Gruyter, 1986), 113

Gardbaum, SA, *The Nature of Preemption* (1993–94) 79 Cornell Law Review 767

Gautier, Y, *La compétence communautaire exclusive*, in *Mélanges en hommage à G Isaac – 50 ans de droit communautaire* (Presses de l'Université des sciences sociales de Toulouse, 2004)

Gellner, E, *Nations and Nationalism* (Wiley Blackwell, 2006)

Geradin, D, *Trade and Environmental Protection: Community Harmonization and National Environmental Standards* (1993) 13 Yearbook of European Law 151

Gericke, HP, *Allgemeine Rechtsetzungsbefugnisse nach Artikel 235 EWG-Vertrag* (L Appel, 1970)

Giardina, A, *The Rule of Law and Implied Powers in the European Communities* (1975) 1 Italian Yearbook of International Law 99

Gierke, O von, *The Development of Political Theory* (Allen & Unwin, 1939)

Goldsmith, JA, *Federal Courts, Foreign Affairs, and Federalism* (1997) 83 Virginia Law Review 1617

—— *Statutory Affairs Preemption*, Chicago John M Olin Law & Economic Working Paper No 116

Golove, DM, *Treaty-Making and the Nation: The Historical Foundations of the Nationalist Conception of the Treaty Power* (1999–2000) 98 Michigan Law Review 1075

Gonzalez, JP, *The Principle of Subsidiarity: (a Guide for Lawyers with a particular community orientation)* (1995) 20 European Law Review 355

Grabitz, E, *Gemeinschaftsrecht bricht nationales Recht* (Appel, 1966)

—— *Der Verfassungsstaat in der Gemeinschaft* (1977) Deutsche Verwaltungsbätter 786

—— & Hilf, M, (eds), *Das Recht der Europäischen Union* (Beck, 1988)

Grimm, D, *Does Europe Need a Constitution?* (1995) 1 European Law Journal 282

—— *Die Verfassung im Prozess der Entstaatlichung* in M Brenner (ed), *Der Staat des Grundgesetzes – Kontinuität und Wandel: Festschrift für Peter Badura* (Mohr Siebeck, 2004), 145

—— *Treaty or Constitution: The Legal Basis of the European Union after Maastricht* in EO Eriksen, JE Fossum & AJ Menéndez (eds), *Developing a Constitution for Europe* (Routledge, 2004), 69

Grodzins, M, *The American System: A New View of Government in the United States* (Transaction Books, 1984)

Groeben, H von der, Thiesing, J & Ehlermann, CD, *Kommentar zum EU-/EG-Vertrag* (Nomos, 1997–99)

—— & Schwarze, J, (eds), *Kommentar zum Vertrag über die Europäische Union* (Nomos, 2003)

Groß, T, *Die Kooperation zwischen europäischen Agenturen und nationalen Behörden* (2005) 40 Europarecht 54

Groux, J & Manin, P, *The European Communities in the International Order* (European Commission, 1985)

Grziwotz, H, *Partielles Bundesrecht und die Verteilung der Gesetzgebungsbefugnis im Bundesstaat* (1991) 116 Archiv des öffentlichen Rechts 588

Gunther, G & Sullivan, M, *Constitutional Law* (Foundation Press, 1997)

Haas, E, *The Uniting of Europe: Political, Social and Economic Forces, 1950–1957* (Stanford University Press, 1968)

Häberle, P, *Das Prinzip der Subsidiarität aus der Sicht der vergleichenden Verfassungslehre* (1994) 119 Archiv des öffentlichen Rechts 169

Habermas, J, *Remarks on Dieter Grimm's 'Does Europe need a Constitution?'* (1995) 1 European Law Journal 303

Hablitzel, H, *Harmonisierungsverbot und Subsidiaritätsprinzip im europäischen Bildungsrecht* (2002) 55 Die öffentliche Verwaltung 407

Häde, U & Puttler, A, *Zur Abgrenzung des Art. 235 EGV von der Vertragsänderung* (1997) 8 Europäische Zeitschrift für Wirtschaftsrecht 13

Halberstam, D, *Comparative Federalism and the Issue of Commandeering* in K Nikolaidis & R Howse (eds), *The Federal Vision: Legitimacy and Levels of Governance in the United States and the European Union* (Oxford University Press, 2001), 213

—— *The Foreign Affairs of Federal Systems: A National Perspective on the Benefits of State Participation* (2001) 46 Villanova Law Review 1015

Hallstein, W, *Zu den Grundlagen und Verfassungsprinzipien der Europäischen Gemeinschaften* in W Hallstein & H-J Schlochauer (eds), *Zur Integration Europas – Festschrift für C.F. Ophüls* (C.F. Müller, 1965), 1

—— *Die Europäische Gemeinschaft* (Econ, 1973)

Hamilton, A, Madison, J & Jay, J, *The Federalist* (ed: T Ball) (Cambridge University Press, 2003)

Hänel, A, *Deutsches Staatsrecht* (Duncker & Humblot, 1892)

Hardy, M, *Opinion 1/76 of the Court of Justice: The Rhine Case and the Treaty-Making Powers of the Community* (1977) Common Market Law Review 561

Hartley, TC, *The Foundations of European Community Law* (Oxford University Press, 1988)

Hay, P, *The Contribution of the European Communities to International Law* (1965) 59 Proceedings of the American Society of International Law 195

Hay, P, *Federalism and Supranational Organisations* (University of Illinois Press, 1966)

Heliskoski, J, *Mixed Agreements as a Technique for Organizing the International Relations of the European Community and its Member States* (Kluwer, 2001)

Henkin, L, *Constitutionalism, Democracy, and Foreign Affairs* (Columbia University Press, 1990)

—— *Foreign Affairs and the Constitution* (Clarendon Press, 1997)

Herrmann, CW, *Common Commercial Policy after Nice: Sisyphus would have done a better Job* (2002) 39 Common Market Law Review 7

Hervey, TK & McHale, JV, *Health Law and the European Union* (Cambridge University Press, 2004)

Hesse, K, *Der unitarische Bundesstaat* (C.F. Müller, 1962)

—— *Aspekte des kooperativen Föderalismus in der Bundesrepublik* in T Titterspach & W Geiger (eds) *Festschrift für Gerhard Müller* (J.C.B. Mohr, 1970), 141

—— *Grundzüge des Verfassungsrechts der Bundesrepublik Deutschland* (C.F. Müller, 1999)

Hill, A, *The Law-Making Power of the Federal Courts: Constitutional Preemption* (1967) 67 Columbia Law Review 1024

Hobbes, T, *Leviathan* (ed: R Tuck) (Cambridge University Press, 1996)

Hobsbawn, FJ, *Nations and Nationalism since 1780: Programme, Myth, Reality* (Cambridge University Press, 1992)

Hoke, SC, *Preemption Pathologies and Civic Republican Values* (1991) 71 Boston University Law Review 685

—— *Transcending Conventional Supremacy: A Reconstruction of the Supremacy Clause* (1991–92) 24 Connecticut Law Review 829

House of Commons, European Scrutiny Committee (Thirty-third Report: 2001–02): *Subsidiarity, National Parliaments and the Lisbon Treaty*, http://www.parliament.the-stationery-office.com/pa/cm200708/cmselect/cmeuleg/563/563.pdf

House of Lords, Select Committee on European Union (Seventh Report: 2001–02): http://www.publications.parliament.uk/pa/ld200102/ldselect/ldeucom/48/4801.htm

Ipsen, HP, *The Relationship between the Law of the European Communities and National Law* (1965) 3 Common Market Law Review 379

—— *Europäisches Gemeinschaftsrecht* (J.C.B. Mohr, 1972)

—— *Europäisches Gemeinschaftsrecht in Einzelstudien* (Nomos, 1984)

—— *Europäische Verfassung – Nationale Verfassung* (1987) 22 Europarecht 195

—— *Zehn Glossen zum Maastricht Urteil* (1994) 29 Europarecht 1

Isaacson, W, *Einstein: His Life and Universe* (Pocket Books, 2008)

Isensee, J, *Subsidiaritätsprinzip und Verfassungsrecht* (Duncker & Humblot, 2001)

—— *Idee und Gestalt des Föderalismus im Grundgesetz* in J Isensee & P Kirchhof (eds), *Handbuch des Staatsrechts der Bundesrepublik Deutschland,* Band IV (C.F. Müller, 2003), 517

Jackson, JH, *World Trade and the Law of GATT* (Bobbs-Merrill, 1969)

Jacot-Guillarmod, O, *Droit communautaire et droit international public* (Librairie de l'université Georg & Cie S.A., 1979)

Jacqué, JP, *La Souveraineté française et l'élection du Parlement Européen au suffrage universel direct* in A Bleckmann & G Ress (eds), *Souveränitätsverständnis in den Europäischen Gemeinschaften* (Nomos, 1980), 71

—— & Weiler, JHH, *On the Road to European Union – A New Judicial Architecture: An Agenda for the Intergovernmental Conference* (1990) 27 Common Market Law Review 185

—— *Droit institutionnel de l'union européenne* (Dalloz, 2003)

Jaenicke, G, *Die Europäische Gemeinschaft für Kohle und Stahl (Montan-Union): Struktur und Funktionen ihrer Organe* (1951/2) 14 Zeitschrift für ausländisches öffentliches Recht und Völkerrecht 727

—— *Der übernationale Charakter der Europäischen Wirtschaftsgemeinschaft* (1958) 19 Zeitschrift für ausländisches öffentliches Recht und Völkerrecht 153

Jans, JH, *European Environmental Law* (Europa Law Publishing, 2000)

Jarass, HD, *Regelungsspielräume des Landesgesetzgebers im Bereich der konkurrierenden Gesetzgebung und in anderen Bereichen* (1996) 15 Neue Zeitschrift für Verwaltungsrecht 1041

—— *Die Kompetenzverteilung zwischen der Europäischen Gemeinschaft und den Mitgliedstaaten* (1996) 121 Archiv des öffentlichen Rechts 173

Jellinek, G, *Allgemeine Staatslehre* (Springer, 1922)

—— *Die Lehre von den Staatenverbindungen* (ed: W Pauly) (Keip, 1996)

Jenks, W, *The Conflict of Law-making Treaties* (1953) 30 British Yearbook of International Law 401

Jestaedt, M, *Bundesstaat als Verfassungsprinzip* in J Isensee & P Kirchhof (eds), *Handbuch des Staatsrechts der Bundesrepublik Deutschland* (C.F. Müller Verlag, 2003), 785

Johnson, SP & Corcelle, G, *The Environmental Policy of the European Communities* (Kluwer, 1995)

Jordan, KA, *The Shifting Preemption Paradigm: Conceptual and Interpretive Issues* (1998) 51 Vanderbilt Law Review 1149

Kadelbach, S, *European Administrative Law and the Law of a Europeanized Administration* in C Joerges & R Dehousse (eds), *Good Governance in Europe's Integrated Market* (Oxford University Press, 2002), 167

Kahl, W, *Umweltprinzip und Gemeinschaftsrecht* (C.F. Müller, 1993)

Kaiser, J, *Grenzen der EG-Zuständigkeit* (1980) 15 Europarecht 97

Kant, J, *Political Writings* (ed: HS Reiss) (Cambridge University Press, 1991)

Kapteyn, PJG & VerLoren van Themaat, P, *Introduction to the Law of the European Communities* (Kluwer, 1998)

Katz, E, *The Development of American Federalism, 1763–1865* in A Bosco (ed), *The Federal Idea* (Volume I) (Lothian Foundation Press, 1992), 39

Keating, M, *Plurinational Democracy: Stateless Nations in a Post-Sovereignty Era* (Oxford University Press, 2001)

Kelsen, H, *Das Problem der Souveränität und die Theorie des Völkerrechts* (Mohr, 1920)

—— *Allgemeine Staatslehre* (Springer, 1925)

—— *General Theory of Law and State* (Russell & Russell, 1945)

Kens, P, *The Source of a Myth: Police Powers of the States and Laissez-Faire Constitutionalism: 1900–1937* (1991) 35 American Journal of Legal History 70

Kewenig, W, *Kooperativer Föderalismus und bundesstaatliche Ordnung* (1968) 93 Archiv des öffentlichen Rechts 433

Kimminich, O, *Der Bundesstaat* in J Isensee & P Kirchhof (eds), *Handbuch des Staatsrechts der Bundesrepublik Deutschland* (Band I) (C.F. Müller, 1987), 1113

Kirchmann, JH von, *Die Wertlosigkeit der Jurisprudenz als Wissenschaft* (Springer, 1848)

Kisker, G, *Kooperation im Bundesstaat: Eine Untersuchung zum kooperativen Föderalismus in der Bundesrepublik Deutschland* (J.C.B. Mohr, 1971)

Klabbers, J, *An Introduction to International Institutional Law* (Cambridge University Press, 2002)

Köck, HF, *Der Gesamtakt in der deutschen Integrationslehre* (Duncker & Humblot, 1978)

Koers, AW, *The External Authority of the EEC in Regard to Marine Fisheries* (1977) 14 Common Market Law Review 269

Kölz, A, *Neue Schweizerische Verfassungsgeschichte* (Volume 1 & 2) (Stämpfli, 1992 and 2004)

Komonchak, JA, *Subsidiarity in the Church: The State of the Question* (1988) 48 The Jurist 298

Koskenniemi, M, *From Apology to Utopia* (Cambridge University Press, 2005)

Kosseleck, R, *Bündnis, Föderalismus, Bundesstaat* in O Brunner, W Conze & R Kosseleck (eds), *Geschichtliche Grundbegriffe: Historisches Lexikon zur politisch-sozialen Sprache in Deutschland* (Klett, 1974–97), 582

Koutrakos, P, *Trade, Foreign Policy and Defence in EU Constitutional Law: The Legal Regulation of Sanctions, Exports of Dual-Use Goods and Armaments* (Hart, 2001)
—— *EU International Relations Law* (Hart, 2006)

Kovar, R, *The Relationship between Community Law and National Law* in EC Commission (ed), *Thirty Years of Community Law* (Office for Official Publications of the EC, 1981), 109

Krajewski, M, *External Trade Law and the Constitution Treaty: Towards a Federal and More Democratic Common Commercial Policy* (2005) 42 Common Market Law Review 91

Kramer, L, *Understanding Federalism* (1994) 47 Vanderbilt Law Review 1485

Krämer, L, *Differentiation in EU Environmental Policy* (2000) 9 European Environmental Law Review 133
—— *Casebook on EU Environmental Law* (Hart, 2002)
—— *EC Environmental Law* (Sweet & Maxwell, 2003)

Krislov, S, Ehlermann, C-D & Weiler, J, *The Political Organs and the Decision-Making Process in the United States and the European Community* in M Cappelletti, M Seccombe & J Weiler (eds), *Integration through Law: Europe and the American Federal Experience* (Volume 1) (de Gruyter, 1986), 3

Krück, H, *Die auswärtige Gewalt der Mitgliedstaaten und die auswärtigen Befugnisse der Europäischen Gemeinschaften als Problem des Souveränitätsverständnisses* in

A Bleckmann & G Ress (eds), *Souveränitätsverständnis in den Europäischen Gemeinschaften* (Nomos, 1980), 155

Kuhn, TS, *The Structure of Scientific Revolutions* (University of Chicago Press, 1997)

Kumm, M, *The Jurisprudence of Constitutional Conflict: Constitutional Supremacy in Europe before and after the Constitutional Treaty* (2005) 11 European Law Journal 262

Kurcz, B, *Harmonisation by means of Directives – never-ending Story?* (2001) 12 European Business Law Review 287

Laband, P, *Das Staatsrecht des Deutschen Reiches* (Scientia, 1964)

Lachmann, P, *Some Danish Reflections on the use of Article 235 of the Rome Treaty* (1981) 18 Common Market Law Review 447

Lauwaars, RH, *Artikel 235 als Grundlage für die flankierenden Politiken im Rahmen der Wirtschafts- und Währungsunion* (1976) 11 Europarecht (Sonderheft) 100

—— *The 'Model Directive' on Technical Harmonization*, in R Bieber, R Dehousse, J Pinder & J Weiler (eds), *1992: One European Market* (Nomos, 1988), 151

Lawson, G & Granger, PB, *The 'Proper' Scope of Federal Power: A Jurisdictional Interpretation of the Sweeping Clause* (1993–4) 43 Duke Law Journal 267

Leleux, P, *Le rapprochement des législations dans la communauté economique européenne* (1968) 4 Cahiers De Droit Européen 129

Lenaerts, K, *Les répercussion des compétences de la communauté européenne sur les compétences externes des états membres et la question de 'preemption'* in P Demaret (ed), *Relations extérieures de la communauté européenne et marché intérieur: aspects juridiques et fonctionnels* (Collège d'Europe No 45, 1986), 39

—— *Le juge et la constitution aux États-Unis d'Amérique et dans l'ordre juridique européen* (Bruyant, 1988)

—— *Constitutionalism and the Many Faces of Federalism* (1990) 38 American Journal of Comparative Law 205

—— *Regulating the Regulatory Process: 'Delegation of Powers' in the European Community* (1993) 18 European Law Review 23

—— *Education in European Community Law after 'Maastricht'* (1994) 31 Common Market Law Review 7

—— & van Ypersele, P, *Le principe de subsidiarité et son contexte: étude de l'article 3b du traité CE* (1994) 30 Cahier de Droit Européen 3

—— *The Principle of Subsidiarity and the Environment in the European Union: Keeping the Balance of Federalism* (1994) 17 Fordham International Law Journal 846

—— *Subsidiarity and Community Competence in the Field of Education* (1994–5) 1 Columbia Journal of European Law 1

—— *Federalism: Essential Concepts in Evolution – The Case of the European Union* (1998) 21 Fordham International Law Journal 746

—— & Geradin, D, *Decentralisation of EC Competition Law Enforcement: Judges in the Frontline* (2004) 27 World Competition 313

—— & van Nuffel, P, *Constitutional Law of the European Union* (Sweet & Maxwell, 2005)

Lerche, P, *Föderalismus als nationales Ordnungsprinzip* (1964) 21 Veröffentlichungen der Vereinigung der Deutschen Staatsrechtslehrer 66

Levitan, DM, *The Foreign Relations Power: An Analysis of Mr. Justice Sutherland's Theory* (1945–6) 55 Yale Law Journal 467

Limpens-Meinertzhagen, A, *La coordination ou l'unification du droit par voie de convention entre les états membres* in D de Ripainsel-Landy et al (eds), *Les instruments du rapprochement des législations dans la communauté économique européenne* (Université Libre de Bruxelles, 1976), 153

Lindberg, LN, *The Political Dynamics of European Economic Integration* (Oxford University Press, 1963)

Livingston, WS, *A Note on the Nature of Federalism* (1952) 67 Political Science Quarterly 81

—— *Federalism and Constitutional Change* (Clarendon Press, 1956)

Locke, J, *Two Treatises of Government* (ed: P Laslett) (Cambridge University Press, 1988)

Louis, J-V, *Quelques réflexions sur la répartition des compétences entre la communauté européenne et ses états membres* (1979) 2 Revue d'intégration européenne 355

—— *The Community Legal Order* (EC Commission, 1980)

Lukas, J, *Bundesstaatliche und gliedstaatliche Rechtsordnung in ihrem gegenseitigen Verhältnis im Rechte Deutschlands, Österreichs und der Schweiz* (1929) 6 Veröffentlichungen der Vereinigung deutscher Staatsrechtslehrer 25

Lüke, G, Ress, G & Will, MR, *Rechtsvergleichung, Europarecht und Staatenintegration: Gedächtnisschrift für Léontin-Jean Constantinesco* (Heymanns, 1983)

Lutter, M, *Die Auslegung angeglichenen Rechts* (1992) 47 Juristenzeitung 593

Maas, HH, *The External Powers of the EEC with Regard to Commercial Policy: Comment on Opinion 1/75* (1976) 13 Common Market Law Review 379

Maccrory, R, *The Amsterdam Treaty: An Environmental Perspective* in D O'Keeffe & P Twomey (eds), *Legal Issues of the Amsterdam Treaty* (Hart, 1999), 171

Mackenzie-Stuart, Lord, *Subsidiarity – A Busted Flush* in D Curtin & D O'Keeffe (eds), *Constitutional Adjudication in European Community and National Law* (Butterworth, 1992), 19

Macleod, J, Hendry, ID & Hyett, S, *The External Relations of the European Communities* (Clarendon Press, 1996)

Manin, P, *The European Communities and the Vienna Convention on the Law of Treaties between States and International Organizations or between International Organizations* (1987) 24 Common Market Law Review 457

Marenco, G, *Les condition d'application de l'article 235 du traité CEE* (1970) 13 Revue du Marché Commun 147

März, W, *Bundesrecht bricht Landesrecht: Eine staatsrechtliche Untersuchung zu Artikel 31 des Grundgesetztes* (Duncker & Humblot, 1989)

Marx, F, *Funktion und Grenzen der Rechtsangleichung nach Art.100 EWG-Vertrag* (Heymann, 1976)

Mason, HL, *The European Coal and Steel Community: Experiment in Supranationalism* (Martinus Nijhoff, 1955)

Mayer, FC, *Die drei Dimensionen der Europäischen Kompetenzdebatte* (2001) 61 Zeitschrift für ausländisches öffentliches Recht und Völkerrecht 577

—— *The Debate on European Powers and Competences: Seeing Trees but not the Forest?*, Walter Hallstein Institut – Working Paper 18/03

McDonald, F, *States' Rights and the Union: Imperium in Imperio, 1776–1876* (University Press of Kansas, 2000)

McGee, A & Weatherill, S, *The Evolution of the Single Market – Harmonisation or Liberalisation* (1990) 53 Modern Law Review 578

McGoldrick, D, *International Relations Law of the European Union* (Longman, 1997)

McMahon, JA, *Law of the Common Agricultural Policy* (Longman, 2000)

—— *EU Agricultural Law* (Oxford University Press, 2007)

Meessen, KM, *The Application of Rules of Public International Law within Community Law* (1976) 13 Common Market Law Review 485

Meier, F, *Die Mitwirkung der Bundesregierung bei der Gesetzgebung der Europäischen Gemeinschaften* (1971) 24 Neue Juristische Wochenschrift 961

Melchior, M, *The Common Agricultural Policy* in Commission of the EC (ed), *Thirty Years of Community Law* (Office for Official Publications of the EC, 1981), 437

Meibom, H von, *Lückenfüllung bei den Europäischen Gemeinschaftsverträgen* (1968) 21 Neue Juristische Wochenschrift 2165

Menzel, J, *Landesverfassungsrecht: Verfassungshoheit und Homogenität im grundgesetzlichen Bundesstaat* (Boorberg, 2002)

Michel, V, *Recherches sur les compétences de la communauté européenne* (L'Harmattan, 2003)

Millon-Delsol, C, *L'état subsidiare* (Presses Universitaires de France, 1992)

Minor, J, *The Lugano Convention: Some Problems of Interpretation* (1990) 27 Common Market Law Review 507

Mitrany, D, *A Working Peace System: An Argument for the Functional Development of International Organization* (National Peace Council, 1946)

Moersch, W, *Leistungsfähigkeit und Grenzen des Subsidiaritätsprinzips: eine rechtsdogmatische und rechtspolitische Studie* (Duncker & Humblot, 2001)

Möllers, C, *Durchführung des Gemeinschaftsrechts* (2002) 37 Europarecht 483

Montesquieu, C de, *Oeuvres Complètes* (Gallimard, 1949)

—— *The Spirit of the Laws* (ed: AM Cohler et al) (Cambridge University Press, 1989)

Moravcik, A, *The Choice for Europe: Social Purpose and State Power from Messina to Maastricht* (Cornell University Press, 1998)

Morgenstern, F, *Judicial Practice and the Supremacy of International Law* (1950) 27 British Yearbook of International Law 42

Mortelmans, K, *Mindestangleichung und Verbraucherrecht* (1988) 1 Europäische Zeitschrift für Verbraucherrecht 1

Mosler, H, *Der Vertrag über die Europäische Gemeinschaft für Kohle und Stahl* (1951–2) 14 Zeitschrift für ausländisches öffentliches Recht und Völkerrecht 1

Müller, K, *Zur Problematik der Rahmenvorschriften nach dem Grundgesetz* (1964) Öffentliche Verwaltung 332

Müller-Graf, P-C, *Die Rechtsangleichung zur Verwirklichung des Binnenmarktes* (1989) 24 Europarecht 107

—— *Binnenmarktauftrag und Subsidiaritätsprinzip* (1995) Zeitschrift für Handelsrecht 34

Needham, W, *The Exclusive Power of Congress over Interstate Commerce* (1911) 11 Columbia Law Review 251

Nelson, C, *Preemption* (2000) 86 Virginia Law Review 225

Nettesheim, M, *Kompetenzen* in A von Bogdandy & J Bast (eds), *Europäisches Verfassungsrecht: theoretische und dogmatische Grundzüge* (Springer, 2003), 415

Neuwahl, NA, *Joint Participation in International Treaties and the Exercise of Power by the EEC and its Member States: Mixed Agreements* (1991) 28 Common Market Law Review 717

—— *The WTO Opinion and Implied External Powers of the Community: A Hidden Agenda* in A Dashwood & C Hillion (eds), *The General Law of E.C. External Relations* (Sweet & Maxwell, 2000), 139

Nicolaysen, G, *Zur Theorie von den implied powers in den Europäischen Gemeinschaften* (1966) 1 Europarecht 129

Niedobitek, M, *Die kulturelle Dimension im Vertrag über die Europäische Union* (1995) 30 Europarecht 349

Note, *Pre-emption as a Preferential Ground: A New Canon of Construction* (1959–60) 12 Stanford Law Review 208

Note, *A Framework for Preemption Analysis* (1978–79) 88 Yale Law Journal 363

Note, *Clear Statement Rules, Federalism, and Congressional Regulation of States* (1993–4) 107 Harvard Law Review 1959

O'Keeffe, D, *Exclusive, Concurrent and Shared Competence* in A Dashwood and C Hillion (eds), *The General Law of E.C. External Relations* (Sweet & Maxwell, 2000), 179

Oliver, P, *Measures of Equivalent Effect: A Reappraisal* (1982) 19 Common Market Law Review 217

—— & Jarvis, M, *Free Movements of Goods in the European Community: under Articles 28 to 30 of the EC Treaty* (Sweet & Maxwell, 2003)

Olmi, G, *The Agricultural Policy of the Community* (1965) 1 Common Market Law Review 118

—— *Politique agricole commune* in J-V Louis et al (eds), *Commentaire Megret: Le droit de la CE et de l'Union européenne* (Volume 2) (Editions de l'Université de Bruxelles, 1991)

Ophüls, CF, *Die Geltungsnormen des Europäischen Gemeinschaftsrechts* in B Aubin, E von Caemmerer, P Meylan, KH Neumayer, G Rinck, W Strauss (eds), *Festschrift für Otto Riese* (C.F. Müller, 1964), 1

—— *Staatshoheit und Gemeinschaftshoheit: Wandlungen des Souveränitätsbegriffs*, in *Recht im Wandel – Festschrift 150 Jahre C. Heymanns Verlag* (Heymanns Verlag, 1966), 519

Oppenheimer, R, *The Relationship between European Community Law and National Law: The Cases* (Volume 1 & 2) (Cambridge University Press, 1994 & 2003)

Panhuys, JHF van, *Conflicts between the Law of the European Communities and Other Rules of International Law* (1965–6) 3 Common Market Law Review 420

Patterson, LA, *Agricultural Policy Reform in the European Community: A Three-level Game Analysis* (1997) 51 International Organization 135

Paulin, B & Foreman, J, *L'élection du parlement européen au suffrage universel direct* (1976) 12 Cahiers de Droit Européen 506

Pauwelyn, J, *Conflict of Norms in Public International Law: How WTO Law Relates to other Rules of International Law* (Cambridge University Press, 2003)

Pechstein, M, *Die Mitgliedstaaten der EG als 'Sachwalter des gemeinsamen Interesses'* (Nomos, 1987)

Pelkmans, J, *The New Approach to Technical Harmonization and Standardization* (1987) 25 Journal of Common Market Studies 249

Pellet, A, *Les fondements juridiques internationaux du droit communautaire* (1994) 5 Collected Courses of the Academy of European Law 211

Pentland, C, *International Theory and European Integration* (Faber and Faber, 1973)

Pernice, I, *Völkerrechtliche Verträge Internationaler Organisationen* (1988) 48 Zeitschrift für ausländisches öffentliches Recht und Völkerrecht 229

—— *Multilevel Constitutionalism and the Treaty of Amsterdam: European Constitution-Making Revisited?* (1999) 36 Common Market Law Review 703

—— *Kompetenzabgrenzung im Europäischen Verfassungsbund* (2000) 50 Juristenzeitung 866

Pernthaler, P, *Kompetenzverteilung in der Krise* (Braumüller, 1989)

Pescatore, P, *Les relations extérieures des communautés européennes: contribution à la doctrine de la personnalité des organisations internationales* (1961) 103 Recueil des Cours de l'Académie de la Haye 1

—— *Remarques sur la nature juridique des 'décisions des représentants des états membres réunis au sein du conseil'* (1966) 14 Sociaal-economische Wetgeving 579

—— *Gemeinschaftsrecht und staatliches Recht in der Rechtsprechung des Gerichtshofs* (1969) 22 Neue Juristische Wochenschrift 2065

—— *Das Zusammenwirken der Gemeinschaftsrechtsordnung mit den nationalen Rechtsordnungen* (1970) 5 Europarecht 307

—— *International Law and Community Law—A Comparative Analysis* (1970) 7 Common Market Law Review 167

—— *The Law of Integration: Emergence of a new Phenomenon in International Relations, based on the Experience of the European Communities* (Sijthoff, 1974)

—— *L'ordre juridique des communautés européennes* (Presse universitaire de Liège, 1975)

Pescatore, P, *External Relations in the Case-Law of the Court of Justice of the European Communities* (1979) 16 Common Market Law Review 615

—— *La carence du législateur communautaire et le devoir du juge* in G Lüke, G Ress, & MR Will (eds), *Rechtsvergleichung, Europarecht und Staatenintegration: Gedächtnisschrift für Léontin-Jean Constantinesco* (Heymanns, 1983), 559

—— *Some Critical Remarks on the 'Single European Act'* (1987) 24 Common Market Law Review 9

—— *Mit der Subsidiarität leben* in O Due et al (eds), *Festschrift für Ulrich Everling* (Volume 2) (Nomos, 1995), 1071

—— *Opinion 1/94 on the 'Conclusion' of the WTO Agreement: Is there an Escape from a Programmed Disaster?* (1999) 36 Common Market Law Review 387

Peters, A, *The Position of International Law within the European Community Legal Order* (1997) 40 German Yearbook of International Law 9

—— *Elemente einer Theorie der Verfassung Europas* (Duncker & Humblot, 2001)

—— *European Democracy after the 2003 Convention* (2004) 41 Common Market Law Review 37

Petersmann, EU, *Artikel 234* in H von der Groeben, J Thiesing, & C-D Ehlermann (eds), *Kommentar zum EWG-Vertrag* (Normos, 1991) 5725

Pietzcker, J, *Zuständigkeitsordnung und Kollisionsrecht im Bundesstaat* in J Isensee & P Kirchhof (eds), *Handbuch des Staatsrechts der Bundesrepublik Deutschland*, Band IV (C.F. Müller, 2003), 693

Popper, K, *The Logic of Scientific Discovery* (Routledge, 2002)

—— *The Poverty of Historicism* (Routledge, 2002)

Pound, E, *ABC of Reading* (New Directions, 1960)

Powell, TR, *Supreme Court Decisions on the Commerce Clause and State Police Power: 1910–1914* (1922) 22 Columbia Law Review 28

—— *Current Conflicts between the Commerce Clause and State Police Power: 1922–1927 (II)* (1927–8) 12 Minnesota Law Review 491

—— *Some Aspects of Constitutionalism and Federalism* (1935–6) 14 North Carolina Law Review 1

Pufendorf, S, *On the Law of Nature and Nations* (trans: CH Oldfather et al) (Volume 2) (Clarendon Press, 1934)

Puissochet, J-P, *La place du droit international dans la jurisprudence de la cour de justice des communautés européennes* in GF Mancini (ed), *Scritti in onore di Giuseppe Federico Mancini* (Milan, Giuffrè, 1998), 779

Raalte, E Van, *The Treaty constituting the European Coal and Steel Community* (1952) 1 International and Comparative Law Quarterly 73

Rabe, H-J, *Das Verordnungsrechts der Europäischen Wirtschaftsgemeinschaft* (L Appel, 1963)

Raeker-Jordan, S, *The Pre-Emption Presumption that Never Was: Pre-emption Doctrine Swallows the Rule* (1998) 40 Arizona Law Review 1379

Ramsay, MD, *The Myth of Extraconstitutional Foreign Affairs Power* (2000–1) 42 William & Mary Law Review 379

Raux, J, *La capacité contractuelle de la communauté européenne en matière environnementale* in J-C Masclet (ed), *La communauté européenne et l'environnement* (La Documentation française, 1997), 159

Raworth, PM, *The Legislative Process in the European Community* (Kluwer, 1993)

Reagan, MD, *The New Federalism* (Oxford University Press, 1972)

Rehbinder, E & Stewart, R, *Environmental Protection Policy* in M Cappelletti, M Seccombe & J Weiler (eds), *Integration through Law* (Volume 2) (de Gruyter, 1985)

Reuter, P, *Le Plan Schuman* (1952) 81 Recueil des Cours de l'Académie de la Haye 519

—— *Organisations Européennes* (Presses Universitaires de France, 1965)

—— *Question of Treaties concluded between States and International Organizations or between two or more International Organizations* (1975) 1 Yearbook of the International Law Commission (Volume 2) (Part I), 119

Rieger, E, *The Common Agricultural Policy* in H Wallace & W Wallace (eds), *Policy-Making in the European Union* (Oxford University Press, 2000), 175

Riker, WH, *The Development of American Federalism* (Kluwer, 1987)

Robertson, AH, *The European Political Community* (1952) 29 British Yearbook of International Law 383

—— *Legal Problems of European Integration* (1957) 91 Recueil des Cours de l'Académie de la Haye 105

—— *European Institutions: Co-Operation, Integration, Unification* (Stevens & Sons, 1973)

Rochère, D de la, *L'ère des compétences partagées de l'étendue des compétences extérieures de la communauté européenne* (1995) 390 Revue Du Marché Commun et de l'Union Européenne 461

Rodgers, RS, *The Capacity of States of the Union to Conclude International Agreements: The Background and some Recent Developments* (1967) 61 American Journal of International Law 1021

Rosas, A, *The European Union and Mixed Agreements* in A Dashwood & C Hillion (eds), *The General Law of E.C. External Relations* (Sweet & Maxwell, 2000), 200

Rosenkrantz, NQ, *Executing the Treaty Power* (2005) 118 Harvard Law Review 1867

Roth, W-H, *Die Harmonisierung des Dienstleistungsrechts in der EWG* (1986) 21 Europarecht 340

Rotunda, RD, *The Doctrine of Conditional Preemption and other Limitations on Tenth Amendment Restrictions* (1983–4) 132 University of Pennsylvania Law Review 289

Salmond, JW, *Citizenship and Allegiance* (1901) 17 Law Quarterly Review 270

Sandalow, T, *The Expansion of Federal Legislative Power* in T Sandalow and E Stein (eds) *Courts and Free Markets: Perspectives from the United States and Europe* (Volume 2) (Oxford University Press, 1982), 49

Sasse, C, *The Common Market: Between International and Municipal Law* (1965–6) 75 Yale Law Journal 695

—— *Zur Auswärtigen Gewalt der Europäischen Wirtschaftsgemeinschaft* (1971) 6 Europarecht 208

Scharpf, FW, *The Joint-Decision Trap: Lessons from German Federalism and European Integration* (1988) 66 Public Administration 239
—— *Kann es in Europa eine stabile föderale Balance geben?* in R Wildenmann (ed), *Staatswerdung Europas? Optionen für eine Europäische Union* (Nomos, 1991), 415
Schermers, HG & Blokker, NM, *International Institutional Law* (Martinus Nijhoff, 2003)
Scheuing, DH, *Umweltschutz auf der Grundlage der Einheitlichen Europäischen Akte* (1989) 24 Europarecht 152
Schilling, T, *A New Dimension of Subsidiarity: Subsidiarity as a Rule and a Principle* (1994) 14 Yearbook of European Law 203
—— *The Autonomy of the Community Legal Order* (1996) 37 Harvard International Law Journal 389
—— *Rejoinder*, Harvard Jean Monnet Working Paper 10/1996
Schima, B, *Das Subsidiaritätsprinzip im Europäischen Gemeinschaftsrecht* (Manz, 1994)
Schlösser, JP, *Die Sperrwirkung sekundären Gemeinschaftsrechts: Mitgliedstaatliche Spielräume im 'harmonisierten' Umweltrecht* (Nomos, 2002)
Schmid, CU, *From Pont d'Avignon to Ponte Vecchio: the Resolution of Constitutional Conflicts between the European Union and the Member States through Principles of Public International Law* (1998) 18 Yearbook of European Law 415
Schmitt, C, *Der Begriff des Politischen* (Duncker & Humblot, 1996)
—— *Verfassungslehre* (Duncker & Humblot, 2003)
Schmitter, P, *Imagining the Future of the Euro-Polity with the Help of New Concepts* in G Marks, W Scharpf, PC Schmitter, & W Streek, *Governance in the European Union* (Sage, 1996), 121
Schmitt von Sydow, H, *The Basic Strategies of the Commission's White Paper*, in R Bieber, R Dehousse, S Pinder, JHH Weiler (eds), *1992: One European Market* (Nomos, 1988), 79
Schneider, H, *Alternativen der Verfassungsfinalität: Föderation, Konföderation – oder was sonst?* (2000) 23 Integration 171
Schönberger, C, *Die Europäische Union als Bund: Zugleich ein Beitrag zur Verabschiedung des Staatenbund-Bundesstaat-Schemas* (2004) 129 Archiv des öffentlichen Rechts 81
—— *Unionsbürger: Europas föderales Bürgerrecht in vergleichender Sicht* (Mohr Siebeck, 2006)
—— *European Citizenship as Federal Citizenship: Some Citizenship Lessons of Comparative Federalism* (2007) 19 European Review of Public Law 61
Schröder, T, *Die Kompetenzverteilung zwischen der Europäischen Wirtschaftsgemeinschaft und ihren Mitgliedstaaten auf dem Gebiet des Umweltschutzes* (Duncker & Humblot, 1992)
Schütze, R, *Organized Change towards an 'Ever Closer Union': Article 308 EC and the Limits to the Community's Legislative Competence* (2003) 22 Yearbook of European Law 79
—— *Parallel External Powers in the European Community: From 'Cubist' Perspectives Towards 'Naturalist' Constitutional Principles?* (2004) 23 Yearbook of European Law 225

—— *Supremacy without Pre-emption? The very slowly emergent Doctrine of Community Pre-emption* (2006) 43 Common Market Law Review 1023

—— *The Morphology of Legislative Power in the European Community: Legal Instruments and the Federal Division of Powers* (2006) 25 Yearbook of European Law 91

—— *EC Law and International Agreements of the Member States—An Ambivalent Relationship?* (2006–7) 9 Cambridge Yearbook of European Legal Studies 387

—— *Lisbon and the Federal Order of Competences—A Prospective Analysis* (2008) 33 European Law Review 708

—— *The European Community's Federal Order of Competences: A Retrospective Analysis* in M Dougan and S Currie (eds), *Fifty Years of the European Treaties—Looking Back and Thinking Forward* (Hart, 2009), 63

—— *Federalism and Foreign Affairs: Mixity as an (Inter)national Phenomenon* in C Hillion & P Koutrakos, *Mixed Agreements Revisited: The EU and its Member States in the World* (Hart, forthcoming)

—— *On 'Federal' Ground: The European Union as an (Inter)national Phenomenon* (2009) 46 Common Market Law Review (forthcoming)

—— *Reforming the CAP: From 'Vertical' to 'Horizontal' Legislation* (2009) 28 Yearbook of European Law (forthcoming)

—— *German Constitutional Federalism: Between* Sein *and* Bewußtsein (in preparation)

Schwartz, IE, *EG-Rechtsetzungsbefugnisse, insbesondere nach Artikel 235 – ausschließlich oder konkurrierend?* (1976) 11 Europarecht (Sonderheft) 37

—— *EG-Kompetenzen für den Binnenmarkt: Exklusiv oder konkurrierend/subsidiär?* in O Due, M Lutter & J Schwarze (eds), *Festschrift für Ulrich Everling* (Nomos, 1995), 1331

Schwarze, J, *European Administrative Law* (Sweet & Maxwell, 2006)

Schwarzenberger, G, *The Frontiers of International Law* (Stevens, 1962)

Schyff, G van der & Leenknegt, G-J, *The Case for a European Senate: A Model for the Representation of National Parliaments in the European Union* (2007) 62 Zeitschrift für öffentliches Recht 237

Seidel, M, *Präventive Rechtsangleichung im Bereich des Gemeinsamen Marktes* (2006) 41 Europarecht 26

Shaw, J, *European Community Law* (Macmillan, 1993)

Shonfield, A, *Journey to an Unknown Destination* (Penguin, 1973)

Simon, D, *Le système juridique communautaire* (Press Universitaires de France, 2001)

Slot, PJ *Technical and Administrative Obstacles to Trade in the EEC* (Sijhoff, 1975)

—— *Harmonisation* (1996) 21 European Law Review 378

Snyder, FG, *Law of the Common Agricultural Policy* (Sweet & Maxwell, 1985)

Soares, AG, *Pre-emption, Conflicts of Powers and Subsidiarity* (1998) 23 European Law Review 132

Spiro, PJ, *Foreign Affairs Federalism* (1999) 70 University of Colorado Review 1233

Stadler, A, *From the Brussels Convention to Regulation 44/2001: Cornerstones of a European Law of Civil Procedure* (2005) 42 Common Market Law Review 1637

Stein, E, *Toward Supremacy of Treaty-Constitution by Judicial Fiat: On the Margin of the Costa Case* (1964–5) 63 Michigan Law Journal 491

—— & Sandalow, T, *On the Two Systems: An Overview* in T Sandalow & E Stein (eds), *Courts and Free Markets: Perspectives from the United States and Europe* (Volume 2) (Oxford University Press, 1982), 3

—— *External Relations of the European Community: Structure and Process* (1990) 1 Collected Courses of the Academy of European Law 115

Steindorff, E, *Grenzen der EG-Kompetenzen* (Recht und Wirtschaft, 1990)

Steiner, J, *Subsidiarity under the Maastricht Treaty* in D O'Keeffe & PM Twomey (eds), *Legal Issues of the Maastricht Treaty* (Wiley Chancery Law, 1994), 49

Stern, K, *Das Staatsrecht der Bundesrepublik Deutschland*, Band I (Beck, 1977)

Stern, RL, *The Commerce Clause and the National Economy, 1933–1946* (1945–6) 59 Harvard Law Review 645

Stettner, R, *Grundlagen einer Kompetenzlehre* (Duncker & Humblot, 1983)

Stewing, C, *Subsidiarität und Föderalismus in der Europäischen Union* (Heymann,1992)

Streinz, R, *Mindestharmonisierung im Binnenmarkt* in U Everling & W-H Roth (eds), *Mindestharmonisierung im Europäischen Binnenmarkt: Referate des 7. Bonner Europa-Symposions vom 27. April 1996* (Nomos, 1997), 9

Swaine, ET, *Subsidiarity and Self-Interest: Federalism at the European Court of Justice* (2000) 41 Harvard International Law Journal 1

Sybesma-Knol, N, *The New Law of Treaties: The Codification of the Law of Treaties concluded between States and International Organizations or between two or more International Organizations* (1985) 15 Georgia Journal of International and Comparative Law 425

Teasdale, AL, *The Life and Death of the Luxembourg Compromise* (1993) 31 Journal of Common Market Studies 567

Timmermans, CWA et al (eds), *Division of powers between the European Communities and their Member States in the Field of External Relations* (Kluwer, 1981)

—— *La libre circulation des marchandises et la politique commerciale commune* in P Demaret (ed), *Relations extérieures de la communauté européenne et marché intérieur: aspects juridiques et fonctionnels* (Collège d'Europe No 45, 1986), 93

—— *Common Commercial Policy (Article 113 EEC) and International Trade in Services*, in F Capotorti, CD Ehlermann, J Frowein, F Jacobs, R Joliet, T Koopmans, R Kovar (eds), *Du droit international au droit de l'integration: Liber Amicorum Pierre Pescatore* (Nomos, 1987), 675

—— *The EU and Public International Law* (1999) 4 European Foreign Affairs Review 181

Tizzano, A, *Lo sviluppo delle competenze materiali delle communita' europee* (1981) 21 Rivista di Diritto Europeo 197

—— *The Powers of the Community* in Commission of the European Communities (ed), *Thirty Years of Community Law* (Office for Official Publications of the EC, 1981), 43

Tocqueville, A de, *Democracy in America* (ed: P Bradley) (Volume 1) (Vintage, 1954)

Toth, AG, *The Principle of Subsidiarity in the Maastricht Treaty* (1992) 29 Common Market Law Review 1079
—— *Is Subsidiarity Justiciable?* (1994) 19 European Law Review 268
—— *A Legal Analysis of Subsidiarity* in D O'Keeffe & PM Twomey (eds), *Legal Issues of the Maastricht Treaty* (Wiley Chancery Law, 1994), 37
Triantaffyllou, D, *Des compétences d'attribution au domaine de la loi* (Bruyant, 1997)
Tribe, LH, *The Puzzling Persistence of Process-Based Constitutional Theories* (1979–80) 89 Yale Law Journal 1063
—— *Taking Text and Structure Seriously: Reflections on Free-Form Method in Constitutional Interpretation* (1994–95) 108 Harvard Law Review 1221
—— *American Constitutional Law* (Volume 1) (Foundation Press, 2000)
Tridimas, T & Eeckhout, P, *The External Competence of the Community and the Case-Law of the Court of Justice: Principles versus Pragmatism* (1994) 14 Yearbook of European Law 143
—— *The General Principles of EC Law* (Clarendon Press, 1999)
Triepel, H, *Unitarismus und Föderalismus im Deutschen Reiche* (Mohr, 1907)
Trüe, C, *Das System der Rechtsetzungskompetenzen der EG und der EU* (Nomos, 2002)
Tschofen, F, *Article 235 of the Treaty Establishing the European Economic Community: Potential Conflicts between the Dynamics of Lawmaking in the Community and National Constitutional Principles* (1991) 12 Michigan Journal of International Law 471
Tushnet, M, *Rethinking the Dormant Commerce Clause* (1979) 1979 Wisconsin Law Review 125
Usher, JA, *The Effects of Common Organizations and Policies on the Powers of a Member State* (1977) 2 European Law Review 428
—— *The Scope of Community Competence: Its Recognition and Enforcement* (1985) 24 Journal of Common Market Studies 121
—— *The Gradual Widening of European Community Policy on the Basis of Articles 100 and 235 of the EEC Treaty* in J Schwarze & HG Schermers (eds), *Structure and Dimension of European Community Policy* (Nomos, 1988), 25
—— *EC Agricultural Law* (Oxford University Press, 2001)
Usteri, M, *Theorie des Bundesstaates* (Polygraphischer Verlag AG Zürich, 1954)
Vandermeersch, D, *The Single European Act and the Environmental Policy of the European Economic Community* (1987) 12 European Law Review 407
Vasey, M, *Decision-making in the Agriculture Council and the 'Luxembourg Compromise'* (1988) 25 Common Market Law Review 725
Vattel, E de, *The Law of Nations* (trans: J Chitty) (Johnson & Co, 1883)
Vázques, CM, *W(h)ither Zschernig?* (2001) 46 Villanova Law Review 1259
Vedder, CW, *Die auswärtige Gewalt des Europa der Neun* (Schwartz & Co, 1980)
Vignes, D, *The Harmonisation of National Legislation and the EEC* (1990) 15 European Law Review 358
Vile, MJC, *The Structure of American Federalism* (Oxford University Press, 1961)
Visscher, C de, *Theory and Reality in Public International Law* (Princeton University Press, 1968)

Vitzthum, W Graf, *Die Bedeutung gliedstaatlichen Verfassungsrechts in der Gegenwart* (1988) 46 Veröffentlichungen der Vereinigung deutscher Staatsrechtslehrer 9

Vogelaar, TW, *The Approximation of the Laws of the Member States under the Treaty of Rome* (1975) 12 Common Market Law Review 211

Voyenne, B, *Histoire de l'idée fédéralist: Les Sources* (Presses d'Europe, 1973)

Waelbroeck, M, *The Emergent Doctrine of Community Pre-emption – Consent and Re-delegation* in T Sandalow & E Stein, *Courts and Free Markets: Perspectives from the United States and Europe* (Volume 2) (Oxford University Press, 1982), 548

Wagner, H, *Grundbegriffe des Beschlussrechts der Europäischen Gemeinschaften* (Heymann, 1965)

Wagner, M, *Das Konzept der Mindestharmonisierung* (Duncker & Humblot, 2001)

Waitz, G, *Das Wesen des Bundesstaates*, in *Grundzüge der Politik* (Homann, 1862)

Walker, DB, *Toward a Functioning Federalism* (Winthrop, 1981)

Walker, N, *Sovereignty and Differentiated Integration in the European Union* (1998) 4 European Law Journal 355

Walz, R, *Rethinking Walt Wilhelm, or the Supremacy of Community Competition Law over National Law* (1996) 21 European Law Review 449

Warren, C, *The Supreme Court in United States History* (Volume 1) (BeardBooks, 1999)

Watts, RL, *Comparing Federal Systems* (McGill-Queen's University Press, 1999)

Weatherill, S, *Beyond Preemption? Shared Competence and Constitutional Change in the European Community* in D O'Keeffe & PM Twomey (eds), *Legal Issues of the Maastricht Treaty* (Wiley Chancery Law, 1994), 13

—— *Law and Integration in the European Union* (Clarendon Press, 1995)

—— *Pre-emption, Harmonisation and the Distribution of Competence to Regulate the Internal Market* in C Barnard & J Scott, *The Law of the Single European Market: Unpacking the Premises* (Hart, 2002), 41

—— *Using National Parliaments to Improve Scrutiny of the Limits of EU Action* (2003) 28 European Law Review 909

Wechsler, H, *The Political Safeguards of Federalism: The Role of the States in the Composition and Selection of the National Government* (1954) 54 Columbia Law Review 543

Weiland, PS, *Federal and State Preemption of Environmental Law: A Critical Analysis* (2000) 24 Harvard Environmental Law Review 237

Weiler, JHH, *The Community System: the Dual Character of Supranationalism* (1981) 1 Yearbook of European Law 267

—— *Supranational Law and Supranational System: Legal Structure and Political Process in the European Community* (EUI Thesis, 1982)

—— *Il sistema comunitario europeo: struttura giuridica e processo politico* (Il Mulino, 1985)

—— *The Transformation of Europe* (1991) 100 Yale Law Journal 2403

—— *Does Europe Need a Constitution: Demos, Telos and the German Maastricht Decision* (1995) 1 European Law Journal 219

—— *The External Legal Relations of Non-Unitary Actors: Mixity and the Federal Principle* in JHH Weiler, *The Constitution of Europe* (Cambridge University Press, 1999), 130

—— *Federalism without Constitutionalism: Europe's Sonderweg* in K Nikolaidis & R Howse (eds), *The Federal Vision: Legitimacy and Levels of Governance in the United States and the European Union* (Oxford University Press, 2001), 54

Weinfeld, AC, *What did the Framers of the Federal Constitution mean by 'Agreements or Compacts'?* (1935–6) 3 University of Chicago Law Review 453

Westerkamp, JB, *Staatenbund und Bundesstaat: Untersuchungen über die Praxis und das Recht der modernen Bünde* (Brockhaus, 1892)

Wheare, KC, *Federal Government* (Oxford University Press, 1953)

Wiederin, E, *Bundesrecht und Landesrecht: Zugleich ein Beitrag zu Strukturproblemen der bundesstaatlichen Kompetenzverteilung in Österreich und Deutschland* (Springer, 1995)

Wildhaber, L, *Sovereignty and International Law* in R St. J Macdonald & DM Johnston (eds), *The Structure and Process of International Law: Essays in Legal Philosophy, Doctrine and Theory* (Martinus Nijhoff, 1983), 425

Wilke, M & Wallace, H, *Subsidiarity: Approaches to Power-sharing in the European Community*, Royal Institute of International Affairs: Discussion Paper 27/1990

Wilkinson, D, *Maastricht and the Environment: The Implications for the EC's Environment Policy of the Treaty on European Union* (1992) 4 Journal of Environmental Law 221

Wils, WPJ, *The Search for the Rule in Article 30 EEC: Much Ado About Nothing?* (1993) 18 European Law Review 475

Winter, G, *Subsidiarität und Deregulierung im Gemeinschaftsrecht* (1996) 31 Europarecht 247

—— *Die Sperrwirkung von Gemeinschaftssekundärrecht für einzelstaatliche Regelungen des Binnenmarkts mit besonderer Berücksichtigung von Art. 130 t EGV* (1998) 51 Die öffentliche Verwaltung 377

Witte, B de, *Rules of Change in International Law: How Special is the European Community?* (1994) 25 Netherlands Yearbook of International Law 299

—— *Direct Effect, Supremacy and the Nature of the Legal Order* in P Craig & G de Búrca, *The Evolution of EU Law* (Oxford University Press, 1999), 177

—— *Old-fashioned Flexibility: International Agreements between Member States of the European Union* in G de Búrca & J Scott (eds), *Constitutional Change in the EU: From Uniformity to Flexibility?* (Hart, 2000), 31

—— *Chameleonic Member States: Differentiation by Means of Partial and Parallel International Agreements* in B de Witte, D Hanf & E Vos (eds), *The Many Faces of Differentiation in EU Law* (Intersentia, 2001), 231

Wittgenstein, L, *Philosophical Investigations* (Blackwell, 2001)

Wohlfarth, E, *Artikel 235* in E Wohlfarth, U Everling, HJ Glaesner, & R Sprung (eds), *Die Europäische Wirtschaftsgemeinschaft* (1960), 608

—— *Anfänge einer Europäischen Rechtsordnung und ihr Verhältnis zum deutschen Recht* (1962–63) 3 Juristisches Jahrbuch 241

Wolfson, P, *Preemption and Federalism: The Missing Link* (1988–1989) 16 Hastings Constitutional Law Quarterly 69

Wuermeling, J, *Kooperatives Gemeinschaftsrecht* (Engel, 1988)

Wyatt, D, *Competence of the Community Internal and External* (1977) 2 European Law Review 41

—— *New Legal Order, or Old?* (1982) 7 European Law Review 147

—— *Subsidiarity and Judicial Review* in D O'Keeffe and A Bavasso (eds), *Liber Amicorum in Honour of Lord Slynn of Hadley* (Kluwer, 2000), 505

—— *Community Competence to Regulate the Internal Market*, Oxford Faculty of Law Research Paper 9/2007

Yandais, D, *La communauté et la pêche* (1978) 14 Cahiers De Droit Européen 158

Young, EA, *Dual Federalism, Concurrent Jurisdiction, and the Foreign Affairs Exception* (2000–2001) 69 George Washington Law Review 139

—— *Two Cheers for Process Federalism* (2001) 46 Villanova Law Review 1349

—— *Protecting Member State Autonomy in the European Union: Some Cautionary Tales from American Federalism* (2002) 77 New York University Law Review 1612

Zoller, E, *Aspects internationaux du droit constitutionnel. Contribution à la théorie de la fédération d'États* (2002) 294 Recueil des Cours de l'Académie de la Haye 43

Zuleeg, M, *Die Kompetenzen der Europäischen Gemeinschaften gegenüber den Mitgliedstaaten* (1970) 20 n.F. Jahrbuch des öffentlichen Rechts 1

—— *Vorbehaltene Kompetenzen der Mitgliedstaaten der Europäischen Gemeinschaft auf dem Gebiete des Umweltschutzes* (1987) 6 Neue Zeitschrift für Verwaltungsrecht 280

—— *Der Rang des europäischen im Verhältnis zum nationalen Wettbewerbsrecht* (1990) 25 Europarecht 123

Zweig, E, *Die Lehre vom Pouvoir Constituant* (Mohr, 1904)

INDEX